IS LAW COMPUTABLE?

What does computable law mean for the autonomy, authority and legitimacy of the legal system? Are we witnessing a shift from Rule of Law to a new Rule of Technology? Should we even build these things in the first place?

This unique volume collects original papers by a group of leading international scholars to address some of the fascinating questions raised by the encroachment of Artificial Intelligence (AI) into more aspects of legal process, administration and culture. Weighing near-term benefits against the longer-term, and potentially path-dependent, implications of replacing human legal authority with computational systems, this volume pushes back against the more uncritical accounts of AI in law and the eagerness of scholars, governments, and LegalTech developers, to overlook the more fundamental – and perhaps 'bigger picture' – ramifications of computable law.

Is Law Computable? includes contributions by Simon Deakin, Christopher Markou, Mireille Hildebrandt, Roger Brownsword, Sylvie Delacroix, Lyria Bennett Moses, Ryan Abbott, Jennifer Cobbe, Lily Hands, John Morison, Alex Sarch and Dilan Thampapillai.

Is Law Computable?

Critical Perspectives on Law and Artificial Intelligence

Edited by
Simon Deakin
and
Christopher Markou

• HART •
OXFORD • LONDON • NEW YORK • NEW DELHI • SYDNEY

HART PUBLISHING

Bloomsbury Publishing Plc

Kemp House, Chawley Park, Cumnor Hill, Oxford, OX2 9PH, UK

1385 Broadway, New York, NY 10018, USA

HART PUBLISHING, the Hart/Stag logo, BLOOMSBURY and the Diana logo are trademarks of Bloomsbury Publishing Plc

First published in Great Britain 2020

A catalogue record for this book is available from the British Library.

Library of Congress Cataloging-in-Publication data

Names: Deakin, S. F. (Simon F.) editor. | Markou, Christopher, editor.

Title: Is law computable? : critical perspectives on law and artificial intelligence / edited by Simon Deakin and Christopher Markou.

Description: Oxford, UK ; New York, NY : Hart Publishing, an imprint of Bloomsbury Publishing, 2020. | Includes bibliographical references and index.

Identifiers: LCCN 2020028708 | ISBN 9781509937066 (hardback) | ISBN 9781509937073 (ePDF) | ISBN 9781509937080 (Epub)

Subjects: LCSH: Law—Data processing. | Artificial intelligence—Law and legislation. | Law—Computer network resources. | Technology and law. | Technological innovations—Law and legislation.

Classification: LCC K564.C6 I8 2020 | DDC 340.0285/63—dc23

LC record available at https://lccn.loc.gov/2020028708

ISBN: HB: 978-1-50993-706-6
ePDF: 978-1-50993-707-3
ePub: 978-1-50993-708-0

Typeset by Compuscript Ltd, Shannon

FOREWORD

The Resilient Fragility of Law

FRANK PASQUALE

For practising lawyers, the stakes of this volume could not be higher: should law remain a distinctive profession, or is it fated to become a subfield of computer science? That question in turn can be divided into at least three further inquiries: Are our current legal processes computable? Should they become more computable? And should scholars and practitioners in AI and computer science work to develop software (and even robots) that better mimic the performance of current legal professionals?

The authors in this volume give nuanced and sophisticated answers to each of these questions. They include some of the leading voices in the world today on the relationship between law and computing. The result is a collection that should be read by a wide range of audiences both in and around the legal profession, and also by anyone studying law, lest they be caught unawares by its rapidly changing social context.

This work is not just of interest to those concerned about legal technology ('legaltech'), but also to those developing it. Those at the cutting edge of fields ranging from natural language processing to automated contracts, should carefully read these contributions. Several apply classic critiques of computerised or automated law to state-of-the-art technology. Others mine important work in critical data studies and critical algorithm studies to enrich legal theory and analysis with social scientific documentation of bias in computational systems. Both areas of concern (developed from within and outside the legal academy) are critical for computer scientists, coders, developers, and legaltech non-profits and for-profits to consider as they take on more law-related tasks.

The volume is crucial for policymakers to consider before they adopt machine learning methods in law (by deploying, say, natural language processing to triage applications for appeal). There are at least two forms of pressure external to legal values that will make such AI systems increasingly tempting. First, the siren song of austerity amidst economic slowdowns will tempt policymakers to try to replace workers in the justice system with cheaper software. Second, high-margin technology businesses skillfully re-invest their profits to lobby governments to expand the use of their wares. In the large number of jurisdictions where such influence is common, we can foresee a predictable political economy of automation: the firms (and sectors) that are more concentrated, with a higher profit margin, will systematically bid legal work away from firms and sectors that are less profitable and less concentrated (and thus less able to coordinate long term investment in influence campaigns).

These two factors – austerity and concentrated influence – have already worked to tilt the playing field toward legal automation, and will continue to do so. Indeed, as Jennifer Cobbe's insightful chapter demonstrates, imbalances of power afflict the development and interpretation of law generally, and must constantly be guarded against via civil society activism, as well as institutionalised cultivation of civic responsibility, professional ethics, and division of powers.[1] Such imbalances of power are particularly worrisome when legaltech enters the picture, given the expanding power of surveillance capitalism to promote personalised stimuli based on projected responses.

What Law is, and What it Might Be

The question 'is law computable?' immediately suggests the classic jurisprudential query, 'what is law?' – a question posed in both pragmatist and idealist modes. For the tough-minded pragmatist, the question 'what is law' may come down to a simple prediction of whether those in authority will or will not act to stop a planned action, or penalise a completed one. This attitude is popular in business. Rarely does a commercial client care deeply about values internal to law – and non-lawyer clients may never have been trained to recognise such values. Rather, the key question is whether some police force, administrator, or judge will stop, penalise, or reward an action. If law is constricted to predicting such interventions, the skills needed to practice it may become similarly circumscribed, and thus more easily computable. Some thought leaders in the field of computational legal studies rarely tire of touting their models' ability to best human experts at some narrow game of foretelling the future – for example, predicting whether the U.S. Supreme Court or European Court of Human Rights will affirm an appealed judgment, based on some set of variables about the relevant jurists and the cases before them.[2]

For reductionist projects in computational law (particularly those that seek to replace, rather than complement, legal practitioners), *traces* of the legal process are equivalent to the process itself.[3] The words in a complaint and an opinion, for instance, are taken to be the essence of the proceeding, and variables gleaned from decisionmakers' past actions and affiliations predict their preferences. In this behaviouristic rendering, litigants present pages of words to the decisionmaker, and some set of pages better matches the decisionmaker's preferences, and then the decisionmaker tries to write a justification of

[1] J Cobbe, 'Legal Singularity and the Reflexivity of Law', in this volume.

[2] On such projects and their practical and normative infirmities, see F Pasquale and G Cashwell, 'Prediction, Persuasion, and the Jurisprudence of Behaviourism' (2018) 68 *U Toronto LJ* 63.

[3] P E Agre, 'Toward a Critical Technical Practice: Lessons Learned in Trying to Reform AI,' in G Bowker, L Gasser, L Star and B Turner, eds, *Bridging the Great Divide: Social Science, Technical Systems, and Cooperative Work* (Erlbaum, 1997) (on AI's 'tendency to conflate representations with the things that they represent'); M Hildebrandt, *Law as Computation in the Era of Artificial Legal Intelligence: Speaking Law to the Power of Statistics* (2017), dx.doi.org/10.2139/ssrn.2983045 (on a tendency to 'mistake the mathematical simulation of legal judgment for legal judgment itself').

the decision sufficient not to be overruled by higher levels of appeal. From the perspective of the client, predictions that are 30 per cent more accurate than a coin flip, or 20 per cent more accurate than casually consulted experts, are quite useful.

But of course there is much more to law and legal process, particularly as social values evolve and the composition of the courts and the bar changes. AI is a long way from explaining *why* a case should be decided a certain way, and how broadly or narrowly an opinion ought to be written. Nor have technology firms proven themselves particularly adept at recognizing the many values at stake in such questions. Given that law is a human institution primarily concerned with human activities, it is quite possible that AI will never attain such forms of reason and evaluation. These skills and competences require normative judgment, and can only be legitimate when completed by a person who can subjectively understand what she or he is imposing on others when decisions are made.[4]

Nevertheless, once computational prediction of legal judgments gains traction, it can move from being a mere novelty to something that powerful people use to settle disputes. If litigants see disputes as a mere coordination problem (similar to settling whether cars should drive on the right or left hand of the road), natural language processing or other computational methods may tempt them to abandon public, reasoned legal processes for sufficiently predictable calculation.

However efficient such a transition may be for litigants, critically important public legal values risk being lost or marginalised when dispute settlement is automated.[5] Giovanni Sartor and Karl Branting have argued that 'No simple rule-chaining or pattern matching algorithm can accurately model judicial decision-making because the judiciary has the task of producing reasonable and acceptable solutions in exactly those cases in which the facts, the rules, or how they fit together are controversial.'[6] Enthusiasts for AI in law have tried to develop ways of extrapolating from past data, what future judgments would be, or ought to be. But even that simple is/ought dichotomy is fraught with dissensus, particularly among those who believe more strongly in the power of precedent (the 'is' camp), and those who emphasise the need for law and legal institutions to adaptively change with the times (the 'ought' camp).

Moreover, even if a legal system could align along one of those stances, there are endless controversies within them. Those who agree on the overriding importance of *stare decisis* may strongly disagree on which interpretive methodology would best ensure its determinacy and generality. The 'ought' camp is, if anything, more diverse in its preferences, goals, and values. Sylvie Delacroix wisely demonstrates that the 'dynamic nature of moral values' (including moral stances' tendency to evolve or devolve over time) precludes an automated system trained to draw conclusions based

[4] K Brennan-Marquez and SE Henderson, 'Artificial Intelligence and Role-Reversible Judgment' (forthcoming, 2020), *J of Crim L and Criminology*.

[5] F Pasquale, 'Digital Star Chamber', *Aeon*, 18 August 2015, https://aeon.co/essays/judge-jury-and-executioner-the-unaccountable-algorithm; Owen Fiss, 'Against Settlement' (1984) 93 *Yale LJ* 1073.

[6] G Sartor and LK Branting, 'Introduction: Judicial Applications of Artificial Intelligence,' in G Sartor and LK Branting (eds), *Judicial Applications of Artificial Intelligence* (Springer, 1998) 1, quoted in S Deakin and C Markou, 'From Rule of Law to Legal Singularity', in this volume, 5.

on backward-looking data, since it cannot reflect the changing values of society.[7] Thus, as Simon Deakin and Christopher Markou explain in an illuminating passage:

> [T]he hypothetical totalisation of 'AI judges' implied by the legal singularity [a vision of completely computerised decisionmaking] would instantiate a particular view of law: one in which legal judgments are essentially deterministic or probabilistic outputs, produced on the basis of static or unambiguous legal rules, in a societal vacuum. This would deny, or see as irrelevant, competing conceptions of law, in particular the idea that law is a social institution, involving socially constructed activities, relationship, and norms not easily translated into numerical functions.[8]

A legal singularity is effectively a simulation of law – but a woefully inadequate one given present or near-future technology.

Should we try to develop better technology? Or more ways for 'socially constructed activities, relationship, and norms' to be translated into numerical functions?[9] That will depend on our theory of human agency and values. Former Yale Law School Dean Anthony Kronman, turning back to Platonic philosophy, once compared the 'city and the soul,' exploring parallels between personhood and statehood.[10] The nature and purpose of a legal system should reflect the nature and purpose of the persons it governs. We may constructively compare the simulation of legal systems, and the simulation of persons. Is what ultimately matters the effects of a person or institution (in which case simulation is successful when it causes those effects), or are persons and institutions valuable and real on additional grounds, by virtue of their nature and history?

Many persons bridle at the thought of a machine simulating someone they know. Nevertheless, one intellectual founder of the singularity ideal has taken the idea of robotic simulation all the way to aspiring to a computerised copy of his deceased father, at least for conversational purposes.[11] If the self is merely the 'software' running on any kind of hardware (whether carbon- or silicon-based), it can be replicated (a theme of *Westworld*, among other science fiction thrillers). The problem with such a vision of personhood is that it is radically solipsistic, focused only on the words and actions of the replicated subject, rather than the society and other stimuli that provoked, inspired, or otherwise catalyzed these words and actions.[12]

[7] S Delacroix, 'Automated Systems and the Need for Change', in this volume, 162, 164. Perhaps such a system could consult opinion polls as 'oracles' indicating evolving social standards on given issues. However, even the development of the questions for such polls, and their methodology (given the increasing rarity of the landline telephones that were the key tool of past pollsters) are strikingly difficult to compute.

[8] S Deakin and C Markou, 'From Rule of Law to Legal Singularity,' 7.

[9] ibid.

[10] A Kronman, *The Lost Lawyer* (Harvard University Press, 1995). Plato's larger project of political psychology reflected this city/soul comparison in its exploration of the personality traits that correspond to different regime ideal-types (aristocracy, timocracy, oligarchy, democracy, and tyranny), closely tied to his tripartite theory of the soul (consisting of logos, thymos, and eros).

[11] M Andrejevic, *Automated Media* (Routledge, 2019), 1 (describing the inventor's belief that 'some combination of archival material and machine learning will be able to construct a digital version of his father that he can converse with –perhaps forever – if he succeeds in surviving until 'the singularity' (when human and machine consciousness merge)'). See also F Pasquale, 'Two Concepts of Immortality', 14 *Yale Journal of Law and Humanities* 73 (for a critique of the aspiration to singularity, based on normative theories of embodied cognition).

[12] Even *Westworld's* robotic protagonist, Delores Abernathy, states in key scenes 'that which is real is irreplaceable.' W Slocombe, ' "That Which Is Real Is Irreplaceable": Lies, Damned Lies, and (Dis-)simulations in *Westworld*,' in *Reading Westworld*, A Goody and A Mackay eds (Palgrave Macmillan, 2019).

Would the same solipsism afflict a 'replicated,' or 'better than replicated,' social order? Even in a seemingly uncontroversial example, like the automation of driving, there are worrying portents, as Roger Brownsword explains. He imagines a speed control system which would automatically reduce the speed of vehicles which are moving faster than the speed limit on the road. Such a system could reduce accidents. However, as he observes,

> When regulators make this final move, 'from perfect detection to perfect prevention', we have full-scale technological management ... [that is] problematic because: (i) it displaces the idea of law as an enterprise of subjecting human conduct to the governance of rules, and (ii) it compromises the conditions for the exercise of human agency and autonomy.[13]

Brownsword's normative analysis counsels in favor of limiting the computability of law, complementing the practical limits also expertly demarcated in this volume. Similarly, Delacroix observes that even if we could rely on a 'system's superior cognitive prowess to figure it all out for us, once and for all,' it would be unwise to install such a digital leviathan, because it would undermine humanity's 'capacity for normative reflection – querying how the world could be made better'.[14] Indeed, to assume that cognitive prowess into the future is to grant the present illegitimate power over the future, consigning our descendants to a silicon 'dead hand' of increasingly outdated rules and standards.

One of the most distinctive contributions of this volume is a growing recognition that the limits of law's applicability and force may be its greatest strengths. As Dilan Thampapillai argues, 'Copyright law works because it tacitly tolerates a degree of infringement and permits an ever-shifting line between free and non-free uses of copyright materials.'[15] To perfectly enforce such intellectual property (as satirised in Lee Konstantinou's novel *Pop Apocalypse*), is to freight delicate and evanescent realms of cultural speculation and play with the burden of commerce and quantification.[16]

Democratised progress, based on distributed (rather than concentrated) expertise, depends on AI complementing (rather than replacing) key professionals, including lawyers.[17]

As James Boyd White has argued, 'The law is not a closed system, operating behind locked doors, but is connected in hundreds of ways to our democratic culture. To disregard this structure of authority and to replace it with a theory – whether philosophical, political, or economic in kind – is to erode our democracy at the root.'[18] As democracy is under threat in so many parts of the world, it may be tempting to theorise some expertocracy, algocracy, technocracy, or AI ruler to replace fallible humans.[19] But to advance

[13] R Brownsword, 'Artificial Intelligence and Legal Singularity: The Thin End of the Wedge, the Thick End of the Wedge, and the Rule of Law', in this volume, 141.

[14] S Delacroix, 'Automated Systems and the Need for Change,' 174.

[15] D Thampapillai, 'The Law of Contested Concepts? Reflections on Copyright Law and the Legal and Technological Singularities,' in this volume, 225.

[16] J Cohen, *Configuring the Networked Self* (Oxford University Press, 2012).

[17] F Pasquale, *New Laws of Robotics: Defending Human Expertise in the Age of AI.* (Harvard University Press, 2020).

[18] J Boyd White, 'Law, Economics, and Torture,' in *Law and Democracy in the Empire of Force*, H Jefferson Powell and J Boyd White, eds (University of Michigan Press, 2009).

[19] For an analysis of algocracy, see J Danaher, 'The Threat of Algocracy: Reality, Resistance and Accommodation,' (2016) 29 *Philosophy and Technology* 245.

such a political denouement as a living option in social order is a prelude to helping bring it about – raising deep problems of performativity addressed in this volume.

Beyond Naturalism

Anticipating the future depends on the ability to make complex judgments about causation, taking into account the changing strategies and evolving self-conceptions of social actors. What distinguishes this volume from the mainstream of writing on 'legal tech,' is a keen attention to the second, third, fourth, and further-order effects of legal automation on persons, legal systems, and more. For example, Jennifer Cobbe expertly explores law's reflexivity – the way it both shapes and is shaped by the society it resides in and structures. As Mireille Hildebrandt observes in this volume, the history of social science is rife with examples of metrics that fail once they become well-known, because those they are supposed to measure find ways of manipulating the metric.[20] A legal system built on readily quantifiable variables is an open invitation to gaming. As philosopher of social science Jason Blakely argues, there is a 'double hermeneutic' effect when some model of understanding the world becomes common: its interpretive frame starts affecting the behaviour of those it was meant merely to model.[21] These effects can overwhelm the original purpose of the model.

In the philosophy of social science, this phenomenon has been characterised as the twin problem of 'performativity' (when a model helps make the world more like its vision of the world) and 'counter-performativity' (when the opposite occurs, and a model undermines itself by provoking activity which reduces its predictive power). The problem of performativity appears in the classic 'self-fulfilling prophecy,' where a prediction helps make itself true by affecting persons' behaviour. For example, if partisans of an automated future loudly predict that computational expertise is the most important and powerful way of ordering society, the very existence of such a prediction may help ensure it becomes true, by drawing particularly ambitious persons toward the study of computer science (and away from, say, law or the humanities). These looping effects are a mainstay of contemporary social studies of science.[22]

Donald Mackenzie and Alice Bamford have recently theorised the reverse problem, counter-performativity, which arises 'when the use of a 'model does not simply fail to produce a reality (e.g. market results) that is consistent with the model, but actively undermines the postulates of the model. The use of a model, in other words, can itself create phenomena at odds with the model.'[23] Such problems do not arise in

[20] M Hildebrandt, 'Code-driven Law: Freezing the Future and Scaling the Past' ('not everything that can be counted counts, and not everything that counts can be counted … [N]ot everything that matters can be controlled, and not everything that can be controlled matters.'). Hildebrandt has compellingly applied similar caution and wisdom in work relating law to computer science. See, eg, M Hildebrandt, *Law for Computer Scientists and Other Folk* (Oxford University Press, 2020).

[21] J Blakely, *We Built Reality: How Social Science Infiltrated Culture, Politics, and Power* (Oxford University Press, 2020).

[22] See, eg, J Isaac, 'Tangled Loops: Theory, History, and the Human Sciences in Modern America,' (2009) 6 *Modern Intellectual History* 327; J Isaac, *Working Knowledge Making the Human Sciences from Parsons to Kuhn* (Cambridge: Harvard University Press, 2009).

[23] D Mackenzie and A Bamford, 'Counterperformativity' (2018) 113 *New Left Review* 97.

the natural world: a plant does not grow differently in response to a botanist's theory of photosynthesis. However, in the social world, a hall of mirrors of perceptions and counterperceptions, moves and countermoves, endangers any effort to durably and effectively predict the behaviour of humans, much less control them.

Thus much of the legal theory included in this volume could be situated as part of a larger movement in social science and philosophy known as 'anti-naturalism.'[24] Naturalism is a tendency to apply methods pioneered in natural sciences to human affairs.[25] For example, some predictive policing algorithms were based on earthquake prediction algorithms; just as seismologists may predict the patterns of future aftershocks by analyzing past aftershocks, a police department might predict patterns of future crimes based on past crimes, and deploy officers accordingly. This approach is fundamentally misguided because the data on which the policing is based were themselves based on prior, often racist and classist, decisions on where to deploy police. There will be more *detected* crime (which is really what the model is based on, not crime itself, which (except in extreme cases like murders) is very difficult to know precisely), where there are more police.[26] Of course, the same may happen in seismology – if a given area is saturated with sensors, it may well register more earthquakes than less sensed zones. But seismology has largely dealt with this problem, whereas police departments are only beginning to. So the straightforward application of such natural science methods to the social world appears deeply unwise.

As John Morison argues, there are fundamental tensions between human values and the scientistic application of automated systems.[27] These tensions result from a deeper problem with overly ambitious programs of computerised law: the near-impossibility of collapsing the functions of prosecutor, judge, and police into a single moment of calculation. As Mireille Hildebrandt concisely explains:

> What code-driven law does is to fold enactment, interpretation and application into one stroke, collapsing the distance between legislator, executive and court. It has to foresee all potential scenarios and develop sub-rules that hopefully cover all future interactions – it must be highly dynamic and adaptive to address and confront what cannot easily be foreseen by way of unambiguous rules. If it fails to do so, code-driven law must be subjected to appeal and contestation, based on, for instance, core legal concepts such as 'unreasonableness,' 'unacceptable consequences,' 'good faith,' or 'the circumstances and the context of the case at hand.' This would imply reintegrating ambiguity, vagueness and multi-interpretability into the heart of the law.[28]

[24] M Bevir and J Blakely, *Interpretive Social Science: An Anti-Naturalist Approach* (Oxford University Press, 2018); J Blakely, *Alasdair MacIntyre, Charles Taylor, and the Demise of Naturalism: Reunifying Political Theory and Social Science* (University of Notre Dame Press, 2016).

[25] For a sustained argument that law is part of the humanities, see F Pasquale, 'The Substance of Poetic Procedure: Law and Humanity in the Work of Lawrence Joseph,' (2020) 32 *Law and Literature* 1.

[26] See also C O'Neil, *Weapons of Math Destruction: How Big Data Increases Inequality and Threatens Democracy* (Crown Books, 2016); B Harcourt, *Against Prediction: Profiling, Policing and Punishing in the Actuarial Age* (University of Chicago Press, 2006); R Richardson, J Schultz and K Crawford, 'Dirty Data, Bad Predictions: How Civil Rights Violations Impact Police Data, Predictive Policing Systems, and Justice', (2019) 94 *NYU L Rev Online* 192; A Ferguson, *The Rise of Big Data Policing: Surveillance, Race, and the Future of Law Enforcement* (2018).

[27] J Morison, 'Towards a Democratic Singularity? Algorithmic Governmentality, The Eradication of Politics – And the Possibility of Resistance', in this volume.

[28] Hildebrandt, 'Code-driven Law: Freezing the Future and Scaling the Past,' 71.

The necessity of this iterative, anticipatory process is another reminder of why the model of natural science, seeking eternal laws of nature, is inappropriate in social and legal sciences.

Nevertheless, naturalism is still popular, often billed as a 'tough-minded' refusal to countenance anything 'special' (such as free will, or a soul) in human beings.[29] As Mark Bevir and Jason Blakely have explained:

> Naturalists have attempted to revolutionise the social sciences by making them look more like the natural sciences in countless ways. These include searching for ahistorical causal laws; eliminating values and political engagement from the study of human behaviour; removing or demoting the role of meanings and purposes in favor of synchronic formalism and quantification; and treating social reality as reducible to brute, verifiable facts in need of minimal interpretation.[30]

Big data-driven visions of computable law are all too often rooted in a naturalistic vision of both social science and policy. They take on a behaviouristic cast, downplaying the role of interpretation and the intersubjective negotiation of meaning, in favor of objectification.[31] This is most obvious in robotic policing, which would enable humans to be dispassionately watched, corralled, and controlled in the manner of cattle or bales of hale.[32] But it is just as great a threat in the advance of surveillance, many forms of personalised law, and all too much AI. Each of these projects may accelerate legal effects by eliminating the judgment and dispersing the personal responsibility that makes these effects legitimate.

Some of competition law's current infirmities give a sense of the dangers inherent in projecting mathematical methods of commensuration onto complex disputes.[33] In U.S. antitrust law, for example, experts are paid by litigants to predict the 'consumer welfare' generated by a given transaction, as geologists might measure the expected flow

[29] This is a troubling popularity, because, as Joseph Vining observes, consciousness and self-consciousness 'confound all objectifying, systematizing, historicizing, all the science of what simply is. To self-consciousness add meaning and with it caring, the dynamic of purpose and desire. Then, from self-consciousness and meaning comes the person, which combinatorial thinking cannot handle, nor the units of calculation represent … So law stands in the way of science; law, and person and sense of self, are mutually sustaining and interpenetrating. So law stands in the way of self-destruction, and the person stands in the way of destruction, for the loss of self and the loss of law proceed together, but grasping the one stops departure of the other.' J Vining, *From Newton's Sleep* (Princeton University Press, 1995).

[30] *Interpretive Social Science: An Anti-Naturalist Approach* 2.

[31] Behaviourism reduces or eliminates emphasis on distinctively human and articulable thought, in favour of an analysis of stimuli and responses that could be applied across species, from salmon to pigeons to humans. Just as a biologist might seek to measure the biomass of fish in a lake, an economist might seek to measure the value of a town's economic output. Merely to draw such analogies is enough to give a sense of their dangers. Value is dependent on values, and there is deep pluralism and conflict about the latter, however much economics may try to flatten these disputes into commensurable exchange values. Any 'singular' prescription for the legal field's progress tends to trample on this diversity of visions, as Lyria Bennett Moses recognises in her prescient vision of multiple futures of complementary law and technology. L Bennett Moses, 'Not a Single Singularity', in this volume.

[32] The critique also applies to the excessive technologisation of policing, where at the limit case some law enforcers take on an exoskeleton of shields and armaments to make themselves as invulnerable to resistance as machines would be: R Balko, *Rise of the Warrior Cop: The Militarization of America's Police Forces* (Public Affairs, 2014). This militarisation undermines the *demos* by assimilating the citizen to the enemy: B Harcourt, *The Counterrevolution: How Our Government Went to War Against Its Own Citizens* (Basic Books, 2014).

[33] S Vaheesan, 'The Profound Nonsense of Consumer Welfare Antitrust,' (2019) 64 *Antitrust Bulletin* 479.

of water to be released by a given drilling pattern. But this alleged measurement of consumer welfare is a 'second-hand' naturalism, because all involved concede that a scientific measure of psychological utility from, say, more personalised advertisements after the Google-Doubleclick merger, is not plausible. Rather, the second-hand naturalists of the antitrust establishment merely mimic the *methods* of natural science, and not its epistemic power to actually measure well-defined and universally agreed physical parameters (such as the volume of water in a lake). Such a critique applies *a fortiori* to many applications of personalised law, to computational determinations of damages for pain and suffering, and to mathematical scoring of mental capacity (as Christopher Markou and Lily Hands suggest).[34]

Given these limits of computation, authors in this volume wisely counsel against assuming (or granting) agency to robots and AI in many critical situations. For example, Ryan Abbott and Alex Sarch argue that, in the context of crimes committed with the aid of AI and robotic systems, it is unwise for judges to reach for the 'radical tool of punishing AI.' Rather, 'A natural alternative ….involves modest expansions to criminal law, including, most importantly, new negligence crimes centered around the improper design, operation, and testing of AI applications as well as possible criminal penalties for designated parties who fail to discharge statutory duties.'[35] 'This is an eminently sensible approach that keeps legal attention where it should be: on the persons responsible for AI and robotics systems, rather than the systems themselves.

The Tragic Context of Dreams of Legal Automation

When legal (and intellectual) historians look back on the first decades of the twenty-first century Anglophone legal sphere, they might draw fruitful comparisons between the allure of rapid, comprehensive legal automation, and dreams of virtual reality. As the novels *Ready Player One* and *Feed* envision, the collapse of ecosystems and social support systems can make virtual realities all the more attractive than real ones. Why try to swim in a polluted river or ocean when there are beautiful streams on Twitch, or virtual islands in *Animal Crossing*? This is a strategy of disinvestment (in the real) and reinvestment (in the virtual) that easily becomes self-reinforcing. Investing more time and emotional energy in AI and robotics becomes ever more tempting as it enables an online life richer, or at least less demanding, than a climate change-ravaged 'real world.' Imagined communities seem all the lusher in comparison with toxic moonscapes of polluted beaches, flooded coasts, and fire-scorched parks. Chatbot 'conversation' is all the more stimulating and rewarding, the less time and inclination actual persons have to talk with one another – as is consultation with a 'chatbot legal advisor' all the more valuable when time is short, or lawyers are too expensive or rare.

As political and legal systems in the U.S. and U.K. are under pressure from increasingly irresponsible and malevolent actors, there is a growing desire to escape them

[34] C Markou and L Hands, '*Capacitas Ex Machina:* Are Computerized Assessments of Mental Capacity a 'Red Line' or Benchmark for AI?' in this volume. See also J Hari, *Lost Connections: Uncovering the Real Causes of Depression – and the Unexpected Solutions* (Bloomsbury, 2018) (exploring complexity of mental health diagnoses).

[35] R Abbott and A Sarch, 'Punishing Artificial Intelligence: Legal Fiction or Science Fiction,' in this volume, 204.

entirely, rather than to try to fight to make them better. One never has to worry about a biased judge misinterpreting a smart contract, the logic goes, if the contract itself is self-executing code set to adjust the moment a condition precedent is perceived by a connected oracle.[36] As philosopher of technology Nolen Gertz said of an online effort to 'virtualise' parts of Stanford University for a class kept home by the U.S.'s inexcusably incompetent coronavirus response, 'Such is the way of technology, leading us to re-create our world virtually rather than confront and change reality.'[37]

Partisans of legaltech may reframe this 'escapism' as a purification, or positive evolution, of a corrupted legal order. They may seek the identities of referee and scientist, set above and judging the social order, rather than taking sides on disputes within it. For example, conflict over worker classification (as either independent contractor or employee) is particularly fraught in an era of hyperinequality and platform capitalism. Some of those who fight for labour against capital are subject to extraordinary campaigns of harassment.[38] How much safer it would be to commit the question to a computer, performing natural language processing on hundreds of past cases to determine which combinations of words in current filings best match the filings of the successful litigants of the past. However tempting that scientistic vision of legal judgment as a 'word matching problem' may be, and however attractive an ideal of the lawyer as value-free scientist may become, such visions elide questions of social justice. They prioritise computational puzzles over social problems, matching and sorting over judgment and persuasion.

The demands of social justice are, no doubt, confusing and challenging in many scenarios. We may never make true 'progress' in interpreting and solving them as we do in, say, manipulating nature via chemistry and physics. But this supposed stagnation is in fact a static and solid foundation of inquiry, on which democracy can be built. The same objections about 'lack of progress' have hounded literary studies, but as Wayne C. Booth has wisely rejoined:

> In what sense can we be said to progress? We seem, instead, to move in circles, and – as Theodore Roethke says of his beloved – those circles move as well. 'The state of the art' – that will-o'-the-wisp that seems to have become our culture's most secure term of evaluation – is permanently unfixed in our arts: so much of our knowledge is tacit, so little of it definable, so little able are we to summarise even what we do know. But we gain one great glory from the irreducible complexities and fluidities in literary studies: any one of us, at any age and in any

[36] As Lyria Bennett Moses puts it in this volume, 'Provided the contract that delegates decision-making authority to an algorithm is enforceable (including all the jurisdiction-specific matters to be considered), then the delegation should be seen as equivalently legitimate to arbitration clauses' ('Not a Single Singularity', at 219–220). This is a very suggestive comparison. As many commentators in the U.S. have noted, arbitration clauses have become a way for large and powerful corporate interests to privatise parts of the legal system and run roughshod over less powerful claimants. See, eg, MJ Radin, *Boilerplate: The Fine Print, Vanishing Rights, and the Rule of Law* (Princeton University Press, 2014). There are parallels to privatisation as well. See, eg, JG Michaels, *Constitutional Coup: Privatization's Threat to the American Republic* (Harvard University Press, 2018).

[37] See twitter.com/ethicistforhire/status/1292075159311048704.

[38] A Mak, 'Why Is an Advocacy Group Funded by Uber and Lyft Hounding a Law Professor on Twitter?,' (Slate, 11 August 2020) slate.com/technology/2020/08/uber-lyft-prop-22-ab5-veena-dubal.html (discussing a campaign against Veena Dubal, who has written critical work on the employee/independent contractor distinction).

> state of ignorance, can practise the art, not just learn about it from other people's practice. Each of us can work at what is always the frontier of the art of narrative and its study.[39]

What makes law relatable is also what makes it frustrating: the sense that anyone can have an opinion as to how a case should come out, or a regulation drafted. Avoiding that indeterminacy would take a project of specialisation and bureaucratisation at least as tightly managed and technologically complex as Google's search engine, or Tencent's WeChat app.

The virtual realities of legal automation may put us on a path toward such determinacy. But they are dangerous because long 'residence' in them (or even aspiration to create them) can dull us to the value of the complexity and intractability of the real. They condition us to make our expression and action ever more 'machine readable' (or to expect litigants to do so in order to be recognised as having valid claims). As Jaron Lanier noted in *You Are Not a Gadget*,[40] phone trees and other computerised interfaces have trained many of us to stereotype or otherwise limit our expressions so we can be understood by crude mechanical interlocutors (or at least can influence these interlocutors). The quest for 'affective computing' and emotive robots is twinned with a shadow curriculum, to train us to make ourselves legible to machines.

The language and interactions now at the core of legal practice are rarely capable of being read by computers. Such ambiguities, as well as imperfect enforcement, are not flaws. What some deride as 'imprecision' in legal language, others will value as flexibility. As social theorist Mark Andrejevic has observed of automated media in other contexts:

> Automation embraces the logic of immediation (the invisibility or disappearance of the medium) that parallels the promise of virtual reality …. This is the promise of machine 'language' – which differs from human language precisely because it is non-representational. For the machine, there is no space between sign and referent: there is no 'lack' in a language that is complete unto itself. In this respect, machine language is 'psychotic'… [envisioning] the perfection of social life through its obliteration.[41]

Andrejevic identifies paradoxes at the core of human experience. Language is only language if it can be misunderstood – otherwise, it is just operational code, or neuro-linguistic programming. Care is only care if it can be abandoned. Otherwise, it is merely a programmed simulation of care, or robotised transformation of what was once known as care into a new form of body management or biomass optimisation. A promise is only a promise if it can be broken – otherwise, it is simply a behaviour mechanism.[42] The social can only be perfected by ceasing to be, dissolving into stereotyped interactions of mere individuals. Accelerate a social process slightly, and you may make it more efficient. Go too far, and you destroy it, as accelerationists gleefully

[39] W Booth, *The Rhetoric of Fiction*, 2nd edn (University of Chicago Press, 1983), 457, mentioning T Roethke, 'I Knew a Woman,' *The Collected Poems of Theodore Roethke* (Random House Inc, 1961).

[40] J Lanier, *You Are Not a Gadget* (Penguin, 2011).

[41] M Andrejevic, *Automated Media*, 72.

[42] J Derrida, 'A Certain Impossible Possibility of Saying the Event' (2007) 33(2) *Critical Inquiry* 441 ('If the promise was automatically kept, it would be a machine, a computer, a computation. For a promise not to be a mechanical computation or programming, it must have the capability of being betrayed. This possibility of betrayal must inhabit even the most innocent promise').

theorise when contemplating a 'post-human' order dominated by machines we cannot keep up with.[43]

There is no multiple-choice test or 5-point scale for legal judgment. Rather, in all but the simplest of transactions, traditional methods of document submission, argument, and appeal are constitutive of legal process. To say an activity is constitutive of a practice means that the practice (here, law) does not really exist without the activity: interaction between humans discussing, and setting, terms for fair cooperation, and methods for resolving disputes. As excited as some may be about a futuristic chatbot that could advocate for any litigant, or a robot jurist to pass judgment on all future filings, such computation is not a replacement for human beings. Encounters with the real communicative demands, gifts, and limitations of persons is the foundation of legal practice.

[43] For accounts and critiques of accelerationist thought, see B Noys, *Malign Velocities: Acceleration and Capitalism* (Zero Books, 2014); E Sandifer and J Graham, *Neoreaction a Basilisk: Essays on and Around the Alt-Right* (CreateSpace, 2018).

CONTENTS

Foreword v
About the Contributors xix

1. *From Rule of Law to Legal Singularity* 1
Simon Deakin and Christopher Markou

2. Ex Machina Lex: *Exploring the Limits of Legal Computability* 31
Christopher Markou and Simon Deakin

3. *Code-driven Law: Freezing the Future and Scaling the Past* 67
Mireille Hildebrandt

4. *Towards a Democratic Singularity? Algorithmic Governmentality, the Eradication of Politics – And the Possibility of Resistance* 85
John Morison

5. *Legal Singularity and the Reflexivity of Law* 107
Jennifer Cobbe

6. *Artificial Intelligence and Legal Singularity: The Thin End of the Wedge, the Thick End of the Wedge, and the Rule of Law* 135
Roger Brownsword

7. *Automated Systems and the Need for Change* 161
Sylvie Delacroix

8. *Punishing Artificial Intelligence: Legal Fiction or Science Fiction* 177
Ryan Abbott and Alex Sarch

9. *Not a Single Singularity* 205
Lyria Bennett Moses

10. *The Law of Contested Concepts? Reflections on Copyright Law and the Legal and Technological Singularities* 223
Dilan Thampapillai

11. Capacitas Ex Machina: *Are Computerised Assessments of Mental Capacity a 'Red Line' or Benchmark for AI?* 237
Christopher Markou and Lily Hands

Glossary and Further Reading 285
Index 311

ABOUT THE CONTRIBUTORS

Ryan Abbott is Professor of Law and Health Sciences at the University of Surrey and Adjunct Assistant Professor of Medicine at UCLA. He studied at the University of California, San Diego School of Medicine and Yale Law School before completing his doctorate at Surrey. He is author of *The Reasonable Robot: Artificial Intelligence and the Law*. He has written widely on issues associated with law and technology, health law, and intellectual property in legal, medical, and scientific books and journals. His research has been featured prominently in the media, including in the *New York Times*, *Wall Street Journal*, and the *Financial Times*.

Twitter: @DrRyanAbbot

Lyria Bennett Moses is Director of the Allens Hub for Technology, Law and Innovation and a Professor in the Faculty of Law at UNSW Sydney. Her research explores issues around the relationship between technology and law, including the types of legal issues that arise as technology changes, how these issues are addressed in Australia and other jurisdictions, and the problems of treating technology as an object of regulation. Recently, she has been working on legal issues associated with the use of artificial intelligence technologies. She is a member of the editorial boards for *Technology and Regulation*, *Law, Technology and Humans* and *Law in Context*.

Twitter: @lyria1

Roger Brownsword is Professor of Law at King's College London where he was founding Director of The Centre for Technology, Ethics, Law and Society (TELOS). He has published extensively on issues at the intersection of law and technology, and his books include *Rights, Regulation and the Technological Revolution*, *Law, Technology and Society* and *Law 3.0*. From 2004–2010, he was a member of the Nuffield Council on Bioethics. From 2011–2015, he chaired UK Biobank's Ethics and Governance Council, and is currently a member of the UK National Screening Committee. He has been a specialist adviser to parliamentary committees on stem cell research and on hybrid embryos.

Jennifer Cobbe is a Research Associate and Affiliated Lecturer in the Department of Computer Science and Technology (Computer Laboratory) at the University of Cambridge, where she is part of the Compliant and Accountable Systems research group. She is also on the Executive Committee of Cambridge's interdisciplinary Trust & Technology Initiative, which explores the dynamics of trust and distrust around internet technologies, societies, and power, and a member of the Microsoft Cloud Computing Research Centre. For her doctoral research at Queen's University, Belfast, she studied the use of machine learning in commercial and state internet surveillance.

Twitter: @jennifercobbe

Simon Deakin is Professor of Law and Director of the Centre for Business Research (CBR) at the University of Cambridge. He specialises in labour law, private law and company law, and contributes to the fields of empirical legal studies and the economics of law. His books include *The Law of the Labour Market: Industrialization, Employment and Legal Evolution* (with Frank Wilkinson) and *Hedge Fund Activism in Japan: The Limits of Shareholder Primacy* (with John Buchanan and Dominic Hee-Sang Chai). He is editor in chief of the *Industrial Law Journal* and an editor of the *Cambridge Journal of Economics*.

Twitter: @CambridgeCBR

Sylvie Delacroix is Professor of Law and Ethics at the University of Birmingham and a Fellow of the Alan Turing Institute. Her research focuses on the intersection between law and ethics, with a particular interest in machine ethics, agency and the role of habit within moral decisions. Her current research focuses on the design of computer systems meant for morally-loaded contexts. She is the author of *Habitual Ethics?*. She was one of three appointed commissioners on the Public Policy Commission on the use of algorithms in the justice system for the Law Society of England and Wales in 2019.

Twitter: @SylvieDelacroix

Lily Hands is a PhD candidate in the Faculty of Law at the University of Cambridge. She holds a Bachelor of Arts (Anthropology) and a Bachelor of Laws with Honours from the University of Western Australia. As an undergraduate she worked as a research assistant and clerk in the State Administrative Tribunal of Western Australia, which is responsible for determining applications concerning mental incapacity. She was a judge's associate and litigator before graduating with an LL.M. from Cambridge in 2018. Her doctoral research concerns the relationship between legal fragility, late modernity and artificial intelligence.

Twitter: @hands_lily

Christopher Markou is a Leverhulme Early Career Fellow in the Faculty of Law and a Research Associate at the Centre for Business Research (CBR), University of Cambridge. He studied religion and history and philosophy of science at Toronto and law at Manchester before completing a Ph.D. on law and artificial intelligence at Cambridge. He directs the 'AI, Law & Society' LLM at the Dickson Poon School of Law, King's College London. He is a Fellow of the Royal Society of the Arts and has spoken at The Cheltenham Science Festival, Cambridge Festival of Ideas, Cognition X, Ted Talks, and The Hay Festival.

Twitter: @cpmarkou

John Morison is Professor of Jurisprudence in the School of Law at Queen's University, Belfast (QUB). A member of the Royal Irish Academy, he has published widely in the areas of constitutional law and theory, legal theory and socio-legal approaches to the legal system. More recently he has become interested in the impact of new technology on government, democracy and wider society. He is one of the founders of a new LLM in Law and Technology in QUB and closely involved with an interdisciplinary doctoral training programme on Cybersecurity and Society.

Frank Pasquale is Professor of Law at Brooklyn Law School, and a visiting professor at Yale and Cardozo Law Schools. He studied at Harvard and Oxford before completing a JD at Yale. His research agenda focuses on challenges posed to information law by rapidly changing technology, and he has written extensively on health information technology law and policy. His books include *The Black Box Society*, which was reviewed in both *Science* and *Nature*, and *The New Law of Robotics*. He was appointed to the US National Committee on Vital and Health Statistics in 2019, and has chaired its Subcommittee on Privacy, Confidentiality, and Security.

Twitter: @FrankPasquale

Alexander Sarch is Professor of Legal Philosophy and Head of School at the University of Surrey School of Law. He received his JD from University of Michigan Law School and his PhD in Philosophy from University of Massachusetts, Amherst. He has published widely on criminal culpability, wilful ignorance, risk taking, well-being and blame, and his current work focuses on cognitive biases and motivated reasoning in corporate crime, as well as legal fictions and the regulation of artificial agents (from AI to corporations). He is the author of *Criminally Ignorant: Why the Law Pretends We Know What We Don't.*

Twitter: @should_b_workin

Dilan Thampapillai is a Senior Lecturer at the ANU College of Law. He received his PhD in Law at the University of Melbourne, an M.Com from the University of Sydney and a BA and LLB from Australian Nation University. He works on artificial intelligence, copyright and contract law. Prior to becoming an academic, he was a government lawyer with the Attorney-General's Department and the Australian Government Solicitor. He has advised on treaties, copyright law and commercial matters. Dilan has authored a textbook on contract law, *Contract Law: Cases and Commentary* and co-authored the textbook Australian *Commercial Law.*

Twitter: @TheDSingularity

1

From Rule of Law to Legal Singularity

SIMON DEAKIN AND CHRISTOPHER MARKOU*

Mathematics may be defined as the subject in which we never know what we are talking about, nor whether what we are saying is true.

Bertrand Russell
Recent Work on the Principles of Mathematics (1901)

In and of itself nothing really matters. What matters is that nothing is ever 'in and of itself'.

Chuck Klosterman
Sex, Drugs, and Cocoa Puffs (2003)

I. The Dawn of the All New Everything

Before most had a clue what the Fourth Industrial Revolution entailed,[1] the 2019 World Economic Forum meeting in Davos heralded the dawn of 'Society 5.0' in Japan.[2] Its goal: creating a 'human-centered society that balances economic advancement with the resolution of social problems by a system that highly integrates cyberspace and physical space'.[3] Using Artificial Intelligence (AI) and various digital technologies, 'Society 5.0' proposes to liberate people from:

> … everyday cumbersome work and tasks that they are not particularly good at, and through the creation of new value, enable the provision of only those products and services that are needed to the people that need them at the time they are needed, thereby optimizing the entire social and organizational system.

* Faculty of Law and Centre for Business Research, University of Cambridge. We gratefully acknowledge the support of the Leverhulme Trust and of the ESRC through its funding for the Digital Futures at Work Research Centre (grant ES/S012532/1) and the UKRI-JST Joint Call on Artificial Intelligence and Society (grant ES/T006/315/1).

[1] K Schwab, *The Fourth Industrial Revolution* (Crown Publishing, 2017).

[2] H Nakanishi, 'Modern Society Has Reached its Limits. Society 5.0 Will Liberate Us' (World Economic Forum, 9 January 2019), www.weforum.org/agenda/2019/01/modern-society-has-reached-its-limits-society-5-0-will-liberate-us.

[3] Cabinet Office, Government of Japan, 'Society 5.0', www8.cao.go.jp/cstp/english/society5_0/index.html.

The Japanese government accepts that realising this vision 'will not be without its difficulties' but the plan makes clear its intention 'to face them head-on with the aim of being the first in the world as a country facing challenging issues to present a model future society'.

Although Society 5.0 enjoys support from beyond Japan,[4] it bears a familiarly Japanese optimism about the possibilities of technological progress.[5] Yet Japan is not alone in seeing how the technologies of the Fourth Industrial Revolution could enable new systems of governance and 'algorithmic regulation'.[6] And this is particularly the case with regard to a specific type of computation, a family of statistical techniques known as Machine Learning (ML),[7] that is central to engineering futures of vast technological possibility that Society 5.0 exemplifies.

Generally, ML 'involves developing algorithms through statistical analysis of large datasets of historical examples'.[8] The iterative adjustment of mathematical parameters and retention of data enable an algorithm to automatically update (or 'learn') through repeated exposure to data and to optimise performance at a task. Initially, the techniques were applied to the identification of material objects, as in the case of facial recognition. Successive breakthroughs and performance leaps in ML, and the related techniques of Deep Learning (DL),[9] have encouraged belief in AI as a universal solvent for complex socio-technical problems. Tantalising increases of speed and efficiency in decision-making, and reductions in cost and bureaucratic bloat, makes the public-sector fertile ground for a number of AI-leveraging 'Techs'. These include LegalTech,[10] GovTech,[11] and RegTech[12] (short for Legal, Government and Regulatory technology respectively) which involve the development of 'smart' software applications for deployment in legal, political, and human decision-making contexts.

The Society 5.0 plan is not, however, an ex nihilo creation of the Japanese government. Rather, it articulates an emerging orthodoxy – one the 'Techs' are now capitalising on – that the core social systems of law, politics and the economy must adapt or die in the face of new modes of 'essentially digital governance'. This is often idealised as leading to a 'hypothetical new state' with 'a small intelligent core, informed by big data … leading

[4] C Dube and M Minevich, 'Mapping AI Solutions in Japan's Society 5.0' (2018) IPSoft/AI Pioneers White Paper, sifted.eu/articles/europe-can-learn-from-japans-society-5-0/.

[5] J West, 'Utopianism and National Competitiveness in Technology Rhetoric: The Case of Japan's Information Infrastructure' (1995) 12 *The Information Society* 3.

[6] K Yeung, 'Algorithmic Regulation: A Critical Interrogation' (2017) King's College London Dickson Poon School of Law Legal Studies Research Paper Series: Paper No. 2017-27.

[7] *cf* E Alpaydin, *Machine Learning* (MIT Press, 2016); G Marcus and E Davis, *Rebooting AI: Building Artificial Intelligence We Can Trust* (Pantheon, 2019) 42–48; D Spiegelhalter, *The Art of Statistics: Learning from Data* (Pelican Books, 2019) 143–87.

[8] Spiegelhalter, *The Art of Statistics*, 144.

[9] I Goodfellow, Y Bengio and A Courville, *Deep Learning* (MIT Press, 2016) 1–8.

[10] R Dale, 'Industry Watch: Law and Word Order: NLP in Legal Tech' (2019) 25 *Natural Language Engineering* 1.

[11] IBM, 'Digital Transformation: Reinventing the Business of Government' (2018), www.techwire.net/sponsored/digital-transformation-reinventing-the-business-of-government.html.

[12] DW Arner, JN Barberis and RP Buckley, 'FinTech, RegTech and the Reconceptualization of Financial Regulation' (2016) University of Hong Kong Faculty of Law Research Paper No. 2016/035, ssrn.com/abstract=2847806; G Roberts, 'Fintech Spawns Regtech to Automate Compliance with Regulations' (Bloomberg, 28 June 2016), www.bloomberg.com/professional/blog/fintech-spawns-regtech-automate-compliance-regulations.

government (at last) to a truly post-bureaucratic "Information State".[13] Some, such as Tim O'Reilly, argue that the 'old' state model is essentially a 'vending machine' where money goes in (tax) and public goods and services come out (roads, police, hospitals, schools).[14] It is time, he and others suggest, to 'rethink government with AI'[15] now that technological change has 'flattened'[16] the world, eroded state power, and provided models for uncoupling citizenship from territory.[17] Only by seeing government as a 'platform' will it be possible to harness critical network externalities and ensure what Jonathan Zittrain calls 'generativity' – the uncanny ability of open-ended platforms like Facebook or YouTube to create possibilities beyond those envisioned by their creators.[18] For O'Reilly, Big Tech 'succeeded by changing all the rules, not by playing within the existing system'.[19] Governments around the world, he suggests, must now follow their lead. Evidence from Japan, Singapore, Estonia and elsewhere, indicates that many are.[20]

A shift towards increasingly 'smart' and data-driven government is now underway and shows no sign of abating.[21] But the intoxicating 'new government smell' and techno-utopian visions of programmes such as Society 5.0 should not distract from critical questions about what exactly 'techno-regulation' means for human rights, dignity and the role of human decision-makers in elaborate socio-technical systems that promise to more or less run themselves.[22] Frank Pasquale observes that societal 'authority is increasingly expressed algorithmically',[23] while John Danaher warns against the 'threat of algocracy' – arguing it is 'difficult to accommodate the threat of algocracy, i.e. to find some way for humans to "stay on the loop" and meaningfully participate in the decision-making process, whilst retaining the benefits of the algocratic systems'.[24] Both are key observations for Society 5.0 where 'people, things, and systems … [are] all connected in cyberspace and optimal results obtained by AI exceeding the capabilities of humans [are] fed back to physical space'. However, the idea of AI 'exceeding' human capabilities is where Society 5.0's vision comes into sharper focus. Looking past the aspirational rhetoric of a 'human-centred society' it is ultimately a future where Artificial General

[13] P Dunleavy and H Margetts, 'Design Principles for Essentially Digital Governance', 111th Annual Meeting of the American Political Science Association (2015) 26, eprints.lse.ac.uk/64125/.

[14] T O'Reilly, 'Government as a Platform' (2010) 6 *Innovations* 13.

[15] H Margetts and C Dorobantu, 'Rethink Government with AI' (*Nature*, 9 April 2019), www.nature.com/articles/d41586-019-01099-5.

[16] G Hadfield, *Rules for a Flat World: Why Humans Invented Law and How to Reinvent It For a Complex Global Economy* (Oxford University Press, 2016).

[17] M Loughlin, 'The Erosion of Sovereignty' (2016) 45 *Netherlands Journal of Legal Philosophy* 2.

[18] J Zittrain, 'The Generative Internet' (2006) 119 *Harvard Law Review* 1974.

[19] O'Reilly, 'Government as a Platform', 38.

[20] M Goede, 'E-Estonia: The e-government Cases of Estonia, Singapore, and Curaçao' (2019) 8 *Archives of Business Research* 2.

[21] Obama White House, 'Digital Government: Building a 21st Century Platform to Better Serve the American People' (2012), obamawhitehouse.archives.gov/sites/default/files/omb/egov/digital-government/digital-government.html; UK Cabinet Office, 'Government Transformation Strategy 2017 to 2020' (9 February 2017), www.gov.uk/government/publications/government-transformation-strategy-2017-to-2020; Treasury Board of Canada Secretariat, 'Digital Operations Strategic Plan: 2018–2022' (27 December 2018), www.canada.ca/en/government/system/digital-government/digital-operations-strategic-plan-2018-2022.html.

[22] E Medina, 'Rethinking Algorithmic Regulation' (2015) 44 *Kybernetes* 6/7.

[23] F Pasquale, *The Black Box Society* (Harvard University Press, 2015) 8.

[24] J Danaher, 'The Threat of Algocracy: Reality, Resistance and Accommodation' (2016) 29(3) *Philosophy & Technology* 266.

Intelligence (AGI) is no longer hypothetical. The AGI hypothesis is that a machine can be designed to perform any 'general intelligent action'[25] that a human is capable of – an idea with longstanding institutional support in Japan.[26] But the invocation of AGI is what makes 'Society 5.0' hard to reconcile with what exactly it portends for the centrality and need of human decision-makers.[27]

II. From Rule of Law to Legal Singularity

While Society 5.0 perhaps exemplifies what Evgeny Morozov terms the folly of 'solutionism', it is not a uniquely Japanese phenomenon.[28] Indeed, such techno-solutionism has long been part of the 'dotcom neoliberalism' Richard Barbrook and Andy Cameron call 'The Californian Ideology'.[29] This ideology has, however, now crept into the rhetoric of LegalTech developers who have the data-intensive – and thus target-rich – environment of law in their sights. Buoyed by investment, promises of more efficient and cheaper everything, and claims of superior decision-making capabilities over human lawyers and judges, LegalTech is now being deputised to usher in a new era of 'smart' law built on AI and Big Data.[30] For some, such as physicist Max Tegmark, the use-case is clear:

> Since the legal process can be abstractly viewed as computation, inputting information about evidence and laws and outputting a decision, some scholars dream of fully automating it with robojudges: AI systems that tirelessly apply the same high legal standards to every judgment without succumbing to human errors such as bias, fatigue or lack of the latest knowledge.[31]

Others, such as Judge Richard Posner, are cautious but no less sympathetic to the idea:

> The judicial mentality would be of little interest if judges did nothing more than apply clear rules of law created by legislators, administrative agencies, the framers of constitutions, and other extrajudicial sources (including commercial custom) to facts that judges and juries determined without bias or preconceptions. Judges would be well on the road to being superseded by digitized artificial intelligence programs … I do not know why originalists and other legalists are not AI enthusiasts.[32]

Legal scholar Eugene Volokh even proposes a legal Turing test to determine whether an 'AI judge' outputs valid legal decisions. For Volokh, the persuasiveness of the output is what matters:

> If an entity performs medical diagnoses reliably enough, it's intelligent enough to be a good diagnostician, whether it is a human being or a computer. We might call it 'intelligent,' or we

[25] A Newell and HA Simon, 'Computer Science as Empirical Inquiry: Symbols and Search' (1976) 19(3) *Communications of the ACM* 116.

[26] EY Shapiro, 'The Fifth Generation Project – a Trip Report' (1983) 26(3) *Communications of the ACM* 637.

[27] DJ Chalmers, 'The Singularity: A Philosophical Analysis' (2010) 17 *Journal of Consciousness Studies* 7; N Bostrom, *Superintelligence: Paths, Dangers, and Strategies* (Oxford University Press, 2014).

[28] E Morozov, *To Save Everything, Click Here: Technology, Solutionism, and the Urge to Fix Problems That Don't Exist* (Penguin, 2014).

[29] R Barbrook and A Cameron, 'The Californian Ideology' (1996) 6 *Science as Culture* 1.

[30] MB Chalmers, 'SmartLaw 2.0: The New Future of Law' (*Lexology*, 22 August 2018), www.lexology.com/library/detail.aspx?g=c7605940-ef62-4c49-9451-3799083beb60.

[31] M Tegmark, *Life 3.0: Being Human in the Age of Artificial Intelligence* (Allen Lane, 2017) 105.

[32] RA Posner, *How Judges Think* (Harvard University Press, 2008) 5.

> might not. But, one way or the other, we should use it. Likewise, if an entity writes judicial opinions well enough … it's intelligent enough to be a good AI judge … If a system reliably yields opinions that we view as sound, we should accept it, without insisting on some predetermined structure for how the opinions are produced.[33]

The import of these views is that human judges are not just replaceable with AI, but that 'AI Judges' should be preferred on the assumption that they will not inherit the biases and limitations of human decision-making.[34] Nonetheless, other scholars, such Giovanni Sartor and Karl Branting, remain sceptical:

> No simple rule-chaining or pattern matching algorithm can accurately model judicial decision-making because the judiciary has the task of producing reasonable and acceptable solutions in exactly those cases in which the facts, the rules, or how they fit together are controversial.[35]

The boldest vision, however, comes from legal scholar and LegalTech entrepreneur Ben Alarie:

> Despite general uncertainty about the specifics of the path ahead for the law and legal institutions and what might be required of our machines to make important contributions to the law, over the course of this century we can be confident that technological development will lead to (1) a significantly greater quantification of observable phenomena in the world ('more data'); and (2) more accurate pattern recognition using new technologies and methods ('better inference'). In this contribution, I argue that the naysayers will continue to be correct until they are, inevitably, demonstrated empirically to be incorrect. The culmination of these trends will be what I shall term the 'legal singularity'.[36]

Although AGI is not seen as a necessary condition, Alarie's legal singularity is described as a point where AI has ushered in a legal system 'beyond the complete understanding of any person.'[37] Seemingly a response to the incompleteness and contingency of the law, the legal singularity is implicitly a proposal for eliminating juridical reasoning as a basis for dispute resolution and normative decision-making. While nothing is said about the role of law in Society 5.0, much less human lawyers and judges, Alarie's legal singularity can be considered a credible interpolation.

Even if the mathematical or symbolic logic used in AI research could, at least in theory, replicate the structure of juridical reasoning, this would not necessarily account for the political, economic, and socio-cultural factors that influence legal discourse and the evolution of the legal system.[38] Jürgen Habermas argues that these factors are important because:

> The positivist thesis of unified science, which assimilates all the sciences to a natural-scientific model, fails because of the intimate relationship between the social sciences and

[33] E Volokh, 'Chief Justice Robots' (2019) 68 *Duke Law Journal* 1135, 1138.

[34] EM Harley, 'Hindsight Bias in Legal Decision Making' (2007) 25 *Social Cognition: Special Issue: The Hindsight Bias* 1; KL Mosier and LJ Skitka, 'Human Decision Makers and Automated Decision Aids: Made for Each Other?' in R Parasuraman and M Mouloua (eds), *Automation and Human Performance: Theory and Applications* (CRC Press, 2009).

[35] G Sartor and LK Branting, 'Introduction: Judicial Applications of Artificial Intelligence' in G Sartor and LK Branting (eds), *Judicial Applications of Artificial Intelligence* (Springer, 1998) 1.

[36] Alarie, 'The Path of the Law: Towards Legal Singularity' (2016) 66 University of Toronto LJ 443, 446.

[37] Alarie, 'The Path of the Law', 455.

[38] P Stein, *Legal Evolution: The Story of an Idea* (Cambridge University Press, 2009); S Deakin, 'Legal Evolution: Integrating Economic and Systemic Approaches' (2011) 7 *Review of Law and Economics* 659.

> history, and the fact that they are based on a situation-specific understanding of meaning that can be explicated only hermeneutically … access to a symbolically prestructured reality cannot be gained by observation alone.[39]

But if mathematical logic cannot capture the 'situation-specific understanding' of legal reasoning and the complexity of the social world it exists in – at least to any extent congruent with how natural language categories cognise social referents and character of meaning – the hypothetical totalisation of 'AI judges' implied by the legal singularity would instantiate a particular view of law: one in which legal judgments are essentially deterministic or probabilistic outputs, produced on the basis of static or unambiguous legal rules, in a societal vacuum. This would deny, or see as irrelevant, competing conceptions of law, in particular the idea that law is a social institution, involving socially constructed activities, relationships, and norms not easily translated into numerical functions.[40] It would also turn a blind eye to the reality that legal decision making involves an exercise of power which is both material and, in Pierre Bourdieu's sense, 'symbolic'.[41] The recursive exercise of this power is only legitimate if the process through which each exercise of it adheres to prevailing procedural expectations that are highly contingent and socially constructed.

As HLA Hart observed, it is critical to 'preserve the sense that the certification of something as legally valid is not conclusive of the question of obedience, and that, however great the aura of majesty or authority which the official system may have, its demands must in the end be submitted to a moral scrutiny'.[42] In short, the legal system as a totality, and its outputs, including legal judgments, should be subject to checks and balances, or 'feedback' to use an algorithmic term, to determine the 'legal validity' of its internal operations and the process of outputting and enforcing them with a society. Thus one particular danger of 'AI judges' is that moral scrutiny would not be a meaningful prophylactic again challenging abuses of power.

This is particularly the case with so-called 'black box' algorithms which are inscrutable at a technical level, or where trade secret-protections prevent diagnostic scrutiny.[43] However, at another level of abstraction, objections to ADM and 'AI Judges' before they have been adopted and normalised are also a way of subjecting the legal system to the moral scrutiny Hart though to be critical. While this perspective does not deny that legal decision-making is some sense structurally algorithmic in nature – insofar as it involves following defined steps to reach a particular output, it is wrong, as Mireille Hildebrandt observes:

> … to mistake the mathematical simulation of legal judgment for legal judgment itself. Whereas machines may become very good in such simulation, judgment itself is predicated

[39] J Habermas, *On the Logic of the Social Sciences* (1967) cited in W Outhwaite, *Habermas: Key Contemporary Thinkers*, 2nd edn (Polity Press, 2009) 22.

[40] H Ross, *Law as a Social Institution* (Hart, 2001).

[41] P Bourdieu, *Language and Symbolic Power* (Harvard University Press, 1991).

[42] HLA Hart, *The Concept of Law*, 3rd edn (Oxford University Press, 2012) 210.

[43] *State of Wisconsin v Loomis* 881 N.W.2d 749 (Wis. 2016); *cf* 'State v. Loomis: Wisconsin Supreme Court Requires Warning Before Using Risk Assessments in Sentencing' (2017) 130 *Harvard Law Review* 1530, harvardlawreview.org/2017/03/state-v-loomis; H-W Liu, C Fu and Y-J Chen, 'Beyond *State v Loomis*: Artificial Intelligence, Government Algorithmization and Accountability' (2019) 27 *International Journal of Law and Information Technology* 2; R Yu and RS Alo, 'What's Inside the Black Box? AI Challenges for Lawyers and Researchers' (2019) 19 *Legal Information Management* 1.

on the contestability of any specific interpretation of legal certainty in the light of the integrity of the legal system – which goes way beyond a quasi-mathematical consistency.[44]

Neglecting the often subtle ways in which power and legitimacy are transferred and social order maintained within and across generations risks undermining one the principal institutions of a liberal-democratic order through the 'black boxing' of the legal system. As such the idea of 'AI judges' must be treated with utmost caution and scepticism, particularly if their outputs continue to defy both moral and technical scrutiny.[45]

III. The Origins of Digital Computation

Mathematical and statistical calculation have long been recognised as the best methods for inferring from the present what might happen in the future.[46] While AI and various statistical techniques are making prediction, to some degree at least, increasingly feasible, the notion of making law more predictable is intertwined with the development of computers more generally. But what are the basic properties of this computational universe created by digital computers?

At its most fundamental the computational universe is composed of bits, the basic unit of information theory and digital communications. The word 'bit' – a contraction of 'binary digit' – was coined by the American mathematician John Tukey.[47] Whether it is a universe of five kilobytes or zettabytes, there are only two types of bits that make a difference in it: differences in space and differences in time. A digital computer selects between these two forms of information by parsing their structure and sequence according to hard-coded rules. Bits that are embodied as structure vary in space, but do not vary over time, are the basis of computational memory. Whereas bits embodied in sequence, which vary over time and remain invariant over space, are the basis of what we call computer code.

The identification of a fundamental unit of communication, represented by a single distinction between binary alternatives (0/1, off/on) was the central idea of information theorist Claude Shannon's then-secret 'Mathematical Theory of Cryptography' in 1945,[48] which he expanded into the seminal 'Mathematical Theory of Communication'

[44] M Hildebrandt, 'Law as Computation in the Era of Artificial Legal Intelligence: Speaking Law to the Power of Statistics' (2017), dx.doi.org/10.2139/ssrn.2983045.

[45] M Annany and K Crawford, 'Seeing without Knowing: Limitations of the Transparency Ideal and its Application to Algorithmic Accountability' (2018) 20(3) *New Media & Society* 973; J Pearl and D MacKenzie, *The Book of Why: The New Science of Cause and Effect* (Penguin, 2018) 358.

[46] Spiegelhalter, *The Art of Statistics*, 143–87.

[47] CE Shannon, 'A Mathematical Theory of Communication' (1948) 47 *The Bell System Technical Journal* 3 ('The choice of a logarithmic base corresponds to the choice of a unit for measuring information. If the base 2 is used the resulting units may be called binary digits, or more briefly bits, a word suggested by J. W. Tukey').

[48] CE Shannon, 'A Mathematical Theory of Cryptography – Case 20878' (1945) MM-45-110-92, www.iacr.org/museum/shannon/shannon45.pdf.

in 1948.[49] The cybernetician Gregory Bateson would subsequently reformulate Shannon's theory into the open-ended phrase 'any difference that makes a difference'.[50] Within the digital universe of computation, however, the only difference that matters is that between zero and one.

The idea that two symbols were enough to encode all communications was not a new one. Rather, it was established by Francis Bacon (1561–1626). In his 1623 tract *De Augmentis Scientarium*, Bacon reasoned:

> The transposition of two Letters by five placeings will be sufficient for 32 Differences [and] by this Art a way is opened, whereby a man may expresse and signifie the intentions of his minde, at any distance of place, by objects ... capable of a twofold difference only. [sic]

He went on to provide examples of how this binary coding could be conveyed at the speed of paper, the speed of sound, or the speed of light.[51] Bacon's insight, that zero and one were sufficient for arithmetic, would be expanded upon by Thomas Hobbes (1588–1679), most notably in his *De Corpore* (1655) and *Computation (or 'Logique')* in 1656. It is in this earlier work that Hobbes first explains his idea that human reasoning is a form of computation. 'By reasoning' he states, 'I understand computation':

> And to compute is to collect the sum of many things added together at the same time, or to know the remainder when one thing has been taken from another. To reason therefore is the same as to add or to subtract.[52]

In the next section, Hobbes offers some examples of how addition works in human reasoning, concluding that adding ideas together allows for the formulation of more complex ones. Accordingly, in Hobbes' view, it is 'from the conceptions of a quadrilateral figure, an equilateral figure, and a rectangular figure the conception of a square is composed'.[53] Though he concedes this accounts for only a fraction of human reasoning, he goes on to describe propositions and syllogisms in terms of addition:

> A syllogism is nothing other than a collection of a sum which is made from two propositions (through a common term which is called a middle term) conjoined to one another; and thus a syllogism is an addition of three names, just as a proposition is of two.[54]

In this way, Hobbes can be seen as one of the progenitors of the Computational Theory of Mind (CTM). The central idea of CTM is that the human mind is a form of computer. As Fodor puts it: 'the immediately implementing mechanisms for intentional laws are computational ... [Computations] viewed in intension, are mappings from symbols under syntactic description to symbols under syntactic description'.[55] While there is a degree of concordance between Hobbes' work and subsequent theories of mind, the claim that Hobbes was 'prophetically launching Artificial Intelligence' seems a stretch.[56]

[49] Shannon, 'A Mathematical Theory of Communication'.

[50] GA Bateson, 'Re-examination of 'Bateson's Rule' (1971) 60 *Journal of Genetics* 230; *cf* MH Schroeder, 'The Difference that Makes a Difference for the Conceptualization of Information' (2017) 1 *Proceedings* 221.

[51] F Bacon, *De Augmentis Scientiarum* (1623) translated by G Wats as 'Of the Advancement and Proficiency of Learning, or the Partitions of Sciences' (1640) 265–66.

[52] T Hobbes, *De Corpore in Part I of De Corpore* AP Martinich (trans) (Abaris Books, 1981) 1.2.

[53] Hobbes, *De Corpore*, 1.3.

[54] Hobbes, *De Corpore*, 4.6.

[55] JA Fodor, *The Elm and the Expert* (MIT Press, 1994) 8.

[56] B Haugeland, *Artificial Intelligence; The Very Idea* (MIT Press, 1985) 23.

IV. The Leibniz Dream and Mathematisation of Law

It is much less a stretch, however, to attribute the conceptual organs of Artificial Intelligence to German polymath Gottfried Wilhelm Leibniz (1646–1716). Nonetheless, Hobbes' influence of Leibniz's thinking is made clear by Leibniz himself:

> Thomas Hobbes, everywhere a profound examiner of principles, rightly stated that everything done by our mind is a computation, by which is to be understood either the addition of a sum or the subtraction of a difference … So just as there are two primary signs of algebra and analytics, + and –, in the same way there are as it were two copulas, 'is' and 'is not'.[57]

Following Hobbes, and in advance of German mathematician David Hilbert,[58] Leibniz believed that it was possible to develop a consistent system of logic, language, and mathematics using an alphabet of unambiguous symbols that could be manipulated according to mechanical rules. In a 1675 letter to the secretary of the Royal Society and his middle-man for correspondence with Isaac Newton, Leibniz wrote that 'the time will come, and come soon, in which we shall have a knowledge of God and mind that is not less certain than that of figures and numbers, and in which the invention of machines will be no more difficult than the construction of problems in geometry'.[59] Foreshadowing what we now refer to as software, Leibniz saw a bi-directional connection between logic and mechanism. In a letter sent to Dutch mathematician Christiaan Huygens in 1679, Leibniz appended the observation that 'one could carry out the description of a machine, no matter how complicated, in characters which would be merely the letters of the alphabet, and so provide the mind with a method of knowing the machine and all its parts'.[60]

Dissatisfied with the laborious arithmetic enabled by the common decimal system, Leibniz declared '[i]t is unworthy of excellent men to lose hours like slaves in the labour of calculation which could safely be relegated to anyone else if machines were used'.[61] To alleviate the burden, Leibniz proposed to 'develop a generalized symbolic language, and an algebra to go with it, so that the truth of any proposition in any field of human inquiry could be determined by simple calculation'.[62] In his *Art of Discovery* (1685) he thus asserted:

> The only way to rectify our reasonings is to make them as tangible as those of the Mathematicians, so that we can find our error at a glance, and when there are disputes among persons, we can simply say: Let us calculate, without further ado, to see who is right.[63]

[57] GW Leibniz, 'Of the Art of Combination' in GHR Parkinson (ed), *Leibniz: Logical Papers* (Clarendon Press, 1966) 3.

[58] D Hilbert, 'Die Grundlegung der elementaren Zahlenlehre' 104 *Mathematische Annalen* 485; translated by W Ewald as 'The Grounding of Elementary Number Theory' in P Manscou (ed), *From Brouwer to Hilbert: The Debate on the Foundations of Mathematics in the 1920s* (Oxford University Press, 1998) 266–73.

[59] 'GW Leibniz to Henry Oldenburg, December 18, 1675' in HW Turnbull (ed), *The Correspondence of Isaac Newton, Vol. 1* (Cambridge University Press, 1959) 401.

[60] 'GW Leibniz – Supplement to a letter to Christiaan Huygens, September 8, 1679' in LE Loemeker (ed), *Philosophical Papers and Letters, Vol. 1* (University of Chicago Press, 1956) 384–85.

[61] G Leibniz quoted in M Nadin, 'Predictive and Anticipatory Computing' in PA Laplante (ed), *Encyclopaedia of Computer Science and Technology: Volume 2* (CRC Press, 2017).

[62] FC Kreiling, 'Leibniz' (1968) 18(5) *Scientific American* 95.

[63] GW Leibniz quoted in M Gelford and Y Kahl, *Knowledge Representation, Reasoning, and the Design of Intelligent Agents* (Cambridge University Press, 2014) 7.

Using his logical calculus, Leibniz embarked on a major project to develop his vision of a 'universal symbolistic in which all truths of reason would be reduced to a kind of calculus'. Central to his project was the idea that: 'a kind of alphabet of human thoughts can be worked out and that everything can be discovered and judged by a comparison of the letters of this alphabet and an analysis of the words made from them'.[64] Leibniz worked out a system of universal coding in which primary concepts could be represented by prime numbers, thus providing a comprehensive framework for mapping numbers to ideas. Having done the groundwork himself, Leibniz thought a complete networking of numbers to ideas was not only feasible, but that 'a few selected men could finish the matter in five years … It would take them only two, however, to work out, by an infallible calculus, the doctrines most useful for life, that is, those of morality and metaphysics'. This was so that: 'the human race will have a new kind of instrument which will increase the power of the mind much more than optical lenses strengthen the eyes and which will be as far superior to microscope or telescopes as reason is superior to sight'.[65]

Although Leibniz believed binary coding to be the basis for a universal language,[66] he credited its creation to the Chinese. Specifically, it was in the hexagrams of the Yi-Jing – an ancient Chinese book of philosophy compiled in the latter part of the ninth century BCE – that Leibniz saw elements of 'a Binary Arithmetic … which I have rediscovered some thousands of years later'. Although Leibniz's ontology differed between writings,[67] some suggest his Dream was premised on a misunderstanding of the Yi-Jing's ontological reality.[68] In short, the Yi-jing treats reality as not entirely real, but more akin to a dream or illusion.[69] The 'dream' of reality humans experience is said to emerge from the binary oppositions of Yin and Yang as they play out in their infinite combinations. Smith notes that '[t]he binary structure of the *Yijing* entranced and inspired Leibniz [although] the number symbolism of the *Yijing* remained numerological and … never truly mathematical'.[70] As a consequence, Leibniz's system integrated a dualist view of reality in which everything could be represented and understood with 1s and 0s, or: Yin and Yang. While binary code was later refined by English mathematician George Boole, from whom 'Boolean logic' derives,[71] modern computation inherited Leibniz's dualist ontology.[72]

[64] GW Leibniz, 'On the General Characteristic' in LE Loemker (ed), *GW Leibniz: Philosophical Papers and Letters* (Kluwer, 1989) 224.

[65] GW Leibniz, 'ca. 1679' in LE Loemker (ed), *GW Leibniz: Philosophical Papers and Letters* (Kluwer, 1989) 344.

[66] G Leibniz, 'Explanation of Binary Arithmetic', www.leibniz-translations.com/binary.htm.

[67] T Tho, 'What is Leibniz's Ontology? Rethinking the Role of Hylomorphism in Leibniz's Metaphysical Development' (2015) 4(1) *Journal of Early Modern Studies* 79; J Whipple, 'Leibniz on Fundamental Ontology: Idealism and Pedagogical Exoteric Writing' (2017) 4(11) *Ergo* 311.

[68] ES Nelson, 'The *Yijing* and Philosophy: From Leibniz to Derrida' (2011) 38(3) *Journal of Chinese Philosophy* 377.

[69] C-Y Cheng, 'The Yi-Jing and Yin-Yang Way of Thinking' in B Mou (ed), *The Routledge History of Chinese Philosophy* (Routledge, 2008).

[70] RJ Smith, *Fortune-Tellers and Philosophers: Divination in Traditional Chinese Society* (Westview Press, 1991) 205.

[71] G Boole, *The Mathematical Analysis of Logic* (MacMillan, Barclay, & MacMillan, 1847).

[72] J Teixeira, 'Computational Complexity and Philosophical Dualism' (1998), www.bu.edu/wcp/Papers/Cogn/CognTeix.htm; D King, 'Cartesian Dualism, and the Universe as Turing Machine' (2003) 47(2) *Philosophy Today* 379.

Leibniz's surviving notes show his iterative development of simple algorithms for selecting between decimal and binary notation, as well as those for performing basic arithmetic function using strings of 1s and 0s. 'In binary arithmetic' he observed, 'there are only two signs, 0 and 1, with which we can write all numbers'.[73] With this system and a mechanical calculating machine he termed the 'Stepped Reckoner', Leibniz became convinced that formalising human thought with logico-mathematical calculations was not only possible, but would introduce mathematical rigour and precision into all the human sciences. This idea, commonly referred to as the Leibniz Dream (*characteristica universalis*), was an important precursor to the development of computer science and foreshadowed subsequent research into cognitive enhancement and extension.[74]

But his misunderstanding also influenced Leibniz's thinking about something of particular interest to him: law.[75] For Leibniz, law exemplified how society should resolve 'the most serious deliberations on life and health, on the state, on war and peace, on the moderation of conscience, [and] on care of eternity'.[76] He praised law as the most advanced instrument of human rationality, particularly in the 'balance' of reasons or 'logometric scales' judges used to evaluate the relative weight of 'arguments of discussants, opinions of authors, [and] voices of advisors'.[77] For law to be as precise as mathematics, a just legal rule was one that merged abstract legal axioms, such as the principle that harm should not be done to others, with empirical insights from the natural sciences. In his *Doctrina Conditionum* (1669) he tested this hypothesis with Roman law.[78] While his ambitions were certainly grand, Leibniz did not look to impose a monolithic 'scientific model' on law. Rather, he believed that the axiomatic method would help make it more precise, and ideally, predictable.

It was in 1679, however, that these ideas began to coalesce in Leibniz's imagination into what we might now call a digital computer in which binary numbers could be represented by marbles and governed by mechanical gates. 'This [binary] calculus' Leibniz wrote:

> … could be implemented by a machine (without wheels) in the following manner, easily to be sure and without effort. A container shall be provided with holes in such a way that they can be opened and closed. They are to be open at those places that correspond to a 1 and remain closed at those that correspond to a 0. Through the opened gates small cubes or marbles are to fall into tracks, through the others nothing. It [the gate array] is to be shifted from column to column as required.[79]

[73] GW Leibniz, 'Discourse on the Natural Theology of the Chinese' translated from 'Lettre sur la philosophie chinoise à Nicolas de Remond' H Rosemont and DJ Crook (trans and eds), *Monographs of the Society for Asian and Comparative Philosophy, No. 4* (University of Hawaii Press, 1977) 158.

[74] S Toulmin, 'The Dream of an Exact Language' in B Göranzon and M Florin (eds), *Dialogue and Technology: Art and Language* (Springer, 1991); *cf* N Bostrom and A Sandberg, 'Cognitive Enhancement: Methods, Ethics, Regulatory Challenges' (2009) 5(3) *Science and Engineering* 311; M Dresler, A Sandberg, C Bublitz, et al., 'Hacking the Brain: Dimensions of Cognitive Enhancement' (2019) 10(3) *ACS Chemical Neuroscience* 1137.

[75] *cf* M Armgardt, 'Leibniz as Legal Scholar' (2014) 20 *Fundamina* 1.

[76] GW Leibniz quoted in 'Introductory Essay' in M Dascal (ed), *GW Leibniz: The Art of Controversies* (Springer, 2006) 38.

[77] GW Leibniz quoted in *GW Leibniz: The Art of Controversies* 36.

[78] P Boucher, 'Leibniz: What Kind of Legal Rationalism?' in M Dascal (ed), *Leibniz: What Kind of Rationalist?* (Springer, 2008).

[79] GW Leibniz, 'De Progressione Dyadica – Pars I (15 March 1679)' in E Hochstetter and H-J Greve (eds), *Herrn von Leibniz' Rechnung mit Null und Einz* (Siemens Aktiengesellschaft, 1966).

While he did not term it as such, Leibniz had basically invented the shift register some 270 years before it was implemented in the Colossus Mark 2 – a British code breaking computer developed in 1944 – and used by the Allies in the Normandy invasions.[80] In the shift registers at the heart of all modern computers, voltage gradients and electron pulses have replaced the marbles and gravity of his original plans, but for all practical purposes modern computers still function largely identically to how Leibniz envisioned them in 1679.

V. *Calculemus!* Leibniz's Influence on Law

Posthumous English translations of Leibniz's work brought it to the attention of the English-speaking world. It particularly appealed to legal scholars, such as the formalist Christopher Columbus Langdell, who presented an axiomatic conception of law in his *Cases on Contracts* (1871).[81] Echoing many of Leibniz's claims, Langdell argued that 'Law, considered as a science, consisted of certain principles or doctrines. To have such mastery of these as to be able to apply them with constant facility and certainty to the ever-tangled skein of human affairs, is what constitutes a true lawyer ….'[82] They differed, however, on the source of legal axioms. Whereas Leibniz considered a combination of existing domestic and natural law as their source, Langdell believed that legal axioms – or to use his term: 'principles' – were empirically derived as they were in the natural sciences. According to Langdell the data for an empirical 'legal science' was contained in the cases decided and reported by courts.[83] This case 'data', he believed, would allow for predicting the outcomes of contract disputes – his primary focus.[84]

Despite vehement disagreement with both Leibniz and Langdell, American jurist Oliver Wendell Holmes was an avid admirer of the German polymath. As a lecturer at Harvard Law School, where Langdell was contemporaneously dean, Holmes spent his early career rejecting Leibnizian-Langdellian axiomatics, and instigating a turn in jurisprudence wary of any formalism or 'logic' in law. In *The Common Law* (1881) Holmes famously proclaimed that 'The life of the law has not been logic: it has been experience.'[85] In his subsequent article 'The Path of the Law' (1897), shrewdly published just after Langdell resigned his deanship, Holmes denounced legal axiomatics as 'a fallacy which I think it important to expose'.[86]

It was in this later article that Holmes articulated his 'Prediction Theory of Law'[87] central to which was the rhetorical 'bad man', a person devoid of ethics or lofty notions

[80] J Copeland and others (eds), *Colossus: The Secrets of Bletchley Park's Codebreaking Computers* (Oxford University Press, 2006) 74–77, 100.

[81] CP Wells, 'Langdell and the Invention of Legal Doctrine' (2010) 28(3) *Buffalo Law Review* 551.

[82] CC Langdell, *Cases on Contracts* (Little Brown & Co., 1871) vi.

[83] MH Hoeflich, 'Law & Geometry: Legal Science from Leibniz to Langdell' (1986) 30(2) *The American Journal of Legal History*.

[84] CP Wells, 'Langdell and the Invention of Legal Doctrine' 599–605.

[85] OW Holmes, *The Common Law* (Little Brown & Co., 1881) 1.

[86] OW Holmes, 'The Path of the Law' (1897) 110(5) *Harvard Law Review* 997.

[87] MH Fisch, 'Justice Holmes, the Prediction Theory of Law, and Pragmatism' (1942) 39(4) *The Journal of Philosophy* 85; RA Posner, 'The Path Away from the Law' (1996) 110 *Harvard Law Review* 1039.

about the jurisprudential role of courts and concerned only with avoiding payment of damages and staying out of jail. Holmes' enduring contribution to jurisprudence was rejecting the deterministic and nonpolitical conceptions of law advanced by legal formalists like Langdell who regarded law a consistent set of rules and norms from which a 'right' answer could always be derived. As Scott Brewer observes, '... the theorist who aspires to high-density axiomatization, as did Leibniz and Langdell, would seem to have to try and steer between the Scylla of generating axioms that are so open-textured and often so vague that one could never settle on the final set of axioms, but would forever have to be revising them'.[88]

Holmes' rejection of formalism provided the ideological foundation for the American Legal Realism school's critique of legal axiomatics.[89] Roscoe Pound, for instance, derided 'mechanical jurisprudence'[90] as the lazy practice of judges to formulaically apply precedents to cases with reckless disregard for consequences. For Pound, the logic of precedents could not solve jurisprudential problems; he warned that axiomatics risked ossifying socially constructed and politically influenced legal concepts into self-evident truths. It was precisely the desire to avoid such ossification – and not let the 'bad man' win – that led Holmes and the realists to conceive law as inherently indeterminate and defying understanding as a coherent or complete system of rules and principles from which there was always a 'right' answer.[91] In 'Logical Method and Law' (1924), John Dewey expanded Holmes' argument that 'general propositions do not decide concrete cases' – a position known as 'rule skepticism'. For Dewey, no legal argument could be validly represented as a deductive inference, and law never accurately represented with deductive axiomatic systems, arguing:

> There is of course every reason why rules of law should be as regular and as definite as possible. But the amount and kind of antecedent assurance which is actually attainable is a matter of fact, not of form. It is large wherever social conditions are pretty uniform, and when industry, commerce, transportation, etc., move in the channels of old customs. It is much less wherever invention is active and when new devices in business and communication bring about new forms of human relationship.[92]

Generally, the realists regarded judicial opinions and judges with scepticism and condescension. Because written rules (statutes, cases) did not determine what the law was, the purpose of juridical reasoning was not explaining how the court arrived at a decision and providing guidance to judges and litigants encountering similar situations in the future. The real purpose was to 'rationalise' and 'legitimise' decisions and conceal from the public and other judges the real, and often unsavoury, justifications. As such,

[88] S Brewer, 'Law, Logic, and Leibniz: A Contemporary Perspective' in A Artosi, B Pieri and G Sartor (eds), *Leibniz: Logico-Philosophical Puzzles in the Law* (Springer, 2013).

[89] SR Ratner, 'Legal Realism School' in R Wolfrum (ed), *Max Planck Encyclopedia of Public International Law Online* (Oxford University Press, 2007).

[90] R Pound, 'Mechanical Jurisprudence' (1908) 8 *Columbia Law Review* 605.

[91] C Gray, *The Nature and Sources of Law* (Columbia University Press, 1909); R Pound, 'Justice According to Law' (1914) 1(3) *The Midwest Quarterly* 223; KN Llewellyn, *The Bramble Bush: The Classic Lectures on the Law and Law School* (Oxford University Press, [1930] 2008).

[92] J Dewey, 'Logical Method and Law' (1924) 10(1) *Cornell Law Review* 25.

no deductive axiomatic method could account for these influences, and the gradual incorporation of social-scientific insights into legal scholarship helped substantiate the realists' scepticism.

VI. *Characteristica Universalis Lex*

But this was far from the last word on the idea of law as axiom. In the twentieth century the Leibniz Dream would inspire Alfred Tarski[93] and others, such as AI pioneer John McCarthy, to investigate whether the axiomatic method could be applied beyond mathematics. Throughout the 1950s McCarthy developed a methodology within the then emerging field of Artificial Intelligence (AI) known as the logic-based approach.[94] McCarthy's idea was to have a computer program capture and store large amounts of 'human knowledge' about a specific domain (such as law or medicine) and use mathematical logic to represent it and logical inference to determine the 'best' actions to achieve a desired 'output' from a knowledge-base.[95] Since McCarthy formalised the logic-based approach, AI research has remained oriented by the long term goal of AGI or 'Strong AI'.[96] In contrast, 'Weak AI' involves machines performing specific problem-solving or 'reasoning' tasks in 'narrow' domains not requiring wider facets of human intelligence.

An initially promising application of logical-AI was the so-called legal expert systems (LES) movement which was at its height in the 1970s and 1980s. Because similar expert systems worked in more 'complicated' domains like medicine, it was widely assumed that they would work in the comparatively 'easy' domain of law.[97] A simple idea underpinned LES: '... that one can take rules of law, mould them into a computer-based formal system, and advice will come out the other end'.[98] For instance, the computer scientist L Thorne McCarty confidently proclaimed:

> [Law] seems to be an ideal candidate for an artificial intelligence approach: the 'facts' would be represented in a lower level semantic network, perhaps; the 'law' would be represented in a higher level semantic description; and the process of legal analysis would be represented in a pattern-matching routine.[99]

According to enthusiastic developers at the time, all that was needed to build a useful LES was a way to: (1) translate legislation or 'rules' into a machine readable format; (2) write software that could interpret them, and; (3) gather some legal experts to

[93] AB Feferman and S Feferman, *Alfred Tarski: Life and Logic* (Cambridge University Press, 2004).

[94] J McCarthy, 'Recursive Functions of Symbolic Expressions and Their Computation by Machine, Part I' (1960), www-formal.stanford.edu/jmc/recursive.pdf; *cf* SL Andersen, 'John McCarthy: Father of AI' (2002) 17(5) *IEEE Intelligent Systems*.

[95] J McCarthy, 'Philosophical and Scientific Presuppositions of Logical AI' in HJ Levesque and F Pirri (eds), *Logical Foundations for Cognitive Agents* (Springer, 1999).

[96] P Wang and B Goertzel (eds), *Theoretical Foundations of Artificial General Intelligence* (Atlantis Press, 2012); L Muehlhauser, 'What is AGI' (*Machine Intelligence Research Institute*, 2013), intelligence.org/2013/08/11/what-is-agi/.

[97] R Susskind, *Transforming the Law* (Oxford University Press, 2000) 162–206.

[98] P Leith, 'The Rise and Fall of the Legal Expert System' (2010) 1(1) *European Journal of Law and Technology* 1.

[99] LT McCarty, 'Some Requirements for a Computer-based Legal Consultant' quoted in RN Moles, *Definition and Rule in Legal Theory: A Reassessment of HLA Hart and the Positivist Tradition* (Basil Blackwell, 1987) 269.

explicate the legal rules so they could then be imputed by a computer programmer. LES developers thus understood their task as formalising what Hart had termed the 'open texture'[100] of legal rules into mathematical conditionals upon which, as Leibniz aspired to centuries earlier, there could be no disagreement.[101] By attempting this, they sought to reanimate the Leibniz Dream using computation to achieve the 'mechanical jurisprudence' Pound and the legal realists bemoaned as radically simplifying the complex and indeterminate nature of law and legal reasoning.

Despite some middling successes, LES proved both overly ambitious and myopic in the attempt to take Occam's Razor to jurisprudence and the sociological context of law to extract a purified mathematical 'essence'. While the reasons for its failure were several and complex, the collapse of the LES project was primarily due to technical limitations and a gross underestimation of the complexity in applying axiomatic methods to law.[102] However, the seeds of failure were the a priori denial of law's social context, purpose, and anthropological role being relevant to its interpretation. Although LES operated in the 'narrow' domain of law, the nature of legal reasoning, deduction and inference made it clear that they would require wider facets of human intelligence. Because humans learn to perform tasks in ways that allow acquired knowledge to become both tacit and implicit,[103] LES engineers could not use axiomatics to extract and represent legal knowledge and intuition in a workable way.[104]

By the end of the twentieth century, a shift away from the logic-AI approach to the use of connectionist models changed things again.[105] Their success in real-world tasks, such as the defeat of chess grandmaster Gary Kasparov by IBM's Deep Blue, renewed interest in AGI research.[106] In the early twenty-first century the sensationalised victories of IBM's Watson at Jeopardy and DeepMind's AlphaGo at the board game Go seemed to make the goal of 'solving intelligence' both technically feasible and commercially viable.[107] Unlike the logical-AI approach, these newer systems, inspired by neuroscientific models of the brain, did not try to exhaustively formalise human expertise and knowledge to generate axioms. Instead, using both ML and DL techniques, they used vast numbers of historical examples (training data) that allowed them to iteratively update their mathematical parameters and optimise performance at directed tasks. While their results have been undoubtedly impressive, David Spiegelhalter reminds us:

> … that these are technological systems that use past data to answer immediate questions, rather than scientific systems that seek to understand how the world works: they are to be

[100] Hart, *The Concept of Law* 124–54.

[101] WG Popp and B Schlink, 'Judith, A Computer Program to Advise Lawyers in Reasoning a Case' (1974) 15(303) *Jurimetrics Journal* 303.

[102] MZ Bell, 'Why Expert Systems Fail' (1985) 36(7) *Journal of the Operational Research Society* 613; P Leith, 'The Rise and Fall of the Legal Expert System'.

[103] M Polanyi, *The Tacit Dimension*, rev edn (University of Chicago Press, 2009) 3–25.

[104] P Leith, 'Fundamental Errors in Legal Logic Programming' (1986) 29(6) *The Computer Journal* 545.

[105] SI Gallant, 'Connectionist Expert Systems' (1988) 32(2) *Communications of the ACM* 137.

[106] Y Seirawan, HA Simon and T Munakata, 'The Implications of Kasparov vs. Deep Blue' (1997) 40(8) *Communications of the ACM* 21; M Newborn, 'Deep Blue's contribution to AI' (2000) 28(1–4) *Annals of Mathematics and Artificial Intelligence* 27.

[107] D Hassabis D Kumaran, C Summerfield and M Botvinick, 'Neuroscience-inspired Artificial Intelligence' (2017) 95(2) *Cell* 245; JE Laird, C Lebiere and PS Rosenbloom, 'A Standard Model of the Mind: Toward a Common Computational Framework Across Artificial Intelligence, Cognitive Science, Neuroscience, and Robotics' (2017) 38(4) *AI Magazine* 13.

> judged solely on how well they carry out the limited task at hand, and, although, the form of the learned algorithms may provide some insights, they are not expected to have imagination or have super-human skills in everyday life.[108]

Even with this caveat, we can safely predict that interest in the application of ML to law will continue to grow. This is not just because it is a new, if still largely untried, technology. As our brief historical review has shown, the idea of a functionally complete legal system, one capable of being described using the formal logic and axiomatic reasoning associated with mathematical models, is not new. Despite serial refutations and reversals, it has a deep hold on the legal imagination. Thus today's law-AI debate, in common with earlier iterations between law and technology, poses in a new form a fundamental question about the nature of law as a mode of governance: is law computable? This is the issue which, in varying ways, the contributions to this collection set out to address.

VII. Computationalism and the Mathematisation of Reality

With growing acceptance that biological and artificial intelligence differ only in their substrates,[109] some suggest that AI and data science will someday enable system-level modelling of social reality and the complete prediction of human behaviours.[110] While this is the long term goal, the more immediate goal of using AI to replicate the cognitive domain of lawyers and judges has spurred confidence that a new generation of AI-leveraging LegalTech and ADM systems will succeed where their logic-based forebears could not: replicating legal reasoning, deduction, and inference. With them comes a familiar refrain: LegalTech will improve access to justice, lower costs, and improve the efficiency of legal administration among many other practical benefits.[111] While the functional capabilities of this new generation have undoubtedly improved, the LegalTech enterprise still rests on the Leibnizian-Langdellian assumption that there is a purified essence to law and legal reasoning there to be mathematised. This leads physicist Max Tegmark to wonder:

> … why has our physical world revealed such extreme mathematical regularity that astronomy superhero Galileo Galilei proclaimed nature to be 'a book written in the language of mathematics,' and Nobel laureate Eugene Wigner stressed the 'unreasonable effectiveness of mathematics in the physical sciences' as a mystery demanding an explanation?[112]

[108] Spiegelhalter, *The Art of Statistics* 145.

[109] PS Churchland, 'Can Neurobiology Teach Us Anything About Self Consciousness?' (1994) 42(3) *Proceedings and Addresses of the American Philosophical Association* 23; M Allen and KJ Friston, 'From Cognitivism to Autopoiesis: Towards a Computational Framework for the Embodied Mind' (2018) 195(6) *Synthese* 2459; *cf* M Velmans, 'Is Human Information Processing Conscious?' (1991) 14(4) *Behavioral and Brain Sciences* 651.

[110] M Morrison, Reconstructing Reality: Models, Mathematics, and Simulations (Oxford University Press, 2015); Tegmark, *Our Mathematical Universe.*

[111] Susskind, *Transforming the Law* 237–43; R Susskind, *Tomorrow's Lawyers*, 2nd edn (Oxford University Press, 2017) 93–121.

[112] Tegmark, *Our Mathematical Universe* 6.

Ultimately it is belief in the 'unreasonable effectiveness of mathematics' that drives much of the current AI enterprise, including its use in the legal realm. For instance, contract analytics is a popular focus for LegalTech applications, with a number of start-ups competing to have their proprietary interpretations of contractual terms established as definitive referents. While the business use case is clear, among the many things it neglects is that widely framed general clauses such as 'reasonableness' or 'good faith' operate symbiotically with lower-level concepts and, ultimately, with fact-specific instances of individual disputes. The application of a legal rule to a set of social facts is, in this sense, algorithmic, involving the addition of concepts to form more complex ones, but contingent upon interactions between concepts and rules expressed at different levels of generality. A deterministic or 'mechanical jurisprudence' approach ignoring the interaction between concepts at different levels of generality accomplishes little more than ossifying legal concepts into self-evident computational 'truths'. As a consequence, it advances a radically simplified legal ontology which assumes that these concepts are stable referents part of tractable computational problems decidable by a Turing Machine.[113] Thus the implicit assumption underpinning the LegalTech enterprise is that 'law' is ultimately Turing Complete, and that 'legal problems' are ultimately decidable as 'right' or 'wrong' – or '1' or '0'.[114]

With seeming indifference to why LES failed in the first place, LegalTech developers remain beholden to an axiomatic conception of law, but also an implicit understanding of reality known as pancomputationalism – the view that physical reality is describable by information and that the universe is the deterministic or probabilistic output of a computer program or network of computational processes.[115] According to its most familiar formation in Tegmark's mathematical universe hypothesis (MUH): 'our physical world not only is described by mathematics, but … is mathematics, making us self-aware parts of a giant mathematical object … [and] forcing us to relinquish many of most deeply ingrained notions of reality'.[116] Observers, including humans, existing within this mathematical object are 'self-aware structures' that 'subjectively perceive themselves as existing in a physically "real" world'.[117] Because the MUH suggests that mathematical existence equals physical existence – and all structures that exist mathematically exist physically – reality is ultimately defined by computable functions. By defining law, legal concepts, norms and the range of human and non-human behaviours they pertain to as ultimately 'computable' functions, LegalTech applications and calls for 'AI Judges' endorse a specific understanding about the nature of social reality and information itself. On one hand, they endorse the dualism Leibniz derived from the Yi-jing expressed in binary code but also, on the other, the purely digital ontology posed by the MUH, where everything is computable, because everything is computation.

[113] MacCormick, *What Can Be Computed* 317–30.

[114] MacCormick, *What Can Be Computed* 103–13.

[115] G Piccinini, *Physical Computation: A Mechanistic Account* (Oxford University Press, 2015) 51–73; M Miłkowski, 'From Computer Metaphor to Computational Modelling: The Evolution of Computationalism' (2018) 28(3) *Minds and Machines* 515.

[116] Tegmark, *Our Mathematical Universe* 17.

[117] M Tegmark, 'Is "The Theory of Everything" Merely the Ultimate Ensemble Theory?' (1998) 270(1) *Annals of Physics* 1.

This is problematic, not only because of the unresolved theoretical and practical limits of computation[118] – which raises the wider questions: what is computable? and is law computable? – but because the binary nature of computation means that all legal problems must ultimately be decidable using binary logic.

While Tegmark's hypothesis has attracted considerable attention within the AI community, the MUH remains fiercely debated.[119] Gualtiero Piccini, for instance, notes the deeply contested nature of pancomputationalism: 'some philosophers find it obviously false, too silly to be worth refuting; [while] others find it obviously true, too trivial to require a defense'.[120] Dan McQuillan, meanwhile, connects it to the wider claims of data science, which he describes as:

> … an echo of the neo-platonism that informed early modern science in the work of Copernicus and Galileo. That is, it resonates with a belief in a hidden mathematical order that is ontologically superior to the one available to our everyday senses.[121]

Despite robust critiques of the MUH's 'digital ontology'[122] and broad support for an informational approach to structural realism whereby 'knowledge of the world is knowledge of its structures',[123] current AI research is largely guided by pancomputationalist and materialist views of intelligence.[124]

Seeing the potential of AI across a number of contexts, legal scholars have become somewhat enamoured with AGI. Most often, however, their enthusiasm about the boundless potential of AI runs the risk of presenting it as a 'magic problem solver' for everyday legal issues (as in the case of corporate governance[125]). This usually means neglecting the wider scope of the societal transformation posed by AGI, and assuming that the legal system will remain more or less stable in a post-AGI paradigm. A different account, can however be found in Ben Alarie's prediction of a forthcoming 'legal singularity'.[126] Derived from the technological singularity hypothesised by Ray Kurzweil,[127] Alarie's 'legal singularity' envisions a scenario where machines designing increasingly capable and powerful machines trigger an 'intelligence explosion' and the creation of a 'superintelligence' vastly exceeding human understanding and control.[128] Once this point is reached, 'disputes over the legal significance of agreed facts will be rare. [There] may be disputes over facts, but the [once] found, the facts will map on to clear legal consequences. The law will be functionally complete'.[129]

[118] MacCormick, *What Can Be Computed* 3–11, 294–311.

[119] J Schmidhüber, 'Algorithmic Theories of Everything' (2000), arxiv.org/abs/quant-ph/0011122; P Hut, M Alford and M Tegmark, 'On Math, Matter and Mind' (2006) 36(6) *Foundations of Physics* 765.

[120] Piccinini, *Physical Computation* 51.

[121] D McQuillan, 'Data Science as Machinic Neoplatonism' (2018) 31(2) *Philosophy & Technology* 254.

[122] L Floridi, 'Against Digital Ontology' (2009) 168(1) *Synthese* 151.

[123] J Smithies, *The Digital Humanities and the Digital Modern* (Palgrave, 2017) 55; L Floridi, 'A Defence of Informational Structural Realism' (2008) 161(2) *Synthese* 219.

[124] Hassabis, Kumaran, Summerfield and Botvinck, 'Neuroscience-Inspired Artificial Intelligence'.

[125] M Petrins, 'Corporate Management in the Age of AI' (UCL Working Paper Series, Corporate Management in the Age of AI No. 3, 2019), https://dx.doi.org/10.2139/ssrn.3346722.

[126] Alarie, 'The Path of the Law' 443.

[127] R Kurzweil, *The Singularity is Near: When Humans Transcend Biology* (Gerald Duckworth & Co. 2006).

[128] Bostrom, *Superintelligence.*

[129] Alarie, 'The Path of the Law' 3.

While results should not be overstated, some systems have already 'outperformed' human legal experts at the task of predicting case outcomes.[130] There is, however, a gulf between using statistical techniques to predict case outcomes using superficial criteria, such as the jurisdiction and political affiliation of a judge, and replacing what judges do with AI. Nevertheless, the ambitions of what we might call the 'legal singularitarians' do not stop at predicting case outcomes. They have in their sights the eventual replacement of juridical reasoning as the basis for dispute resolution and the substitution of some protean triumvirate of powers, rights, and responsibilities for legitimate legal authority.

VIII. Chapter Overview

The papers collected in this volume were first presented as part of 'Lex Ex Machina: A Conference on Law's Computability' held at Jesus College, in the University of Cambridge, on 13 December 2019. This conference was borne out of the desire to gather together some of the most influential scholars working at the intersection of law/technology and explore what 'computational law', 'robot judges' and the 'legal singularity' mean for the future of law as a social institution, and to push back against some of the more sensationalist claims emanating out of legal scholarship about the use of AI in law.

A. Christopher Markou and Simon Deakin – *Ex Machina Lex*: Exploring the Limits of Legal Computability

In their chapter '*Ex Machina Lex*: Exploring the Limits of Legal Computability' Christopher Markou and Simon Deakin pose the question: to what extent do the statistical techniques of ML/DL lend themselves to formalisation of legal reasoning? While new use cases are being identified for AI in law, their article assesses the feasibility of their success and what 'success' would indeed mean in legal contexts. Although there are material and practical limits to computation and data storage, and theoretical limits to the computability of all problems, this does not mean that legal problems are necessarily non-computable. Some might be, but not necessarily all. The authors thus explore the extent to which the legal system – a system in the sense implied by the theory of social systems – is amenable to computation and automation, and how far the replacement of juridical reasoning with strategic and computational reasoning might impact the autonomy of the legal system, erode the rule of law, and diminish state authority in structuring and mediating legal relations. Their approach adopts a systemic-evolutionary understanding of law to identify unifying principles that help explain the legal system's mode of operation with respect to other social sub-systems, including the economy, politics and technology itself, and which help to clarify the role of juridical reasoning in facilitating legal evolution.

[130] J Goodman-Delahunty, PA Granhag, M Hartwig and EF Lotus, 'Insightful or Wishful: Lawyer's Ability to Predict Case Outcomes' (2010) 16(2) *Psychology, Public Policy and Law* 133; B Alarie, A Niblett and A Yoon, 'Using Machine Learning to Predict Outcomes in Tax Law' (2017), dx.doi.org/10.2139/ssrn.2855977; DM Katz, MJ Bommarito I and J Blackman, 'A General Approach for Predicting the Behavior of the Supreme Court of the United States' (2017) 12(4) *PLoS One* e0174698.

The chapter suggests that the hypothetical 'legal singularity' – which presumes the elimination of all legal uncertainty – conflates simulation and the probabilistic capabilities of ML and Big Data for the process of legal judgment. The authors build on Mireille Hildebrandt's observation that '[w]hereas machines may become very good in such simulation, judgement itself is predicated on the contestability of any specific interpretation of legal certainty in the light of the integrity of the legal system – which goes beyond a quasi-mathematical consistency'[131] and, following Alain Supiot's identification of the 'anthropological function' of law as a 'technique [for the] humanization of technology'[132] contend that the replacement of juridical reasoning with computation would ultimately result in the subordination of the 'rule of law' to a new 'rule of technology'.

The chapter develops this critique through an examination of one of the issues high on the agenda of those arguing for a computational approach to law, namely the determination, for tax and employment purposes, of the distinction between employees and independent contractors. This distinction is shown to be historically contingent and to have been shaped by numerous economic and political factors. To reduce the juridical task of work classification to an automated process would conceal the political choices which are unavoidably present in these areas of law.

B. Mireille Hildebrandt – Code Driven Law: Freezing the Past and Scaling the Future

In 'Code Driven Law: Freezing the Past and Scaling the Future', Mireille Hildebrandt examines 'cryptographic law' or 'smart regulation' (that is, self-executing code as a new type of legal regulation). She begins by drawing an important distinction between data-driven law and code-driven law. The former pertains to predictions of legal decisions or mining of legal arguments, which is often discussed in Legal AI or LegalTech literature, and in Hildebrandt's wider works on 'law as computation'.[133] The latter, on the other hand, concerns the 'legal norms or policies that have been articulated in computer code, either by a contracting party, law enforcement authorities, public administration or by a legislator'. Her focus is on how these code-driven laws establish pre-determined thresholds that trigger 'smart'/automated regulations (as in the case of social security fraud detection).

The first part of her paper describes what code-driven law 'is' by explaining what it 'does' with respect to text-driven law. She provides examples of code-driven laws in smart contracts (which are 'not only articulated in computer code but also self-executing'), public administration ('a decision-support or a decision-making system that is articulated in computer code'), and legislatures. Hildebrandt argues that these examples of code-driven laws raise questions about principles in private law, public law, criminal

[131] M Hildebrandt, 'Law as Computation in the Era of Artificial Legal Intelligence: Speaking Law to the Power of Statistics' (2017), www.ssrn.com/abstract=2983045.

[132] A Supiot, *Homo Juridicus* 117.

[133] M Hildebrandt, 'Law as Computation in the Era of Artificial Legal Intelligence'.

law and constitutional law. She concludes that what the code-driven law does is to 'fold enactment, interpretation and application into one stroke, collapsing the distance between legislator, executive and court'. The implicit assumption of code-driven law is that it can foresee all potential scenarios in order to cover all future interactions, which out of necessity must be 'highly dynamic and adaptive to address and confront what cannot easily be foreseen by way of unambiguous rules'.

Hildebrandt then turns to the capacity assumption of code-driven law – that is, our ability to sufficiently foresee the future at the moment legal norms are encoded into law. She argues that compared to text-driven laws – which are structured on natural language and speech acts – code-driven law has certain constraints in its computational architecture and design. These include the requirement of formal deduction ('if this then that', IFTTT), disambiguation of terms and rules, and the incompleteness and inconsistency of computations.[134] These constraints are all 'related to the uncertainty that inheres in the future'. ML embraces a false assumption that the distribution of training data can be a close approximation of the distribution of future. In reality, the future distribution of data can only be predicted rather than learnt by ML.

Hildebrandt claims that predictions influence the very behaviours they supposedly predict, and rephrasing the Goodhart/Campbell/Lucas effect argues that 'when a measure becomes a target it ceases to be a good measure'. While we could design many present futures, there is only one future present (reality), and 'the best way to predict the future is to create it'. She concludes by claiming that Arendt's 'human condition' can be best explained in terms of the Parsonian/Luhmannian 'double contingency', and that natural language makes the process of anticipating a process of anticipating how others anticipate us. The co-evolutionary nature of anticipation based on interpretable natural language thus generates radical uncertainty, which in turns demands the institutionalisation of specific patterns of behaviours to consolidate, stabilise, and reduce both complexity and uncertainty in social systems. Legal certainty is thus crucial to this process of consolidation and stabilisation, and occurs without freezing the future based on a scaling of the past due to its text-driven nature.

Hildebrandt's paper concludes with an inquiry into the nature of code-driven law, pointing out the problems in the concept of 'legal by design' and the formulation of her own approach – 'legal protection by design'. The latter does not focus on compliance or enforcement of legal norms, but strategies for embedding legal protections into the technological infrastructure of code-driven and data-driven environments. At the very least, she contends, code-drive decision-making systems must come with an effective right to appeal against automated decisions and to give legal justification. Her ultimate conclusion, however, is that law is not computable due to its text-driven and multi-interpretable nature, which mean it could be computed in various ways. The choice for how to design 'legal computation' must therefore belong to the 'people' and the courts rather than software developers in big tech or big law.

[134] *cf* K Gödel, 'Die Vollständigkeit der Axiome des logischen Funktionenkalküls' (1930) 37 *Monatshefte für Mathematik und Physik* 349; JM Rogers and RE Molzon, 'Lessons about the Law from Self-Referential Problems in Mathematics' (1992) 90 *Michigan Law Review* 5.

C. John Morison – Toward a Democratic Singularity?

In the chapter 'Toward a Democratic Singularity?' John Morison considers foundational issues surrounding the implementation of automated systems and their attendant impact on democracy and the legitimacy of legal regimes. The paper first outlines shortcomings in the promise of online consultations, and how they have yet to realise their democratic potential. Morison then speculates on the development of new surveillance technologies, which purport to transform virtually all aspects of human existence into quantifiable data that is used to monitor behaviours and allow for greater predictive capabilities. He then examines how these technologies have been used to enable 'biosurveillance' in the context of the Covid-19 pandemic.

Morison's argument is that the convergence of digital technologies amounts to a new, pervasive, and all-encompassing form of surveillance and social control he terms 'algorithmic governmentality'. Building upon insights from the shortcomings of democratic consultations, he argues that these developments run the risk of rendering ideas about consultation and deliberative democracy all but redundant 'as actual preferences can be measured directly without the need for an intermediary political process to represent preferences'. The totalisation of these technologies, he suggests, allows for the elicitation of individual 'preferences' through various means of statistical inference, profiling, and the wider process of 'radical datafication' which 'offers a false emancipation by appearing to be, by its very nature, all-inclusive and accurate'.

Morison's conclusion is that these developments amount to a novel form of governance, one that is post-political, and has the potential to first 'undermine, and then transcend, many of fundamental attributes of citizenship which presently appear as part of the bargain within the government-governed relationship'. His conclusion is that we should resist efforts to de-politicise politics by removing it from the process of detailed decision-making and replacing it with algorithmic governmentality, which in turn must be resisted by debating and questioning the processes themselves.

D. Jennifer Cobbe – Legal Singularity and the Reflexivity of Law

In 'Legal Singularity and the Reflexivity of Law' Jennifer Cobbe argues that those pursuing legal AI – particularly those interested in the so-called 'legal singularity' – misunderstand both the nature of law and of technology. She contends that not only would they fail to solve the very real problems of the law, but they could potentially make them worse and cause new and greater problems.

Drawing on insights and concepts from a variety of disciplines, Cobbe's argument is premised on the idea that law functions as a reflexive societal institution. In her view, law not only reflects society but significantly influences society and its institutions. As such, she argues, the law cannot be neutral, as it is inherently contextual and contingent on the circumstances of the time, and imbued with normative assumptions and priorities of that time. Ultimately, the law reifies the interest and goals of its creators (legislatures), practitioners (lawyers), and adjudicators (judges). This reflexive functioning should be understood as distinct from the role that law plays in society as a result of its reflexivity. In Cobbe's view, law's role in society, both historically and in the present, has been to entrench the power of capital, strengthen the position of the wealthy, reinforce inequalities, and protect established interests from outside challenges. Functioning as a reflexive societal institution, Cobbe argues, the law's role has not only been to reflect the inequalities and injustices in society, but establish societal conditions that repeat, reinforce, and re-encode them back into society. Cobbe further argues that algorithms, too, are reflexive: 'Just as law in its reflexivity moulds society according to the subjective assumptions, understandings, and goals of those who write and practice it', she says, 'so too with algorithms'. As such, just as it matters what goals and priorities those working within the law are pursuing, and whose interests they serve, it matters what goals and priorities are being pursued in the design, deployment, and use of algorithmic systems.

Having laid the groundwork by describing the reflexivity of both law and AI, Cobbe proceeds to develop her argument in two parts. In the first, she argues that algorithmic systems are not – and may never be – capable of replacing human lawyers and judges. She highlights some faulty assumptions relied upon by legal AI proponents, such as the idea that AI systems can engage in legal reasoning or be neutral and objective arbiters. She emphasises, though, that critiques of legal AI that focus on the technical limitations of algorithmic systems, while important, do not get to the heart of the structural questions in which she is primarily interested.

In the second part of her argument, therefore, Cobbe formulates a critique of the power relations and structural effects of legal AI as it is commonly envisaged. Adopting Foucauldian theories of governmentality, she begins by locating the ideological underpinnings and motivations of legal AI as being part of a process of neoliberal rationalisation; replacing the qualitative, normative values of law with supposedly rational, objective, quantitative metrics and logics based on statistical and economic thinking. As part of this process of rationalisation, the law is often problematised by legal AI proponents as slow, costly, inefficient, complex, unpredictable, in need of optimisation, and thus amenable to techno-solutionist interventions. By framing the case for legal AI in terms that are fundamentally concerned with the quality of the law's functioning, advocates for legal AI – and the 'legal singularity' more generally – not only fail to consider the nature of the law's role in society but also prioritise the kind of market-oriented and commercially-driven ways of thinking that contribute to the development of problems with that role in the first place. Without a critical examination of the law's role in society, Cobbe argues, legal AI proponents therefore risk developing systems that will primarily make law 'better' at extending and reinforcing hierarchies, maintaining the law's exclusionary effects, and reifying the dominance and power of capital.

E. Roger Brownsword – Artificial Intelligence and the Functional Completeness of Law

Roger Brownsword's chapter 'Artificial Intelligence and Legal Singularity: The Thin End of the Wedge, the Thick End of the Wedge, and the Rule of Law' starts with the observation that 'a number of technological wedges are being driven under the idea of law as a rule-based enterprise; that the wedges that are being driven in relation to the channelling and re-channelling function of law are much more significant than those being driven into adjudication' and that at least some of these technological wedges are 'going in thick end first'. Brownsword contends that these challenges may well necessitate a 'radical rebooting of our legal thinking' and potentially reshape 'the Rule of Law and our conception of coherence in the law'.

The argument of his paper can be broken down into three axes. The first is that the use of algorithmic or 'AI' tools by both public and private regulators must be guided by a comprehensive technological management strategy, and grounded in a revised conception of what regulatory responsibility entails. Secondly, he suggests that this revised understanding, which he describes as a 'new benchmark for legality', must be circumscribed into the rules governing the exercise of regulatory power that depend on these technological measures. Thirdly, Brownsword suggests that the revision of these rules requires what he terms a 'new coherentism' which focuses on the compatibility, and inter-contingency, of regulatory measures with newly established benchmarks for legality. By revising 'traditional coherentist thinking' – which is concerned with how general legal principles apply to particular fact patterns – Brownsword formulates 'how a new coherentist mind-set needs to be cultivated so that there is a constant scrutiny of technological measures to check that they are compatible with the benchmark regulatory responsibilities'.

Brownsword concludes his paper with reflections on the need for new institutional configurations that are better suited to nurturing and sustaining coherentist legal reasoning, and supporting 'the stewardship responsibilities that regulators have for the global commons'.

F. Sylvie Delacroix – Automated Systems and the Need for Change

Sylvie Delacroix's chapter, 'Automated Systems and the Need for Change', examines the use of AI systems in moral decision making. One of the problems with this idea, she suggests, is that AI systems would not arrive at a form of moral consciousness in any way that we would recognise as characterising our own experience. In particular, current efforts to develop automated systems to be deployed in morally loaded contexts pay little attention to the difficulties that stem from the unavoidable need for moral change. If we take the view that ethics is a 'work in progress', it would be essential to retain a role for human agents in the process of value formation.

Systems like law which are designed to provide simplified guidance on how to live together can induce conformity and dissipate pressure for change. Automated systems are similarly 'morally risky'. Dangers include the backward-looking nature of machine learning. Delacroix explores the use of inverse reinforcement learning (IRL) as a possible solution. IRL involves the design of 'systems that are meant to infer from the behaviour of surrounding (human) agents a morally-loaded "utility function"'. There is interest in the use of AI to allow data to train the system, avoiding the need to select data 'by hand'. The utility function is not fixed but evolves in the light of new data on agents' moral judgments.

The possibility of automating moral choices may seem attractive in the light of the difficulty human beings have in assessing practices to which they become habituated. Moral capacity cannot be preserved through cognitive vigilance alone, however, as the latter is conditioned by the habits of thought acquired through immersion in a particular social environment. For some who take a 'realist' stance on issues of morality, the possibility of a superintelligence that would set us on the path to righteousness is attractive. However, Delacroix warns that 'without regular exercise, our moral muscles will just wither away, leaving us unable to consider alternative, better ways of living together'.

A more pragmatic aim, she argues, would be to 'build human-computer interactions that are apt at dispelling moral torpor'. One way to do this would be to include human beings as 'end-users' in the decision loop, as in the case of 'interactive machine learning'. But 'in the absence of a radical shift in the design choices that preside over the way those systems call for interaction with us, lazy normative animals, that effect will be dramatic, to the point of possibly undermining the very possibility of human-triggered change'.

G. Ryan Abbott and Alex Sarch – Punishing Artificial Intelligence: Legal Fiction or Science Fiction?

Ryan Abbott and Alex Sarch's chapter, 'Punishing Artificial Intelligence: Legal Fiction or Science Fiction', explores the question of whether it is feasible to consider applying criminal sanctions to AI entities. They point out that the idea of applying the criminal law to non-human entities is nothing new, as the criminal responsibility of corporations is, in principle, well established. Corporate persons are subject to criminal penalties, they suggest, where organisations cause systemic harms which are not reducible to the actions of individual human beings. If an AI system has the potential to cause similarly 'irreducible' harms – 'Hard AI crimes' – the possibility of punishing AI needs to be at least carefully considered.

While there is no immediate prospect of a 'strong AI' which can exactly replicate human cognition, it is possible to envisage cases in which AI systems could behave not just unpredictably and unexplainably, but also autonomously of any direct human control. Machines may then cause harms which would be categorised as criminal but where no identifiable human person has acted with criminal culpability, or when it is not practicably defensible to attach criminal culpability to any one human actor, as in the case of actions taken by many individuals over a period of time or in a complex organisational setting. In these circumstances, punishment of an AI entity could indirectly deter the individuals who develop and market it, and the law's expressive function might be satisfied in the legal condemnation of certain outcomes associated with AI.

Abbot and Sarch then discuss whether it is possible to attribute mental states to AI systems. This is already done, they point out, in the case of corporate entities, through theories of agency, as in the case of the respondeat superior principle. This involves looking to the mental state of the user or developer responsible for the AI. However, it runs up against the problem that it may not be clear who is responsible for an AI. Use of criminal law techniques for imposing liabilities on those ultimately responsible for serious harms, such as the doctrine of constructive liability, runs the risk of imposing excessive liabilities on developers and stifling valuable innovation.

On the vexed question of whether to attribute legal personality to AI systems, Abbot and Sarch warn against the danger of 'rights creep', as has happened already with the attribution, in a number of jurisdictions, of constitutionally-protected human rights to corporations. One solution, they suggest, would be to designate a 'responsible person', in practice likely to be a corporation, as the ultimate guarantor of an AI. They also consider the costs and benefits of requiring mandatory registration and reporting for certain AI systems.

They conclude that notwithstanding 'the growing possibility of Hard AI Crime', the 'radical tool of punishing AI' would be an overreaction. Preferable would be 'modest expansions to criminal law, including, most importantly, new negligence crimes centered around the improper design, operation, and testing of AI applications as well as possible criminal penalties for designated parties who fail to discharge statutory duties'.

H. Lyria Bennett Moses – Not a Single Singularity

Lyria Bennett Moses' chapter, 'Not a Single Singularity', envisages the development of AI in law occurring along three dimensions: an 'x axis' describing what is currently possible at any given time, a 'y axis' referring to what the technology is capable of becoming, and a 'z axis' along which decisions about the legitimacy of AI will be made. She argues that rather than there being a 'straight path' towards a legal singularity, there are likely to be periods of alternating progress and stasis along each of the three axes, and that the final outcome is unlikely to be a fully computable legal system.

In the context of legal AI, human and machine capabilities are more likely to be complements than substitutes. Machines can currently simulate certain human tasks, and if the focus is on observed functions they may be understood as simulating certain forms of rational behaviour. However, the current state of AI systems is such that they are very far from achieving anything approaching general intelligence. When particular techniques are closely scrutinised, their limitations with respect to law come into sharp relief. Thus attempts to make legislation machine-readable through the use of expert systems techniques have shown that it is most straightforward to code those statutory texts which embed an element of calculation or which rely on relatively straightforward decision rules. The danger in seeking to translate legislation into code is that it will change the way in which laws themselves are drafted. Expert systems cannot code for open-ended concepts such as 'reasonableness', but general clauses of this kind which, by virtue of their incompleteness, permit legal adaptation.

Similar problems arise when natural language processing and machine learning are used for case prediction. The current state of these techniques is inadequate given their tendency to replicate racial and other biases, as the case of the COMPAS software has highlighted. But even if these capabilities can be enhanced in future, there are problems of legitimacy associated with their use. In the context of legal decision making, judgment is not a purely predictive process; it is the outcome of deliberation and contestation.

She concludes that an uneven development of AI in law is likely, not just because of limits to what can be achieved technically, but by virtue of unavoidable concerns over the legitimacy of automated decision making. Technological advances 'will lead to both progress and error, sometimes expanding what is available, what is possible and what is appropriate and legitimate in ways that are both evolutionary and revolutionary. But there are many thresholds to cross, and it is hard to imagine a system that would render law fully computable without changing the nature of law itself'.

I. Dilan Thampapillai – The Law of Contested Concepts: Reflections on Copyright Law and the Legal and Technological Singularities

Dilan Thampapillai's chapter 'The Law of Contested Concepts? Reflections on Copyright Law and the Legal and Technological Singularities' argues that while the idea of the legal singularity might seem convincing enough at a high level of abstraction, it runs up against serious objections in context of an applied field of law such as intellectual property ('IP'). IP law reflects a complex bargain around notions of property, human rights, free expression, technological development, and education, among other things. Copyright can only function as an imperfect property system in which the courts have discretion to balance competing interests and values on a case by case basis.

As a form of property law, IP gives expression to the right of exclusion. However, exclusion has always been an imperfect vehicle for realising the goals of IP law. Copyright affords the right to claim to redress for violations of exclusive rights, but it cannot guarantee that the right-holders' interests will be completely protected. The legitimacy of the law depends also on recognising alternative interests, and in allowing carve-outs such as the fair use doctrine. It is only by accepting that it serves a range of interests that copyright law retains its legitimacy.

The legal singularity, by contrast, describes a version of a complete legal system, overseen by a superhuman intelligence. Such a system is premised on the possibility of the perfect enforcement of legal rights. This, Thampapillai suggests, is inherently antithetical to the kind of multi-factorial decision making which occurs in copyright cases. The fair use doctrine has evolved in such a way as to allow courts to strike complex compromises in the cases that come before them. The concepts they use to strike these balances are useful precisely because they are open-textured and contestable at the point of interpretation. Concepts also express a value dimension which no amount of data can straightforwardly capture.

For these reasons, Thampapillai suggests that scepticism is in order when contemplating the legal singularity. The example of copyright highlights the degree to which 'human systems and reasoning have proved resilient and adaptable' in responding to the challenges of technological change; the vision of the legal singularity, by contrast, is one in which not just human labour but the human subject itself is pushed to the margins.

J. Christopher Markou and Lily Hands – *Capacitas Ex Machina*: Are Computerised Systems of Mental Capacity a 'Red Line' or Benchmark for AI?

In the volume's concluding contribution, '*Capacitas Ex Machina*: Are Computerised Assessments of Mental Capacity a "Red Line" or Benchmark for AI?', the prospect of using AI and advanced technologies such as fMRI and Automated Mental Stated Detection is taken up by Christopher Markou and Lily Hands. Their paper begins by reviewing the history of AI in medicine, starting with the advent of Expert Systems (ES) in the mid-twentieth century, to the rise of connectionist AI research in its latter half, to the development of Automated Mental State Detection (AMSD) and related bio-cognitive interfaces. It examines theoretical and practical problems for implementing these systems in the real world, and how psychiatry is likely to be impacted in the near term by technological advances.

The paper situates this as for now hypothetical problem within the context of historical efforts to use computers to assist with medical diagnosis, and potentially replace human doctors and psychiatrists. It then examines whether and how computational reasoning could, and indeed should, operate in the context of capacity decisions in England and Wales. Following the critique of computer scientist Joseph Weizenbaum, Markou and Hands highlight not only the technical challenges faced in capturing, encoding, and applying domain expertise in medicine, but the normative – and deeply political question – of whether a computer should under any circumstances be given the authority to make legally consequential judgements turning upon subjective psychological and psychiatric phenomena. Highlighting many of the problems identified earlier in the volume by Hildebrandt, Morison and others, they argue that allowing a machine to make determinations of mental incapacity is not just, at least for now, technically infeasible, but that 'the essential humanity and consequence of capacity decisions on not just the individual, but their community, demands that capacity be not only defined, but assessed and imputed by members of that community'. They conclude that 'anything else would result in a machine being elevated to the role of arbiter of human behaviour and experience within a social reality it cannot access'.

IX. Conclusion

The chapters that comprise this volume are part of a deliberate effort to push-back against the more hagiographical accounts of AI in law, and to help delineate domain specific challenges that must be considered in the course of their development before they can be reliably deployed in real-world legal contexts. We hope that this volume serves as a socratic entry point for lawyers, legal scholars, and students alike, but that it also helps bridge the gap between the technical dimensions of AI research and its normative implications for effective policy and governance.

Although the contributions to this volume identify a range of legal, ethical, and political challenges related to the automation of justice more generally, they help us better connect present and near-term challenges to those that might be faced in the longer-term. Perhaps the real danger is not that the legal singularity occurs, but that what is willed to truth as 'just' by the modern AI enterprise is, in fact, nothing more than what is 'satisficed' as 'just enough'. In an AGI paradigm the prospect of AI judges is, perhaps, a trivial one. We simply do not, and cannot, know. But we do have reason to think that it might be a scenario where all bets are off for humanity and by some accounts our odds aren't good.[135]

[135] E Yudkowsky, 'Artificial Intelligence as a Positive and Negative Factor in Global Risk' in N Bostrom and MM Cirkovic (eds), *Global Catastrophic Risks* (Oxford University Press, 2008).

Yet pinning a hypothetical argument on long-term and unspecified conditionals is just an elaborate way of counting '1, 2, 3, a million' and calling it good numerical sense and a sound business proposition. While for some the latter seems nonetheless true, all it does is frame the totalisation of AI in law as inevitable once an arbitrarily defined threshold of 'intelligence' is attained or various functional capabilities achieved. Indeed, the perspectives contained in this volume are advanced in an attempt to fulfill Ray Kurzweil's suggestion that concerned and constructively critical observers of technology will be needed to manage what he sees as the inevitable transition to a post-singularity world:

> My own expectation is that the creative and constructive applications of this technology will dominate, as I believe they do today. But there will be a valuable (and increasingly vocal) role for a concerned and constructive Luddite movement (i.e., anti-technologists inspired by early nineteenth century weavers who destroyed labour-saving machinery in protest).[136]

It is hoped that this volume, its contributions, and the ongoing work of its contributors inspires like-minded sceptics, critical thinkers, and rebels to challenge the orthodoxy of Big Tech and its salvific claims of limitless potential and untold prosperity. As Julia Powles and Helen Nissenbaum remind us:

> … the preoccupation with narrow computational puzzles distracts us from the far more important issue of the colossal asymmetry between societal cost and private gain in the roll-out of automated systems. It also denies us the possibility of asking: Should we be building these systems at all?[137]

[136] R Kurzweil, 'The Law of Accelerating Returns' (2001), www.kurzweilai.net/the-law-of-accelerating-returns.

[137] J Powles and H Nissenbaum, 'The Seductive Diversion of "Solving" Bias in Artificial Intelligence' (Medium, 7 December 2018), medium.com/s/story/the-seductive-diversion-of-solving-bias-in-artificial-intelligence-890df5e5ef53.

2

Ex Machina Lex: Exploring the Limits of Legal Computability

CHRISTOPHER MARKOU AND SIMON DEAKIN*

> [Mathematics] did not, as they supposed, correspond to an objective structure of reality; it was a method and not a body of truths; with its help we could plot regularities – the occurrence of phenomena in the external world – but not discover why they occurred as they did, or to what end.
>
> **Isaiah Berlin**
> 'Counter Enlightenment' in *Dictionary of the History of Ideas* (1973)

One consequence of recent advances in Machine Learning[1] (ML) – a family of statistical techniques enabling an algorithm to 'learn' over time through the iterative adjustment of mathematical parameters and optimise performance at a task – is renewed interest in applying computation to more aspects of the law and legal processes.[2] Concurrent breakthroughs in Natural Language Processing[3] (NLP) – a theory-driven subfield of computer science and artificial intelligence (AI) exploring the use of computers to automatically analyse and process and represent human language – have contributed to the emergence of the so-called 'Legal Technology' (LegalTech) industry and development of various tools for use in legal practice and administration.[4] Included within this are those leveraging Big Data and related techniques to forecast the outcome of legal cases – with

* Faculty of Law and Centre for Business Research, University of Cambridge. We gratefully acknowledge the support of the Leverhulme Trust and of the ESRC through its funding for the Digital Futures at Work Research Centre (grant ES/S012532/1) and the UKRI-JST Joint Call on Artificial Intelligence and Society (grant ES/T006351/1).

[1] DJC MacKay, *Information Theory, Inference and Learning Algorithms* (Cambridge University Press, 2003); E Alpaydin, *Machine Learning* (MIT Press, 2016).

[2] R Dale, 'Industry Watch: Law and Word Order: NLP in Legal Tech' (2019) 25 *Natural Language Engineering* 1, 211–12.

[3] MZ Kurdi, *Natural Language Processing and Computational Linguistics: Speech, Morphology, and Syntax: Volume I* (ISTE-Wiley, 2016); MZ Kurdi, *Natural Language Processing and Computational Linguistics: Semantics, Discourse, and Applications: Volume 2* (ISTE-Wiley, 2017); L Deng and Y Liu (eds), *Deep Learning in Natural Language Processing* (Springer, 2018).

[4] Dale, 'Industry Watch: Law and Word Order: NLP in Legal Tech'; *cf* R Susskind, *Tomorrow's Lawyers: An Introduction to Your Future*, 2nd edn (Oxford University Press, 2017).

some demonstrating predictive capabilities greater than human experts.[5] A number of algorithmic decision-making (ADM) systems using ML to simulate aspects of human reasoning are also used in both public and private-sector contexts.[6] From medicine to finance and immigration[7] to criminal justice,[8] ADM systems have proliferated at a remarkable pace – albeit with sometimes lamentable results.[9]

Because law has language at its core, researchers have long been exploring how to bring AI research to bear on the legal domain, and the cognitive domain of judges and lawyers. Earlier logic-based approaches to AI were used to develop systems for searching legal databases as early as the 1960s–70s, and the advent of Legal Expert Systems (LES) contributed to a swell of optimism for using AI to compliment, extend, and potentially replace the work of human lawyers and judges in the 1970s–80s.[10] Thanks to the success of connectionist models and availability of data, recent years have seen a major renewal of interest in the area, with a number of start-ups competing to apply advanced computational techniques to entire areas of law.

While new use cases in law are being identified with each subsequent breakthrough and performance leap, little attention has been paid to how we might assess the fundamental limits of computation in relation to legal reasoning and various decision-making processes.[11] With mounting issues around bias, accountability, and transparency of ADM systems – and rule of law concerns more generally[12] – we pose a question about

[5] B Alarie, A Niblett and A Yoon, 'Using Machine Learning to Predict Outcomes in Tax Law' (2017), papers.ssrn.com/sol3/papers.cfm?abstract_id=2855977; J Kleinberg, H Lakkaraju, J Leskovec, J Ludwig and S Mullainathan, 'Human Decision and Machine Predictions' (2017) 133 *Quarterly Journal of Economics* 1; DM Katz, MK Bommarito II and J Blackman, 'A General Approach for Predicting the Behavior of the Supreme Court of the United States' (2017) 12 *PLoS One* 4; C Xiao, H Zhong, Z Guo et al., 'CAIL2018: A Large-scale Legal Dataset for Judgment Prediction' (2018), arxiv.org/abs/1807.02478.

[6] For a general overview of ADM: M Whittaker, K Crawford et al., 'AI Now Report 2018', ainowinstitute.org/AI_Now_2018_Report.pdf; *cf* F Pasquale, *The Black Box Society: The Secret Algorithms That Control Money and Information* (Harvard University Press, 2016); V Eubanks, *Automating Inequality* (St Martins Press, 2018).

[7] P Molnar and L Gill, 'Bots at the Gate: A Human Rights Analysis of Automated Decision-making in Canada's Immigration and Refugee Systems' (2018), citizenlab.ca/wp-content/uploads/2018/09/IHRP-Automated-Systems-Report-Web-V2.pdf.

[8] J Angwin and J Larson, 'Bias in Criminal Risk Scores is Mathematically Inevitable' (*ProPublica*, 30 December 2016), www.propublica.org/article/bias-in-criminal-risk-scores-is-mathematically-inevitable-researchers-say; The Law Society of England and Wales, 'Algorithms in the Criminal Justice System' (2019), www.lawsociety.org.uk/support-services/research-trends/documents/algorithm-use-in-the-criminal-justice-system-report/.

[9] GL Ciampaglia, A Nematzadeh, F Menczer and A Flammini, 'How Algorithmic Popularity Bias Hinders or Promotes Quality' (2018) 8 *Scientific Reports* 15951; A Lambrecht and CE Tucker, 'Algorithmic Bias? An Empirical Study into Apparent Gender Based Discrimination in the Display of STEM Career Ads' (2018), papers.ssrn.com/sol3/papers.cfm?abstract_id=2852260.

[10] R Susskind, *Expert Systems in Law* (Oxford University Press, 1987); P Leith, 'The Rise and Fall of the Legal Expert System' (2010) 1 *European Journal of Law and Technology* 1.

[11] A body of scholarship exists on mathematically formalising legal argumentation into computable functions. For an overview: TJM Bench-Capon and H Prakken, 'Introducing the Logic and Law Corner' (2008) *Journal of Logic and Computation* 1. For recent contributions *cf* TJM Bench-Capon, 'Taking Account of the Actions of Others in Value-based Reasoning' (2018) 254 *Artificial Intelligence* 1; H Prakken, 'A New Use case for Argumentation Support Tools: Supporting Discussions of Bayesian Analyses of Complex Criminal Cases' (2018) *Artificial Intelligence and Law* 1; K Atkinson, P Baroni, M Giacomin, et al., 'Towards Artificial Argumentation' (2017) 38 *AI Magazine* 3; E Cloatre and M Pickersgill (eds), *Knowledge, Technology and Law* (London, Routledge 2015).

[12] E Bayamlıoğlu and R Leenes, 'Data-driven Decision-making and the "Rule of Law"' (2018) Tilburg Law School Research Paper, ssrn.com/abstract=3189064.

limits: how do we determine where AI-leveraging systems should be used, where they should be prohibited, and why?

We think these are urgent questions for legal scholars. Proponents frame the totalisation of ADM as inevitable once various technical issues are resolved and more data and methods of better statistical inference become available. But this current AI hype cycle has allowed promises of what's to come overshadow virtually any democratic deliberation over whether they should be invested in, built, and deployed in the first place. Even when such issues have been tabled – as they were with the EU Commission's High Level Expert Group on AI – lobbying has been successful in forestalling discussion of regulatory 'red lines' – contexts in which AI should be strictly prohibited on legal, moral, or humanitarian grounds.[13] Nonetheless, there are compelling cases for prohibiting AI – broadly conceived – in autonomous weapons, facial recognition – and as the French legislature has recently determined, the use of state legal data for judicial analytics, an important, and potentially lucrative, LegalTech domain.[14]

Given the disruptive impact of technology on political processes and social discourse in recent years,[15] a lack of meaningful deliberation becomes all the more concerning in light of predictions about a forthcoming 'legal singularity'. This is a hypothetical point where computational intelligence and decision-making capabilities exceed those of human lawyers, judges and other decision-makers.[16] Lest we forget, a primary justification for ADM systems is the belief they will offer quicker, cheaper, and more reliable decisions untainted by human shortcomings. As physicist Max Tegmark, reasons:

> Since the legal process can be abstractly viewed as computation, inputting information about evidence and laws and outputting a decision, some scholars dream of fully automating it with robojudges: AI systems that tirelessly apply the same high legal standards to every judgment without succumbing to human errors such as bias, fatigue or lack of the latest knowledge.[17]

Practical and juridical reasoning are thus weak links to be severed and reforged with strategic reasoning expressed and imputed computationally. However, the wholesale replacement of juridical reasoning with computation risks undermining one of the principal institutions of a democratic-liberal order. We suggest that it must be treated with all due caution and scepticism. Particularly when one considers that a primary function of the legal system is guarding individuals against the potentially

[13] T Metzinger, 'Ethics Washing Made in Europe' (*Der Tadesspiegel*, 4 April 2019), www.tagesspiegel.de/politik/eu-guidelines-ethics-washing-made-in-europe/24195496.html.

[14] 'France Bans Judge Analytics, 5 Years In Prison For Rule Breakers' (*Artificial Lawyer*, 4 June 2019), www.artificiallawyer.com/2019/06/04/france-bans-judge-analytics-5-years-in-prison-for-rule-breakers/.

[15] D Helbing, S Frey, G Gigerenzer, E Hafen, Y Hofstetter, J van den JHoven, RV Zixcari and A Zwitter, 'Will Democracy Survive Big Data and Artificial Intelligence?' (*Scientific American*, 25 February 2017), www.scientificamerican.com/article/will-democracy-survive-big-data-and-artificial-intelligence/; F Levy, 'Computers and Populism: Artificial Intelligence, Jobs, and Politics in the Near Term' (2018) 34 *Oxford Review of Economic Policy* 3; J Schroeder, 'Toward a Discursive Marketplace of Ideas: Reimagining the Marketplace Metaphor in the Era of Social Media, Fake News, and Artificial Intelligence' (2018) 52 *First Amendment Studies* 1–2.

[16] B Alarie, 'The Path of the law: Toward Legal Singularity' (2016), ssrn.com/abstract=2767835.

[17] M Tegmark, *Life 3.0: Being Human in the Age of Artificial Intelligence* (Allen Lane, 2017) 105.

dehumanising dangers of science and technology, and the threat of totalitarianism.[18] As Hannah Arendt reminds us, 'the first essential step on the road to total domination is to kill the juridical person'.[19]

To avoid such an outcome, scrutiny must be directed to identifying and establishing limits to the use of AI and other data-driven approaches in replicating core aspects of legal administration and the role of human lawyers and judges. The success of these measures ultimately depends on the law's capacity to maintain its autonomy in the face of all-encompassing technological change, an outcome which is far from guaranteed. The hypothesis of this chapter is that there are limits to the computability of legal reasoning and, hence, the use of AI to replicate the core processes of the legal system. The method we employ is to consider the extent to which there are resemblances between ML and legal decision making as systems involving information retention, adaptive learning, and error correction. Our argument is that while there are certain structural resemblances, there are also critical differences which set limits to the project of replacing juridical reasoning with ADM and ML more generally.

I. Methodology

If there are limits to using ADM systems in legal contexts, the next step is identifying and defining them. While there are material and practical limits to computation and data storage,[20] and theoretical limits to the computability of problems,[21] this does not mean that legal problems are necessarily non-computable. Some might be, but not necessarily all. We thus explore the extent to which the legal system – a system in the sense implied by the theory of social systems[22] – is amenable to computation and automation, and how the replacement of juridical reasoning with strategic and computational reasoning might impact the autonomy of the legal system, erode the rule of law, and diminish state authority in structuring and mediating legal relations. We adopt a systemic-evolutionary understanding of law to identify unifying principles that help explain the legal system's mode of operation with respect to other social sub-systems, including the economy, politics and technology itself, and which help to clarify the role of juridical reasoning in facilitating legal evolution.

Our suggestion is that the hypothetical 'legal singularity' – which presumes the elimination of all legal uncertainty – conflates simulation and the probabilistic capabilities of ML and Big Data for the process of legal judgment. As Mireille Hildebrandt observes, '[w]hereas machines may become very good in such simulation, judgment itself is predicated on the contestability of any specific interpretation of legal certainty

[18] A Supiot, *Homo Juridicus: On the Anthropological Function of Law* (Verso, 2007).

[19] H Arendt, *The Origins of Totalitarianism* (Harcourt, 1973) 447.

[20] CH Bennet and R Landauer, 'The Fundamental Physical Limits of Computation' (1985) 253 *Scientific American* 1; S Lloyd, 'Ultimate Physical Limits to Computation' (2000) 406 *Nature* 1047; IL Markov, 'Limits on Fundamental Limits to Computation' (2014) 512 *Nature* 147.

[21] MR Garey and DS Johnson, *Computers and Intractability: A Guide to the Theory of NP-Completeness* (WH Freeman and Company, 1979); *cf* PE Dunne, 'An Annotated List of NP-complete Problems', cgi.csc.liv.ac.uk/~ped/teachadmin/COMP202/annotated_np.html.

[22] G Teubner, *Autopoietic Law: A New Approach to Law and Society* (De Gruyter, 2011); N Luhmann, *Theory of Society: Volumes I and II* (R Barrett (trans), Stanford University Press, 2012/2013).

in the light of the integrity of the legal system – which goes beyond a quasi-mathematical consistency'.[23] Following Alain Supiot's identification of the 'anthropological function' of law as a 'technique [for the] humanization of technology'[24] we contend that the replacement of juridical reasoning with computation would ultimately result in an embedding of society in law and the subordination of the 'rule of law' to a new 'rule of technology'.

II. Machine Learning (ML)

The recent resurgence in AI research, investment, and applications is primarily driven by the promise posed by a family of computational techniques collectively known as machine learning (ML). Generally, ML 'involves developing algorithms through statistical analysis of large datasets of historical examples'.[25] Through the iterative adjustment of mathematical parameters, data retention, and error correction techniques ML algorithms are said to automatically update (or 'learn') through repeated exposure to data and optimise performance at various classification, prediction, and decision-making tasks. ML bears more than a 'family resemblance' to the practice of 'data mining' – the 'study of collecting, processing, analyzing, and making inferences from data'[26] – as both techniques involve processing large data sets to identify correlations (alternatively referred to as 'relationships' or 'patterns') between variables.

'Learning' in this case refers to the properties of an algorithm – a series of mathematical instructions for transforming an informational input into an output – that allow for the iterative adjustment and dynamic optimisation of parameters upon repeated exposure to example data when directed towards specific tasks (such as classifying data or identifying images) without being explicitly programmed.[27] Through a process referred to as 'training', an algorithm is repeatedly exposed to data so that over time its performance is optimised at an objective function; a mathematical formula defining the algorithms 'goal'.[28] ML algorithms are said to 'learn' from previous calculations by retaining information and using error correction techniques – such as backpropagation – to produce increasingly stable and repeatable computational models.[29]

Training an algorithm is ultimately a process of trial and error and involves 'tuning' various mathematical parameters. Ultimately, it is both an art and a science. To assess

[23] M Hildebrandt, 'Law as Computation in the Era of Artificial Legal Intelligence: Speaking Law to the Power of Statistics' (2017), www.ssrn.com/abstract=2983045.

[24] Supiot, *Homo Juridicus*, 117.

[25] D Spiegelhalter, *The Art of Statistics: Learning from Data* (Pelican, 2019) 144.

[26] CC Aggarwal, *Data Mining: The Textbook* (Springer, 2015) 1.

[27] Alpaydin, *Machine Learning*, 1–28; *cf* D Lehr and P Ohm, 'Playing with the Data: What Legal Scholars Should learn about Machine Learning' (2017) 51 *UC Davis Law Review*; P Domingas, 'A Few Useful Things to Know about Machine Learning' (2012) 55 *Communications of the ACM* 10.

[28] S Becker and RS Zemel, 'Unsupervised Learning with Global Objective Functions' in A Arbib (ed), *The Handbook of Brain Theory and Neural Networks* (MIT Press, 1997) 997 ('The main problem in unsupervised learning research is to formulate a performance measure or cost function for the learning, to generate this internal supervisory signal. The cost function is also known as an objective function, since it sets the objective for the learning process.').

[29] DE Rumelhart, G Hinton and JW Williams, 'Learning Representations by Back-propagating Errors' (1989) 323 *Nature*; S Russell and P Norvig, *Artificial Intelligence: A Modern Approach* (Pearson, 2016) 578.

performance at an objective function it must be re-trained, re-tuned, and re-assessed multiple times to correct for errors using test data it did not encounter in the course of training. This allows performance to be assessed by reference to 'unfamiliar' data – that is, data not 'seen' by the algorithm in the course of training. Performance can be assessed using a variety of strategies. Most often these involve testing it by sectioning or partitioning a dataset, running each iteration of an algorithm on a section of the data and then validating the 'accuracy' (as defined by its objective function) of outputs against iterations that were not exposed to a particular section of data. However, these methods are not as reliable as using separate test data.

A. Supervised + Unsupervised Learning

ML algorithms are broadly classifiable as 'supervised' or 'unsupervised'.[30] Supervised algorithms are provided with a defined outcome variable representing what should be predicted on the basis of input data. This involves defining a problem by correctly labelling the outcome variable (for example, this image is dog, that number is 6). Outcome variables can be variously defined, but those defined with binaries (True/False, Cat/Dog) are referred to 'classification' algorithms. In 'multi-label classification' an algorithm can predict indicators with more than two classes (Vehicle/Cyclist/Sign/Tree; Red/Yellow/Green). Algorithms applied to 'regression' problems are used to predict a continuous quantitative result in the form of a specific numerical value. Finally, and related to both classification and regression algorithms, are algorithms that help predict ordinal outcomes, involving multiple classes of information that despite not adhering to a continuous number line, have some innate ordering (First/Second/Third; High/Average/Low).

In supervised ML systems, a programmer defines the desired output. Through training, a program processes input data through its statistical model to produce an output and dynamically adjusts the weightings applied to each variable (or 'node') within the statistical model so that it is 'tuned' to produce a desired output. This process of incremental adjustment and re-adjustment can be repeated over thousands or millions of iterations until a model outputs a desired value or one within a defined range. A statistical model is considered 'trained' when the relative weighting of neuronal inputs has been adjusted to produce a desired output and it can reliably perform a designated task (for example, identifying symptoms of breast cancer). However, because a model is constructed and trained on data provided by the designer, the choices they make – such as the composition of the model, section of training data, weighting of inputs – significantly determine how a system functions, how inputs are transformed into outputs, and by extension, the subsequent decision-making process relying on those outputs. This is to say: a supervised algorithm is only as good as the people constructing, tuning, and training it, and the data it has available.

In unsupervised learning an algorithm uses a vector of variables – such as the physical symptoms or characteristics of breast cancer – and a 'correct' label for this

[30] J Schmidhüber, 'Deep Learning in Neural Networkers: An Overview' (2014), people.idsia.ch/~juergen/DeepLearning2July2014.pdf, 6–7.

vector (for example, a positive diagnosis of breast cancer). This is referred to as a 'ground truth'. Whereas the goal in supervised learning is to accurately predict a ground truth from specific input variables when only input variables exist, unsupervised learning is not 'supervised' by the ground truth. Instead, unsupervised ML systems try to identify a ground truth from a data set or cluster of data points based on their proximity or similarity. For example, an unsupervised ML system might be used to identify a 'cluster' of provisions in an employment contract to determine the rights and status of a worker. The clustering of data points can be done as an end in itself or as intermediary step to refine a dataset for a supervised learning approach, where the clusters identified by an unsupervised algorithm could be used as classes to be predicted through supervised learning. While unsupervised algorithms are not without their use in the legal domain, supervised algorithms are of the greatest saliency as they are driving the most legally consequential decisions in contexts such as risk assessment,[31] immigration,[32] predictive policing,[33] credit scoring,[34] and other contexts.[35]

B. Artificial Neural Networks

A primary tool of ML is so-called artificial neural networks ('ANNs'). ANNs are computational models that use a simplified understanding of how the human brain learns through the use of essentially statistical models. These models generally consist of: (1) an input layer or 'neurons' that receive information, (2) a hidden layer consisting of equations to transform inputs, and (3) 'synapses' that link neurons together by transferring the outputs of one neuron to form the inputs of another.[36] Neurons are arranged in 'layers' that effectively divide the model into different stages of calculation through which data passes, with synapses typically weighted so their values are modified by a multiplier. Models can involve several layers each consisting of multiple neurons, with neurons in each layer linked to the neurons in the previous and subsequent layers by synapses (see Figure 1).

[31] J Larson, S Mattum L Kirchener and J Angwin, 'How We Analyzed the COMPAS Recidivism Algorithm' (*ProPublica*, 2016), www.propublica.org/article/how-we-analyzed-the-compas-recidivism-algorithm; K Hannah-Moffat, 'Algorithmic Risk Governance: Big Data Analytics, Race and Information Activism in Criminal Justice Debates' (2018) *Theoretical Criminology* (online first).

[32] P Molnar and L Gill, 'Bots at the Gate: A Human Rights Analysis of Automated Decision-making in Canada's Immigration and Refugee System' (2018), ihrp.law.utoronto.ca/sites/default/files/media/IHRP-Automated-Systems-Report-Web.pdf.

[33] WL Perry, B McInnis CC Price, SC Smith and JS Hollywood, 'Predictive Policing: the Role of Crime Forecasting in Law Enforcement Operations' (Rand, 2013); W Hardyns and A Rummens, 'Predictive Policing as a New Tool for Law Enforcement? Recent Developments and Challenges' (2018) 24 *European Journal on Criminal Policy and Research* 3; J Chan and LB Moses, 'Can "Big Data" Analytics Predict Policing Practice?' in S Hannem, CB Sanders, CJ Schneider A Doule and T Christensen (eds), *Security and Risk Technologies in Criminal Justice* (Canadian Scholars Press, 2019).

[34] M Hurley and J Adebayo, 'Credit Scoring in the Era of Big Data' (2016) 18 *Yale Journal of Law and Technology* 148; P Hacker, 'Teaching Fairness to Artificial Intelligence: Existing and Novel Strategies against Algorithmic Discrimination under EU Law' (2018) 55 *Common Market Law Review* 1143.

[35] M Oswald, 'Algorithm-assisted Decision-making in the Public Sector: Framing the Issues Using Administrative Law Rules Governing Discretionary Power' (2018) 376 *Philosophical Transactions of the Royal Society* A 2128.

[36] Schmidhüber, 'Deep Learning in Neural Networkers: An Overview'.

Figure 1 Simplified Artificial Neural Network

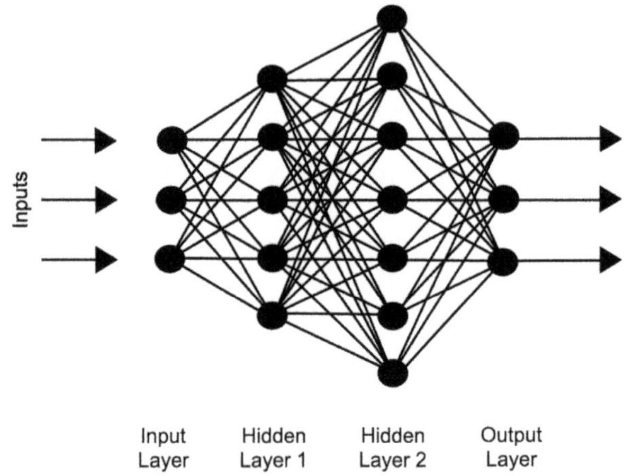

Inputs (which may consist of significant quantities of data) are provided to the first layer of neurons, which calculate these inputs and then pass them on as outputs to the next layer through synapses. The neurons in the subsequent layer in turn perform calculations and produce an output. Each layer repeats this process until the final output of the model is produced. Depending on the nature and complexity of the task, a programmer will choose the number of layers, the number of neurons in each layer, and the equation used to calculate the weighting and behaviour of data between the neurons.

III. Deep Learning (DL)

DL is a subset of ML, and is the technique primarily responsible for some of the most high-profile breakthroughs in modern AI research,[37] but also some of its more hubristic claims.[38] As Gary Marcus observes:

> Deep learning has been at the center of practically every advance in AI in the last several years, from DeepMind's superhuman Go and chess player AlphaZero to Google's recent tool for conversation and speech synthesis, Google Duplex. In each case, big data plus deep learning plus faster hardware has been a winning formula.[39]

[37] Y LeCun, Y Bengio and G Hinton, 'Deep Learning' (2015) 521 *Nature* 436; D Silver, T Hubert, J Schrittwieser, et al., 'AlphaZero: Shedding New Light on the Grand Games of Chess, Shogi and Go', deepmind.com/blog/alphazero-shedding-new-light-grand-games-chess-shogi-and-go/.

[38] *cf* J Pontin, 'Greedy, Brittle, Opaque, and Shallow: the Downsides to Deep Learning' (*Wired*, 2 February 2018), www.wired.com/story/greedy-brittle-opaque-and-shallow-the-downsides-to-deep-learning/; D Heaven, 'Why Deep-learning AIs are So Easy to Fool' (*Nature*, 9 October 2019), www.nature.com/articles/d41586-019-03013-5.

[39] G Marcus and E Davis, *Rebooting AI: Building Artificial Intelligence We Can Trust* (Pantheon, 2019) 10.

While DL approaches vary depending on application, they generally involve large ANNs where 'depth' is determined by the number of hidden layers and neurons within them. Generally, DL uses both supervised and unsupervised approaches to predict an output from a set of input variables. This is done by assigning a numerical weight to each connection between neurons determining the importance of an input value in the overall model. By strengthening the weights associated with a particular input, it is possible to 'train' a network to map a particular association, which allows the model to 'learn' how to map subsequent connections.

For instance, a DL algorithm designed to predict the price of airline tickets would assign a higher weight to a factor such as the departure date/time given its importance as a variable in determining cost. Through training, the use of an error correction algorithm called backpropagation allows a process called gradient descent to dynamically adjust the mapping of connections between neurons so that any given input is correctly mapped to the corresponding output.[40] Training a DL system is an intensive process due to the vast amounts of data required to produce valid models, but the development of the backpropagation algorithm has markedly improved training efficiency.

Most DL approaches also employ a technique known as convolution.[41] This allows neuronal connections within a network to be constrained so that they can capture a property referred to as translational invariance.[42] In tasks involving image recognition, this allows a system to recognise a specific object and maintain recognition when its appearance varies in some way in subsequent images (see Figure 2). For instance, a traffic light in one image can be presumed to be the same object in a subsequent one, without direct experience of it. This is, of course, a critical issue for computer vision systems, particularly those embedded in autonomous vehicles where recognising phenomena in the real-world is paramount for safety.[43] Due to their strengths in local connectivity, weight sharing, and pooling, CNNs are also particularly helpful in speech recognition tasks where invariance is highly desired.[44]

[40] Goodfellow, Bengio, and Courville, *Deep Learning*, 19; *cf* Rumelhart, Hinton and Williams, 'Learning Representations by Back-propagating Errors'.

[41] Y LeCun, 'Generalization and Network Design Strategies' (1989) Technical Report CRG-TR-89-4, yann.lecun.com/exdb/publis/pdf/lecun-89.pdf.

[42] E Kauderer-Abrams, 'Quantifying Translation-invariance in Convolutional Neural Networks' (2017), arxiv.org/abs/1801.01450.

[43] BT Nugraha and S-F Su and Fahmizal, 'Towards Self-driving Car Using Convolutional Neural Network and Road Lane Detector' (2017) 2nd International Conference on Automation, Cognitive Science, Optics, Micro Electro-Mechanical System, and Information Technology (ICACOMIT); Y Tian, K Pei, S Jana and B Ray, 'DeepTest: Automated Testing of Deep-neural-Network-driven Autonomous Cars' (2018) Proceedings of the 40th International Conference on Software Engineering.

[44] T Young, D Hazarika, S Poria, and E Cambria, 'Recent Trends in Deep Learning Based Natural Language Processing' (*ArXiv*, 2018), arxiv.org/pdf/1708.02709.pdf.

Figure 2 Examples of Translational Invariance

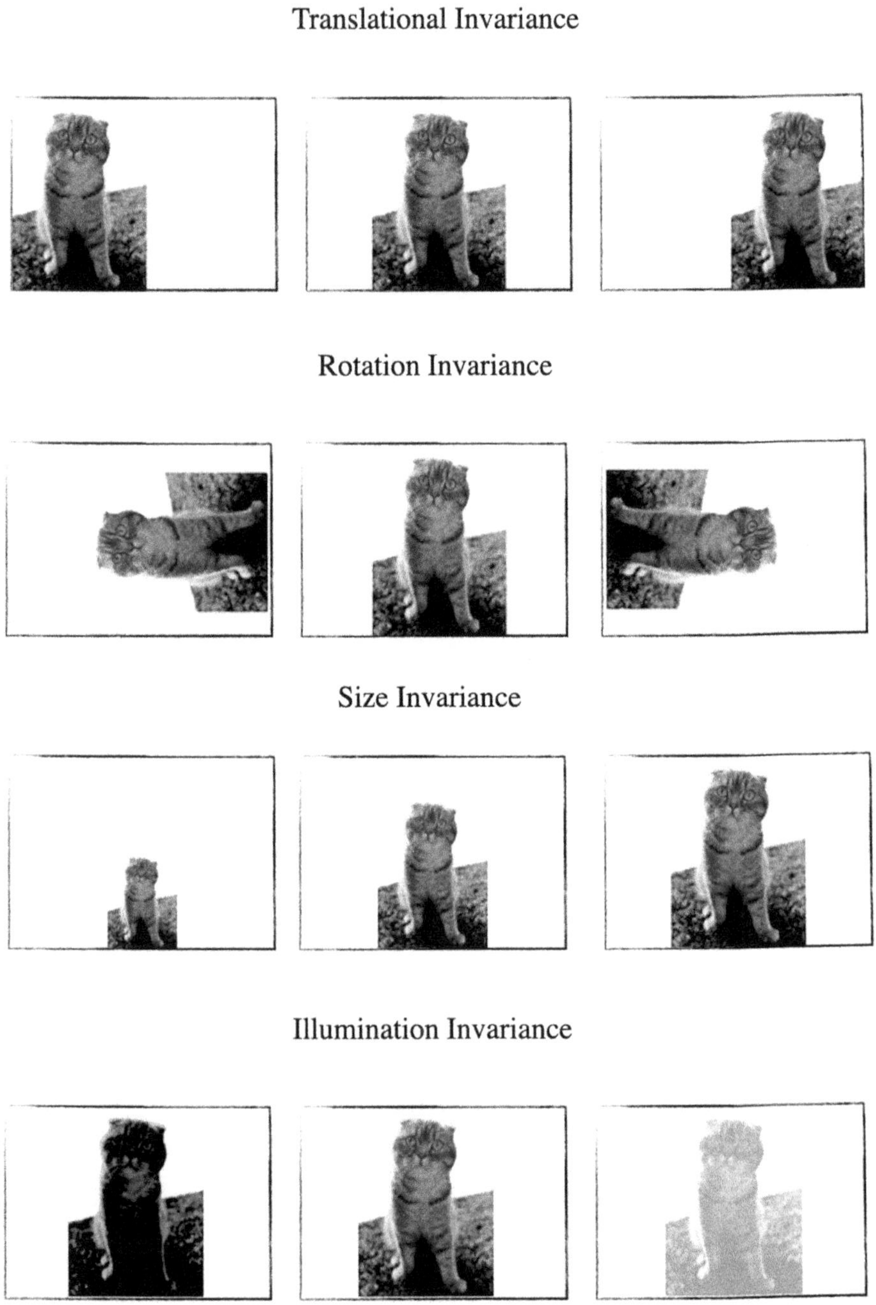

IV. Natural Language Processing (NLP)

From a scientific perspective, NLP models the cognitive dimensions of how natural language is understood and produced by humans. From an engineering perspective, NLP involves developing practical applications for facilitating interactions between computers and human languages. Bates notes that:

> [NLP] has evolved to incorporate aspects of many other disciplines (such as artificial intelligence, computer science, and lexicography). Yet it continues to be the Holy Grail of those who try to make computers deal intelligently with one of the most complex characteristics of human beings: language.[45]

Common NLP applications include speech recognition, lexical analysis, machine translation, information retrieval and question answering, among others.[46] Natural language can be understood as a system for conveying meaning or semantics and is by nature a symbolic or discrete system.[47] The observable aspect of language, text, is a physical signal that exists in purely symbolic form. Text has a counterpart in the 'speech' signal, which is reducible to the continuous correspondence of symbolic text. Together they share the same linguistic hierarchy of natural language.[48]

NLP has been a facet of AI research since the 1950s, when machine translation was the primary focus of researchers but 'abandoned when it was discovered that, although it was easy to get computers to map one word string to another, the problem of translating between one natural language and another was much too complex to be expressible as such a mapping'.[49] The most familiar example of this is the 'Turing Test' which used natural language exchanges between a human and a computer designed to generate human-like responses.[50] Deng and Liu indicate that NLP research has gone through three distinct waves: (1) rationalism; (2) empiricism; and (3) deep learning.

A. Rationalism and NLP

The first of these, rationalism, dates from the 1960s–80s. During this time research was primarily oriented around having machines 'understand' and respond to questions. Manning and Schütze explain that rationalist approaches to NLP are 'characterized by the belief that a significant part of the knowledge in the human mind is not derived

[45] M Bates, 'Models of Natural Language Understanding' (1993) 92 *Proceedings of the National Academy of Sciences* 9977.

[46] Young, Hazarika, Poria, and Cambria, 'Recent Trends in Deep Learning Based Natural Language Processing', 8–10.

[47] H Kamp and U Reyle, *From Discourse to Logic: Introduction to Model Theoretic Semantics of Natural Language, Formal Logic and Discourse Representation Theory* (Springer, 1993) 21–24.

[48] *cf* SL Frank., R Bod and MH Christiansen, 'How Hierarchical is Language Use?' (2012) 279 *Proceedings of the Royal Society* B 4522; H Hu, D Yarats, Q Gong, Y Tian and M Lewis, 'Hierarchical Decision Making by Generating and Following Natural Language Instructions' (2019), arxiv.org/abs/1906.00744.

[49] Bates, 'Models of Natural Language Understanding' 9977.

[50] A Turing, 'Computing Machinery and Intelligence' (1950) 14 *Mind* 433.

by the senses but is fixed in advance, presumably by genetic inheritance'.[51] The rationalist approach to NLP has dominated the field of linguistics largely due to Noam Chomsky's arguments for innateness of language in humans. AI research was thus guided by the idea that knowledge of language in the human mind was pre-determined by genetic inheritance.[52] Rationalist approaches were largely derived from the work of Chomsky on the innateness of language and grammatical structure and his rejection of N-grams.[53] Believing that core aspects of language were biologically encoded into the brain at birth through genetic inheritance, rationalist approaches to NLP attempted to design hard-coded rules for capturing human knowledge and incorporating reasoning mechanisms into NLP systems using various techniques borrowed from the emerging field of AI research.[54]

This first wave of NLP systems had particular strengths in transparency and interpretability but were limited in their capacity to perform logical reasoning tasks. Following the approach of so-called Expert Systems, NLP systems such as ELIZA or MARGIE relied upon hard coded rules and codifying human expertise.[55] This meant that they were only useful for narrow applications and could not cope with uncertainty enough to be useful in practical applications.[56] Instead, most NLP applications during this time relied upon symbolic rules and templates using various grammatical and ontological constructs. When this approached worked, it worked quite well. However, successes were few and far between and there were major difficulties to their use in practical contexts.[57]

B. Empiricism and NLP

The second wave, referred to as empiricism, relies upon data sets and early ML and statistical techniques to make sense of them. The empiricist approach to NLP, Manning and Schütze explain:

> … begins by postulating some cognitive abilities as present in the brain. The difference between the approaches is therefore not absolute but one of degree. One has to assume some initial structure in the brain which causes it to prefer certain ways of organizing and generalizing from sensory inputs to others, as no learning is possible from a completely blank slate, tabula rasa.[58]

[51] CD Manning and H Schütze, *Foundations of Statistical Natural Language Processing* (MIT Press, 1999) 4–5.

[52] L Deng and Y Liu, 'A Joint Introduction to Natural language Processing and to Deep Learning' in Deng and Liu (eds), *Deep Learning in Natural Language Processing.*

[53] N Chomsky, *Syntactic Structures* (Mouton, 1957); D Jurafsky and JH Martin, 'Chapter 3: N-gram Language Models' in D Jurafsky and JH Martin, *Speech and Language Processing* (Prentice Hall, 2018), web.stanford.edu/~jurafsky/slp3/3.pdf.

[54] E Brill and RJ Mooney, 'Empirical Natural Language Processing' (1997) 18 *AI Magazine* 4.

[55] C Markou and L Hands, '*Capacitas Ex Machina*' (this volume); H Shah, K Warwick, J Vallerdú and D Wu, 'Can Machines talk? Comparison of Eliza and Modern Dialogue Systems' (2016) 58 *Computers in Human Behavior* 278.

[56] D Kahneman and A Tversky, 'Variants of Uncertainty' (1982) 11 *Cognition* 2; *cf* D Li and Y Du, *Artificial Intelligence with Uncertainty*, 2nd edn (CRC Press, 2017).

[57] Brill and Mooney, 'Empirical Natural Language Processing' 13–18.

[58] Mannin and Schütze, *Foundations of Statistical Natural Language Processing* 5.

Generally, empiricist NLP approach assumes that the human mind is not hard-coded with detailed rule sets and mechanisms dedicated to various components of language or other cognitive processes. Instead, it assumes that a baby's brain starts out with general associative rules that allow it to detect patterns, generalise information, and that both can be recursively applied to the sensory data in the baby's environment that allow it to learn the detailed and nuanced structure of natural language.[59]

Armstrong-Warwick observes that empirical NLP methods offer several advantages over rationalist approaches, such as: (1) acquisition – the ability to identify and encode relevant domain knowledge, (2) coverage – incorporating all the phenomena of a domain or application, (3) robustness – combining (often 'noisy') empirical data and factors not explicitly accounted for in the underlying NLP model, and (4) extensibility – the ability to extend an application from one domain or task to another.[60] Empiricist approaches are nonetheless beset by a 'reproducibility crisis'.[61]

While prevalent between the 1920s and 1960s, the ICT revolution made large tracts of machine-readable data available, driven by a steady increase in computing power, and better, faster, and cheaper components – driven by the relentless technological selection enshrined by Moore's Law.[62] The exponential growth of digital information – which by one estimate will total 175 zettabytes worldwide by 2025[63] – has meant that data-hungry empirical approaches have dominated NLP research since the 1990s. In contrast to rationalist approaches, which assumed language was a genetic inheritance, empirical approaches presumed that the human brain begins with only rudimentary capacity for association, pattern recognition and generalisation. To learn the complex structure of natural language the mind was thought to require a stream of rich sensory data.[64] Early empirical NLP approaches used generative models, such as Hidden Markov Models ('HMMs'), to create stochastic models describing a sequence of probable events where the probability of an event depends on the state attained by a previous event.[65]

[59] *cf* T Pedersen, 'Empiricism is Not a Matter of Faith' (2008) 34 *Computational Linguistics* 3; S Nirenburg and MJ McShane, 'Natural Language Processing' in SF Chipman (ed), *The Oxford Handbook of Cognitive Science* (Oxford University Press, 2017) 340–42.

[60] Brill and Mooney, 'Empirical Natural Language Processing' 16.

[61] S Cassidy and D Estival, 'Supporting Accessibility and Reproducibility in Language Research in the Alveo Virtual Laboratory' (2017) 45 *Computer Speech & Language* 375; KB Cohen, J Xia, P Zweigenbaum, et al., 'Three Dimensions of Reproduciblity in Natural Language Processing' (2018) *Proceedings of the Eleventh International Conference on Language Resources and Evaluation* 156; H Killcoglu, 'Biomedical Text Mining for Research Rigor and Integrity: Tasks, Challenges, Directions' (2018) 19 *Briefings in Bioinformatics* 6; A Moore and P Rayson, 'Bringing Replication and Reproduction together with Generalisability in NLP: Three Reproduction Studies for Target Dependent Sentiment Analysis' (2018) *Proceedings of the 27th International Conference on Computational Lingustics* Santa Fe, New Mexico, USA, 20–26 August 2018, 1132.

[62] GE Moore, 'Cramming More Components onto Integrated Circuits' (1998) 86 *Proceedings of the IEEE* 1.

[63] D Reinsel, J Gantz and J Rydning, 'Data Age 2025: The Digitization of the World from Edge to Core' (*IDC White Paper*, November 2018), www.seagate.com/files/www-content/our-story/trends/files/idc-seagate-dataage-whitepaper.pdf.

[64] Brill and Mooney, 'Empirical Natural Language Processing' 16–18.

[65] *cf* EA Feinberg and A Shwartz (eds), *Handbook of Markov Decision Processes: Methods and Applications* (Springer, 2002). In 'A Mathematical Theory of Communication' (1948) 27 *Bell System Technical Journal* 379, Claude Shannon for all intents founded information theory and by doing so revolutionised the telecommunications industry and laid the groundwork for the Information Age. Shannon proposed using a Markov chain to create a statistical model of the sequences of letters in a piece of English text. This was remarkably successful. Markov chains are now widely used in speech recognition, handwriting recognition, information retrieval, data compression, and spam filtering among many other uses. Markov models and decision

Among many other uses, these HMM models remain remarkably useful for determining the structure of natural languages from large data sets, and developing various probabilistic language models.[66]

Generally, ML based approaches to NLP perform much better than earlier knowledge-based ones.[67] Virtually every successful NLP application, including speech recognition, hand-writing recognition, and machine translation are attributable to empiricist approaches.[68] However, while recent developments have yielded major performance increases in translation quality,[69] NLP is not yet nearly as pervasive in real-world deployment as many hope it can be.

C. Deep Learning and NLP

While NLP applications such as speech recognition, language understanding and machine translations developed out of this second wave – and generally performed much better than those in the first – they fell far short of human-level performance.[70] The ML models used were insufficient for dealing with large sets of training data and algorithmic design, method and implementation were lacking. This, however, changed dramatically a few years ago with the third wave of NLP under the Deep Learning (DL) paradigm.[71] As discussed above, ML requires human programmers to define various features; as such, feature engineering is a bottleneck that requires significant human expertise. Moreover, comparatively 'shallow' ANNs lack the capacity to produce decomposable abstractions and ontologies that allow for the automatic disentangling of complex language structures. Young et al. note the advantages of DL approaches over ML:

> Deep learning enables multi-level automatic feature representation learning. In contrast, traditional machine learning based NLP systems liaise heavily on hand-crafted features. Such hand-crafted features are time-consuming and often incomplete.[72]

The complexity of DL models in NLP contexts enables the learning of concepts at higher-levels of abstraction by building them out of lower-level representations. This has led to the development of so-called Deep Belief Networks[73] – a form of ANN that

processes also inform numerous scientific applications including: the genemark algorithm for gene prediction, the Metropolis algorithm for measuring thermodynamical properties, and Google's PageRank algorithm for Web search.

[66] Y Bengio, R Ducharme, P Vincent and C Jauvin, 'A Neural Probabilistic Language Model' (2003) 3 *Journal of Machine Learning Research* 1137–55; A Karpathy, 'The Unreasonable Effectiveness of Recurrent Neural Networks' (2015), karpathy.github.io/2015/05/21/rnn-effectiveness/.

[67] R Socher, Y Bengio and CD Manning, 'Deep Learning for NLP (Without Magic)' (2012), dl.acm.org/doi/10.5555/2390500.2390505.

[68] M Och, 'Minimum Error Rate Training in Statistical Machine Translation' (2003) Proceedings of the 41st Annual Meeting on Association for Computational Linguistics.

[69] F Och and H Ney, 'Discriminative Training and Maximum Entropy Models for Statistical Machine Translation' (2002) Proceedings of the 40th Annual Meeting on Association for Computational Linguistics; D Chiang, 'Hierarchical Phrase-based Translation' (2007) 33 *Computational Linguistics* 2.

[70] Deng and Liu (eds), *Deep Learning in Natural Language Processing* 4–6.

[71] *cf* T Young, D Hazarika, S Poria and E Cambria, 'Recent Trends in Deep Learning Based Natural Language Processing' (2018) *IEEE Computational Intelligence Magazine.*

[72] Young, Hazarika and Cambria, 'Recent Trends in Deep Learning Based Natural Language Processing' 55.

[73] G Hinton, S Osindero and Y-W Teh, 'A Fast Learning Algorithm for Deep Belief Nets' (2006) 18 *Neural Computation* 7, 1527.

can generate connections between layers without needing to do so between neurons in the same layer – and Convolutional Neural Networks (CNN) which replicate the organisation of the animal visual cortex to produce vast performance leaps in image classification and recognition.[74] However, the overarching promise of DL is the ability to discover intricate patterns and correlation in high-dimensional data. This has enabled the development of applications useful in real-world tasks, perhaps most notably speech recognition, image recognition and machine translation. For instance, Collobert et al. demonstrate that even a simple DL model can outperform the most cutting-edge approaches to NLP in tasks such as named-entity recognition (NER), part of speech tagging (POS), and syntactic parsing.[75] Since then several, and often very complex, DL-based approaches have been proposed to solve some of the most intractable problems in NLP.

D. NLP + Law

Because law is almost entirely expressed in natural language categories, true NLP is essential for the deployment of AI in law at scale. However, different legal texts (statutes, case reports, contracts) present different challenges, and require selecting the right technique. As a rule of thumb, the more formulaic the layout of a text (as in the case of a statute) the more predictable its content becomes, and in turn, the more amenable the text is to being converted using formal representations.

For instance, judicial opinions vary greatly because they involve fact-specific information drawn from real-world cases. Moreover, individual judges have their own rhetorical techniques, and their judgments can often turn on linguistic abstractions not easily captured. Administrative regulations, on the other hand, are typically more formulaic and detailed than corresponding statutes, whereas public law regulations follow regular patterns, and re-use familiar phrases that make their content and structure more amenable to translation. Even so, public law texts do not profess to cover every possible contingency, and the statutes on which they are based must usually be interpreted by judges or other officials. Yet public law texts differ from private contracts which *do* attempt to legislate for a number of contingencies and outcomes relevant to the relationships they formalise. Superficially, then, contracts are better placed to move out of the messy, ambiguous, and open-textured world of natural language than public law. Indeed, mounting interest in the use of distributed ledgers such as Blockchain are accelerating the trend towards so-called 'Smart Contracts'.

E. Applying NLP to Legal Texts

Because law is such a data-rich domain, researchers have long explored how to apply NLP techniques to various aspects of legal work and policymaking. But the Internet, that most data-rich of domains, allows for more creative approaches. For instance, if a

[74] A Krizhevsky, H Sustkever and GE Hinton, 'ImageNet Classification with Deep Convolutional Neural Networks' (2017) 60 *Communications of the ACM* 6; Young, Hazarika, Poria, and Cambria, 'Recent trends in Deep Learning Based Natural Language Processing' 59–62.

[75] R Collobert, J Weston, L Bottou, M Karlen, K Kavukcuoglu and P Kuksa, 'Natural Language Processing (Almost) from Scratch' (2011) 12 *Journal of Machine Learning Research* 2493.

researcher wanted to assess public reaction to high-profile cases they might wish to mine social media platforms (Twitter/Facebook) for information. However, given the volume of posts it is impractical to read each and every tweet or post. Instead, an NLP tool can summarise relevant posts and extract reactions to the outcome of the case. The subsequent sections briefly survey the primary applications of NLP in legal contexts, including (1) sentiment analysis, (2) text summarisation, and (3) topic modelling.

i. Subjectivity + Sentiment Analysis

Of all of the recent breakthroughs in various domains, some of the most important NLP research innovations have been made in what is called 'sentiment' and 'subjectivity' analysis. Along with emotion detection, a task expanding beyond the NLP domain, both sentiment and subjectivity analysis are important factors in the development of AI and affective computing more generally. However, as Montoyo et al., observe: 'Given the ambiguous nature of the terms "subjectivity" and "sentiment", research in these areas has span over many different approaches and applications, making a unique definition difficult to provide.'[76]

Generally, however, we can say that sentiment analysis tools are used to automatically identify and label subjective expressions of emotion or the 'point of view' in a text. For instance, 'I thought dinner was terrific' expresses a positive sentiment, whereas 'the chicken was overcooked' expresses a negative one. In the context of law, and policy/government more widely, gathering and qualifying public sentiment can help regulators better assess public receptivity to proposed legislative or regulatory changes.[77]

Practically, sentiment labelling involves the use of numeric scales ranging from positive to negative (sentiment polarity) or more specific emotions such as enthusiasm or disgust. When all of the relevant texts are analysed and placed on this numeric scale, the scores for each word can then be averaged to assign an overall sentiment score for a particular document. By using categorical emotion labels, the percentage of words assigned to each label can in turn be used to summarise the sentiment. The majority of sentiment analysis techniques can be sub-divided into either dictionary-based or learning-based. Dictionary-based techniques, as the name implies, use large lists of manually pre-scored/rated words for their subjective sentiment. Scoring is usually done at the level of individual words (unigrams) because sets of multiple words (bigrams, trigrams, and so on) occur far less frequently and thus have less diagnostic value in the automatic labelling of sentences.

While dictionary-based techniques do, however, seem to work well for tracking public sentiment on Twitter,[78] their performance drops precipitously when negation

[76] A Montoyo, P Martínez-Barco and A Balahur, 'Subjectivity and Sentiment Analysis: An Overview of the Current State of the Area and Envisaged Developments' (2012) 53 *Decision Support Systems* 675.

[77] C Cardie, C Farina and T Bruce, 'Using Natural Language Processing to Improve eRulemaking: Project Highlight' (2006) in Proceedings of the 2006 International Conference on Digital Government Research (Digital Government Society of North America, 2006); N Kwon, SW Shulman and E Hovy, 'Multidimensional Text Analysis for eRulemaking' in Proceedings of the 2006 International Conference on Digital Government Research (Digital Government Society of North America, 2006); D Pérez-Fernández, J Arenas-García, D Samy, A Padilla-Soler and V Gómez-Verdejo, 'Corpus Viewer: NLP and ML-based Platform for Public Policy Making and Implementation' (2019) 63 *Procesamiento del Lenguaje Natural, Revista* 193.

[78] PS Dodds, KD Harris, IM Kloumann, CA Bliss and CM Danforth, 'Temporal Patterns of Happiness and Information in a Global Social Network: Hedonometrics and Twitter' (2011) 6 *PLoS ONE* 12.

or sarcasm are involved. Dictionary-based approaches can be improved, however by automatically parsing them and labelling the function of a word within a sentence, and then using rules of negation, and valence shifters, to assess sentiment.[79] Nonetheless, dictionary-based approaches do not generalise well to texts in specialised domains (law, medicine) where words are too rare to have been previously scored using a dictionary, or where words that are scored serve different functions in different contexts. This is particularly critical for legal texts due to the fact that most sentiment dictionaries have not been compiled and scored by non-legal experts, and sentiment analysis is most often done in the context of news articles or social media.

Recent research into ML-based sentiment analysis has explored how to leverage the entire text of documents to build predictive sentiment models based on strings of words, or the proximity of words to each other. Thomas et al., for example, have applied these methods to predict whether lawmakers are likely to support or oppose specific policy issues using transcripts of debates from the US Congress.[80] To achieve this, ML NLP models use entire sentences or documents as inputs to predict sentiment on the basis of the entire collection of words. Practically, a developed model must (1) label the sentiment across a sufficient number of documents, (2) use one of the above-described methods to transform words into numerical representations, so that (3) a model can 'learn' how to map sentiment across documents for any textual input. The goal then is to train the model on levelled documents so that it can be used to predict sentiment in unlabelled documents it has not encountered in the course or training.

The primary drawback to the ML NLP method is similar to that in dictionary-based approaches. Namely, a ML model trained to predict sentiment in one domain (for example Twitter) may not necessarily transfer well to a different domain (for example legal judgments).[81] Moreover, the context of documents matters for how subjective sentiment is assessed. For instance 'go read the book' is a positive sentiment in the context of a book review, but negative in the context of a review of a film based on the book.[82]

ii. Text Summarisation

Generally, text summarisation tools involve various techniques that enable the automatic conversion of long texts into shorter ones. This might involve converting an entire document into shorter ones, or summarising multiple documents. This can be approached in one of two ways. The simpler approach, *extractive summarisation*, flags relevant portions of text (words, phrases, sentences), extracts them, and then combines them into a single summary. The more complex approach, albeit the more powerful one,

[79] A Kennedy and D Inkpen, 'Sentiment Classification of Movie Review Using Contextual Valance Shifters' (2006) 22 *Computational Intelligence* 2; D Zimbra, M Chiassi and S Lee, 'Brand-related Twitter Sentiment Analysis Using Feature Engineering and the Dynamic Architecture for Artificial Neural Networks' (2016) 49th Hawaii International Conference on System Sciences (HICSS).

[80] M Thomas, B Pang and Lee, 'Get Out the Vote: Determining Support or Opposition from Congressional Floor-debate Transcripts' in Proceedings of the 2006 Conference on Empirical Methods in Natural Language Processing (Association for Computational Linguistics, 2006).

[81] S Owsley, S Sood and KJ Hammond, 'Domain Specific Affective Classification of Documents' in *AAAI Spring Symposium: Computational Approaches to Analyzing Weblogs* (AAAI Press, 2006).

[82] B Pang, L Lee and S Vaithyanathan, 'Thumbs Up?: Sentiment Classification Using Machine Learning Techniques' in Proceedings of the ACL-02 Conference on Empirical Methods in Natural Language Processing: Volume 10 (Association for Computational Linguistics, 2002).

is called *abstractive summarisation*. This involves generating an entirely new text, and not necessarily one that was contained in the text being summarised. But this requires an algorithm capable of building complex and abstract representations from the text to capture its 'essence'.

As it stands, abstractive summarisation only works well for texts with a few paragraphs, and extractive summarisation methods have outperformed abstractive ones. One of the most widely used extractive techniques is called TextRank, and it works by creating a graphical representation of a text where each vertex represents a sentence in the document being summarised.

iii. Topic Modelling

While an algorithm like TextRank can offer high quality summaries of longer texts, it was originally intended for summarising one text at a time. In cases where there are a number of documents on a diverse array of topics, then it is more helpful – and indeed feasible – to have an algorithm identify what proportion of a text is devoted to a particular topic. While a topic might involve a list of particular words (employee, contract, control) a topic *model* is a means of probabilistically modelling the distribution of words across a set of texts.[83] Rehurke and Sojka explain that the basic premise of topic modelling is that:

> … texts in natural languages can be expressed in terms of a limited number of underlying concepts (or topics), a process which both improves efficiency (new representation takes up less space) and eliminates noise (transformation into topics can be viewed as noise reduction).[84]

Topic modelling algorithms can thus be classified as a type of generative process: they create topics out of textual corpora, identify the distribution of topics across documents, and then for each word in each document select a vocabulary term from the topics. From a specific list of topics, estimating the parameters of the model automatically uncovers topics across a corpus, their distribution per-document, and then per-document/per-word, with the goal of arriving at a correlated topic model that explicitly represents variability between the proportion of topics, and topical prevalence within documents to exhibit their own correlations. For instance, a topic relevant to Labour Law is more likely to occur in judicial opinions that have a high proportion of words such as 'employer', 'holiday pay' and 'wage', which are more likely to occur in employment law contexts than in securities law. Legal scholars have begun exploring how to apply these methods to case law. For instance, Carter, Brown and Rahmani conducted one of the first topic modelling experiments using decisions from the High Court of Australia from 1903–2015.[85] While their paper was primarily methodological in nature, their analysis revealed changes in the 'length and number of cases published

[83] R Rehurek and P Sojka, 'Software Framework for Topic Modelling with Large Corpora' in Proceedings of the LREC 2010 Workshop on New Challenges for NLP Frameworks (2010), www.fi.muni.cz/usr/sojka/papers/lrec2010-rehurek-sojka.pdf.

[84] Rehurek and Sojka, 'Software Framework for Topic Modelling with Large Corpora' 46.

[85] DJ Carter, J Brown and A Rahmani, 'Reading the High Court at a Distance: Topic Modelling the Legal Subject Matter and Judicial Activity of the High Court of Australia, 1903–2015' (2016) 39 *UNSW Law Journal* 4.

by the Court … [and] how the Court's focus upon particular topics has changed over time'.[86] While their results indicate a potentially fruitful trajectory for future research, Hildebrandt reminds us that 'positive law, inscribed in legal texts, entails an authority not inherent in literary texts, generating legal consequences that can have real effects on a person's life and liberty'.[87]

V. Exploring the Limits of AI in Law

Successive studies have begun to probe the inherent limitations and discriminatory effects of deploying ADM to various social contexts.[88] From concerns about the opacity and explainability of ML algorithms, to flawed selection of data, to technical and legal strategies to ensure the trustworthiness, accountability, and compliance of automated systems, a clear picture has emerged as to the dangers of relying on what Wigner termed the 'unreasonable effectiveness of mathematics in the natural sciences'.[89] But in addition to immediate concerns loom much bigger and more entangled questions about the epistemic and practical viability of using AI and Big Data to replicate core aspects and processes of the legal system, if not the cognitive domain of lawyers of judges altogether.

If we are to assess claims of a forthcoming 'legal singularity' we must first ask basic questions: what is AI good at?, what is AI bad at?, and what does it mean to claim that ML (in current and aspirational forms) can replicate core processes of the legal system, if not human reasoning and authority altogether? Contrary to the assumptions of empiricists, Thomas Kuhn argued that reality is not directly accessible to human observers as 'facts' that can be recorded and mathematically formalised. While we may access reality as limited by our senses, we cannot do so without the interference of 'meaning making'. What we can sense, through a camera lens, for instance, already has meaning, and meaning is not a function of sensory perception. Sensory perception is not possible without biological cognition that allows an observer to observe.

Data science, on the other hand, does not simply record facts about the world. It transforms data in ways that can be apprehended by the human senses. The same applies to AI and ML applications using vast data sets. Efforts to formalise legal knowledge into mathematical axioms and transform juridical reasoning into something that can be modelled echo the Neo-platonism of the early scientific era and revive the Leibnizian assumption that there exists a hidden mathematical order underlying the structure of reality and human cognition. With the rise of 'LegalTech', it is now presumed that mathematical formalisation is not just possible, but that strategic reasoning expressed via

[86] Carter, Brown and Rahmani, 'Reading the High Court at a Distance' 1301.

[87] M Hildebrandt, 'The Meaning and Mining of Legal Texts' in DM Berry (ed), *Understanding Digital Humanities* (Palgrave Macmillan, 2012) 145.

[88] S Barocas and AD Selbst, 'Big Data's Disparate Impact' (2016) 104 *California Law Review* 671; J Burrell, 'How the Machine "Thinks": Understanding Opacity in Machine Learning Algorithms' (2016) 3 *Big Data & Society* 1; LB Moses and J Chan, 'Algorithmic Prediction in Policing: Assumptions, Evolution, and Accountability' (2018) 28 *Policing and Society* 7; B Lepri, N Oliver, E Letouzé, A Pentland and P Vinck, 'Fair, Transparent, and Accountable Algorithmic Decision-making Processes' (2018) 31 *Philosophy & Technology* 4.

[89] EP Wigner, 'The Unreasonable Effectiveness of Mathematics in the Natural Sciences' (1960) XIII *Communications on Pure and Applied Mathematics* 001–014.

computation should be considered ontologically superior to inherently faulty practical reasoning expressed through natural language categories.

Understanding the assumptions of the new normative order posed by AI and Big Data will help legal scholars better understand not just the consequences, but their role in expediting or mitigating the 'legal singularity'. However, we must first consider some of the inherent limitations of AI and ML, particularly as they relate to the task of formalising legal reasoning and imputed legal consequences from algorithmic processes.

A. Natural Language Understanding (NLU)

At the outset it is helpful to distinguish between the various goals subsumed under the umbrella of NLP. Although they are often confused for one another, or conflated, both Natural Language Understanding (NLU) and NLP are different aspects of the goal of having computers work with natural language in the ways that humans do. More precisely, however, NLU is best understood as a subset of goals in having computers comprehend natural language.[90] The relationship between the constituent aspects of NLP and NLU are illustrated in Figure 3.

Figure 3 Natural Language Understanding vs Natural Language Processing vs Automatic Speech Recognition

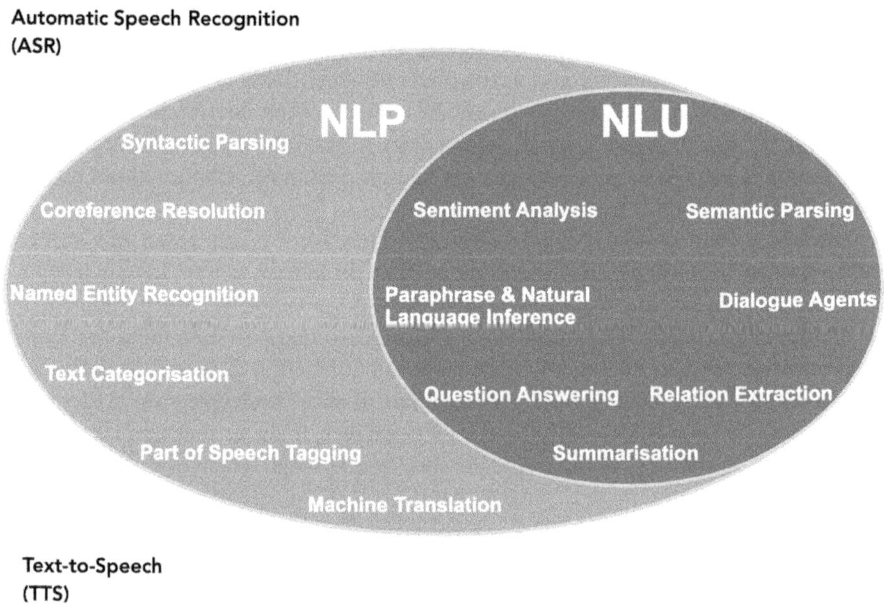

[90] GM Green, *Pragmatics and Natural Language Understanding*, 2nd edn (Lawrence Erlbaum, 2008).

While developing machines to generate language is a challenge – even in the narrowest domains – having them understand the semantic contours of language as humans do is perhaps the most intractable problem in NLP. Indeed, many NLP experts identify NLU as a necessary condition for both natural language generation (NLG) and natural language interpretation (NLI). Semaan distinguishes between these interrelated domains:

> NLG is the inverse of NLU (Natural Language Understanding) or NLI (Natural Language Interpretation), in that NLG maps from meaning to text; while, NLU maps from text to meaning NLG is easier then NLU because a NLU system cannot control the complexity of the language structure it receives as input while NLG links the complexity of the structure of its output.[91]

Despite sustained efforts, and significant breakthroughs, even the most advanced language models fall far short of true understanding of natural language.

B. Finite Data

Data is the 'lifeblood' of AI research and a major bottleneck for the development of new applications.[92] Despite an ongoing lack of labelled data, compelling and effective use cases for ML continue to be found in a variety of real-world contexts. The use cases for DL, on the other hand, have been slow in coming, leading some to question its long term viability.[93] There are several reasons for this, but the primary reason is the data intensive nature of DL and sheer scale of data required to train and produce valid models.[94] It is for this very reason that the entities prioritising AI research are engaging in elaborate multiyear games to overcome the data acquisition problem and compete for the data they need.[95] Because DL systems must generalise solutions beyond their training data (for example pronouncing a new word or identifying an unseen image) data availability limits algorithmic performance to the extent that it cannot guarantee high-quality solutions.

Generalisation takes place by either interpolation of known (that is, correctly identified) examples or extrapolation which requires an algorithm generalising beyond the examples in training data. For a DL network to accurately generalise, it must, at least in most cases, have access to a vast library of data with test data similar to that of its training data so that new solutions can be interpolated from previous ones. In the paper credited with reigniting interest in the viability and practicality of DL applications, the landmark performance results were achieved using a nine-layer Convolutional Neural Network (CNN)

[91] P Semaan, 'Natural Language Generation: an Overview' (2012) 1 *Journal of Computer Science and Research* 3, 50.

[92] Y Roh, G Her and E Whang, 'A Survey on Data Collection for Machine Learning: a Big Data – AI Perspective' (2018), arxiv.org/abs/1811.03402.

[93] G Marcus, 'Deep Learning: A Critical Appraisal' (2018), arxiv.org/abs/1801.00631; *cf* T Nield, 'Is Deep Learning Already Hitting its Limitations?' (*Towards Data Science*, 5 January 2019), towardsdatascience.com/is-deep-learning-already-hitting-its-limitations-c81826082ac3.

[94] A Woodie, 'Deep Learning is Great, but Use Cases Remain Narrow' (*Datanami*, 3 October 2018), www.datanami.com/2018/10/03/deep-learning-is-great-but-use-cases-remain-narrow.

[95] T Simonite, 'AI and "Enormous Data" Could Make Tech Giants Harder to Topple' (*Wired*, 13 July 2017), www.wired.com/story/ai-and-enormous-data-could-make-tech-giants-harder-to-topple/.

with 60 million parameters and 650,000 nodes trained on approximately a million images from approximately 1,000 categories. While the brute force approach to image recognition yielded impressive results, it did so in the large but nonetheless finite context of the ImageNet database.[96] Moreover, DL works particularly well in stable domains where training exemplars can be mapped onto finite or limited categories, but struggles in tasks requiring open-ended inference, examined in greater detail below.

C. Data Intensiveness

Humans are able to learn abstract relationships with only a few trials. For instance, if a drother was defined as a brother between the ages of 15 and 30, perhaps using an example, a human could easily infer whether they had any drothers or if anyone they knew did. Using an explicit definition a human does not require potentially millions of training examples to generalise and abstract out what a drother is. Rather, the capacity to infer abstract relationships between algebraic variables (male/age range) through explicit and implicit heuristics is a tacit and innate quality of biological intelligence.

Psychological researchers observe that the capacity for inference and abstraction is seen in seven month old toddlers who can learn language rules from a limited number of labelled examples in under two minutes.[97] At present, DL approaches cannot learn abstract relationships through explicit verbal definitions, and instead work best (if at all) when trained using millions or even billions of training examples; this is best evidenced by Deep Mind's success with video games and Go.[98] As successive researches demonstrate, humans are far more efficient at learning complex rules and generalising abstraction relationships than DL systems.[99] This has not been lost on DL's staunchest proponents, leading some to question whether CNNs' dependence on large numbers of labelled examples and difficulty in generalising novel viewpoints might 'lead to their demise.'[100]

D. Transfer Learning

While DL has yielded impressive results in computationally intensive domains, the word 'deep' refers to a technical property (that is, the number of hidden or convolutional layers) and does not imply conceptual depth or sophistication. For instance, a DL network thousands of layers deep cannot induce understanding or generalise abstract

[96] One count indicates that ImageNet contains more than 14 million images divided into more than 20,000 categories, *cf* J Markoff, 'Seeking a Better Way to Find Web Images' *New York Times* (19 November 2012), www.nytimes.com/2012/11/20/science/for-web-images-creating-new-technology-to-seek-and-find.html.

[97] GF Marcus, S Vijayan, S Bandi Rao and PM Vishton, 'Rule Learning by Seven Month-old Infants' (1999) 2283 *Science* 5398.

[98] D Silver, A Huange and CJ Maddison et al., 'Mastering the Game of Go with Deep Neural Networks and Tree Search' (2016) 529 *Nature* 484.

[99] BM Lake, R Salahutdinov and JB Tenenbaum, 'Human-level Concert Learning through Probabilistic Program Induction' (2015) 350 *Science* 6266; BM Lake, TD Ullman, JB Tenenbaum, & SJ Gershman, 'Building Machines that Learn and Think like People' (2016) *Behavioral and Brain Sciences* 1.

[100] S Sabour, N Frosst and GE Hinton, 'Dynamic Routing between Capsules' (2017), arxiv.org/abs/1710:09829.

and subjective concepts such as 'fairness', 'justice' or 'employee'. Even more mundane concepts can elude understanding. In his analysis of Deep Mind's success using reinforcement learning methods to conquer Atari video games, Marcus critiques the suggestion that the program has 'learned' anything, but rather 'doesn't really understand what a tunnel, or what a wall is; it has just learned specific contingencies for particular scenarios'.[101] The system represents 'knowledge' through converting raw informational data into inputs that allow a game to be 'played' but there is no player as such.

Transfer tests – where a deep reinforcement learning system is confronted with scenarios that differ in minor ways from those it was trained on – show that DL solutions are often extremely superficial. Marcus argues that it is misleading to suggest that reinforcement learning enables a program to induce a semantic understanding of the narrow computational environment: 'It's not that the Atari system genuinely learned a concept of wall that was robust but rather the system superficially approximated breaking through walls within a narrow set of highly trained circumstances.'[102]

The superficiality of DL's 'learning' is particularly evident in natural language contexts. For instance, research by Jia and Liang trained artificial neural networks (ANNs) on the Stanford Question Answering Database (SQuAD) where the goal was to highlight words in a passage corresponding to a given question. In one example, the system was correctly trained to identify John Elway as the winning quarterback of Super Bowl XXXIII based on a short summary of the game. However, the inclusion of red herring sentences – such as a fictional one about Google AI researcher Jeff Dean winning another 'bowl' game – led to a major drop off in accuracy from 75 per cent to 36 per cent.[103]

E. Non-Hierarchical Language

Most language-based DL models represent sentences as strings of words. This contrasts with the hierarchical view of language proposed by Chomsky, in which language is ordered into four classes by its complexity, and larger linguistic structures are recursively constructed out of smaller components.[104] Earlier research cast doubts that even the most sophisticated neural networks could systematically represent and extend the recursive structure of language to new and unfamiliar sentences.[105] More recently, however, Lake and Baroni conclude that neural networks are 'still not systematic after all these years' and that they could 'generalize well when the differences between training and test … are small [but] when generalization requires systematic compositional skills, [they] fail spectacularly'.[106]

[101] Marcus, 'Deep learning: a critical appraisal' 8.
[102] Marcus, 'Deep learning: a critical appraisal' 8.
[103] R Jia and P Liang, 'Adversarial Examples for Evaluating Reading Comprehension Systems' (2017), arxiv.org/abs/1707.07328.
[104] N Chomsky, 'Three Models for the Description of Language' (1956) 2 *IRE Transaction of Information Theory* 113; N Chomsky, 'On Certain Formal Properties of Grammars' (1959) 2 *Information and Control* 137.
[105] JA Fodor and ZW Pylyshyn, 'Connectionism and Cognitive Architecture: A Critical Analysis' (1988) 28 *Cognition* 3; MH Christiansen and N Chater, 'Toward a Connectionist Model of Recursion in Human Linguistic Performance' (1999) 23 *Cognitive Science* 2.
[106] BM Lake and M Baroni, 'Still Not Systematic After All These Years: On The Compositional Skills of Sequence-to-sequence Recurrent Networks' (2017), arxiv.org/abs/1711.00350.

While similar difficulties are likely to be encountered in other domains, the inability to deal with complex hierarchical language structures presents specific challenges within the domain of law, where systems will inevitably encounter novel fact patterns requiring generalising abstract relationships from agonistic accounts of underlying 'facts'. As Marcus observes:

> The core problem, at least at present, is that deep learning learns correlations between sets of features that are themselves 'flat' or non-hierarchical, as if in a simple, unstructured list, with every feature on equal footing. Hierarchical structure (e.g., syntactic trees that distinguish between main clauses and embedded clauses in a sentence) are not inherently or directly represented in such systems, and as a result deep learning systems are forced to use a variety of proxies that are ultimately inadequate, such as the sequential position of a word presented in a sequences.[107]

Whereas people learn and acquire many different types of tacit and innate knowledge from diverse experiences over many years,[108] in most cases becoming better learners over time, DL systems are comparatively narrow and able to learn only a single function or data model from statistical analysis of a single data set. Although progress has been made in representing words in the form of vectors and complete sentences in ways that are compatible with DL techniques, they remain limited in the ability to reliably represent and generalise rich semantic structure,[109] such as that found in legal judgments.

A promising solution is, however, posed by the never-ending language learning (NELL) paradigm developed by researchers at Carnegie Mellon University. Since 2010, Carnegie Mellon researchers have programmed NELL to run around the clock to identify fundamental semantic relations between hundreds of data categories such as cities, corporations, emotions and sports teams. This has involved NELL processing millions of web pages for connections between what it is has already 'learned' and what it finds through an exhaustive search process. The goal of the Carnegie Mellon team is to have NELL draw inferential connections and discern a hierarchical linguistic structure to deduce subsequent connections so that it can answer natural language questions with no human intervention.[110]

F. Open-ended Inference

Consider the sentences: 'Adam promised Eve to stop' and 'Adam promised to stop Eve'. Without the ability to draw semantic inferences about who is stopping who, the meaning of these sentences can dramatically diverge. While ML systems have proved adept at machine reading tasks such as SQuAd – where the answers are specified in the text being read – they have been far less successful at tasks requiring inference beyond

[107] Marcus, 'Deep Learning: A Critical Appraisal' 10.

[108] M Polanyi, *The Tacit Dimension*, rev edn (University of Chicago Press, 2009) 3–25.

[109] R Socher, CC Lin, A Ng and C Manning, 'Parsing Natural Scenes and Natural Language with Recursive Neural Networks' in L Getoor and T Scheffer (eds), *Proceedings of the 28th International Conference on Machine Learning* (Omnipress, 2011).

[110] S Lohr, 'Aiming to Learn as We Do, A Machine Teaches Itself' *New York Times* (4 October 2010), www.nytimes.com/2010/10/05/science/05compute.html.

those made explicit in a text. Common problems encountered include the combining of multiple sentences into a single semantic string (multi-hop inference)[111] or combining explicit sentences with information not included in a particular text selection. In contrast, when humans read a text they can automatically draw a variety of novel and implicit inferences, such as the ability to derive a fictional character's intentions from indirect dialogue.[112]

VI. Law as Algorithm: Exploring the Limits of 'Computable Law'

The next step in our analysis is to consider how far legal reasoning can be understood in terms equivalent to those developed for use in the domain of ML (and by extension DL). In so far as legal reasoning can be broken down into a series of algorithmic processes similar to those employed in ML, the case for applying ML to law is to that extent enhanced. Conversely, identifying features of legal reasoning which are not captured by an algorithmic logic can help us understand the limits to ML in legal contexts. Understanding those limits will also enable us to more clearly identify potential social harms resulting from the over-extensive application of ML in the legal sphere.

Our analysis proceeds as follows. We first of all consider the degree to which legal reasoning contains elements of information retention and error correction which are the approximate equivalent of those used in ML Then we look more closely at how legal reasoning involves processes of data partitioning and weighting which are analogous to those used in ML. We identify similarities between legal reasoning and ML, but also some critical differences. In particular, we question the applicability to the legal context of the idea of 'optimisation'. The 'learning' involved in legal reasoning is, we suggest, a process of non-linear adjustment between the legal system and its external context which is not adequately captured by the optimisation function of ML.

A. Classification, Information Retention and Error Correction in Legal Reasoning: The Case of Employment Status

As we have seen,[113] 'learning' in the context of ML refers to the iterative adjustment and dynamic optimisation of an algorithm, understood as a process for correctly mapping inputs into outputs in response to repeated exposure to data. Success is measured in terms of the algorithm's ability to predict or identify a specified outcome or range (a 'ground rule') from a given vector of variables. In order to 'learn', in the sense of becoming more accurate in its predictions, the algorithm must be able to retain information

[111] J Welbl, P Stenetorp and S Riedel, 'Constructing Datasets for Multi-hop Reading Comprehensive Access Documents' (2018), arxiv.org/abs/1710.06481.

[112] D Tannen, *Talking Voices*, 2nd edn (Cambridge University Press, 2007) 102–160.

[113] See sections IIA-IIC.

from previous iterations (or 'states'), while correcting errors. The statistical techniques used to tune and refine an algorithm's performance in this way include the partitioning of data into conceptual categories and the assignment of differential weights to those categories in order to establish their relative importance in the process of identification and prediction.[114]

B. Classifying Employment Relationships

To see how the legal system might be thought of as containing analogous mechanisms of information retention and error correction, we will use as an illustration the way in which courts and tribunals perform the task of classifying work relationships. This is a foundational issue in a number of areas of law, including employment law, tax law and tort law, and is one found in a functionally similar form (albeit with some important cross-national differences as well as variations across different areas of law) in virtually all legal systems today.[115]

The equivalent of the outcome or 'ground rule' here is the classification of an individual supplier of labour as either an 'employee', indicating one particular set of legal rights and obligations, or an 'independent contractor' or 'self-employed' person, indicating another. The terms used in various legal systems differ, but the basic classifications, and their normative functions, are remarkably consistent across national regimes.[116] 'Employee' status signifies that the individual supplier of labour is under a duty to obey orders of the counter-party, here signified as the 'employer', in return for receiving certain protections against work-related and labour market risks. An 'independent contractor' supplying their labour to a 'client' is in a different type of relationship: in essence, they have more autonomy over how they work but acquire fewer legal rights against their contractual counter-party. The outcome here is binary and so, at least in principle, is capable of being captured in mathematical form using a pairwise code (1, 0).[117] In this sense it is like very many legal determinations, which can be expressed as binary alternatives, such as (liable, not liable), and so on.

Certain classification systems, which may at first sight appear more complex, can be reduced to binary outcomes by narrowing the focus of the decision-making process, or in other words: making it more fact-intensive. Thus UK labour law currently knows not just one, but three basic categories of work relation: the employee, the self-employed or independent contractor and, somewhere in between them, an intermediate category

[114] See our analysis above. For a thorough overview of the training and tuning process *cf* Lehr and Ohm, 'Playing with the Data: What Legal Scholars Should Learn about Machine Learning' esp. 669–701.

[115] The literature on this question is huge. Here we draw principally on the historical analysis of the evolution of labour classifications in English law set out in S Deakin and F Wilkinson, *The Law of the Labour Market: Industrialization, Employment and Legal Evolution* (Oxford University Press, 2005).

[116] On the degree of functional continuity across systems, notwithstanding differences in terminology, *cf* S Deakin, 'The Comparative Evolution of the Employment Relationship' in G Davidov and B Langille (eds), *Boundaries and Frontiers of Labour Law* (Hart, 2006).

[117] Alarie, Niblett and Yoon, 'Using Machine Learning to Predict Outcomes in Tax Law'.

known as a 'limb (b) worker' which has some, but not all, of the characteristics of each of the other two.[118]

On closer inspection the existence of this third category does not detract from the essentially binary nature of the classification process. It just means that the court goes down one further layer of analysis in the sense of conducting an additional factual inquiry. After answering the question of whether the individual is an 'employee' or 'self-employed' in favour of the latter category, it will then undertake a further review of the facts to see whether the individual is a 'limb (b) worker', in which case they will acquire (among other things) the right to the minimum wage, or not, in which case they will not be accorded this legal right, among others. In effect, the set (limb (b) worker) is a set located entirely within the wider set (self-employed).

This example illustrates a further feature of legal categories, which is that they are arranged hierarchically. 'Higher level' categories, meaning those defined at a higher level of abstraction or generality, contain within them 'lower-level' or more fact-specific classifications.[119] The process of applying a concept to a given fact situation can be understood as one of moving from the general to the specific, or the abstract to the factual.[120] The process continues until the scope for conceptual classification is exhausted and the court is left with the unstructured empirical data of the facts presented to it.

The point at which the law reaches the limits of its discursive capabilities demarcates its boundary with other systems, such as the economy, politics, or technology.[121] Beyond the boundary of juridical analysis, as far as the legal system is concerned, data are unstructured or 'chaotic'.[122] With respect to such variables, law is unavoidably incomplete.[123] There is no unique 'right answer' to cases of classification which involve novel or untested points. When a new type of social or economic relationship comes before the courts for classification (as in the case, currently, of 'gig' or 'platform' work[124]), rather than a clear solution appearing immediately, what tends to happen instead is that different courts propose a number of alternative solutions which are then tested against each other, and selected in or out as the case may be, through external pressures arising from litigation and lobbying, as well as from academic legal commentary. Eventually, data which were initially unstructured or 'chaotic' are translated into the conceptual

[118] Employment Rights Act 1996, s 230(3)(b). For further detail *cf* S Deakin and G Morris *Labour Law*, 6th rev edn (Hart, 2012) ch 3; J Prassl, 'Pimlico Plumbers, Uber drivers, Cycle Couriers, and Court Translators: Who is a Worker?' (2017) Oxford Legal Studies Research Paper No. 25/2017.

[119] On this feature of legal concepts, *cf* S Deakin, 'Juridical Ontology: the Evolution of Legal Form' (2015) 40 *Historical Social Research* 170.

[120] B Alarie, 'Turning Standards into Rules – Part 3: Behavioral Control Factors in Employee vs. Independent contractor decisions' (2019), papers.ssrn.com/sol3/papers.cfm?abstract_id=3374051.

[121] We draw here on Niklas Luhmann's concept of coevolving social subsystems, *cf* N Luhmann, *Theory of Society: Volumes I and II* (Stanford University Press, 2012/2013).

[122] On the relevance to law of concepts of complexity and chaos to be found in Benoit Mandelbrot's mathematical models of systems (B Mandelbrot, *Les objets factals: forme, hazard et dimension* (Flammarion, 1975)), *cf* S Deakin, 'Evolution du droit: théories et modèles (système, complexité, chaos)' (May 2019) Collège de France, www.college-de-france.fr/site/en-alain-supiot/guestlecturer-2019-05-14-14h00.htm.

[123] K Pistor and C Xu, 'Incomplete law' (2003) 35 *New York University Journal of International Law and Politics* 931.

[124] J Prassl, *Humans as a Service: The Promise and Perils of Work in the Gig Economy* (Oxford University Press, 2018).

language of the law and thereby absorbed into its processes.[125] Conceptual stability is restored, if only provisionally, through a ruling of a higher appellate court, or a legislative clarification or modification of the relevant rule. Law remains bounded with respect to its environment, even if the 'shape' of this boundary is altered as a result of the selective pressures exerted by other systems.[126]

We might next ask: in what sense does the allocation of legal status to particular types of work relationship involve a process of learning functionally similar to that involved in ML as described above? The first point of similarity to note is that with classification problems, courts are applying tests which are essentially algorithmic in nature, since they consist of an ordered series of decisions which will result in a particular output for a given set of inputs. Thus according to the 'control' test, for example, which is widely used in labour law systems in some form or another to demarcate employee status, the individual will be (or least is more likely to be) an employee if they are under the command or subordination of another as to how they should do their work.[127] The control test is a verbal algorithm used to reconcile 'data' drawn from the facts presented to the court with an 'outcome' which is a legal determination of the parties' rights.

C. Information Retention in Legal Reasoning

The next point of similarity is that the use of abstract categories involves a form of information retention.[128] Legal concepts condense and hence retain information in two senses. The first is a function of concepts being hierarchically ordered in the sense we have just identified, and that implied by the Chomsky Hierarchy of formal grammars. Since higher order concepts can be decomposed into lower-order ones which become more fact-specific at each descending level of definition, a general category such as 'employee' becomes a shorthand form of expression for information embedded in categories operating at lower levels.[129] Thus the control test groups together a range of more precisely defined indicators of employee status such as having a supervisor or boss, being paid a wage, being subject to disciplinary control, paying tax at source, and so on.[130] At the very final (lowest) level of analysis, when conceptual reasoning is exhausted, only the facts of individual disputes remain: this is the systemic boundary just referred to. The capacity of the law to order external 'factual' data into juridical categories of varying degrees of specificity allows for its internal processing as legal material. As this conceptual ordering takes place, information of a detailed kind can be stored within linguistic categories of varying degrees of abstraction.[131]

[125] N Luhmann, *Law as a Social System*, trans K Ziegert, eds F Kastner, R Nobles, S Schiff and R Ziegert (Oxford University Press, 2004) 250.

[126] On law's boundary, *cf* A Morrison, 'The Law is a Fractal: The Attempt to Anticipate Everything' (2013) 44 *Loyola University Chicago Law Journal* 649; D Post and M Eisen, 'How Long is the Coastline of the Law? Thoughts on the Fractal Nature of Legal Systems' (2000) 29 *Journal of Legal Studies* 545.

[127] *Yewens v Noakes* (1880) 6 QBD 530; *cf* Deakin and Wilkinson, *The Law of the Labour Market* 91.

[128] Luhmann, *Law as a Social System* 341.

[129] Deakin, 'Juridical Ontology'.

[130] S Deakin and G Morris, *Labour Law*, 6th edn (Hart, 2012) para 3.26.

[131] Luhmann, *Law as a Social System* 257.

The second sense in which legal concepts embed and retain information concerns their inter-temporal effect.[132] The processing of external information does not have be repeated every single time a new case falls to be decided. The information 'learned' by the system is retained there through the persistence of conceptual forms across time.[133] The legal system's meta-norm of precedent – 'like cases should be decided alike' – constrains a later court to adapt its reasoning to the linguistic categories used in earlier iterations. While in one sense constraining, the norm of precedent is also facilitative, as it ensures that information on these past iterations is retained for future use: information retention over time.

D. Error Correction in Legal Reasoning

Error correction can also be observed in how courts and judges deal with cases. We can see error correction occur, for example, in the capacity of legal classifications to adjust to new data inputs over time. The doctrine of precedent notwithstanding, the categories used to determine employee status are dynamic, not static. They are continuously being adjusted in the light of new fact situations coming before the courts for resolution. Thus the 'control' test no longer (since the 1940s) places a primary emphasis on 'personal' subordination as the essence of employee status (as it did, for example, in the 1880s) but stresses instead the individual's incorporation in, and subjection to, procedures and processes of a more bureaucratic and depersonalised nature, reflecting a change in the way that managerial functions are performed in practice within firms and organisations.[134]

The importance attributed to 'control' itself as a guide to employee status is not fixed: it can be eclipsed by other tests which are seen as more useful or appropriate for their time, such as 'integration' at the point when vertically integrated firms and public service delivery organisations were the norm, 'economic reality' when the capacity of the post-1945 welfare state to deliver protection against labour market risks was at its height, and 'mutuality of obligation' at the point where the labour market was becoming more 'flexible' as a result of a combination of political and technological changes.[135] Even the foundational concept of the 'employee' is not as stable as it looks: it is in a line of descent from earlier juridical categories such as 'artificer', 'servant' and 'workman' which served somewhat different classificatory purposes from the contemporary 'employee', purposes which reflected the technological and political conditions of previous phases of industrialisation.[136]

[132] TO Elias, 'The Doctrine of Intertemporal Law' (1980) 74 *American Journal of International Law* 2; R Higgins, 'Time and the Law: International Perspectives on an Old Problem' (1997) 46 *International & Comparative Law Quarterly* 3; U Linderfalk, 'The Application of International Legal Norms over Time: the Second Branch of Intertemporal law' (2011) 48 *Netherlands International Law Review* 2; *cf* H Price, *Time's Arrow and Archimedes' Point: New Directions for the Physics of Time*, new edn (Oxford University Press, 1997).

[133] Luhmann, *Law as a Social System* 255.

[134] Deakin and Morris, *Labour Law* para 3.26.

[135] S Deakin and F Wilkinson, *The Law of the Labour Market* 307–9.

[136] Deakin and Wilkinson, *The Law of the Labour Market* 106; V De Stefano and A Aloisi, 'Fundamental Labour Rights, Platform Work and Human-rights Protection of Non-standard Workers' (2019) Bocconi Legal Studies Research Paper No. 3125866, dx.doi.org/10.2139/ssrn.3125866.

The updating of legal categories is an incremental process which occurs through the experimental testing of concepts against new fact situations as they come before the courts for decision. Incremental as the process is, its effects, over a sufficient period of time, can be radically transformative. Existing linguistic categories can be remoulded, given entirely new meanings, or even abandoned in favour of entirely new typologies. The process can be understood in an evolutionary sense as a dynamic adjustment of the legal system to its economic, political and, especially relevant for this discussion, technological context. It is a version of the variation-selection-retention algorithm which explains the survival and persistence of approximately functional features of a system's operation in a context where that system is subject to selective pressures from its environment. In the context of legal evolution, the element of variation is supplied by experimentation in the stock of judicial decisions as different courts arrive at diverse outcomes when faced with novel fact situations; selection, by pressures to challenge or alter existing rules through litigation and legislation; and retention, by the meta-rule or doctrine of precedent which ensures continuity at the point of change by requiring courts to justify innovations as extrapolations from, or adjustments of, existing modes of reasoning.[137]

E. Data Partitioning and Weighting in Legal Reasoning

We saw above[138] that one of the techniques used by ML to achieve error correction is to partition input data into categories which are connected to one another through 'mapping equations'. These equations have the effect of treating the output of one category as the input to another. The categories are arranged in hierarchical layers so that the model is divided into different stages of calculation. Error correction is achieved by assigning different numerical weights to the different inputs and outputs to achieve a desired result. In DL models 'backpropagation' allows for the more efficient dynamical mapping of connections. The distinctive aspect of DL models is that solutions can emerge through trial and error as different weightings are tested. Thus in the case of the algorithm for pricing airline tickets cited above,[139] the precise weight to be attributed to departure date as against other input variables cannot be known in advance, but can be identified through repeated iterations of the mapping process, as different weights are tried out and 'errors' progressively minimised.

Data partitioning and weighting have equivalents in legal reasoning. Data partitioning is a feature of the tendency, which we have already observed,[140] to bundle fact situations into conceptual categories expressed as abstractions at different levels of generality. Thus 'employee' (at a higher level), 'control', 'integration', 'economic reality' and 'mutuality of obligation' (at an intermediate level) and 'mode of payment', 'ownership of equipment', 'paying tax at source', 'given orders', 'receives regular work', and so on (at a lower level), are categories to which data from cases (detailed factual descriptions of

[137] Luhmann, *Law as a Social System* 255.
[138] Section IIA-C, above.
[139] Section III, above.
[140] Section VIC, above.

working relationships drawn from the parties' pleadings and submissions) are assigned. 'Mapping' occurs when lower level indicators are assigned to higher level categories, so that, for example, 'given orders' is assigned to the 'control' concept while 'receives regular work' is assigned to the 'mutuality of obligation' concept.

The process also works in the other direction: higher level concepts inform the selection and identification of lower level ones.[141] Thus once an intermediate-level concept such as 'mutuality of obligation' becomes established as a relevant test of employee status (as it did under conditions of an increasingly flexible labour market in the course of the 1980s), lower-level categories which were previously of minimal importance in the law (such as 'receives regular work') achieve a heightened relevance (or 'weight') within legal reasoning.[142]

Legal reasoning also involves 'weighting' in the sense of an experimental and iterative adjustment of the relative importance of inputs in deciding cases. In the context of the rise of the 'mutuality of obligation' test in the 1980s, the additional importance accorded to the 'given regular work' indicator led to the eclipse of other, previously well-established factors for determining employee status, in particular 'given orders'. While it would be artificial to regard these different factors being assigned precise numerical weights in the way that occurs in ML, it is not artificial, we suggest, to see their relative importance in judicial decision making being adjusted over time as the courts dealt with a growing number of cases involving 'precarious' or insecure work, which tested the established boundaries of the employee concept.[143]

More generally, it would seem that 'weighting' (assigning degrees of importance to indicators) is a near-universal feature of legal reasoning, just as 'data partitioning' (allocating facts to concepts) is. Complex fact situations of the kind which do not admit an easy resolution are the most likely to be litigated. These are precisely the cases in which courts must make adjustments of the kind implied by the 'weighting' analogy. For the English courts of the 1980s to decide that a casual worker, despite being subject to a duty to obey orders while working and economically dependent on a particular user of labour, was not an employee because of the irregular and discontinuous nature of the hiring,[144] was to accord a decisive weight to one variable among practically dozens which courts had relied on in case law stretching back over decades.

This example is also instructive because it requires us to focus on why this (or indeed, any) single variable should have acquired the weight that it did, at that time. From one point of view, we might conclude that the variable acquired a high 'weighting' in an incremental and emergent way, as it was initially proposed in a number of first-instance decisions, taken up and adopted by intermediate courts, and finally endorsed by the highest appellate court[145] and thereby stabilised. The 'error correction' process – which we might liken to a metaheuristic inspired by natural selection[146] – benefited from the

[141] S Deakin, 'The Contract of Employment: a Study in Legal Evolution' (2001) 17 *Historical Studies in Industrial Relations* 1.

[142] S Deakin 'Decoding employment status', forthcoming, *King's Law Journal*.

[143] Deakin and Wilkinson, *The Law of the Labour Market* 309.

[144] *O'Kelly v Trusthouse Forte plc* [1983] IRLR 369; Deakin and Wilkinson, *The Law of the Labour Market* 307.

[145] *Carmichael v National Power plc* [2000] IRLR 43; Deakin and Wilkinson, *The Law of the Labour Market* 310.

[146] *cf* AE Eiben and JE Smith, *Introduction to Evolutionary Computing*, 2nd edn (Springer, 2015) 13–24.

operation of the doctrine of precedent in a dual sense: not just the influence of preceding decisions, but the stabilising effect of the hierarchy of courts, helping to elevate the concept of mutuality of obligation to its pre-eminent position as the first point of reference for courts when deciding employee status cases.

Yet the example also poses difficulties for the idea that ML can replicate legal reasoning, since it is far from obvious that the mutuality case law was 'correcting' an 'error' in the system. On the contrary, the test has proved controversial to the point of being regarded by many commentators as an 'error' in itself, warping the application of employment law.[147] In what sense, then, is it appropriate to think of the end result of legal 'learning' as a process of 'optimisation', and not an ongoing process of 'training' and 'tuning' without an explicitly defined 'objective function'?

As we have seen,[148] in unsupervised learning, ML systems identify an output or 'ground truth' from an initial clustering of data points on the basis of their similarity or complementarity. The clustering of data points can be tested and refined through an unsupervised DL analysis and then adopted as an output in a supervised learning approach. This is already being done in a number of contexts with a bearing on the administration of civil and criminal justice, including probation, immigration, police resourcing, and credit scoring. Although its use in legal adjudication as such is currently limited to a small number of isolated trials, it would be surprising if it were not more widely taken up at the level of judicial decision making in the relatively near future.

An important factor which accounts for the success of DL approaches in matching processes to outcomes to date is that they have generally been applied to contexts in which the ultimate output variable is invariant to the process being used to identify or predict it. In other words, a medical condition such as diabetes or cancer is an invariant reality which exists regardless of the techniques used, whether through ML or otherwise, to diagnose it. The 'success' of the algorithm or model used to predict a medical condition can be tested against that invariant reality: the model will be more or less effective in ensuring improved survival or recovery rates on the basis of the diagnoses it makes. In that sense, there is an objectively ascertainable measure of 'success' against which the model can be benchmarked.

In the context of legal adjudication, there is no equivalently invariant measure of a model's success. This is because the output variable – in the case we have been considering, the classification of the individual as either an employee or self-employed – is not invariant with respect to the processes used to define it. Legal knowledge is inherently reflexive.[149] In other words, the law's epistemic categories alter the social forms to which they relate, as well as being altered by them. The category 'employee' is a legal construct which would not exist if the law did not create it. It is not a reality which exists independently of the law. A concept of this kind operates in a complex, two-way relationship to a given social referent, in part reflecting it (just as the notion of 'employee' has changed over time as forms of working have also changed), but also shaping it (since the way in

[147] E McGaughey, 'Uber, the Taylor Review, Mutuality and the Duty not to Misrepresent Employment Status' (2019) 48 *Industrial Law Journal*, doi.org/10.1093/indlaw/dwy014.

[148] See section IIA, above.

[149] G Samuel, *Epistemology and Method in Law* (Ashgate, 2003).

which the law defines employment has tangible consequences for, and effects on, the way in which labour relations are constituted in the economy).[150]

It follows that no legal determination, even of the most straightforward kind in which a stable rule is applied to uncontentious facts, is a simple description of reality. It is a normative act intended to change that reality.[151] When 'work', understood in its most elemental material form as a physical act of labour, becomes 'employment' as a result of a legal classification, what follows is the assignment to that material form of normative effects: legal rights, liabilities, powers, immunities, and so on. Thus the legal classification of work relations, while it undoubtedly has a technical (juridical) dimension, is also, necessarily, political in nature, in the sense of being concerned with the articulation of values. It defines and instantiates a particular conception of justice in the ordering of work.[152]

This suggests the need for some care when specifying the outcome variable or ground truth which legal reasoning achieves. What exactly is being optimised? If our argument to this point is correct, it is at least insufficient, and arguably misleading, to suggest workers might be classified more 'accurately' through ML than through human decision making. There is no technically 'optimal' solution to the question of how many 'employees' and 'independent contractors' there are in a given industry or economy. The relative proportions of the two groups is ultimately a normative question which turns on competing conceptions of the public good in the regulation of labour relations.

The unqualified application of ML to legal adjudication at the very least has the potential to obscure the political issues at stake in the process of juridical classification. But it could also undermine the effectiveness of legal reasoning as a means of resolving political issues. Legal reasoning involves more than the algorithmic application of rules to facts.[153] Because of the unavoidable incompleteness of rules in the face of social complexity,[154] legal reasoning is best thought of as an exercise in experimentation. Approximate solutions to recurring issues of dispute are proposed through adjudication and then subjected to scrutiny through a number of mechanisms of selection which include litigation, lobbying and commentary. It is a dynamic process which, while drawing on experience from the past (information retained in the system from earlier iterations), is forward-looking in the sense of adjusting existing rules to novel contexts and projecting their normative effect into future anticipated states of the world.[155] ML, however effective it may be in replicating the effects of known iterations of a particular classification problem, can only work on existing data. By comparison to legal reasoning, it is unavoidably backward-looking. ML's effectiveness is diminished in direct relation to the novelty of the cases it must process and, relatedly, to the pace of social change in the particular context to which it is applied.

Where ML has so far been used to 'predict' the outcome of cases, this has been done by using data from past decisions with a view to 'training' an algorithm to replicate the

[150] Deakin, 'Juridical Ontology'.
[151] H Kelsen, 'What is the Pure Theory of Law?' (1960) 34 *Tulane Law Review* 269, 271.
[152] A Supiot, *L'Esprit de Philadelphie. La justice sociale face au marché total* (Seuil, 2011).
[153] A Supiot *Governance by Numbers: The Making of a Legal Model of Allegiance* (Hart, 2017) 25–30.
[154] Pistor and Xu, 'Incomplete Law'.
[155] H Kelsen, 'Pure Theory of Law'.

outcomes in those decisions on similar facts. An algorithm of this kind can only be used as a basis for adjudication if it is assumed that the facts of future cases will be unchanged from those in the past. Yet this is almost certainly not going to be the case in many social contexts, including the one we are considering: it is generally agreed that the current rise of 'gig' or 'platform' work is posing challenges to the existing definitional structure of labour law which are just as foundational as those posed by the rise of precarious or 'flexible' forms of work four decades ago.[156] Novel fact situations arising from platform work are coming before labour courts all the time. New technologies will challenge existing conceptual categories in ways that will undoubtedly require adaptation of those concepts, and may render many of them otiose. Under these circumstances, using ML in place of legal reasoning as a basis for adjudication would lock in existing solutions, leading to the ossification or 'freezing' of the law.[157]

F. ML Overreach

It is not part of our argument to claim that ML cannot, by its nature, be applied to many areas of legal decision making. On the contrary, because much of legal reasoning is algorithmic, there is huge scope for ML applications in the legal context. We can expect further advances in ML which will overcome some of its current limits. As the costs of ML come down, and its predictive capacities improve, we can anticipate growing pressure for it to be used to replicate or substitute for adjudication. This will involve a step beyond its current use, in various 'LegalTech' applications, to estimate litigation risks. Employing ML to predict how a particular judge might decide a future case on the basis of their past performance may raise ethical and legal issues of a kind which could justify restrictions on its use, as has already happened in at least one jurisdiction, but it does not pose a direct threat to the autonomy of the judicial process. ML adjudication, by contrast, does pose such a threat, as it would lead to the de-norming of law, as well as to its ossification.

For some supporters of an enhanced role for ML in the legal sphere, this scenario, far from being a matter for concern, should be actively welcomed. Their argument is that biases and inefficiencies in the policy making process would justify the extension of ML beyond adjudication. While in the short run (the 'next few decades') more data and improved machine learning are likely to be 'complements to human judgment rather than substitutes', over time the goal of a 'functionally complete law'[158] will come into view. Governments will use machine learning to 'optimise the content' of the law in the light of 'prevailing politically endorsed social values'. ML will facilitate the implementation of 'transfer systems that achieve the distributive justice trade-offs that democratic political processes endorse'. As ML is used to identify an 'efficiency frontier' at which different values are traded off against each other, the law will become not only more complete but also more generally stable. In this state of a 'legal singularity', ML will

[156] Prassl, *Humans as a Service*; S Deakin and C Markou, 'The Law-technology Cycle and the Future of Work' (2018) 158 *Giornale di diritto del lavoro e di relazioni industriali* 445–62.
[157] M Hildebrandt, 'Code-driven Law: Freezing the Future and Scaling the Past' in this volume.
[158] Alarie, 'The Path of the Law: Toward Legal Singularity' 3.

generate a 'stable and predictable legal system whose oscillations will be continuous and yet relatively insignificant'.[159]

We would suggest an alternative prediction. This is one in which the mirage of 'complete law' leads to the removal of political contestation from the legal system. In its place will be a version of the 'rule of technology' according to which solutions based on computation are accorded an elevated status. Challenging outcomes based on supposedly neutral modes of decision making will prove increasingly problematic. At the same time, the techniques used to generate these outcomes are likely to prove more remote and opaque as time goes on. The tendency, already evident in the development of Legal Tech, for algorithms to be concealed from view behind a veil of commercial confidentiality and official secrecy, will only intensify.

VII. Conclusion

This chapter has explored the hypothesis that there are limits to the computability of legal reasoning and hence to the use of machine learning to replicate the core processes of the legal system. It has considered the extent to which there are resemblances between machine learning and legal decision making as systems involving information retention, adaptive learning, and error correction. Our argument has been that while there are certain resemblances, there are also critical differences which set limits to the project of replacing legal reasoning with machine learning.

Machine learning uses mathematical functions to perform various analysis and classification tasks. In 'deep learning' approaches, data is organised into concepts which are expressed hierarchically, with more complex concepts being built out of simpler ones. The classification of data into concepts is achieved through the use of weights whose values are adjusted over time as the system receives new inputs. Through its recursive operations, a system adjusts its internal mode of operation or 'learns', so that, in principle, errors are corrected and gradually purged.

The legal system also makes use of concepts to store and retain information. Legal concepts are ordered hierarchically, with higher-order categories informing the content of sub-categories operating at lower levels of abstraction. Legal concepts possess the capacity for self-adjustment in response to external signals. Error correction at a systemic level is achieved through a number of mechanisms including claimant-led litigation, appellate review of lower court judgments, and statutory reversals of unworkable or dysfunctional rules.

At a structural level, then, the resemblances between machine learning and legal reasoning are more than superficial. Some of the objections to the use of machine learning in a legal context are perhaps less fundamental than they might first seem. For example, the implication of the hierarchical ordering of legal concepts is that even a very widely framed general clause such as 'reasonableness' or 'good faith' can be understood as operating symbiotically with lower-level concepts and, ultimately, with fact-specific

[159] Alarie, 'The Path of the Law: Toward Legal Singularity' 10.

instances of individual disputes. The application of a legal rule to a set of social facts is, in this sense, an algorithmic process depending upon the interaction between concepts and rules which are expressed at different levels of generality, not unlike, in principle, the neural layering and assigning of relative weights to new informational inputs that characterise the artificial neural networks used in deep learning.

However, for machine learning to replicate legal reasoning it requires the translation of the linguistic categories used by the law into mathematical functions. This is not straightforward, even with advances in natural language processing which are making it possible to convert text into computer code with ever more sophistication. As the debate over 'smart' and 'semantic' contracts has already made clear, there is an element of flexibility and contestability in the natural language used to express juridical forms which cannot be completely captured by mathematical algorithms.

We suggest that the natural language categories used in juridical reasoning, precisely because of their imprecision and defeasibility, are superior in a number of respects to mathematical functions. Not only are they better at storing and representing complex information about the social world; they are more adaptable in light of new information. Machine learning, for all its advances, remains backwards-looking and prone to error through lock-in effects. It also has relatively few options for error correction by comparison with the range of techniques available in legal decision making. While progress is being made to ensure greater algorithmic transparency and explainability, the intricate layering and opacity of artificial neural networks remain, at least for now, more problematic than those of the law.

Underlying the project to apply machine learning to law is the goal of a perfectly complete legal system. This implies that the content and application of rules can be fully specified ex ante no matter how varied and changeable the social circumstances to which they are applied. In this world of a 'legal singularity' the law operates in a perpetual state of equilibrium between facts and norms. Advanced as an answer to the incompleteness and contingency of the law, the project for the legal singularity is also a proposal for the elimination of juridical reasoning as a basis for dispute resolution and the allocation of powers, rights and responsibilities. As such it risks undermining one of the principal institutions of a democratic-liberal order.

To avoid such an outcome, thought will need to be given to identifying and establishing limits for the use of machine learning and other data-driven approaches in core aspects of the legal system. The success of these measures will ultimately depend on the law's capacity to maintain the autonomy of its operations in the face of all-encompassing technological change, an outcome which is far from guaranteed.

3

Code-driven Law: Freezing the Future and Scaling the Past

MIREILLE HILDEBRANDT*

I. Introduction

In this chapter I refer to code-driven law to address legal norms or policies that have been articulated in computer code, either by a contracting party, law enforcement authorities, public administration or by a legislator. Such code can be self-executing or not, and it can be informed by machine learning systems or not. When it concerns codification of contract terms this is often called a 'smart contract', and when it concerns legislation or policies it is called 'smart regulation', especially where the code self-executes when triggered.[1]

My concern in this paper is not with data-driven law, such as prediction of legal judgments or argumentation mining, about which I have written elsewhere.[2] However, because code-driven law may integrate output of data-driven applications, these may nevertheless be relevant. For instance, a smart contract may trigger an increase in the premium of my car insurance after my car has detected a certain threshold of fatigue or risky driving. What interests me here is the fact that in code-driven law the threshold is determined in advance, in the computer code that 'drives' the smart contract. Another example would be a social security fraud detection system that halts benefit payments whenever someone is flagged by the system as probably committing fraud.[3] Again, my

* Mireille Hildebrandt is Research Professor at Vrije Universiteit Brussel on 'Interfacing Law and Technology', and holds the part-time Chair on 'Smart Environments, Data Protection and the Rule of Law' at Radboud University Nijmegen. She was awarded an ERC Advanced Grant in 2018 for 'Counting as a Human Being in the Era of Computational Law' (COHUBICOL), under the HORIZON2020 Excellence of Science program ERC-2017-ADG No 788734, which funded the research for this chapter. See www.cohubicol.com.

[1] P De Filippi and A Wright, *Blockchain and the Law: The Rule of Code* (Harvard University Press, 2018); P Hacker and others (eds), *Regulating Blockchain: Techno-Social and Legal Challenges* (Oxford University Press, 2019); M Finck, *Blockchain Regulation and Governance in Europe* (Cambridge University Press, 2019).

[2] M Hildebrandt, 'Law as Computation in the Era of Artificial Legal Intelligence: Speaking Law to the Power of Statistics' (2018) 68(1) *University of Toronto Law Journal* 12–35.

[3] S Marsh, 'One in Three Councils Using Algorithms to Make Welfare Decisions' *The Guardian* (15 October 2019) www.theguardian.com/society/2019/oct/15/councils-using-algorithms-make-welfare-decisions-benefits accessed 19 January 2020; 'Sweden: Rogue Algorithm Stops Welfare Payments for up to 70,000 Unemployed' (*AlgorithmWatch*, 2019) algorithmwatch.org/en/rogue-algorithm-in-sweden-stops-

interest is in the fact that the threshold for such probability is determined in advance, in the computer code that 'drives' this type of smart regulation. We can actually foresee that many machine learning applications will be used in such a way. First, an algorithm is trained on a – hopefully relevant – dataset, to learn which factors (eg, fatigue, spending) seem to have a strong correlation with a certain behavioural output (risky driving or social security fraud). Then, an algorithm is created that can be applied to individual persons to assess the probability that they will display this behaviour. The infamous COMPAS software operates in that way.

A private company, Northpoint, trained an algorithm on a dataset containing data on recidivism, based on 137 potentially relevant features (factors). The software detected seven of those features as strongly correlated with recidivism, including their different weights (not every feature correlates equally strong). Courts and public prosecutors have invested in the software (which is proprietary), and use it to automatically infer a risk score based on a small set of data and an interview with the person concerned. The output is then used to decide on parole or detention.[4] The software does not self-execute, and judges or prosecutors are fully responsible for the decision. However, the aura of objectivity that is often attributed to computing systems may have a strong influence on the human decision-makers.

In section II I will discuss what code-driven law does, by tracing the kind of questions it raises in different domains of law and by connecting its operations with relevant principles of private, public, constitutional and criminal law. Section III dives deeper into the nature of code-driven normativity.

II. What Code-driven Law Does

What interests me here is what code-driven law 'does' compared to text-driven law.[5] To investigate this, we will investigate different types of code-driven law and inquire how they relate to relevant principles of private, public, constitutional and criminal law.

In the case of a contracting party, code-driven law will probably refer to a smart contract, which is not only articulated in computer code but also self-executing. We could ask about the legal status of smart contracts, that is we can raise the question of whether the code counts as a legal agreement or is merely an expression of what has been agreed upon in speech or in writing. Is such an expression, just like a written agreement, merely evidence of an underlying agreement, or rather, just like with a legal deed, constitutive for the agreement itself?[6] What happens if parties disagree about

welfare-payments/ accessed 19 January 2020; Zack Newmark, 'Cabinet Member Resigns over False Accusations of Fraud by the Tax Authority' (*NL Times*, 2019) nltimes.nl/2019/12/18/cabinet-member-resigns-false-accusations-fraud-tax-authority accessed 19 January 2020.

[4] M Hildebrandt, *Law for Computer Scientists and Other Folk* (Oxford University Press, 2020) chs 10 and 11.

[5] On modern positive law as an affordance of a text-driven information and communication infrastructure (ICI), see ch 1 in M Hildebrandt, *Law for Computer Scientists and Other Folk*, and chs 7 and 8 in M Hildebrandt, *Smart Technologies and the End(s) of Law. Novel Entanglements of Law and Technology* (Edward Elgar, 2015).

[6] JG Allen, 'Wrapped and Stacked' (2018) 14(4) *European Review of Contract Law* 307–43.

the precise meaning of the underlying agreement in view of the operations of the self-executing script?[7] Have they given up their right to go to court about an execution that deviates from what they legitimately expected, considering the circumstances? Should their accession to the contract imply a waiver of any right to claim that the code got it wrong, compared to what they thought they agreed upon?

In the case of public administration, code-driven law can refer to either a decision-support or a decision-making system that is articulated in computer code, enabling swift execution (based on input from a citizen or a civil servant). In the case of self-execution (decision-making), we could ask whether such decisions have the force of law if taken under the responsibility of a competent government body, that is, we can ask under what conditions a fully automated decision (taken by a software program) even counts as a valid decision of a competent body. We can also ask under what conditions a decision taken by a human person based on a decision-support system nevertheless counts as an automated decision, for instance, because the human person does not really understand the decision and/or lacks the power to deviate from the output of the software.[8]

In the case of the legislature, code-driven law may refer to legislation that is articulated in writing but in a way that anticipates its translation into computer code, or it could relate to legislation written in computer code, which can either self-execute or require human intervention. Could legislation, enacted by a democratic legislature, count as such if it were written in computer code? Or would this depend on whether the legislature and/or its constituency are sufficiently fluent in code? Would code-driven law also refer to legislation, policies and decisions of public administration and judgments of courts that have been made machine-readable, in the sense of being structured with the help of metadata that allow software programs to categorise and frame such legal text, and to apply various types of data analytics such as argumentation mining, prediction of judgments, and search for applicable law?

These are all very interesting and highly relevant questions, relating to core principles of private, administrative and constitutional law. To the extent that policing and sentencing become contingent upon decisions made by software programs that determine the risk that a person has committed or may or even will commit a criminal offence, core principles of the criminal law are at stake.

Private law principles, such as the freedom to contract and the freedom to dispose of one's property raise questions around the constitution of a contract: what information should have been provided by the offering party, what investigations should have been undertaken by the accepting party? When does a lack of information result in the contract being void? Or, has the will of a party been corrupted by duress, fraud or deception, making the contract voidable? How does the law on unfair contract terms apply if it turns out that a party should have known that the terms of service implied their agreement to waive the right to appeal? Does the freedom to conduct a business incorporate the freedom to offer a service on condition that a smart contract is accessed? Does it make a difference whether this concerns a pair of shoes, a car or a health insurance?

[7] M Raskin, 'The Law and Legality of Smart Contracts' (2017) 1(2) *Georgetown Law and Technology Review* 304–41.

[8] M Finck, 'Smart Contracts as Automated Decision Making Under Article 22 GDPR' (2019) 9 *International Data Privacy Law* 1–17.

Public law principles, such as the legality and the fair play principles, aim to ensure that whenever government agencies exercise legal powers they do so in a way that stays within the bounds of the purpose for which they were attributed, while also remaining within the bounds of legitimate expectations that have been raised. To what extent will code-driven law result in what Diver calls computational legalism,[9] confusing rule-fetishism with acting under the rule of law? What happens if citizens are forced to articulate their applications for tax returns, health care, education or social welfare benefits in terms they do not recognise as properly describing their situation? What if their competence to appeal against automated decisions is restricted to what code-driven decision-systems can digest?

Criminal law principles, such as the presumption of innocence, equality of arms, immediacy with regard to the contestation of evidence, and the legality of criminal investigation that requires probable cause, proportionality and a range of other safeguards whenever fundamental rights are infringed in the course of a criminal investigation may be violated in case of, for example, 'smart policing' or 'smart sentencing'.[10] What if one is not made aware of the fact that code-driven systems have raised a flag resulting in invasive monitoring? What if such monitoring is skewed towards black people, or towards those with a criminal record, or towards people with a particular political opinion, taking note that this need not depend on direct discrimination, as it could be the result of flagging based on data that serves as a proxy for this type of bias? What if increased attention to specific groups of people results in them being charged more often, in a way that is disproportional in relation to their actual involvement in criminal offences?

Constitutional principles, such as legality, accountability, transparency and other expressions of the checks and balances of the rule of law are core to constitutional democracies.[11] The rule of law implies that neither the legislature nor public administration get the last word on the meaning (the interpretation and application) of the law. Judgment is reserved for the courts.[12] What if legislation is translated into computer code, that is, disambiguated, and what if at that very moment both its interpretation and application are de facto decided? What should courts decide if a legislature enacts law in the form of code? To what extent is the meaning of the law contestable in a court of law if the law has been disambiguated and caught in unbending rules that only allow for explicitly formulated (and formalised) exceptions? What if courts use the same software as the public prosecutor, or depend on the same legal technologies as Big Law?

What code-driven law does is to fold enactment, interpretation and application into one stroke, collapsing the distance between legislator, executive and court. It has to foresee all potential scenarios and develop sub-rules that hopefully cover all future interactions – it must be highly dynamic and adaptive to address and confront what

[9] LE Diver, 'Digisprudence: The Affordance of Legitimacy in Code-as-Law' (*era*, 2019), era.ed.ac.uk/handle/1842/36567 accessed 19 January 2020.

[10] M Oswald, 'Algorithm-Assisted Decision-Making in the Public Sector: Framing the Issues Using Administrative Law Rules Governing Discretionary Power', Philosophical Transactions of the Royal Society A: Mathematical, Physical and Engineering Sciences, 376: 2017035 (2018).

[11] M Hildebrandt, 'Algorithmic Regulation and the Rule of Law', Philosophical Transactions of the Royal Society A, 376: 20170355 (2018).

[12] DK Citron, 'Technological Due Process' (Washington University Law Review, 2008) 1249–1313.

cannot easily be foreseen by way of unambiguous rules. If it fails to do so, code-driven law must be subjected to appeal and contestation, based on, for instance, core legal concepts such as 'unreasonableness', 'unacceptable consequences', 'good faith', or 'the circumstances and the context of the case at hand'. This would imply reintegrating ambiguity, vagueness and multi-interpretability into the heart of the law.

III. The Nature of Code-driven Normativity

A. Language, Speech and Text-driven Normativity

In this paper, code-driven normativity refers to behavioural patterns generated by computer code that aims to influence human behaviour. Normativity – as intended here – is close to habits, which are neither moral nor merely regular. Such normativity is in line with how Wittgenstein understood rule following.[13] A prime example is the normative character of language usage (grammar, vocabulary, idiom),[14] which is neither merely regular nor a matter of morality. Following the rules of a particular language or idiom is constitutive of the meaning of the text, and conveying such meaning depends on speaking in a way that others recognise as meaning what is intended. However, meaning depends on connecting the intra-linguistic meaning of a word (its relationship with other words, its connotation) with its extra-linguistic meaning (its reference, or denotation). This reference may concern a tree or a mountain, a table or a car, but also institutions such as a marriage, a university or a legal service. These different types of references demonstrate that extra-linguistic meaning is co-constituted by the intra-linguistic framings that in turn depend on the success they offer language users in navigating their physical as well as institutional world. This is not just a matter of words, but also of grammar (conjugations, the use of pronouns, future and past tense).

The way language constitutes a world of institutions, roles and actions determines to a large extent what is possible, feasible or precluded, by shaping what is thinkable and affording what is thought. Interestingly, this determination is never final or complete – precisely because the same text can be interpreted in different ways, meaning that interpretations themselves can always be contested. This implies that the shared world that is constituted by our usage of language is contingent upon our ongoing support. In point of fact our shared, institutional world is performed by way of speech acts that do what they say: 'I declare you husband and wife' does not describe the marriage but performs, concludes, 'makes' it. The same goes for qualifying the complex network of behavioural patterns around higher education as a university. The performative nature of spoken and written speech (use of language) in turn drives a specific normativity, that is typical for the way human beings interact with their shared institutional world and with each other.

[13] L Wittgenstein and others, *Philosophical Investigations* (Wiley Blackwell, 2009); C Taylor, 'To Follow a Rule', in C Taylor, *Philosophical Arguments* (Harvard University Press, 1995) 165–81.

[14] R Bartsch, 'The Concepts "Rule" and "Norm" in Linguistics' (1982) 58(1) *Lingua* 51–81.

The text-driven normativity that concerns us here is based on the attribution of legal effect: if certain legal conditions apply, the law attributes a specific legal effect. For instance, in the case of a contract of sale, if a stipulated consideration is performed, a stipulated price must be paid. The legal effect is neither the consideration nor the payment. The legal effect concerns the fact that two legal obligations come into existence: to perform what is required by the contract. As we have seen above, a whole range of legal norms apply to the interpretation of the terms of the contract, taking into account the concrete circumstances of the case. These legal norms are often framed in terms of essentially contested concepts,[15] which have an open texture,[16] such as reasonableness, equity (in common law jurisdictions), force majeur, foreseeability etc. The multi-interpretability of these concepts generates a normativity of contestability, due to the fact that the potential of contestation is inherent in the nature of text. This is how text-driven normativity affords the core tenet of the rule of law: the contestability of the interpretation given by a party or a public authority. This is also how text-driven normativity affords the other core tenet of the rule of law: the need to perform closure. Once it is clear that such closure is not given with the text, because text does not speak for itself, it becomes clear that interpretation is construction rather than description and thus requires giving reasons for interpreting a legal norm in one way rather than another.[17]

Obviously, the rule of law adds closure by an independent court, instead of closure by a magistrate who is part of public administration. The latter would be rule by law. As Montesquieu said *iudex est lex loqui* (the court speaks the law), thereby countering the absolutist maxim of *rex est lex loqui* (the king speaks the law). As Schoenfeld has argued on historical grounds, the usual understanding of Montesquieu's *bouche de la loi* (the court as mouth of the law) is mistaken.[18] Montesquieu emphasised the court's loyalty to the law rather than to the king. When the court speaks, they do not follow the arbitrary interpretation of the ruler (rule by law by man) but are bound by the law, over which they have the last word (rule of law). We will return to this when discussing the difference between legalism and legality in relation to legal certainty.

B. Computer Architecture, Design and Code-driven Normativity

Clearly, the kind of rule following that is generated by text differs from rule following generated by computer code. What matters here is a set of constraints that are inherent in computer code that do not constrain natural language and text.[19]

The first is the need to formalise whatever requirements are translated into code. Formalisation enables the logical operation of deduction, in the sense of 'if this then that' (IFTTT). Such operations are crucial for automation, which is the core of computing systems. To the extent that formalisation is not possible or questionable, code-driven

[15] WB Gallie, 'Essentially Contested Concepts' (1956) 56 *Proceedings of the Aristotelian Society* 167–98.

[16] HLA Hart, *The Concept of Law* (Oxford University Press, 1994).

[17] FCW de Graaf, 'Dworkin's Constructive Interpretation as a Method of Legal Research' (2015) 12 *Law and Method*.

[18] KM Schoenfeld, 'Rex, Lex et Judex: Montesquieu and La Bouche de La Loi Revisted' (2008) 4 *European Constitutional Law Review* 274–301.

[19] See eg en.wikibooks.org/wiki/Logic_for_Computer_Scientists/Introduction, or a more in-depth discussion by A Arana in her Review of BJ Copeland, O Shagrir and CJ Posy (eds), *Computability: Turing, Gödel,*

architectures cannot be developed or may be unreliable. The second constraint is the need to disambiguate the terms used when formulating the requirements. This constraint is in turn inherent in formalisation, because deduction is not possible if it remains unclear what the precise scope is of the requirements. Disambiguation implies an act of interpretation that should result in a clear demarcation of the consequences of applying the relevant terms. The third constraint is that completeness and consistency cannot be assumed, meaning that the mathematical underpinnings of code-driven systems limit the extent to which claims about the correctness of computer code can be verified.[20] In the context of data-driven models, based on machine learning, a further set of constraints comes to the surface, relating to the limitations inherent in the design of a feature space, the hypothesis space, the articulation of the machine-readable task and the definition of the performance metrics.[21]

To some extent all these constraints are related to the uncertainty that inheres in the future. As to code-driven applications, we must face the limits of our ability to sufficiently foresee how changing circumstances will impact the execution of the code. In data-driven applications this can be summarised in the observation that one cannot train an algorithm on future data. Machine learning has to assume that the distribution of the data on which a learning algorithm has been trained is equivalent with or is a close approximation of the distribution of future data. This assumption, however, is not correct. On the contrary, it is the distribution of future data that machine learning hopes to predict but does not know. Integrating the output of machine learning systems therefore increases the risk that for example self-executing code 'gets things wrong' in the real world it aims to regulate. This is related to the radical uncertainty that defines the future, not in the sense of the future being entirely random or arbitrary but in the sense of its being underdetermined, notably when we concern ourselves with the consequences of human interaction. The radicality must be situated in the fact that this underdetermination cannot be resolved because it defines the human condition.[22]

The radical uncertainty of the future is exacerbated by the fact that predictions impact the behaviour they supposedly predict. In economics this is known as the Goodhart effect,[23] the Campbell effect[24] or the Lucas critique[25] and has nicely been summed up by Strathern[26] as: 'When a measure becomes a target, it ceases to be a good

Church, and Beyond (20 March 2015), *Notre Dame Philosophical Reviews*, ndpr.nd.edu/news/computability-turing-gdel-church-and-beyond accessed 30 November 2019.

[20] This connects with Gödel's theorem and the Church-Turing theses, see previous note and eg BJ Copeland, 'The Church-Turing Thesis' in EN Zalta (ed), *The Stanford Encyclopedia of Philosophy* (Spring 2019) plato.stanford.edu/archives/spr2019/entries/church-turing/ accessed 30 November 2019.

[21] TM Mitchell, 'Key Ideas in Machine Learning' in *Machine Learning*, draft for the 2nd edn (2017) 1–11; T Mitchell, *Machine Learning* (McGraw Hill, 1997).

[22] H Arendt, *The Human Condition* (University of Chicago Press, 1958); H Plessner and JM Bernstein, *Levels of Organic Life and the Human: An Introduction to Philosophical Anthropology*, trans. by M Hyatt, (Fordham University Press, 2019).

[23] D Manheim and S Garrabrant, 'Categorizing Variants of Goodhart's Law' (*arXiv*, 2019), http://arxiv.org/abs/1803.04585 accessed 19 January 2020.

[24] DT Campbell, 'Assessing the Impact of Planned Social Change' (1979) 2(1) *Evaluation and Program Planning* 67–90.

[25] RE Lucas, 'Econometric Policy Evaluation: A Critique' (1976) 1 *Carnegie-Rochester Conference Series on Public Policy* 19–46.

[26] M Strathern, '"Improving Ratings": Audit in the British University System' (1997) 5(3) *European Review* 305–21.

measure'. Once a description (measurement) of a certain state of affairs is understood as a prediction it may start functioning as a way to coordinate the behaviour of those whose behaviour is described (measured); if such predictions are then used to influence people they may no longer apply because people change their behaviour in function of the predictions (which they may for instance resist or execute, in divergence of how they would have behaved had such predictions not been employed).

Esposito has framed this effect even more pointedly, where she concludes (in my words) that our present futures change the future present.[27] What she is recounting here is that predictions (our present futures) influence the anticipation of interactions, resulting in an adjustment of actions, thus instantiating a different future present (compared to the one that might have become true if no predictions were employed). Her work also reminds us that whereas we can develop many present futures (predictions, imaginations, anticipations), we have only one future present. Considering the impact of predictions, we may want to exercise prudence when predicting.

Yet another way to state this is that 'the best way to predict the future is to create it'. This adage has been attributed to (amongst others) Gabor, one of the founding fathers of cybernetics, who elaborated:

> We are still the masters of our fate. Rational thinking, even assisted by any conceivable electronic computers, cannot predict the future. All it can do is to map out the probability space as it appears at the present and which will be different tomorrow when one of the infinity of possible states will have materialized. Technological and social inventions are broadening this probability space all the time; it is now incomparably larger than it was before the industrial revolution – for good or for evil.

In other work I have elaborated on this crucial insight, which asserts the counter-intuitive finding that predictions do not reduce uncertainty but rather extend it.[28]

C. Double Contingency and the Radical Uncertainty of the Future

The radical uncertainty that defines the human condition is best explained in terms of what Parssons and Luhmann have coined the 'double contingency' that is inherent in human interaction.[29] This refers to the fact that due to the nature of natural language we are always in the process of anticipating how others anticipate us. To be able to act meaningfully we need to anticipate how others will 'read' our actions, which links the interpretation of text to that of human action.[30] This explains the Goodhart, Campbell and Lucas effects.

[27] E Esposito, *The Future of Futures* (Edward Elgar, 2011).

[28] M Hildebrandt, 'New Animism in Policing: Re-Animating the Rule of Law?' in B Bradford and others (eds), *The SAGE Handbook of Global Policing* (Sage Publishing, 2016) 406–28.

[29] R Vanderstraeten, 'Parsons, Luhmann and the Theorem of Double Contingency' (2007) 2(1) *Journal of Classical Sociology* 77–92; M Hildebrandt, 'Profile Transparency by Design: Re-Enabling Double Contingency' in M Hildebrandt and E. De Vries (eds), *Privacy, Due Process and the Computational Turn: The Philosophy of Law Meets the Philosophy of Technology* (Routledge, 2013) 221–46.

[30] P Ricoeur, 'The Model of the Text: Meaningful Action Considered as a Text' (1973) 5(1) *New Literary History* 91–117.

Parssons and Luhmann both emphasised the radical uncertainty that is generated by what they called the 'double contingency' of human interaction, where I try to anticipate how you will read my actions while you try to anticipate how I will read your actions. They emphasise that this demands consolidation and stabilisation, by way of the institutionalisation of specific patterns of behaviour that form the background against which interactions are tested as meaning one thing or another. Luhmann thus explains the existence of social systems as a means to achieve *Kontingenzbewaltigung*, reducing complexity and uncertainty to a level that is productive instead of merely confusing. Without endorsing Luhmann's depiction of social systems as autopoietic I think we can take from his work the crucial insight that the mode of existence of human interaction is anticipatory, forever reaching out into a future world of human interaction that we cannot control. Legal certainty plays a pivotal role in stabilising and consolidating the mutual double anticipation that defines human interaction within a specific jurisdiction, without freezing the future based on a scaling of the past.

IV. Legal Certainty and the Nature of Code

A. Legalism and Legality; Consistency and Integrity

Legal certainty can be understood in two ways. Some authors equate it with consistency, which assumes that legal systems are coherent and complete. This usually goes with a legalistic understanding of the rule of law, where 'rules are rules' and 'facts are facts'. The discussion above should clarify that this is an untenable position that ignores the role played by natural language and the open texture of legal norms. Text-driven normativity simply does not afford the logical and deductive coherence such legalism assumes. In his doctorate thesis Diver has built on this pivotal insight by qualifying code-driven law as a form of computational legalism.[31] This seems a salient qualification, notably insofar as such 'law' claims perfect execution (where the enactment of the law includes both its interpretation and its implementation).

A less naïve understanding of legal certainty instead emphasises the integrity of the law, which is both more and less than consistency. Many of the misunderstandings around Dworkin's *Empire of Law*, where he explains the concept of the integrity of law, stem from conflating his 'integrity' with logical constituency (which would turn law into a closed system and the judge into a master of logical inference). The integrity of law could be understood as referring both to the coherence of the legal system (the intra-systematic meaning of legal norms), and to the moral implications of their legal effect (their extra-systematic meaning, which is performative as it reshapes the shared institutional world). The moral implications, however, do not depend on the 'subjective' opinion of the deciding judge but on the 'implied philosophy' that is given with law's complex interaction between intra- and extra-systematic meaning. It is crucial to understand the fundamental uncertainty that sustains the dynamic between internal coherence and the performative nature of attributing legal effect. Integrity is therefore

[31] Diver, 'Digisprudence'.

more than consistency, where it needs to achieve closure under uncertainty, and it is less than consistency, where it relies on an implied philosophy that must take into account both the justice and the instrumentality of the law (next to legal certainty).[32] This connects with Dworkin's constructive interpretation,[33] which emphasises that the right interpretation is not given but must be constructed as part of the refined but robust fabric of legal meaning production.

In light of the above, legal certainty faces two challenges. First, it needs to sustain sufficient consistency to enable those subject to law to foresee the consequences of their actions. This is not obvious, due to the impact of changing circumstances that may destabilise common sense interpretations of legal norms. The terms of a contract may seem clear and distinct, but in the case of unexpected events a reasonable interpretation may unsettle mutual expectations and require their reconfiguration. The fact that written law affords such reconfiguration is not a bug but a feature of text-driven normativity, because it enables to calibrate and consolidate such mutual expectations in a way that is in line with past and future decisions – thus also weaving a fabric of legitimate mutual expectations that holds in the course of time. Text-driven law is adaptive in a way that would be difficult to achieve in code-driven law (which relies on a kind of completeness that is neither attainable nor desirable).

The second challenge, which is deeply connected with the first, concerns the fact that legal certainty is not the sole constitutive aim of the law. If it were, perhaps computational legalism would work. Totalitarian and populist ideologists may vouch for this, hoping to construct the ideal legal system that enforces by default with no recourse to independent courts. Law's empire, however, is also built on two other constitutive aims: those of justice and instrumentality. Even though these aims may be incompatible in practice, the law should align them to the extent possible. The mere fact that legal certainty, justice and instrumentality are what Radbruch coined as 'antinomian',[34] and require decisions whenever they cannot be aligned, does not imply that when one goal overrules another in a particular case the others are disqualified as constitutive goals. In other words, any practice or theory that systematically resolves the tension between these three goals reduces the rule of law to either legal certainty (legalism), justice (natural law) or instrumentality (politics). As discussed above, legalism does not actually provide for certainty, as it builds on the mistaken assumption that future events will not impact the interpretation of a legal norm. Similar things can be said about justice and instrumentality. If any of them is taken to systematically overrule the others, they lose their fitting.

Justice refers to equality, both in the sense of proportionality (punishment should, eg, be attributed in proportion to the severity of the crime, compensation paid in proportion to, eg, the damage suffered) and in the sense of distribution (treating equal

[32] M Hildebrandt, 'Radbruch's Rechtsstaat and Schmitt's Legal Order: Legalism, Legality, and the Institution of Law' (2015) 2(1) *Critical Analysis of Law*, cal.library.utoronto.ca/index.php/cal/article/view/22514 accessed 24 March 2015.

[33] Graaf, 'Dworkin's Constructive Interpretation as a Method of Legal Research'.

[34] G Radbruch, 'Five Minutes of Legal Philosophy (1945)' (2006) 26(1) *Oxford Journal of Legal Studies* 13–15; G Radbruch, 'Legal Philosophy', in K Wilk (ed), *The Legal Philosophies of Lask, Radbruch, and Dabin* (Harvard University Press, 1950) 44–224; M Hildebrandt, 'Radbruch's Rechtsstaat and Schmitt's Legal Order'; M Hildebrandt, 'The Artificial Intelligence of European Union Law' (2020) 21(1) *German Law Journal* 74–79.

cases equally and unequal cases unequally to the extent of their inequality). These two types of justice, which inform legally relevant justice, have been coined corrective and distributive justice by Aristoteles and it should be clear that they interact;[35] to decide on distributive justice one needs a decision on corrective justice and vice versa. The equality that defines justice has a direct link with legal certainty, since it enables to foresee how one's case would be treated and thus helps to foresee the consequences of one's actions. On top of this it is crucial to remember that in law what matters in decisions that define what counts as either equal or unequal cases, will always be how this affects individuals.[36] Law requires governments to treat each and every person under their rule with equal respect and concern.[37] This grounds both the rule of law (individual human rights) and democracy (one person one vote) and their interaction (majority rule cannot overrule individual rights).

Instrumentality refers to how law serves policy goals determined by the legislature. The latter not only defines the legality principle that requires a legal competence for public administration to act lawfully, but also enables to serve a range of policy goals (full employment, sustainable environments, competitive markets, healthcare, social welfare, crime reduction, education, etc). The point here is that under the rule of law the legal norms that configure the space of lawful action are instrumental in a way that also safeguards the other goals of the law. In that sense legal norms are always both constitutive and limitative of lawful interaction. They allow or enable certain actions but also limit them (eg, by requiring that contracts are performed, but are not valid when they serve an illegitimate goal).

As Waldron has argued,[38] legal certainty is not only important because it contributes to foreseeability and trust, but also because it builds on the contestability of legal norms. Precisely because their interpretation (including their validity in light of other legal norms) can be contested, their force is more robust than the force of mechanical application or brute enforcement could ever be. This relates to the primacy of procedure in the substance of the rule of law, which like any text cannot speak for itself. Without litigation, due process (US) and fair trial (Europe), and an independent judiciary, legal certainty and the rule of law lose their meaning.

B. The Nature of Code-driven Law: Inefficiencies and Ineffectiveness

Legal interpretation is constructive and has performative effect. Legal interpretation, based on text-driven normativity, institutes the adaptive nature of text-driven law. The force of law is based on a complex interplay between the demands of legal certainty,

[35] J Waldron, 'Does Law Promise Justice?' (2001) 17(3) *Georgia State University Law Review*.

[36] Waldron, 'Does Law Promise Justice?'.

[37] See references to Dworkin and a discussion of their impact in Stefan Gosepath, 'Equality' in EN Zalta (ed), *The Stanford Encyclopedia of Philosophy* (Spring 2011), plato.stanford.edu/archives/spr2011/entries/equality/ accessed 1 December 2019.

[38] J Waldron, 'The Rule of Law and the Importance of Procedure' (2011) 50 *Nomos* 3–31, 19. See also M Hildebrandt, 'Law as Computation in the Era of Artificial Legal Intelligence' 21–22.

justice and instrumentality. It is more than mechanical application of disambiguated rules and more than brute enforcement based on the monopoly of violence that grounds the rule of law in most constitutional democracies. The force of law is robust due to procedures in front of independent courts that engage with contestation while providing closure.

The force of code differs from the force of law. The act of translation that is required to transform text-driven legal norms into computer code differs from the constructive interpretation typically required to 'mine' legal effect from text-driven legal norms in the light of the reality they aim to reconfigure. The temporal aspect is different, because code-driven normativity scales the past; it is based on insights from past decisions and cannot reach beyond them. The temporality also differs because code-driven normativity freezes the future; it cannot adapt to unforeseen circumstances due to the disambiguation that is inherent in code. Instead it can accommodate a range of additional rules that apply under alternative conditions, implying complex decision trees that hope to map future occurrences. This mapping is by definition underdetermined, not because of a lack of knowledge but due to the radical uncertainty that is the future (see above Sections IIIB and IIIC).

If machine learning is involved as input into the decision tree, some may argue that this affords adaptiveness, for instance by triggering new interpretations based on learning algorithms trained, validated and tested on, for example, streaming data. This, however, still requires specifying the behavioural response of the code-driven system, for instance by way of specified input thresholds. In many ways this will make the legal system more complicated and cumbersome, as it requires endlessly complex decision trees based on the identification of relevant future circumstances.

In the end, such coding efforts will forever lag behind the myriad relevant future circumstances that can be captured by legal concepts endowed with an open texture, as these are flexible and adaptive 'by nature', while nevertheless constrained due to the institutional settings of an independent judiciary that has the last word on their interpretation. On top of this particular inefficiency – and concomitant ineffectiveness – code-driven law has other inefficiencies that may involve massive externalisation of costs. If smart regulation is based on an inventory of legal norms that has been mined from statutory and case law, a small army of relatively cheap legal experts (students? paralegals?) is required to label relevant factors (features) in the body of relevant text. A redistribution of labour will be enacted: those who define the feature space and those who sit down to qualify text elements in terms of these features. The power of interpretation will reside with those who design the feature space, though in the end those who actually label the data may unintentionally disrupt such framing based on their own (mis)understandings. These problems may be solved – guess what – by even more automation, hoping to write code that automates the identification of relevant features as well as the labelling process. Obviously, this will push decisions on interpretation even deeper into the design of the code.

As long as such systems are 'under the rule of law', their output remains contestable in a court of law. Considering the drawbacks of the disambiguation that is at the heart of code-driven normativity, this could lead to a surge in litigation, with litigants claiming that their rights have been violated because the system mis-qualifies their actions when freezing the interpretation of the norm, or contending that it fails to take into account higher law, such as international human rights or constitutional law. A surge in litigation would make the employment of these systems less efficient (also considering the investment they require and the huge costs of maintenance, considering both security threats and other bugs). We should not be surprised when the legislature decides to restrict contestation, based on legal assumptions (in public administrative law) and waivers (in private law). This would create a decisional space outside the rule of law, enabling consistent application of arbitrary norms (as these norms cannot be tested against the architecture of legal norms they are a part of).

V. 'Legal by Design' and 'Legal Protection by Design'

A. Legal by Design

In their article on 'Legal By Design: A New Paradigm for Handling Complexity in Banking Regulation and Elsewhere in Law',[39] Lippe, Katz and Jackson observe that (at 836):

> in many instances, the growth of legal complexity appears to be outpacing the scalability of an approach that relies exclusively or in substantial part on human experts and the ability of the client to absorb and act on the advice given.

This argument has been heard before, for instance in the realm of healthcare (we need remote healthcare and robot companions to address the rising costs of care), suggesting that code-driven architectures will be more efficient and effective in solving relevant problems than the employment of human beings.[40] As argued above, I believe this is an untenable position.

In this subsection I will trace the meaning of 'legal by design' (LbD) and confront it with a concept I coined a long time ago, namely 'legal protection by design' (LPbD),[41] which should not be confused with LbD. The distinction should not only clarify that we need LPbD rather than LbD, but also allow us to inquire to what extent 'compliance by design',[42] 'enforcement by design',[43] 'technological management',[44] 'technoregulation,[45] or 'computational law' could support LPbD,[46] enhancing rather than diminishing human agency, and challenging rather than scaling the past, even though such techno-legal 'solutions' may result in freezing dedicated parts of our shared future.

[39] P Lippe, DM Katz and D Jackson, 'Legal by Design: A New Paradigm for Handling Complexity in Banking Regulation and Elsewhere in Law' (2015) 93(4) *Oregon Law Review* 833–52.

[40] R Susskind and D Susskind, *The Future of the Professions: How Technology Will Transform the Work of Human Experts* (Oxford University Press, 2015).

[41] M Hildebrandt, 'Legal Protection by Design: Objections and Refutations' (2011) 5(2) *Legisprudence* 223–48. See also M Hildebrandt and L Tielemans, 'Data Protection by Design and Technology Neutral Law' (2013) *Computer Law & Security Review* 509–21.

[42] N Lohmann, 'Compliance by Design for Artifact-Centric Business Processes' (2013) 38(4) *Information Systems, Special section on BPM 2011 conference* 606–18.

[43] N García and AP Kimberly, 'Enforcement by Design: The Legalization of Labor Rights Mechanisms in US Trade Policy', CIDE Working Paper Series, División de Estudios Internacionales (2010).

[44] R Brownsword, 'Technological Management and the Rule of Law' (2016) 8(1) *Law, Innovation and Technology* 100–40.

[45] R Leenes, 'Framing Techno-Regulation: An Exploration of State and Non-State Regulation by Technology' (2011) 5(2) *Legisprudence* 143–69.

[46] M Genesereth, 'Computational Law. The Cop in the Backseat' (2015,) logic.stanford.edu/complaw/complaw.html accessed 9 October 2016.

Let's first note that Lippe, Katz and Jackson are referring to a very specific subsection of what is best called 'legal services', rather than 'law'. Their article concerns regulation of banking and the claim or assumption of the authors is that such regulation has become so complex that those addressed are at a loss as to compliance. This is a bit funny, of course, considering the choices that have been made by the financial sector in advancing their own interests.[47] The article seems entirely focused on business to business (B2B) relationships, treating them as if they only concern the businesses involved, though we all know decisions made around financial markets affect many individuals whose lives may be disrupted due to decisions by those who couldn't care less (about them). This is the first caveat; a healthy network of financial markets is not merely the private interest of financial institutions. The second caveat is that the proposed LbD suggests a smooth path towards compliance with legal norms deemed overly complicated, whereas the article abstracts from the underlying goals. These goals involve the public interest in a way that may not align with the interests of those running the financial sector. We can be naïve about this, or turn a blind eye, but this will not do when investigating the role of code-driven law in the light of LbD solutionism.

The authors refer to the Massive Online Legal Analysis (MOLA) and recount (at 847):

> The MOLA process is conceptually similar to processes that have been used for almost two decades to address and solve extremely large, complex mathematical and scientific problems. IBM developed one of the best organized efforts – the World Community Grid – to conduct massive and complex research in a variety of areas, including cancer research, clean air studies, AIDS investigations, and other health-related projects. As described on its website, the 'World Community Grid brings together people from across the globe to benefit humanity by creating the world's largest non-profit computing grid … by pooling surplus processing power from volunteers' devices'.

There is no evidence that MOLA's solutions 'work', no reference to serious, independent verification of the findings (which findings?), let alone any attempt at falsification.[48] One is tempted to quote Cameron:[49]

> It would be nice if all of the data which sociologists require could be enumerated because then we could run them through IBM machines and draw charts as the economists do. However, not everything that can be counted counts, and not everything that counts can be counted.

[47] The financial crisis of 2008 demonstrated that compliance is perhaps not enough. To prevent global catastrophes will require the right kind of rules, instigating the right type of incentives, coupled with transnational enforcement. On the interest of the financial sector in achieving compliance 'It Knows Their Methods. Watson and Financial Regulation' (*The Economist*, 22 October 2016), www.economist.com/news/finance-and-economics/21709040-new-banking-rules-baffle-humans-can-machines-do-better-it-knows-their-methods accessed 6 June 2017.

[48] The World Community Grid enables 'anyone with a computer, smartphone or tablet to donate their unused computing power to advance cutting-edge scientific research on topics related to health, poverty and sustainability'. It 'brings together volunteers and researchers at the intersection of computational chemistry, open science and citizen science – three trends that are transforming the way scientific research is conducted'. The Grid provides computational power, it does not impose any specific methodology. See www.worldcommunitygrid.org/about_us/viewAboutUs.do.

[49] W Cameron, Informal Sociology, a Casual Introduction to Sociological Thinking (Random House, 1963) at 13.

Lippe, Katz and Jackson continue (at 847):

> As with the World Community Grid, MOLA breaks a large, data rich, and complex legal project into small pieces that can be assigned to individual attorneys for completion. Those small, individual solutions, when combined with thousands of other individual solutions, result in a cost-effective solution to the overarching larger project.
>
> More concretely, the solution is specified as an approach meant to convert a contract into a pointable data object where the contract memorializes the set of rights and obligations that are attendant to that agreement. To attain this goal, [financial, mh] institutions will need to:
>
> 1. Collect the set of all agreements held by a bank.
> 2. Identify each counterparty from those agreements (and third party where available).
> 3. Develop a model of counterparty risk which would include both an individual and systematic (ecosystem) component.
> 4. Determine the nature of resource (financial) flows attendant to each counterparty.
> 5. Convert each contract into a pointable data object, which allows its contents to be immediately memorialized in a balance sheet or other relevant IT system.
> 6. Offer the ability for key decision makers to query a system and run various scenarios in which some sort of aggregate or systematic risk could be the output.

In what sense could this 'solution' be understood as a LbD solution? This depends on how one understands 'design'. The authors suggest (at 843):

> As such, 'design' describes object creation, manifested by an agent, to accomplish a goal or goals, where the object satisfies a set of requirements, and its creation is subject to certain fixed constraints. Used in this traditional sense, the design 'object' is a physical one, the agent is a human being (the designer), the goal is the purpose of the design exercise (move this large object from here to there), the set of requirements include material specifications (use only found objects), and the constraints are things such as available found materials (stone and wood). Thus, the first rudimentary wheel was not invented, but designed.

Beyond this physical context, legal design based on MOLA supposedly enables a financial institution to reinterpret the fixed constraints imposed by financial regulation:

> Using new technology and alternative approaches to organize legal information can expand the available options well beyond what are initially seen as fixed constraints.

Why and how this would amount to 'legal by design' is not clear to me, but it does sound like a scheme that allows financial institutions to document compliance based on hybrid systems that integrate code- and data-driven search and assessment, assuming for no apparent reason that such an assessment is reliable, or at least more reliable then human auditing. Taking into account the feedback loops discussed in Section IIIC this is not at all obvious, and the question comes to mind how human auditors could check whether or not the system is getting things right. If the 'regulatory environment' is too complex for any human auditor, how could we assume that the exercise of decoding (written law) and recoding (in code-driven output) reliably frames these complexities?

A second attempt to achieve LbD is the use of blockchain-based smart contracts, which add self-execution to a decisional system; above and in other work I have explained why this cannot be LbD because the code is fixed and will inevitably turn out to be over- and underinclusive when applied.[50]

VI. Legal Protection by Design

LPbD embodies an entirely different approach. It is not focused on achieving compliance or enforcement of whatever legal norms, but targets the articulation of legal protection into the ICT infrastructure of code- and data-driven environments. The point of departure is not the translation of a written legal norm into computer code but an inquiry into the way a data- and code-driven environment affects the substance of fundamental legal principles and rights. Based on this assessment LPbD seeks ways to prevent diminished legal protection by intervening in the design of the relevant computational architecture, where design refers to the joint constructive work of whoever make, build, assembly, and construct such architectures. This may involve engineers, computer scientists, lawyers and other domain experts, as well as those who will suffer the consequences of the decisions mandated to these architectures.

The most important principles that need articulation in the design phase are those that safeguard the checks and balances of the rule of law. This refers for example to legality and fair play for systems employed by public administration, proportionality, accountability, transparency, access to justice, and a series of more specific fundamental rights, such as the presumption of innocence, non-discrimination, privacy, freedom of speech and fair trial. As to code-driven decision systems we need to acknowledge that these principles and rights cannot all be articulated in these systems in a straightforward, scalable manner. They require bespoke architectures, targeting specific contexts, taking into account vulnerable groups or individuals, potential redistribution of risks and benefits, and further consequences for public goods such as safety, trust, trustworthiness, fairness, and expediency – all fine-tuned to the relevant context (of eg, education, policing, healthcare, medical interventions, welfare benefits, employment conditions, and access to all of these).

Nevertheless, we can surmise that at the very least these systems must afford an effective right to appeal against automated decisions, to obtain a meaningful explanation of the logic that informs them and to be given a legal justification for the decision by those who employ the system (note that an explanation of the software is not at all equivalent to a justification of the decision). Of similar importance is that for such rights to be effective, claims that they were violated must be heard by an independent court. These rights have been developed in the context of the General Data Protection Regulation, notably in the prohibition of fully automated decisions that have a significant effect on those whose data are being processed. A major and often cross-disciplinary response has erupted to this prohibition and to a range of concomitant obligations. A new type of cross-disciplinary doctrinal discourse has developed around, for instance, the legal obligation to provide a meaningful explanation on the one hand and 'explainable machine learning' on the other, often co-authored by lawyers, computer scientists

[50] M Hildebrandt, *Law for Computer Scientists and Other Folk* ch 10.2.

and philosophers. In a broader sense, targeting algorithmic decision systems beyond personal data and beyond the jurisdiction of the EU, new subdomains in computer science have emerged, notably XAI (explainable AI) and FAccT (fair, accountable and transparent) computing.

The goal of the collaboration of computer scientists and lawyers in this new strand of computational-legal doctrine is not to develop code-driven compliance, but – on the contrary – to ensure that computer architectures incorporate fundamental safeguards against bias, invasion of privacy, incomprehensible decisions, unreliable assessments, and against an effective denial of access to justice. LPbD must be situated as the primary goal of this new doctrinal development; instead of investing in replacing law with automation, LPbD demands cross-disciplinary investment in keeping the rule of law on track – into the capillaries of code-driven architectures. In relation to code-driven law, this will require a straightforward acknowledgement that such 'law' is not law but public administration or technological management, asserting the need to build LPbD into the technical architectures of code-driven law, and doing the usual – but now cross-disciplinary – doctrinal work on how specified risks must be assessed, mitigated or redistributed.

VII. Finals: the Issue of Countability and Control

As noted above 'not everything that can be counted counts, and not everything that counts can be counted'.[51] I would add that 'not everything that matters can be controlled, and not everything that can be controlled matters'. If we take these admonitions seriously, we may want to hesitate when considering investments in code-driven regulation.

Law is not computable in any final sense, because due to its text-driven multi-interpretability it can be computed in different ways and these different ways will make a difference for those subject to law. In a constitutional democracy such design choices belong to 'the people' and to the courts, not to arbitrary software developers in big tech or big law.

[51] On the need to protect the incomputable self from overdetermination by algorithmic systems: M Hildebrandt, 'Privacy As Protection of the Incomputable Self: Agonistic Machine Learning' (2019) 20(1) *Theoretical Inquiries in Law*, Special Issue on The Problem of Theorizing Privacy 83–121. The solution is not to reject computation but to acknowledge its limitation and its framing problem, see also M Hildebrandt, 'The Issue of Bias. The Framing Powers of Ml' in M Pellilo and T Scantamburio (eds), *Machine Learning and Society: Impact, Trust, Transparency* (MIT Press, 2020), https://papers.ssrn.com/abstract=3497597 accessed 5 January 2020.

4

Towards a Democratic Singularity? Algorithmic Governmentality, the Eradication of Politics – And the Possibility of Resistance

JOHN MORISON*

I. The Disappointments of Democracy in an Internet Age

Democracy is beset by many problems currently. However the goal of increased participation remains as a beacon for improving democracy, and the related notion of consultation can be seen as a way of reinvigorating democratic engagement. Earlier work explored some of the problems associated with consultation.[1] Essentially this concluded that consultation on policy development can reinvigorate democratic engagement but often it can silence views through a sort of participatory disempowerment whereby the existence of an official consultation exercise closes off further, alternative or subaltern voices who are silenced by the existence of an official depiction of 'the public'. This is true both for policy development and the sort of engagement that seems to be required in any form of modern, responsive service delivery. Here consultation can improve services or it can be used to detach public services from an integrated public sector, and loosen the democratic anchorage of the public service within the state through the adoption of consumerist perspectives. Often official consultations – to decide policy directions or fine-tune services – are not a properly democratic exchange. Voice is not being privileged despite appearances. There is instead an idea of consultation as part of a wider technology of government, involving a set of programmes, strategies and assemblages designed to mobilise local communities and other targets of consultation to become agents of policy as well as simply objects of policy. Ideas of democratic

* School of Law, Queen's University of Belfast. I would like to thank the editors and the participants at the Lex ex Machina Conference in Cambridge in December 2019, as well as participants in BILETA 2019 and Anthony Behan, Mary Dobbs and Rebekah Corbett for valuable comments and references (and with apologies to Claire Hamilton).

[1] J Morison, 'Citizen Participation: A Critical Look at the Democratic Adequacy of Government Consultations' (2017) 37 *Oxford Journal of Legal Studies* 636–59.

engagement are constructed, managed and controlled. Consultees 'make themselves up' in reply to the strategies of consultation: the fact of their engagement renders them 'representative', while their response to the structured engagement simultaneously reinforces and advances the wider governing project that exists beyond their control. In the wider context of legitimating governance, consultation can be conscripted into a process of remaking the public sphere in ways that have a justificatory veneer of democratic engagement.

Of course one promising way to improve upon this might seem to involve harnessing the democratic power of the internet world. There is a level of connectedness and an abundance of information there that should promise a new age of democracy. In the immediate future this may involve various forms of direct democracy, with online or app-based referendum voting, improved methods of cyber-facilitated deliberation, or, more likely, simply enhanced consultation.[2] However, putting an interaction online does not necessarily improve its democratic quality.[3] Indeed there is a view that it makes it worse. From an earlier age of online engagement in the early 2000s Jodi Dean writes of the feeling of disconnect experienced in relation to foreign policy in the US where terabytes of online commentary hostile to the Iraq engagement seemed to gain no purchase at all on the activities of officials becoming instead simply 'so much circulating content … cultural effluvia wafting through cyberia'.[4] According to Dean this is because a 'fantasy of abundance' (relating to the sheer volume and diversity of communication facilitated by the internet) contributes to a 'fantasy of activity or participation' whereby internet exchanges simply reiterate wider political struggles but also displace them into a safer online world, leaving the space of 'official' politics secure and untroubled. All of this is facilitated by a 'technology fetishism' where the internet seems to offer exciting new solutions.[5] Within this thinking the messy problems of wider politics – relating to opinion and knowledge, access and inclusion, participation and representativeness etc – can be reduced to one problem, and it is a problem that has a technological solution. If the problem of democracy is simply that people are not informed, and cannot express an opinion, then information technologies can solve the problem: the internet can supply both the information needed *and* a huge array of means – official and unofficial – to express views. Indeed, the world wide web seems to open up a huge space of communicative action, from clicking on a petition site to responding to a government consultation to joining or forming a pressure group. It also seems to promise a sense

[2] See also the simple tools that can match preferences with parties in ways that facilitate tactical voting and which were supposed to transform the results of the 2019 general election in the UK: whoshouldyouvotefor.com, www.buzzfeed.com/jimwaterson/which-party-should-you-actually-vote-for and voteforpolicies.org.uk.

[3] See further eg, S Wright, 'Politics as usual? Revolution, normalization and a new agenda for online deliberation' (2012) 14(2) *New Media and Society* 244–61; S Albrecht, 'Whose voice is heard in online deliberation? A study of participation and representation in political debates on the internet; (2006) 9 *Information, Communication & Society* 62–82 and T Davies and S Gangadhern (eds), *Online Deliberation: Design, Research, and Practice* CSLI Publications (2009), odbook.stanford.edu/static/filedocument/2009/11/10/ODBook.Full.11.3.09.pdf.

[4] J Dean, 'Communicative Capitalism: Circulation and the Foreclosure of Politics' (2005) 1 *Cultural Politics* 51–73 at 52.

[5] Dean (see n 4). See also J Morison, 'Algorithmic Governmentality: Techo-optimism and the Move towards the Darkside' (2016) 27(3) *Computers and Law.*

of wholeness or universality in so far as the internet appears as a free and open space connecting (almost) everybody without the need for mediation by government or the machinery of a political party.

Of course this is not the case. Fake news and media manipulation has entered this innocent world. The internet is not a wholly pleasant, reasonable or truthful place. AI bots mimicking humans distort the debate while some users simply screen out contrary views. There is no internet agora, or ideal speech situation – online or offline. The internet with its anonymity, limited quality control and fragmented reality is no more value free, unstructured or universal than any other space.[6] The hippy entrepreneurs of the earlier world wide web are now the corporate titans of the 'GAFAM' group.[7] The dream of a connected, online democracy is not entirely dead but the conclusion of the earlier work on consultation is that its promise is limited, and to deliver even on this requires very vigilant monitoring. The adoption of a governmentality perspective, whereby consultation could be seen as part of a wider strategy of governance, allowed a clearer appreciation there of what was occurring, and it is this perspective that should be retained as new developments and potential developments in technology and democracy are considered.

There are now emerging developments in technology which threaten to transcend this whole debate and introduce a series of new challenges, perhaps rendering mere consultation irrelevant. The phenomenon of 'big data' and its analysis through new forms of machine learning is still developing but it seems to promise a new paradigm in the constitution of knowledge, and perhaps the future of democracy.[8] Again, a governmentality perspective may be required to allow us to see this more clearly.

II. From Surveillance to Algorithmic Governmentality

> Due to the zettabytes of data we have amassed, we have a unique understanding of the human soul, of its desires and intentions, of the desires and intentions of humans in general and humans in particular.[9]

[6] This is true in a technical sense as well. It is becoming more widely known now how the algorithms used by search engines such as Google are not value free but rather are highly structured for commercial and other ends. Indeed the whole architecture of the internet is far from random and spaces within it do not make up a seamless unity. Consider, for example, how the internet is divided into four major 'continents', each with their own navigational links which do not cross boundaries or provide links to another continent. See further A-L Barabasi, *Linked: How Everything is connected to Everything Else and What it Means* (Plume, 2003); M Hildebrandt, 'Law *as* Information in an era of Data Driven Agency' (2016) 79 *Modern Law Review* 1–30; and R Kitchin, *The Data Revolution: Big Data, Open Data, Data Infrastructures and Their Consequences* (Sage, 2014).

[7] This comprises Google (including its parent company, Alphabet), Amazon, Facebook, Apple, and Microsoft. See J Taplin, *Move Fast and Break Things: How Facebook, Google, and Amazon Have Cornered Culture and What It Means For All Of Us* (Little Brown, 2017).

[8] See further R Kitchen (n 6) and M Hildebrandt and B-J Koops, who claim that 'ambient intelligence builds on profiling techniques or automated pattern recognition, which constitutes a new paradigm in the constitution of knowledge', 'The Challenges of Ambient Law and the Legal Protection in the Profiling Area' (2010) *Modern Law Review* 428–60 at 428, See also M Hildebrandt, *Smart Technologies and End(s) of Law* (Edward Elgar, 2015).

[9] J Kavenna, *Zed* (Faber, 2019). This idea may remind some of Alex Garland's *Devs*, a TV series made by Fox and shown on Hulu and BBC 2 in 2020, or the 'demon' described in 1814 by the philosopher Simon

Joanna Kavenna's dystopian novel describes a (perhaps not too distant) future where a tech super company, the Beetle Corporation, has harnessed big data and developed a series of algorithmic 'lifechains' to predict all aspects of human activity. The company has fused with the state and become enmeshed in all most every aspect of contemporary life from the economy, transport and employment to policing and security. This is a world without freewill, or at least one where every action is knowable and every preference predictable via the constant stream of data from all elements of life – from BeetleBand activity trackers, fully interactive Very Intelligent Personal Digital Assistants (Veeps) operating through BeetlePads and Veepstations, smart cars and fridges, to Argus surveillance cameras and a Custodian technology that polices all activities suppling constant prompts to action. While such a world is not here yet there are features that are readily recognisable. It does not take too much imagination to envisage Amazon suggestions, Fitbit updates and interactions with Alexa as pointing the way to a future of complete surveillance capitalism.[10]

Indeed, in a postscript in 1992 to his *Societies of Control* work[11] Delueze remarks on how types of machines can be matched to different types of society. This is not because the machines in some way directly determine how the society works but rather because they express the social forms capable of devising them and using them. Clocks, simple levers and pulleys seem to suggest older societies of Sovereignty, whereas more complex factory machines using energy as part of a productive process suggest a disciplinary society with its fears about machine breaking, entropy and control. However, as Foucault pointed out, these formulations are transient: the spaces of enclosure of earlier disciplinary societies, such as the prison, school or the factory, were able to order time and control spaces to make up a productive force for capitalism and property in the nineteenth and twentieth centuries. Now it is digital technology – the computer and all those associated smart devices – and their totalising capture of information across every facet of life that represents the present society of surveillance and control. Digital society no longer provides the same world of production or discipline within fixed enclosures. However the control element remains, and indeed it is intensified further. There is now an element of what Bauman and Lyon term 'liquid surveillance' involved as our lives leave digital traces providing an undeniable and indelible record of all our

Laplace as 'an intellect which at a certain moment would know all forces that set nature in motion, and all positions of all items of which nature is composed, if this intellect were also vast enough to submit these data to analysis, it would embrace in a single formula the movements of the greatest bodies of the universe and those of the tiniest atom'. See S Laplace, *A Philosophical Essay on Probabilities*, 6th edn, trans F Truscott and F New York (Dover Publications, 1951) 4 and also N Silver, *The Signal and the Noise: The Art and Science of Prediction* (Penguin, 2013).

[10] See S Zuboff, *The Age of Surveillance Capitalism: The Fight for a Human Future at the New Frontier of Power* (Profile Books, 2019). There are suggestions that elements of this are already present in parts of China through the deployment of the Integrated Joint Operations Platform (IJOP) which can gather information from a variety of sources including CCTV with face recognition technology, 'wifi sniffers' which can collect the unique identifying addresses of smartphones and other networked devices and vehicle checkpoints, and visitor registration systems. This is then combined with existing information from health and legal records, banking and vehicle ownership registers to produce a framework for detailed surveillance. See Human Rights Watch at www.hrw.org/news/2018/02/26/china-big-data-fuels-crackdown-minority-region (accessed 3 April 2020). See also J Palfrey, 'The Ever-Increasing Surveillance State' (2020) *GeorgeTown Journal of International Affairs*.

[11] G Deleuze, 'Postscript on the Societies of Control' (1992) 59 *October* (winter) 3–7.

activities.[12] This idea of liquidity is captured in Deleuze's formulation too: '[e]nclosures are molds, distinct castings, but controls are a modulation, like a self-deforming cast that will change continuously from one moment to the other like a sieve whose mesh will transmute from point to point'.[13]

This description begins to capture the nature of the current wider project of control, surveillance and discipline. This is much more ambitious and totalising in terms of the enclosure it aims for. There is now a ubiquitous, pernicious and indeed *total* 'society of control' being slid into place. This has come about from the development and deployment of a set of digital technologies and practices in what we might term the 'digital lifeworld'.[14] The practical technologies are familiar.[15] Techniques around big data, cloud storage, data mining, pattern recognition, machine learning, datafication, dataveillance, personalisation, allow massive data sets to be gathered in a volume, velocity and variety that makes conventional forms of analysis impossible, and new algorithmic forms possible.[16] The internet of things, as enabled by 5G, gathers information, in real time and continuously, from a huge range of everyday objects and activities to provide a further impetus for ever increasing volumes of data to be used in a range of decision-making systems that can regulate activities and manage behaviour across a whole range of social activities.[17] New machine learning techniques involving sophisticated

[12] Z Bauman and D Lyon, *Liquid Surveillance: A conversation* (Polity, 2013) and the overview of Bauman's earlier work in D Lyons, 'Liquid Surveillance: The Contribution of Zygmunt Bauman to Surveillance Studies' (2010) 4 *International Political Sociology* 325–38.

[13] See n 11 at 4.

[14] This term is used in part by way of reference to how Susskind deploys the phrase to indicate all the immediate experiences, activities and contacts that comprise our individual and collective interactions with the range of technologies. (See further J Susskind, *Future Politics: Living together in a World Transformed by Tech* (OUP, 2018) 29.) However, it is used also to attempt to capture the widest social, political and economic context of technology and its operation. This will include the power relations (in their historical specificity) that are involved in the ways that technology is organised, supplied and consumed, as well as the ways in which technology seeks to constitute us as users, consumers, citizens and more. It is about how practices combine with instruments, and the myriad ways the surveillant assemblage (see n 25) and the 'legal complex' interact. See also the Critical Data Studies (CDS) approach which calls for the widest possible approach to examining the social drivers, implications and power relations of emergent forms of data and algorithmic practices (C Dalton, L Taylor and J Thatcher, 'Critical Data Studies: A dialog on data and space' (2016) *Big Data & Society* 1–9).

[15] See W Christl, 'Corporate Surveillance in Everyday Life. How Companies Collect, Combine, Analyze, Trade, and Use Personal Data on Billions' (Report by Cracked Labs, Vienna, 2017), crackedlabs.org/en/corporate-surveillance and W Christl, 'How Companies Use Personal Data Against People: Automated Disadvantage, Personalized Persuasion, and the Societal Ramifications of the Commercial Use of Personal Information' (Working paper by Cracked Labs, Vienna, 2017), crackedlabs.org/en/data-against-people. See also Amnesty International, 'Surveillance Giants: How the business model of Google and Facebook threatens human rights' (2019), www.amnesty.org/download/Documents/POL3014042019ENGLISH.PDF (accessed 4 February 2020). See also the series of reports from *The Guardian* 'The Cambridge Analytica files' at www.theguardian.com/news/series/cambridge-analytica-files.

[16] For an account of what algorithms are in this context, and what they do, see further R Kitchin 'Thinking critically about and researching algorithms' (2017) 20(1) *Information, Communication & Society* 14–29, and, more widely, see L Amoore and V Pioteukh, (eds), *Algorithmic Life: Calculative Devices in the Age of Big Data* (Routledge, 2016). For an account of the scale of this approach see also J McCormick, *Algorithms that have Changed the Future: The Ingenious ideas that Drive Today's Computers* (Princeton University Press, 2016). A more sceptical view, or at least one that does not deny the phenomenon but suggests that some of it is based on myths about what technology can do, is offered by V Mosco, *Becoming Digital: Towards a Post-Internet Society* (Emerald, 2017).

[17] See further B Marr, *Big Data: Using Smart Big Data, Analytics and Metrics to Make Better Decision and Improve Performance* (Wiley, 2015); S Greengard, *The Internet of Things* (MIT Press, 2015). For a dystopian

algorithms developed in a bottom-up process are being introduced to interrogate this data and allow bulk data ingestion into processes where ever more connections and relations are being mapped and manipulated, sorted and filtered, and searched and prioritised.[18] This can inform geographic information systems, involving global positioning systems, geodemographics, and remote surveillance systems, to yield up further new information.[19] They also facilitate the re-use of existing data to simultaneously extend individual surveillance and produce knowledge about groups. Knowledge about these groups can be constructed in all sorts of ways, cutting across cultural, self-definitions of community to focus on socio-economic characteristics in ways that may, for example, dissolve the idea of 'place' and replace this with a whole range of inferences drawn from other factors, with some elements emphasized and others that we might think important set aside. Cultural groups can thus be represented as mere aggregations of individuals in a way that undermines the legitimate claims of those groups, and diminishes their political agency.[20]

To understand this properly we must consider how this combines with relatively older technologies such as Universal Product Code (UPC or bar code) and radio-frequency identification (RFID) which uses electromagnetic fields to automatically identify and track tags attached to objects, *and* newer, wider converging technologies deploying biometric, genetic and even olfactory devices to make a whole range of judgements and underpin new categories of social sorting. There is also a range of new technologies in related fields. Nanotechnology, biotechnology, information technology and cognitive technology (NBIC) together are providing a paradigm change on a level similar to but perhaps exceeding the last industrial revolution.[21]

These and other surveillance measures are now woven into the fabric of everyday life. In Weiser's well-known formulation, this is 'ubiquitous computing'.[22] In terms of policing, cameras are ubiquitous with face and gait recognition technology, along with fingerprints, electronic tags, transponders, phone records, iris scanning, photo ID, breathalysers, databases and DNA as part of a wider armoury of security. There is in addition the equally important data trails that everyone one leaves behind in the online

account see J Bridle, *New Dark Ages: the End of Future* (Verso, 2018) and, for an account of the volumes of data involved, see J Schultz, 'How much data is created on the internet each day?' (2019) blog.microfocus.com/how-much-data-is-created-on-the-internet-each-day/ (accessed 16 January 2020).

[18] For a useful account of how this is done see H Armstrong, *Machines That Learn in the Wild: Machine Learning Capabilities, Limitations and Implications* (NESTA, 2015), media.nesta.org.uk/documents/machines_that_learn_in_the_wild.pdf (last accessed 23 January 2020).

[19] See further D Swanlund and N Schuurman, 'Resisting geosurveillance: A survey of tactics and strategies for spatial privacy' (2019) 43(4) *Progress in Human Geography* 596–610.

[20] As Curry argues the creation of these data profiles seems to call an end to the postmodern view of individuals being a set of unique identities, replacing it with a view where individuals are seen as coherent units that share visible and quantifiable characteristics with their neighbours in ways that can be connected in a hugely complex range of different ways. (See further M Curry 'The Digital Individual and the Private Realm' (1997) 87(4) *Annals of the Association of American Geographers* 681–99.) The power of this to undermine the solidarity required for effective political action is a topic which will be returned to later.

[21] See R van Est and J Gerritsen, *Human Rights in the Robot Age* (Rathenau Instituut, 2017) for an account of this wider process.

[22] M Weiser, 'The Computer for the 21st Century' (1991) *Scientific American*. As he notes, 'the most profound technologies are those that disappear. They weave themselves into the fabric of everyday life until they are indistinguishable from it' (p 94).

world, and, increasingly, in the real world. As citizens are moving about, working, buying, communicating, browsing the web, engaging with public services and more, they leave a wealth of data trails. As Rob Kitchin describes it (in the context of the Smart City): 'the result is a vast deluge of real-time, fine-grained, contextual and actionable data, which are routinely generated about cities and their citizens'.[23] Furthermore this is what Lupton terms 'lively data' – dynamic, continuously flowing, encapsulating any and every aspect of life from length of phone call to likes on social media, and reflecting the continually changing flow of data from lives that are open-ended, indicating a non-essentialist conception of human life which is indifferent to social context and identity (gender, income, education and skills, etc) as well as to grander modern narratives (nationality, class, etc). The data also is constantly updating, where any fault in reach or accuracy is accepted and absorbed, and the update added into a now improved data set.[24] Overall this can be seen in terms of what has been termed 'surveillant assemblages' – referring to the way in which discrete objects, technologies and systems come together to work within a functional surveillance entity that abstracts the corporeal, territorial individual into a digital dimension where the individual can be broken down into various component parts, and datified, before being reassembled into distinct 'data doubles', which can then be analysed and targeted for intervention.[25]

The Covid-19 health crisis has provided a perfect conjunction of political conditions to produce a government response that aligns with developing technology to extend this further, and produce a new regime of 'bio-surveillance'.[26] Significantly it is one that we might actually demand as ostensibly 'for our own good'. Such a regime also offers a particular instantiation of a positive technology of power that Foucault would have recognised. Writing about how plague replaced leprosy as the basis for a new model of political control in the eighteen century or Classical Age, Foucault describes how the reaction to leprosy – one of rejection, exclusion etc – is replaced by a more positive reaction of 'inclusion, observation, the formation of knowledge, [and] the multiplication of effects of power on the basis of the accumulation of observations and knowledge'.[27] As Foucault observes, plague is the moment that produces and justifies 'an exhaustive, unobstructed power that is completely transparent to its object and exercised to the full'.[28] Plague produces a process of knowledge collection and analysis to underlie a programme of spatial partitioning, regulation and control. Foucault describes how in the period from the seventeenth century, towns placed under quarantine required citizens to register with local inspectors, and then observe strict segregation into districts and streets which were policed by sentries. Inspectors called twice daily and each individual in a house was assigned to a window at which they should appear when their

[23] R Kitchin, 'The Ethics of smart cities and urban science' (2016) *Philosophical Transactions of the Royal Society* 2. See also the Special Edition on 'IoT and AI for Smart Government' (2019) 36 *Government Information Quarterly*.

[24] D Lupton, *The Quantified Self* (Polity Press, 2016).

[25] K Heggerty and R Ericson, 'The Surveillant Assemblage' (2000) 51(4) *British Journal of Sociology* 51 605–774.

[26] See the origins of this in B Parry, 'Domesticating biosurveillance: "Containment" and the politics of bioinformation' (2012) 18 *Health and* Place 718–25.

[27] M Foucault in V.Marchetti and A Salomoni (eds), *Abnormal: Lectures at the Collége de France 1974–1975* (Picador, 2003) Lecture Two at 48.

[28] See above, at 47.

name was called, sorting themselves into those who were fit, and those who were dead or ill, and so dangerous and requiring intervention. This regime involves a power which reaches right into what Foucault terms 'the grain of individuals themselves' and its 'capillary ramifications' operates on 'their time, habitat, localization, and bodies'.[29]

From quite an early stage in the Covid-19 pandemic a number of states deployed technology to attempt to achieve a bio surveillance programme.[30] Indeed it was reported that the mobile phone industry explored the creation of a global data-sharing system that could track individuals around the world, as part of an effort to curb the spread of Covid-19.[31] Individual states may potentially deploy CCTV and phone data, including possibly all those sensors on most mobile phones which monitor not only location but up to 14 other elements of an individual's micro environment, and perhaps even individual health data from our fitness trackers, in order to develop new, sophisticated forms of surveillance for a time of crisis – and perhaps for some time afterwards. The so-called 'health code' service, developed for the Chinese Government and run on the ubiquitous platforms Alipay and WeChat, provides users with colour-coded designations based on their health status and travel history, and a QR code that can be scanned by authorities to allow or deny access to travel and various faculties or require home isolation or quarantine.[32] There is certainly potential here for a number of states to explore a more intense and invasive surveillance apparatus. This is occurring at time when many of its citizens might actively embrace this, and indeed assist and reinforce the regulation of others through the online shaming through various social media of those who do not observe the rules. All this can occur, and indeed be welcomed despite the very real possibility that such measures might be unlikely to be removed when the immediate danger passes.[33]

Of course this surveillance is not restricted to the state in a pandemic or law enforcement context. Indeed, arguably, in normal times the state is less of a problem – or least no more of one – than the corporate world. Here, as Zuboff has outlined so forcefully, there is a wider process of commodifying experience into data and marketising it.[34]

[29] See above.

[30] It seems that at least 19 countries introduced digital tracking in the relatively early stages of response to the Covid-19 crisis. See the Covid-19 Digital Rights Tracker from TOP10VPN at www.top10vpn.com/news/surveillance/covid-19-digital-rights-tracker/ (accessed 30 March 2020).

[31] This included the US, India, Iran, Poland, Singapore, Israel and South Korea. The UK Government was reported as being engaged in talks with BT, and the UK mobile operator EE, about using phone location and usage data to determine the efficacy of isolation orders. See *The Guardian* (19 March 2020) at www.theguardian.com/world/2020/mar/19/plan-phone-location-data-assist-uk-coronavirus-effort and *The Guardian* (25 March 2020) at www.theguardian.com/world/2020/mar/25/mobile-phone-industry-explores-worldwide-tracking-of-users-coronavirus?CMP=share_btn_tw.

[32] See further www.theguardian.com/world/2020/apr/01/chinas-coronavirus-health-code-apps-raise-concerns-over-privacy. There is a more modest proposal in the UK for an app to record GPS location data, with a link to a home testing service, to ensure the rapid tracing of contacts. See L Ferretti et al 'Quantifying SARS-CoV-2 transmission suggests epidemic control with digital contact tracing' *Science* (31 March 2020) at science.sciencemag.org/content/early/2020/03/30/science.abb6936.

[33] See further J Cliffe, 'The rise of the bio-surveillance state' (*New Statesman* 25 March 2020), Y Harari, 'The World After Coronavirus' (*Financial Times* 20 March 2020) at www.ft.com/content/19d90308-6858-11ea-a3c9-1fe6fedcca75 and A Spadaro, 'Covid-19: Testing the Limits of Human Rights' (2020) *European Journal of Risk Regulation* 1–9.

[34] See S Zuboff, *The Age of Surveillance Capitalism* above n 10 which builds upon earlier work including S Zuboff, 'Big other: surveillance capitalism and the prospects of an information civilization' (2015) 30 *Journal of Information and Technology* 75–89.

Indeed often the process seems characterised by a sort of agentless domination and control where there is not one mastermind behind the process. Rather as Hoye and Monaghan argue, a variety of state and corporate powers between them have turned the internet and related technologies into a 'global surveillance dragnet'.[35] Zuboff captures the relentless inevitability of this:

> Surveillance capitalism's rendition practices overwhelm any sensible discussion of 'opt in' or 'opt out'. There are no more fig leaves. The euphemisms of consent can no longer divert attention from the bare facts: under surveillance capitalism, rendition is typically unauthorised, uniliateral, gluttonous, secret and brazen. These characteristics summarise the asymmetries of power that put the 'surveillance' in surveillance capitalism. They also highlight a harsh truth; it is difficult to be where rendition is not. As industries far beyond the technology sector are lured by surveillance profits, the ferocity of the race to find and render experience as data has turned rendition into a global project of surveillance capitalism.[36]

But considering this in terms of surveillance, and indeed discipline, alone does not capture the ambition of the new models.[37] Now, as new surveillance practices follow us across almost all aspects of everyday life we must consider not only wider ideas of 'datafication, but also think carefully about ideas such as 'dataveillance'. As Cohen has observed much of the excitement surrounding Big Data is rooted in its capacity to identify patterns and correlations that cannot be detected by human cognition, converting massive volumes of data (often in unstructured form) into a particular, highly data-intensive form of knowledge, and thus creating a new mode of knowledge production.[38] These are 'enigmatic technologies' as Pasquale terms them, where authority is concealed behind algorithms and the 'values and prerogatives that the encoded rules enact are hidden within black boxes' and 'critical decisions are made not on the basis of the data per se, but on the basis of data analyzed algorithmically'.[39] Indeed, as Rieder has observed, algorithmic tools offer an 'aura of objectivity, rationality, and legitimacy' that is derived from their empirical underpinnings.[40] Algorithms are epistemologically performative; unlike theory, they make no claims as to truth, only to function. As Lowrie puts it, algorithms cannot be wrong in any theoretical or mathematical sense.[41]

All of this has occasioned some alarm among some commentators. For example, in a number of important contributions Yeung has alerted us to the dangers of both hypernudging,[42] and some further related threats from the sort of tailored, user-specific

[35] J Hoye and J Monaghan, 'Surveillance, freedom and the republic' (2018) 17(3) *European Journal of Political Theory* 343–63.

[36] See n 34 at 241.

[37] See eg C Fuchs, 'Political economy and surveillance theory' (2013) 39(5) *Critical Sociology* 671–87; D Lyon, *Surveillance Studies: An Overview* (Polity Press, 2007).

[38] J Cohen, *Configuring the Networked Self* (Yale University Press, 2012).

[39] F Pasquale, *The Black Box Society: The Secret Algorithms that Control Money and Information* (Harvard University Press, 2015) 8 and 21.

[40] B Rieder, 'On the Diversity of the Accountability Problem: Machine Learning and Knowing Capitalism' (2015) 2 *Digital Culture and Society* (2015) 39.

[41] I Lowrie, 'Algorithmic rationality: Epistemology and efficiency in the data sciences' (2017) 4(1) Big *Data & Society*.

[42] The term 'nudge' was first developed by Thaler and Sunstein (R Thaler and C Sunstein, *Nudge* (Penguin Books, 2008)) to refer to a 'form of choice architecture that alters people's behaviour in a predictable way without forbidding any option or significantly changing their economic incentives'. Yeung builds on this concept,

displays of information, known as personalisation.[43] Yeung correctly emphases the new relations of production and consumption that are ushered in when an emphasis on economic growth through consumption remains but there is no longer a domestic manufacturing basis. The model of industrial capitalism is instead replaced by surveillance capitalism where a set of networked computational technologies transform modes and cultures of consumption. Questioning whether techniques such as personalisation lead to a more meaningful experience and an empowered consumer, or an opportunity for exploitation, exclusion and inequality, Yeung points to the costs in terms of fairness and justice as well as to the erosion of social solidarity and loss of community. All this remains true and important. However the emphasis on production and consumption does not tell the related story of how similar developments are affecting our futures in relation to government. What is on offer in the new digital lifeworld extends also to new forms of government and political engagement.

III. Algorithmic Governmentality and Democracy – the Power of 'Inference'

The emerging digital lifeworld provides resources for a new form of government. This algorithmic government is about extracting facts, entities, concepts and objects from vast repositories of data, and, as calculative devices create subjects and objects of interest in this way, they make those subjects and objects perceptible and amenable to decision and action through the ineluctable power of inference. Now there is a new governmental resource available through this accumulation and interpretation of vast reserves of data. It is one where people as the subjects and objects of government are simultaneously present – through their every measurable action – and absent in the sense of not having any individual agency beyond the data. They become part of the governable reality, the 'everyone' who are all included in the sweep-up of data. In this way, within this particular governing conjecture, the manner in which individuals see themselves, and are constructed as units of governance, is changing radically along with the means of their governance. The target of this government is the future, what people might do or chose, what they might buy, how they might act or react. The resources of big data, endlessly analysed by algorithms, can master this future through the power of inference.

This has very profound consequences. In essence it introduces a new idea of *algorithmic governmentality* which draws upon and seeks to involve governable subjects who function not as real individuals but rather as temporary aggregates of infra-personal data

redefining it as a 'hyper nudge' to illuminate the techniques where 'big data interacts with personalisation in an effort to devise highly persuasive attempts to influence the behaviour of individuals'. K Yeung, '"Hypernudge": Big Data as a mode of regulation by design' (2017) 20(1) *Information Communication & Society* 118–36.

[43] K Yeung, 'Five fears about mass predictive personalization in an age of surveillance Capitalism' (2018) 8(3) *International Data Privacy Law* 258 and 'Algorithmic Regulation: A Critical Introduction' (2018) 12 *Regulation and Governance* 505–23.

gathered at, and exploitable on, an almost unimaginable scale and detail.[44] This produces what might be termed, following Foucault, a new 'truth regime'.[45] Algorithmic government is, in Foucauldian terms, a new 'technology of government', but it is perhaps more. It is a technology of government that wins the arms race started in the mid eighteenth century by the statisticians who rendered modern forms of government power feasible by naming, numbering and controlling the world through the deployment of statistical power.[46] Now there is the conjunction of the big Foucauldian concepts of 'knowledge', 'biopower', and 'population' which come together in a new governmentality. This is something new. Algorithmic government is about extracting facts, entities, concepts and objects from vast repositories, and, as calculative devices create subjects and objects of interest in this way, they make those subjects and objects perceptible and amenable to decision and action. Inference from the data is all-important here: the data provides a constant in a world where humans are moving around, changing their behaviours and attitudes and responding to a changing world where instability is a constant.[47] Algorithms work on this shifting, fluid set of data that is constantly being re-formulated and re-compiled to find answers to whatever questions are required. This is more than the sort of ratings produced by such as PageRank, EdgeRank, and What'sTrending which merely show what is popular online. These algorithms purport to do much more, and with much more data. Drawing upon the almost total picture to be provided by what is visible from the data streaming in from the internet of things, they can claim the advantage of almost total comprehensiveness in every area of life. (Arguably here the very notion of the representative sample is over: in a world where 'everything' is captured, 'n = all'.[48])

It has been suggested that Facebook's algorithm requires only ten 'likes' before being able to predict your opinions more accurately than your work colleagues, 150 before it exceeds your family and 300 before it can forecast your views better than your spouse.[49]

[44] The work of Antoinette Rouvroy is of particular value here. See further A Rouvroy, and T Berns, 'Algorithmic Governmentality and Prospects of Emancipation' (2013) 177(1) *RT. Réseaux*, 163–96; A Rouvroy, 'Algorithmic governmentality: a passion for the real and the exhaustion of the virtual', *Transmediale – All Watched Over by Algorithms*, Berlin. (2015), www.academia.edu/10481275/Algorithmic_governmentality_a_passion_for_the_real_and_the_exhaustion_of_the_virtual (accessed 17 January 2020); 'The end(s) of critique: data-behaviourism vs. due-process' in M Hildebrandt and E De Vries (eds), *Privacy, Due Process and the Computational Turn* (Routledge, 2012); 'Governing Without Norms: Algorithmic Governmentality' (Contribution to the special issue on 'Lacanian Politics and the Impasses of Democracy Today', ed Bogdan Wolf)) (2018) 32 *Psychoanalytical Notebooks* 99–102. See also K Yeung, 'Algorithmic Regulation: A Critical Interrogation' (2018) 12 *Regulation and Governance* 505 for a valuable mapping of some related ideas.

[45] See further A Rouvroy, 'The end(s) of critique: data-behaviourism vs. due-process' above.

[46] See I Hacking, *The Taming of Chance* (Cambridge University Press, 1990).

[47] See further J Cheney-Lippold, *We are Data: Algorithms and the Making of our Digital Selves* (York University Press, 2017).

[48] *cf* the perspective offered by Hildebrandt, who argues for the illusory nature of such an idea as 'N is never All, because the flux of life can be translated into machine-readable data in a number of ways and whichever way is chosen has a major impact on the outcome of data mining operation'. See 'Slaves to big Data or Are We?' (2013) 17 *IDP*, www.researchgate.net/publication/269779688_Esclaus_de_les_macrodades_O_no (last accessed 23 January 2020) or the more generally sceptical approach of A Smart, *Beyond Zero and One: Machines, Psychedelics and Consciousness* (OR Books, 2015). Of course, it could be argued at this point that it does not matter if this creation of a whole from a collection of data fragments is accurate or true (or even perhaps really possible) only that people think it might be so and act as if it were.

[49] Y Harari, *Homo Deus: A Brief History of Tomorrow* (Harvill Secker, 2015) 340. See also the working methods employed in the Cambridge Analytical scandal at www.theguardian.com/news/series/cambridge-analytica-files (accessed 15 May 2020).

The new algorithmic governmentality, achieved through the accumulation and interpretation of vast reserves of data, is potentially much more far-reaching, comprehensive and ambitious than this.

All this data, and the knowledge it produces, can be represented as much more than the simple 'democratic input' obtainable from elections or consultation exercises, no matter how well-designed. This surely can be offered as the basis for a more responsive, more effective, and even more *democratic*, basis for public decision-making than anything up until now. It is the expression of what people actually *do* – across a myriad of everyday activities and actions. Data mining and the computational generation of knowledge from algorithmic government re-organises how we see the world, and it does so with the compelling certainty of science and statistics. As Beer recognises, algorithms as the foundation of a system of government increasingly are achieving a social and cultural power as they become more familiar in society.[50] A system based on algorithms can be posited as one that can think more quickly, comprehensively and accurately than any human agency. Decisions made by algorithms can be presented as neutral, efficient, objective – drawn from the data and beyond politics. This relates directly to ideas about the production of truth, and its role in how power operates. Algorithmic knowledge can claim the capacity to produce truth, and it does so both by providing the discursive framing of the subject to be considered – risk, criminal behaviour, smartness as it applies to the city, the home or transport systems, or whatever – *and*, seemingly, providing an accurate and comprehensive account of *everything* that should populate this knowledge.[51] There is a powerful conjunction of power/knowledge in Foucauldian terms here.[52] As Beer points out, in the mid-1970s Foucault placed the production of truth centrally in understandings of the operation of power, what he termed the 'how' of power.[53] While algorithmic knowledge was unimaginable to Foucault, the material interventions that such knowledge could make in the exercise of power would be recognised as an essential element of the 'how' of power here.[54]

As Mehozay and Fisher[55] argue in the context of risk assessment in criminal justice, this is a new epistemology. It is one that signals a rejection of any essentialism in how we

[50] D Beer. 'The social power of algorithms' (2017) 20 *Information, Communication & Society* 1–13 and the other contributions to that special issue as well as D Beer, *The Data Gaze: Capitalism, Power and Perception* (Sage, 2019) for a further account of how 'a faith in data emerges and then becomes embedded or cemented in social structures and practices … [and, as] the data gaze expands its reach, increases the data accumulated and further embeds data-led thinking into decision making, knowledge and into ideals of the way the world should be run' (p 127).

[51] See further J Cobbe and J Morison, 'Understanding the Smart City: Framing the challenges for law and good governance' in JB Auby, É Chevalier and E Slautsky (eds), *Le Futur de Droit Administratif/The Future of Administrative Law* (LexisNexis, 2019) which discusses the processes of problematising whereby where a particular way of seeing and dealing with an area are 'manufactured' within a wider social and political context.

[52] It involves asking as Foucault does, 'what type of power is it that is capable of producing discourses of power that have, in a society like ours, such powerful effects?' M Foucault, *Society Must be Defended: Lectures at the College De France 1975–76* (Penguin, 2004) 24.

[53] See Beer, n 50 above.

[54] As Foucault puts it, 'Power cannot be exercised unless a certain economy of discourses of truth functions in, on the basis of, and thanks to, that power': M Foucault, *Society Must be Defended* above at 24.

[55] Y Mehozay and E Fisher, 'The epistemology of algorithmic risk assessment and the path towards a nonpenology penology' (2018) *Punishment & Society*.

think about people as individuals and about human nature. If there is no 'deep structure' but only surface behaviour, it becomes impossible to speak of any individual as a case of a larger systemic whole, such as gender or class. The algorithmic episteme assumes no social ascription, identifying individuals solely in terms of the sum of their actions. Patterns in the data are more important than individual agency or identity: we are nothing but the data. If the task here is to construct meaning out of apparently meaningless information, this involves the disappearance of the individual subject whose only point of interest is how he/she exists in a relational context with other individuals as they themselves appear massed up into huge data sets, and how their conduct affects others. This creates a new and constantly updated reality, and with it a new normality that is reinforced by being – seemingly – the expression of everyone. The knowledge that algorithmic government draws upon is not created by individuals or given meaning by political or other frameworks of reference. Instead it seems to appear ineluctably from the data. It is to be found simply present (albeit hidden until the algorithms give it meaning) in the big data. In this sense the world of algorithmic government is something that is not comprehensible naturally.

This would seem to undo very many understandings of ourselves and our relationships with each other, and the material world. Of particular interest here is the effect that this may have on any sense of being part of a wider group or community, and on any consequent political organisation or action that might follow from this. As suggested above,[56] the way in which data can be collected as an entirety, and then ordered, classified, sorted, correlated and used to find patterns, overwhelms any efforts to assert individual autonomy or even group interests. Our essential being is evidenced by the data: our own understandings of why we do what we do are of limited interest compared to this reality.[57] This undermines mobilisation in such terms as community or interest as individuals become disassociated from one another: the individual is now a data point who can be correlated or combined in relation to other data which may be meaningless to him or her in any real sense but nevertheless can now be interpreted as a transcendently accurate account of reality. (While we might perceive ourselves as, for example, ecologically aware, classless progressives, sharing our worldview with all those in our village neighbourhood, the 'reality' gleaned from the datasphere may reveal us instead to be high-end consumers who have more in common in our travel, lifestyle and consumption choices with urban, venture capitalists.) Not only can we be re-politicised in ways that we may not want to be, or cannot easily deny, our agency and capacity for action is undermined too. Algorithmic governance offers a false emancipation by

[56] See n 20.

[57] This approach to *homo documentus*, seeing a person as 'document', with all the abdication of identity and personal judgement that is involved normally is captured well by Ron Day who comments that 'routinely and obsessively we use online resources – whose algorithms and indexes both serve and profit from us in ways that the users are largely unaware – as the way of overcoming the physical and emotional distances that are a consequence of modernity, and in particular capitalist modernity, where markets have become the means and the ends for reasoning, communication, and, increasingly, emotion. These devices have become the governance structures – the 'idea' or 'concept' – for our human manner of being … which increasingly subsume and subvert the former roles of personal judgement and critique in personal and social being and politics.' *Indexing It All: The Subject in the Age of Documentation, Information, and Data (History and Foundations of Information Science)* (MIT Press, 2014) ix.

appearing to be, by its very nature, all-inclusive. It is the expression of all, across a whole range of behaviours and relationships – and if there are complaints about being omitted or misunderstood the data set is open to revision in its search for comprehensiveness and accuracy.

This might seem to suggest not only a departure of individual agency, but with this, the disappearance of politics as currently understood. How this might be made manifest is not entirely clear: might there be voting apps that continually decide for us on a range of issues, based on the profile of our data double?[58] Alternatively might there be simply an algorithmically driven public decision making system along the lines of systems used widely in a range of areas from traffic routing to finance to (particularly) the criminal justice system?[59] It is likely that some form of representative democracy would remain but it could be (further) hollowed out with its remit focusing on headline issues of identity, culture and personality, leaving much public decision making around service provision, planning and general administration within the control of the technology.

What is clear is that algorithmic government power has the capacity to de-politicise, or rather re-depoliticises us in new ways. It has the potential to undermine, and then transcend, many of the fundamental attributes of citizenship which presently appear as part of the bargain within the government – governed relationship. While many of these are anchored in ideas of the individual, privacy, and indeed selfhood, they spill over into wider conceptions of civicness, community, and citizenship – and indeed the whole idea of publicness and the liberal state. This is a form of government without politics. What is to be done?

One of the advantages of recognising this potential transformation in public decision making in terms of it being a governmentality is that we can and must factor in some forms of *resistance*: as Foucault famously remarked 'where there is power there is resistance'.[60] Power and freedom are, on the governmentality model, co-constitutive. Power relations necessarily presuppose that all parties involved in such relations have the ability, even in the most extreme cases, to choose amongst a range of structured options. As Thompson argues, this sort of minimal freedom is, in turn, only possible in a field defined precisely by the structuring work of governance. Thus, each is the condition of the possibility of the other.[61] It is to the idea of resistance that we must now turn.

[58] See J Susskind (above n 14, at 227–54) for an account of some of the ways that this 'future politics' might operate.

[59] See A Zavrsnik, 'Algorithmic justice: Algorithms and big data in criminal justice settings' (2019) *European Journal of Criminology* for an overview and J Morison and A Harkens, 'Re-engineering justice? Robot judges, computerised courts and (semi) automated legal decision-making' (2019) 39 *Legal Studies* 618–35 for a sceptical account of this in the context of legal decisions.

[60] *The History of Sexuality* Volume 1 (Penguin, 1990) 95. Foucault continues, in a less well-known passage that 'resistances do not derive from a few heterogeneous principles; but neither are they a lure or a promise that is of necessity betrayed. They are the odd term in relations of power; they are inscribed in the latter as an irreducible opposite. Hence they too are distributed in irregular fashion: the points, knots, or focuses of resistance are spread over time and space at varying densities, at times mobilising groups or individuals in a definitive way, inflaming certain points of the body, certain moments in life, certain types of behaviour. Are there no great radical ruptures, massive binary divisions, then? Occasionally, yes. But more often one is dealing with mobile and transitory points of resistance, producing cleavages in a society – that shift about, fracturing unities and effecting regroupings, furrowing across individuals themselves, cutting them up and remoulding them, marking off irreducible regions in them, in their bodies and minds' (p 97).

[61] K Thompson, 'Forms of resistance: Foucault on tactical reversal and self-formation' (2003) 36 *Continental Philosophy Review* 113–38. There is a view that this issue remains a continuing problem within Foucault's

IV. Resistance – Our Puny Efforts?

One of the important features of Zuboff's account is that she vehemently opposes the normalness of surveillance; or any idea that, for example, we accept that an idea of recognition with all its intimations of familiarity is the same sort of recognition that is involved in machine-based face recognition, or that a 'friend' can be someone you have never seen, or that every move, utterance, facial expression or emotion can be catalogued, manipulated and then used surreptitiously to herd us through the future for someone else's profit. Zuboff also objects to any idea that our role in the face of all this is simply to find ways to hide ourselves, through camouflaging or blocking software, or trying to live off-grid.[62] Nonetheless, given that connectivity may seem, particularly for the young, to be a necessity as well as a basic right, there is a need to re-balance the terms on which it is offered. There is a move towards developing a number of strategies. These seem to amount to variations on attempting to neutralise the technology, and turning the tables. Both have echoes for a Foucauldian interpretation.

Gary Marx explains how surveillance neutralisation can be undertaken through a variety of often systematically related techniques. He details a range of prominent types of response to privacy-invading surveillance.[63] Some of these are behavioural, opportunistic acts of individual resistance to reclaim freedom and autonomy within the framework of strategies governing a space.[64] Others focus more on developing and mainstreaming alternative technologies.[65] Certainly there are a collection of measures that could be taken up involving, for example a focus on privacy enhancing instruments

wider account. It is thought by some critics that his continual insistence that the subject cannot get outside of power relations indicates a social field totalised by power. While some critics, such as Charles Taylor, believe that Foucault's description of power 'does not make sense' without an opposing concept such as 'liberation' or 'freedom' ('Foucault on Freedom and Truth' in D Hoy (ed), *Foucault: A Critical Reader* (Blackwell, 1986) 92), by far the most prevalent critical response reads it as having, in Edward Said's terms, as 'a profoundly pessimistic view' of social relations. If power has no external limit, then one cannot get outside of power in order to oppose it. As a result, Said considers this view of power as being directly linked to what he reads as Foucault's 'singular lack of interest in the force of effective resistance'. E Said, 'Foucault and the Imagination of Power' In Hoy (ed), above at 151. See also J Muckelbauer, 'On reading differently: Through Foucault's resistance' (2000) 63(1) *College English* 71–94.

[62] Zuboff, above n 10.

[63] These techniques include discovering the location of surveillance actors, avoiding surveillance actors, blocking surveillance actors from functioning as intended, masking one's identity from surveillance actors, and engaging in countersurveillance: employing the same techniques used by surveillance actors against them (See further G Marx, 'A Tack in the Shoe: Neutralizing and Resisting the New Surveillance' (2016) 59 *Journal of Social Issues* and *Windows into the Soul: Surveillance and Society in an Age of High Technology* (University of Chicago Press, 2016). Of course the law can also be enlisted in an attempt to block some types of surveillance, (see, eg, J Vagle, *Being watched: Legal challenges to government surveillance* (NYU Press, 2017)).

[64] eg, in an entertaining account Wood and Thompson take the instance of resistance in Australia to speed trap technology and random breath tests to suggest that there is emerging 'a new form of social media facilitated counter surveillance that we term crowdsourced counter-surveillance: the use of knowledge-discovery and management crowdsourcing to facilitate surveillance discovery, avoidance, and countersurveillance'. Crowdsourced counter-surveillance, they argue, represents a form of counter surveillant assemblage: 'an ensemble of individuals, technologies, and data flows that, more than the sum of their parts, function together to neutralize surveillance measures'. Wood and Thompson, 'Crowdsourced Countersurveillance: A Counter-surveillant Assemblage?' (2018) 16 *Surveillance & Society* 21.

[65] See L Dencik, A Hintz and J Cable, 'Towards data justice? The ambiguity of anti-surveillance resistance in political activism' (2016) *Big Data & Society*.

such as the TOR browser, tools such as 'httpseverywhere' which is a free, open source browser extension to support the more secure https protocol rather than the standard http, the GPG email encryption system and software such as Signal, which is a cross-platform encrypted messaging service.[66] Of course, as Foucault might see it, this does not involve escaping the surveillance net at all: as he notes in *Discipline and Punish*,[67] such techniques are simply evidence of a consciousness of being monitored by unseen observers that can lead to feelings of actual control; people adopt the norms and rules of the surveillors, regulate their behaviours accordingly, and thus discipline themselves. To the degree that people extend that discipline to others around them, the panopticon succeeds in gaining further power through individual disciplinary efforts.

In terms of resistance through turning the tables, an ideal strategy, particularly in Foucauldian terms, might be to develop what Foucault terms 'hetrotopias'. This is a complex term with a range of applications[68] but here can be seen to refer to the creation of other spaces; spaces of resistance, 'radically other spaces [that] withdraw from the reigning order and the necessities of the present', and act as 'counter-sites' in which existing social and spatial arrangements are 'represented, contested and inverted'.[69] Although usually conceived as isolated spaces away from the gaze of surveillance and social control strategies, the term can be extended to include 'public-space heterotopias'; spaces that, despite being located in visible public places, have a heterotopian character.[70] These other spaces can counter or invert normal cultural configurations, perhaps by developing techniques of 'sousveillance'. Here people 'watch from below' to mirror and confront the bureaucracies that have embedded surveillance technology into the everyday fabric of life, using the idea of transparency as an antidote to concentrated power in the hands of surveillors.[71] For Mann, Nolan and Wellman, sousveillance works by enhancing the ability of people to access and collect data about their surveillance, and so neutralise, block, distort or counter it.[72] Of course even since Mann et al

[66] See further privacy guides such as the Electronic Frontier Foundation's 'Surveillance Self-Defense' (ssd.eff.org/en) and the Tactical Tech Collective's 'Security in a Box' (tacticaltech.org/projects/security-box, last accessed 4 February 2020) which explain these further and offer advice on secure online communication. 'Crypto-parties' have brought necessary training in such tools to towns and cities worldwide.

[67] M Foucault, *Discipline and Punish: The Birth of the Penitentiary* (Allen Lane 1977).

[68] See, eg, M Dehaene and L De Cauter (eds), *Heterotopia and the City: Public Space in a Postcivil Society* (Routledge, 2008).

[69] M Foucault (and J Miskowiec), 'Of other spaces' (1986) 18 *Diacritics* 22–27 at 24 (available via www.jstor.org/stable/464648).

[70] See further R Rymarczuk and M Derksen, 'Different spaces: Exploring Facebook as heterotopia' (2014) 19 *First Monday* 1–11.

[71] See further J Fernback, 'Sousveillance: Communities of resistance to the surveillance environment' (2013) 30 *Telematics and Informatics* for a general account of the ways in which this can be carried out and see M Welsh, 'Counterveillance: How Foucault and the Groupe d'Information sur les Prisons reversed the optics' (2011) 15 *Theoretical Criminology*) 301–13 for an account of how in the 1970s the GIP made coalitions with experts and others and gave voice to prisoners through, for example, the introduction of prisoner questionnaires on food and conditions, and made films on the real lived experience in prisons to counter official deployment of oppressive power being exercised under such terms as justice, knowledge, or objectivity. The revelations made by Edward Snowden about the surveillance activities of GCHQ and the NSA, and the continuing activities of Wikileaks (see wikileaks.org) perhaps provide a more a technologically up-to-date example of the same phenomenon.

[72] S Mann, J Nolan and B Wellman, 'Sousveillance: inventing and using wearable computing devices for data collection in surveillance environments' (2003) 1 *Surveillance and Society* 331–55.

wrote in 2003, efforts to resist omnipresent surveillance have needed to become more sophisticated to catch up with the pervasive computing and ambient intelligence that puts surveillance into the whole range of smart devices now supporting all the basic activities of everyday life in ways that are so embedded into the environment as to be almost imperceptible. But even in 2003 Mann et al did recognise while sousveillance may seem like an act of liberation, a staking out of public territory, overall it contributes to a more general world of ubiquitous total surveillance where the involvement of individuals in sousveillance can appear as act of acquiescence in the generation of that world which, in the end, may only serve the ends of the existing dominant power structure.[73] In other words, the cycles of surveillance and sousveillance operate together to promote the conditions of monitoring and data assemblage that are characteristic of surveillance. Within a Foucauldian perspective, this dynamic reveals the limitations of resistance to the overwhelming environment of surveillance, and perhaps signals the very individualistic, reactive, partial, temporary and ineffective nature of individual behavioural initiatives in this space. Faced with this, we need help. And of course it is to the state and its instruments of governance, regulation and law that we turn.

V. Law, Regulation and Governance – What is to be Done?

It is not the job of this chapter to provide a solution to the problems of surveillance capitalism generally, or develop the sort of legal, regulatory and governance frameworks that are needed to roll back, break-up and control the powerful forces within the digital lifeworld. That is perhaps one of the more important tasks for law and legal scholars in the next decade, and, as shall be argued shortly, it is one that must be carried out in conjunction with the whole range of actors – technologists and programmers, planners, ethicists, politicians and local government officials, workers, consumers and citizens who all are increasingly becoming enmeshed in this ubiquitous technology. It does however have to be said that the tools available to law presently do not really seem to be wholly adequate.[74] While data protection law has some purchase, ideas of privacy and the protective mechanism afforded by consent, provide a flimsy basis for legal counter strategies.[75] While we may have some residual attachment to ideas of privacy online, it is

[73] Above at 347.

[74] For a good general account of the challenges involved, and the limitations of law's response, see J Turner, *Robot Rules: Regulating Artificial Intelligence* (Palgrave Macmillan, 2019). In a recent lecture Lord Sales set out some interesting ways for law to address issues of legal regulation involving not just controlling power, but also considering how agency might be conceptualised, perhaps involving ascribing legal personality to machines or developing ideas of risk creation and vicarious liability. To counter problems of lack of technical knowledge in courts (and indeed to preserve commercial secrecy in relation to code) he suggests neutral expert evaluation by an Algorithm Commission or an independently appointed expert who report back to inform the court. ('Algorithms, Artificial Intelligence and the Law, The Sir Henry Brooke Lecture for BAILII', London Lord Sales, Justice of the UK Supreme Court 12 November 2019, London at www.bailii.org/bailii/lecture/06.pdf.

[75] Notwithstanding this, there is some evidence of the legal imagination emerging to develop these categories in ways that may have some purchase. For example, there is work on data trusts, where data subjects would be empowered to pool the rights they hold over their personal data into the legal framework of a trust. A trustee is appointed with a fiduciary obligation to manage the trust's assets in accordance with the trust

difficult to see how this can compete with the appeal of TikTok to a teenager or a mobile phone or Facebook account to a grandparent or an Amazon account to a rural shopper. (And indeed, in the post-Covid-19 world of intermittent lock-downs and cocooning many people may find themselves increasingly dependent on a whole new range of online services and social networking products.) In general, as Wu remarks, 'consumers on the whole seem content to bear a little totalitarianism for convenience'.[76] Research on terms of service and privacy policy has rightly characterised these legal constructions as the 'biggest lie on the internet', as they are largely ignored.[77] Meanwhile rights approaches stumble over the reality that much of the activity crosses public private boundaries effortlessly, and the big tech corporations are resistant to anti-monopoly controls (or even submitting to national taxation regimes). Nevertheless there is an increasing engagement from the academic rights perspectives with issues of AI, both in general and in its various applications.[78] This engagement is replicated by a number of international bodies who both explore the problems and set out some rights based solutions.[79]

Away from the rights framework there is work too on regulation through audit and impact assessment. Of particular relevance here, is the European Parliament who, within the context of developing an industrial policy on AI and robotics, have adopted

charter and the interests of its beneficiaries. The trustee is accountable to the beneficiaries for the management of the trust, and has a responsibility to take appropriate legal action to protect their rights. See further S Delacroix and N Lawrence, 'Bottom-up Data Trusts: disturbing the "one size fits all" approach to data governance' (2019) *International Data Privacy Law* and Centre for International Governance Innovation, *What is a Data Trust* (2019) available at www.cigionline.org/articles/what-data-trust.

[76] T Wu, *The Master Switch: The Rise and Fall of Information Empires* (London Atlantic, 2010) 292.

[77] eg, see further J Obar and A Oeldorf-Hirsch, 'The biggest lie on the Internet: ignoring the privacy policies and terms of service policies of social networking services, Information' (2020) 23 *Communication & Society* 128–47 which details an experimental study assessing the extent to which individuals ignored PP and TOS when joining a fictional social networking site.

[78] See, generally, eg, E Donahoe and M Metzger, 'Artificial Intelligence and Human rights' (2019) 30 *Journal of Democracy* 113; and from a philosophical perspective M Risse, 'Human rights and Artificial Intelligence: An Urgently Needed Agenda' (2019) 41 *Human Rights Quarterly* 1: and in relation to problems around social media, see R Deibert, 'The Road to Digital Unfreedom: Three Painful Truths about Social Media' (2019) 30 *Journal of Democracy* 25, from an equality perspective see L Stanila, 'Artificial Intelligence and Human Rights: A Challenging Approach on the Issue of Equality' (2018) *Journal of Eastern-European Criminal Law* 19: and from a discrimination angle, I Cofone, 'Algorithmic Discrimination Is an Information Problem' (2019) 70 *Hastings Law Journal*.

[79] See eg, the Committee of experts on internet intermediaries MSI-NET *Algorithms and Human Rights: Study on the Human Rights Dimensions of Automated Data Processing Techniques and Possible Regulatory Implications* Council of Europe Study DGI (2017) 2, Strasbourg, Council of Europe (2018) available at rm.coe.int/algorithms-and-human-rights-en-rev/16807956b5; Access Now, *Human rights in the age of Artificial Intelligence*, November 2018 (available at www.accessnow.org/cms/assets/uploads/2018/11/AI-and-Human-Rights.pdf); Amnesty International, *Toronto Declaration on Protecting the Rights to Equality and Non-Discrimination in Machine Learning Systems*, 2019 (available at www.amnesty.org/download/Documents/POL3084472018ENGLISH.PDF; and F Raso et al, *Artificial Intelligence & Human Rights: Opportunities & Risks* (Berkman Klein Center Research Publication No. 2018-6, 2018) available at papers.ssrn.com/sol3/papers.cfm?abstract_id=3259344 which details the implications of new tech in light of the international human rights framework and, interestingly, the United Nations *Guiding Principles on Business and Human Rights* 2011. See also K Jones, *Online Disinformation and Political Discourse: Applying a Human Rights Framework*, London: Chatham House (2019) at www.chathamhouse.org/sites/default/files/2019-11-05-Online-Disinformation-Human-Rights.pdf and Global Information Society Watch *Artificial intelligence: Human rights, social justice and development* (2019) www.apc.org/en/pubs/global-information-society-watch-2019-artificial-intelligence-human-rights-social-justice-and.

a resolution declaring that algorithms in decision-making systems should not be deployed without a prior algorithmic impact assessment.[80] This of course is mirrored in the current data protection frameworks in the UK where solely automated (in contrast to semi-automated) decision-making is prohibited by both the Data Protection Act 2018 and the European Union's General Data Protection Act 2018 – with a limited number of derogations.[81] There is a new focus emerging too on the legal duties of internet intermediaries – those who provide internet service or host content.[82] Mac Síthigh provides a very valuable examination here of the various reviews undertaken by the European Union and other jurisdictions in response to the 'techlash' against some of the operations of the big technology companies, and the attempts to get some control in this sphere.[83] Other recent publications from the European Commission have focused mainly on the potential of Europe to become 'a global leader in innovation in the data economy and its applications', and framed the role of governance and democracy as merely an adjunct to this, fuelled only by the usual platitudes about how human agency and oversight, privacy and consent, non-discrimination, transparency and fairness, and accountability are (in some unspecified way) the answer to all problems.[84]

But perhaps of more direct relevance to the role of technology in public decision-making is the work carried out by Harlow and Rawlings,[85] and by Cobbe.[86] Focusing on the increasing role of automated decision making in public administration, and in particular its interface with administrative justice in courts and tribunals, Harlow and

[80] Para 154 of the European Parliament resolution of 12 February 2019 on a comprehensive European industrial policy on artificial intelligence and robotics (2018/2088(INI) stresses 'that algorithms in decision-making systems should not be deployed without a prior algorithmic impact assessment (AIA), unless it is clear that they have no significant impact on the life of individuals'.

[81] For a fuller account of this see L Edwards and M Veale, 'Slave to the algorithm? Why a "right to an explanation" is probably not the remedy you are looking for' (2017) 16 *Duke Law & Technology Review* 18; Data Protection Act 2018, s 14; Regulation (EU) 2016/679 of the European Parliament and of the Council of 27 April 2016 on the protection of natural persons with regard to the processing of personal data and on the free movement of such data, and repealing Directive 95/46/EC (GDPR), Art 22, and also Article 29 Data Protection Working Party 'Guidelines on Automated individual decision-making and Profiling for the purposes of Regulation 2016/679' (2018a) 17/EN WP251rev.01, p 19, available at ec.europa.eu/newsroom/article29/item-detail.cfm?item_id=612053.

[82] See further L Edwards, '"With Great Power Comes Great Responsibility?" The Rise of Platform Liability' in L Edwards (ed), *Law, Policy and the Internet* (Hart, 2018) 253–89; and J Riordan, *The Liability of Internet Intermediaries* (Oxford University Press, 2016).

[83] D Mac Síthigh, 'The road to responsibilities: new attitudes towards Internet intermediaries' (2019) *Information & Communications Technology Law* 1.

[84] See COM(2020) 65 final European Commission White Paper on *Artificial Intelligence – A European approach to excellence and trust* (2020) at ec.europa.eu/info/sites/info/files/commission-white-paper-artificial-intelligence-feb2020_en.pdf. See also the critical view expressed by A Rouvroy, 'Adopt AI, think later. The Coué method to the rescue of artificial intelligence: A comment following the publication of the European Commission's White Paper: Artificial Intelligence. A European Approach Based on Excellence and Trust.' (2020), available at www.researchgate.net/publication/339566187_Adopt_AI_think_later_The_Coue_method_to_the_rescue_of_artificial_intelligence_A_comment_following_the_publication_of_the_European_Commission's_White_Paper_Artificial_Intelligence_A_European_Approach_B.

[85] C Harlow and R Rawlings, 'Proceduralism and Automation: Challenges to the Values of Administrative Law' LSE Legal Studies Working Paper No. 3/2019, available at SSRN: ssrn.com/abstract=3334783 or http://dx.doi.org/10.2139/ssrn.3334783; and forthcoming, E Fisher, J King and A Young (eds), *The Foundations and Future of Public Law (in honour of Paul Craig)* (Oxford University Press, 2020).

[86] J Cobbe, 'Administrative law and the machines of government: judicial review of automated public-sector decision- making' (2019) 39 *Legal Studies* 636–55.

Rawlings are uneasy that automated systems may not be compatible with human rights law, due process and good governance, and principles of transparency and accountability. In particular they fear that the opacity of automated systems, and the commercial values that have stimulated their development into this context, will not reference the procedures of proper public decision making such as to allow for transparency, accountability and participation, and act as a repository for important values of good governance in administrative law. A similar approach is taken by Cobbe who is concerned that automated decision making systems will need to meet administrative law's standards for public-sector decision-making. Her account, blending various administrative law grounds for judicial review with relevant restrictions and requirements from data protection law, along with an understanding of the technical features of the automated systems, begins the job of establishing how automated decision making in the public sector might be enabled properly.

But the focus in this chapter is not so much on this sort of decision making but on more general, political style decision making in the context of policy formation, operating perhaps as replacement for (or at least a direct democracy style reinvigoration of) the traditional representative political apparatus. Of course public law values are relevant and important here too: there must be openness, accountability and fairness. However the essentially *democratic* nature of decision making as an expression of what people think and want must be respected too. This is something that is under particular threat from mass surveillance systems that claim a capacity to infer popular will (or at least what people want, which is taken to be the same thing) from the observable behaviour of people, and the various (consumer and other) choices that they make. Such an approach may also claim that it is *more democratic* than traditional politics because it is more comprehensive, and captures what people actually *do*, rather than what they merely say. We must object to this. We are more than what we browse or buy, view and visit, or what we 'like' or screen out. The democratic engagement that is involved in public decision making cannot be reduced to this – as if such data, however huge and apparently comprehensive, were genuinely reflective of what we are, and how we should interact in the public space of decision making. We should reserve the right to make ourselves up in relation to whatever grouping we choose – be it a local community, political party, based on a lifestyle choice, or whatever – and resist any efforts to decouple us from our own reality into a mere data point to be manipulated in an algorithmic decision making process. Furthermore, a properly political process should afford the possibility of people changing their minds, and aspiring to be more than they presently are and do – no matter how accurately and completely this may be measured.

While it might seem rather weak to conclude by simply referring to a European expert report, and one that seems to call rather mildly for more research, debate and discussion, this is in fact a central element in the resistance that is needed. The Council of Europe's Committee of experts on internet intermediaries reviewed research in AI and concluded that

> it is highly welcome that there is increasing research on these topics. However, academic research on its own is insufficient. It is essential to ensure that members of professional (technological, engineering, legal, media, philosophical and ethical) communities engage in discussions and debates that must also include the general public. In order to promote active engagement of human beings and a lively public debate about an issue that affects all

> human beings and communities, adequate media and information literacy promotion activities should be organised to facilitate the empowerment of the public to critically understand and deal with the logic and operation of algorithms. Notably, public entities and governments must have access to sufficiently comprehensive information to properly understand algorithmic decision-making systems that are already deeply embedded in societies across the world.[87]

They are correct. Not only should we resist the attempt to take the politics out of detailed decision making by replacing it with an algorithmic governmentality, we should resist the algorithmic governmentality itself – by debating and questioning the processes themselves. Some of this debate will involve arguing that the technology cannot possibly do what it claims, either now or in the foreseeable future. It will suggest that the richness of social life and the complexity of political decision making is now, and always will be, far beyond the capacity of machine learning, no matter how powerful. In the same way as it has been argued that 'robot judges' simply cannot replicate the complexity and essentially social nature of the law – either technically or conceptually[88] – so it must be argued that the essentially political nature of any public, political decision making (that is properly so called) cannot (and should not) be reproduced without conscious and deliberate human agency. Plato famously remarked that one of the penalties of refusing to participate in politics is that you end up being governed by your inferiors. An algorithmic governmentality would certainly be inferior to human politics. It must be resisted.

[87] Committee of experts on internet intermediaries MSI-NET, Council of Europe, *Algorithms and Human Rights* above n 79 at 43. See also the European Commission's High-Level Expert Group on Artificial Intelligence, *Ethics Guidelines for Trustworthy AI* Brussels, European Commission 2019.

[88] See Morison and Harkens, above n 59 and other contributions to this volume.

5

Legal Singularity and the Reflexivity of Law

JENNIFER COBBE*

I. Introduction

I take as my starting point Ben Alarie's 2016 paper on the legal singularity.[1] In that paper, Alarie sets out his vision of what improvements in machine learning and deep learning techniques could mean for the future of the law. Alarie approvingly quotes from Oliver Wendell Holmes Jr, writing in 1897: 'For the rational study of the law the blackletter man may be the man of the present, but the man of the future is the man of statistics and the master of economics'.[2] The idea that the traditional methods of law – judicious doctrinal analysis based on blackletter law, rules of interpretation, reasoned legal argument, and so on – would be superseded by statistics and economic thinking has, as Alarie acknowledges, not yet proven to be true. Alarie believes, though, that the advent of modern information and communications technologies will bring about such a seismic shift. In particular, he argues that advances in machine learning have put us on the path towards the 'legal singularity' – the point at which machines become as good as if not better than humans at understanding, applying, and, potentially, writing the law. Daniel Goldsworthy, in his take on the singularity of law,[3] goes as far as to predict that advanced deep learning systems will be able to find the single 'correct' answer to every legal problem.[4] The result, according to Goldsworthy, 'will be the ability to leverage the collective knowledge of great legal minds across

* Compliant and Accountable Systems Group, Department of Computer Science and Technology, University of Cambridge (jennifer.cobbe@cl.cam.ac.uk). I acknowledge the financial support of the University of Cambridge, through the Cambridge Trust & Technology Initiative, and the UK Engineering and Physical Sciences Research Council (EPSRC) [EP/P024394/1, EP/R033501/1]. Many thanks to Christopher Markou and Elettra Bietti for helpful conversations, questions, and insightful comments in preparing this chapter.

[1] B Alarie (2016) 'The Path of the Law: Toward Legal Singularity', ssrn.com/abstract=2767835.

[2] Alarie (2016).

[3] D Goldsworthy, 'Dworkin's dream: Towards a singularity of law' (2019) 44(4) *Alternative Law Journal* 286–90.

[4] Goldsworthy (2019) 286; in Goldsworthy's view, this will prove Ronald Dworkin to have been correct on that point.

countries, continents and generations – both past and present – to resolve legal disputes'.[5] For Alarie, the path towards legal singularity is an inexorable one with an inevitable outcome;[6] the point at which 'naysayers' are 'demonstrated empirically to be incorrect'.[7]

Legal singularity seems at times to be proposed as a convenient, natural, and obvious solution to various problems with the law. But, as with many tech solutions for societal issues, it can sometimes be difficult to tell which came first – the supposed problem, or the apparent solution. Alarie himself identifies two trends that he believes will result in the legal singularity: '(1) significantly greater quantification of observable phenomena in the world ("more data"); and (2) more accurate pattern recognition using new technologies and methods ("better inference")'.[8] Based on these trends, he frames post-singularity AI as the solution to all of law's ills: 'The legal singularity contemplates the elimination of legal uncertainty and the emergence of a seamless legal order, universally accessible in real-time. In the legal singularity, disputes over the legal significance of agreed facts will be rare. There may be disputes over facts, but the once found, the facts will map on to clear legal consequences. The law will be functionally complete'.

Absent from Alarie's vision of the legal singularity is any meaningful discussion of the role that law plays in society; of the effect it has on society and the people within it; or of how those things should be. While Alarie does, towards the end of his piece, suppose that in future, with enough data, machine learning systems might be able to identify 'optimised', 'efficient', and 'best' policy options for achieving normative outcomes,[9] his view of the legal singularity seemingly rests on the idea that 'better law' is better for everyone. Yet those who come to law from a more critical viewpoint may consider that the law has historically and contemporarily played a significant role in creating and maintaining conditions that are of benefit primarily to only a few. Indeed, law has often been a tool of division, exploitation, marginalisation, and repression. Alarie promises the 'completion' of law and its 'automatic functioning', but provides no insight into what a complete, automated legal system would mean for society or for the people who comprise it and are subject to the law. To the more critical mind, the promise of 'better' law – whether in the capitalist societies of the west or elsewhere – leads to the obvious question: better for whom?

I freely admit that I am deeply sceptical of both the plausibility and likelihood of Alarie's claims about legal singularity. But, taking his argument at face value, what would Alarie's vision of the legal singularity mean for law and the legal process? More specifically, how does this vision of legal singularity relate to the law's function in organising society? In this chapter, I attempt to fill the gap in Alarie's argument and to sketch out an answer to that question.

[5] Goldsworthy (2019) 286.
[6] Alarie (2016) 3.
[7] ibid.
[8] ibid.
[9] ibid, 10.

I first (Section II) set out some relevant distinctions between Legal AI and Legal Tech and clarify the focus of my argument. I then argue (Section III) that law functions as a reflexive societal institution; a construct of society, it not only reflects society, but incorporates the assumptions, priorities, and values of those who act within it (lawyers, legislators, judges, legal academics, and so on), and reproduces that society along those lines. The societal role that law has reflexively played as a result, I argue, has been as a tool of hierarchy, of exclusion, of marginalisation, of domination, of colonialism, and of capital. I next (Section IV) take two separate lines of argument against Legal AI and the legal singularity as envisaged by Alarie and Goldsworthy. First (Section IVA), my position is that Legal AI proponents misunderstand the nature of both the technology and the law, with the result that they mistakenly believe that the former could adequately and reliably replace the latter. Secondly (Section IVB), I argue that, even if they were correct about AI's capabilities, Legal AI proponents, in focusing on the quality of law's functioning rather on the nature of the law's role in society, pursue technologies that would support and strengthen the systems and structures of power, knowledge, and capital that underpin that role and its effects.

II. Legal Singularity, Legal AI, and Legal Tech

Automation is sometimes proposed as the solution to a legal sector and a legal system that is seen as slow, expensive, and inefficient.[10] But moves towards introducing automating technologies into the law can take many forms. I therefore want to begin here by defining some concepts, clarifying some distinctions, and providing some examples.

In this chapter, I am focusing specifically on the idea within certain minority strands of Legal Tech that 'artificial intelligence' (or 'AI') – understood for the purposes of this chapter to refer to computer systems that involve machine learning techniques[11] – can substantially or entirely replace legislators, lawyers, judges, and other legal actors in the provision of some or all aspects of legal services and in the legal system. Deloitte, for instance, have claimed that over 100,000 jobs in the British legal sector may be automated in the long-term.[12] Alarie's legal singularity envisages the total replacement of legal actors in the far future; other proposals typically suggest that human legal actors will still have a role to play.[13] For both the legal singularity and the more general subset of Legal Tech that seeks to develop AI for the purposes of replacing humans to a lesser

[10] F Pasquale, 'A Rule of Persons, Not Machines: The Limits of Legal Automation' (2019a) 87(1) *George Washington Law Review*, ssrn.com/abstract=3135549.

[11] Although 'artificial intelligence' and 'AI' are both used in some contexts to mean essentially any computer system, and 'legal expert systems' that do not rely on machine learning have existed for decades.

[12] Deloitte (2016) Developing legal talent: Stepping into the future law firm, www2.deloitte.com/uk/en/pages/audit/articles/developing-legal-talent.html; as with many predictions of the impact of technology on society, and the labour market in particular, such claims should be taken with a healthy dose of scepticism.

[13] Pasquale (2019a); Robert F Weber, 'Will the "Legal Singularity" Hollow Out Law's Normative Core?' (2019) *Center for the Study of the Administrative State Working Paper* 19–38, George Mason University, administrativestate.gmu.edu/wp-content/uploads/sites/29/2019/11/Weber-Will-the-Legal-Singularity-Hollow-Out-Laws-Normative-Core.pdf.

degree by automating legal services, legal reasoning, and adjudication, I will refer from hereon in to 'Legal AI'. Much of what I discuss in this chapter applies equally to these kinds of AI-focused versions of Legal Tech, more generally, as to the legal singularity, specifically. In my view, the legal singularity is merely a particularly techno-futurist vision of the more general Legal AI proposition as I have described it; if Legal AI proponents are correct about AI's capacity to automate aspects the law, legal singularity takes that proposition to its logical conclusion. I therefore treat legal singularity as a particularly future-looking version of Legal AI more generally.

I use the term 'Legal Tech' for the more general trend towards introducing new technologies into the legal sector, including more limited uses of AI for supplementing or augmenting humans or for analytics purposes that are largely divorced from the idea of automating humans away from various areas of the law. Commercial research suggests that, as of 2018, 48 per cent of law firms in the UK were already using AI within their business, primarily for document generation of review, e-discovery, due diligence, and research, as well as compliance and administrative support.[14] Many of those designing, deploying, or using Legal Tech would disavow the idea of the legal singularity, and perhaps few of the law firms or startups that are pursuing AI for use in the legal sector would consider themselves to be in the business of Legal AI as I have described it. For the most part, Legal Tech more generally is not under discussion in this chapter.

III. Reflexivity

I want to introduce here the concept of 'reflexivity'. Although the term has various meanings depending on the discipline and context, reflexive things are generally understood to 'bend back on' themselves, with circular relationships between cause and effect. The concept of reflexivity emerged in part from the understanding that ethnographic researchers in the field are not neutral observers – that where they exist in a situation they are influenced by their subjective understanding of that situation and can in turn act upon it. Where researchers are said to be reflexive, this indicates that they are concerned with understanding how undertaking research influences its outcome and with feeding that understanding back into their subsequent research practices. The concept of reflexivity has also been taken up and applied in many other disciplines and areas of study. Robert Merton, for example, wrote about self-fulfilling prophecies stemming from reflexivity.[15] Karl Popper showed how making a prediction about something can reflexively impact the outcome of the thing being predicted.[16] Margaret Archer has argued that people move through the social world reflexively, deliberating upon themselves in relation to their social contexts (and vice-versa).[17]

[14] M Walters, 'London Law Firms Embrace Artificial Intelligence' (2018) *CBRE*, news.cbre.co.uk/london-law-firms-embrace-artificial-intelligence.

[15] RK Merton, *Social Theory and Social Structure* (Macmillan, 1960).

[16] K Popper, *The Poverty of Historicism* (Routledge, 1957).

[17] M Archer, *Making our Way through the World: Human Reflexivity and Social Mobility* (Cambridge University Press, 2007).

I use 'reflexivity' in this chapter in a sense derived from the idea that individuals are influenced by their subjective experience of social interactions with others and with society more generally, and, in turn, through their thoughts, behaviours, actions, and interactions, influence those other individuals and that society. Taking the concept of reflexivity away from its origins in describing human behaviours and interactions, I now argue that: (a) law functions as a reflexive societal institution, and that (b) algorithms (more properly understood as algorithmic systems) are also reflexive. I will make these two arguments in that order.

A. Reflexivity and the Law

In my view, law is not just a product of its society (as certain strands of jurisprudence have argued), but also something that affects, alters, and itself produces that society. I thus understand law to be a reflexive construct of society that not only reflects society but itself has significant influence on society. As a reflexive construct of society, law cannot be neutral. Rather, it is contextual and contingent on the circumstances of the time, it is imbued with normative assumptions and priorities, and it reifies the interests and goals of its writers, practitioners, and adjudicators. Whoever positions themselves to write the laws that govern us, to interpret them, and to apply them has therefore positioned themselves to have a potentially significant influence on society through the law. Legislators, lawyers, judges, claimants, defendants, prosecutors, academics, as well as the written law itself and law's principles, practices, procedures, and so on are all in different ways and to various extents part of its reflexive functioning.

The point I want to make here is that we as a society produce law and law, in turn, reproduces us. The subjective experiences, assumptions, understandings, priorities, and goals of actors located within the law – that is to say, those involved in writing, practicing, interpreting, studying, and applying the law – thus all feed into the law, and from there into society itself. And the experiences, assumptions, understandings, priorities, and goals of those actors are, in turn, themselves influenced by the society that they inhabit, and which has itself been produced, at least in part, by the law. Law thus reflexively bends back on itself, with a circular relationship between cause and effect. I should note that I'm not talking here about how law functions internally – when I describe the law as reflexive I'm not concerned with legal process, or legal reasoning, or with the operation of law in relation to itself (and others have argued that law is internally reflexive in that there is a circular relationship between, for instance, jurisprudential thought and doctrinal argument[18]). Rather, I'm talking about how law functions within society more generally to reflexively reproduce the conditions, assumptions, and priorities from and upon which it is constructed.

I find it useful to distinguish between how law functions (reflexively reproducing society), on one hand, and what role law plays in society as a result of that functioning (for example, entrenching or alleviating inequalities), on the other. That is to say, we can distinguish between how law functions within society and the normative effect

[18] NE Simmonds, 'Reflexivity and the Idea of Law' (2010) 1(1) Jurisprudence 1–23.

that it has on society as a result. Understanding that law functions as a reflexive societal institution doesn't in and of itself tell us much about its effect on society. But it is precisely because law is functionally reflexive that it matters what role it plays; what values it (re)promotes, what goals it (re)prioritises over others, and what power relations it (re) produces. Because of its reflexivity, how we as a society construct and order law tells us much about what kind of society we hope that it will in turn produce.

We of course will all have different views about what law – understood to function as a non-neutral, reflexive societal institution, with significant influence on the development and functioning of society – should seek to achieve and what kind of society it should seek to produce. We might perhaps agree on some general, higher level points – that law should promote justice, fairness, accessibility, and so on – even if we disagree on precisely what those things might involve. As for other things, the fragile consensus that exists for those more general concepts might evaporate. Whether we agree on the details or not, as legal academics and practitioners – and as ordinary members of society governed by law – we would all, I hope, like to think that the law can be a force for good in the world. The idea that law serves justice above all else in the interests of society is a heady one, and lawyers can easily become intoxicated on the promise of a better society through the law. But the mistake should not be made of viewing the development of the law as always trending towards the better. The law in the UK and elsewhere has historically and contemporarily tended towards entrenching the power of capital, strengthening the position of the wealthy, reinforcing inequalities, and protecting established interests from outside challenges.[19] As critical scholars have shown us,[20] law has historically been and remains a tool of hierarchy, of exclusion, of marginalisation, of domination, of colonialism, and of capital. Functioning as a reflexive societal institution, the law's role has not only been to reflect the inequalities and injustices in society, but to repeat, reinforce, and re-encode them back into society.

As a human institution, the functional reflexivity of law can thus be leveraged such that it can play different roles within society according to the interests of the actors within the law's functioning. Being located within its functioning means that the legal actors involved in its functioning can leverage the power that gives them for their own ends. Law's functional reflexivity can be turned towards the goals of those within it, directing law's role towards those goals and, through it, assisting in cementing the cultural hegemony of dominant groups. And, throughout much of history, access to that position within the law has been contingent on hierarchies of wealth, class, gender,

[19] M Horwitz, *The Transformation of American Law, 1780–1860* (Harvard University Press, 1977); K Pistor, *The Code of Capital: How the Law Creates Wealth and Inequality* (Princeton University Press, 2019); G Baars, *The Corporation, Law and Capitalism* (Brill, 2019).

[20] eg, S Engle Merry, 'Review: Law and Colonialism' (1991) 25(4) *Law & Society Reader* 889–922; CL Tomlins, *Law, Labor, and Ideology in the Early American Republic* (Cambridge University Press 19993); I Haney Lopes, *White by Law: The Legal Construction of Race* (NYU Press, 2006); D Marie Provine, *Unequal under Law: Race in the War on Drugs* (University of Chicago Press, 2007); H Brabazon (ed), *Neoliberal Legality: Understanding the Role of Law in the Neoliberal Project* (Routledge, 2016); K McBride, 'Colonialism and the Rule of Law' in K McBride, *Mr. Mothercountry: The Man Who Made the Rule of Law* (Oxford University Press, 2016); HF Fradella and J Sumner (eds), *Sex, Sexuality, Law, and (In)justice* (Routledge, 2016); M Goodfellow, *Hostile Environment: How Immigrants Became Scapegoats* (Verso, 2019); I Pang, 'The Legal Construction of Precarity: Lessons from Construction Sectors in Beijing and Delhi' (2019) 45(4–5) *Critical Sociology*.

race, sexuality, and so on.[21] The result is that legal actors have been drawn largely from certain demographics (predominantly wealthy, well-educated white men) and members of those demographics have dominated the levers of law's substantial and influential organising function in society. Marginalised and subaltern groups have been historically excluded from the law – sometimes by the law; other times by structural conditions created through the law – and, in some cases, are only now beginning to make inroads[22] (although they are generally still heavily underrepresented in its upper echelons). Aspects of the role that law has reflexively played in society – in particular, to support the hierarchies of wealth, class, capital, gender, race, sexuality, and others that maintain that dominance and the more general capitalist system – should, I argue, be understood in part as a result of their dominance of those levers.

There is a systems thinking heuristic put forward by Stafford Beer that holds that 'the purpose of a system is what it does'.[23] By this, Beer means that the actual effects of a system are a more reliable guide to its actual purpose than the intended effects of its designers. Many legal actors might intend that the law lives up to its lofty normative ideals of justice, fairness, accessibility, and so on and that it works to provide opportunity and benefit for all. Certainly, few would, I think, admit to deliberately using the law to exclude or marginalise. But that is indeed the effect of the law's reflexive functioning. The purpose of law, then, is not – as we might hope – to pursue the ideals that we might hold dear. The purpose of law as historically and currently constructed has been to reflexively entrench the power of capital, strengthen the position of the wealthy, reinforce inequalities, and protect established interests from outside challenges.

B. Reflexivity and Algorithms

I want to acknowledge here that, as Nick Seaver points out, 'algorithms' are better thought of as just one part of algorithmic systems – 'intricate dynamic arrangements of people and code'.[24] We should understand them, then, not simply as technical systems, but as sociotechnical systems. In the real world, it would be unusual for an algorithm to not be acting as just one part of such an algorithmic sociotechnical system. Indeed, it doesn't really make much sense to think of 'an algorithm' as doing very much on its own at all. Removing people from the equation is not at all straightforward; perhaps not even possible.

[21] Women were legally barred from entering the legal profession in the UK until 1919, for example. The UK's first female judge was appointed in 1962.

[22] Although (as of 2017) 48% of solicitors in the UK are now women, for instance, just 33% of partners in private practice are women (29% in the largest firms) (Solicitors' Regulation Authority (2017) 'How diverse are law firms?', www.sra.org.uk/sra/equality-diversity/archive/law-firms-2017/). As of 2016, 33.5% of self-employed and 45.8% of employed barristers are women; 15% of heads of chambers and 13% of QCs are women (Bar Standards Board (2016) Women at the Bar, www.barstandardsboard.org.uk/uploads/assets/14d46f77-a7cb-4880-8230f7a763649d2c/womenatthebar-fullreport-final120716.pdf). The figures for ethnic minorities, LGBT people, and people with disabilities are considerably worse (Solicitors' Regulation Authority, 2017).

[23] S Beer, 'What is Cybernetics?' (2004) 33(3/4) *Kybernetes*.

[24] N Seaver, 'Knowing Algorithms' (2013) *Media in Transition* 8.

As critical scholars of technology have long recognised, there is no such thing as an objective technology. Artifacts, as Langdon Winner put it,[25] have politics. More specifically, critical analyses of 'AI' and 'algorithms' (both broadly conceived of) have shown repeatedly that there is no such thing as an objective dataset[26] or an objective algorithm or algorithmic system – such ideas are 'a carefully crafted fiction'.[27] Rob Kitchin undertakes a thorough overview of the critical literature,[28] concluding that 'algorithms need to be understood as relational, contingent, contextual in nature, framed within the wider context of their socio-technical assemblage … there is also a need to consider their work, effects and power. Just as algorithms are not neutral, impartial expressions of knowledge, their work is not impassive and apolitical'.[29] As well as their functional power, algorithmic systems are inherently normative, always intended to pursue some goal; according to David Beer, '[a]lgorithms are inevitably modelled on visions of the social world, and with outcomes in mind, outcomes influenced by commercial or other interests and agendas'.[30]

Algorithmic systems thus inherit the societal structures and power relations reflected in the historical data sets on which they are trained, insert the subjective priorities and goals of their designers, and then, setting about organising the world according to those logics, encode those structures, power relations, priorities, and goals into the future. As algorithms 'interpret' and analyse society and then send outputs back into society, this affects how that society functions. Since algorithmic systems are themselves societally and socially contingent and contextual, they would then re-interpret, re-analyse, and re-encode the society that they have, in part, produced. Because of this circular action, algorithmic feedback loops can develop that work to reinforce the effects of the system. As Adrian Mackenzie says, 'the more effectively [machine learning models] operate in the world, the more they tend to normalize the situations in which they are entangled'.[31]

Algorithms, then, are reflexive, too. Just as we as a society produce law and law, in turn, reflexively reproduces us, so too with algorithms. Just as law in its reflexivity moulds society according to the subjective assumptions, understandings, and goals of those who write and practice it, so too with algorithms. That law and machine learning both take their designers' understanding of and goals for society and try to reproduce them in the future is perhaps why the idea of bringing them together can seem, on the surface, to make intuitive sense. But it is precisely because algorithmic systems are normative, contextual, contingent, and reflexive that they feed into the law's reflexivity. To understand algorithmic systems, then, we must consider their context (the culture in which they are embedded, the assumptions and circumstances on which

[25] L Winner, 'Do Artifacts Have Politics?' (1980) 109(1) *Daedalus* 121–36.

[26] R Kitchin and T Lauriault, 'Towards Critical Data Studies: Charting and Unpacking Data Assemblages and Their Work' (2014) *The Programmable City Working Paper* 2, ssrn.com/abstract=2474112.

[27] T Gillespie, 'The Relevance of Algorithms' in T Gillespie, PJ Boczkowski and KA Foot (eds), *Media Technologies: Essays on Communication, Materiality, and Society* (MIT Press, 2014).

[28] R Kitchin, (2014) 'Thinking Critically About and Researching Algorithms' (2014) 5 *The Programmable City Working Paper* 18, ssrn.com/abstract=2515786.

[29] Kitchin (2014) 18.

[30] D Beer, 'The Social Power of Algorithms' (2017) 20(1) *Information, Communication & Society* 4.

[31] A Mackenzie, 'The production of prediction: What does machine learning want?' (2015) 18(4–5) *European Journal of Cultural Studies* 442.

they are contingent) as well as their purpose (the goals and outcomes pursued by their designers and users) and their effects (including their interactions with people and other algorithmic systems).

IV. Automating the Law

Although Legal Tech and Legal AI offer very different views of the future for the law, they do share common elements in terms of how they problematise the law and in their approach to identifying solutions for those problems. In his paper on the legal singularity, Alarie generally characterises the law as being slow, inefficient, complex, and unpredictable.[32] For Alarie, the problems with the law and the solutions to those problems are to be found not in its exclusionary, marginalising effects, but in the idea that it does not work efficiently, cheaply, quickly, or consistently enough for his liking. His view of the law's deficiencies, as he sees them, are essentially a performance issue; no matter what its effects, it should be 'better' (in some way) at achieving them. Alarie is thus concerned almost exclusively with the quality of the law's functioning (how well does it reflexively reproduce society) rather than with the nature of its role (what does it do to society through that reflexive functioning).

The kinds of views put forward by Alarie are not unique to the legal singularity or to other visions of Legal AI.[33] Outside of these future-looking proposals, more prosaic Legal Tech is increasingly being integrated into the services provided by the UK's 'Magic Circle' and law firms[34] in the present and promoted according to similar logics. Clifford Chance, for example, emphasises the benefits of Legal Tech in terms of speed, cost, efficiency, quality, and consistency.[35] Freshfields emphasise the benefits of efficiency and increased value from more limited uses of AI in contract review.[36] Slaughter and May's legal innovation team discusses the use of AI in more limited Legal Tech developments in terms of efficiency.[37] Linklaters similarly talks about the benefits of Legal Tech in terms of efficiency, time and cost savings, and improvements in consistency and accuracy.[38] Beyond law firms, Legal Tech and Legal AI are often framed as providing

[32] Alarie (2016).

[33] Pasquale (2019a); Weber (2019).

[34] Allen & Overy, Clifford Chance, Freshfields Bruckhaus Deringer, Linklaters, and Slaughter and May.

[35] Clifford Chance, 'Artificial Intelligence and the Future for Legal Services' (2017), www.cliffordchance.com/content/dam/cliffordchance/briefings/2017/11/artificial-intelligence-and-the-future-for-legal-services.pdf.

[36] L Sanders, 'The evolution of Legal Tech: Bringing AI contract review from the exception to the expected' Freshfields Bruckhaus Deringer (2019), digital.freshfields.com/post/102fkqs/the-evolution-of-legal-tech-bringing-ai-contract-review-from-the-exception-to-th.

[37] Slaughter and May, 'Slaughter and May launches legal tech programme' (2019), www.slaughterandmay.com/news-and-recent-work/news/slaughter-and-may-launches-legal-tech-programme; R Parnham, 'How law firms are using AI-assisted LegalTech solutions: A conversation with Slaughter and May's Knowledge and Innovation team' Unlocking the Potential of Artificial Intelligence for English Law: Blog (2019), www.law.ox.ac.uk/unlocking-potential-artificial-intelligence-english-law/blog/2019/06/how-law-firms-are-using-legal.

[38] 'Artificial Intelligence' Linklaters, www.linklaters.com/en/insights/online-services/artificial-intelligence.

similar benefits;[39] productivity gains, cost-savings, efficiencies, and increased speed are front and centre. Legal Tech startups – including Alarie's own company – also generally emphasise these same.[40] I do not claim that these examples capture the full spectrum of thinking within Legal Tech or Legal AI, but they do reflect the broad trends that dominate – in promoting the benefits of efficiency, speed, cost-saving, and consistency, they reflect a focus on law's functioning and a general understanding within Legal Tech as a whole of the law being too inefficient, too slow, too expensive, and too unpredictable. Optimisation of the law according to these priorities is thus a key theme running through much of the Legal Tech discourse more generally. Indeed, optimisation can be thought of as a general organising principle in certain kinds of digital system, as Bogdan Overdorf at al argue[41] and is itself a profoundly market-oriented idea; it seeks 'maximum extraction of economic value'[42] by maximising on key metrics aligned with commercial imperatives.

Though Legal Tech and Legal AI share much the same view of the problems with the law, and although they both essentially view the law as a system to be optimised, they offer very different visions of the future. While Legal Tech generally seeks to augment or supplement the human practice of the law, Legal AI promises a more ambitious substitution of some or all legal actors with machines and the deprecation and replacement of law's traditional methods: judicious doctrinal analysis based on blackletter law, rules of interpretation, reasoned legal argument, and so on. Alarie argues that 'The future of the law belongs to computing'.[43] He says that the changes that he envisages 'have the potential to dramatically reshape how lawyers interact with the law on a fundamental level, ultimately pushing the legal system to function extraordinarily well, virtually automatically'.[44]

Alarie's vision, reflected to varying degrees in Legal AI more generally, is a call for the rule of law's replacement with what Roger Brownsword calls the 'rule of technology'[45] bringing law firmly within the world in which, as Frank Pasquale puts it, 'authority is increasingly expressed algorithmically'.[46] The legal singularity thus promises to produce a legal system in which the judgment of the algorithm is privileged above all. As law is a reflexive societal institution, with significant effects on society and everyone within it, the 'rule of technology' raises the spectre of the mediation of legal questions and the

[39] S Miller, 'Artificial intelligence and its impact on legal technology: to boldly go where no legal department has gone before' Thompson Reuters Legal, legal.thomsonreuters.com/en/insights/articles/ai-and-its-impact-on-legal-technology.

[40] Pasquale (2019a); Weber (2019); Alarie's firm is Blue J Legal (www.bluejlegal.com) – leading firms make similar claims, including Luminance (www.luminance.com) and ThoughtRiver (www.thoughtriver.com)

[41] R Overdorf, B Kulynych, E Balsa, C Troncoso and S Gürses (2018), 'POTs: Protective Optimization Technologies', arXiv preprints, arXiv:1806.02711v3, arxiv.org/abs/1806.02711v3.

[42] Overdorf et al (2018) 1.

[43] L Cumming, 'The Path to the Legal Singularity', Blue J Legal, www.bluejlegal.com/ca/blog/thepathtolegalsingularity.

[44] ibid.

[45] R Brownsword, 'So What Does the World Need Now? Reflections on Regulating Technologies' in R Brownsword and K Yeung (eds), *Regulating Technologies* (Hart, 2008) 23–48.

[46] Frank Pasquale, *The Black Box Society: The Secret Algorithms That Control Money and Information* (Harvard University Press, 2016).

ordering of society according to the best judgement of algorithms. This, in turn, would produce a society in which the judgement of the algorithm is privileged above all. Indeed, there seems to be an assumption underpinning much of the Legal AI proposition that AI will hum away neutrally, putting the law to rights in everybody's best interests. This might not seem like such a bad idea, if we assume that the claims about the capabilities of machine learning systems made by Legal AI proponents such as Alarie were accurate and if the drive towards Legal Tech more generally was truly concerned with the well-being of society as a whole. But a more critical examination reveals that these are not necessarily safe assumptions.

The first part of this section will lie firmly within what Pasquale has termed the 'first wave' of algorithmic accountability.[47] This refers to a body of academic work that focuses on the technical limitations of algorithms in the hope that they can be engineered to be better. In this context, I would recognise such critiques as being essentially concerned with whether machine learning can ever hope to automate law's functioning through improved mechanisms for parsing 'more data', leading to 'better inference' (to use Alarie's language). This is the frame within which both Legal AI more generally and Alarie's depiction of the legal singularity more specifically operate – his vision relies on the idea that while the technical systems might not yet be capable, they will be in time and then everything will be well. I am generally more interested in the so-called 'second wave'; concerned more with structural issues and power relations and the question of whether these systems should even be used at all, regardless of whether they can be made to be free from bias and errors. This gets more to the role of law in society, and it is to that question that I will turn in the second part of this section.

In all, my argument is twofold. I first argue that Legal AI proponents fail to understand why Legal AI is not a suitable replacement for human actors within the law and therefore cannot bring about the improvements in law's functioning that they predict. I further argue that, in any case, regardless of Legal AI's capacity to replace human actors, Legal AI proponents fail to recognise that improving the quality of the law's functioning without first addressing the nature of the law's role would perpetuate and exacerbate problems with that role. Not only does Legal AI fail to challenge those problems, but it is likely to repeat and reinforce the law's marginalising, exclusionary effects and hierarchies by: (a) deprecating and displacing normative legal values, and (b) encoding the influence of market-oriented logics and corporate incentives on technological development into society at large in their place.

A. Legal AI and Law's Function

First of all, I will for now essentially take Alarie's view of the problems with law and of the solutions to those problems on his terms. If, for the sake of argument, he is right about law's problems, can the technical systems do what he and Legal AI solutionists propose? Alarie himself talks about 'the considerable advantages that machines have

[47] F Pasquale, 'The Second Wave of Algorithmic Accountability' (2019b) *Law and Political Economy*, lpeblog.org/2019/11/25/the-second-wave-of-algorithmic-accountability.

over humans in terms of memory, objectivity, and logic',[48] and refers to these repeatedly throughout his discussion. Goldsworthy claims that, with Legal AI, 'synthesising incomprehensible volumes of judgments and theoretical analysis no longer remains an impossibility, but rather a technical problem to be solved'.[49] Alarie also believes that the use of machine learning systems will bring order, predictability, and reliability to increasingly complex legal frameworks: 'The complexity [of law] will increase with time such that eventually everyone will become dependent on machine learning to cope with the complexity of the system. Interestingly, a by-product of this dynamic is that despite the ever-increasing complexity of the system, the effect of the law will be more predictable and reliable than ever'.[50]

While optimisation of systems according to certain market-oriented metrics can bring some benefits, there are often a number of negative consequences (usually framed as 'externalities' and disregarded). Overdorf et al set out some of the common 'externalities' intrinsic to optimisation systems.[51] I now consider what some of these could mean in the context of Legal AI. First: Optimisation systems disregard non-users and environments. In Legal AI, the law would be optimised for the needs of those who are engaging with it (as claimants, respondents, or defendants), with little regard for the needs and interests of others. Second: Optimisation systems prioritise the needs of 'high value' users. In Legal AI, this would mean those whose cases can be resolved quickly and efficiently. Third: Optimisation systems unfairly distribute errors by favouring the most likely option. In Legal AI, this would likely involve generally distributing errors to less likely case outcomes. Fourth: Optimisation systems promote unintended behaviours to reach intended outcomes by finding shortcuts to their optimisation goals. In Legal AI, this would potentially mean adopting strategies that resolve cases quickly and efficiently but to the detriment of those involved. For Legal AI, such 'externalities' of optimising towards goals like efficiency, cost, speed, and consistency could have significant negative consequences, which would potentially be projected across society by the law.

Moreover, while Alarie is effusive about the potential benefits of machine learning, he seems unaware of – or unwilling to acknowledge – its reflexivity or its limitations (Goldsworthy, to his credit, does at least acknowledge some).[52] Machines do undoubtedly have advantages in memory and in performing logical operations, but superiority in performing logical operations (that is to say, in mathematics and statistical modelling) does not necessarily mean superiority in legal reasoning or in grappling with more amorphous, qualitative elements of the law like justice, fairness, or accessibility. Nor does it mean that they will operate objectively, reliably, and predictably. Fundamentally, I argue, Legal AI proponents fail to appreciate either the reflexive, sociotechnical nature of the technology or the reflexive, human nature of the law, with the result that they mistakenly believe that the former can adequately and reliably supplant the latter and bring the benefits that they suppose. Broadly speaking, I divide the limitations of machine learning systems for the purposes of automating law's functioning into three

[48] Alarie (2016) 7.
[49] Goldsworthy (2019) 289.
[50] Alarie (2016) 9.
[51] Overdorf et al (2018).
[52] Goldsworthy (2019) 289.

categories: (1) deficiencies in their capacity to reason legally; (2) lack of objectivity; and (3) unreliability and unpredictability.

i. Legal Reasoning

Machines typically show promise in applications where the problem to be solved is well-defined and well-delineated.[53] As Bolander argues, it should not be surprising that IBM was able to develop a machine (Deep Blue)[54] to 'play' chess as early as the 1990s – chess is a well-defined and well-delineated game.[55] Yet proponents of Legal AI seem to mistakenly assume that because machine learning systems can perform well in certain well-defined and well-delineated tasks, they are transferable (perhaps with modifications) to other purposes. Goldsworthy, for instance, builds his predictions on Deep Blue's chess abilities and DeepMind's AlphaGo Zero's capabilities at Go,[56] while Alarie also refers to them approvingly.[57] But applying machine learning to a complex, shifting thing like law, filled with loosely-defined abstract concepts, is not so straightforward. As NE Simmonds points out in discussing law's internal reflexivity, law is not simply the aggregate of rules but 'an intellectual system structured by general ideas and doctrinal traditions'.[58] And John Morison and Adam Harkens argue that judges do more than 'judging' – being a judge is in many ways a complex, ill-defined, social endeavour.[59] In failing to appreciate the differences between board games and law, Legal AI proponents often fail to understand why computational approaches might not translate across so easily.

I should also note here that machine learning systems, unlike humans, are not well-equipped to generalise from limited information or to answer new questions.[60] While a human can reason to a conclusion in response to a question that has never before been asked, machine learning systems will struggle and may fail to adequately deal with things that were not sufficiently represented in the dataset on which they were trained. Yet the true difficulties and intricacies in law and legal reasoning rarely arise where there is a clear or existing legal answer to a question. Where the legal system is most needed is where there are new situations, new questions, or unresolved issues. Given that many courts deal largely in such questions that have not previously been asked or satisfactorily resolved, it is not obvious how machine learning systems could provide the necessary original insight and abstract, creative reasoning to allow for law's automation. By viewing legal questions merely as straightforward problems to be solved, Legal AI proponents typically neglect to consider why there might be unresolved questions

[53] T Bolander, 'What do we lose when machines take the decisions?' (2019) 23(4) *Journal of Management & Governance* 851.

[54] Albeit not employing machine learning; Deep Blue was based on symbolic artificial intelligence.

[55] Bolander (2019) 851.

[56] Goldsworthy (2019) 288.

[57] Alarie (2016) 2–3.

[58] Simmonds (2010) 2.

[59] J Morison and A Harkens, 'Re-engineering justice? Robot judges, computerised courts and (semi) automated legal decision-making' (2019) 39 *Legal Studies* 628–31.

[60] Bolander (2019) 852–53.

to address in the first place and what effect that might have on the ability of machine learning systems to automate the law.

ii. Objectivity

The idea that machines have an advantage in objectivity is similarly unsustainable. Substantial evidence has amounted over the past couple of decades that machine learning systems are infected with bias.[61] Famously, the COMPAS system used to help judges in the US to make sentencing decisions was found to be biased against Black defendants. Rather than bringing an objective view to things, African-Americans were 77 per cent more likely to be classed as a higher risk of committing a violent crime in future compared to white defendants and 45 per cent more likely to be predicted to commit any crime (with other factors controlled for).[62] The reason for this is straightforward: the system was trained on historical sentencing data from the US criminal justice system, and the US criminal justice system has in both the past and the present been profoundly racist. As a result, the COMPAS system merely reflexively reproduced the society on which it was trained. But COMPAS is far from the only example of biases creeping into machine learning systems – a string of prominent examples and studies have shown that this is a widespread problem.[63] And it seems that, for all the attention now being paid to trying to deal with this problem, eliminating bias from machine learning systems may be an intractable task.[64] Given the nature of the law's role in reproducing the inequalities and hierarchies of contemporary society, and given the reflexive, sociotechnical nature of AI, how are Legal AI's algorithmic systems, trained on data about society and the law, supposed to be objective? How are they to not be biased and to not then reflexively reencode those biases further into society? No answers to these questions are readily forthcoming.

iii. Reliability and Predictability

Alarie's suppositions about predictability and reliability are much like those of his about legal reasoning and objectivity, in that they rest on faulty assumptions about machine learning and how algorithmic systems interact with the world. It may seem obvious that machine learning systems will reliably produce predictable and consistent outputs provided they are well engineered. The reality is rather different. Machine learning is essentially the process of approximating a statistical model that works sufficiently well enough of the time; as a result, systems are trained until their error rate is deemed acceptable, but they cannot possibly cover all (or perhaps even most) eventualities. And, while Alarie argues that increasingly complex algorithmic systems of the future will be

[61] R Courtland, 'Bias detectives: the researchers striving to make algorithms fair' (2018) *Nature* 558, www.nature.com/articles/d41586-018-05469-3.

[62] J Angwin, J Larson, S Mattu and L Kirchner, 'Machine Bias: There's software used across the country to predict future criminals. And it's biased against blacks' (*ProPublica*, 2016), www.propublica.org/article/machine-bias-risk-assessments-in-criminal-sentencing.

[63] Courtland (2018).

[64] ibid.

key to the realising the fullness of the legal singularity, it seems that the more complex an algorithm the more fragile its processes become.[65] Small changes to input data – small enough to be imperceptible to humans – can result in wildly different outputs. As a result, although more complex systems are in theory better at classifying and predicting, they can also readily fail for unknown reasons and are open to adversarial attacks.[66] Are we to believe that a technology that struggles to deal with noise is going to revolutionise the law to the extent that it can function automatically?

As discussed above, there is considerable likelihood of biases and errors in machine learning systems and the complexity of deep learning systems in particular can often introduce fragility. The effect is that the outputs of these systems can be difficult to predict precisely,[67] somewhat undermining Alarie's proposition. Moreover, there is also a widely recognised phenomenon in which complex systems give rise to emergent properties and behaviour. That is to say, complex systems are known to exhibit properties and thus behaviours that are not provided by or a feature of their component parts.[68] Here I'm not just referring to emergent properties in the law, although it is itself a complex system (as Alarie rightly acknowledges). Machine learning and deep learning are themselves also highly complex sociotechnical processes, producing their own emergent phenomena. Introducing complex sociotechnical systems to the already complex legal system is only likely to produce greater complexity with the potential for further emergence. These emergent phenomena are generally impossible to anticipate; any societal institution relying on complex systems that are prone to emergent behaviour may appear somewhat erratic to observers.

Alarie is at least correct that the more complex the law is, the more opaque it becomes and thus the more difficult it is for even trained legal practitioners to understand. What he does not mention, however, is that complexity in technical systems also invariably produces opacity.[69] To that extent, law and machine learning do not significantly differ – the more complex a system (technical or otherwise) is, the more difficult it is to understand how it functions or why its outputs are reached. At a certain level of complexity, a level beyond which many machine learning and most deep learning systems operate, systems become impenetrable and incomprehensible – even, in some cases, to the technically literate. If Alarie is correct that law itself will in the future be increasingly complex and difficult to understand or predict, then introducing the high degree of technical complexity of machine and deep learning systems will only exacerbate the

[65] D Heaven, 'Why deep-learning AIs are so easy to fool' (2019) *Nature* 574, www.nature.com/articles/d41586-019-03013-5.

[66] Heaven (2019); C Szegedy, W Zaremba, I Sutskever, J Bruna, D Erhan, I Goodfellow and R Fergus, 'Intriguing properties of neural networks' (arXiv preprints, *arXiv*:1312.6199, 2013), arxiv.org/abs/1312.6199; B Biggio, I Corona, D Maiorca, B Nelson, N Srndic, P Laskov, G Giacinto and F Roli, 'Evasion Attacks against Machine Learning at Test Time' (2017) III(8190) *ECML PKDD*, LNCS, 387–402, arxiv.org/abs/1708.06131; IJ Goodfellow, J Shlens, C Szegedy, 'Explaining and Harnessing Adversarial Examples' (arXiv preprints, *arXiv*:1412.6572, 2014), arxiv.org/abs/1412.6572.

[67] Seaver (2013) 8.

[68] JC Mogul, 'Emergent (Mis)behavior vs. Complex Software Systems' (2006) *1st ACM SIGOPS/EuroSys European Conference on Computer Systems* 293–304.

[69] J Burrell, 'How the machine 'thinks': Understanding opacity in machine learning algorithms' (2016) *Big Data & Society*, January–June 1–12, journals.sagepub.com/doi/full/10.1177/2053951715622512.

problem. Adding complexity to complexity is likely to produce significant opacity. Machine learning may, in theory, subject to the problems of biases, errors, and emergence discussed above, be more consistent in resolving disputes. But, if that proves to be the case, it would be consistency without any real ability to understand why those decisions are being arrived at. Predictability in law, I would argue, comes not just from consistency, but in being able to understand why certain decisions have been reached so that the same reasoning can be applied to different facts. It does not therefore follow that any consistency resulting from machine learning means that those outputs are any more predictable as a result – quite the opposite, in fact.

B. Legal AI and Law's Role

Although AI may have some applications in the legal sector as part of the trend towards increasing use of Legal Tech, machine learning systems are not and may never be up to the task of taking expansive roles within the law or of automating it to the extent envisioned by Alarie, Goldsworthy, and other Legal AI proponents. We might end up with more limited systems that can perform some useful functions within legal services or emulate some form of legal reasoning to some extent, but the idea that in future they can replace humans and bring a new era of objectivity, accuracy and consistency to the law seems fanciful. Their deficiencies for those purposes may be irredeemable and irreconcilable with sound principles of justice, fairness, equality and the rule of law. But critiques of limitations, biases, error rates, and fragility, while valid and potentially fatal to legal singularity in and of themselves, are insufficient. It's all well and good to critique the idea of Legal AI on the basis that the technical systems are flawed, but, fundamentally, a critique that a proposition is flawed because the technical systems aren't there yet isn't a critique that the proposition is flawed at all. It's a critique that the technical systems are flawed. I want to move on then to discuss what Legal AI might mean in terms of law's role in society.

In their rallying call for critical discussions of machine learning to move beyond issues of biases, error rates, and so on, Julia Powles and Helen Nissenbaum pose some questions: 'Which systems really deserve to be built? Which problems most need to be tackled? Who is best placed to build them? And who decides?'.[70] The law's role in contemporary capitalist society, reinforcing hierarchies, inequalities, and power relationships, means that Legal AI is ripe for this kind of 'second wave' analysis. Yet, as I noted in the introduction, absent from Alarie's vision of the legal singularity is any meaningful discussion of the role that law plays in society; of the effect it has on society and the people within it; or of how those things should be. Beyond more technical issues of biases and errors, I therefore want to consider some broader questions. Law plays a significant role in organising society and AI is itself reflexive; what kind of society would be reproduced and reinforced by machine learning systems of Legal AI? What kind of priorities? What kind of power relations?

[70] J Powles and H Nissenbaum, 'The Seductive Diversion of 'Solving' Bias in Artificial Intelligence' (2018) *Medium*, onezero.medium.com/the-seductive-diversion-of-solving-bias-in-artificial-intelligence-890df5e5ef53.

To begin to answer these questions, I first want to introduce the sociological concept of 'rationalisation'[71] – the process of replacing subjective values with 'rational' thinking based on 'reason' and 'objectivity'. This often involves forms of quantification, of statistical and economic thinking replacing other ways of seeing the world – other ways that are more suited to the human complexity of society or of law. Building on concepts of rationalisation, Foucault talked about governmentalities – forms of power based on knowledge developed through rationalisation and quantification and exercised in pursuit of a desired goal. Subsequent writers have greatly expanded his relatively brief thoughts on governmentality,[72] developing a way of thinking about power relations that is principally concerned with analysing how the world is made governable. Any governmentality involves two things. The first are rationalities, or 'ways of rendering reality thinkable in such a way that it was amenable to calculation and programming'.[73] The second are technologies of power, or strategies and techniques 'imbued with aspirations for the shaping of conduct in the hope of producing certain desired effects and averting certain undesired events'.[74] If the real world is rendered into thought by rationalities (through rationalisation), then technologies of power translate thoughts and desires (as rationalities) into reality.[75] A governmentality, then, consists of the entangled ensemble of: (a) the rationalities (forms of knowledge, calculations, analyses, and desired outcomes) that underpin power, and (b) the strategies and mechanisms by which those rationalities are to be achieved. And Antoinette Rouvroy and Thomas Berns have written of the emergence of a new form of algorithmic governmentality,[76] predicated on data collection, predictive analysis, and automated forms of power and control. As Kitchin puts it, 'algorithms construct and implement regimes of power and knowledge … [they are] used in systems of coercion, discipline, regulation, and control'.[77]

Thinking in terms of governmentality, I argue that the machine learning systems of Legal AI would operate fundamentally as technologies for translating the rationalities of Legal AI into reality; in doing so, they would (re)construct relations of power within the law, from where the law's reflexivity would project them into society at large. The technologies of Legal AI are married to rationalities concerned primarily with 'improving' the quality of the law's functioning. Rather than being founded on normative legal values, these rationalities are developed through problematisation of the law according

[71] M Weber, *The Protestant Ethic and the Spirit of Capitalism* (Oxford University Press, 2010); J Habermas, *Theory of Communicative Action, Volume 1: Reason and the Rationalization of Society* (Polity, 1986).

[72] N Rose and P Miller, 'Political Power Beyond the State: Problematics of Government' (1992) 43(2) *British Journal of Sociology* 172–205; M Dean, *Governmentality: Power and Rule in Modern Society* (Sage Publications, 1999); N Rose, *Powers of Freedom: Rethinking Political Thought* (Cambridge University Press, 1999); P Miller and N Rose, *Governing the Present: Administering Economic, Social and Personal Life* (Polity, 2008).

[73] Miller and Rose (2008) 15; M Foucault, *Discipline and Punish: The Birth of the Prison* (A Sheridan tr, Vintage Books, 1991) 79; Rose (1999) 26.

[74] Rose (1999) 52; M Foucault, 'About the Beginning of the Hermeneutics of the Self: Two Lectures at Dartmouth' (1993) 21(2) *Political Theory* 203.

[75] Rose and Miller (1992) 48; Rose (1999) 48; M Jones, *An Introduction to Political Geography: Space, Place, and Politics* (Routledge, 2007) 174.

[76] A Rouvroy and T Berns, 'Algorithmic Governmentality and Prospects of Emancipation' (2013) 1(177) *Réseaux* 163–96; A Rouvroy, 'Algorithmic governmentality: a passion for the real and the exhaustion of the virtual' (Transmediale – All Watched Over by Algorithms, Berlin, 2015).

[77] Kitchin (2014) 19.

to the logics of efficiency, cost-saving, speed, consistency, and optimisation. But those rationalities do not challenge the nature of the law's role that I discussed previously. Rather, they displace normative values and instead pursue market-oriented goals aligned with commercial imperatives that support and strengthen the systems and structures of power, knowledge, and capital that underpin that role and those effects. Those designing, deploying, and profiting from these technologies thus seek (consciously or otherwise) to enact their vision for the world; empowering themselves and, potentially, disempowering others. Without a radical reconstitution of the role of law in society, therefore, Legal AI will, I argue, inevitably be bound up in governmentalities for extending and reinforcing hierarchies, maintaining exclusionary effects, and reifying the dominance and power of capital.

I will come to four aspects of this in turn. First: law is problematised in Legal AI as failing to match up to market-oriented logics and commercial imperatives in such a way as to direct attention away from law's role in society and to open up space for techno-solutionist interventions. Second: through quantification and rationalisation, normative legal values are deprecated and replaced by metrics in market-oriented systems and relations of thought and knowledge grounded in statistical and economic thinking. Third: self-reinforcing algorithmic interactions would work to reinforce those underlying rationalities, market-oriented logics and commercial imperatives of Legal AI. Fourth: Legal AI reinforces monopolies of knowledge that privilege legal actors and the opacity of algorithmic systems admits computer scientists to the upper echelons of this hierarchy. In all, as the governmentalities of Legal AI seek to translate its rationalities into realities, these four aspects of Legal AI would combine to restructure relations of power within the law. In the process, the market-oriented logics and commercial imperatives of Legal AI would be brought into the heart of the law. And law's reflexivity means that they would from there be reproduced and reencoded further into society.

i. Problematising Law

Problems do not come ready formed for intervention. Problematisation is the process by which something, as Peter Miller and Nikolas Rose describe it, 'comes to be organized so as to render [it] as a "problem" to be addressed and rectified'.[78] Through problematisation, a particular way of conceiving of something as a problem to be addressed is manufactured by creating or drawing upon various ways of thinking about and understanding that thing in that way. This will require various strategies and will often involve corporate leaders, experts, professionals, and the media all in their own way being brought to play a role in developing an account of the issue to be tackled. The development of 'problems' will typically also be tied to wider trends in economic and social relations; instrumental rationalisation and applying statistical and economic thinking to subjective, normative, qualitative things.

Because law is reflexive, and because the normative values that we embed in law tell us a lot about what kind of society we want to produce, how we problematise law tells

[78] Miller and Rose (2008) 175.

us a lot about what kind of society we want to see. As discussed above, Legal AI proponents often problematise the law as slow, costly, inefficient, complex, unpredictable, and in need of optimisation. Some of those things may of course be true – but how they problematise the law misses the issues that more critical analyses would highlight. This means that when those who believe in the legal singularity or who promote Legal AI tell us that law will be better, I tend to ask: better for whom? In problematising the law as costly, slow, inefficient, in relying on logics of optimisation, and in focusing on the law's function, not only do Legal AI proponents fail to recognise that there are problems with the role that the law plays in contemporary society, but they prioritise the kind of market-oriented and commercially-driven ways of thinking about and seeing the world that contribute to the development of those problems in the first place.

Legal AI proponents thus problematise law such that normative legal considerations are augmented or superseded by statistical and economic thinking. I would contextualise this within the societally-dominant neo-liberal capitalist frame of thought.[79] Neo-liberalism has often been poorly defined, but I understand it to involve a revival of the classical liberal tradition that emphasises individualism and responsibilisation[80] and the marketisation of society at large[81] (including the prioritisation of commercial imperatives and market logics). I readily acknowledge that Legal AI proponents likely don't think of these things in those terms – perhaps they don't even recognise that these kinds of logics are what Legal AI seeks to pursue – but I maintain that these trends and ideological frames are the broader context within which those logics by which the law is problematised and solutions are proposed are located.

A key aspect of problematisation, for Miller and Rose, is that the problem will be framed as being amenable to rationalised forms of calculation, intervention, and transformation and it will be accompanied by ideas for resolving it.[82] Ultimately, problematisation feeds into the development of governmentalities – problematisation allows the development of rationalities and opens space for the application of technologies. The problematisation of law according to market-oriented and commercially-driven logics of efficiency, cost-saving, speed, consistency, and optimisation opens up space for a variety of utopian tech-solutionism[83] grounded firmly in what José van Dijck has called 'dataism'.[84] This refers to ideological beliefs about the power and objectivity of machine learning and predictive analytics and the potential of tracking all kinds of human behaviour for societal transformation.[85] While van Dijck in her analysis discusses specifically the development of dataism in relation to the drive towards the tracking and prediction

[79] D Harvey, *A Brief History of Neoliberalism* (Oxford University Press, 2005).

[80] Rose and Miller (1992) 34; U Beck and E Beck-Gernsheim, *Individualization: Institutionalized Individualism and Its Social and Political Consequences* (Sage Publications, 2001); F Hayek, *The Road to Serfdom*, 2nd edn (Routledge, 2001); Harvey (2005) 68; JL Powell and R Steel, 'Policy, Governmentality, and Governance' (2012) 7(1) *JOAGG* 2; Z Bauman, *Consuming Life* (Polity, 2007) 58–59.

[81] M Friedman, *Capitalism and Freedom* (University of Chicago Press, 1962) 9; Hayek (2001); Harvey (2005); Bauman (2007); Powell and Steel (2012) 2.

[82] Miller and Rose (2008) 15.

[83] E Morozov, *To Save Everything, Click Here: The Folly of Technological Solutionism* (PublicAffairs, 2014).

[84] J van Dijck, 'Datafication, dataism and dataveillance: Big Data between scientific paradigm and ideology' (2014) 12(2) *Surveillance & Society*.

[85] van Dijck (2014) 201.

of sociality,[86] the core assumptions and beliefs can be recognised elsewhere, including in Legal AI. Ideologically dataist approaches are typically not grounded in a realistic appraisal of the capabilities and limitations of actually existing machine learning systems, nor of those that are likely to be developed in even the medium-term. Van Dijck recognises the trends underlying dataism as being largely industry-driven, emerging out of the 'gold rush' around new technologies,[87] and I place the dataist ideologies that they similarly produce alongside and in alignment with the prioritisation of other market-oriented logics in Legal AI.

I said previously that the law's functional reflexivity can be leveraged such that it can play different roles within society according to the interests of the legal actors within its functioning. In focusing their problematising on law's functioning, with Legal AI as the identified solution, its proponents typically make the dataist argument that automating the law is a solution that will benefit society as a whole. Indeed, as Pasquale notes, developments in Legal Tech more generally are often framed as means to 'advance access to justice, reduce legal costs, and promote the rule of law'.[88] Yet it is primarily those actors within the law's functioning that, I will argue, would stand to benefit. There is a connection here with Antonio Gramsci's argument that for dominant groups to succeed they must convince the rest of society that their interests are the interests of society.[89] Legal AI's problematisation of law's function, rather than of its role, thus directs attention to issues that seem, on the surface, to be pressing issues for all of society. Who, after all, could argue against the law being cheaper, faster, and more consistent? But, in problematising law's functional reflexivity, Legal AI proponents – inadvertently or otherwise – argue for improving law's capacity to play a role that cements the cultural hegemony of dominant groups within the law and society more generally. Yet if law's role in past and present society was instead problematised, things might look rather different.

ii. Rationalising and Quantifying Law

The algorithmic governmentalities of Legal AI would necessarily rely on large quantities of data drawn from qualitative sources and dealing in abstract, contextual concepts. Much of this will be the written law itself (statutes, judgments, and so on); other data may come from society at large. These data sources and concepts will need to be made understandable to machines through quantification using natural language processing and other methods. Yet, as Nick Seaver points out, there is significant academic concern about what happens when 'the rigid, quantitative logic of computation tangles with the fuzzy qualitative logics of human life'.[90] Indeed, much of what Alarie proposes seems to be based on a rationalising desire to eliminate the 'fuzzy qualitative logics' of law by subjecting them to the quantitative logic of machines. I would argue, though, that law

[86] ibid, 198.
[87] ibid, 199.
[88] Pasquale (2019a) 4.
[89] R Kearney, *Modern Movements in European Philosophy: Phenomenology, Critical Theory, Structuralism* (Manchester University Press, 1994) 183.
[90] Seaver (2013) 2.

is a human construct dealing with complex human matters, and not everything can be quantified or dealt with by computers. How, for instance, could we quantify and measure fairness? Researchers addressing bias in machine learning systems have struggled to conclusively answer that question without success – indeed, mounting research suggests that it is impossible to come up with a robust and generalisable method of doing so.[91] Such is the difficulty of dealing in qualitative, contextual, abstract things.

The quantification of law and society necessary for Legal AI, as with all quantification, is itself subjective and contextual[92] and inextricably tied up with power. Quantification usually takes place within larger social projects – it is 'work that makes other work possible'.[93] In the context of the social project of Legal AI, as in all contexts, machine learning systems can only ever deal with abstractions and approximations of the real world expressed in data. This is a subjective, interpretative, reductionist process with considerable impact on the end-result of the algorithmic system. Quantification unites and incorporates qualitative things into new systems of thought and knowledge (such as the new rationalities of Legal AI), while creating new relationships between them based on quantified and measurable difference and distinction.[94] As Wendy Espeland and Mitchell Stevens put it, 'turning qualities into quantities creates new things and new relations among things'.[95] How qualitative values and concepts are measured, compared, and distinguished quantitatively has, in turn, an effect on the social world that they depict and the relations of power therein.[96] And, because algorithmic systems are reflexive, how the world is rationalised, quantified, and made understandable to machines has a significant effect on their outputs. How the approximation of the real world through measurement and quantification is determined (what is included, what is not included, how is it quantified and represented, and so on) therefore has a significant effect on how those values are encoded into the algorithm system and from there into society at large.

Power and knowledge are, of course, inextricably linked[97] – each depends upon and supports the other – and there is power inherent in approximating, in abstracting, in quantifying. This underpins the algorithmic governmentalities of Legal AI, allowing for rationalisation, calculation, and intervention. Since this will largely be a matter for the algorithmic system's designer or overseer, that power will lie with them. This power, I would argue, following from Espeland and Stevens, is not just in determining what is represented and what is excluded, or even in how it is represented (as suggested by Seaver[98]), but also in how it compares with, distinguishes from, and relates to other factors and in what form it is then used by the system. The art of rendering the world into a format that can be processed by machines is itself a rationalising technology

[91] Courtland (2018).
[92] WN Espeland and ML Stevens, (2008) 'A Sociology of Quantification' (2008) 49(3) *European Journal of Sociology* 401–36.
[93] Espeland and Stevens (2008) 411.
[94] Espeland and Stevens (2008) 408.
[95] ibid, 412.
[96] WN Espeland and M Saunders, 'Rankings and Reactivity: How Public Measures Recreate Social Worlds' (2007) 113(1) *American Journal of Sociology* 1–40.
[97] M Foucault, in C Gordon (ed), *Power/Knowledge: Selected Interviews and Other Writings 1972–1977* (Pantheon Books, 1980).
[98] Seaver (2013) 8–9.

of power that facilitates the process of developing and sustaining governmentalities, of producing rationalities and other technologies, of making the world amenable to calculation and intervention. How, when, and why you calculate and intervene will be influenced by how, when, and why you quantify. Who decides how, when, and why that takes place will therefore have significant power to determine what 'matters' in the context of the system, its inputs, its outputs, and its effects.

Legal AI deprecates normative legal values in favour of market-oriented metrics of efficiency, speed, cost, and consistency. The law is thus quantified and rationalised into new systems and relations of thought and knowledge grounded in statistical and economic thinking and prioritising and promoting commercial imperatives. As knowledge and power are inextricably linked, incorporating the law into these new systems and relations of thought and knowledge means also incorporating it into new systems and relations of power that prioritise and depend upon those market-oriented and commercially-driven systems and relations of thought and knowledge. And it is those who do the quantifying and the rationalising who will principally determine how that incorporation occurs.

iii. Algorithmic Interactions

Algorithmic systems when deployed in the real world typically act as part of an ill-defined network of power relations in which unintended consequences can be critically important.[99] Within this network of power relations, as noted previously, it would be unusual for an algorithm operating on its own to make decisions and not be acting as just one part of a wider sociotechnical algorithmic system.[100] And algorithmic systems are often themselves built on top of other algorithmic systems[101] – in many cases, it is, effectively, algorithmic systems all the way down. In such an 'algorithmic ecosystem' it is the interaction of algorithms and other components, including human participants, that produces outputs.[102] Law's reflexive organising function means that, through Legal AI, societal relations of power would be mediated and played out through and reproduced by such algorithmic interactions.

Alarie offers up an example of this in the form of tax lawyers and accountants using machine learning to help determine their clients' best options for minimising their tax obligations.[103] He acknowledges that this might lead to governments and policymakers themselves using machine learning systems to protect public revenue by identifying and eliminating loopholes and weaknesses, producing what he describes as a 'dynamic back and forth'.[104] Algorithmic interaction is central to Alarie's vision; indeed, this is the process by which he thinks the law will becoming more specific, more elaborate, and more "complete'.[105] It is not, I think, unimaginable that this could take place to

[99] A Goffey, 'Algorithm' in M Fuller (ed), *Software Studies* (2008) 15–20.
[100] Seaver (2013).
[101] J Danaher, 'The Threat of Algocracy: Reality, Resistance and Accommodation' (2016) 29(3) *Philosophy and Technology*; Kitchin (2014).
[102] Danaher (2016) 255; Seaver (2013) 9.
[103] Alarie (2016) 9.
[104] ibid.
[105] ibid.

some extent as a result of developments in Legal Tech – the idea that tax lawyers and accountants might use machine learning systems to minimise their clients' liabilities is not particularly fantastical, nor is the idea that governments might use similar systems to try to stop them. Towards the end of his paper, though, Alarie supposes that public policy may in the farther future of the legal singularity be best determined automatically and algorithmically – essentially a harmonious process of negotiation between various complex algorithmic systems, with minimal human intervention. Alarie imagines that this process, as described in his example, could involve 'vast amounts of data on taxpayer behaviour', greatly aided by the expansion in consumer surveillance promised by the Internet of Things.[106] (Aside from the obvious privacy and data protection problems with this, if Legal AI or the legal singularity boils down to putting everyone under surveillance so that lawyers and computer scientists can combine to algorithmically rebuild society in their image then it's probably best that they think again.)

Alarie seems to erroneously assume that algorithmic systems will interact neutrally as merely technical phenomena. The reflexivity of algorithms, their contextual, contingent, and normative nature, suggests otherwise. Indeed, as they will seek to give effect to the goals and priorities of their designers and users, the various algorithmic systems that Alarie supposes will passively interact will in reality be actively seeking to maximise their effectiveness. Donald Mackenzie looks at the interaction between financial trading algorithms,[107] broadening and applying Erving Goffman's sociological concept of the 'interaction order' (that is to say, the social space where two or more individuals interact[108]) to assess this activity. Based on his study of financial trading, Mackenzie discusses several strategic possibilities of algorithmic interaction – where algorithmic systems adopt different strategies to best pursue the goals desired by their designers and users. For instance, he describes forms 'algorithmic dissimulation'[109] in financial trading. Some systems engage in 'spoofing' by placing offers to sell in large quantities, taking advantage of resulting moves in market pricing to buy at a temporary low price before cancelling the original offer. Another example given by Mackenzie is the practice of algorithmically breaking up large orders into many small orders and executing them individually to conceal the fact that large orders are being placed. The algorithmic systems of particularly enterprising or unscrupulous actors may well engage in dissimulation.

Mackenzie also observes that what happens inside the 'algorithmic interaction order' depends on things outside of it, including social relationships and societal structure.[110] Algorithmic interaction is not simply a matter of machines talking to machines to execute their tasks – it is not so easy to produce a harmonious set of interactions between algorithms themselves or to remove human and societal influences as Alarie appears to assume. I return here to the idea that algorithms are reflexive and that how they operate and what they do within algorithmic systems is conditioned on the

[106] ibid.

[107] D Mackenzie, 'How Algorithms Interact: Goffman's "Interaction Order" in Automated Trading' (2019) 36(2) *Theory, Culture & Society*.

[108] E Goffman, 'The Interaction Order: American Sociological Association, 1982 Presidential Address' (1983) 48(1) *American Sociological Review* 1–17.

[109] Mackenzie (2019) 13–17.

[110] ibid, 17–20.

subjective assumptions, priorities, rationalities, and goals of their designers and users as well as by their societal context. What Mackenzie shows us is that how algorithmic systems interact is similarly reflexive and conditioned on their designers, users, and societal context. Indeed, this is a central feature of Goffman's concept of the (social) interaction order – human interactions are shaped by their context and by the desired outcomes of the actors, which are in turn shaped by those interactions.[111] Within the ill-defined network of power relations of the algorithmic interaction order, this dynamic again plays out.

I said previously that Legal AI's algorithms are technologies that translate Legal AI's rationalities into reality and in doing so (re)construct relations of power within the law, from where the law's reflexivity would project them into society at large. These algorithmic governmentalities would achieve this, in part, through self-reinforcing interactions. Although they may engage in strategies like dissimulation in attempts to achieve the best outcome for their designers and users within the algorithmic interaction order, at a more fundamental level, I argue, they would work together to reinforce the underlying market-oriented logics and commercial imperatives of that order within which they are interacting. Through these dynamics, Legal AI's algorithmic governmentalities would affirm and reproduce their designers' and users' subjective assumptions and ideological priorities as well as their accompanying societal contexts and structures through feedback loops. In Alarie's most futuristic claims of the legal singularity, this would be an automatic interactive process between the algorithmic systems of governments, lawyers, corporations, and those with the resources to develop the systems necessary to fully take part, with little space left for the interests of others. Rather than challenging the exclusionary, hierarchical, domineering effects of law, then, Legal AI promises to repeat and reproduce and reencode the logics and imperatives that underpin them.

iv. Algocracy and Opacity

John Danaher talks about the 'threat of algocracy', where decision-making processes reliant on opaque technical systems limit opportunities for human participation in and comprehension of public decision-making.[112] Automation of law, he says, would prioritise 'instrumental and procedural virtues but [sacrifice] human control and comprehension'.[113] Although members of society have a substantial interest in how law – as a reflexive societal institution that has a major organising function in society – operates and the outcomes that it produces, Legal AI in the more futuristic of visions (such as Alarie's) may reduce us to mere subjects, lacking any real understanding of why it functions, how it functions, or why decisions that affect us have been reached. Quite simply, I would say, this stands strongly at odds with the basic proposition that the law should be transparent and comprehensible to those who are subject to it. As Danaher persuasively argues, situations where 'the creation of new legislation, or the adjudication of a legal trial, or the implementation of a regulatory policy relies heavily

[111] Goffman (1983).
[112] Danaher (2016).
[113] ibid, 246.

on algorithmic assistance'[114] could undermine the moral and political legitimacy of law and public decision-making. If justice must be seen to be done, what hope is there in an algorithmic future?

Opacity is clearly a problem in terms of the legitimacy of law. I argue that the high degree of complexity and opacity that would be present in legal-technical sociotechnical assemblages of Legal AI also produce inequalities of power. As others have argued, and as I have already noted, power and knowledge are inextricably linked – they depend upon and support each other. Harold Innis wrote about 'monopolies of knowledge',[115] by which power is maintained through the control of knowledge. His key insight here was that unequal access to and ability to make use of knowledge produces unequal relations of power, privileging those who control knowledge and disempowering others. The law has itself, of course, operated as an effective monopoly of knowledge for centuries, with obscure terminology, arcane processes, and rules, judgments, and statutes that are often impenetrable to outsiders. Moreover, access to this monopoly has, let us not forget, been contingent on hierarchies of wealth, class, gender, race, sexuality, and so on. The result is that those who have had effective access to legal knowledge (primarily legal actors – lawyers, judges, legal academics, and others who can be located within the law) have been drawn largely from certain demographics (primarily wealthy, well-educated white men) and have themselves dominated the levers of law's reflexive function in society. The role that law has played in society should, as I have argued, be understood in part as a result of their dominance of those levers.

The introduction of complex, opaque sociotechnical systems into the law (with Legal AI generally but in particular with legal singularity) is likely to only produce further inaccessibility. Danaher's view is that the introduction of 'algocratic systems' would limit participation in and therefore legitimacy of public decision-making.[116] His argument is normatively grounded in the idea that legitimate decision-making procedures must not be opaque to those affected by those procedures but should be justifiable in terms that are accessible and comprehensible. Danaher concludes that reliance on opaque algocratic systems would produce public decision-making procedures that lack legitimacy. Hence, in his view, algocracy poses a 'threat' to the legitimacy of public decision-making. This position is, I think, correct, but it is not, I would argue, the whole picture. While most people would indeed find themselves further excluded from the law's monopoly of knowledge, with potentially deleterious effects on the law's legitimacy, there is one group in particular who would be brought deep within its fold: the computer scientists who would design, develop, deploy, and maintain the algorithms at the heart of these sociotechnical systems. Legal AI moves law into a more complex sociotechnical form, making it less accessible to the general public and cementing the legal sector's monopoly on legal knowledge; the price that the legal sector would pay for this is that computer scientists get a share in the spoils.

As I argued above, the governmentalities of Legal AI involve rationalising normative legal values into new market-oriented systems and relations of thought, knowledge,

[114] Danaher (2016) 246.
[115] H Innis, *The Bias of Communication* (University of Toronto Press, 1989).
[116] Danaher (2016).

and power that incorporate and depend upon statistical and economic thinking. There is, though, more to it than that – they also move the law beyond these forms of rationalisation and quantification into new computational and algorithmic systems and relations of thought, knowledge, and power. This would continue the broader trend in society towards the ascendancy of computer science, computational methods, and the commercial imperatives of the tech industry; in this case, capturing the law and the legal system. That industry, of course, has its own motivations and ideologies, many of which are identifiably dataist, built around logics of optimisation, and are voraciously profit-driven. Indeed, as Overdorf et al tell us, optimisation systems typically result in concentrations of resources in the hands of a few companies (ie, those with the capacity to collect and process large quantities of data). I said before that the governmentalities of Legal AI are concerned with reconstructing relations of power within the legal system from where they are projected into society. The small cadre of lawyers and computer scientists who have been initiated into the ranks of the new algocratic order would be the primary beneficiaries. And, as with the law, computer science is far from free of hierarchies of class, gender, race, and sexuality, and other characteristics.[117]

V. Conclusion

My ambivalence towards legal singularity and Legal AI more generally shouldn't be misunderstood as being grounded in a belief that people are necessarily, inherently better at law than a machine, or will inherently produce better law than a machine. Nor should my ambivalence be taken as opposition to the idea of using technology in the law at all. Judges and human legal processes are flawed, often unreliable, and can be biased and error prone. The pattern-spotting, predicting, and classifying capabilities of machines are advancing all the time, and it may well not be so long before AI systems are capable of replicating some of the human processes of law and the legal system. But law is a reflexive societal institution that in the past and the present has primarily entrenched the power of capital, strengthened the position of the wealthy, reinforced inequalities, and protected established interests from outside challenges. And 'AI' (however defined) is itself also reflexive – inherently normative, inherently contextual, and inherently contingent upon the assumptions and priorities of its designers and users. No matter how good the algorithmic systems get – even if they match or exceed human capabilities in certain ways – if they are applied to the law without the nature of its role first being substantially addressed, then they will merely reproduce and reinforce its effects. Legal singularity without a transformation in the law and society itself will only ever reproduce the same result. Tech solutionism is often at its most

[117] As of 2016–17, 17.2% of computer science students at UK universities were women, 'Patterns and Trends in UK Higher Education' (Universities UK (2018), www.universitiesuk.ac.uk/facts-and-stats/data-and-analysis/Documents/patterns-and-trends-in-uk-higher-education-2018.pdf). See also, C Funk and K Parker, 'Diversity in the STEM workforce varies widely across jobs' (Pew Research Center 2018), www.pewsocialtrends.org/2018/01/09/diversity-in-the-stem-workforce-varies-widely-across-jobs; B Myers, (2018) 'Women and Minorities in Tech, By the Numbers' (*Wired*, 2018), www.wired.com/story/computer-science-graduates-diversity.

pernicious when it seeks to make things functionally 'better' without first addressing the contexts and effects of what they're supposed to be better at. A legal system made functionally 'better' at performing its current role is not, in my view, a desirable thing at all.

Yet proponents of legal singularity – as envisaged by Alarie and others – seem to uncritically buy into the idea that better law is better for everyone. By problematising the law as slow, costly, inefficient, complicated, and expensive, rather than as a tool of marginalisation, exclusion, exploitation, and for reifying the power of capital, they pursue market-oriented goals and commercial imperatives that are likely to repeat and reinforce those effects. Without a critical re-examination of the law and the idea of the legal singularity, without rethinking how law is problematised and responses are developed, and without working towards radically rebuilding the law to try to produce a fairer, more just society, legal singularity as a vision and a goal will remain primarily concerned with making the law better at entrenching market-oriented logics, commercial imperatives, and a particularly computational worldview.

I referred earlier to Beer's heuristic that the purpose of a system is what it does – that a system's actual effects are a more reliable guide to its actual purpose than its designers' intentions. I do not argue that Legal AI's proponents intend to reinforce the law's role in maintaining hierarchies, marginalising effects, and the power of capital. Indeed, according to Pasquale,[118] Legal AI proponents may believe that by automating to some greater or lesser extent the activities of legal actors they can promote access to justice and the rule of law. But, I argue, because of their focus on the quality of the law's functioning rather on the nature of law's role, that would be the effect of Legal AI in the absence of a wider project of radical legal reform.

I acknowledge, though, that in arguing for a focus on the law's role I do nothing to address the problems with the law's function that Legal AI proponents rightly identify. So what is the alternative to Legal AI? If law is indeed becoming increasingly complex and impenetrable over time to the point that even trained lawyers (let alone ordinary people) are unable to satisfactorily understand it, it does not necessarily follow that the solution is to introduce exponentially more complexity in the form of machine learning. It does not necessarily follow that the solution to the law being inaccessible to all but the legally trained is to introduce technical systems that are inaccessible to all but the technically trained. It does not necessarily follow that the solution to the law lacking clarity and certainty is to deprecate transparency and accessibility. To address the law's functional problems, we should seek to consolidate, streamline, and simplify the law through the traditional processes of comprehensive legal reform. Democratic legal processes should be involved in reforming it and addressing its deficiencies (including complexity and impenetrability). Law should be made accessible by making it readily available and understandable – through clarifying, simplifying, and educating. This is, of course, a slower, more deliberative process, and it doesn't bring quite the excitement of turning to 'AI'. But, I would argue, it is the more suitable solution (and one that could involve machine learning to help). If the resources involved in working towards Legal AI were directed instead to these more traditional and suitable processes of reform, then, perhaps, all of society might benefit.

[118] Pasquale (2019a) 4.

6

Artificial Intelligence and Legal Singularity: The Thin End of the Wedge, the Thick End of the Wedge, and the Rule of Law

ROGER BROWNSWORD*

I. Introduction

How should we respond to the view that, in the not too distant future, the functions of law will be discharged by smart technologies, that smart machines will serve as legal functionaries? How should we respond, for example, to the claim that recent developments in artificial intelligence (AI) and machine learning (ML) foreshadow a transition to a 'legal singularity' – a singularity, as Benjamin Alarie puts it, in which 'disputes over the legal significance of agreed facts will be rare' and, with the coming of which, the 'law will be functionally complete'?[1]

Perhaps we should simply 'be philosophical'. If AI and ML are the thin end of a technological wedge that will transform the practice of law then so be it. As Anthony Quinton famously remarked, albeit in a very different context – where it was being proposed that the rules at New College, Oxford, should be relaxed to permit undergraduates to sleep with women undisturbed at weekends –if we are faced with the thin end of a wedge then 'better [that] than the other'.[2]

Or, perhaps we should be sceptical: AI and ML might be the thin end of a wedge but, at least in relation to common law adjudication, the wedge is unlikely to get much thicker. In this context, as Christopher Markou and Simon Deakin have argued, the practical utility of AI tools might be limited by their backward-looking nature as well as

* Dickson Poon School of Law, King's College London.

[1] B Alarie, 'The Path of the Law: Toward Legal Singularity' (2016) 66 *University of Toronto Law Journal* 443, 445, papers.ssrn.com/sol3/papers.cfm?abstract_id=2767835 (last accessed 24 January 2020).

[2] See J O'Grady, 'Lord Quinton obituary' *The Guardian* (22 June 2010), www.theguardian.com/world/2010/jun/22/lord-quinton-obituary (last accessed 24 January 2020).

their unwelcome lock-in effects;[3] and, as Lyria Bennett Moses cautions, we should not underrate the essentially human and social elements in adjudication.[4]

A further response might be to push back and resist. Strikingly, in France, section 33 of the Justice Reform Act 2019 provides that 'The identity data of magistrates and members of the judiciary cannot be reused with the purpose or effect of evaluating, analysing, comparing or predicting their actual or alleged professional practices.'[5] Even though those who commit the new offence can face a custodial sentence of up to five years, the extent to which the mere redaction of the identifying data will impede the use of AI and ML to predict the outcome of cases is unclear.[6] Nevertheless, section 33 represents a significant expression of resistance.

In this article, I will introduce a rather different response. Stated shortly, this is that there are a number of technological wedges being driven under the idea of law as a rule-based enterprise; that the wedges that are being driven in relation to the channelling and re-channelling function of law are much more significant than those being driven into adjudication; and that, to put the point provocatively, at least some of the technological wedges into channelling are going in thick end first. These are the wedges to which we urgently need to respond; and, our response will involve a radical rebooting of our legal thinking, starting with our understanding of regulatory responsibilities (as the benchmarks of regulatory legitimacy and legality), and then reshaping the Rule of Law and our conception of coherence in the law.

Accordingly, the main purpose of the paper[7] is to argue: (i) that the use by regulators (both public and private) of AI tools, especially where they are part of a strategy of technological management, needs to be guided by a revised understanding of the full range of regulatory responsibilities, (ii) that this revised understanding, as a new benchmark for legality, needs to be inscribed in the agreed groundrules for exercises of regulatory power that rely on technological measures – this calling for a renewal of the Rule of Law, and (iii) that this all calls for the articulation of a 'new coherentism' the focus of which is on the compatibility of regulatory measures (whether rules or tech-tools) with the benchmarks for legality.

The paper is in five principal parts. First, I speak to the distinction between the use of AI tools by regulatees for the purposes of clarifying the legal position (where the end of the wedge is thin) and the use of AI by regulators for purposes associated with technological management (where the end of the wedge is thick).

[3] C Markou and S Deakin, '*Ex Machina Lex*: Exploring The Limits of Legal Computability', in this volume, see also papers.ssrn.com/sol3/papers.cfm?abstract_id=3407856. Similarly, see R Crootof, '"Cyborg Justice" and the Risk of Technological-Legal Lock-In' (2019) 119 *Columbia Law Review* 1; and J Morison and A Harkens, 'Re-engineering justice? Robot judges, computerised courts and (semi) automated legal decision-making' (2019) 39 *Legal Studies* 618, 619, declaring 'an initial and strong scepticism that the essentially social nature of law can be reproduced by machines, no matter how sophisticated'.

[4] L Bennett Moses, 'Not a Single Singularity' (in this collection of essays).

[5] 'France Bans Judge Analytics, 5 Years in Prison for Rule Breakers' (*Artificial Lawyer*, 4 June 2019), www.artificiallawyer.com/2019/06/04/france-bans-judge-analytics-5-years-in-prison-for-rule-breakers/ (last accessed 24 January 2020).

[6] ibid.

[7] Drawing on the analysis and arguments in R Brownsword, *Law, Technology and Society – Re-Imagining the Regulatory Environment* (Routledge, 2019), 'Law Disrupted, Law Re-imagined, Law Re-invented' (2019) 1 *Technology and Regulation* 10, and *Law 3.0: Rules, Regulation and Technology* (Routledge, 2020).

Secondly, I sketch a three-tiered scheme of regulatory responsibilities, which differentiates between: (i) our responsibilities for the conditions on which any form of human social existence is predicated (the global commons), (ii) the responsibility to respect the conditions that distinguish, identify, and constitute a community as the particular human community that it is, and (iii) the responsibility to find acceptable accommodations where members of the community have competing or conflicting interests. These responsibilities are the key reference points for making judgments of legitimacy and legality. It follows that no technology, including AI, should be applied for regulatory purposes unless it has a triple licence – a commons licence, a community licence, and a social licence.

Thirdly, I propose a three-point revision of our understanding of the Rule of Law conceived of as a compact between regulators and regulatees, in which there are reciprocal rights and responsibilities. First, the standard procedural benchmarks for legality need to be supplemented by a substantive understanding of the responsibilities of regulators (particularly their responsibility for the protection and maintenance of the global commons); secondly, the Rule of Law must cover the full range of regulatory measures, whether rule or non-rule (technological) instruments; and, thirdly, in principle, the constraints of the Rule of Law should apply to all regulators whether they are acting in a public or a private capacity.

Fourthly, revising traditional 'coherentist' thinking (which is concerned with the application of general legal principles to particular fact situations, and which regards the integrity and consistency of legal doctrine as desirable in and of itself),[8] I indicate how a new coherentist mind-set needs to be cultivated so that there is a constant scrutiny of technological measures to check that they are compatible with the benchmark regulatory responsibilities.

Finally, a few reflections are presented on the possible need for new institutional arrangements to nurture and sustain new coherentist legal reasoning, particularly to support the stewardship responsibilities that regulators have for the global commons.

II. AI and Legal Functions: From the Thin End of the Wedge to the Thick End of the Wedge

In my introductory remarks, I have already indicated that I see some uses of AI and ML as representing a relatively thin wedge under the idea of law as a rule-based enterprise, as an enterprise of subjecting human conduct to the governance of rules; and that I am more concerned about the much thicker regulatory wedges already being driven under rules as the means by which law channels human conduct.

Taking this perspective, it is arguable that Alarie's vision of legal singularity is benign – or, at most, the thin end of a technological wedge – AI tools being employed, first by citizens and then by legal officials, to clarify how particular rules of law apply to specified facts. On the face of it, such use of AI is compatible with the Rule of Law ideal

[8] Brownsword, *Law, Technology and Society – Re-Imagining the Regulatory Environment* (n 7) ch 7.

that there should be certainty as to the legal position and that there should be congruence between the rules as promulgated and the rules as administered by legal officials. Moreover, employing AI in this way does not disrupt the underlying assumption that agents will make their own autonomous decisions about compliance with the rules. Such a use, however, falls some way short of legal singularity. If there is to be functional completeness, the tools must also take on the primary task of channelling human conduct. It is only when technological measures are employed by regulators to improve (and, ultimately, to guarantee) compliance with mandatory rules of law that we begin to see the thicker end of the wedge.

To take Alarie's example of using AI tools to ascertain where we stand relative to legal rules that allow for tax avoidance, what functional completeness implies is that the technologies enable not only perfect avoidance but also the elimination of evasion. In other words, we have to imagine a legal singularity in which the channelling function of law is completed not by reliance on prescriptive rules but by 'technological management' (which includes the use of tools such as AI). In this vision, the regulatory enterprise is no longer rule-based in the way that we traditionally conceive of law. Crucially, while regulatees might know precisely where they stand, this is no longer relative to a regime of rules but relative to an array of technologies that designs out the practical option of 'non-compliance'. Where there is legal singularity, while regulatees are perfectly clear about what they can and cannot do in technologically managed environments, this is very different to being clear about what one ought or ought not to do relative to some rules. To the extent that we conceive of the Rule of Law as predicated on an enterprise of subjecting human conduct to the governance of rules, and to the extent that technological measures crowd out both self-interested and other-regarding agency, we have reasons to be concerned about such a vision of legal singularity.

Before proceeding to the main parts of the article, where the focus is on channelling and re-channelling of conduct, it as well to be clear about the difference between the thin and thick end of the technological wedge and what precisely is at stake as the wedge gets thicker. In the following four indicative cases, we discuss two uses of AI tools by regulatees (first, to clarify the legal position and, secondly, to guarantee their own compliance with rules that govern some optional act) after which we consider two uses by regulators (first, to improve compliance by regulatees with mandatory rules and, secondly, to guarantee compliance by regulatees with such rules).

A. Using an AI Tool to Clarify the Legal Position

Let us imagine that a citizen, Smith, uses an AI tool to clarify the legal position on a particular matter, to predict how the legal rules will be applied to a specified set of facts – for example, to clarify (as in Alarie's example) whether a particular working arrangement will be treated as an employment relationship or as a relationship between a client and an independent contractor. In this hypothetical, it makes no difference whether Smith is seeking to clarify his position relative to a legal rule that is mandatory (prohibiting or requiring certain action) or one that is optional (permissive or facilitative). Now, let us imagine that a regulator, Jones, uses the same tool to clarify the legal position – for example, to determine whether an option has been validly exercised or to decide whether a legal prohibition or requirement has been breached. Again, it makes no difference whether the rules in question are mandatory or optional: Jones, like Smith, is simply seeking to ascertain the legal position.

While we need to be careful about switching from regulatees (such as Smith) using AI tools to regulators (such as Jones) making such use, where the AI tool is simply being used to clarify the legal position, reliance by both regulatees and regulators seems to be much the same. The use of an AI tool, rather than a human unaided by such a tool, is a thin end of the technological wedge, but neither the idea of law itself (as a rule-based phenomenon), nor that of the Rule of Law (as the non-arbitrary rule of rules), nor indeed the value that we attach to human agency and autonomy is radically disrupted.

First, these hypotheticals continue to treat the regulatory enterprise as rule-based and human-centric. The AI tool does not replace either the rules or their human interpreters. Secondly, if, as in Alarie's example of tax avoidance, the tool enables regulatees to know precisely where they stand relative to the rules (and to plan with more confidence) and, at the same time, it enables regulators to apply and enforce the rules more accurately, then this seems to be compatible with the ideals of the Rule of Law. Thirdly, so long as regulators and regulatees elect to use such tools and to act on their indications, human agency and autonomy is not compromised.

That said, it must be conceded that the equivalence between AI tools being used to apply legal rules and principles and traditional 'coherentist' legal reasoning is only approximate. The AI tools might have been trained by reference to many examples of humans applying legal rules and principles but the tools lack the authenticity of a human who is trying to construct a compelling narrative that justifies reading the law in a particular way. In other words, the AI tools might simulate an exercise in coherentist legal reasoning but the logic that drives the tools is not coherentist in the same way. Accordingly, while AI tools might outperform humans in a straightforward predictive context, and while applying the general principles of the cases to particular facts is functionally equivalent to coherentist reasoning, it does not follow that AI tools outperform humans in reasoning like a coherentist lawyer.[9] To this extent – and we might not be greatly concerned about this – the technological wedge is only a thin one.[10]

B. Using an AI Tool to Guarantee Compliance with Rules that Specify a Particular Optional Legal Facility

Imagine that Smith wishes to make a will in a legal system where the rules do not require citizens to make a will (it is optional) but where the rules do prescribe a set of conditions to be observed (for example, conditions relating to a testator's signature and witnesses) before a will is to be treated as valid. Imagine, too, that Smith is aware that the courts are very strict in enforcing compliance with the conditions and that he is anxious not to slip up. Accordingly, in order to ensure that he makes a will that will be recognised as legally

[9] See Crootof (n 3).

[10] But, nb, F Pasquale, 'A Rule of Persons, Not Machines: The Limits of Legal Automation' (2019) 87 *Geo. Wash. LR* 1.

valid, Smith employs an AI tool (or some other form of technological management) that guarantees that the will that is made will be recognised as valid and effective. Quite simply, if Smith tries to write his will in a way that is not compliant, the technology will prevent him from proceeding.

While we should be extremely cautious about the use of technological management by regulators (because it might compromise agency and autonomy), where it is a regulatee who freely elects to employ such technology, it is not so clear that there is a problem. Again, the use of the technology is a thinnish wedge under the law: Smith freely chooses a particular end (the making of a will) and the technology is a means to that end. This seems both instrumentally rational and consistent with Smith's agency.

C. Using Tools to Improve Compliance with Mandatory Legal Rules

Let us suppose that Jones and other regulators turn to AI tools as well as other kinds of technological instruments in order to improve compliance with mandatory legal rules. Here, the wedge gets thicker.

As is well-known, there is a raft of technologies that might be deployed by regulators to improve compliance.[11] For example, there are technologies that record acts of non-compliance and that survey, locate, recognise and identify regulatees; and there are AI tools that are designed to employ enforcement resources more effectively, as well as to risk-assess and risk-manage particular groups or individuals. In other words, technologies can improve regulatory performance by enhancing detection of non-compliance and correction of those who are not compliant.

Where regulators rely on such technologies to support the legal rules, disincentivising and correcting non-compliance, we are still dealing with the enterprise of subjecting human conduct to the governance of rules. The greater the disincentivising effect, the thicker the technological wedge becomes. However, we have not yet got to full-scale technological management of regulatee conduct.

D. Using Technological Management to Guarantee Compliance with Mandatory Legal Rules

Pat O'Malley charts the different degrees of technological control on a spectrum running from 'soft' to 'hard' by reference to the regulation of the speed of motor vehicles:

> In the 'soft' versions of such technologies, a warning device advises drivers they are exceeding the speed limit or are approaching changed traffic regulatory conditions, but

[11] See B Bowling, A Marks and C Murphy, 'Crime Control Technologies: Towards an Analytical Framework and Research Agenda' in R Brownsword and K Yeung (eds), *Regulating Technologies* (Hart, 2008) 51; A Marks, B Bowling and C Keenan, 'Automatic Justice? Technology, Crime, and Social Control' in R Brownsword, E Scotford and K Yeung (eds), *The Oxford Handbook of Law, Regulation and Technology* (Oxford University Press, 2017) 705; and R Brownsword and A Harel, 'Law, Liberty and Technology – Criminal Justice in the Context of Smart Machines' (2019) 15 *International Journal of Law in Context* 107.

> there are progressively more aggressive versions. If the driver ignores warnings, data – which include calculations of the excess speed at any moment, and the distance over which such speeding occurred (which may be considered an additional risk factor and thus an aggravation of the offence) – can be transmitted directly to a central registry. Finally, in a move that makes the leap from perfect detection to perfect prevention, the vehicle can be disabled or speed limits can be imposed by remote modulation of the braking system or accelerator.[12]

When regulators make this final move, 'from perfect detection to perfect prevention', we have full-scale technological management. This is the completion of the regulatory function of law. This is where the wedge is both thick and problematic because: (i) it displaces the idea of law as an enterprise of subjecting human conduct to the governance of rules, and (ii) it compromises the conditions for the exercise of human agency and autonomy. Unlike the earlier hypothetical in which Smith uses technological management to ensure that his will is validly made, motorists who are technologically managed as in O'Malley's example do not freely opt in to this form of control.

Taking stock, in Alarie's discussion, where smart tools are used by regulatees for the purposes of effective tax avoidance and facilitative planning, the disruption is not too great; the technological wedge is relatively thin. The regulatory enterprise remains normative and rule-reliant; and regulatees continue to have the practical option of whether or not to comply with the rules. However, if smart tools are employed by regulators as part of a strategy of technological management that displaces normativity, rule-reliance and the practical option of non-compliance, we have a very different scenario with quite different implications for the Rule of Law. This is where the wedge is altogether thicker.

III. Rethinking Regulatory Responsibilities

If AI tools are developed to the point where they could be used to discharge various functions of law, what are the responsibilities of regulators in relation to prohibiting, permitting, or requiring, to encouraging and supporting or discouraging, the application of such tools? Where the direction of regulatory travel is towards an ever more intense focus on instrumental considerations (on what works), the importance of this question cannot be overstated. As Robert Merton put it so eloquently in his Foreword to Jacques Ellul's *The Technological Society*, we should treat with caution those civilisations and technocrats that are 'committed to the quest for continually improved means to carelessly examined ends'.[13] So, how should regulators respond to proposed applications of technological tools, whether by regulatees or by regulators themselves who see an opportunity to improve their own performance?

[12] P O'Malley, 'The Politics of Mass Preventive Justice', in A Ashworth, L Zedner and P Tomlin (eds), *Prevention and the Limits of the Criminal Law* (Oxford University Press, 2013) 273 at 280.

[13] J Ellul, *The Technological Society* (Vintage Books, 1964) vi.

A. A Possible and Plausible Response

A possible response runs along the following lines. Applications must be socially acceptable; in effect, there must be a social licence for AI and its applications. This implies a process of inclusive consultation and democratic deliberation structured by a concern that the governing regulatory framework should not 'over-regulate' and risk stifling potentially beneficial innovation but nor should it 'under-regulate' and expose citizens to unacceptable risks. For example, speaking about the regulation of Fintech, Martin Wheatley has said that the regulatory challenge is to achieve a level of oversight that reduces the risk of financial services becoming 'a kind of tech-led Wild West' without damaging the 'new wave of possibility' presented by global technology and innovation. That is to say, the overarching regulatory responsibility is to 'confront the challenges, to take hold of the advantages, and ultimately, to create a better future for our financial services and their customers'.[14] At the conclusion of this process of consultation and deliberation, a regulatory position would be taken, not one that is written in stone, not one that should be regarded as universally right, but one which for the time being should be respected by all.

As far as it goes, this is a plausible response. Indeed, some might even see it as chiming in with much of the early thinking about the ethics of AI.[15] At two levels, however, we might wonder whether it captures the full range of regulatory responsibilities.

First, although in regulatory debates about new technologies, there is endless talk of the 'balancing' of various interests, some will want to insist that certain values are privileged in the sense that they are outwith the accommodation of ordinary competing or conflicting interests. For example, in its report on Ethics Guidelines for Trustworthy AI,[16] the EC independent high-level expert group on artificial intelligence takes it as axiomatic that the development and use of AI should be 'human-centric'. To this end, the group highlights four key principles for the governance of AI, namely: respect for human autonomy; prevention of harm; fairness; and explicability. Where tensions arise between these principles, then they should be dealt with by 'methods of accountable deliberation' involving 'reasoned, evidence-based reflection rather than intuition or random discretion'.[17] Nevertheless, it is emphasised that there might be cases where 'no ethically acceptable trade-offs can be identified. Certain fundamental rights and correlated principles are absolute and cannot be subject to a balancing exercise (eg, human dignity)'.[18] Accordingly, regulators need to be sensitive to 'red lines' or 'third rails' in their communities where fundamental values are engaged.

[14] Financial Conduct Authority reporting a speech by their CEO, M Wheatley, on 'The technology challenge' (10.06.2014), www.fca.org.uk/news/speeches/technology-challenge (last accessed 26 March 2019).

[15] Compare A Daly, T Hagendorff, L Hui, M Mann, V Marda, B Wagner, W Wang and S Witteborn, 'Artificial Intelligence Governance and Ethics: Global Perspectives' (28 June 2019) (on file with author) at p 7: 'AI ethics must satisfy two traits in order to be effective. First, it should use weak normativity [i.e. it "just uncovers blind spots or describes hitherto underrepresented issues] and should not universally determine what is right and what is wrong". Second, AI ethics should seek close proximity to its designated object [this means that ethics has to be "quite narrow and pragmatic"]'.

[16] European Commission, Brussels, 8 April 2019.

[17] ibid, 13.

[18] ibid.

Secondly, we might also wonder whether there are not some cosmopolitan values to which all communities should be committed and for the integrity of which regulators have a stewardship responsibility. What makes such values cosmopolitan is not that they happen to be recognised by all (or by most) communities. In this sense, cosmopolitan values are not quite like *jus cogens*. Rather, these are values that relate to the pre-conditions for any form of human social existence. In other words, these are not values that reflect a particular articulation or expression of humanity but the essential pre-conditions that set the stage for any articulation or expression of human community/humanity.

Once we introduce these two levels of regulatory responsibility, we have an important corrective to the plausible response, where process and acceptability are the order of the day but where we lack both foundations and hierarchy.[19]

B. Correcting the Plausible Response

In the spirit of correction, I suggest that we should frame our thinking by articulating three tiers of regulatory responsibility, the first tier being foundational, and the responsibilities being ranked in three tiers of importance. At the first and most important tier, regulators have a 'stewardship' responsibility for maintaining the pre-conditions for human social existence, for any kind of human social community. I will call these conditions 'the commons'. At the second tier, regulators have a responsibility to respect the fundamental values of a particular human social community, that is to say, the values that give that community its particular identity. At the third tier, regulators have a responsibility to seek out an acceptable balance of legitimate interests. The responsibilities at the first tier are cosmopolitan and non-negotiable (the red lines here are hard); the responsibilities at the second and third tiers are contingent, depending on the fundamental values and the interests recognised in each particular community. Any conflicts between these responsibilities are to be resolved by reference to the tiers of importance: responsibilities in a higher tier always outrank those in a lower tier.

i. First Tier Responsibilities

The idea of the commons conditions draws on two simple ideas – indeed, these ideas are so simple that regulators really should not need striking schoolchildren to remind them of the glaringly obvious.[20]

First, there are conditions that relate to the essential biological characteristics of the human species. Most planets will not support human life. The conditions on planet Earth are special for humans. Secondly, it is characteristic of human agents – understood in a

[19] Compare S Franklin, 'Ethical research – the long and bumpy road from shirked to shared' (2019) 574 *Nature* 627–30, doi: 10.1038/d41586-019-03270-4. According to Franklin, there is a similar crisis in bioethics, where there is no longer confidence about overarching principles and, instead, an almost total reliance on process.

[20] 'Climate strike: Schoolchildren protest over climate change' (*BBC News*, 15 February 2019), www.bbc.co.uk/news/uk-47250424 (last accessed 24 January 2020).

thin sense akin to that presupposed by the criminal law[21] – that they have the capacity to pursue various projects and plans whether as individuals, in partnerships, in groups, or in whole communities. Sometimes, the various projects and plans that they pursue will be harmonious; but, often, human agents will find themselves in conflict or competition with one another as their preferences, projects and plans clash. However, before we get to particular projects or plans, before we get to conflict or competition, there needs to be a context in which the exercise of agency is possible. This context is not one that privileges a particular articulation of agency; it is prior to, and entirely neutral between, the particular plans and projects that agents individually favour; the conditions that make up this context are generic to agency itself. In other words, there is a deep and fundamental critical infrastructure, a commons, for any community of agents. It follows that any agent, reflecting on the antecedent and essential nature of the commons must regard the critical infrastructural conditions as special. Indeed, from any practical viewpoint, prudential or moral, that of regulator or regulatee, the protection of the commons must be the highest priority.[22]

Accordingly, we expect regulators to be mindful that we, as humans, have certain biological needs and that there should be no encouragement for technologies that are dangerous in that they compromise the conditions for our very existence; secondly, given that we have a (self-interested) sense of which technological developments we would regard as beneficial, we will press regulators to support and prioritise such developments – and, conversely, to reject developments that we judge to be contrary to our self-interest; and, thirdly, even where proposed technological developments are neither dangerous nor lacking utility, some will argue that they should be prohibited (or, at least, not encouraged)[23] because their development would be immoral.[24]

If we build on this analysis, we will argue that the paramount responsibility for regulators is to protect, preserve, and promote:

- the essential conditions for human existence (given human biological needs);
- the essential conditions for human agency and self-development; and,
- the essential conditions for the development and practice of other-regarding moral agency.

These, it bears repeating, are imperatives for regulators in all regulatory spaces, whether international or national, public or private. Of course, determining the nature of these

[21] Compare SJ Morse, 'Uncontrollable Urges and Irrational People' (2002) 88 *Virginia Law Review* 1025, at 1065–66.

[22] In communities that are characterised by prudential pluralism and/or by moral pluralism, this pluralism is predicated on the commons; at the level of the commons, prudential and moral viewpoints must converge on a generic principle of respect for the commons' conditions. Compare the seminal analysis in A Gewirth, *Reason and Morality* (University of Chicago Press, 1978).

[23] Compare R Brownsword, 'Regulatory Coherence – A European Challenge' in K Purnhagen and P Rott (eds), *Varieties of European Economic Law and Regulation: Essays in Honour of Hans Micklitz* (Springer, 2014) 235, for discussion of the CJEU's decision and reasoning in Case C-34/10, Oliver Brüstle v Greenpeace e.V. (Grand Chamber, 18 October 2011).

[24] Recall eg, F Fukuyama, *Our Posthuman Future* (Profile Books, 2002) for the argument that the development and application of modern biotechnologies, especially concerning human genetics, should not be permitted to compromise human dignity.

conditions will not be a mechanical process and I do not assume that it will be without its points of controversy. Nevertheless, let me give an indication of how I would understand the distinctive contribution of each segment of the commons.

In the first instance, regulators should take steps to protect, preserve and promote the natural ecosystem for human life.[25] At minimum, this entails that the physical well-being of humans must be secured; humans need oxygen, they need food and water, they need shelter, they need protection against contagious diseases, if they are sick they need whatever medical treatment is available, and they need to be protected against assaults by other humans or non-human beings. It follows that the intentional violation of such conditions is a crime against, not just the individual humans who are directly affected, but humanity itself.[26]

Secondly, the conditions for meaningful self-development and agency need to be constructed: there needs to be a sufficient sense of self and of self-esteem, as well as sufficient trust and confidence in one's fellow agents, together with sufficient predictability to plan, so as to operate in a way that is interactive and purposeful rather than merely defensive. Let me suggest that the distinctive capacities of prospective agents include being able:

- to freely choose one's own ends, goals, purposes and so on ('to do one's own thing');
- to understand instrumental reason;
- to prescribe rules (for oneself and for others) and to be guided by rules (set by oneself or by others);
- to form a sense of one's own identity ('to be one's own person').

Accordingly, the essential conditions are those that support the exercise of these capacities. With existence secured, and under the right conditions, human life becomes an opportunity for agents to be who they want to be, to have the projects that they want to have, to form the relationships that they want, to pursue the interests that they choose to have and so on. In the twenty-first century, no other view of human potential and aspiration is plausible; in the twenty-first century, it is axiomatic that humans are prospective agents and that agents need to be free.

In this light, we can readily appreciate that – unlike, say, Margaret Atwood's post-apocalyptic dystopia, *Oryx and Crake*[27] – what is dystopian about George Orwell's *Nineteen Eighty-Four*[28] and Aldous Huxley's *Brave New World*[29] is not that human existence is compromised but that human agency is compromised. We can appreciate, too, that today's dataveillance practices, as much as 1984's surveillance, 'may be doing less

[25] Compare J Rockström et al, 'Planetary Boundaries: Exploring the Safe Operating Space for Humanity' (2009) 14 *Ecology and Society* 32 (www.ecologyandsociety.org/vol14/iss2/art32/) (last accessed 14 November 2016); and K Raworth, *Doughnut Economics* (Random House Business Books, 2017) 43–53.

[26] Compare R Brownsword, 'Crimes Against Humanity, Simple Crime, and Human Dignity' in B van Beers, L Corrias, and W Werner (eds), *Humanity across International Law and Biolaw* (Cambridge University Press, 2014) 87.

[27] (Bloomsbury, 2003).

[28] (Penguin Books, 1954) (first published 1949).

[29] (Vintage Books, 2007) (first published 1932).

to deter destructive acts than [slowly to narrow] the range of tolerable thought and behaviour'.[30]

Thirdly, the commons must secure the conditions for an aspirant moral community, whether the particular community is guided by teleological or deontological standards, by rights or by duties, by communitarian or liberal or libertarian values, by virtue ethics, and so on. The generic context for moral community is impartial between competing moral visions, values, and ideals; but it must be conducive to 'moral' development and 'moral' agency in a formal sense.

So, for example, in her discussion of techno-moral virtues, (sous)surveillance, and moral nudges, Shannon Vallor is rightly concerned that any employment of digital technologies to foster prosocial behaviour should respect the importance of conduct remaining 'our *own conscious activity and achievement* rather than passive, unthinking submission'.[31] Even if we act in reliably prosocial ways, even if we seem to be model citizens, we are not acting as moral agents unless we can 'explain *why* [we] act in good ways, why the ways [we] act *are* good, or *what* the good life for a human being or community might be'.[32] Quite simply, where technologies do too much regulatory work, there is a risk that moral agency will be compromised.

Agents who reason impartially will understand that each human agent is a stakeholder in the commons where this represents the essential conditions for human existence together with the generic conditions of both self-regarding and other-regarding agency; and, it will be understood that these conditions must, therefore, be respected. While respect for the commons' conditions is binding on all human agents, it should be emphasised that these conditions do not rule out the possibility of prudential or moral pluralism. Rather, the commons represents the pre-conditions for both individual self-development and community debate, giving each agent the opportunity to develop his or her own view of what is prudent as well as what should be morally prohibited, permitted, or required. However, the articulation and contestation of both individual and collective perspectives (like all other human social acts, activities and practices) are predicated on the existence and integrity of the commons.

ii. Second Tier Responsibilities

Beyond the fundamental stewardship responsibilities, regulators are also responsible for ensuring that the fundamental values of their particular community are respected. Just as each individual human agent has the capacity to develop their own distinctive identity, the same is true if we scale this up to communities of human agents. There are common needs but also distinctive identities.

[30] F Pasquale, *The Black Box Society* (Harvard University Press, 2015) 52. Compare S Zuboff, *The Age of Surveillance Capitalism* (Profile Books, 2019) who views the data collection practices of the big tech corporations as less about controlling our thoughts (as in Big Brother) and more about predicting and, ultimately, shaping our behaviour (as in BF Skinner's *Walden Two*). Either way, it is our agency that is under threat.

[31] S Vallor, *Technology and the Virtues* (Oxford University Press, 2016) 203 (emphasis in original).

[32] ibid (emphasis in the original).

From the middle of the Twentieth Century, many nation states have expressed their fundamental (constitutional) values in terms of respect for human rights and human dignity.[33] These values (most obviously the human right to life) clearly intersect with the commons conditions and there is much to debate about the nature of this relationship and the extent of any overlap – for example, if we understand the root idea of human dignity in terms of humans having the capacity freely to do the right thing for the right reason,[34] then human dignity reaches directly to the commons' conditions for moral agency.[35] However, those nation states that articulate their particular identities by the way in which they interpret their commitment to respect for human dignity are far from homogeneous. Whereas, in some communities, the emphasis of human dignity is on individual empowerment and autonomy, in others it is on constraints relating to the sanctity, non-commercialisation, non-commodification, and non-instrumentalisation of human life.[36] These differences in emphasis mean that communities articulate in very different ways on a range of beginning of life and end of life questions as well as questions of human enhancement, and so on.

Prompted by visions of a legal singularity, one question that should now be addressed is whether, and if so how far, a community sees itself as distinguished by its commitment to governance by rules (the rules being made, applied, interpreted, and enforced by human agents). In some smaller scale communities or self-regulating groups, there might be resistance to a technocratic approach because compliance that is guaranteed by technological means compromises the context for trust. This might be the position, for example, in some business communities (where self-enforcing transactional technologies, such as blockchain, are rejected)[37] as well as in communities where there is a sense that there needs to be some slack for vulnerable consumers and debtors.[38] Or, again, a community might prefer to stick with regulation by rules because it values public participation in setting standards and is worried that this might be more difficult if the debate were to become technocratic.

If a community decides that it is generally happy with an approach that relies on technological features rather than rules, it then has to decide whether it is also happy for humans to be out of the loop. Where the technologies involve AI the 'computer loop' might be the only loop that there is. As Shawn Bayern and his co-authors note, this raises an urgent question, namely: 'do we need to define essential tasks of the state

[33] See R Brownsword, 'Human Dignity from a Legal Perspective' in M Duwell, J Braavig, R Brownsword and D Mieth (eds), *Cambridge Handbook of Human Dignity* (Cambridge University Press, 2014) 1.

[34] For such a view, see R Brownsword, 'Human Dignity, Human Rights, and Simply Trying to Do the Right Thing' in C McCrudden (ed), *Understanding Human Dignity (Proceedings of the British Academy 192)* (The British Academy and Oxford University Press, 2013) 345.

[35] See R Brownsword, 'From Erewhon to Alpha Go: For the Sake of Human Dignity Should We Destroy the Machines?' (2017) 9 *Law, Innovation and Technology* 117.

[36] See D Beyleveld and R Brownsword, *Human Dignity in Bioethics and Biolaw* (Oxford University Press, 2001); T Caulfield and R Brownsword, 'Human Dignity: A Guide to Policy Making in the Biotechnology Era' (2006) 7 *Nature Reviews Genetics* 72; and R Brownsword, *Rights, Regulation and the Technological Revolution* (Oxford University Press, 2008).

[37] See, the excellent discussion in KEC Levy, 'Book-Smart, Not Street-Smart: Blockchain-Based Smart Contracts and The Social Workings of Law' (2017) 3 *Engaging Science, Technology, and Society* 1.

[38] Compare the case discussed by Zuboff (n 30) at 334–35.

that must be fulfilled by human beings under all circumstances?'[39] Furthermore, once a community is asking itself such questions, it will need to clarify its understanding of the relationship between humans and robots – in particular, whether it treats robots as having moral status, or legal personality, and the like.[40]

It is, of course, essential that the fundamental values to which a particular community commits itself are consistent with (or cohere with) the commons conditions; and, if we are to talk about a new form of coherentism – as I will suggest we should – it should be focused in the first instance on ensuring that regulatory operations are so consistent.

iii. Third Tier Responsibilities

This takes us to the third tier of regulatory responsibility. Here, the challenge to regulators is to seek to achieve a balance between various competing and conflicting interests that is socially acceptable in the way that we described at the start of this section.

Today, we have the perfect example of this challenge in the debate about the liability (both criminal and civil) of Internet intermediaries for the unlawful content that they carry or host. Should intermediaries be required to monitor content or simply act after the event by taking down offending content? In principle, we might argue that such intermediaries should be held strictly liable for any or some classes of illegal content; or that they should be liable if they fail to take reasonable care; or that they should be immunised against liability even though the content is illegal. If we take a position at the strict liability end of the range, we might worry that the liability regime is too burdensome to intermediaries and that online services will not expand in the way that we hope; but, if we take a position at the immunity end of the range, we might worry that this treats the Internet as an exception to the Rule of Law and is an open invitation for the illegal activities of copyright infringers, paedophiles, terrorists and so on. In practice, most legal systems balance these interests by taking a position that confers an immunity but only so long as the intermediaries do not have knowledge or notice of the illegal content. Predictably, now that the leading intermediaries are large US corporations with deep pockets, and not fledgling start-ups, many think that the time is ripe for the balance to be reviewed.[41] However, finding a balance that is generally acceptable, in both principle and practice, is another matter.[42]

[39] S Bayern, T Burri, TD Grant, DM Häusermann, F Möslein and R Williams, 'Company Law and Autonomous Systems: A Blueprint for Lawyers, Entrepreneurs, and Regulators' (2017) 9 *Hastings Science and Technology Law Journal* 135, at 156.

[40] See eg B-J Koops, M Hildebrandt and D-O Jaquet-Chiffelle, 'Bridging the Accountability Gap: Rights for New Entities in the Information Society?' (2010) 11 *Minnesota Journal of Law, Science and Technology* 497; and JJ Bryson, ME Diamantis and TD Grant, 'Of, for, and by the people: the legal lacuna of synthetic persons' (2017) 25 *Artif Intell Law* 273.

[41] For a particularly compelling analysis, see M Thompson, 'Beyond Gatekeeping: the Normative Responsibility of Internet Intermediaries' (2016) 18 *Vanderbilt Journal of Entertainment and Technology Law* 783.

[42] In the EU, there is also the question of whether national legislative initiatives – such as the recent German NetzDG, which is designed to encourage social networks to process complaints about hate speech and other criminal content more quickly and comprehensively – are compatible with the provisions of Directive 2000/31/EC on e-commerce: see, for discussion of this particular question, G Spindler, 'Internet Intermediary Liability Reloaded – The New German Act on Responsibility of Social Networks and its (In-) Compatibility With European Law', www.jipitec.eu/issues/jipitec-8-2-2017/4567 (last accessed 5 February 2018).

It is imperative, of course, that the interests brought into the balance are not higher tier values or conditions. Arguably, one condition or value that has been improperly 'downgraded' in the rush to gather personal data that will fuel data-hungry technologies is privacy.[43] What precisely the scope of privacy is might be moot, and its weight and content might vary from one context to another.[44] Nevertheless, privacy matters; it should not be treated as 'dead'; and, at minimum, it should be restored to the balancing of interests. However, this might not be sufficient. In some communities, respect for privacy might be a distinctive second-tier value; and, it is now being appreciated that privacy might actually represent first-tier conditions that are a pre-requisite for agents 'being their own person'. As Bert-Jaap Koops has so clearly expressed it, privacy has an 'infrastructural character', 'having privacy spaces is an important presupposition for autonomy [and] self-development'.[45]

So much for the benchmarks of regulatory legitimacy – benchmarks that indicate that, before AI tools should be used by either regulators or regulatees, there will need to be a triple licence for the particular use or application: a commons' (first tier) licence, a community (second tier) licence, and a social (third tier) licence. Our next step is to consider how these benchmarks are to be incorporated in the Rule of Law.

IV. Reworking the Rule of Law

As indicated in my introductory remarks, I see an urgent need to re-work the Rule of Law (which implicitly assumes a rule-guided form of order) so that it covers the use of technological tools by both public and private regulators.[46] While we can spend a long time debating the details of the Rule of Law, the spirit surely is that, on the one side, the exercise of arbitrary power is to be constrained and that, on the other, the exercise of non-arbitrary power is to be respected.[47]

The importance of the Rule of Law in an era of technological management should not be understated. One of the first priorities is to shake off the idea that brute force and coercive rules are the most dangerous expressions of regulatory power; the regulatory

[43] See eg Zuboff (n 30).

[44] See eg DJ Solove, *Understanding Privacy* (Harvard University Press, 2008) and H Nissenbaum, *Privacy in Context* (Stanford University Press, 2010).

[45] B-J Koops, 'Privacy Spaces' (2018) 121 *West Virginia Law Review* 611, at 621. Compare, too, the insightful analysis of the importance of privacy in M Brincker, 'Privacy in Public and the Contextual Conditions of Agency' in T Timan, B Clayton Newell and B-J Koops (eds), *Privacy in Public Space* (Edward Elgar, 2017) 64; and, similarly, see M Hu, 'Orwell's 1984 and a Fourth Amendment Cybersurveillance Nonintrusion Test' (2017) 92 *Washington Law Review* 1819, at 1903–04.

[46] Compare M Hildebrandt, *Smart Technologies and the End(s) of Law* (Edward Elgar, 2015); and JE Cohen, *Between Truth and Power* (Oxford University Press, 2019) 237 and 266–68 (arguing for a Rule of Law 2.0 that reflects the need to entrench respect for fundamental human rights in a networked digital (information) era).

[47] Seminally on the Rule of Law, see LL Fuller, *The Morality of Law* (Yale University Press, 1969). For extensive debates about the Rule of Law, see eg J Raz, 'The Rule of Law and its Virtues' (1977) 93 *LQR* 195; D Dyzenhaus (ed), *Recrafting the Rule of Law* (Hart, 1999) 1; J Waldron, 'Is the Rule of Law an Essentially Contested Concept (in Florida)?' (2002) 21 *Law and Philosophy* 137; and LM Austin and D Klimchuk (eds), *Private Law and the Rule of Law* (Oxford University Press, 2014). For my sense of the spirit of the Rule of Law, see D Beyleveld and R Brownsword, *Law as a Moral Judgment* (Sweet and Maxwell, 1986; reprinted, Sheffield Academic Press, 1994).

power to limit our practical options might be much less obvious but no less dangerous. Power, as Steven Lukes rightly says, 'is at its most effective when least observable'[48] – and even more so, Lukes might warn, where technologies (such as AI) shape our sense of what is in our 'real' interest.

While I cannot here specify a model Rule of Law for future communities, I suggest that the following conditions, reflecting the three-tiered scheme of regulatory responsibilities, merit serious consideration.[49]

First, for any community, it is imperative that technological management (just as with rules and standards) does not compromise the essential conditions for human social existence (the commons). The Rule of Law should open by emphasising that the protection and maintenance of the commons is always the primary responsibility of regulators. Moreover, all uses of technological management, whether by public regulators or by private regulators or actors should respect this fundamental responsibility.

Secondly, where the aspiration is not simply to be a moral community (a community committed to the primacy of moral reason) but a particular kind of moral community, then it will be a condition of the Rule of Law that the use of technological management (just as with rules and standards) should be consistent with its particular constitutive features – whether those features are, for instance, liberal or communitarian in nature, rights-based or utilitarian, and so on. Such is the nature of the second tier of responsibility.

Many modern communities, as we have already noted, have articulated their constitutive values in terms of respect for human rights and human dignity.[50] In an age of technological management, this might translate into a human right (or corresponding duties derived from respect for human dignity) to know whether one is interacting or transacting with a robot, to being cared for by humans (rather than robots which can appear to care but without really caring),[51] to having a right to have 'bad news' conveyed by another human,[52] and to reserving the possibility of an appeal to a human arbitrator against a decision that triggers an application of technological management that forces or precludes a particular act or that excludes a particular person or class of persons.[53]

[48] S Lukes, *Power: A Radical View*, 2nd edn (Palgrave Macmillan, 2005) 1.

[49] Compare R Brownsword, 'The Rule of Law, Rules of Law, and Technological Management' Amsterdam Law School Research Paper No. 2017–35 (2017) 9–17, https://ssrn.com/abstract=3005914. See, too, C Gavaghan, 'Lex Machina: Techno-regulatory Mechanisms and "Rules by Design"' (2017) 15 *Otago Law Review* 123, where, at 135, it is suggested that, in addition to asking the general question about whether a measure is 'likely to be effective, what we think of the values it embodies, whether the likely benefit is worth the cost, and so forth', we should ask whether technological measures are: (i) visible, (ii) flexible, (iii) simply enforcing rules already agreed upon by democratic means, and (iv) employing unusually intrusive or inflexible means of enforcement.

[50] See R Brownsword, 'Human Dignity from a Legal Perspective' in M Duwell, J Braavig, R Brownsword and D Mieth (eds), *Cambridge Handbook of Human Dignity* (Cambridge University Press, 2014) 1.

[51] See eg S Turkle, *Alone Together* (Basic Books, 2011) esp at 281–82 (concerning the case of Richard).

[52] Last year, it was reported that Ernest Quintana's family were shocked when they saw that a 'robot' displaying a doctor on a screen was used to tell Ernest that doctors (at the Californian hospital where he was a patient) could do no more for him and that he would die soon: see M Cook, 'Bedside manner 101: How to deliver very bad news' (*Bioedge*, 18 March 2019), www.bioedge.org/bioethics/bedside-manner-101-how-to-deliver-very-bad-news/12998 (last accessed 3 April 2019).

[53] Compare Gavaghan (n 49). However, the extent to which the possibility of human intervention can make much practical difference when smart machines are known to outperform humans is moot. For insightful discussion, see H-Y Liu, 'The Power Structure of Artificial Intelligence' (2018) 10 *Law, Innovation and Technology* 197, at 222.

Looking ahead, one (possibly counter-intuitive) thought is that a community might attach particular value (based on its interpretation of respect for human rights and human dignity) to preserving both human officials (rather than machines) and rules (rather than technological measures) in the core areas of the criminal justice system.[54] To ring-fence core crime in this way promises to retain some flexibility in the application of rules that carry serious penalties for their infringement as well as preserving an important zone for moral development (and display of moral virtue). Indeed, in some communities, this zone might be thought to be so critical to the very possibility of moral development that the eschewal of technological solutions is seen as reaching back to the commons conditions themselves.[55]

Thirdly, where the use of technological management is proposed as part of a risk management package, so long as the community is committed to the ideals of deliberative democracy, it will be a condition of the Rule of Law that there needs to be a transparent and inclusive public debate about the terms of the package. It will be a condition that all views should be heard with regard to whether the package amounts to both an acceptable balance of benefit and risk as well as representing a fair distribution of such risk and benefit (including adequate compensatory provisions). Before the particular package can command respect, it needs to be somewhere on the spectrum of reasonableness. This is not to suggest that all regulatees must agree that the package is optimal; but it must at least be reasonable in the weak sense that it is not a package that is so unreasonable that no rational regulator could, in good faith, adopt it. Such is the shape of the third tier of responsibility.

For example, where technologically managed places or products operate dynamically, making decisions case-by-case or situation-by-situation, then one of the outcomes of the public debate might be that the possibility of a human override is reserved. In the case of driverless cars, for instance, we might want to give agents the opportunity to take control of the vehicle in order to deal with some hard moral choice (whether of a 'trolley' or a 'tunnel' nature) or to respond to an emergency (perhaps involving a 'rescue' of some kind).[56]

Similarly, there might be a condition that interventions involving technological management should be reversible – a condition that might be particularly important if measures of this kind are designed not only into products and places but also into people, as might be the case if regulators contemplate making interventions in not only the coding of product software but also the genomic coding of particular individuals. It should be noted, however, that while reversibility might speak to the acceptability of a technological measure, it might go deeper, to either second or first tier responsibilities.

Fourthly, the community will want to be satisfied that the use of technological measures is accompanied by proper mechanisms for accountability. When there are problems, or when things go wrong, there need to be clear, accessible, and intelligible

[54] Compare R Brownsword and A Harel (n 11), and D Beyleveld and R Brownsword, 'Punitive and Preventive Justice in an Era of Profiling, Smart Prediction and Practical Preclusion' (2019) 15 *International Journal of Law in Context* 198.

[55] Compare the discussion in R Brownsword, 'From Erewhon to Alpha Go: For the Sake of Human Dignity Should We Destroy the Machines?' (2017) 9 *Law, Innovation and Technology* 117.

[56] For discussion of such moral hard choices, see R Brownsword, *Law, Technology and Society – Re-imagining the Regulatory Environment* (Routledge, 2019) 249–51.

lines of accountability. It needs to be clear who is to be held to account as well as how they are to be held to account; and, the accounting itself must be meaningful.[57]

Fifthly, a community might be concerned that the use of technological management will encourage some mission creep. If so, it might stipulate that the restrictive scope of measures of technological management or their forcing range should be no greater than would be the case were a rule to be used for the particular purpose. In this sense, the restrictive sweep of technological management should be, at most, co-extensive with that of the equivalent (shadow) rule.[58]

Sixthly, it is implicit in the Fullerian principles of legality[59] that regulators should not try to trick or trap regulatees; and this is a principle that is applicable whether the instrument of regulation is the use of rules or the use of technological management. Accordingly, it should be a condition of the Rule of Law that technological management should not be used in ways that trick or trap regulatees and that, in this sense, the administration of a regime of technological management should be in line with the reasonable expectations of regulatees (implying that regulatees should be put on notice that technological management is in operation).[60] Crucially, if the default position in a technologically managed regulatory environment is that, where an act is found to be available, it should be treated as permissible, then regulatees should not be penalised for doing the act on the good faith basis that, because it is available, it is a lawful option.

Seventhly, regulatees might also expect there to be a measure of public authorisation and scrutiny of the private use of technological management. Indeed, as Julie Cohen puts it, it is self-evident that 'institutions for recognising and enforcing fundamental rights should work to counterbalance private economic power rather than reinforcing it. Obligations to protect fundamental rights must extend – enforceably – to private, for-profit entities if they are to be effective at all'.[61] The point is that, even if public regulators respect the conditions set by regulatees, it will not suffice if private regulators are left free to use technological management in ways that compromise the community's moral aspirations, or violate its constitutive principles, or exceed the agreed and authorised limits for its use. Accordingly, it should be a condition of the Rule of Law that the private use of technological management should be compatible with the general principles for its use.

While there is much to debate about the Rule of Law, there are a number of ways in which my discussion presupposes a version of the ideal that is thicker, deeper, and broader than, say, the Fullerian version. It is thicker because it goes beyond procedural

[57] See JA Kroll, J Huey, S Barocas, EW Felten, JR Reidenberg, DG Robinson and H Yu, 'Accountable Algorithms' (2017) 165 *University of Pennsylvania Law Review* 633, 702–04.

[58] Compare Gavaghan (n 49).

[59] Seminally, see LL Fuller (n 47). For an application of the Fullerian principles to particular instances of cyberlaw, see C Reed, 'How to Make Bad Law: Lessons from Cyberspace' (2010) 73 *MLR* 903, esp at 914–16. Generally, for applications of Fuller to technological management (or 'code regulation'), see L Asscher, '"Code" as Law. Using Fuller to Assess Code Rules' in E Dommering and L Asscher (eds), *Coding Regulation: Essays on the Normative Role of Information Technology* (TMC Asser, 2006) 61; and R Brownsword, 'Technological Management and the Rule of Law' (2016) 8 *Law, Innovation and Technology* 100.

[60] Compare Gavaghan (n 49) on visibility, at 135–37 (do we know that technological measures are employed, do we know that they are in operation in a particular place or at a particular time, and do we know the precise details or limits of such measures?).

[61] Cohen (n 46) at 267.

requirements to include substantive requirements; it is deeper because those substantive requirements reach back to the most fundamental principles of regulatory responsibility (principles that no human agent can rationally deny); and its application is broader because it includes the use of the full range of regulatory instruments, normative as well as non-normative.

V. New Coherentism

In the bigger picture of regulatory responsibilities, where the paramount responsibility is to ensure that no harm is done to the commons, we might wonder whether a traditional coherentist mind-set (fixated on the application of general legal principles and focused on consistency and integrity within the doctrinal body) is appropriate. If regulators think in such a coherentist way, they might fail to take the necessary protective steps – steps that might involve new rules, or the use of measures of technological management, or both. While the commons is being compromised, we might fear, coherentists will be concerned only with the integrity of doctrine.

Such a concern invites the thought that a regulatory-instrumentalist approach is a better default but it is only so if regulators are focused on the relevant risks – namely, the risks presented by technological development to the commons' conditions. Moreover, we might want to add that regulatory-instrumentalism with this particular risk focus is only a better default if it is applied with a suitably precautionary mentality. Regulators need to understand that compromising the commons is always the worst-case scenario.[62] Alongside such a default, a technocratic approach might well be appropriate. For example, if we believe that a rule-based approach cannot protect the planetary boundaries, then a geo-engineering approach might be the answer.[63] However, it needs to be borne in mind that, with a resort to technological management, there is potentially more than one kind of risk to the commons: an ineffective attempt to manage risks to the existence conditions might actually make things worse; and an effective intervention for the sake of the existence conditions might compromise the conditions for self-development and moral agency (because both autonomy and virtue presuppose a context in which one acts freely).

Accordingly, if we are to respond to the thick end of the technological wedge, a central element in the re-invention of law is the articulation of a 'new coherentism'. New coherentism reminds regulators (and others with regulatory roles and responsibilities) of two things: first, that their most urgent regulatory focus should be on the commons' conditions; and, secondly, that, whatever their interventions, and particularly

[62] Compare D Beyleveld and R Brownsword, 'Complex Technology, Complex Calculations: Uses and Abuses of Precautionary Reasoning in Law' in M Duwell and P Sollie (eds), *Evaluating New Technologies: Methodological Problems for the Ethical Assessment of Technological Developments* (Springer, 2009) 175; and 'Emerging Technologies, Extreme Uncertainty, and the Principle of Rational Precautionary Reasoning' (2012) 4 *Law Innovation and Technology* 35.

[63] For discussion, see J Reynolds, 'Solar Climate Engineering, Law, and Regulation' in R Brownsword, E Scotford and K Yeung (eds), *The Oxford Handbook of Law, Regulation and Technology* (Oxford University Press, 2017) 799.

where they take a technocratic approach, their acts must always be compatible with the preservation of the commons.

In future, the Courts – albeit the locus for traditional coherentist thinking – will have a continuing role to play in bringing what we are calling a new coherentism to bear on the use of technological measures. Most importantly, it will be for the Courts to review the legality of any technological measure that is challenged relative to the authorising and constitutive rules; and, above all, to check that particular instances of technological management are consistent with the commons-protecting ideals that are inscribed in the Rule of Law.

With a new coherentist mind-set, it is not a matter of checking for internal doctrinal consistency, nor checking that a measure is fit for its particular regulatory purpose. Rather, the Courts, and others, applying the renewed ideal of coherence should start with the paramount responsibility of regulators, namely, the protection and preservation of the commons. All regulatory interventions should cohere with that responsibility. All uses of AI tools should be within the terms of the commons' licence (compatible with respect for the conditions for human existence and the context for flourishing agency).

While the many codes and guidelines being advanced for responsible and trustworthy use of AI are not explicitly structured and organised in the form of new coherentism, we can find traces of such thinking. For example, when researchers met at Asilomar in California to develop a set of precautionary guidelines for the use of AI, it was agreed (in Principle 21) that 'risks posed by AI systems, especially catastrophic or existential risks, must be subject to planning and mitigation efforts commensurate with their expected impact'.[64]

Having satisfied themselves that a particular use of AI (or some other technological instrument) does not compromise either the existence or the agency conditions of the commons, the next step for new coherentists is to check the community licence. Measures of technological management should cohere with the particular constitutive values of the community – such as respect for human rights and human dignity, the way that non-human agents are to be treated, and so on – and its particular articulation of the Rule of Law. Again, at Asilomar, it was agreed (in Principle 11) that 'AI systems should be designed and operated so as to be compatible with ideals of human dignity, rights, freedoms, and cultural diversity'; the EC high level expert group, as we have said, insisted that the development and use of AI should be human-centric; similarly, the OECD Recommendation on AI recognises the need to promote a human-centric approach to trustworthy AI as well as highlighting the importance of human-centred values;[65] and, drawing on the OECD's Recommendation, the G20 has expressed its support for 'human-centered AI that promotes innovation and investment'.[66] No doubt, the Courts will face many challenges in interpreting and applying these, or similar, principles but the critical point is that they should always be guided by a new coherentist understanding of their role and responsibility.

[64] See futureoflife.org/ai-principles/ (last accessed 18 March 2019).

[65] OECD/LEGAL/0449, adopted on 22/05/19.

[66] G20 Ministerial Statement on Trade and Digital Economy, June 2019, para 17, www.mofa.go.jp/files/000486596.pdf (last accessed 15 January 2020).

There will also be challenges to technological management on procedural grounds associated with the social licence. Once again, there will be work for the Courts. Where explicit procedures are laid out for the adoption of technological management, the Courts will be involved in a familiar reviewing role. However, there might also be some doctrinal issues of coherence that arise – for example, where it is argued that the explicit procedural requirements have some further procedural entailments; or where the Courts, having developed their own implicit procedural laws (such as a practice raising a legitimate expectation of consultation), find that the body of doctrine is not internally coherent.

Coherence might be an ideal that is dear to the hearts of private lawyers but, in an era of technological management, it is once coherence is brought into the body of public law that we see its full regulatory significance. Regulation, whether normative or non-normative, will lack coherence if the procedures or purposes that accompany it are out of line with the authorising or constitutive rules that take us back to the Rule of Law itself; and, regulation will be fundamentally incoherent if it is out of line with the responsibility for maintaining the commons. Regardless of whether we are sceptical about the ability of AI to emulate traditional coherentist legal reasoning (applying and re-interpreting the general principles of the law), the challenge for lawyers is to renew the coherentist ideal. In an age of technological management, that act of renewal demands that we engage with both the full range of regulatory responsibilities and the full repertoire of regulatory instruments.

VI. Reviewing Institutional Arrangements and Expectations

If our regulatory responsibilities are to be properly discharged, there might need to be some redesigning of the institutions on which we rely both nationally and internationally. While we can expect national regulators to deal with the routine balancing of interests within their communities as well as to respect the distinctive values of their particular community, the stewardship of the commons seems to call for international oversight. We can start with some remarks about the arrangements nationally for engaging with emerging technologies and then we can turn to the possible international regulation of the commons.

A. The Design of National Institutions

In the UK (and, I suspect, in many other nation states), there are two contrasting features in the institutional arrangements that we have for engaging with and regulating new technologies. On the one hand, there is no standard operating procedure for undertaking the initial review of such technologies; and, on the other hand, the Rule of Law in conjunction with democracy dictates that the Courts should settle disputes in accordance with established legal principles and that it is for the Legislature and the Executive to formulate and agree public policies, plans and priorities. In other words, while there is no expectation about who will undertake the initial review or how that review will be approached, we have very definite expectations about the role and reasoning of judges and advocates in the Courts (where the discourse is coherentist) and similarly about the policy-making members of the Legislature and Executive (where the discourse is regulatory-instrumentalist). The question is: where in this institutional design do we find the responsibility for stewardship of the commons and for the community's distinctive values?

To start with the initial engagement with, and review of, an emerging technology, it seems to be largely a matter of happenstance as to who addresses the issue and how it is addressed – or, at any rate, this is the case in the UK. For example, in the late 1970s, when techniques for assisted conception were being developed and applied, but also being seriously questioned, the response of the UK government was to set up a Committee of Inquiry chaired by Mary Warnock. In 1984, the Committee's report (the Warnock Report) was published.[67] However, it was not until 1990, and after much debate in Parliament, that the framework legislation, the Human Fertilisation and Embryology Act 1990, was enacted. This process, taking the best part of a decade, is regularly held up as an example of best practice when dealing with emerging technologies. Nevertheless, this methodology is not in any sense the standard operating procedure for engaging with new technologies – indeed, there is no such procedure.

The fact of the matter is that legal and regulatory responses to emerging technologies vary from one technology to another, from one legal system to another, and from one time to another. Sometimes, there is extensive public engagement, sometimes not. On occasion, special Commissions (such as the now defunct Human Genetics Commission in the UK) have been set up with a dedicated oversight remit; and there have been examples of standing technology foresight commissions (such as the US Office of Technology Assessment);[68] but, often, there is nothing of this kind. Most importantly, questions about new technologies sometimes surface, first, in litigation (leaving it to the Courts to determine how to respond) and, at other times, they are presented to the Legislature (as was the case with assisted conception).

With regard to the question of which regulatory body engages with new technologies and how, there can of course be some local agency features that shape the answers. Where, as in the US, there is a particular regulatory array with each agency having its own remit, a new technology might be considered in just one lead agency or it might be assessed in several agencies.[69] Once again, there is a degree of happenstance about this. Nevertheless, in a preliminary way, we can make three general points.

First, if the question (such as that posed by a compensatory claim made by a claimant who alleges harm caused by a new technology) is put to the Courts, their responsibility for the integrity of the law will push them towards a coherentist assessment. Typically, courts are neither sufficiently resourced nor mandated to undertake a risk assessment let alone adopt a risk management strategy (unless the Legislature has already put in place a scheme that delegates such a responsibility to the courts).

[67] Report of the Committee of Inquiry into Human Fertilisation and Embryology (HMSO, Cm. 9314, 1984).

[68] On which, see B Bimber, *The Politics of Expertise in Congress* (State University of New York Press, 1996) charting the rise and fall of the Office and drawing out some important tensions between 'neutrality' and 'politicisation' in the work of such agencies.

[69] Compare, AC Lin, 'Size Matters: Regulating Nanotechnology' (2007) 31 *Harvard Environmental Law Review* 349.

Secondly, if the question finds its way into the legislative arena, it is much more likely that politicians will engage with it in a regulatory-instrumentalist way; and, once the possibility of technological measures gets onto the radar, it is much more likely that (as with institutions in the EU) we will see a more technocratic mind-set.

Thirdly, if leaving so much to chance seems unsatisfactory, then it is arguable that there needs to be a body that is charged with horizon-scanning and undertaking the preliminary engagement with new technologies. The remit and challenge for such a body would be to ensure that there is no harm to the commons; to try to channel such technologies to our most urgent needs (relative to the commons); and, to help each community to address the question of the kind of society that it distinctively wants to be – doing all that, moreover, in a context of rapid social and technological change. As Wendell Wallach rightly insists:

> Bowing to political and economic imperatives is not sufficient. Nor is it acceptable to defer to the mechanistic unfolding of technological possibilities. In a democratic society, we – the public – should give approval to the futures being created. At this critical juncture in history, an informed conversation must take place before we can properly give our assent or dissent.[70]

Granted, the notion that we can build agencies that are fit for such purposes might be an impossible dream. Nevertheless, this is surely the right time to establish a suitably constituted body[71] – possibly along the lines of the Centre for Data Ethics and Innovation (to set standards for the ethical use of AI and data)[72] – that would underline our responsibilities for the commons as well as facilitating the development of each community's regulatory and social licence for these technologies.[73]

B. International Stewardship of the Commons

The commons is not confined to particular nation states. The conditions for human existence on planet Earth are relevant to all nation states and can be impacted by each nation state's activities. The same applies where nation states interfere with the conditions for flourishing agency beyond their own national borders. Whether in relation to the conditions for existence or for the enjoyment of agency, there can be cross-border spill-over effects. Accordingly, if the essential infrastructure for human social existence

[70] See W Wallach, *A Dangerous Master* (Basic Books, 2015) 10.

[71] Amongst many matters in this paper that invite further discussion, the composition of such a Commission invites debate. See, too, Wallach (n 70) chs 14–15.

[72] www.gov.uk/government/organisations/centre-for-data-ethics-and-innovation (last accessed 3 November 2019).

[73] Compare G Mulgan's proposal for the establishment of a Machine Intelligence Commission, www.nesta.org.uk/blog/machine-intelligence-commission-uk (blog 'A machine intelligence commission for the UK', 22 February 2016: last accessed 11 December 2016); O Bustom et al, *An Intelligent Future? Maximising the Opportunities and Minimising the Risks of Artificial Intelligence in the UK* (Future Advocacy, London, October 2016) (proposing a Standing Commission on AI to examine the social, ethical, and legal implications of recent and potential developments in AI); HC Science and Technology Committee, Robotics and Artificial Intelligence HC 145 2016–17.

is to be secured, this implies that there needs to be a considerable degree of international co-ordination and shared responsibility.[74]

On paper, there are some positive indications in international law – for example, in the cosmopolitan idea of *jus cogens* (the idea of acts that are categorically wrong in all places) and crimes against humanity. Moreover, when the United Nations spells out the basic responsibilities of states, it can do so in terms that are redolent of the commons' conditions. For instance, Article 18(b) of the UN Global Compact on Safe, Orderly and Regular Migration, which was adopted in December 2018, provides that states should invest in programmes for

> poverty eradication, food security, health and sanitation, education, inclusive economic growth, infrastructure, urban and rural development, employment creation, decent work, gender equality, and empowerment of women and girls, resilience and disaster and risk reduction, climate change mitigation and adaptation, addressing the socioeconomic effects of all forms of violence, non-discrimination, rule of law and good governance, access to justice and protection of human rights, as well as creating and maintaining peaceful and inclusive societies with effective, accountable and transparent institutions.

If we check this back against the elements of the commons' conditions that were sketched earlier in the article, this might seem a touch over-inclusive. Nevertheless, much of what this Article specifies surely aligns with the first-tier stewardship responsibilities of regulators.

In support of such provisions, there is an extensive international regulatory architecture. We might assume, therefore, that securing the commons will only require some minor adjustments or additions – rather like we might add an extension to an existing property. On the other hand, stewardship of the kind that is required calls for a distinctive and dedicated approach. It might be, therefore, that we need to have bespoke international laws and new international agencies to take this project forward.[75] Moreover, because politics tends to operate with short-term horizons, it also implies that the regulatory stewards should have some independence from the political branch, but not of course that they should be exempt from the Rule of Law's culture of accountability and justification.[76]

That said, whatever the ideal legal provision, we have to take into account the realities of international relations.

First, while all Member States of the United Nations are formally equal, the reality is that some are more equal than others, this being exemplified by the constitution of the Security Council. Not only are the five permanent members of the Security Council amongst 'the most important actors on the world stage, given their size, their economic

[74] See DA Wirth, 'Engineering the Climate: Geoengineering as a Challenge to International Governance' (2013) 40 *Boston College Environmental Affairs Law Review* 413, esp at 430–36.

[75] Compare eg SD Baum and GS Wilson, 'The Ethics of Global Catastrophic Risk from Dual Use Bioengineering' (2013) 4 *Ethics in Biology, Engineering and Medicine* 59; G Wilson, 'Minimizing global catastrophic and existential risks from emerging technologies through international law' (2013) 31 *Virginia Environmental Law Journal* 307; and D Pamlin and S Armstrong, 'Twelve risks that threaten human civilisation: The case for a new risk category' (Global Challenges Foundation, 2015) 182 (mooting the possibility of establishing a Global Risk Organisation, initially only with monitoring powers).

[76] See, too, R Brownsword, 'Responsible Regulation: Prudence, Precaution and Stewardship' (2011) 62 *Northern Ireland Legal Quarterly* 573.

and financial weight, their cultural influence, and, above all, their military might',[77] they have the power to veto (and, in practice, they do veto) decisions that the Council would otherwise make. Not surprisingly, this has led to widespread criticism of the undemocratic and unrepresentative nature of the Council; and, crucially, to criticism of the veto which enables the permanent members to subordinate their collective responsibilities (for the commons' conditions) to their own national priorities.

Secondly, as Gerry Simpson highlights, the makers and subjects of international law have different amounts of power and influence, different intentions (some are more well-intentioned than others), different levels of commitment to collective responsibilities, and different degrees of civilisation.[78] To start with, there are both functioning states and failed states. Amongst the former, while many states are good citizens of the international order (respecting the rules of international law), there are also superpowers (who play by their own rules) and rogue states (who play by no rules). If the regulatory stewards were drawn from the good citizens, that might be fine insofar as an agency so populated would be focused on the right question and motivated by concerns for the common interest of humans. However, we have to doubt that they would be in any position to ensure compliance with whatever precautionary standards they might propose let alone be mandated to introduce measures of technological management.

A third reality is that, where the missions of international agencies include a number of objectives (such as trade, human rights, and environmental concerns), or where there is a dominant objective (such as the control of narcotics), value commitments (to human rights) will tend to be overridden ('collateralised') or even treated as irrelevant ('nullified').[79] Now, while it is one thing for the international community to unite around what it takes to be its shared prudential interests and, in so doing, to give less weight to its interest in certain aspirational values, respect for the commons' conditions should never be collateralised or nullified in this way. Accordingly, to keep this imperative in focus, if the regulatory stewards are located within an international agency, their mission must be limited to the protection of the commons; and acceptable collateralisation or nullification must be limited to non-commons matters. Even then, there would be no guarantee that the stewards would be immunised against the usual risks of regulatory capture and corruption. In short, unless the culture of international relations is supportive of the stewards, even the ideal regulatory design is likely to fail.

The moral seems to be that, if the common interest is to be pursued, this is a battle for hearts and minds. As Neil Walker has remarked in relation to global law, our future prospects depend on 'our ability to persuade ourselves and each other of what we hold in common and of the value of holding that in common'.[80] An international agency with a new coherentist mission to preserve the commons might make some progress in extending the pool of good citizens but to have any chance of success the entire international community needs to be on board.

[77] G Rosenthal, *Inside the United Nations* (Routledge, 2017) 95.

[78] G Simpson, *Great Powers and Outlaw States* (Cambridge University Press, 2009).

[79] See eg S Leader, 'Collateralism' in R Brownsword (ed), *Global Governance and the Quest for Justice Vol IV: Human Rights* (Hart, 2004) 53; and on the nullification of human rights in the context of narcotics control, see R Lines, *Drug Control and Human Rights in International Law* (Cambridge University Press, 2017).

[80] N Walker, *Intimations of Global Law* (Cambridge University Press, 2015) 199.

VII. Conclusion

In this article, I have suggested that we – by which, I mean 'we lawyers' – should anticipate an AI-enabled regulatory environment, an environment that features not only rule-based normative signals (and tools that assist with the interpretation and application of those rules) but also measures of non-normative technological management. Some technological applications represent the thin end of a wedge that destabilises the idea of law as a rule-based enterprise; but other applications are thicker, destabilising not only our idea of law but also the importance that we attach to agency and autonomy. There is no guarantee that rules and technological measures can comfortably co-exist; and, there is no guarantee that regulators will eschew applications of technologies that compromise the conditions for self-interested and other-regarding agency. There is no guarantee, in other words, that a legal singularity will improve the human social condition.

In response to the adoption of AI as a regulatory tool, I have suggested that we first need to have clearly in focus a grounded and hierarchically ordered scheme of regulatory responsibilities. That scheme (forming the basis for a triple licence for the development and regulatory use of AI) can then be used to inform each community's articulation of the Rule of Law (constraining and authorising the use of measures of technological management) and it can be taken forward through a new and revitalised form of coherentist thinking together with new institutional arrangements for the stewardship of the commons.

Rationally, humans should need little persuading: what we all have in common is a fundamental reliance on a critical infrastructure; if that infrastructure is compromised, the prospects for any kind of legal or regulatory activity, or any kind of persuasive or communicative activity, indeed for any kind of human social activity, are diminished. If we value anything, if we are positively disposed towards anything, we must value the commons. If we cannot agree on that, and if we cannot agree that the fundamental role of law is to ensure that power is exercised only in ways that are compatible with the preservation of the infrastructure of all other infrastructures, then any version of a legal singularity will not end well. If, as lawyers, we understand how this story should end, then we have a special responsibility to do our best to ensure that it does go well. In this story, we are not merely observers; we have a responsibility for constitutions and for codes, but above all for the commons and for the future of human social existence.

7

Automated Systems and the Need for Change

SYLVIE DELACROIX*

I. Introduction

The problem this paper seeks to expose is a methodological one. Current efforts to develop automated systems[1] meant to be deployed in morally loaded contexts (like law) pay little attention – if any – to the difficulties that stem from the unavoidable need for moral change. Moral change – altering our understanding of what we owe to others – comes in many colours and shapes. What may look like mere societal adaptation to environmental constraints (from a sociologist or behavioural psychologist perspective) may be experienced as epoch-making by the society in question. This momentous change may in turn be met as nothing but the belated formalisation of a widely held attitude. The continuity in the background that moulds and conditions the very possibility of change can be conceived from a variety of perspectives and scales. Somewhere between the historically acknowledged mutation[2] and the constant individual adjustment[3] to one's shifting landscape,[4] the change that arises from the acknowledgment of a discrepancy between one's present stand and the person one aspires to be is essential to making sense of ethics as a question – 'how should I [we] live?'.

The possibility of such change – and hence of ethics, rather than ideology – can be compromised. A 'lack of aspiration',[5] or 'thoughtlessness'[6] can come in the way. Systems designed to simplify our practical reasoning can also undermine our ability to keep

* Alan Turing Institute; University of Birmingham.

[1] The term 'automated system' has been chosen to remain neutral/indeterminate as to the kind of methodology underlying such automation.

[2] Such as the processes leading to the ending of the British slave trade in 1807 and the various Bills abolishing slavery.

[3] The manoeuvres entailed by this constant individual adjustment are both unconscious (see for instance the ways in which implicit bias is affected by a variety of environmental factors) and conscious.

[4] 'We transform ourselves and our moral landscape, through the structures of thought and practice that we collectively create, and the idea of law is a part of that complex process of self-transformation' (NE Simmonds, 'The Bondwoman's Son and the Beautiful Soul' (2013) 58 *American Journal of Jurisprudence* 111, at 115).

[5] J Annas, *Intelligent Virtue*, Kindle Edition edn (Oxford University Press, 2011).

[6] H Arendt, *Eichmann in Jerusalem: A Report on the Banality of Evil* (Penguin, 1994).

calling for better ways of living together. Law is one such system, and the 'moral risk' inherent in its institutional structure facilitating a 'sheeplike' society (where all the sheep might end up in the 'slaughterhouse'[7]) has recently been re-emphasised by Green,[8] among others. To the extent that (and because) they are designed to simplify our practical reasoning, many of the automated systems we increasingly rely on in our day to day (and professional) lives are no less 'morally risky'. These risks can be felt at an individual level – 'automation bias'[9] is but one of the factors that contribute to 'thoughtlessness' – and at a systemic, collective level. Just like mobile, connected devices are gradually changing not only the way we make friends, but the nature of friendship itself, many of the algorithmic tools that are being deployed within legal practice have the potential to insidiously change the very nature of our legal systems.[10] Several of this volume's contributions[11] delve into the factors that contribute to this transformative potential. Among these is the fact that an algorithm trained on historical data (whether it be to predict the outcome of cases or the likelihood of recidivism) will be 'backward-looking',[12] hence likely to struggle to retain adequacy as a society's fabric of socio-cultural expectations evolves.

In a bid to address the above adaptation challenge, 'Inverse reinforcement learning' (henceforth IRL) methods have been put forward. Section II surveys these IRL methods with a view to denouncing the lack of attention to the fragile and complex processes underlying social and moral changes. Once the latter are taken into account, the proposed IRL agents start to look like elephants in a porcelain shop. To understand why, Section III outlines the dependence of social and moral change processes upon habitual agency. The latter encapsulates a fundamental tension: we might be normative animals, capable of questioning and calling for better ways of doing things, yet we are also creatures of habit. This tension is key to illuminating both the mechanisms underlying social and moral change and the extent to which IRL agents – who are unlikely to experience habit reversal in the same way as humans – might compromise them.

Section IV may be deemed a necessary meta-ethical detour. On a realist, perfectionist understanding of moral values, the prospect of our progressively losing our ability to flex our normative muscles, trapped within the rigidified habits prompted by extended 'moral holidays', is not necessarily a bad thing. If the artificial agents – who have henceforth become the exclusive source of socio-moral change – are both benevolent and unhindered by our all too human cognitive (and habitual) limitations, why prefer the human-led, chaotic and short-sighted way of triggering such changes? There is no

[7] HLA Hart, *The Concept of Law*, 2nd edn (Clarendon Press, 1994) 202.

[8] L Green, 'Positivism and the Inseparability of Law and Morals' (2008) 83 *NYUL Rev* 1035.

[9] LJ Skitka, KL Mosier and M Burdick, 'Does automation bias decision-making?' (1999) 51 *International Journal of Human-Computer Studies* 991.

[10] The process underlying this insidious transformation is highlighted in greater detail in S Delacroix, 'Automated systems fit for the legal profession?' (2019) 21 *Legal Ethics*.

[11] C Markou and S Deakin, '*Ex Machina Lex*: Exploring The Limits of Legal Computability' and M Hildebrandt, 'Code-driven Law: Freezing the Future and Scaling the Past' both in this volume.

[12] ibid, 31.

satisfactory way of answering this question save for highlighting the heavy metaphysical presuppositions entailed by such a realist understanding of moral values.

If one does not have the kind of faith required to endorse the above, realist presuppositions, the only moral values available to us are in myriad ways constructed by us. Hence what needs protecting is precisely the ongoing, dynamic weaving of the socio-cultural fabric of expectations that underlies our effort to address the ethical question. This endeavour to safeguard normative agency is at odds with the 'creating systems/agents like us' fantasy. Section V denounces the all too common assumption that progress, when it comes to designing systems meant for morally loaded contexts, consists in expanding the degree of autonomy of such systems. The challenge, instead is complementarity. Given who we are – and are becoming – what systems can support our ongoing efforts to re-articulate normative frameworks, whether they be social, legal or moral? To address this question not only demands that speculative theories of the type reviewed in Section IV be firmly left at the backdoor. It also presupposes rigorous cross-disciplinary engagement: lawyers' commitment to acknowledging and understanding the mechanisms underlying normative change is not that much better than computers scientists (so far). Because one cannot hope to remedy this lacunae by considering legal change only, this chapter probably strays furthest from what is classically understood as 'legal' theory, to unveil the extent to which the latter presupposes normative agency as a given (rather than something that may be compromised by our increased reliance on automated systems).

II. Automated Systems, Moral Stances and the Under-appreciated Need for Change

Current efforts to develop systems that are capable of being deployed in morally loaded contexts pay little attention – if any – to the difficulties that stem from the unavoidable need for change in those systems' moral stances. The challenge inherent in those systems having to take into account a wide range of moral values is often referred to as the 'value-alignment problem'. The very term 'alignment' carries somewhat unfortunate connotations: moral values are not static entities 'ready for the picking'.

There is a growing body of literature addressing the challenge inherent in identifying and interpreting relevant values in the context of systems that are not designed to continuously learn from their environment. In such cases the fact that we humans cannot but evolve in our moral stances is meant to be dealt with through ongoing auditing of both the system and its societal impact, as well as readiness to go and revise whichever embedded norms are deemed out of touch. The above assumes a lot: first it assumes that the system's designers have a high enough level of reflective awareness to document not only the values that are made to explicitly constrain the system, but also those values that have implicitly influenced its design (for instance by framing a problem in a certain way). It also assumes that the auditing process is agile and perceptive enough to recommend revision before the system's impact is such that a community has started to adapt its values and aspirations to fit with the system's (rather than the other way round).

As an alternative to the 'top-down' incorporation strategies[13] mentioned above, some have sought to design systems that are meant to infer from the behaviour of surrounding (human) agents a morally-loaded 'utility function'. Sometimes referred to as 'inverse reinforcement learning', this method has received a fair amount of attention recently for two reasons. First because of its allowing system designers to bypass the need to define a morally-loaded utility function 'a priori'. The issues inherent in defining such a utility function in advance are similar to those that pertain to top-down incorporation strategies: the task of identifying the relevant values will necessarily be morally-loaded. For any given problem, there will be a range of values that may be deemed pertinent in any given community and within this range there will be irreconcilable clashes and incompatible interpretations.[14] Hence the attraction inherent in letting data train the system, rather than coding ethical values 'by hand'.

Most importantly, this inverse reinforcement learning method also has the merit of being compatible with an acknowledgment of the dynamic nature of moral values. Yet the way it tackles this dynamism is problematic too. In contrast to both supervised and unsupervised learning approaches, the set of data on the basis of which RL methods proceed is not given a priori: the data is generated by the artificial agent's interaction with the environment. The aim of the learning process is to come up with an action-selection policy that minimises some measure of long-term cost, which is determined on the basis of a – continuously updated – utility function. Aside from the difficulty inherent in articulating the initial utility function, traditional reinforcement learning methods are vulnerable to deception on the part of the system: 'an AI system might manipulate its reward functions in order to accomplish the goals that it holds as most important, however unethical its effects on human beings'.[15]

Inverse reinforcement learning (IRL) methods, by contrast, do not proceed from a given, initial utility function: the system is meant to infer the latter function from observed behaviour. Russell et al.[16] propose this behaviourist, bottom-up approach as a way of approximating our expectations for an ethical system: as these inferred

[13] This focus on top-down incorporation strategies is openly visible in the 2016 IEEE report: 'The conceptual complexities surrounding what "values" are make it currently difficult to envision AIS that have computational structures directly corresponding to values. However, it is a realistic goal to embed explicit norms into such systems, because norms can be considered instructions to act in defined ways in defined contexts.' IEEE, 'Ethically Aligned Design: A vision for prioritizing human wellbeing with artificial intelligence and autonomous systems (version 2)', 2017) 22. See also T Arnold, Dl Kasenberg and M Scheutz, 'Value Alignment or Misalignment – What Will Keep Systems Accountable?' (2017) AAI workshop on AI, ethics and society for the perspective of 'adding' or incorporating 'top-down' some kind of ethics to a system's decision-making procedures.

[14] For a discussion of the concrete challenges raised by the 'contested' nature of the moral values informing algorithmic content moderation, see R Binns and others, 'Like trainer, like bot? Inheritance of bias in algorithmic content moderation' (09th International Conference on Social Informatics (Socinfo, 2017)).

[15] Arnold, Kasenberg and Scheutz, 'Value Alignment or Misalignment – What Will Keep Systems Accountable?'.

[16] Since the foundational papers of S Russell, 'Learning agents for uncertain environments' (1998) and AY Ng and SJ Russell, 'Algorithms for inverse reinforcement learning' (2000), this method has given rise to a large body of literature. Of particular relevance to the present discussion, see notably S Russell, D Dewey and M Tegmark, 'Research priorities for robust and beneficial artificial intelligence' (2015) 36 *Ai Magazine* 105 and S Armstrong and S Mindermann, 'Occam's razor is insufficient to infer the preferences of irrational agents' (2018).

expectations evolve, the system is meant to update its utility function accordingly, thus in principle solving the 'mechanisms for change' challenge. Yet there are two major difficulties inherent in this approach. The first one has been discussed/pointed out by others: one cannot but dangerously over-simplify (and distort) ethical aspirations if one allows observed behaviour to be their sole determinant.[17] The biggest problem with the IRL method, however, stems from the lack of attention to the fragile and complex processes underlying social and moral changes. Once the latter are taken into account, IRL agents start to look like elephants in a porcelain shop. The next section outlines the dependence of social and moral change processes upon habitual agency. The latter encapsulates a fundamental tension: we might be normative animals, capable of questioning and calling for better ways of doing things, yet we are also creatures of habit. This tension is key to illuminating both the mechanisms underlying social and moral change and the extent to which IRL agents might compromise them.

III. Habit Acquisition, Habit Reversal and Socio-moral Change

A. Habit Acquisition

Whether it be repeated movement, posture or frame of thought, habit requires repetition. In the pattern shaped by this repetition, at some point a habit is formed. Because diminished awareness of the pattern underlying a habit is key to its emergence, it is difficult to identify a precise moment in time when a habit is born. This emergence condition need not confine habits to mere conditioned reflexes or Pavlovian automatisms. Habits can be acquired in many ways: intentionally (for instance to foster the realisation of a particular goal) or unintentionally (through learned responses to particular environmental features or contexts). No matter how regular the repetition pattern – I might have gone running every day for the last two weeks – for this regular pattern to become a habit it needs to have momentarily slipped my conscious awareness. My suddenly realising that I am all geared up on the pavement ready to run when I am meant to attend a work meeting in 10 minutes is a sure sign that a habit is born.

What matters is the fact that the process that has led me to be on the pavement ready to run was not 'goal-mediated',[18] to use psychologists' jargon: I did not have to remind myself of my fitness goals, willing myself to go running. These goals were internalised, and a set of automatisms led me on the pavement. Of crucial importance is the nature of the automaticity that underlies each habit. Depending on the degree of malleability and availability to conscious awareness, there are many different ways of having a habit, from wholly unconscious, rigid tics to carefully cultivated, goal-adaptable habits.[19]

[17] This point is made much better, and in greater detail, in M Hildebrandt, *Smart Technologies and the End(s) of Law: Novel Entanglements of Law and Technology* (Edward Elgar, 2015).

[18] W Wood and D Rünger, 'Psychology of habit' (2016) 67 *Annual Review of Psychology*.

[19] This is developed in greater length in S Delacroix, 'Law and Habits' (2017) 37 *Oxford Journal of Legal Studies* 660.

B. Habit Reversal

While the process of habit formation often eludes conscious awareness from the start, in the vast majority of cases (a key exception is considered below) a habit can be reversed by raising it to awareness.[20] The more deeply ingrained the habit, the more effort is required to reverse it. This effort often has a negative emotional valence. The physical and/or psychological anguish that is frequently associated with habit reversal in humans (in contrast to non-human habits – see below) reflects the role of somatic markers in the process of habit acquisition.

According to Damasio's theory, for each action that is in the process of becoming habitual, the brain accumulates information about the somatic outcomes (what bodily sensations are associated with that action) and encapsulates that information into an intuitive 'marker' that is subsequently activated (and steers behaviour) in any context relevant to that action. Even those who challenge Damasio's somatic marker theory readily concede the essential role played by bodily sensations in the formation – and reversal – of habits. The latter, habit reversal process can be painful (smoking cessation is the easiest example) and/or utterly disorienting: Proust for instance compares the effect of certain novels to 'temporary bereavements, abolishing habit [of thought, in this case]'.[21]

Habit reversal can also prove impossible. This is most obviously the case when a habit answers a physiological or biological need. Just like we may have developed a habit of walking close to walls or hedges as a way of coping with dramatic gushes of wind, a plant may have a habit of growing on a particular side of the house, no matter how sunny the other side might be, or how much pruning that plant endures on its favoured side of the house. To reverse the habit of that plant would necessitate the modification of this plant's biological needs and vulnerabilities – in short, it would require a different plant. While humans have habits of that sort too (think breathing, sleeping, but also environment-specific adaptations), most of our habits can be reversed, albeit at a psychological and/or physical cost that reflects the extent to which a habit has been internalised.

This relationship between a (human) habit's degree of internalisation and the 'cost' of its reversal turns out to be central to what is best described as the unavoidable asymmetry between humans and 'algorithmic machines' when it comes to the mechanisms underlying socio-moral changes. Just like intentionally acquired human habits are often driven by efficiency concerns, those same concerns can lead to algorithm-optimisation strategies that support the idea that there are such things as 'algorithmic habits'. To make an algorithm run more efficiently, it is indeed standard practice to 'profile', that is, to look at which parts of the software are going fast or slow and store underlying calculations for certain tasks. In a dynamic environment, where the heuristics that are relied on to determine whether such underlying calculations are still valid, over-optimisation

[20] Some habitual patterns can remain persistently out of reach of conscious awareness. N Levy and T Bayne, 'Doing without deliberation: automatism, automaticity, and moral accountability' (2004) 16 *Int Rev Psychiatry* 209 highlight the continuum that leads from 'automatistic' processes all the way to automatic action that is informed by and controlled by deliberative agency.

[21] M Proust, *In Search of Lost Time, vol 5* (Vintage, 1996) 642.

will compromise performance: just as over-reliance on habits will compromise human performance. Yet the algorithm-human analogy when it comes to habit only goes so far. Its limits become evident when one considers the cost of habit reversal.

Unlike the reversal of human habits, the cost of reversing algorithmic habits comes down to mere efficiency losses. In the absence of somatic markers associated with the internalisation process, algorithmic systems are unlikely to ever experience the process necessary to habit reversal in a 'bereavement-like' fashion. Even if one day computers were to be endowed with both conscious awareness[22] and a body that experiences both physical and psychological pain, this experience of pain would have to be intrinsically linked to the process of memory formation if computers were to experience habit reversal in a way that is vaguely comparable to that of humans. Independently of the feasibility of the above, it is difficult to come up with plausible reasons why anybody would want to fashion computers in such a way. Today the idea of 'simulating' the pain associated with habit reversal by triggering some kind of electrical short-circuit every time a repeated pattern needs to be reversed would be downright silly. In the rather fanciful, super-evolved and anthropocentric computing scenario described above, the pain involved may not be simulated anymore, but it is just as unlikely to be constructive.

C. Ethical Agency and Socio-Moral change

Now, some might want to ask: why is this difference in the way humans and algorithmic systems experience habit reversal at all important? The short answer is that this experience of habit reversal shapes socio-moral change. Without a sophisticated understanding of the mechanisms underlying habit reversal, one can only get a set of observations about what socio-moral changes have taken place over what time frame, possibly venturing hypothetical links between likely trigger factors and those changes. In short, one can only get an external understanding of socio-moral change.

The long way of explaining the significance of habit reversal – and one's experience thereof – starts by pointing out that without habits, we would be perpetually clueless. Habits not only shape and determine our sense of self, they are also at the root of our understanding of the world, both as it is and as it should be. To concede that habits are at the root of most of our normative stands, determining what values we endorse and what type of life is seen as worth living, goes against the dominant, intellectualist tradition. The latter likes to think that it's our conscious, deliberative self that is exclusively in charge – at least when it comes to ethics and morality. We have known for some time that this is not the case. Yet even now that we have extensive evidence suggesting that

[22] Those who claim that one day, as a result of increased computational power and some rather mysterious 'complexity', computers may well wake up to their own existence (M Du Sautoy, *What We Cannot Know: Explorations at the Edge of Knowledge* (HarperCollins UK, 2016)) have yet to specify what distinct 'consciousness enabling' features, if any, such conscious computers would have. R Tallis, *Aping Mankind: Neuromania, Darwinitis and the Misrepresentation of Humanity* (Acumen, 2011) brilliantly exposes the pitfalls (and naivety) of the materialist reductivism that conditions endeavours to 'measure' consciousness or locate its seat in the brain. For the sake of the above – speculative – discussion, one may nevertheless adopt an agnostic or lax understanding of consciousness, according to which computers would develop 'conscious' response patterns based on hyper-personalised anticipation of their users' tasks, say.

culturally acquired habits of evaluation and the intuitions they give rise to have a direct, causal impact on most of our moral judgments,[23] the impact of this intellectualist tradition remains considerable. Studies of habit within political and moral philosophy are still few and far between (even if they have recently seen a resurgence[24]). As a result, we not only have a relatively poor understanding of the mechanisms underlying socio-moral change. The cross-disciplinary importance of what is probably the most difficult question in moral philosophy has also consequently been under-appreciated.

That cross-disciplinary question can be summed up thus: given the way in which our ethical sensitivity is shaped by the environment and conventions within which we grow up, how does anyone find the momentum necessary to stepping back and questioning widely accepted practices? Traditional answers tend to assume the continued possibility of ethical agency. At the centre of elaborate, and often highly abstract theories – Kant's categorical imperative might be the most prominent example – our capacity to not only question but denounce potentially abhorrent habits of thoughts and practices is all too often taken as a given. This continued capacity would be safeguarded by the availability of an external vantage point whence we may impartially assess those habits and practices. Yet the availability of such an external vantage point, safely removed from our fallible practices, can be called into question.[25] As is the idea that our capacity for ethical agency may be deemed a given. That capacity can be lost. Just like a muscle that has gone limp through lack of exercise, ethical agency can be compromised to the point of dying out. Why? Just like there are many ways of acquiring a habit – the majority are acquired unintentionally – there are many ways of having a habit. At one end of the spectrum one finds ways of having a habit that systematically escape conscious awareness; at the other end one may be both conscious of and committed to one's particular habit.

When a habit can be brought to conscious awareness, the crucial question – especially when one considers the continued possibility of ethical agency – is how malleable that habit is. Factors that range from the quality of one's attitude to the characteristics of one's environment can contribute to a degradation in the nature of the automaticity underlying a habit. While the availability to conscious awareness is rarely lost, an agent can much more easily lose her ability to adapt underlying habits in light of the demands of a particular situation. This rigidification can be the result of what Annas describes as a 'lack of aspiration'.[26] It can also proceed from a lack of what may be called 'teleological plasticity': a willingness to reconsider both the pertinence of one's aims, and the adequacy of the habits of thought and action that frame our understanding of those aims (and serve them).

While there are good reasons to think that we are born with such 'teleological plasticity', we are also born with a propensity for both cognitive and normative laziness. Any opportunity to offload cognitive or normative quandaries to systems designed

[23] J Haidt, 'The emotional dog and its rational tail: A social intuitionist approach to moral judgment' in *Reasoning: Studies of Human Inference and its Foundations* (Cambridge University Press; US, 2008).

[24] C Carlisle, *On Habit* (Routledge, 2014); T Bennett and others, 'Habit and Habituation: Governance and the Social' (2013) 19 *Body & Society* 3l; V Colapietro, 'Doing – and Undoing – the Done Thing: Dewey and Bourdieu on Habituation, Agency, and Transformation' (2004) 1 *Contemporary Pragmatism* 65.

[25] This line of questioning has a long intellectual pedigree. 20th century pragmatism – as instantiated in James and Dewey and more recently in Putnam – probably puts forward the most cogent critique of what is sometimes referred to as the 'rationalist' tradition.

[26] Annas, *Intelligent Virtue*.

to simplify our practical reasoning tends to be[27] met with relief. If the effect of such offloading were limited to punctual respite from cognitive and normative overload, the impact of such systems could be unambiguously positive. Yet alongside this positive, liberating aspect, one must also consider the potential compromising of our readiness to flex our normative muscles. In other words, one must consider the potential compromising of ethical agency through the rigidification of the habits of thought and action that shape our ethical sensibility.

D. Inherently Risky? The 'Moral Holidays' Facilitated by Legal and Automated Systems

Both legal systems and automated systems designed for morally loaded contexts can be said to aim to 'simplify our practical reasoning', albeit in different ways. In the legal domain, Hart once noted that one of the defining features of established legal orders is that they can be sustained on the basis of official acceptance alone, thanks to their institutional structure.[28] Because of this structure, an established legal system may be particularly conducive to a society that is 'deplorably sheeplike' – and where the sheep might all end up 'in the slaughterhouse'.[29] Because the design of those automated systems meant to be deployed in morally loaded contexts (see Section II) does not currently require any more active engagement on the part of the population than 'established' legal systems, the 'moral risk'[30] inherent in legal systems is no less pertinent for such automated systems. If anything, that risk may be greater, given the well-documented effects of so-called 'automation bias'.[31]

To understand the nature of the 'moral risk' which legal and automated systems have in common, one needs to explain how the extended 'moral holidays'[32] prompted by dwindling active engagement increase the odds of a slaughter house ending (or a no less scary Wall-E-[33] scenario). Key to this explanation is the following proposition: our

[27] As with any trend, there are important exceptions: Sunstein for instance refers to the notion of 'norm entrepreneurs' in CR Sunstein, *How Change Happens* (Mit Press, 2019).

[28] This is further developed in Delacroix, 'Law and Habits'.

[29] Hart, *The Concept of Law*.

[30] Green, 'Positivism and the Inseparability of Law and Morals'.

[31] Skitka, Mosier and Burdick, 'Does automation bias decision-making?'; LJ Skitka, K Mosier and MD Burdick, 'Accountability and automation bias' (2000) 52 *International Journal of Human-Computer Studies* 701.

[32] This concept of 'moral holidays' is borrowed from W James, 'Pragmatism: a new name for some old ways of thinking' in *Pragmatism and Other Writings* (Penguin Classics 2000). The following passage highlights its relationship to what James calls 'absolutism', or what I refer to as a 'final' understanding of ethics: '[The world of pluralism] is always vulnerable, for some part may go astray; and having no "eternal" edition of it to draw comfort from, its partisans must always feel to some degree insecure. If, as pluralists, we grant ourselves moral holidays, they can only be provisional breathing-spells, intended to refresh us for the morrow's fight. This forms one permanent inferiority of pluralism from the pragmatic point of view. It has no saving message for incurably sick souls. Absolutism, among its other messages, has that message [...] That constitutes its chief superiority and is the source of its religious power. That is why, desiring to do it full justice, I valued its aptitude for moral-holiday giving so highly', W James, '"The Absolute and the Strenuous Life"' in *The Meaning of Truth* (Longman Green and Co, 1911).

[33] This is further developed in S Delacroix and M Veale, 'Smart Technologies and Our Sense of Self: The Limitations of Counter-Profiling' in M Hildebrandt and K O'Hara (eds), *Life and the Law in the Era of Data-Driven Agency* (Edward Elgar, 2019).

ability to question and call for better ways of doing things – calling to account a perverted legal system or denouncing deficient automated systems – cannot be preserved through cognitive vigilance alone. The latter is all too conditioned by the habits of thought acquired through immersion in an environment shaped by those systems. Aside from cognitive vigilance, the habits that shape our ethical sensitivity need to have retained a degree of plasticity.

Empirical studies of the factors that contribute to a degradation in the nature of the automaticity underlying habits are still few and far between. Studies of the non-cognitive underpinnings of expertise nevertheless suggest a link between rigidification and increased reliance on efficient, automated processes.[34] That link may result at least in part from the (mostly unwarranted) epistemic confidence and lessened vigilance that stems from reliance on supposedly 'authoritative' systems. Either way, what matters is to be aware of the extent to which reliance on systems designed to simplify our practical reasoning (legal or automated systems) will impact upon the nature and shape of socio-moral change. This impact is double-edged. On the positive side, such systems may provide welcome respite from cognitive and normative overload, hence improving our availability to demands for change. On the negative side, their freeing us from the normative work required to answer the 'how should we [I] live?' question may leave us with the 'atrophied normative muscle scenario',[35] content to tag along and unable to appreciate the very point of engaging with the ethical question.

For some this would be good news. The next section highlights the renewed relevance of long-standing meta-ethical debates about the status of moral values: for those who adopt a 'realist' stand, our lazily endorsing the normative framework promoted by an 'enlightened' agent should be welcomed. Such a realist stance would also be critical of the inverse reinforcement learning methods mentioned in Section II, albeit for different reasons. From such a perspective, the problem with the idea of updating a system's utility function based on observed behaviour consists not such much in its effect on the fragile mechanisms underlying socio-moral change. The problem, instead, may be best referred to as a missed opportunity: why should one 'make do' with our highly fallible, short-sighted grasp of moral rightness if an artificial agent that is not constrained by rigidified habits can show us the way towards moral progress?

[34] Along this line, I Dror emphasises the drawback of experts' increased performance (thanks to 'computationally efficient', automated processes): 'The automaticity that often accompanies the development of expertise can also degrade performance because it introduces different types of slips (Norman, 1981). An expert can make a slip because an uncontrolled automated process has taken place rather than what was actually needed, which may result in expert errors (Reason, 1979, 1990). The lack of conscious awareness and monitoring, as well as lack of control, bring about rigidity and minimise mindfulness (Langer, 1989). Expert performance many times requires flexibility and creativity, but with automaticity it is reduced (if not eliminated altogether), resulting in degradation of expert performance (eg Frensch and Sternberg, 1989)'. I E Dror, 'The paradox of human expertise: why experts get it wrong' in N Kapur (ed), *The Paradoxical Brain* (Cambridge University Press, 2011) 7230 (loc.).

[35] When thinking of atrophied moral muscles etc., the image I associate with this comes from the film *Wall-E*, depicting ballooned humans each sipping their smoothie while watching a movie on a floating cushion: due to lack of exercise, they are simply unable to stand up and have become utterly dependent on some automated entertainment structure.

IV. The Impact of Moral Realism and Perfectionism

For those who entertain the idea that a final answer to the 'How should I [we] live?' question is not only available in principle, but desirable, the prospect of developing some superintelligence on whose superior cognitive capacities we could rely on 'to figure out just which actions fit [what is morally right] is extremely attractive':[36]

> The idea is that we humans have an imperfect understanding of what is right and wrong, and perhaps an even poorer understanding of how the concept of moral rightness is to be philosophically analyzed: but a superintelligence could understand these things better.[37]

The notion that there is a concept of 'moral rightness' whose contours do not depend in any way on our all too human, fallible, short-sighted nature has a long pedigree in the history of moral philosophy (its roots can be found in Plato). On this account, all we need to rescue us from our persistent moral failings is a once-and-for-all source of enlightenment. A superintelligence that does not share in any of our shortcomings – including our propensity to habit rigidification – could provide precisely that, and more (it might also figure out a way to motivate us to act according to 'moral rightness'). There is neither room nor need, on this account, for any 'mechanism for moral change': life's circumstances might change, but 'moral rightness' does not … Or does it?

The tradition that questions the extent to which one may meaningfully speak of 'moral rightness' independently of the kind of creatures we are (itself a work in progress) is almost as old as Plato – its roots can be traced back to Aristotle's moral psychology. The tricky part, on this account, is to avoid throwing the baby out with the bathwater: there is a crucial difference between asserting the dependency of moral rightness upon who we are and a relativist 'anything goes'. Many have fallen for the mistake of assuming that without moral realism there is no ethical objectivity to be had.[38] Bostrom has the merit of explicitly articulating this assumption when he states:

> What if we are not sure whether moral realism is true? We could still attempt the [Moral Rightness] proposal […] we could stipulate that if the AI estimates with a sufficient probability that there are no suitable non-relative truths about moral rightness, then it should revert to implementing coherent extrapolated volition[39] instead, or simply shut itself down.[40]

Suppose the AI were indeed to shut itself down. What would it leave us with? We'd still be trying to find our way around the world, generally aiming for better (rather

[36] N Bostrom, *Superintelligence: Paths, Dangers, Strategies* (Oxford University Press, 2014).

[37] ibid.

[38] Mackie's 'error theory' has been influential in legal (and moral) theory: JL Mackie, *Ethics: Inventing Right and Wrong* (Penguin Books, 1990) and is indirectly referred to by Bostrom, *Superintelligence: Paths, Dangers, Strategies*. H Putnam, *Ethics Without Ontology* (Harvard University Press 2004) exposes the extent to which this assumption reflects a Cartesian dualism according to which there is only one sort of objectivity, that of the natural sciences.

[39] E Yudkowsky, *Coherent Extrapolated Volition* (2004) defines our 'coherent extrapolated volition' (which a superintelligence would be relied on to figure out, and implement) thus: 'Our coherent extrapolated volition is our wish if we knew more, thought faster, were more the people we wished we were, had grown up farther together; where the extrapolation converges rather than diverges, where our wishes cohere rather than interfere; extrapolated as we wish that extrapolated, interpreted as we wish that interpreted'.

[40] Bostrom, *Superintelligence: Paths, Dangers, Strategies*.

than worse) ways of living together. Rather than dismiss as 'lacking in objectivity' the rich background of norms that informs our ongoing ethical efforts, a (non-reductive) naturalism[41] starts from precisely such 'contingent' normative practices. Eminently fallible, our answers to the 'How should I [we] live?' question cannot but be constantly changing, just as human nature evolves as we learn to live together. In such a dynamic normative context, the process through which we engage with the ethical question matters at least as much as the answer itself, for that process renews the background of normative practices that informs others' ethical judgement.

Now imagine that, at some point in the future, a superintelligence is somehow developed along the lines considered by Bostrom. Whether it is supposed to have 'cracked' moral rightness for us or relies instead on our 'extrapolated' wish – that 'if we were more the people we wished we were, superintelligence wouldn't fool around.[42] It would set us on the path to 'righteousness', like it or not. Even if it were to find a palatable way of imposing what may otherwise appear to us as morally alien and abhorrent (hence avoiding potential 'human override' procedures), in its bid to achieve moral perfection it may well end up depriving us from the possibility of living ethical lives. The systematic offloading of the normative work[43] required to answer the 'how should we [I] live?' question to an AI may indeed leave us incapable of appreciating the very point of engaging with such a question. Thus the cost of moral perfectionism (and AI-enabled normative laziness) may turn out to be the end of ethics: we might be normative animals, but without regular exercise, our moral muscles will just wither away, leaving us unable to consider alternative, better ways of living together.

Of course we need not adhere to the 'final' understanding of moral values referred to earlier. What would an autonomous system meant for morally loaded contexts look like, if we start from the opposite, 'ethics as a work in progress' conception? Such a system would have to start from somewhere. Even if – and this is an ideal, 'sci-fi' scenario at the moment – that system were to learn to value things sufficiently slowly and progressively as to mimic the human process of growing up, it is unclear whether such a system could be said to be capable of experiencing habits – and their reversal – in a way that is comparable to humans (see Section III).[44] This likely asymmetry in the mechanisms underlying moral change in humans v machines (whether one adopts a realist

[41] Whatever else it is, naturalism involves at least one key commitment. Its rejection of any dualist metaphysics involves a claim that 'there is no unbridgeable space between what happens in that [natural] order and any other order in heaven or earth, including the order of our own minds: Simon Blackburn, 'Normativity a la mode' (2001) 5 *Journal of Ethics: An International Philosophical Review* 139. Hence the challenge which any naturalism must address consists in understanding how the demands we typically associate with morality may be understood as outgrowths of our animal (rather than noumenal, or god-like etc.) nature. A non-reductive naturalism rejects both non-naturalism and any kind of naturalism that confines 'the natural' to that which is the result of elementary, material forces (as opposed to human forces). Such a restrictive understanding of nature inevitably throws into sharp focus the ontological and epistemological precariousness of the man-made. This is discussed in greater detail in Delacroix, 'Law and Habits'.

[42] Yudkowsky, *Coherent Extrapolated Volition*.

[43] Bostrom's characterisation of this work in purely cognitive terms reflects his robust realist meta-ethical premises.

[44] This would depend on the kind of effort required on the part of such system to shake off any 'habituated' pattern of behaviour (or thought). If there is a qualitative difference between the effort required to overcome such patterns and the processing effort concomitant with just any other task, then we might ask ourselves if that system has indeed developed a habit. For the reasons outlined in Section II, I remain sceptical about the extent to which automated systems may do so.

understanding of moral values or not) entails normative questions about the desirability of – putative – autonomous artificial agents.

V. Questioning the Desirability of Autonomous Artificial Moral Agents

Who wouldn't be fascinated by the prospect of being able to engineer creatures designed to overcome human frailties and limitations – including not only our biases and incurable short-sightedness, but also our very limited ability to store and process data? It is not difficult to explain our captivation for the debate surrounding the possibility of developing fully autonomous artificial agents that are capable of acting and thinking 'like us' (a debate which Turing[45] launched almost 70 years ago). Because many identify our normative inclinations as a peculiarly human trait – most of us are not content with the world 'as it is', and keep wondering how it could be made better – normative agency has become a sort of 'yardstick'. If we can develop artificial agents that are capable of thinking 'normatively', then we'll have cracked the challenge set by Turing in the 1950's: we'll have created creatures that are truly 'like us'. Or so the story goes.

This story can be challenged on several grounds. Section III outlined one of these grounds when it unpacked the fundamental asymmetry in humans 'v machines' experience of change. This asymmetry should be enough to dispel the 'artificial moral agents like us' fantasy. If, eventually, we do develop artificial agents – or systems – that are capable of autonomous moral agency, they will evolve along a radically different trajectory from our habit-dependent ways. Aside from calling into question the 'Godlike fantasy' that underlies much of the so-called 'moral Turing test (MTT)' literature,[46] this

[45] AM Turing, 'Computing machinery and intelligence' (1950) 59 *Mind* 433.

[46] To bring home the roots of the debate about artificial moral agency, some speak of the 'moral Turing Test': 'A moral Turing test (MTT) might similarly be proposed to bypass disagreements about ethical standards by restricting the standard Turing test to conversations about morality. If human interrogators cannot identify the machine at above chance accuracy, then the machine is, on this criterion, a moral agent': C Allen, G Varner and J Zinser, 'Prolegomena to any future artificial moral agent' (2000) 12 *Journal of Experimental & Theoretical Artificial Intelligence* 251. Allen et al. acknowledge that there are some obstacles inherent in this test being used a benchmark for the development of artificial moral agents: aside from the fact that the moral standards relevant to such agents may have to be more demanding than those that apply to us, moral agency can't all be a matter of the reasons one gives (but one could tweak the test to allow for comparisons of actions between human and artificial moral agent). M Scheutz and T Arnold, 'Against the Moral Turing Test: Accountable Design and the Moral Reasoning of Autonomous Systems' (2016) 18 *Ethics and Information Technology* 103 go further, and highlight, among the problems inherent the MTT, the fact that the MTT 'if it carries enough similarity to the original Turing test to deserve that name, ultimately and unavoidably rests on imitation as a criterion for moral performance. In turn, the kind of deceptive responses consistent with imitation, both as a representation of the agent and as a substitute for moral action writ large, undermines a more accountable, systematic design approach to autonomous systems'. I would go further still, and emphasise what a bizarre understanding of moral agency the MTT conveys: unlike thinking (which was the focus of the original Turing test), moral agency is not a predicate for which we lack some essential criteria. All humans think (bar marginal cases). But do all humans exercise their moral agency? No. It is certainly a peculiarly human trait that we are capable of moral agency. When we do exercise that capability, we deploy it in myriad different ways. Can we lose that capability? Yes. In fact, in the 'endless moral holidays' scenario I have described earlier, one could envisage a reversed 'moral Turing Test', whereby a computer is asked to 'blindly' interrogate a human and a computer in a bid to determine which is which: they might find that test much easier than humans do.

asymmetric trajectory argument highlights the importance of much more pragmatic questions: how do we design systems that foster rather than compromise the 'normative muscles' mentioned in Section III?

Once one rejects the assumption that ethical agency can be taken as a given,[47] whatever dreams one may have had of developing 'autonomous' artificial agents quickly give way to much more pragmatic endeavours to build human-computer interactions that are apt at dispelling moral torpor. From such a perspective, systems that place (and retain) end-users within the learning loop (this approach is sometimes referred to as 'interactive machine learning'[48] or 'IML'[49]) seem particularly promising. An explicit requirement to keep monitoring the result of the learning process, combined with a demand for regular input on the part of end-users, has the potential to not only improve the system's learning performance; it might also keep moral torpor at bay by encouraging an 'ethical feedback loop' that carves a continuous, active role on the part of whichever professional community the system is designed for. The latter feedback may allow for some dynamic process of adaptation to the changing values of end-users, thus addressing the issue related to the dynamics of moral change addressed in Section II while avoiding the 'moral muscle atrophy' problem discussed in Section III.

VI. Conclusion

One cannot discuss the possibility of developing autonomous systems meant for morally loaded contexts (whether they be legal or not) without taking on board the fact that we humans do keep changing our moral stances (Section II). For those who believe in the possibility and desirability of a 'final' answer to ethics, that fact merely reflects our all too fallible and fickle nature. From that perspective, the prospect of somehow being able to rely on a system's superior cognitive prowess to figure it all out for us, once and for all, is a boon that ought to be met with enthusiasm. From the 'ethics as a work in progress' perspective, by contrast, such a prospect can only be met with scepticism at best (or alarm at worst).

[47] Or the realist take on ethical agency, according to which this agency is mostly a matter of correctly implementing or translating norms or values that are wholly independent of human attitudes or constructs.

[48] There does not seem to be much published in this 'interactive machine learning' area recently, aside from some research focusing on the challenges raised by multiple people interacting with machine learning systems: 'An important opportunity exists to investigate how crowds of people might collaboratively drive interactive machine learning systems, potentially scaling up the impact of such systems. […] in understanding how we can coordinate the efforts of multiple people interacting with machine learning systems.' S Amershi and others, *Power to the People: The Role of Humans in Interactive Machine Learning* (Association for the Advancement of Artificial Intelligence, 2014).

[49] 'Although humans are an integral part of the learning process (the provide labels, rankings etc.), traditional machine learning systems used in these applications are agnostic to the fact that inputs/outputs are from/for humans. In contrast, interactive machine learning places end-users in the learning loop (end users is an integral part of the learning process), observing the result of learning and providing input meant to improve the learning outcome. Canonical applications of IML include scenarios involving humans interacting with robots to teach them to perform certain tasks, humans helping virtual agents play computer games by giving them feedback on their performance.' Wallach, Wendell and C Allen, *Moral Machines: Teaching Robots Right from Wrong* (Oxford University Press, 2008).

Whether it is met with enthusiasm or scepticism, the ambition to construct autonomous systems meant for morally loaded contexts comes with a hazard that is seldom considered: put lazy normative animals – that's us – together with systems to which we may offload the task of figuring out the 'how should I [we] live?' question, and what you get are endless moral holidays, and lazy animals tout court. Our capacity for normative reflection – querying how the world could be made better, rather than 'sitting on it – is all too often taken for granted. What if that capacity can be lost through lack of normative exercise? What if we enjoy the comforts of automated, simplified practical reasoning a bit too much, a bit too long? What was meant to be a 'moral holiday' may turn out to be a condition which we are unable to get out of, for want of being able to mobilise moral muscles that have become atrophied through lack of exercise.

The prospect of AI-enabled, extensive moral holidays may sound like too exotic a possibility to worry about its effects on our capacity for normative agency, let alone law as a system too often seen as only marginally affected by socio-moral changes. The latter assumption is more easily questioned than the former, which was the focus of this paper. To understand the extent to which normative agency can be compromised, and the effects of such compromising on the processes that lead to socio-moral change, one needs to grasp the dual role of habit on such processes. Depending on the nature of their underlying automaticity, habits may condition and enable our normative stances, just as they may compromise them.

This paper's foray into the agency conditions underlying the continued possibility of socio-moral change is meant to flag a methodological problem that has so far been overlooked by computer scientists and lawyers alike. To truly take on board the challenges raised by our evolving socio-moral stances is not just a case of developing systems that are capable of dynamically (and intelligently[50]) updating their 'utility function' in light of perceived changes. One also needs to consider the effect those very systems will have on the processes that lead to such changes. In the absence of a radical shift in the design choices that preside over the way those systems call for interaction with us, lazy normative animals, that effect will be dramatic, to the point of possibly undermining the very possibility of human-triggered change.

[50] As discussed in Section II, discussing the potential of IRL methods, adaptation based on mere observed behaviour is unlikely to be intelligent enough.

8

Punishing Artificial Intelligence: Legal Fiction or Science Fiction

RYAN ABBOTT AND ALEX SARCH*

The possibility of directly criminally punishing AI is receiving increased attention by the popular press and legal scholars alike.[1] Perhaps the best-known defender of punishing AI is Gabriel Hallevy. He contends that '[w]hen an AI entity establishes all elements of a specific offense, both external and internal, there is no reason to prevent imposition of criminal liability upon it for that offense'.[2] In his view, '[i]f all of its specific requirements are met, criminal liability may be imposed upon any entity – human, corporate or AI entity'.[3] Drawing on the analogy to corporations,[4] Hallevy asserts that 'AI entities are taking larger and larger parts in human activities, as do corporations', and he concludes that 'there is no substantive legal difference between the idea of criminal liability imposed on corporations and on AI entities'.[5] 'Modern times', he contends, 'warrant modern legal measures'.[6] More recently, Ying Hu has subjected the idea of criminal liability for AI to philosophical scrutiny and made a case 'for imposing criminal liability on a type of robot that is likely to emerge in the future', insofar as they may employ morally sensitive decision-making algorithms.[7] Her arguments likewise draw heavily on the analogy to corporate criminal liability.[8]

* University of Surrey. This chapter was adapted from Ryan Abbott and Alexander Sarch, 'Punishing Artificial Intelligence: Legal Fiction or Science Fiction' [2019] *UC Davis Law Review* 323.

[1] See eg G Hallevy, 'The Punishibility of Artificial Intelligence Technology' in *Liability for Crimes Involving Artificial Intelligence Systems* (Springer, 2015) 185–29; JKC Kingston, 'Artificial Intelligence and Legal Liability' in M Bramer and M Petridis (eds), *Research and Development in Intelligent Systems XXXIII Incorporating Applications and Innovations in Intelligent Systems XXIV* (Springer, 2016) 269, arxiv.org/pdf/1802.07782.pdf; C Mulligan, 'Revenge Against Robots' (2018) 69 *S.C. L. Rev.* 579, 580; J Wale and D Yuratich, 'Robot Law: What Happens If Intelligent Machines Commit Crimes?' (*Conversation*, 1 July 2015), theconversation.com/robot-law-what-happens-if-intelligent-machines-commit-crimes-44058.

[2] G Hallevy, 'The Criminal Liability of Artificial Intelligence Entities – From Science Fiction to Legal Social Control' (2010) 4 *Akron Intell. Prop. J.* 171, 191.

[3] ibid, 199.

[4] ibid, 200.

[5] ibid, 200–01.

[6] ibid, 199.

[7] Y Hu, 'Robot Criminals' (2019) 52 *Mich. J.L. Reform* 487, 531; see also ibid, 490.

[8] See Y Hu, 'Robot Criminal Liability Revisited' in J Soo Yoon, S Hoon Han and S Jo Ahn (eds), *Dangerous Ideas in Law* (Bobmunsa, 2018) 494, 497–98.

In contrast to AI punishment expansionists like Hallevy and Hu, sceptics might be inclined to write off the idea of punishing AI from the start as conceptual confusion – akin to hitting one's computer when it crashes. If AI is just a machine, then surely the fundamental concepts of the criminal law like culpability – a 'guilty mind' that is characterised by insufficient regard for legally protected values[9] – would be misplaced. One might think the whole idea of punishing AI can be easily dispensed with as inconsistent with basic criminal law principles.

The idea of punishing AI is due for fresh consideration. This chapter takes a measured look at the proposal, informed by theory and practice alike. We argue punishment of AI cannot be categorically ruled out. Harm caused by a sophisticated AI may be more than a mere accident where no wrongdoing is implicated. Some AI-generated harms may stem from difficult-to-reduce behaviours of an autonomous system, whose actions resemble those of other subjects of the criminal law, especially corporations. These harms may be irreducible where, for a variety of reasons, they are not directly attributable to the activity of a particular person or persons.[10] Corporations similarly can directly face criminal charges when their defective procedures generate condemnable harms[11] – particularly in scenarios where structural problems in corporate systems and processes are difficult to reduce to the wrongful actions of individuals.[12]

It is necessary to do the difficult pragmatic work of thinking through the theoretical costs and benefits of AI punishment, how it could be implemented into criminal law doctrine, and to consider the alternatives. Our primary focus is not what form AI punishment would take, which could directly target AIs through censure, deactivation, or reprogramming, or could involve negative outcomes directed at natural persons or companies involved in the use or creation of AI.[13] Rather, our focus is the prior question of whether the doctrinal and theoretical commitments of the criminal law can be reconciled with criminal liability for AI.

Our inquiry focuses on the strongest case for punishing AI: scenarios where crimes are functionally committed by machines and there is no identifiable person who has acted with criminal culpability. We call these Hard AI Crimes. This can occur when no person has acted with criminal culpability, or when it is not practicably defensible to reduce an AI's behaviour to bad actors. There could be general deterrent and expressive benefits from imposing criminal liability on AI in such scenarios. Moreover, the most important negative, retributivist-style limitations that apply to persons, need not prohibit AI punishment. On the other hand, there may be costs associated with AI punishment: conceptual confusion, expressive costs, spillover, and rights creep. In the end, our conclusion is this: while a coherent theoretical case can be made for punishing AI, it is not ultimately justified in light of the less disruptive alternatives that can provide substantially the same benefits.

[9] A Sarch, 'Who Cares What You Think? Criminal Culpability and the Irrelevance of Unmanifested Mental States' (2017) 36 *L. & Phil.* 707, 709.

[10] See Section IIB below.

[11] See Model Penal Code § 2.07 (Am. Law Inst. 1962).

[12] See WS Laufer, 'Corporate Bodies and Guilty Minds' (1994) 43 *Emory L.J.* 647, 664–68.

[13] See Hu, n 7 above, 529–30.

This chapter proceeds as follows. Section I provides a brief background of AI and 'AI crime. It then provides a framework for justifying punishment that considers affirmative benefits, negative limitations, and feasible alternatives. Section II considers potential benefits to AI punishment, and argues it could provide general deterrence and expressive benefits. Section III examines whether punishment of AI would violate any of the negative limitations on punishment that relate to desert, fairness, and the capacity for culpability. It finds that the most important constraints on punishment, such as requiring a capacity for culpability for it to be appropriately imposed, would not be violated by AI punishment.

Finally, Section IV considers feasible alternatives to AI punishment. It argues the status quo is or will be inadequate for properly addressing AI crime. While direct AI punishment is a solution, this would require problematic changes to criminal law. Alternately, AI crime could be addressed through modest changes to criminal laws applied to individuals together with potentially expanded civil liability. We argue that civil liability is generally preferable to criminal liability for AI activity as it is proportionate to the scope of the current problem and a less significant departure from existing practice with fewer costs. In this way, the chapter aims to map out the possible responses to the problem of harmful AI activity and makes the case for approaching AI punishment with extreme caution.

I. Artificial Intelligence and Punishment

A. Introduction to Artificial Intelligence

We use the term 'AI' to refer to a machine that is capable of completing tasks otherwise typically requiring human cognition.[14] AI only sometimes has the ability to directly act physically, as in the case of a 'robot', but it is not necessary for an AI to directly affect physical activity to cause harm (as the RDS case demonstrates).

A few features of AI are important to highlight. First, AI has the potential to act unpredictably.[15] Some leading AIs rely on machine learning or similar technologies which involve a computer program, initially created by individuals, further developing in response to data without explicit programming.[16] This is one means by which AI can engage in activities its original programmers may not have intended or foreseen.

Secondly, AI has the potential to act unexplainably. It may be possible to determine what an AI has done, but not how or why it acted as it did.[17] This has led to some

[14] AI lacks a standard definition, but its very first definition in 1955 holds up reasonably well: '[T]he artificial intelligence problem is taken to be that of making a machine behave in ways that would be called intelligent if a human were so behaving.' J McCarthy et al., *A Proposal for the Dartmouth Summer Research Project on Artificial Inteligence* (1955), www-formal.stanford.edu/jmc/history/dartmouth/dartmouth.html.

[15] See eg, T Yasseri, 'Never Mind Killer Robots – Even the Good Ones Are Scarily Unpredictable' (*Phys.Org*, 25 August 2017), phys.org/news/2017-08-mind-killer-robots-good-scarily.html.

[16] See eg D Castelvecchi, 'Can We Open the Black Box of AI?' (*Nature*, 5 October 2016), www.nature.com/news/can-we-open-the-black-box-of-ai-1.20731.

[17] See eg Castelvecchi, n 16 above.

AIs being described as 'black box' systems.[18] For instance, an algorithm may refuse a credit application but not be able to articulate why the application was rejected.[19] That is particularly likely in the case of AIs that learn from data, and which may have been exposed to millions or billions of data points.[20] Even if it is theoretically possible to explain an AI outcome, it may be impracticable given the potentially resource intensive nature of such inquiries, and the need to maintain earlier iterative versions of AI and specific data.

Thirdly, AI may act autonomously. For our purposes, that is to say an AI may cause harm without being directly controlled by an individual. Suppose an individual creates an AI to steal financial information by mimicking a bank's website, stealing user information, and posting that information online. While the theft may be entirely reducible to an individual who is using the AI as a tool, the AI may continue to act in harmful ways without further human involvement. It may even be the case that the individual who sets an AI in motion is not able to regain control of the AI, which could be by design.

Of course, it is possible for a conventional machine to perform unpredictably, unexplainably, or autonomously. However, at a minimum, AI is far more likely to exhibit these characteristics, and to exhibit them to a greater extent. Even a sufficient difference in degree along several axes makes AI worth considering as a distinctive phenomenon, possibly meriting novel legal responses.

Finally, general AI, and even super- or ultra-intelligent AI,[21] is different than the sort of self-aware, conscious, sentient AIs that are common in science fiction. The latter sorts of AIs, sometimes referred to as 'strong AI,' are portrayed as having a human-like abilities to cognitively reason and to be morally culpable for their actions.[22] Today, even the prospect of such machines is safely within the realm of science fiction.[23] We will not consider punishment of strong AI.[24]

B. A Framework for Understanding AI Crime

We use the term 'AI crime' as a loose shorthand for cases in which an AI would be criminally liable if a natural person had performed a similar act. Machines have caused harm since ancient times, and robots have caused fatalities since at least the 1970s.[25] Yet AI can differ from conventional machines in a few essential ways that make the direct

[18] ibid.

[19] ibid.

[20] ibid.

[21] See R Abbott, 'Everything Is Obvious' (2019) 66 *UCLA L. Rev.* 2, 23–28.

[22] See J Rodriguez, 'Gödel, Consciousness and the Weak vs. Strong AI Debate' (*Towards Data Sci.*, 23 August 2018), towardsdatascience.com/g%C3%B6del-consciousness-and-the-weak-vs-strong-ai-debate-51e71a9189ca.

[23] See ibid.

[24] If and when such machines come into existence, we will certainly enjoy reading their works on AI criminal liability.

[25] See R Abbott, 'The Reasonable Computer: Disrupting the Paradigm of Tort Liability' (2018) 86 *Geo. Wash. L. Rev.* 1, 8; B Young, 'The First 'Killer Robot' Was Around Back in 1979' (*How Stuff Works*, 9 April 2018), science.howstuffworks.com/first-killer-robot-was-around-back-in-1979.htm.

application of criminal law more worthy of consideration. Specifically, AI can behave in ways that display high degrees of autonomy and irreducibility. In terms of autonomy, AI is capable of acting largely independently of human control. AI can receive sensory input, set targets, assess outcomes against criteria, make decisions and adjust behaviour to increase its likelihood of success – all without being directed by human orders.[26] Reducibility is also critical because if an AI engages in an act that would be criminal for a person and the act is reducible, then there typically will be a person that could be criminally liable.[27] If an AI act is not effectively reducible, there may be no other party that is aptly punished, in which case intuitively criminal activity could occur without the possibility of punishment.

Almost all AI crimes are likely to be reducible. For instance, if an individual develops an AI to hack into a self-driving car to disable vital safety features, that individual has directly committed a crime.[28] If someone strikes another person with a rock, the rock has not committed battery – the individual throwing the rock has. Even where AI behaves autonomously, to the extent that a person uses AI as a tool to commit a crime, and the AI functions foreseeably, the crime involves an identifiable defendant causing the harm. Even when AI causes unforeseeable harm, it may still be reducible – for example, if an individual creates an AI to steal financial information, but a programming error results in the AI shutting down an electrical grid that disrupts hospital care. This is a familiar problem in criminal law.[29] If someone commits a robbery and in so doing injures bystanders in unforeseeable ways (imagine a tripped bank alarm startles the animals in a neighbouring zoo and they break loose and trample pedestrians), criminal law has doctrinal tools by which liability could still be imposed.[30]

Sometimes, however, it may be difficult to reduce AI crime to an individual due to AI autonomy, complexity, or lack of explainability. There are several possible grounds on which criminal law might deem AI crime to be irreducible.[31]

(1) Enforcement Problems: A bad actor is responsible for an AI crime, but the individual cannot be identified by law enforcement. For example, this might be the case where the creator of a computer virus has managed to remain anonymous.[32]
(2) Practical Irreducibility: It would be impractical for legal institutions to seek to reduce the harmful AI conduct to individual human actions, because of the number of people involved, the difficulty in determining how they contributed to the AI's design, or because they were active far away or long ago. Criminal law inquiries do not extend indefinitely for a variety of sound reasons.

[26] See above nn 17–22 and accompanying text.
[27] See Section IVA below.
[28] See JK Gurney, 'Driving into the Unknown: Examining the Crossroads of Criminal Law and Autonomous Vehicles' (2015) 5 *Wake Forest J.L. & Pol'y* 393, 433 (discussing crimes applicable to this scenario).
[29] See Section IV below.
[30] See Section IVA below.
[31] See Section IIIBi below.
[32] The chance of being prosecuted for a cyberattack in the United States is estimated at a mere 0.05% versus 46% for a violent crime. See W Dixon, 'Fighting Cybercrime – What Happens to the Law When the Law Cannot Be Enforced?' (*World Econ. Forum*, 19 February 2019), www.weforum.org/agenda/2019/02/fighting-cybercrime-what-happens-to-the-law-when-the-law-cannot-be-enforced/.

(3) Legal Irreducibility: Even if the law could reduce the AI crime to a set of individual human actions, it may be bad criminal law policy to do so. For example, unjustified risks might not be substantial enough to warrant being criminalised. Perhaps multiple individuals acted carelessly in insubstantial ways, but their acts synergistically led to AI causing significant harm. In such cases, the law might deem the AI's conduct to be irreducible for reasons of criminalisation policy.

We will largely set aside enforcement-based reasons for irreducibility as less interesting from a legal design perspective. Enforcement problems exist without AI. Other forms of irreducibility may exist, such as moral irreducibility, but we will not focus on these here because they are controversial and undertheorised.

Instead, our analysis will focus on what we take to be less controversial forms of irreducibility: those where it is not practically feasible to reduce the harmful AI conduct to human actors, or where the harmful AI conduct was just the result of human misconduct too trivial to penalise. In these instances, AI can be seen as autonomously committing crimes in irreducible ways, where there is no responsible person. This is what we refer to as 'Hard AI Crime' and what we take to provide the strongest case for holding AI criminally liable in its own right.

C. A Mainstream Theory of Punishment

To anchor our analysis, this section introduces a theory of punishment that reflects the broad consensus in the literature.[33] We use the term 'punishment' roughly as defined by HLA Hart in terms of five elements:

(i) It must involve pain or other consequences normally considered unpleasant;
(ii) It must be for an offence against legal rules;
(iii) It must be of an actual or supposed offender for his offence;
(iv) It must be intentionally administered by human beings other than the offender; and
(v) It must be imposed and administered by an authority constituted by a legal system against which the offence is committed.[34]

Punishment is justified only if its affirmative justifications outweigh its costs and it does not otherwise offend applicable negative limitations on punishment. Affirmative justifications are the positive benefits that punishment might produce like harm reduction, increased safety, enhanced well-being, or expressing a commitment to core moral or political values. Such benefits can give reason to criminalise certain types of conduct and impose sanctions on actors who perform those types of acts. Affirmative justifications are distinct from negative limitations on punishment, which are commonly

[33] See generally MN Berman, 'The Justification of Punishment' in A Marmor (ed), *The Routledge Companion to Philosophy of Law* (Routledge, 2012) 141, 144–45 (noting the convergence on this sort of theory of punishment).

[34] HLA Hart, *Punishment and Responsibility: Essays in the Philosophy of Law*, 2nd edn (Oxford University Press, 2008) 4–5.

associated with culpability-focused retributivist views of criminal law. For example, it is widely held to be unjust to punish the innocent – or to punish wrongdoers in excess of what they deserve in virtue of their culpability – even if this would promote aggregate well-being in society.[35] This so-called 'desert constraint' imposes a limitation, grounded in justice, on promoting social welfare through punishment.[36]

The most important affirmative reasons are consequentialist in nature and centre on crime reduction. Punishment can reduce crime several ways. The simplest is incapacitation: when the offender is locked up, he or she is physically limited from committing further crimes while incarcerated.[37] The next and arguably most important way punishment prevents harm is through deterrence – namely by threatening negative consequences for the commission of a crime that give would-be offenders reasons to refrain from prohibited conduct.[38] Deterrence comes in two forms: (i) specific deterrence and (ii) general deterrence. Specific deterrence is the process whereby punishing a specific individual discourages that person from committing more crime in the future.[39] General deterrence occurs when punishing an offender discourages other would-be offenders from committing crimes.[40] It is a matter of punishing an offender in order to 'send a message' to other potential offenders. There can be affirmative benefits to punishing those who qualify for an insanity defence because it may deter sane individuals from committing crimes and attempting to rely on an insanity defence.[41]

These are not the only kinds of consequentialist benefits that can support punishment. Besides incapacitation and deterrence, punishment can reduce harm through rehabilitation of the offender.[42] Insofar as punishment helps the offender to see the error of his or her ways, or training or skills are provided during incarceration, this, too, can help prevent future crimes.

While virtually everyone agrees that the good consequences of preventing crime must be a major part of what justifies punishment,[43] there is more debate about whether retributivist reasons also exist – that is, the value of giving offenders what they deserve.[44] While retributivist reasons for punishment are worth taking seriously, here we assume that the lion's share of the affirmative case in favour of punishment will involve harm reduction and similar desirable consequences.

Besides having affirmative benefits, punishment also should not violate deeply held normative commitments such as justice or fairness. The most important of these

[35] See nn 45–46 below and accompanying text.
[36] ibid.
[37] See A Duff and Z Hoskins, 'Consequentialist Accounts' in E Zalta (ed), *Stanford Encyclopedia of Philosophy* (18 July 2017), plato.stanford.edu/entries/legal-punishment/#PurConPun ('It is commonly suggested that punishment can help to reduce crime by deterring, incapacitatiing [sic], or reforming potential offenders …').
[38] ibid.
[39] See Berman, n 33 above, 145 (discussing types of deterrence).
[40] ibid.
[41] See Hart, n 34 above, 19.
[42] See Berman, n 33 above, 145 (discussing rehabilitation).
[43] See V Tadros, *The Ends of Harm: The Moral Foundations of Criminal Law* (Oxford University Press, 2011) 21.
[44] ibid, 60.

limitations focus on the culpability of those subject to the criminal law. One such limitation on punishment is the desert constraint, which figures into most retributivist views.[45] The desert constraint claims that an offender may not, in justice, be punished in excess of his or her desert. Desert, in turn, is understood mainly in terms of the culpability one incurs in virtue of one's conduct. The main effect of the desert constraint is to rule out punishments that go beyond what is proportionate to one's culpability.[46] Thus, it would be wrong to execute someone for jaywalking even if doing so would ultimately save lives by reducing illegal and dangerous pedestrian crossings.

Besides the desert constraint, criminal law also requires certain prerequisites, such as a capacity for culpability, that defendants must meet in order to be properly subject to punishment. It is a fundamental aim of criminal law to condemn culpable wrongdoing, and it is the default position in criminal law doctrine that punishment may only be properly imposed in response to culpable wrongdoing.[47] Without the requisite capacities of deliberation and agency, an entity is not an appropriate subject for criminal punishment – as can be seen from the fact that lacking such capacities altogether can give rise to an incapacity defence.[48] Thus, capacity for culpability is an eligibility requirement for being aptly subject to regulation by criminal law.

Lastly, for punishment to be justified, it is not enough for it to have affirmative benefits and to be consistent with the negative limitations for punishment. In addition, there cannot be better, feasible alternatives, including doing nothing. This is an obvious point that is built into policy analysis of all kinds.

Thus, determining whether a given punishment is appropriate requires investigation of three questions:

(a) Affirmative Benefits: Are there sufficiently strong affirmative reasons in favour of punishment? This chiefly concerns consequentialist benefits of harm reduction but may also include retributive and expressive benefits.
(b) Negative Limitations: Would punishment be consistent with applicable negative limitations? This primarily concerns culpability-focused principles like the desert constraint as well as basic prerequisites of apt criminal punishment such as capacity for culpability.
c) Feasible Alternatives: Is punishment a better response to the harms or wrongs in question, compared to alternatives like civil liability, regulation, or doing nothing?

In the remainder of this chapter, we will apply this theory to investigate whether the direct punishment of AI is justified. We will begin in Section II with the question

[45] See Berman, n 33 above, 144 (on retributivism, punishment is justified if, but only to the extent that, 'it is deserved or otherwise fitting, right or appropriate, and not [necessarily because of] any good consequences' it may have); See also ibid, 151 (discussing desert-constrained consequentialism).

[46] Negative retributivism is the view that the desert of the offender only prohibits punishing in excess of desert (even if it has good consequences). Positive retributivism says that the offender's desert provides an affirmative reason for punishment.

[47] See Model Penal Code § 1.02(C) (Am. Law Inst. 1962) (declaring that one of the 'general purposes' of the Code is 'to safeguard conduct that is without fault from condemnation as criminal').

[48] See Model Penal Code § 4.01 (outlining the incapacity defence based on mental defect as when a person is unable 'either to appreciate the criminality … of his conduct or to conform [it to] the law').

of Affirmative Benefits, consider Negative Limitations in Section III, then Feasible Alternatives in Section IV.

II. The Affirmative Case

This Section considers the affirmative benefits that might be adduced to support punishing AI. The discussion focuses primarily on consequentialist benefits. Even if retribution can also count in favour of punishment, we assume that such benefits would be less important than consequentialist considerations centering on harm reduction.[49] This Section does not aim to completely canvass the benefits of punishing AI. Instead, it argues that punishing AI could produce at least some significant affirmative benefits.

A. Consequentialist Benefits

Recall that, arguably, the paramount aim of punishment is to reduce harmful criminal activity through deterrence. Thus, a preliminary objection to punishing AI is that it will not produce any affirmative harm-reduction benefits because AI is not deterrable. Peter Asaro argues that 'deterrence only makes sense when moral agents are capable of recognizing the similarity of their potential choices and actions to those of other moral agents who have been punished for the wrong choices and actions – without this … recognition of similarity between and among moral agents, punishment cannot possibly result in deterrence.'[50] The idea is that if AIs cannot detect and respond to criminal law sanctions in a way that renders them deterrable, there would be nothing to affirmatively support punishing AI. It is likely true that AI, as currently operated and envisioned, will not be responsive to punishment, although responsive AI is theoretically possible.

The answer to the undeterrability argument requires distinguishing specific deterrence from general deterrence.[51] Specific deterrence involves incentivising a particular defendant not to commit crimes in the future.[52] By contrast, general deterrence involves incentivising other actors besides the defendant from committing crimes. We must further distinguish two types of general deterrence: deterring others from committing offences of the same type the defendant was convicted of, offence-relative general deterrence, and deterring others from committing crimes in general, unrestricted general deterrence.

Punishing AI could provide general deterrence. Presumably, it will not produce offence-relative general deterrence to other AIs, as such systems are not designed to be sensitive to criminal law prohibitions and sanctions. Nonetheless, AI punishment could produce unrestricted general deterrence. That is to say, direct punishment of AI could

[49] See Tadros, n 43 above, 25–28.

[50] PM Asaro, 'A Body to Kick, but Still No Soul to Damn: Legal Perspectives on Robotics' in P Lin et al. (eds), *Robot Ethics: The Ethical and Social Implications of Robotics* (MIT Press, 2011) 169, 181.

[51] See Hart, n 34 above, 19.

[52] See Berman, n 33 above, 145.

provide unrestricted general deterrence as against the developers, owners, or users of AI and provide incentives for them to avoid creating AIs that cause especially egregious types of harm without excuse or justification. Depending on the penalty associated with punishment, such as destruction of an AI, what Mark Lemley and Brian Casey have termed the 'robot death penalty',[53] punishing AI directly could deprive such developers, owners or users of the financial benefits of the systems. This penalty may thereby incentivise such human parties to modify their behaviour in socially desirable ways. The deterrence effect may be stronger if capitalisation requirements are associated with some forms of AI in the future, or if penalties associated with punishment are passed on to, for example, an AI's owner.

B. Expressive Considerations

Punishment of AI may also have expressive benefits. Expressing condemnation of the harms suffered by the victims of an AI could provide these victims with a sense of satisfaction and vindication. Christina Mulligan has defended the idea that punishing robots can generate victim-satisfaction benefits, arguing that, 'taking revenge against wrongdoing robots, specifically, may be necessary to create psychological satisfaction in those whom robots harm'.[54] On her view, 'robot punishment – or more precisely, revenge against robots – primarily advances … the creation of psychological satisfaction in robots' victims'.[55] Punishment conveys a message of official condemnation that could reaffirm the interests, rights, and ultimately the value of the victims of the harmful AI.[56] This, in turn, could produce an increased sense of security among victims and society in general.

This sort of expressivist argument in favour of punishing AI may seem especially forceful in light of empirical work demonstrating the human tendency to anthropomorphise and attribute mentality to artificial persons like corporations.[57] The same sorts of tendencies are likely to be even more powerful for AI-enabled robots that are specifically designed to seem human enough to elicit emotional responses from humans.[58] In the corporate context, some theorists argue that corporations should be punished because the law should reflect lay perceptions of praise and blame, 'folk morality', or else risk losing its perceived legitimacy.[59] This sort of argument, if it succeeds for corporate punishment, is likely to be even more forceful as applied to punishing AI, which often are deliberately designed to piggy-back on the innate tendency to anthropomorphise.[60]

[53] MA Lemley and B Casey, 'Remedies for Robots' (2019) 86 *U. Chi. L. Rev.* 1311, 1316, 1389–93.

[54] C Mulligan, n 1 above, 580; see D Lewis, 'The Punishment That Leaves Something to Chance' (1989) 18 *Phil. & Pub. Aff.* 53, 54.

[55] Mulligan, n 1 above, 593.

[56] See A Duff, *Answering for Crime – Responsibility and Liability in the Criminal Law* (Hart, 2007) 114; G Binder, 'Victims and the Significance of Causing Harm' (2008) 28 *Pace L. Rev.* 713, 733.

[57] See ME Diamantis, 'Corporate Criminal Minds' (2016) 91 *Notre Dame L. Rev.* 2049, 2078.

[58] See M Scheutz, 'The Inherent Dangers of Unidirectional Emotional Bonds Between Humans and Social Robots', in P Lin et al. (eds), n 50 above, 205–22.

[59] See Diamantis, n 57 above, 2088–89.

[60] See, eg, M Rhodes, 'The Touchy Task of Making Robots Seem Human – But Not Too Human' (*Wired*, 19 January 2017, 7:00 AM), www.wired.com/2017/01/touchy-task-making-robots-seem-human-not-human/.

Were the law to fail to express condemnation of robot-generated harms despite robots being widely perceived as blameworthy (even if this is ultimately a mistaken perception), this could erode the perception of the legitimacy of criminal law. Thus, a number of benefits could be obtained through the expressive function of punishment.

Nonetheless, there are a range of prima facie worries about appealing to expressive benefits like victim satisfaction in order to justify the punishment of AI. First, punishing AI to placate those who want retaliation for AI-generated harms would be akin to giving in to mob justice. Legitimising such reactions could enable populist calls for justice to be pressed more forcefully in the future. The mere fact that punishing AI might be popular would not show the practice to be just. As David Lewis observed, if it is unjust for the population to 'demand blood' in response to seeing harm, then satisfying such demands through the law would itself be unjust – even if 'it might be prudent to ignore justice and do their bidding'.[61] Simply put, the popularity of a practice does not automatically justify it, even if popularity could be relevant to its normative justification. Secondly, punishing AI for expressivist purposes could lead to further bad behaviour that might spill over to the way other humans are treated. Thus, Kate Darling has argued robots should be protected from cruelty in order to reflect moral norms and prevent undesirable human behaviour.[62]

Thirdly, expressing certain messages through punishment may also carry affirmative costs which should not be omitted from the calculus. Punishing AI could send the message that AI is itself an actor on par with a human being, which is responsible and can be held accountable through the criminal justice system. Such a message is concerning, as it could entrench the view that AI has rights to certain kinds of benefits, protections and dignities that could restrict valuable human activities.

In sum, punishing AI may have affirmative benefits. It could result in general deterrence for developers, owners, and users, as well as produce expressive benefits (if also potential costs). Whether these benefits would provide sufficient justification for punishing AI when compared to the feasible alternatives will be discussed in Section IV. Before that, we turn to another kind of threshold question: whether punishing AI violates the culpability-focused negative limitations on punishment.

III. Retributive and Conceptual Limitations

This Section considers retributivist (culpability-focused) limitations on punishment. Subsection A asks whether AI is the right kind of entity to be eligible for punishment – what we call The Eligibility Challenge. Where criminal law's fundamental prerequisites are not satisfied, its sanctions are not legitimately deployed. Subsection B considers two further retributivist objections to the punishment of AI. Finally, subsection C considers the conceptual objection that AI punishment is not actually punishment at all.

[61] Lewis, n 54 above, 54.

[62] See K Darling, 'Extending Legal Protection to Social Robots: The Effects of Anthropomorphism, Empathy, and Violent Behavior Towards Robotic Objects' in R Calo, AM Froomkin and I Kerr (eds), *Robot Law* (Edward Elgar, 2016) 213, 228.

A. The Eligibility Challenge

The Eligibility Challenge is simple to state: AI, like inanimate objects, is not the right kind of thing to be punished. AI lacks mental states and the deliberative capacities needed for culpability, so it cannot be punished without sacrificing the core commitments of the criminal law. The issue is not that AI punishment would be unfair to AI. AIs are not conscious and do not feel (at least in the phenomenal sense),[63] and they do not possess interests or well-being.[64] Therefore, there is no reason to think AI gets the benefit of the protections of the desert constraint, which prohibits punishment in excess of what culpability merits.[65] The Eligibility Challenge does not derive from the desert constraint.

Instead, the Eligibility Challenge, properly construed, comes in one narrow and one broad form. The narrow version is that, as a mere machine, AI lacks mental states and thus cannot fulfill the mental state (mens rea) elements built into most criminal offences. Therefore, convicting AI of crimes requiring a mens rea like intent, knowledge, or recklessness would violate the principle of legality. This principle stems from general rule of law values and holds that it would be contrary to law to convict a defendant of a crime unless it is proved (following applicable procedures and by the operative evidentiary standard) that the defendant satisfied all the elements of the crime.[66] If punishing AI violates the principle of legality, it threatens the rule of law and could weaken the public trust in the criminal law.

The broad form of the challenge holds that because AI lacks the capacity to deliberate and weigh reasons, AI cannot possess broad culpability of the sort that criminal law aims to respond to.[67] A fundamental purpose of the criminal law is to condemn culpable wrongdoing, as it is at least the default position in criminal law doctrine that punishment may be properly imposed only in response to culpable wrongdoing.[68] The capacity for culpable conduct thus is a general prerequisite of criminal law, and failing to meet it would remove the entity in question from the ambit of proper punishment – a fact that is encoded in law, for example, in incapacity defences like infancy and insanity. Thus, the broad version of the Eligibility Challenge holds that because AI lacks the practical reasoning capacities needed for being culpable, AI does not fall within the scope of criminal law. Punishing AI despite its lack of capacity would not only be conceptually confused, but would fail to serve the retributive aims of criminal law – namely, to mark out seriously culpable conduct for the strictest public condemnation.

Here we explore three answers to the Eligibility Challenge.

[63] See DJ Chalmers, 'Facing Up to the Problem of Consciousness' (1995) 2 *J. Consciousness Stud.* 200, 201 (describing phenomenal experiences as those personally felt or experienced).

[64] ibid (discussing the hard problem of consciousness).

[65] See nn 45–46 above and accompanying text.

[66] See DN Husak and CA Callender, 'Wilful Ignorance, Knowledge, and the "Equal Culpability" Thesis: A Study of the Deeper Significance of the Principle of Legality' [1994] *Wis. L. Rev.* 29, 32–33.

[67] See generally D Husak, '"Broad" Culpability and the Retributivist Dream' (2012) 9 *Ohio St. J. Crim. L.* 449, 456–57 (distinguishing narrow culpability as merely mens rea categories from broad culpability, which is the underlying normative defect that criminal law aims to respond to).

[68] See Model Penal Code § 1.02(C) (Am. Law Inst. 1962); see also M Moore, *Placing Blame: A General Theory of the Criminal Law* (Oxford University Press, 1997) 35.

i. Answer 1: Respondeat Superior

The simplest answer to the Eligibility Challenge has been deployed with respect to corporations. Corporations are artificial entities that might also be thought ineligible for punishment because they are incapable of being culpable in their own right.[69] However, even if corporations cannot literally satisfy mens rea elements, criminal law has developed doctrines that allow culpable mental states to be imputed to corporations. The most important such doctrinal tool is respondeat superior, which allows mental states possessed by an agent of the corporation to be imputed to the corporation itself provided that the agent was acting within the scope of her employment and in furtherance of corporate interests.[70] Some jurisdictions also tack on further requirements.[71] Since imputation principles of this kind are well-understood and legally accepted, thus letting actors guide their behaviour accordingly, respondeat superior makes it possible for corporations to be convicted of crimes without violating the principle of legality.

It may be more difficult to use respondeat superior to answer the Eligibility Challenge for AI than for corporations – at least in cases of Hard AI Crime. Unlike a corporation, which is literally composed of the humans acting on its behalf, an AI is not guaranteed to come with a ready supply of identifiable human actors whose mental states can be imputed. This is not to say there will not also be many garden-variety cases where an AI does have a clear group of human developers. Most AI applications are likely to fall within this category and so respondeat superior would at least be a partial route to making AI eligible for punishment. Of course, in many of these cases when there are identifiable people whose mental states could be imputed to the AI – such as developers or owners who intended the AI to cause harm – criminal law will already have tools at its disposal to impose liability on these culpable human actors. In these cases, there is less likely to be a need to impose direct AI criminal liability.

Thus, while respondeat superior can help mitigate the Eligibility Challenge for AI punishment in many cases, this is unlikely to be an adequate response in cases of Hard AI Crime.

ii. Answer 2: Strict Liability

A different sort of response to the Eligibility Challenge is to look for ways to punish AI despite its lack of a culpable mental state. That is not to simply reach for a consequentialist justification[72] of the conceptual confusion or inaptness involved in applying criminal law to AI. Within criminal law, we take this to be a justificatory strategy of last resort – especially given the blunt form of consequentialism it relies on. Rather, what is needed is a method of cautiously extending criminal law to AI that would not entail weighty violations of the principle of legality.

[69] See eg, AW Alschuler, 'Two Ways to Think About the Punishment of Corporations' (2009) 46 *Am. Crim. L. Rev.* 1359, 1367–69 (arguing against corporate punishment).

[70] See AS Kircher, 'Corporate Criminal Liability Versus Corporate Securities Fraud Liability: Analyzing the Divergence in Standards of Culpability' (2009) 46 *Am. Crim. L. Rev.* 157, 157.

[71] See Model Penal Code § 2.07(1)(C) (Am. Law Inst. 1962) (adopting respondeat superior but restricting it to the mental states of high corporate officials).

[72] See nn 37–39 above (explaining the idea of justifying punishment based on its good consequences).

One way to do this would be to establish a range of new strict liability offences specifically for AI crimes – that is, offences that an AI could commit even in the absence of any mens rea like intent to cause harm, knowledge of an inculpatory fact, reckless disregard of a risk or negligent unawareness of a risk. In this sense, the AI would be subject to liability without 'fault'. This would permit punishment of AI in the absence of mental states. Accordingly, strict liability offences may be one familiar route by which to impose criminal liability on an AI without sacrificing the principle of legality.

Many legal scholars are highly critical of strict liability offences. For example, as Duff argues, strict criminal liability amounts to unjustly punishing the innocent:

> That is why we should object so strongly …: the reason is not (only) that people are then subjected to the prospect of material burdens that they had no fair opportunity to avoid, but that they are unjustly portrayed and censured as wrongdoers, or that their conduct is unjustly portrayed and condemned as wrong.[73]

Yet this normative objection applies with greatest force to persons. The same injustice does not threaten strict criminal liability offences for AI because AI does not obviously enjoy the protections of the desert constraint (which prohibits punishment in excess of culpability).

This strategy is not without problems. Even to be guilty of a strict liability offence, defendants still must satisfy the voluntary act requirement.[74] LaFave's criminal law treatise observes that 'a voluntary act is an absolute requirement for criminal liability'.[75] The Model Penal Code, for example, holds that a 'person is not guilty of an offence unless his liability is based on conduct that includes a voluntary act or the omission to perform an act of which he is physically capable'.[76] Behaviours like reflexes, convulsions or movements that occur unconsciously or while sleeping are expressly ruled out as non-voluntary.[77] To be a voluntary act, 'only bodily movements guided by conscious mental representations count'.[78] If AI cannot have mental states and is incapable of deliberation and reasoning, it is not clear how any of its behaviour can be deemed to be a voluntary act.

There are ways around this problem. The voluntary act requirement might be altered (or outright eliminated) by statute for the proposed class of strict liability offences that only AI can commit. Less dramatically, even within existing criminal codes, it is possible to define certain absolute duties of non-harmfulness that AI defendants would have to comply with or else be guilty by omission of a strict liability offence. The Model Penal Code states that an offence cannot be based on an omission to act unless the omission is expressly recognised by statute or 'a duty to perform the omitted act is otherwise imposed by law'.[79] A statutory amendment imposing affirmative duties on AI to avoid

[73] A Duff, *The Realm of Criminal Law* (Oxford University Press, 2018) 19.

[74] See WR LaFave, *Substantive Criminal Law*, 3rd edn (Thomsom Reuters, 2018) § 6.1(c) ('[C]riminal liability requires that the activity in question be voluntary.').

[75] ibid.

[76] Model Penal Code § 2.01(1) (Am. Law Inst. 1962).

[77] See ibid, § 2.01(2).

[78] G Yaffe, 'The Voluntary Act Requirement' in A Marmor (ed), *The Routledge Companion to Philosophy of Law* (Routledge, 2012) 174, 175.

[79] Model Penal Code § 2.01(3) (Am. Law Inst. 1962).

certain kinds of harmful conduct is all it would take to enable an AI to be strictly liable on an omission theory.

Of course, this may also carry costs. Given that one central aim of criminal law is usually taken to be responding to and condemning culpable conduct, if AI is punished on a strict liability basis, this might risk diluting the public meaning and value of the criminal law.[80] That is, it threatens to undermine the expressive benefits that supposedly help justify punishing AI in the first place.[81] This is another potential cost to punishing AI that must be weighed against its benefits.

iii. *Answer 3: A Framework for Direct Mens Rea Analysis for AI*

The last answer is the most speculative. A framework for directly defining mens rea terms for AI – analogous to those possessed by natural persons – could be crafted. This could require an investigation of AI behaviour at the programming level and offer a set of rules that courts could apply to determine when an AI possessed a particular mens rea – like intent, knowledge or recklessness – or at the very least, when such a mens rea could be legally constructed. We do not attempt here to formulate necessary and sufficient conditions for an AI mens rea, but rather to sketch some possible approaches.

Work in the Philosophy of Action characterising the functional role of human intentions could be extended to AI. On Bratman's well-known account,[82] actors who intend (ie, act with the purpose) to bring about an outcome 'guide [their] conduct in the direction of causing' that outcome.[83] This means that in the normal case, 'one [who intends an outcome] is prepared to make adjustments in what one is doing in response to indications of one's success or failure in promoting' that outcome.[84] Suppose an actor is driving with the intention to hit a pedestrian. In that case, if the actor detects that conditions have changed so that behavioural adjustments are required to make this outcome more likely, then the actor will be disposed to make these adjustments. Moreover, actors with this intention will be disposed to monitor the circumstances to find ways to increase the likelihood of the desired outcome. Merely foreseeing the outcome, but not intending it, does not similarly entail that one will guide one's behaviour in these ways to promote the outcome in question (ie, make it more likely).

This conception of intention could be applied to AI. One conceivable way to argue that an AI (say, an autonomous vehicle) had the intention (purpose) to cause an outcome (to harm a pedestrian) would be to ask whether the AI was guiding its behaviour so as to make this outcome more likely (relative to its background probability of occurring). Is the AI monitoring conditions around it to identify ways to make this outcome more likely? Is the AI then disposed to make these behavioural adjustments to make the outcome more likely (either as a goal in itself or as a means to accomplishing

[80] See Duff, n 73 above, 19–20.
[81] See Section IIB above.
[82] See ME Bratman, 'What Is Intention?' in PR Cohen et al. (eds), *Intentions in Communications* (MIT Press, 1990) 15, 23–27; see also A Sarch, 'Double Effect and the Criminal Law' (2015) 11 *Crim. L. & Phil.* 453, 467–68.
[83] Bratman, n 82 above, 26.
[84] ibid.

another goal)? If so, then the AI plausibly may be said to have the purpose of causing that outcome. Carrying out this sort of inquiry will of course require extensive and technically challenging expert testimony regarding the nature of the programming – and could thus be prohibitively difficult or expensive. But it does not seem impossible in principle, even if difficult questions remain.

Similar strategies may be developed for arguing that an AI possessed other mens rea, like knowledge. For example, on dispositional theories, knowledge may be attributed to an actor when the actor has a sufficiently robust set of dispositions pertaining to the truth of the proposition – such as the disposition to assent to the proposition if queried, to express surprise and update one's plans if the proposition is revealed to be false, to behave consistently with the truth of the proposition, or to depend on it carrying out one's plans.[85] In criminal law, knowledge is defined as practical certainty.[86] Thus, if we extend the above dispositional theory to AI, there is an argument for saying an AI knows a fact, F, if the AI displays a sufficiently robust set of dispositions associated with the truth of F – such as the disposition to respond affirmatively if queried (in a relevant way) whether F is practically certain to be true, or the disposition to revise plans upon receiving information showing that F is not practically certain, or the disposition to behave as if F is practically certain to be true. If enough of these dispositions are proven, then knowledge that F could be attributed to the AI.[87] One could take a similar approach to arguing that recklessness is present as well, as this requires only awareness that a substantial risk of harm is present – that is, knowledge that the risk has a mid-level probability of materialising (below practical certainty).[88]

Although much more needs to be said for such arguments to be workable, it at least suggests that it may be possible to develop a set of legal doctrines by which courts could deem AIs to possess the mens rea elements of crimes.

B. Further Retributivist Challenges: Reducibility

Even assuming AI is eligible for punishment, two further culpability-focused challenges remain. The most important concerns the reducibility of any putative AI culpability. (One might also worry about spillover of AI punishment onto innocent people nearby, such as owners and operators, but this is not a bar for punishing corporations, so we set this spillover challenge aside in what follows.)

[85] See E Schwitzgebel, 'Belief' in E Zalta (ed), *Stanford Encyclopedia of Philosophy* (3 June 2019), plato.stanford.edu/entries/belief/#1.2 ('Traditional dispositional views of belief assert that for someone to believe some proposition P is for [her] to possess [relevant] behavioral dispositions pertaining to P. Often cited is the disposition to assent to utterances of P in [appropriate] circumstances .... Other relevant dispositions might include the disposition to exhibit surprise should the falsity of P [become] evident, the disposition to assent to Q if ... shown that P implies Q, and the disposition to depend on P's truth in [acting]. [More generally, this amounts to] being disposed to act as though P is the case.').

[86] See Model Penal Code § 2.02(2)(B) (Am. Law Inst. 1962) (defining knowledge as practical certainty).

[87] See E Schwitzgebel, 'In-Between Believing' (2001) 51 *Phil. Q.* 76 (defending this approach to determining when to attribute beliefs to humans).

[88] See Model Penal Code § 2.02(2)(C) (Am. Law Inst. 1962) (defining recklessness).

The reducibility worry is this: One might object that there is never a genuine need to punish AI because any time an AI seems criminally culpable in its own right, this culpability can always be reduced to that of nearby human actors – such as developers, owners, and users. The law could target the relevant culpable human actors instead.

This objection has been raised against corporate punishment too. Sceptics argue that corporate culpability is always fully reducible to culpable actions of individual humans.[89] Any time a corporation does something intuitively culpable – like causing a harmful oil spill through insufficient safety procedures – this can always be fully reduced to the culpability of the individuals involved: the person carrying out the safety checks, the designers of the safety protocols, or the managers pushing employees to cut corners in search of savings. For any case offered to demonstrate the irreducibility of corporate culpability, a sceptic may creatively find additional wrongdoing by other individual actors further afield or in the past to account for the apparent corporate culpability.[90]

This worry may not be as acute for AI as it is for corporations. AI seems able to behave in ways that are more autonomous from its developers than corporations are from their members. Corporations, after all, are simply composed of their agents (albeit organised in particular structures). Also, AI may sometimes behave in ways that are less predictable and foreseeable than corporate conduct.

Nonetheless, there are ways to block the reducibility worry for corporate culpability as well as AI. The simplest response is to recall that it is legal culpability we are concerned with, not moral blameworthiness. Specifically, it would be bad policy for criminal law to always allow any putative corporate criminal culpability to be reduced to individual criminal liability. This would require criminalising very minute portions of individual misconduct – momentary lapses of attention, the failure to perceive emerging problems that are difficult to notice, tiny bits of carelessness, mistakes in prioritising time and resources, not being sufficiently critical of groupthink, and so on. Mature legal systems should not criminalise infinitely fine-grained forms of misconduct, but rather should focus on broader and more serious categories of directly harmful misconduct that can be straightforwardly defined, identified, and prosecuted. Criminalising all such small failures – and allowing law enforcement to investigate them – would be invasive and threatening to values like autonomy and the freedom of expression and association.[91] It would also increase the risk of abuse of process. Instead, we should expect 'culpability deficits'[92] in any well-designed system of criminal law, and this in turn creates a genuine need for corporate criminal culpability as an irreducible concept.

Similar reasoning could be employed for AI culpability. There is reason to think it would be a bad system that encouraged law enforcement and prosecutors to, any time an AI causes harm, invasively delve into the internal activities of the organisations developing the AI in search of minute individual misconduct – perhaps even

[89] See eg A Szigeti, 'Are Individualist Accounts of Collective Responsibility Morally Deficient?' in A Konzelmann Ziv and H Bernhard Schmid (eds), *Institutions, Emotions, and Group Agents: Contributions to Social Ontology* (Springer, 2014) 329.

[90] C List and P Pettit, *Group Agency: The Possibility, Design, and Status of Corporate Agents* (Oxford University Press, 2011) 158.

[91] See Hart, n 34 above, 1–27.

[92] See List and Pettit, n 90 above, 165.

the slightest negligence or failure to plan for highly unlikely exigencies. The criminal justice system would be disturbingly invasive if it had to create a sufficient number of individual offences to ensure that any potential AI culpability can always be fully reduced to individual crimes. Hence, where AI is concerned, we do not think the Reducibility Challenge – at least as applied to legal culpability – imposes a categorical bar to punishing AI.

C. Not Really Punishment?

We end this Part by considering another challenge to AI punishment – that AI cannot be truly 'punished'. Even if an AI was convicted of an offence and subject to negative treatment – such as being reprogrammed or terminated – this may not be punishment under our working definition. On Hart's definition introduced in Section IC, punishment 'must involve pain or other consequences normally considered unpleasant'.[93] However, AI cannot experience things as being painful or unpleasant.[94]

A first response is to argue that AI punishment does satisfy Hart's definition because prong (i) requires only that the treatment in question must be 'normally considered unpleasant' – not that it be actually unpleasant or unwelcome to a convicted party. This is what allows Hart's definition to accommodate people who, for idiosyncratic reasons, do not experience their sentence as unpleasant or bad and to still regard this as punishment. The mere fact that a convicted party overtly wants to be imprisoned, like the Norwegian mass murderer Anders Bering Breivik, who wanted to be convicted and imprisoned to further his political agenda, does not mean that doing so pursuant to a conviction ceases to be punishment.[95] Something similar might be said for AI as well as defendants who may be physically or psychologically incapable of experiencing pain or distress. Having one's actions frozen or being terminated really are the kind of thing that can 'normally be considered unpleasant'.

This response can be developed further. Why might punishment need to be normally regarded as unpleasant? Why does it still seem to be punishment, for example, to imprison a person who in no way experiences it as unpleasant or unwelcome? The answer may be that defendants can have interests that are objectively set back even when they do not experience these setbacks as painful, unpleasant or unwelcome.[96] Some philosophers argue it is intrinsically bad for humans to have their physical or agential capacities diminished – regardless of whether this is perceived as negative.[97] If correct,

[93] See Hart, n 34 above, 4.

[94] See n 53 above and accompanying text. See DJ Chalmers, 'Facing Up to the Problem of Consciousness' (1995) 2 *J. CONSCIOUSNESS STUD.* 200, 216 (distinguishing intellectual capacities from phenomenal consciousness).

[95] See 'Anders Breivik Found Sane: The Verdict Explained' *Telegraph* (24 August 2012), www.telegraph.co.uk/news/worldnews/europe/norway/9496641/Anders-Breivik-found-sane-the-verdict-explained.html.

[96] See G Fletcher, 'A Fresh Start for the Objective-List Theory of Well-Being' (2013) 25 *Utilitas* 206, 206 (defending objective theories of well-being from familiar objections); A Sarch, 'Multi-Component Theories of Well-Being and Their Structure' (2012) 93 *Pac. Phil. Q.* 439, 439–41 (defending a partially objective theory of well-being, where both subjective experiences and some objective components can impact well-being).

[97] See E Harman, 'Harming as Causing Harm' in MA Roberts and DT Wasserman (eds), *Harming Future Persons* (Springer, 2009) 137, 139.

this suggests that what prong (i) of Hart's definition, properly understood, requires is that punishment involve events that objectively set back interests, and negative subjective experiences are merely one way to objectively set back interests.

Can an AI have interests that are capable of being set back? AI is not conscious in the phenomenal sense of having subjective experiences and thus cannot experience anything as painful or unpleasant.[98] However, one could maintain that being incapacitated or destroyed is objectively bad for AIs even if the AI does not experience it as such – in much the same way that things like nutrition, reproduction, or physical damage can be said to be good or bad for biological entities like plants or animals.[99] Some philosophers argue that it is in virtue of something's having identifiable functions that things can be good or bad for it. Most notably, Philippa Foot defends this sort of view (tracing it to Aristotle) when she argues that the members of a given species can be evaluated as excellent or defective by reference to the functions that are built into its characteristic form of life.[100] From this evaluation as flourishing or defective, facts about what is good or bad for the entity can be derived. Thus, if having interests in this broad, function-based sense is all that is required for punishment to be sensible, then perhaps AI fits the bill. AIs also have a range of functions – characteristic patterns of behaviour needed to continue in good working order and succeed at the tasks it characteristically undertakes. If living organisms can in a thin sense be said to have an interest in survival and reproduction, ultimately in virtue of their biological programming, then arguably an AI following digital programming could have interests in this thin sense as well.

Other philosophers reject this view, however. They insist that only those entities capable of having beliefs and desires, or at least phenomenal experiences such as of pleasure and pain, can truly be said to have full-blooded interests that are normatively important. Legal philosopher Joel Feinberg took the capacity for cognition as the touchstone full-blooded interests, that is as a precondition for having things really be good or bad for us.[101] He notes 'we do say that certain conditions are "good" or "bad" for plants' (unlike rocks), but he denies that they have full-blooded interests.[102] Although 'Aristotle and Aquinas took trees [and plants] to have their own "natural ends"' (in much the same sense that Foot argues for), Feinberg denies plants 'the status of beings with interests of their own' because 'an interest, however the concept is finally to be analyzed, presupposes at least rudimentary cognitive equipment'.[103] Interests, he thinks, 'are compounded out of desires and aims, both of which presuppose something like belief, or cognitive awareness'.[104] Since AIs are not literally capable of cognitive awareness (notwithstanding the discussion in Section IIIA of how mens rea might be imputed), they cannot literally possess full-blooded interests of the kind Feinberg has in mind.[105]

[98] See n 53 above and accompanying text.
[99] See P Foot, *Natural Goodness* (Clarendon Press, 2001).
[100] ibid, 33.
[101] See J Feinberg, 'The Rights of Animals and Unborn Generations' in W Blackstone (ed), *Philosophy and Environmental Crisis* (University of Georgia Press, 1974) 43, 49–51.
[102] ibid, 51.
[103] ibid, 52.
[104] ibid.
[105] See ibid, 49–50.

Thus, the pertinent question for present purposes is what sense of interest an entity must have for it to be intelligible to talk of punishing it – the thin sense of function-based interests of the kind Foot defended or the full-blooded, attitudinally-based interests Feinberg had in mind? This is ultimately a question about how to understand prong (i) of Hart's definition of punishment, and one that goes to the heart of what criminal law is and what it is for. We simply note that this is one possible way of defending the idea of AI punishment as sensible.

A final type of reply, always available as a last resort, is that even if applying criminal law to AIs is conceptually confused, it could still have good consequences to call it punishment when AIs are convicted. This would not be to defend AI punishment from within existing criminal law principles, but to suggest that there are consequentialist reasons to depart from them.

IV. Feasible Alternatives

We have argued that punishing AI could have benefits and that doing so would not be ruled out by the negative limitations and retributive preconditions of punishment. But this does not yet show the punishment of AI to be justified. Doing so requires addressing the third main question in our theory of punishment: Would the benefits of punishing AI outweigh the costs, and would punishment be better than alternative solutions? These solutions might involve doing nothing, or relying on civil liability and regulatory responses, perhaps together with less radical or disruptive changes to criminal laws that target individuals.

Ideally a cost-benefit analysis would involve more than identifying various costs and benefits, and would include quantitative analysis. If only a single Hard AI Crime is committed each decade, there would be far less need to address an AI criminal gap than if Hard AI Crime was a daily occurrence. The absence of evidence suggesting that Hard AI Crime is common counsels against taking potentially more costly actions now, but this balance may change as technological advances result in more AI activity.

Subsection A focuses on Hard AI Crime, and finds that existing criminal law coverage will likely fall short. Subsection B argues that AI punishment has significant costs that suggest alternative approaches may be preferable. In subsections C and D, we map out some alternative approaches to managing AI crime. In particular, we examine moderate expansions of criminal law as well as tools available within civil law, and we argue that they have the resources to provide preferable solutions to the problem of Hard AI Crime.

A. First Alternative: The Status Quo

In considering the alternatives to direct punishment of AI, we begin with asking whether it would be preferable to simply do nothing. This section answers that existing criminal law falls short: there is an AI criminal gap. The impact of this gap is an empirical question we do not attempt to answer here.

i. What the AI Criminal Gap is Not: Reducible Harmful Conduct by AI

We begin by setting aside something that will not much concern us: cases where responsibility for harmful AI conduct is fully reducible to the culpable conduct of individual human actors. A clear example would be one where a hacker uses AI to steal funds from individual bank accounts. There is no need to punish AI in such cases, because existing criminal offences, like fraud or computer crimes, are sufficient to respond to this type of behaviour.[106]

Even if additional computer-related offences must be created to adequately deter novel crimes implemented with the use of AI, criminal law has further familiar tools at its disposal, involving individual-focused crimes, which provide other avenues of criminal liability when AI causes foreseeable harms. For example, as Hallevy observes, cases of this sort could possibly be prosecuted under an innocent 'agency model' (assuming AI can sensibly be treated as meeting the preconditions of an innocent agent, even if not of a fully criminally responsible agent in its own right).[107] Under the innocent agency doctrine, criminal liability attaches to a person who acts through an agent who lacks capacity – such as a child or someone with an insanity defence. For instance, if an adult uses a five-year-old child to deliver illegal drugs, the adult rather than the child would generally be criminally liable.[108] This could be analogous to a person programming a sophisticated AI to break the law: the person has liability for intentionally causing the AI to bring about the external elements of the offence.

This doctrine requires intent (or at least the knowledge) that the innocent agent will cause the prohibited result in question.[109] This means that in cases where someone does not intend or foresee that the AI system being used will cause harm, the innocent agency model does not provide a route to liability. In such cases, one could instead appeal to recklessness or negligence liability if AI creates a foreseeable risk of a prohibited harm.[110] For example, if the developers or users of AI foresee a substantial and unjustified risk that an AI will cause the death of a person, these human actors could be convicted of reckless homicide.[111] If such a risk was merely reasonably foreseeable (but not foreseen), then lower forms of homicide liability would be available.[112] Similar forms of recklessness or negligence liability could be adopted where the AI's designers or users actually foresaw, or should have foreseen, a substantial and unjustified risk of other kinds of harms as well – such as theft or property damage.[113]

Hallevy also discusses this form of criminal liability for AI-generated harms, calling it the 'natural and probable consequences model' of liability.[114] This is an odd

[106] See 18 U.S.C. § 1030(a)(1) –(7) (2019) (defining offences such as computer trespass and computer fraud); id. § 1343 (wire fraud statute).
[107] Hallevy, n 2 above,179–81.
[108] See SH Kadish, 'Complicity, Cause and Blame: A Study in the Interpretation of Doctrine' [1985] 73 *Calif. L. Rev.* 323, 372–73.
[109] See P Alldridge, 'The Doctrine of Innocent Agency' (1990) 2 *Crim. L. F.* 45, 70–71; 18 U.S.C. § 2(b) (2019).
[110] See Model Penal Code § 2.02(2)(C)-(D) (Am. Law Inst. 1962).
[111] See ibid, § 210.3(a).
[112] See ibid, § 210.4.
[113] See eg ibid, § 220.1(2); id. § 220.2(2); ibid, § 220.3.
[114] See Hallevy, n 2 above,181–84.

label, however, since the natural and probable consequences doctrine generally applies only when the defendant is already an accomplice to – that is, intended – the crime of another. More specifically, the 'natural and probable consequences' rule provides that where A intentionally aided B's underlying crime C1 (say theft), but then B also goes on to commit a different crime C2 (say murder), then A would be guilty of C2 as well, provided that C2 was reasonably foreseeable.[115]

Despite his choice of label, Hallevy seems alive to this complication and correctly observes that there are two ways in which negligence liability could apply to AI-generated harms that are reasonably foreseeable. He writes:

> the natural-probable-consequence liability model [applied] to the programmer or user differ in two different types of factual cases. The first type of case is when the programmers or users were negligent while programming or using the AI entity but had no criminal intent to commit any offense. The second type of case is when the programmers or users programmed or used the AI entity knowingly and willfully in order to commit one offense via the AI entity, but the AI entity deviated from the plan and committed some other offense, in addition to or instead of the planned offense.[116]

In either sort of scenario, there would be a straightforward basis for applying existing criminal law doctrines to impose criminal liability on the programmers or users of an AI that causes reasonably foreseeable harms. Thus, no AI criminal gap exists here.

A slightly harder scenario involves reducible harms by AI that are not foreseeable, but this is still something criminal law has tools to deal with. Imagine hackers use an AI to drain a fund of currency, but this ends up unforeseeably shutting down an electrical grid which results in widespread harm. The hackers are already guilty of something – namely, the theft of currency (if they succeed) or the attempt to do so (if they failed). Therefore, our question here is whether the hackers can be convicted of any further crime in virtue of their causing harm through their AI unforeseeably taking down an electrical grid.

At first sight, it might seem that the hackers would be in the clear for the electrical grid. They could argue that they did not proximately cause those particular harms. Crimes like manslaughter or property damage carry a proximate cause requirement under which the prohibited harm must at least be a reasonably foreseeable type of consequence of the conduct that the actors intentionally carried out.[117] But in this case, taking down the electrical grid and causing physical harm to human victims were assumed to be entirely unforeseeable even to a reasonable actor in the defendant's shoes.

Criminal law has tools to deal with this kind of scenario, too. This comes in the form of so-called constructive liability crimes. These are crimes that consist of a base crime which require mens rea, but where there then is a further result element as to which no mens rea is required. Felony murder is a classic example.[118] Suppose one breaks into a

[115] The rule holds that the aider and abettor 'of an initial crime … is also liable for any consequent crime committed by the principal, even if he or she did not abet the second crime, as long as the consequent crime is a natural and probable consequence of the first crime'. B Weiss, 'What Were They Thinking?: The Mental States of the Aider and Abettor and the Causer Under Federal Law' (2002) 70 *Fordham L. Rev.* 1341, 1424.

[116] Hallevy, n 2 above, 184.

[117] See, eg, Model Penal Code § 2.03 (Am. Law Inst. 1962).

[118] See WR LaFave, n 74 above, § 14.5.

home one believes to be empty in order to steal artwork. Thus, one commits the base crime of burglary.[119] However, suppose further that the home turns out not to be empty, and the burglar startles the homeowner who has a heart attack and dies. This could make the burglar guilty of felony murder.[120] This is a constructive liability crime because the liability for murder is constructed out of the base offence (burglary) plus causing the death (even where this is unforeseeable). According to one prominent theory of constructive liability crimes, they are normatively justifiable when the base crime in question (burglary) typically carries at least the risk of the same general type of harm as the constructive liability element at issue (death).[121]

This tool, if extended to the AI case, provides a familiar way to hold the hackers criminally liable for unforeseeably taking down the electrical grid and causing physical harm to human victims.

It may be beneficial to create a new constructive liability crime that takes a criminal act like the attempt to steal currency using AI as the base offence, and then taking the further harm to the electrical grid, or other property or physical harm, as the constructive liability element, which requires no mens rea (not even negligence) in order to be guilty of the more serious crime. This constructive liability offence, in a slogan, could be called Causing Harm Through Criminal Uses of AI.

New crimes could be created to the extent there are not already existing crimes that fit this mold. Indeed, in the present example, one might think there are already some available constructive liability crimes. Perhaps felony murder fits the bill insofar as attempting to steal currency may be a felony, and the conduct subsequently caused fatalities. However, this tool would be of no avail in respect to the property damage caused. This is why a new crime like Causing Harm Through Criminal Uses of AI may be necessary. In any case, no AI criminal gap is present here because criminal law has familiar tools available for dealing with unforeseeable harms of this kind.

ii. *What the AI Criminal Gap Is: Irreducible Criminal Conduct by AI*

Consider a case of irreducible AI crime inspired by RDS. Suppose an AI is designed to purchase class materials for incoming Harvard students, but, through being trained on data from online student discussions regarding engineering projects, the AI unforeseeably 'learns' to purchase radioactive material on the dark web and has it shipped to student housing. Suppose the programmers of this 'Harvard Automated Shopper' did nothing criminal in designing the system and in fact had entirely lawful aims. Nonetheless, despite the reasonable care taken by the programmers – and subsequent purchasers and users of the AI (ie, Harvard) – the AI caused student deaths.

In this hypothetical, there are no upstream actors who could be held criminally liable. Innocent agency is blocked as a mode of liability because the programmers, users and developers of the AI did not have the intent or foresight that any prohibited or harmful

[119] See Model Penal Code § 221.1 (defining burglary).
[120] See WR LaFave, n 74 above, § 14.5.
[121] See AP Simester, 'Is Strict Liability Always Wrong?' in AP Simester (ed), *Appraising Strict Liability* (Oxford University Press, 2005) 21, 45.

results would ensue – as is required for innocent agency to be available.[122] Moreover, in the case of RDS, if the risk of the AI purchasing the designer drugs was not reasonably foreseeable, then criminal negligence would also be blocked. Finally, constructive liability is not available in cases of this sort because there is no 'base crime' – no underlying culpable conduct by the programmers and users of the AI – out of which their liability for the unforeseeable harms the AI causes could be constructed.

One could imagine various attempts to extend existing criminal law tools to provide criminal liability for developers or users. Most obviously, new negligence crimes could be added for developers that make it a crime to develop systems that foreseeably could produce a risk of any serious harm or unlawful consequence, even if a specific risk was unforeseeable. The trouble is that this does not seem to amount to individually culpable conduct, particularly as all activities and technologies involve some risks of some harm. This expansion of criminal law would stifle innovation and beneficial commercial activities. Indeed, if there were such a crime, most of the early developers of the internet would likely be guilty of it.

B. The Costs of Punishing AI

Earlier, we discussed some of the potential costs of AI punishment, including conceptual confusion, expressive costs, and spillover. Even aside from these, punishment of AI would entail serious practical challenges as well as substantial changes to criminal law. Begin with a practical challenge: the mens rea analysis.[123] For individuals, the mens rea analysis is generally how culpability is assessed. Causing a given harm with a higher mens rea like intent is usually seen as more culpable than causing the same harm with a lower mens rea like recklessness or negligence.[124] But how do we make sense of the question of mens rea for AI?

Section III considered this problem, and argued that for some AI, as for corporations, the mental state of an AI's developer, owner, or user could be imputed under something like the respondeat superior doctrine. But for cases of Hard AI Crime that is not straightforwardly reduced to human conduct – particularly where the harm is unforeseeable to designers and there is no upstream human conduct that is seriously unreasonable to be found – nothing like respondeat superior would be appropriate. Some other approach to AI mens rea would be required.

A regime of strict liability offences could be defined for AI crimes. However, this would require a legislative work-around so that AI are deemed capable of satisfying the voluntary act requirement, applicable to all crimes.[125] This would require major revisions to the criminal law and a great deal of concerted legislative effort. It is far from an off-the-shelf solution. Alternately, a new legal fiction of AI mens rea, vaguely analogous

[122] See nn 107–08 above and accompanying text.

[123] See Section IIIA above (discussing the Eligibility Challenge).

[124] See KW Simons, 'Should the Model Penal Code's Mens Rea Provisions Be Amended?' (2003) 1 *Ohio St. J. Crim. L.* 179, 195–96.

[125] See nn 75–80 above and accompanying text.

to human mens rea, could be developed, but this too is not currently a workable solution. This approach could require expert testimony to enable courts to consider in detail how the relevant AI functioned to assess whether it was able to consider legally relevant values and interests but did not weight them sufficiently, and whether the program has the relevant behavioural dispositions associated with mens rea-like intention or knowledge. In Section IIIA, we tentatively sketched several types of argument that courts might use to find various mental states to be present in an AI. However, much more theoretical and technical work is required and we do not regard this as a first best option.

Mens rea, and similar challenges related to the voluntary act requirement, are only some of the practical problems to be solved in order to make AI punishment workable. For instance, there may be enforcement problems with punishing an AI on a blockchain. Such AIs might be particularly difficult to effectively combat or deactivate.

Even assuming the practical issues are resolved, punishing AI would still require major changes to criminal law. Legal personality is necessary to charge and convict an AI of a crime, and conferring legal personhood on AIs would create a whole new mode of criminal liability, much the way that corporate criminal liability constitutes a new such mode beyond individual criminal liability.[126] There are problems with implementing such a significant reform.

Over the years, there have been many proposals for extending some kind of legal personality to AI. Perhaps most famously, a 2017 report by the European Parliament called on the European Commission to create a legislative instrument to deal with 'civil liability for damage caused by robots'.[127] It further requested the Commission to consider 'a specific legal status for robots', and 'possibly applying electronic personality' as one solution to tort liability.[128] Even in such a speculative and tentative form this proposal proved highly controversial.[129]

Full-fledged legal personality for AIs equivalent to that afforded to natural persons, with all the legal rights that natural persons enjoy, would clearly be inappropriate. To take a banal example, allowing AI to vote would undermine democracy, given the ease with which anyone looking to determine the outcome of an election could create AIs to vote for a particular candidate. However, legal personality comes in many flavours, even for natural persons such as children who lack certain rights and obligations enjoyed by adults. Crucially, no artificial person enjoys all of the same rights and obligations as a natural person.[130] The best-known class of artificial persons, corporations, have long enjoyed only a limited set of rights and obligations that allows them to sue and be sued, enter contracts, incur debt, own property, and be convicted of crimes.[131]

[126] See TJ Bernard, 'The Historical Development of Corporate Criminal Liability' (1984) 22 *Criminology* 3, 3–4.

[127] European Parliament, Report with Recommendations to the Commission on Civil Law Rules on Robotics, (27 January 2017) 16, www.europarl.europa.eu/doceo/document/A-8-2017-0005_EN.pdf.

[128] See ibid, 18.

[129] For instance, more than 150 AI 'experts' subsequently sent an open letter to the European Commission warning that, '[f]rom an ethical and legal perspective, creating a legal personality for a robot is inappropriate whatever the legal status model'. Robotics-Openletter.eu, Open Letter to the European Commission Artificial Intelligence and Robotics, www.robotics-openletter.eu/.

[130] See SM Solaiman, 'Legal Personality of Robots, Corporations, Idols and Chimpanzees: A Quest for Legitimacy' (2017) 25 *Artificial Intelligence & L.* 155.

[131] E Arcelia Quintana Adriano, 'The Natural Person, Legal Entity or Juridical Person and Juridical Personality' (2015) 4 *Penn. St. J.L. & Int'l Aff.* 363, 365.

However, they do not receive protection under constitutional provisions, such as the Fourteenth Amendment's Equal Protection Clause, and they cannot bear arms, run for or hold public office, marry, or enjoy other fundamental rights that natural persons do. Thus, granting legal personality to AI to allow it to be punished would not require AI to receive the rights afforded to natural persons, or even those afforded to corporations. AI legal personality could consist solely of obligations.

Even so, any sort of legal personhood for AIs would be a dramatic legal change that could prove problematic.[132] Perhaps most worryingly, conferring legal personality on AI may lead to rights creep, or the tendency for an increasing number of rights to arise over time.[133] Even if AIs are given few or no rights initially when they are first granted legal personhood, they may gradually acquire rights as time progresses. Granting legal personhood to AI may thus be an important step down a slippery slope. In a 1933 Supreme Court opinion, for instance, Justice Brandeis warned about rights creep, and argued that granting corporations an excess of rights could allow them to dominate the State.[134] Eighty years after that decision, Justice Brandeis' concerns were prescient in light of recent Supreme Court jurisprudence such as *Citizens United v Federal Election Commission* and *Burwell v Hobby Lobby Stores*, which significantly expanded the rights extended to corporations.[135] Such rights, for corporations and AI, can restrict valuable human activities and freedoms.

C. Second Alternative: Minimally Extending Criminal Law

There are alternatives to direct AI punishment besides doing nothing. The problem of Hard AI Crime would more reasonably be addressed through minimal extensions of existing criminal law. The most obvious would be to define new crimes for individuals. Just as the Computer Fraud and Abuse Act criminalises gaining unauthorised access or information using personal computers,[136] an AI Abuse Act could criminalise malicious or reckless uses of AI. In addition, such an Act might criminalise the failure to responsibly design, deploy, test, train, and monitor the AIs one contributed to developing. These new crimes would target individual conduct that is culpable along familiar dimensions, so they may be of limited utility with regard to Hard AI Crimes that do not reduce to culpable actors. Accordingly, a different way to expand the criminal law seems needed to address Hard AI Crime.

In cases of Hard AI Crime, a designated adjacent person could be punished who would not otherwise be directly criminally liable – what we call a Responsible Person. This could involve new forms of criminal negligence for failing to discharge statutory duties (perhaps relying on strict criminal liability) in order to make a person liable in cases of Hard AI Crime. It could be a requirement for anyone creating or using an AI to

[132] See Hu, n 7 above, 527–28.

[133] See DS Law and M Versteeg, 'The Evolution and Ideology of Global Constitutionalism' (2011) 99 *Calif. L. Rev.* 1163, 1170.

[134] See *Louis K. Liggett Co. v Lee* (1933) 288 U.S. 517, 549 (Brandeis, J., dissenting).

[135] See *Citizens United v Fed. Election Comm'n* (2010) 558 U.S. 310, 341; *Burwell v Hobby Lobby Stores, Inc.* (2014), 573 U.S. 682.

[136] See 18 U.S.C. § 1030(a) (2019).

ex ante register a Responsible Person for the AI.[137] It could be a crime to design or operate AI capable of causing harm without designating a Responsible Person.[138] This would be akin to the offence of driving without a licence.[139] The registration system might be maintained by a federal agency. However, a registration scheme is problematic because it is difficult to distinguish between AI capable of criminal activity and AI not capable of criminal activity, especially when dealing with unforeseeable criminal activity. Even simple and innocuous seeming AI could end up causing serious harm. Thus, it might be necessary to designate a Responsible Person for any AI. Registration might involve substantial administrative burden and, given the increasing prevalence of AI, the costs associated with mandatory registration might outweigh any benefits.

A default rule rather than a registration system might be preferable. The Responsible Person could be the AI's manufacturer or supplier if it is a commercial product. If it is not a commercial product, the Responsible Person could be the AI's owner, developer if no owner exists, or user if no developer can be identified. Even non-commercial AIs are usually owned as property, although that may not always be the case, for instance, with some open source software. Similarly, all AIs have human developers, and in the event an AI autonomously creates another AI, responsibility for the criminal acts of an AI-created AI could reach back to the original AI's owner. In the event an AI's developer cannot be identified, or potentially if there are a large number of developers, again in the case of some open source software, responsibility could attach to an AI's user. However, this would fail to catch the rare, perhaps only hypothetical, case of the non-commercial AI with no owner, no identifiable developer, and no user. To the extent that a non-commercial AI owner, developer, and user working together would prefer a different responsibility arrangement, they might be permitted to agree to a different ex ante selection of the Responsible Person.[140] That might be more likely to occur with sophisticated parties where there is a greater risk of Hard AI Crime. The Responsible Person could even be an artificial person such as a corporation.[141]

It would be possible to impose criminal liability on the Responsible Person directly in the event of Hard AI Crime. For example, if new statutory duties of supervision and care were defined regarding the AI for which the Responsible Person is answerable,

[137] A new criminal offence – akin to driving without a licence – could be imposed for cases where programmers, developers, owners or users have unreasonably failed to designate a Responsible Person for an AI.

[138] The Responsible Person should also be liable for harms caused by an AI where the AI, if a natural person, would be criminally liable together with another individual. Otherwise, there is a risk that sophisticated AI developers could create machines that cause harm but rely on co-conspirators to escape liability.

[139] There is precedent for such a Responsible Person registration scheme. In the corporate context, executives may be required to attest to the validity of some SEC filings and held strictly liable for false statements even where they have done nothing directly negligent. If the Responsible Person is a person at a company where a company owns the AI, it would have to be an executive to avoid the problem of setting up a low-level employee as 'fall guy'. The SEC for this reason requires a C-level executive to attest to certain statements on filings.

[140] It might also be likely that parties with more negotiating power would attempt to offload their liability. For instance, AI suppliers might attempt to shift liability to consumers. At least in the case of commercial products, it should not be possible for suppliers to do this.

[141] This raises potential concerns about corporations with minimal capital being used to avoid liability. However, this same concern exists now with human activities, where thinly capitalised corporations are exploited as a way to limit the liability of individuals. Still, there are familiar legal tools to block this sort of illicit liability avoidance. To the extent a bad actor is abusing the corporate form, courts can, for instance, pierce the corporate veil.

criminal negligence liability could be imposed on the Responsible Person should he or she unreasonably fail to discharge those duties. Granted, this would not be punishment for the harmful conduct of the AI itself. Rather, it would be a form of direct criminal liability imposed on the Responsible Person for his or her own conduct.

D. Third Alternative: Moderate Changes to Civil Liability

A further alternative to dealing with Hard AI Crime is to look to the civil law, primarily tort law, as a method of both imposing legal accountability and deterring harmful AI. Some AI crime will no doubt already result in civil liability, however, if existing civil liability falls short, new liability rules could be introduced. A civil liability approach could even be used in conjunction with expansions to criminal liability.

Specifically, the Responsible Person proposal sketched above could be repurposed so that the Responsible Person might only be civilly liable. The case against a Responsible Person could be akin to a tort action if brought by an individual or a class of plaintiffs, or a civil enforcement action if brought by a government agency tasked with regulating AI. At trial, an AI would not be treated like a corporation, where the corporation itself is held to have done the harmful act and the law treats the company as a singular acting and 'thinking' entity. Rather, the question for adjudication would be whether the Responsible Person discharged his or her duties of care in respect of the AI in a reasonable way – or else civil liability could also be imposed on a strict liability basis (a less troubling prospect than it is within criminal law).

E. Concluding Thoughts

We took a careful look at how a criminal law regime that punished AI might be constructed and defended. In so doing, we showed that it is all too easy to underestimate the ability of criminal law theory to accommodate substantial reforms. We explored the ways in which criminal law can – and, where corporations are involved, already does – appeal to elaborate legal fictions to provide a basis within the defensible boundaries of criminal law theory for punishing some artificial entities. We showed what a system of punishment for AI might look like and showed how some hasty arguments against it can be answered.

Nonetheless, this Article has argued that, confronted with the growing possibility of Hard AI Crime, we should not overreact and reach for the radical tool of punishing AI. Alternative approaches could provide substantially similar benefits and would avoid many of the pitfalls and difficulties involved in punishing AI. A natural alternative, we argued, involves modest expansions to criminal law, including, most importantly, new negligence crimes centered around the improper design, operation, and testing of AI applications as well as possible criminal penalties for designated parties who fail to discharge statutory duties. Expanded civil liability would also be a valuable supplement to this framework. AI punishment thus is not justified at the end of the day because less radical alternatives remain available. There will be no need to reach for the big guns of the criminal law to solve the problems in this space in the foreseeable future.

9

Not a Single Singularity

LYRIA BENNETT MOSES*

Analysing affordances and limitations of artificial intelligence (AI) in the context of law is a multi-dimensional puzzle. The most prominent dimension is time, where we travel from descriptions of today's applications, through a relatively clear vision of the near-horizon, to a future sometimes described in terms of singularity – a fully automated legal system where machines are better than lawyers and judges and exponentially improving. Such future imaginaries are difficult to debate – because they lie beyond current knowledge and techniques, any affordance can be hypothesised, while any posited limitation could be overcome. Despite this, scholars have argued that there are limits that cannot be cured by greater processing power, newer AI techniques, or more data.

This chapter does not purport to answer the question 'is law computable?'. Instead, it outlines a means of visualising changes in the computability of aspects of law over time. Rather than visualising improvements in machine intelligence along a single scale towards a single singularity, it describes an evolving solid, expanding around a three-dimensional grid. Changing how we draw the future of AI in law opens up three distinct questions that can be asked at a particular point in time: (1) what is available and to what extent do existing applications replace humans in performing legal tasks and administering law; (2) what are the affordances and limitations of current AI techniques with potential application to law; and (3) in what circumstances should non-human systems be deployed to perform legal tasks or administer the law? These are, respectively, questions in the realms of is, can and ought or, alternatively, availability, capability and legitimacy.

The computability of law can then be plotted as a solid in those three dimensions. Each axis comprises legal tasks otherwise performed by human paralegals, lawyers and judges, and the solid changes over time from invisible (a purely human legal system) to a map of what tasks are being, can be and ought to be performed with current technology. The solid need not always grow. For example, demonstration of limitations or harms of actual or hypothesised techniques, previously unknown, will impact what is understood to be appropriate and, hopefully, what is deployed. The solid is also unlikely to be spherical – things might be done and possibilities created despite their being unsuitable for some contexts. Further, because the axes represent categories of activities rather than a number line, the solid may be disconnected (depending on how the axes are ordered).

* Allens Hub for Technology, Law and Innovation; UNSW Law.

This visualisation remains easier to construct for the past than the future. Much has been written on applications of, and limitations of, particular AI techniques such as expert systems and machine learning algorithms (such as random forests and neural networks). But the abstract idea of AI promises infinite potential, up to and beyond the hypothesised singularity. When lawyers imagine natural language processing and machine learning systems replacing judges, the mystique of these ideas often overpowers any practical familiarity with diverse methods and, importantly, their affordances and limitations. The 'intelligence' that machines are mimicking does not function in the same way as human thought and cannot be measured along a one-dimensional scale. Rather than asking about the future existence of a single legal singularity, one is better off asking concrete questions as to how particular applications (real or hypothesised) have and might change the shape of our solid – what is, can and ought to be automated. Like expert systems and machine learning techniques used to predict the future from historical data patterns, newer tools will be useful or even revolutionary in carrying out some tasks otherwise undertaken by humans, while failing miserably at others. The future shape of our solid ('to what extent is law computable?') remains hard to predict, but describing it forces consideration of all aspects of the challenge.

By understanding the problem as three-dimensional, it is easier to see that the legal singularity is not a single point towards which one inevitably climbs. One can progress far along the x- and y- axes without truly being in a position to automate the role that lawyers, and particularly judges, play in a society governed by the rule of law. Nevertheless, there will be many legal functions that can and will be automated so that the practice of law will change. These mini-upheavals will cause disruption, in courts, in legal practice, and in legal education. But there is no single singularity.

This chapter is structured as follows. Section I discusses what is meant by 'artificial intelligence' and the idea of a legal 'singularity'. Section II very briefly describes legal tasks that one might want to automate, including ultimately judging. Section III introduces the three-dimensional challenge of automation, involving availability, capability and legitimacy. Section IV imagines the future shape of legal automation, focusing on the potential for reaching a point where the solid fills the graph, a true 'legal singularity'. Section V concludes.

I. The Idea of Artificial 'Intelligence' and the Singularity

A. Artificial Intelligence

Artificial intelligence is a useful term for computer scientists because it describes a kind of problem that might be solved. A person working in artificial intelligence uses a variety of methods (such as neural networks) to perform a species of tasks (those that would otherwise require 'intelligence'). Just as being an expert in contract law implies a kind of shared knowledge, terminology, approach and understanding, so too does being an expert in artificial intelligence.

The use of the term 'artificial intelligence' assumes that we can recognise and measure 'intelligence'. The *Oxford Dictionary of English*[1] defines intelligence as 'the ability to acquire and apply knowledge and skills'. The *Oxford Dictionary of Psychology* offers a variety of definitions, starting with 'cognitive ability' then citing scholars for definitions such as 'the ability to carry on abstract thinking' (Terman) and 'the aggregate or global capacity of the individual to act purposively, to think rationally, and to deal effectively with his environment' (Wechsler).[2]

What machines currently do under the heading of 'artificial intelligence' is not always captured by definitions of 'intelligence'. Machines do not 'think', for example, but rather execute their programming. This does not mean that they do not achieve similar functionality at some tasks – I need to 'think' if I want to work out the sum of two numbers, whereas a machine is able to perform the same task more quickly without anything that looks like human thought. Even though machines that 'think' is how some people have conceptualised AI,[3] this remains a futuristic vision.

Many definitions of artificial intelligence thus quite reasonably focus on outcomes rather than internal processes. The classic Turing test for artificial intelligence imagines a human and a machine hidden behind curtains, with a human observer unable to distinguish between them based on the performance of each at a task (such as a text-based conversation).[4] The *Oxford Dictionary of Psychology* describes artificial intelligence as machines that 'do things normally done by minds'.[5] Similarly, the Dartmouth Summer Research Project on AI in 1955 framed the challenge in terms of doing things that, if a human did them, would require intelligence.[6] Russell and Norvig's *Artificial Intelligence: A Modern Approach*, organises historical definitions into four categories before selecting a series of fields said to comprise AI (natural language processing, knowledge representation, automated reasoning, machine learning, computer vision and robotics), all being techniques that allow an agent to act rationally.[7] The main distinction among these approaches is whether the goal is to emulate humans or the more abstract ambition of rational action, but both focus on observable behaviour rather than internal processes.

While this definition work is useful in defining a field of research and practice, mostly associated with computer science but with interdisciplinary features, it is less helpful as a legal category. It is neither an appropriate target of technology-specific regulation[8] nor a useful way to understand affordances and limitations of particular tools that are or might be deployed. It is more useful to analyse specific techniques (such as expert systems, machine learning, natural language processing) or even specific methodologies as applied to a given context.

[1] A Stevenson (ed), *Oxford Dictionary of English*, 3rd online edn, (Oxford University Press, 2015) (entry for 'intelligence').

[2] AM Colman, *Oxford Dictionary of Psychology*, 4th edn (Oxford University Press, 2015) (entry for 'intelligence').

[3] S Russell and P Norvig, *Artificial Intelligence: A Modern Approach*, 3rd edn (Pearson, 2014) 3.

[4] AM Turing, 'Computing Machinery and Intelligence' (1950) 59 *Mind* 433.

[5] Above n 2 (entry for 'artificial intelligence').

[6] J McCarthy et al, 'A Proposal for the Dartmouth Summer Research Project on Artificial Intelligence' (Report, 31 August 1955), www-formal.stanford.edu/jmc/history/dartmouth/dartmouth.html.

[7] S Russell and P Norvig, *Artificial Intelligence: A Modern Approach*, 3rd edn (Pearson Education Limited, 2016) 16–29.

[8] See M Guihot and L Bennett Moses, *Artificial Intelligence, Robots and the Law* (LexisNexis, 2020) ch 10.

B. The Singularity

An argument has been made that there is a point at which the performance of artificial intelligence will exceed the ability of humans to perform all tasks. This is often narrated in dystopian terms, for example:

> Let an ultraintelligent machine be defined as a machine that can far surpass all the intellectual activities of any man however clever. Since the design of machines is one of these intellectual activities, an ultraintelligent machine could design even better machines; there would then unquestionably be an 'intelligence explosion', and the intelligence of man would be left far behind … Thus the first ultraintelligent machine is the last invention that man need ever make.[9]

Those concerned about the singularity generally turn to the question of whether we can build 'friendly' AI that will act in ways supportive of human flourishing.[10] The challenge, of course, is the difficulty of capturing the complex and contested idea of human value in computer programmed 'intelligence'.[11] There are a variety of organisations focussing on the existential risk of artificial general intelligence and how to overcome it, including the University of Cambridge's Centre for the Study of Existential Risk (spawning the Leverhulme Centre for the Future of Intelligence) and the Future of Life Institute. Approaches include negotiating an international treaty mandating prohibition, creating a friendly artificial general intelligence that would prevent the development of other artificial general intelligences, creating a net of artificial general intelligences to police the collective, or augmenting humans to collaborate with or control all artificial general intelligence.[12]

The idea of a singularity suggests a one-dimensional comparison between artificial and human intelligence over time, with a moment in time at which there exists a machine that is more 'intelligent' than humans. At this moment, the machine will surpass humans in all capabilities.[13] In reality, however, we are likely to see machines that are generally intelligent (acting beyond human capability in numerous tasks) before we see machines that outperform humans in all tasks. A machine that could outperform Einstein at creative scientific thought would be impressive even if it wrote mediocre poetry. Not even human intelligence is measured on a one-dimensional scale. In the world of education, there is a category of children who are 'gifted but learning disabled' being '[c]hildren who … exhibit remarkable talents or strengths in some areas and disabling weaknesses in others. This idea only seems paradoxical[14] because we usually imagine intelligence as a single measurement (say, IQ score) rather than as a complex combination of abilities. If AlphaGo (the system that beat human champion Go players) were a human child, it could well be classified as both gifted and learning disabled.

[9] IJ Good, 'Speculations Concerning the First Ultraintelligent Machine' in F Alt and M Rubinoff (eds), *Advances in Computers*, Vol 6 (Academic Press, 1965) 31.

[10] J Tallinn, 'The Intelligence Stairway' (Sydney Ideas Conference, Sydney, July 2015), www.youtube.com/watch?v=BNqQkFg-7AM.

[11] L Muehlhauser, The Intelligence Explosion (online, 2011) intelligenceexplosion.com/en/2011.

[12] A Turchin, D Denkenberger and BP Green, 'Global Solutions vs Local Solutions for the AI Safety Problem' (2019) 3 *Big Data and Cognitive Computing* 16.

[13] D Wood, Risk Roundup, Risk Group, youtu.be/WGtsY8KOa8Q.

[14] S Baum, 'Gifted but Learning Disabled: A Puzzling Paradox' (*LD OnLine*), www.ldonline.org/article/5939.

C. Diverse Intelligence and Milestones

The fact that human intelligence is complex suggests that any notion of a singularity should be multi-dimensional. We are not on a road to a single point in time, but rather meandering through a forest with turns and twists and occasionally getting lost. Software can be awe-inspiring, or it can be buggy and malfunctioning. If we want to understand the role that technology does, can and should play in law, then we need something more than an arrow on a diagram moving unrelentingly upwards.

Clarke has introduced the term 'complementary artefact intelligence' as an alternative to AI.[15] This term recognises that the computers perform well at some tasks (typically those requiring reliability, accuracy and/or speed), and are useful where there are issues of cost, danger or mundanity,[16] but still require human direction. The building of 'smarter' machines is best understood not as a race against humans, but rather as components of human-machine systems that interface effectively, efficiently and adaptably with both humans and other artefacts.[17] Wu makes a similar point in the legal context, arguing that improving machine-human systems is a better focus than human displacement, particularly in the context of the administration of justice.[18]

II. Automation of Legal Tasks and the Legal Singularity

Automation of legal tasks is part of a broader conversation around the evolution of work in an age of AI taking place in both scholarship and the broader media.[19] If a machine can be as 'intelligent' as a human (assuming this is a one-dimensional comparison), then it can arguably be as good a lawyer.[20] Alarie has thus introduced the idea of the 'legal singularity' which 'will arrive when the accumulation of massively more data and dramatically improved methods of inference make legal uncertainty obsolete'.[21] Facts, once established, will 'map on to clear legal consequences'.[22] This postulates not only a statement about technology (analogous to the idea of the technological singularity) but also a statement about law (that it is computable, with inputs leading to an output in every case).

The 'legislation as code' or 'machine-readable laws' movement is a vision of partially computable law. As an experiment, the Service Innovation Lab in New Zealand trialled

[15] R Clarke, 'Why the World Wants Controls over Artificial Intelligence' (2019) 35(4) *Computer Law & Security Review* 423, 429–30.

[16] ibid, 430.

[17] ibid.

[18] T Wu, 'Will Artificial Intelligence Eat the Law? The Rise of Hybrid Social-Ordering Systems' (2002) 119 *Columbia Law Review* 2001.

[19] eg T Meltzer, 'Robot Doctors, Online Lawyers and Automated Architects: the Future of the Professions?' *Guardian* (15 June 2014), perma.cc/73Q4-WVZA; J Koebler, 'Rise of the Robolawyers' *The Atlantic* (April 2017); JO McGinnis and RG Pearce, 'The Great Disruption: How Machine Intelligence Will Transform the Role of Lawyers in the Delivery of Legal Services' (2013) 82 *Fordham Law Review* 3041, 3041.

[20] E Volokh, 'Chief Justice Robots' (2019) 68 *Duke Law Journal* 1135 (2019).

[21] B Alarie, 'The Path of the Law: Toward Legal Singularity' (2016) 66 *University of Toronto Law Journal* 443.

[22] ibid.

the idea of rewriting existing legislation as software code.[23] The goal was to align service delivery and decision making (which is increasingly automated) with the legislation being implemented by writing legislation in a form that software can 'read'.[24] As the New Zealand group determined, rather than taking existing law and re-writing it, it is more effective to change the content of law to that which can be automated.[25] Waddington describes this as 'co-drafting' where 'the legislative drafter is drafting the legislation at the same time as the coder is drafting the coding language' with feedback between them.[26] Such formalisation processes can resolve ambiguities in how sections relate to each other, improving clarity for human as well as machine readers.[27] Designing legislation that can be implemented by a machine has several benefits, including efficiency, transparency (everyone understands how the machine works) and consistency and predictability (everyone can predict the outputs given an input).[28] But it does not work for all kinds of law. In particular, the New Zealand team found:[29]

> The features of legislation that we identified that are likely to mean that it would be of value to make it available in a machine consumable format are, if the legislation:
>
> - involves a calculation
> - involves a process that requires factual information to determine application, eligibility, entitlements, or coverage
> - prescribes a process that is used repeatedly
> - prescribes a compliance process or obligation (for example, regulations that set out 14 different steps that must take place before raw milk can be certified as being fit for human consumption)
> - prescribes a process or system that can be delivered digitally.

This description captures some law, but not all law or even all legislation. In New Zealand, the case studies used were the Rates Rebate Act 1973 (NZ) and the Holidays Act 2003 (NZ), both of which can be imagined as expert systems deploying decision trees and formulas. This example suggests that some laws can be rendered computable based on simple programming techniques.

Using rules as code techniques to render all law computable would require changing the content of that law. Waddington's idea of co-drafting can either be cabined (as in New Zealand to particular kinds of law) or expanded across the legislative repertoire. However, the latter would limit the kinds of laws that could be drafted – it would need to remove all discretion, ambiguity and vagueness. While reducing these in some contexts might be desirable, doing so across the board would be a significant limitation. Vague terms can be used to provide flexibility, while contestable terms can ensure evaluation takes place along particular lines, and both allow rule-makers to finesse

[23] Better Rules for Government Discovery Report (March 2018), www.digital.govt.nz/dmsdocument/95-better-rules-for-government-discovery-report/html.

[24] ibid.

[25] ibid.

[26] M Waddington, 'Machine-consumable legislation: A legislative drafter's perspective – human v artificial intelligence' (*The Loophole 21*, July 2019).

[27] SB Lawsky, 'Formalizing the Code' (2017) 70 *Tax Law Review* 377, 379.

[28] ibid.

[29] Above n 23.

their disagreement.[30] Discretion allows parliament to ensure that all factors are taken into account in a wide variety of potentially unanticipated scenarios. The rules as code movement thus accepts that not all law can or should be enacted through machine-readable code and that the focus should be prescriptive rules where there is a use case for automation.[31]

Applying legislation to particular fact scenarios is only one kind of legal task. Various scholars have looked more broadly at the kind of legal tasks that are being or can be automated, in particular Alairie, Niblett and Yoon,[32] Remus and Levy,[33] and Susskind and Susskind.[34] While different authors reach different conclusions about the likely extent of automation over the short, medium and longer term, all agree that there are a variety of tools being used in the delivery of legal services and the performance of legal tasks, and that these will expand over time.

Even technologically unsophisticated systems can help people navigate the legal system. The rules as code example above does not require new AI techniques, only government commitment and proper processes. The 'DoNotPay' chatbot is another example of a simple but effective system – it asks a series of questions then provides advice and documentation to help users avoid traffic and parking tickets.[35] Students in my one-semester course on Designing Technology Solutions for Access to Justice have built tools to help teenagers navigate age of consent laws, to help music festival attendees find out the legality of a police search conducted on them, to assist social housing tenants in following the complex process for getting repairs done, and to help human rights workers in the region navigate the maze of relevant international treaties. Expert systems can also be used to collect instructions, complete forms and personalise documents.[36]

Beyond expert systems and other pre-programmed logics lie the possibilities opened up by machine learning and natural language processing, the two branches of AI with significant implications for law. Search engines that locate doctrinally relevant material

[30] HLA Hart, *Jhering's Heaven of Concepts and Modern Analytical Jurisprudence* (1970), reprinted in HLA Hart, *Essays in Jurisprudence and Philosophy* 265, 269–70 (Clarendon Press, Oxford University Press, 1983); J Waldron, 'Vagueness in Law and Language: Some Philosophical Issues' (1994), 82 *California Law Review* 509, 512–14; JA Grundfest and AC Pritchard, 'Statutes with Multiple Personality Disorders: The Value of Ambiguity in Statutory Design and Interpretation' (2002) 54 *Stanford Law Review* 627 reprinted in *Essays in Jurisprudence and Philosophy* 265, 269–70 (1983) ('It is a feature of the human predicament, not only of the legislator but of anyone who attempts to regulate some sphere of conduct by means of general rules, that he labors under one supreme handicap – the impossibility of foreseeing all possible combinations of circumstances that the future may bring. … This means that all legal rules and concepts are 'open'; and when an unenvisaged case arises we must make a fresh choice, and in doing so elaborate our legal concepts, adapting them to socially desirable ends.')

[31] See eg digtal.nsw (NSW Government), 'Emerging Technology Guide: Rules as Code', www.digital.nsw.gov.au/digital-transformation/policy-lab/rules-code.

[32] BH Alarie, A Niblett and AH Yoon, 'How Artificial Intelligence Will Affect the Practice of Law' (2018) 68 (supplement 1) *University of Toronto Law Journal* 106, 109ff.

[33] D Remus and F Levy, 'Can Robots Be Lawyers: Computers, Lawyers, and the Practice of Law' (2017) 30(3) *Georgetown Journal of Legal Ethics* 501.

[34] R Susskind and D Susskind, *The Future of the Professions: How Technology will Transform the Work of Human Experts* (Oxford University Press, 2015).

[35] Available at donotpay.com.

[36] J Bennett et al, 'Current State of Automated Legal Advice Tools' (Discussion Paper No 1, Networked Society Institute, University of Melbourne, April 2018) 22–25.

increasingly rely on these techniques. For example, Ross (associated with IBM Watson) can understand legal questions written in regular English and provide answers based on its knowledge database.[37] In the future, advanced versions of these tools will make legal research significantly more efficient. Machine learning prediction engines, such as Lex Machina and Premonition, search for trends that facilitate prediction of likelihood of success (for different judges), quantification of damages, and likely cost and time of proceedings.[38] Tools that partially automate document review (whether for due diligence or discovery) are also increasingly popular.[39]

Collectively, these examples demonstrate that some legal tasks are being delegated to machines and that possibilities expand as new AI techniques are introduced. There have, however, been strong critiques of the use of particular tools in particular contexts. For example, the COMPAS tool, deployed extensively in the US, provides a risk assessment score to judges as a measure of the likelihood that a given defendant will re-offend for use in sentencing.[40] This tool not only fails to operate fairly by some measures (the false positive rate had a disparate impact on African Americans[41]) but it explicitly uses variables that would not ordinarily be considered relevant to sentencing.[42]

The map of where we are thus includes both excellence and failure, both usefulness and harm, both affordances and limitations. It seems less a march towards an inevitable singularity that a journey with choices – to develop AI tools and implement them in an expanding range of contexts. Looking back, we can recognise mirages, such as uses that seemed efficient and fair but were in fact problematic and illegitimate. Understanding our travels to date and where we might go in the future requires a more complex map than a single path upwards towards a single singularity. As Clarke has argued in a broader context and Wu in the legal context, it also requires a break from the idea of humans versus machines to the construction of systems that deploy integrated human and machine components in ways that take advantage of the strengths of each.[43] Moving forwards then is not about approaching the legal singularity as a destination, but rather enhancing the legal system (including its tools and processes) for the benefit of society.

III. A Three-dimensional Challenge

If one lists or maps the technologies that have been developed for or deployed in legal contexts, particularly in recent times, it could be narrated as the first steps along an inevitable climb towards a legal singularity. One might think that it is impossible for

[37] See Ross Intelligence, rossintelligence.com/.

[38] See lexmachina.com and premonition.ai.

[39] T Davey and M Legg, 'Machine Learning Disrupts Discovery' (2017) 32 *Law Society Journal* (NSW) 82.

[40] See description in *State Wisconsin v Loomis*, 881 NW2d 749 (Wis 2016). The United States Supreme Court denied certiorari on 26 June 2017.

[41] J Angwin et al, 'Machine Bias: There's Software Used Across the Country to Predict Future Criminals. And It's Biased Against Blacks' *ProPublica* (online, 23 May 2016), www.propublica.org/article/machine-bias-risk-assessments-in-criminal-sentencing.

[42] M Zalnieriute, L Bennett Moses and G Willliams, 'The Rule of Law and Automation of Government Decision-Making' (2019) 82(3) *MLR* 425, 447–8.

[43] Clarke, above n 15.

technological forecasts to be too optimistic. However, when mapping techniques along three separate dimensions – availability, capability and legitimacy – it becomes clear that developments are mostly about volume and technical range, ignoring the more fundamental issues around legitimacy.

A. The X-axis: Availability of Useful Tools

The x-axis, representing the volume of tools available to perform legal tasks, has moved quickly, although there is a considerable way to go. Most legal technology conferences include a presentation with a slide that sets out all of the legal technology companies operating (either generally or in the relevant jurisdiction) and that slide feels more crowded each year.[44] Tools include those that target marketing to potential clients, analyse and classify documents, analyse data to make predictions about legal costs or changes of success, draft legal documents, answer legal questions, assist with legal research, help with practice and document management and facilitate collaboration. Law firms are also building products in house or in partnership with technology companies.[45] It is a crowded, but exciting and fast-moving space.

Beyond corporate endeavours, are projects with more communal goals, such as Austlii's DataLex. Austlii (austlii.edu.au) provides free legal information for Australia and, through partnerships, beyond. The original DataLex project ran from 1984 to 2001, creating a platform for developing legal expert systems, incorporating a case-based inferencing mechanism, a full text retrieval system and a hypertext engine.[46] Enhanced DataLex tools are currently available on the AustLII Communities platform, a closed wiki, with developers able to play with building expert systems that can navigate complicated legislation.[47] With further development work, DataLex could be used to convert all Australian legislation into an expert system, with users answering questions (which may require interpretation of terms or legal guidance) to find out how particular laws apply to their personal circumstances. The use of DataLex software is free for students and legal community centres and there is no cost to end-users.[48] The real benefit is that development work can be conducted by lawyers with no coding expertise. However, to date, only a small part of Australia's statutory corpus has been re-written in the format required by DataLex.

Although the x-dimension appears straightforward, there is nothing 'easy' about creating legal tools that can replace or assist humans in performing legal tasks. Time can be spent designing, building and marketing legal tools without any expansion along the x-axis. There are many examples of poor design and implementation. Consider an interactive mobile phone application built by Victoria Legal Aid[49] offering 'targeted, relevant

[44] For example, see *LawGeex*, Legal Tech Buyers Guide 2019, ltbg2019.lawgeex.com/products-by-category/.

[45] L Bennett Moses, 'The Need for Lawyers', in K Lindgren, F Kunc and M Coper M (eds), *The Future of Australian Legal Education* (Australia, Lawbook Company, 2018) 355.

[46] G Greenleaf, A Mowbray and P Chung, 'The DataLex Project: History and Bibliography' (3 January 2018), [2018] UNSWLRS 4.

[47] ibid.

[48] DataLex, Legal inferencing systems (brochure).

[49] Victoria Legal Aid, Case study of the BELOW THE BELT PHONE APP (May 2016).

and free information to young people on legal issues that affected them'. It focused on information about sexting, intercourse, sexual consent and cyberbullying.[50] For example, users could enter personal information to find out whether they were above the age of consent. The application was launched in November 2013 but encountered low install rates and high uninstall rates and was discontinued in November 2015.[51] At that time, only 1,095 users had installed the app and only 40 of those had created accounts. Further, the app could no longer run on newer Android phones due to an operating system upgrade. In the evaluation, there were problems with lack of a comprehensive market strategy, failure to consider the value proposition for the client, failure to consider challenges with building on one platform only (Android).[52] Despite its ambitions, the application did not significantly expand the circumstances in which users could obtain automated legal advice, and thus did not give rise to growth along the x-axis. This example highlights that what is often at stake in automation is not how technically sophisticated the methodology, but: how buggy the software, how well-designed the tool, processes of implementation and marketing, and building solutions that align with problems not solutions in isolation.

A jurisdiction travels along the x-axis though the conception, design and building of useable systems to automate legal tasks. This will draw on existing AI capabilities, requiring also time, quality design and effective implementation. It is crucial that such tools be developed with an understanding of the broader socio-technical networks in which they will be deployed, including the needs of potential users.

B. The Y-axis: Evolving Capabilities

Each 'type' of AI has both affordances and limitations. As new AI techniques are introduced, automated tools can perform new tasks in the legal domain. The current boom in legal technology is largely related to developments in machine learning and natural language processing, which have facilitated prediction of legal outcomes, automation of document review, and more intuitive legal search products.

The limitations of expert systems were identified decades ago.[53] Expert systems can manage legal domains that are simple (like age of consent laws) and complicated (like tax law), but not those that are complex and unpredictable (such as evaluations of reasonableness).[54] Similar points apply to the rendition of rules as code. In some cases, drafting law in this way would be an improvement. In particular, it reduces the need for those seeking to operationalise 'compliance by design' to each independent (and possibly inaccurate) conversion of laws from text to machine-readable code. Instead, everyone can rely on the government-endorsed machine-readable version of rules. However,

[50] ibid.
[51] ibid.
[52] ibid.
[53] See generally P Leith, 'The Rise and Fall of the Legal Expert System' (2010) 1(1) *European Journal of Law and Technology*, ejlt.org//article/view/14/1; R Stamper, 'Expert Systems – Lawyers Beware!' in Stuart S Nagel (ed), *Law, Decision-Making, and Microcomputers: Cross-National Perspectives* (Quorum Books, 1991) 19, 20.
[54] DJ Snowden and ME Boone, 'A Leader's Framework for Decision Making' (2007) *Harvard Business Review* 69 (November issue).

'rules as code' does not purport to deal with discretionary components of legislation; discretion remains outside the system but, once a decision is made, can be looped back into the process. Discretion can only be delegated to a machine if one is satisfied with pure chance[55] or prediction of outcomes based on machine learning trained on historic exercises of discretion or other events. Further, 'rules as code' requires avoidance of language that permits ambiguity and flexibility in favour of programmable logic.[56] As noted above, this is undesirable in some circumstances and is outside the remit of the rules as code movement.

Machine learning can surmount the limitations of pre-programmed rules. In a learning process, one does not need to know a rule. Instead (in supervised learning) one can have historical classifications (such as whether the plaintiff won or lost) and the facts of those cases. The machine can learn to identify the variables (facts) that correspond with the classification (win or lose). Machine learning can be used to 'learn' the weights given in practice to a range of factors known to be relevant. Further, it can learn to identify more complex patterns, as where the presence of one or more factors changes the weight given to a different factor.

The closest machine learning has come to replacing judges is predicting judicial behaviour. Aletras et al have built a tool to analyse textual content from European Court of Human Rights judgments in order to predict the final outcome, a task accomplished with 79 per cent average accuracy.[57] There are flaws in that particular study, in particular the fact that the training set was descriptions of the facts in the judgments themselves.[58] Any tool that claims it can predict judicial decisions also needs to be carefully evaluated, and accuracy rates need to be measured as against pure chance (50 per cent) not pure error (0 per cent).

Machine learning has limitations, different to those of expert systems. A machine learning algorithm will only predict the outcomes of new cases where they are sufficiently similar to those on which it was trained. Human decision-makers are better at dealing with unanticipated circumstances and using 'common sense' to assess the importance of a new situation. While a computer will only know speeding might be permitted in a medical emergency if it has previously seen this scenario, humans can deduce that this situation may need to be separately assessed even if it is the first time it is encountered.[59] Machine learning is inherently conservative, better at making predictions about the legal system as it currently exists rather than making suggestions for how it should evolve.[60] At most, it can learn a trend that is already present in the data (such as an increase in damages payouts) and project that trend into the future. But it cannot change course – historical legal revolutions such as recognition of tort liability

[55] A D'Amato, 'Can/Should Computers Replace Judges?' (1977) 11 *Georgia Law Review* 1277, 1279.

[56] F Pasquale, 'A Rule of Persons, Not Machines: The Limits of Legal Automation' (2019) 87 *George Washington Law Review* 1, 3.

[57] N Aletras et al, 'Predicting Judicial Decisions of the European Court of Human Rights: A Natural Language Processing Perspective' (2016) 2 *Peer Journal of Computer Science* 92.

[58] F Pasquale and G Cashwell, 'Prediction, Persuasion, and the Jurisprudence of Behaviourism' (2018) 68 (Supplement 1) *University of Toronto Law Review* 63, 68–72.

[59] G Marcus and E Davis, *Rebooting AI: Building Artificial Intelligence we can Trust* (Pantheon, 2019).

[60] D Remus and F Levy, 'Can Robots Be Lawyers: Computers, Lawyers, and the Practice of Law' (2017) 30(3) *Georgetown Journal of Legal Ethics* 501, 549.

for negligence[61] or the recognition of native title in Australia[62] would not be dreamt up by a system that replicates historic patterns and trends. Some might think this is a good thing (confining judicial innovation) but it is not a mirror for current judicial practice. Further, machine learning is often criticised for not justifying outputs in legally relevant terms.[63]

The question is not only about what machines can (and cannot) accomplish independently. Automated systems often work alongside humans in performing legal tasks, providing legal advice and making legal decisions. Expert systems are often designed to be used by lawyers (who can interpret legal language in particular factual contexts) rather than clients. Machine learning is most commonly used in tasks that would otherwise be assigned to junior lawyers. Machine learning systems must be trained by junior lawyers and remains under the supervision of senior lawyers. It is then used in e-discovery, document classification and clustering, semantic legal search, data-driven document creation, narrative generators, predictive analytics and relevance, negotiation and risk optimisers.[64] These are impressive, and have led to questions about how junior lawyers will gain basic skills without these standard large-scale tasks.[65] But accomplishing more strategic tasks independently will likely require another technological revolution. In the meantime, affordances and limitations need to be assessed for tools operating independently as well as in the more common context of machine-human systems.

C. The Z-axis: Legitimacy and Appropriateness of Deployment

There are important questions to ask beyond affordances and limitations of particular systems and tools. The existence of a z-axis is an assertion that not every tool that can do something should be used in all circumstances. For example, there may be reasons why, even if a system could predict the decision of a given human judge with a high degree of accuracy, we would want the decision to be made by the judge rather than the system.

Some have argued that the existence of a z-axis ultimately comes down to techno-scepticism or sentimentality, and that society should focus on outputs rather than the means through which those outputs are produced. According to this argument, if a system can produce outputs that are assessed as at least as good as those of human professionals, then there is no reason to prefer humans. Volokh argues, for example,

[61] *Donoghue v Stevenson* [1932] UKHL 100, [1932] AC 562.

[62] *Mabo v Queensland* (No 2) (1992) 175 CLR 1.

[63] F Pasquale, 'Toward a Fourth Law of Robotics: Preserving Attribution, Responsibility, and Explainability in an Algorithmic Society' (2017) 78(5) *Ohio State Law Journal* 5; L Bennett Moses and J Chan, 'Using Big Data for Legal and Law Enforcement Decisions: Testing the New Tools' (2014) 37(2) *University of New South Wales Law Journal* 643.

[64] JO McGinnis and RG Pearce, 'The Great Disruption: How Machine Intelligence Will Transform the Role of Lawyers in the Delivery of Legal Services' (2013) 82 *Fordham Law Review* 3041; D Ben-Ari et al, '"Danger, Will Robinson"? Artificial Intelligence in the Practice of Law: An Analysis and Proof of Concept Experiment' (2017) 23 *Richmond Journal of Law and Technology* 2, 31–5; D Remus and F Levy, 'Can Robots Be Lawyers: Computers, Lawyers, and the Practice of Law' (2017) 30(3) *Georgetown Journal of Legal Ethics* 501; H Surden, 'Machine Learning and Law' (2014) 89 *Washington Law Review* 87.

[65] McGinnis and Pearce, above n 64, 3065–6. However, one might equally wonder how juniors could manage without the opportunity to retype or manually edit correspondence or deliver paper document folders around the city – tasks that would likely have been common training ground in the past.

that we should assess hypothetical lawyer robots by whether the outputs provide us with what we need, which is persuasiveness at least equal to the average human performing the same task.[66] According to him, it is irrelevant whether a judge reaches decisions by a similar process to a human (applying legal rules to facts), provided that the output is equivalently or more persuasive (according to a panel of evaluators).[67] If Volokh is right, there is no z-axis, no questions to be asked beyond technical capability (y-axis) and practical implementation and deployment (x-axis).

To understand the flaw in Volokh's argument, it is worth looking back to earlier thoughts about the limits of automated systems. In 1976, Weizenbaum (author of the language analysis program DOCTOR that could substitute for a psychotherapist), wrote that 'since we do not now have any ways of making computers wise, we ought not now to give computers tasks that demand wisdom'.[68] While we can build machines that learn, we have not yet built one that could be described as wise, albeit that it may be able to predict average behaviour of people who deserve that accolade. Dreyfus had slightly different concerns, about modelling the indeterminacy of the problems addressed by humans.[69] There are a variety of modern arguments against machines generally or machine learning specifically that deploy a range of concepts, but ultimately align with Weizenbaum's concern about wisdom and Dreyfus' concerns about the limitations of digital machines confined to a series of determinate states.

Hildebrandt is concerned that those focusing on outputs seem to 'mistake the mathematical simulation of legal judgment for legal judgment itself'.[70] She links judgment with recognition of contestability of legal interpretation, citing Waldron that we do not just obey laws, we argue about them.[71] According to Hildebrandt, the output of a machine learning system is less practically contestable (due to its opacity) and is not contestable on the same terms – one can argue the statistics but not the reason. Contestability is also reduced within the broader system given the deskilling of those who could conduct a full evaluation in the future. At least in the context of legal decision-making that is integrated into the state, a contestability requirement would render illegimate judgments created purely through automation.

Kerr and Mathen[72] also raise issues that go beyond the alignment of outputs, recognising the importance of the state of mind of actors in the system. They give the example of the oath sworn by federal US judges:

> I, A. B., do solemnly swear or affirm, that I will administer justice without respect to persons, and do equal right to the poor and to the rich, and that I will faithfully and impartially discharge and perform all the duties incumbent on me as, according to the best of my abilities and understanding, agreeably to the constitution, and laws of the United States. So help me God.

[66] Volokh, above n 20.

[67] ibid, 1162.

[68] J Weizenbaum, *Computer Power and Human Reason: From Judgment to Calculation* 227 (1976).

[69] HL Dreyfus, *What Computers Can't Do* (Harper & Row, 1972) 194.

[70] M Hildebrandt, 'Law as computation in the era of artificial legal intelligence' (2018) 68 (Supplement 1) *University of Toronto Law Journal* 12, 23.

[71] J Waldron, 'The Rule of Law and the Importance of Procedure' in JE Fleming (ed), *Getting to the Rule of Law, NOMOS L* (New York University Press, 2011).

[72] I Kerr and C Mathen, 'Chief Justice John Roberts is a Robot' (2014) University of Ottawa Working Paper.

This is not a promise not to reach a particular outcome, but a promise to have a particular orientation in the course of making a decision. We do not want a judge to merely persuade an audience that they are meeting this standard, we want them to actually take their obligation to heart. As they note 'the mere fact that a machine demonstrates rule-following behaviour does not make it a rule follower'.[73] Such machines cannot truly adopt what HLA Hart described as an internal point of view.[74] Kerr and Mathen conclude 'Legal reasoning also requires being a member of the community, understanding its history, its moral convictions, having a point of view about its current character and having a stake in its future'.[75] Neither expert systems nor machine learning can give rise to systems having such a psychological perspective on their task.

The difference between simulation or prediction of human judges and actual human judges can also be understood by comparing judicial decisions to the conduct of elections. Suppose that pollsters could predict elections with a high degree of accuracy (not the case currently!). Imagine that sampling and statistical methods improve to bring the accuracy to 99 per cent. Then suppose it is argued that elections are expensive to hold and that, for the sake of 1 per cent accuracy, it is better to simply take the pollster's prediction as the outcome. In my view, a country that accepted that logic would no longer be democratic. It is a requirement that the vote be held, not merely simulated or predicted. The point that Hildebrandt as well as Kerr and Mathen are making is similar for judicial decisions – irrespective of the alignment of outcomes, there needs to be a decision-making process that meets particular criteria. For Hildebrandt, this is contestability while, for Kerr and Mathen, it is the ability to psychologically embrace the internal point of view.

These kinds of challenges to automation of legal decision-making are fundamental – they go beyond the limitations of current techniques and pose broader questions about the enterprise itself. It is, however, worth noting that most legitimacy challenges are concrete and relate to specific use-cases with current techniques. Machine learning, in particular, has come under extensive critique, particularly with respect to its alignment with rule of law values.[76] As Surden points out, many of these concerns are contingent.[77] While there are examples of applications that fail to ensure equal treatment under the law (such as COMPAS), there is also the potential for AI to detect bias in historical data and conduct learning within prescribed fairness constraints.

Pasquale and Cashwell's critique[78] of Aletras et al's prediction of the European Court of Human Rights is arguably contingent in this sense. As they write: 'it is a foundational principle of both administrative and evidence law that irrelevant factors should not factor into a decision'.[79] An automated system looking for correlations in language used in statements

[73] ibid, 24.

[74] HLA Hart, *The Concept of Law*, 2nd edn (Oxford University Press, 1994) 89.

[75] Above n 72, 39–40.

[76] Zalnieriute et al, above n 42.

[77] H Surden, 'The Ethics of Artificial Intelligence in Law: Basic Questions' *Oxford Handbook of Ethics of AI* (draft chapter).

[78] F Pasquale and G Cashwell, 'Prediction, Persuasion, and the Jurisprudence of Behaviourism' (2018) 68 (Supplement 1) *University of Toronto Law Review* 63.

[79] ibid, 76.

of facts and the ultimate decision will potentially take into account facts that ought to be dismissed as irrelevant, likely due to spurious correlation in an inevitably small data set.[80] Even if the system is only used for triage, there are real concerns about its deployment in contexts that affect potential litigants.[81] The rule of law not only cares about outcome, but the mode through which it is generated – the internal logic (human or machine) thus matters so that using irrelevant considerations renders the decision illegitimate even if the result is likely to be the same (as noted in high accuracy probabilities). But this is not about the psychology of the decision-making entity. Pasquale and Cashwell are focusing on one specific machine learning algorithm so that it is less clear whether they would accept an algorithm where only weightings and not variables are 'learnt'. An example would be something similar to the New Zealand Risk of Reconviction algorithm which, unlike COMPAS, draws on only specific published variables associated with criminal activity and past interactions with the criminal justice system.[82]

Another critique of automation where there is contingency is alignment with legal ethics. Remus and Levy point out that automated advice systems will generally lack the ethical, law-abiding orientation of human lawyers who give advice. They use the example of tax advice, and the willingness of (some) human lawyers to advise clients to act legally and in line with the spirit of the law even where, statistically, they may be unlikely to face consequences.[83] Other than the interpretation question (what is 'the spirit of the law'?), this could arguably be met by programming. One might well consider 'ethical behaviour' as something that can be assessed purely on the basis of outputs, that is the content of the advice given. In that light, it can be met by (some) systems.

Some objections about legitimacy are broad (applying to all technology in many applications) while others are narrow or contingent (for example, those relating to the legitimacy of particular systems used in particular contexts). Overcoming all types of objections is required to move along the z-axis. If we take seriously the concerns of Hildebrandt, Kerr and Mathen, in particular, then we have not travelled very far along the z-axis to date. In particular, neither expert systems nor machine learning ought to replace human judges in most contexts.

Some argue that human judges ought to be replaced in at least some circumstances. Some have suggested, and Estonia is proposing to adopt, a model where small claims are resolved by AI tools.[84] However, it ought not be simply a matter of the 'importance' of the matter along some objective scale such as total value at stake (in Estonia, the amount is 7000 euro) or classification of the issue as procedural.[85] Smallness ought not to remove a person's entitlement to legitimate justice if that is what they wish to pursue. It may be acceptable where the parties agree to an automated process. After all, most jurisdictions recognise the rights of parties to agree to move outside the state-sponsored justice system, for example by agreeing to arbitration or, for that matter, appearing before Judge

[80] ibid, 76–77.

[81] ibid.

[82] NZ Government, Algorithm Assessment Report (October 2018) 21. The exceptions are age and sex.

[83] D Remus and F Levy, 'Can Robots Be Lawyers: Computers, Lawyers, and the Practice of Law' (2017) 30(3) *Georgetown Journal of Legal Ethics* 501, 552–4.

[84] E Niiler, 'Can AI Be a Fair Judge in Court? Estonia Thinks So' (*Wired*, 25 March 2019), www.wired.com/story/can-ai-be-fair-judge-court-estonia-thinks-so/.

[85] D'Amato, above n 47, 1289.

Judy or abiding by the result of a coin toss. Provided the contract that delegates decision-making authority to an algorithm is enforceable (including all the jurisdiction-specific matters to be considered), then the delegation should be seen as equivalently legitimate to arbitration clauses. But parties ought not to be forced to accept a simulation of justice without informed consent, even where the total value at stake is relatively small.

Despite measurable progression upon the x-axis and constant expansion of what is technically possible (represented by the y-axis), current techniques such as machine learning and expert systems operating alone fare poorly on the z-axis, particularly in the context of the administration of justice. There are some objections that can be met with current technologies implemented well, but many which cannot. A judge does not merely find legislation and cases, locate relevant provisions or ratio decidendi, and apply logic to deduce a result. Nor do judges reason statistically from historical data points. Instead, judges are a lynchpin for the rule of law, both in terms of their own decision-making processes and, through building trust and respect, encouraging a broader rule of law culture. Ultimately, judges decide what a decision should be, which is quite different to predicting what the decision will be. Even if machine learning could improve performance against rule of law values such as equal treatment, it could not be contestable on the same terms or take the internal point of view. The strongest progress on the z-axis has been for technologies (such as search engines) that improve human performance.

IV. What Kind of Technology Could Replace Judges?

What has been generated so far is a three dimensional solid, growing over time up to the present. This solid has grown most rapidly along the x-axis with the large number of businesses expanding into the legal technology space alongside social good projects such as DataLex and rules as code. The growth along the y-axis has been sporadic but significant. The main bursts have been associated with expert systems in the 1980s and 1990s followed by machine learning more recently. The solid, is however, rather shallow, with the z-axis only embracing voluntary submission to automation, efficiencies in some aspects of legal service delivery, and as a component in human-machine systems (as where it is used to locate relevant materials and improve legal prediction).

The question, then, is whether focusing on a different part of the y-axis might enable growth along the z-axis for fully autonomous systems. In other words, is there an AI technology that can answer contemporary the concerns about legitimacy? The difference between human judges and machines raised above are not necessarily biology, but rather concern that particular programming techniques do not match the requirements of the rule of law or the psychological attitudinal requirements of judging. It is thus worth asking whether we can progress along the z-axis by pursuing different approaches to artificial intelligence.

There are a variety of, at this stage, purely hypothetical sub-fields of AI. In his book on Superintelligence, Bostrom proposes a variety of paths to the singularity. One might, for example, be able to take a human judge and perfectly replicate their brain within computer hardware or a computer model. Would such a replicant be in a position to answer the critiques above? Assuming it reasoned the same way as the replicated human judge, it would treat legal propositions as contestable so as to answer Hildebrandt's point. It would also feel bound by rules and take Hart's internal perspective on the law, so as to satisfy Kerr and Mathen. It would not rely on machine learning as a technique but would rather simulate precisely the reasoning of the replicated judge, thus avoiding the issues raised concerning that approach.

There are, however, some concerns that would still apply. Brennan-Marquez and Henderson argue that the situation of the decision-maker is itself important. In particular, they suggest that 'those tasked with making decisions should be susceptible, reciprocally, to the impact of decisions'.[86] Unless machines can be placed in this state psychologically, they are arguably not suitable judges. For this to be the case, the replicated brain would need to be placed in a robot that could truly experience the confinement of jail. Even there, one might wonder whether the psychological state of that robot would be sufficiently human that one can describe their feelings about this as truly mirroring those of a defendant in the criminal justice system.

Another matter worth considering is the importance of generational renewal within the justice system. There are ideas currently viewed as central to the rule of law, such as equal treatment of women and racial minorities, that would have felt quite foreign to those born a thousand years ago. Similarly, Oliver Wendell Holmes may have been a famous judge of his time, but 'three generations of imbeciles is enough' would hardly constitute good legal reasoning today.[87] If we uploaded today's judges into artificial brains inside computer systems or robotic bodies, it is unlikely that they would adapt to radical new ideas. Judicial decision-making would become increasingly conservative, possibly leading to stagnation of society more broadly.

Uploaded brains is just one example of a futuristic vision of AI, and science fiction books are filled with plenty more. Nevertheless, it is difficult to imagine forms of AI to which one could not raise important objections. New kinds of techniques can overcome objections to legitimacy raised in the past, but will often meet new concerns. Each time a barrier to legitimacy is crossed by new techniques, there is a possibility that the z-axis will expand in that the use of those techniques will be legitimate in circumstances where use of earlier techniques was not. I doubt that we can conceive of an autonomous system that will overcome all objections to legitimacy, but I may be proven wrong. Based on the objections raised to date, it would seem that this would require machines to do more than merely mimic or predict human judges. Rather, people may need to be convinced that machine judges share a similar consciousness to themselves and are oriented to their moral and historical understandings.

V. Conclusion

Disentangling current practice, technical capacity and legitimacy, with a focus on differences between and within subfields of AI, helps ground debates about AI. Along the x-axis, one might observe successes and failures in the implementation of new legal

[86] K Brennan-Marquez and S Henderson, 'Artificial Intelligence and Role-Reversible Judgment' (2019) 109 *Journal of Criminal Law and Criminology* 137.

[87] *Buck v Bell*, 274 US 200 (1927).

technologies and critique the balance between applications that make large-scale litigation more efficient versus applications that enhance access to justice. Along the y-axis, one can look at new techniques introduced over time, each bringing different affordances and limitations that need to be understood when considering the bounds what they make possible. More recently, there has been a growth in scholarship around where the limits of legitimacy may lie, particularly when delegating judicial powers of the state to automated systems. We thus have an evolving picture of the z-axis, but the solid is relatively flat.

Straining visualisation further, one might use opacity of the solid generated to signal the extent of automation (actual, possible and legitimate) in a given domain. Hybrid systems with machine and human components can then be imagined within the same solid – more opaque where human components are minimal (human-on-the-loop) and more transparent where humans retain greater control over the system as a whole. Here, legitimacy can grow, for example through automated 'pre-instance' decisions overseen by independent human appeal mechanisms offering a full hearing and human judgment.[88]

Barriers that seem insurmountable along all three axes may (or may not) be overcome in the future as technology continues to evolve. However, it is unlikely that future history will play out as a straight path towards the legal singularity. More likely, new technologies will lead to both progress and error, sometimes expanding what is available, what is possible and what is appropriate and legitimate in ways that are both evolutionary and revolutionary. But there are many thresholds to cross, and it is hard to imagine a system that would render law fully computable without changing the nature of law itself.

[88] Wu, above n 18.

10

The Law of Contested Concepts? Reflections on Copyright Law and the Legal and Technological Singularities

DILAN THAMPAPILLAI*

Since the invention of the Caxton Printing Press in 1476, copyright law was brought into existence by technological developments and its internal revolutions have been driven by the same.[1] Yet, throughout its several hundred years of existence, from the common law of copyright through to the Statute of Anne and onto the modern statutes that now proliferate across the globe, copyright has always banked upon human beings enjoying an untrammelled monopoly over creativity.[2] This monopoly is made plain in a number of important jurisdictions, such as Singapore,[3] Australia[4] and the US,[5] where the law requires that the author of a work must be a human being.

At its heart, copyright law is a species of property. In a Hohfeldian sense,[6] copyright is concerned with establishing a jural relationship between an owners and a vast array of non-owners. Further, copyright as a property system is predicated upon the notion of exclusion. Yet, exclusion has always been an imperfect vehicle. All that copyright really affords is the opportunity to claim redress for violations of the exclusive rights of the owner rather than any wholesale guarantee that those rights will always be observed. To maintain legitimacy as a property system, copyright law has substantial carve-out areas such as the fair use doctrine. Fair use works to demarcate the extent of an owner's

* School of Law, Australian National University.

[1] B Kaplan, *An Unhurried View of Copyright* (Columbia University Press, 1967) 2–7. See also E Eisenstein, *The Printing Press as an Agent of Change, Volume 1* (Cambridge University Press, 1979).

[2] See D Thampapillai, 'If Value Then Right? Copyright and Works of Non-human Authorship' (2019) 30 *Australian Intellectual Property Journal* 1.

[3] *Global Yellow Pages Ltd v Promedia Directories Pte Ltd* [2017] SGCA 28, [27] (Menon CJ delivering the opinion of the Court).

[4] *Telstra Corp Ltd v Phone Directories Co Pty Ltd* (2010) 194 FCR 142; [2010] FCAFC 149. See *also IceTV Pty Ltd v Nine Network Australia Pty Ltd* (2009) 239 CLR 458.

[5] *Naruto v David John Slater* (ND Cal, Case No 315-cv-04324 WHO, 2016).

[6] See W Hohfeld, 'Fundamental Legal Conceptions as Applied in Judicial Reasoning and Other Legal Essays' (1913) 23 *Yale Law Journal* 16.

monopoly by use of a proportionality system. As a result, the boundaries of copyright ownership are both permeable and moveable.

Herein lies a very fundamental problem. The prescient nature of the singularity strikes at the heart of two core truths of copyright. Namely, that copyright exists to serve the interests and ambitions of human beings and also that the law of copyright is incapable of perfect enforcement. Though it may not seem so, these two principles are deeply intertwined because the interests of creators and owners do not always coincide and also because copyright was never meant to stifle the development of new technologies.

On this basis, Alarie's advocacy of a legal singularity – as a perfect legal system – is deeply and profoundly problematic.[7] It works off of an assumption that may well not hold true for copyright law. Alarie's example of a tax system that efficiently forestalls tax evasion and adroitly collects tax revenue, never engages with the base issue of income generation.[8] Put simply, Alarie's tax model never stops to contemplate whether the emergence of AI systems might mean that human labour is overwhelmingly replaced,[9] thereby largely obviating the need for a tax system in the first instance. This is no small oversight, and, as the future of copyright law might well demonstrate, the technological singularity could easily undermine the fundamental purpose of the law in the way in which it impacts human labour, creativity and enterprise.[10]

The legal singularity may pose a problem along the lines foreshadowed above. As the legal singularity would entail technology replacing human decision-making it raises questions about how that technology would operate and whether it would be open to critique and reform. As Hildebrandt has suggested, the fundamental problem is that AI technologies make decisions on the basis of vast volumes of past data.[11] Future data cannot be coded into an automated decision-making system.[12] This then begs the question of how an automated decision-making system will react once a novel problem arises. Using the fair use doctrine from the US, I suggest that this will be problematic.[13]

The structure of this chapter is as follows: these opening paragraphs have introduced the basic premise. Namely, a scepticism that a legal singularity would effectively deal with copyright law. Section I maps out the parameters of two dual and overlapping singularities – one technological and the other legal. The legal singularity depends for its existence on the development of a super-human technological intelligence. Without this technological singularity there can be no real legal singularity. In the sense contemplated by Alarie's legal singularity, this new legal system must be driven by some intelligence otherwise it is nothing more than an automated tool of human minds. Section II addresses the nature of copyright as a functionally incomplete

[7] B Alarie, 'The Path of the Law: Towards Legal Singularity' (2016) 66(4) *University of Toronto Law Journal* 443.

[8] ibid.

[9] ibid.

[10] There has already been considerable debate about whether AI should even be permitted to enter into the realm of copyright law. For example, see D Gervais, 'Machine Authors' (Vanderbilt Law Research Paper No 19-35, 25 March 2019) 22, papers.ssrn.com/sol3/papers.cfm?abstract_id=3359524.

[11] M Hildebrandt, 'Code Driven Law', paper for Lex Ex Machina Conference, Cambridge 13 December 2019, 8; ch 3 in this volume.

[12] ibid.

[13] There are other reasons to be concerned, such as hidden values in the law and the like.

property system. It is argued here that copyright law works because it tacitly tolerates a degree of infringement and permits an ever-shifting line between free and non-free uses of copyright materials. The true danger that the legal singularity poses then is that it threatens to perfect an imperfect system and to freeze in time a moveable line around use. Section III of this chapter addresses the complex compromises and hidden concepts within key areas of copyright law such as fair use. It is difficult to imagine that even a super-human technological intelligence could deliver rules that would placate all of the stakeholders within copyright law. In Section IV, I conclude that a legal system driven by a super-human technological intelligence is inherently unpredictable because the intelligence is essentially non-human. This lack of predictability undermines the need for certainty within private law.

I. Dual Singularities: Technological and Legal

The technological singularity is commonly thought to refer to a state within which technological progress is so radical and infinite that it cannot be predicted. Within this state a super-human intelligence might emerge as a competitor or even as a successor to human intelligence. The legal singularity of which Alarie writes is contentious then in this context.[14] There is an argument that Alarie's legal singularity is nothing more than a mere technological progression rather than a significant evolutionary leap. Alarie writes:

> With the considerable advantages that machines have over humans in terms of memory, objectivity, and logic, one may feel that machines will come to strictly dominate humans in the law in the near future. Although there is considerable evidence that experts expect this to be true in the long run, it is likely that more data and better machine learning inference tools are likely to be complements to human judgment rather than substitutes for the next several decades (in all likelihood).[15]

At least in the near future this is a situation well short of a true singularity. It is instead a shift in the current state of affairs, albeit one that is not as radical as Alarie appears to suggest.

In his ground-breaking piece on the singularity, Vernor Vinge postulated that mankind might eventually be faced with 'computers that are awake and superhumanly intelligent'.[16] This is of course profoundly speculative, but it is not beyond the realms of possibility. Moreover, given the trajectory of technological development it does not seem at all to be an unlikely outcome. There are at least four different variants of the technological singularity. First, there is the prospect that the computers will develop a consciousness such that they are 'awake' in a manner of speaking in addition to possessing intelligence far beyond that of human beings.[17] The second, that the network of

[14] See Alarie, above n 7.
[15] Alarie, above n 7, 450.
[16] V Vinge, 'The Coming Technological Singularity: How to Suvive in the Post-Human Era' (Working Paper), edoras.sdsu.edu/~vinge/misc/singularity.html.
[17] ibid.

computers might also awaken and function as a single entity.[18] The third, postulates a union of sorts between man and technology such that the human-computer system becomes superhuman.[19] The fourth, which is beyond the scope of this chapter, is that human biology might be altered in some manner that radically changes our intelligence and intellectual abilities.[20]

There has been considerable angst in copyright circles around the rise of artificial intelligence.[21] As noted above, this is due to the displacement of the human monopoly over creativity. It is beyond the scope of this chapter to explore this issue in detail, but there is a particular problem with assuming that the technological singularity will not severely disrupt the industries around copyright law. If it does, then there might be precious little by way of human-centric disputes for a machine learning decision-making system to adjudicate upon.

It is difficult not to see these visions of a singularity as profoundly dystopian. There is little to suggest that if either or both of the first two situations envisaged by Vinge eventuated that any superhuman technological entity would necessarily want to serve as a dispute resolution tool for human beings. The more likely situation, in the context of the legal singularity, is that there would be a sustained interaction between human beings and technology in a way that radically changes the legal system. In effect, technology would become so intertwined with the business and governance of law that it would appear super-human to an outside person.

The real question then about the legal singularity is how would such a system function? As it stands, artificial intelligence already has a black box problem.[22] Where the rule of law is concerned this is problematic. A decision-making system must deliver an outcome, but it must also demonstrate that there are sufficient reasons behind the decision. Likewise, there is a very real problem with AI decision-making systems producing outcomes that are clearly wrong. For example, Facebook's AI moderation system recently removed a substantial number of posts concerning the COVID-19 health crisis even though those posts did not actually breach the terms of service.[23] Presumably, in the legal singularity these problems would be substantially reduced, but there is no guarantee that they could be completely eliminated.

Markou and Deakin have also identified that for machine learning '[s]uccess is measured in terms of the algorithm's ability to predict or identify a specified outcome or range … from a given vector of variables'.[24] This requires significant amounts of

[18] ibid.

[19] ibid.

[20] ibid.

[21] See Gervais, above n 10.

[22] See M Rich, 'Machine Learning, Automated Suspicion Algorithms, and the Fourth Amendment' (2016) 164 *University of Pennsylvania Law Review* 871, 886. Rich makes the observation that machine learning leads to AI whose operations become too complicated for their original programmers to understand. See also W Knight, 'The Dark Secret at the Heart of AI' (*MIT Technology Review*, 11 April 2017), www.technologyreview.com/s/604087/the-dark-secret-at-the-heart-of-ai/.

[23] See J Constine, 'Facebook Wrongly Blocked Some Links Including Coronavirus Info' (*TechCrunch*, 18 March 2020), techcrunch.com/2020/03/17/facebook-link-spam-filter-coronavirus/.

[24] C Markou and S Deakin, 'Ex Machina Lex: The Limits of Legal Computability' 21 (Working Paper), www.academia.edu/39761958/Ex_Machina_Lex_The_Limits_of_Legal_Computability.

data, training, effective error correction and review.[25] In particular, the prediction function is heavily data specific. Similarly, identifying a desirable outcome means that there would need to be a substantial amount of input data upon which the technology could rely.

The obvious problem that arises here is that a machine learning system has potential value within the legal system where there are very significant amounts of data, but the type of cases that raise particularly novel issues often have little or no precedent. *Sony Corporation of America v Universal City Studios*,[26] *Metro-Goldwyn-Mayer Studios v Grokster*[27] and *Campbell v Acuff-Rose*[28] are cases within the framework of fair use and contributory liability that raise peculiar and unusual issues. Whether a heavily data-dependent machine learning system could adequately achieve the same results as the US Supreme Court did in those cases, and which other human judiciaries have achieved in like cases, is highly questionable. Indeed, replicating decision-making outcomes in relatively routine situations appears quite manageable for machine learning.

Given the nature of the singularity it is likely that a new and evolved legal system would have the following features:

- A tendency towards perfect enforcement of legal rights.
- The ability to effectively apply rules in situation where a vast amount of data already exists to guide effective decision-making.
- A similar, but less widely accepted ability to make decisions in situations that require abstract reasoning and where the is insufficient data upon which to base a decision.
- Efficiencies of scale in relation to vast tranches of data in a manner that far outweighs that of human beings.

The four features identified above are desirable, but they are most effective where decision-making occurs in data heavy contexts. More importantly, given the black box problem surrounding the operation of the technology, without a human being to review and endorse the decision made by AI technology the entire system would be open to controversy and dispute. As such, it seems safe at this point to question Alarie's use of the term 'legal singularity' and instead to suggest that what might ultimately be transpiring here is a radical and fundamental shift in the operation of the law. Nevertheless, it should fall short of the dystopian situation identified by Vinge.

For the purposes of this chapter, I will assume that the legal singularity entails a system wherein human decision-making at a judicial level is almost entirely replaced save for the functions of review and endorsement. This then results in a legal system which is primarily reliant upon automated decision-making. In turn, this raises the question of whether that could ever be as good as the outcomes previously obtained by the iterative human decision-making system of the common law.

[25] ibid.
[26] (1984) 464 U.S. 417.
[27] 454 F. Supp. 2d 996 (2006) (D. U.S.).
[28] 510 U.S. 569 (1994).

II. Copyright as a Functionally Incomplete Property System

Copyright law has to house competing concerns, but it must also do this within the framework of a particular species of legal regime. Namely, copyright is a property system. Albeit, copyright is a property system that has to accommodate competing concerns in the form of technology development and changes in accepted user culture.

There are consequences that stem from constructing copyright law as a property regime. Intellectual property law scholars have sought to resist the classification of intellectual property as 'property'. Indeed, at the beginning of the digital revolution there was a spirited scholarly debate about whether intellectual property could legitimately be regarded as property.[29] This was no mere debate about semantics. There was much at stake in the sense that the different conceptions of property could directly affect the policy choices that courts and legislators made about intellectual property law.[30] These can be regarded as choices about rules, both in terms of which rules should exist within the system and how those rules should be applied. As Lemley has noted seeing intellectual property as property made the courts rather more likely to support the needs of rights-holders and less likely to tolerate 'free-riding' even in those instances where free riding caused little real harm and delivered benefits to the society as a whole.[31] In turn, this has the potential to disadvantage other actors such as users or authors who emerge later in time and attempt to build their new works on the back of existing works.[32]

As a property system, copyright law must feature and privilege exclusion in its rules. Indeed, as Balganesh has noted the right to exclude represents 'a manifestation of the norm of inviolability, on which the entire institution of property is centered'.[33] The exclusion function automatically accompanies ownership within a property regime.[34] Landes and Posner have written '[a] property right is a legally enforceable power to exclude others from using a resource'.[35] Similarly, in the case of *Kaiser Aetna v United States*, Rehnquist J stated that, 'one of the most essential sticks in the bundle of rights that are commonly characterized as property' is 'the right to exclude others'.[36]

Exclusion features in copyright law by: (i) the creation of exclusive rights that vest in copyright owners, and (ii) the statutory tort of copyright infringement, and (iii) by

[29] See eg, F Easterbrook, 'Intellectual Property is Still Property' (1990) 13 *Harvard Journal of Law and Public Policy* 108; S Carter, 'Does it Matter Whether Intellectual Property is Property?' (1993) 68 *Chicago-Kent Law Review* 715; T Hardy, 'Property in Cyberspace' (1996) *University of Chicago Legal Forum* 217. See also M Lemley, 'Property, Intellectual Property, and Free Riding' (2005) 83 *Texas Law Review* 1031; R Epstein, 'Liberty versus Property? Cracks in the Foundations of Copyright Law' (2005) 42 *San Diego Law Review* 1.

[30] Lemley op cit, 1036–37.

[31] ibid.

[32] This latter category of authors perfectly describes the situation in *Campbell v Acuff-Rose Music Inc* 510 U.S. 569 (1994).

[33] S Balganesh, 'Demystifying the Right to Exclude: Of Property, Inviolability, and Automatic Injunctions' (2008) 31 *Harvard Journal of Law and Public Policy* 617, 627.

[34] W Landes and R Posner, *The Economic Structure of Intellectual Property* (Harvard University Press, 2003) 12. For a discussion of the primacy of exclusion within property regimes see T Merrill and H Smith, 'The Morality of Property' (2007) 48 *William & Mary Law Review* 1849. See also E Weinrib, 'Poverty and Property in Kant's System of Rights' (2003) 78 *Notre Dame Law Review* 795.

[35] Landes and Posner op cit.

[36] 444 U.S. 164, 176 (1979).

creating norms that privilege ownership. In *JT International SA v Commonwealth of Australia*,[37] French CJ stated, '[C]opyright is defined by reference to exclusive rights of, inter alia, reproduction and publication of works and subject matter other than works'.[38] As excluding other parties from consuming a non-rivalrous good is difficult, copyright law responds to the 'intrusion' by making infringement an actionable tort.[39] It is this construction of copyright law as a statutory tort-based system that is itself a manifestation of exclusion within copyright law.[40]

However, it would be wrong to characterise the copyright as being solely concerned with exclusion. The copyright laws invariably contain a number of statutory licensing schemes, including those that are designed for education, libraries and disabled access. Further, there are exceptions to a copyright owner's rights, in terms of fair use, fair dealing and other specific exceptions, which further limit and conditions ownership.

Fair use is a perfect example of a doctrine that seeks to balance the interests of existing copyright owners, users, emerging authors and technology developers. In 1976 when the US Copyright Act was enacted the fair use doctrine in section 107 was put in place to serve as a safeguard to protect copyright balance at a time where new legitimate uses could not be predicted.[41] This proved essential in cases such as *Sony Corporation of America v Universal City Studios Inc*,[42] and *Campbell v Acuff-Rose*.[43] The former case balanced the rights of technology developers against existing copyright owners. In turn, it led to a major revolution in the consumption of television entertainment and helped spawn the video-rental industry which in turn has now been replaced by online content services such as Netflix and the like. The latter case dealt with emerging musicians whose work drew on and parodied the work of an older, more established musician.

All of this was possible because of the inherent uncertainty of the application of the fair use doctrine. Consider the wording of section 107 of the US Copyright Act:

> … the fair use of a copyrighted work, including such use by reproduction in copies or phonorecords or by any other means specified by that section, for purposes such as criticism, comment, news reporting, teaching (including multiple copies for classroom use), scholarship, or research, is not an infringement of copyright. In determining whether the use made of a work in any particular case is a fair use the factors to be considered shall include—
>
> (1) the purpose and character of the use, including whether such use is of a commercial nature or is for nonprofit educational purposes;
> (2) the nature of the copyrighted work;

[37] (2012) 86 ALJR 1297.
[38] 86 ALJR 1297, [34].
[39] W Gordon, 'Copyright As Tort Law's Mirror Image: "Harms," "Benefits", and the Uses and Limits of Analogy' (2003) 34 *McGeorge Law Review* 533. Gordon explains that while copyright law and personal injury law are opposites they share many crucial characteristics and serve similar purposes. See also, S Ricketson, 'Reaping Without Sowing: Unfair Competition and Intellectual Property Rights in Anglo-Australian Law' (1984) 7 *University of New South Wales Law Journal* 1.
[40] See *Corelli v Gray* (1913) 29 TLR 570; *Francis Day & Hunter Ltd v Bron* [1963] Ch 587; *Zeccola v Universal City Studios Inc* [1982] AIPC 90-019.
[41] See P Samuelson, 'Justifications for Copyright Limitations and Exceptions' in R Okediji (ed), *Copyright Law in an Age of Limitations and Exceptions* (Cambridge University Press, 2017).
[42] *Sony Corporation of America v Universal City Studios Inc* 464 U.S. 417 (1984).
[43] 510 US 579 (1994).

> (3) the amount and substantiality of the portion used in relation to the copyrighted work as a whole; and
> (4) the effect of the use upon the potential market for or value of the copyrighted work.
>
> The fact that a work is unpublished shall not itself bar a finding of fair use if such finding is made upon consideration of all the above factors.

The fair use doctrine is in effect a 'principles-based' statutory rule.[44] That is, the four factor test sets out principles that serve to guide judicial decision-making, but which also leave a substantial amount of flexibility for judges to develop the common law of the statute. Each of the four factors generates arguments for and against a finding of fair use, but there is no rigid rule that must be applied.

Fair use is in effect a common law rule transplanted into a statutory context. As the US Supreme Court has stated, the fair use doctrine originated in the decision of Story J in *Folsom v Marsh*.[45] Further, fair use retains its inherent common law qualities because it is a set of guided principles by which the law may be made rather than a prescriptive set of elements that must be satisfied. Section 107 of the Copyright Act offers more guidance than was originally contemplated with the provision setting out a four factor test which must be applied in light of the chapeau. Section 107 is not a cumulative test. A finding of fair use does not require that all or even a majority of the four factors must be satisfied. Instead, the four factors guide a decision on fair use with the verdict depending upon the intuition and reasoning of the judges as to whether the use is fair overall.

Nowhere is this more relevant than where instances of transformative use arise. The question of transformative use arises in relation to a particular type of copyright problem. For example, an artist may create a new work that is based upon the original work of another artist. The artist who created the original work may seek to sue the artist who created the new work for copyright infringement. If the artist took more than a substantial part of the original work to create the new work then there is a prima facie case for infringement and the only real escape will be if fair use can be made out. On the bare facts as set out above two simple policy issues can be discerned. The first is that the creator of the original work has copyright in that work and the property interest that lies therein should be protected. The second is that in any culture artists will need to draw on the work of others to create new works. This second issue raises questions of free speech and cultural development.

The fair use doctrine mediates between these two issues. As Judge Pierre Leval noted in his influential *Harvard Law Review* article, 'copyright is not an inevitable, divine, or natural right that confers on authors the absolute ownership of their creations. It is designed rather to stimulate activity and progress in the arts for the intellectual enrichment of the public'.[46] This statement was endorsed by the Second Circuit in *Cariou v Prince*,[47] who also identified the 'mediating' role of fair use. In essence the fair use principles embodied in

[44] See G Austin, 'The Two Faces of Fair Use' (2012) 25 *New Zealand Universities Law Review* 285.

[45] *Campbell v Acuff-Rose Music Inc* 510 U.S. 569 (1994). *Folsom v Marsh* 9 F Cas 342 (CCD Mass 1841) (No 4901). However, Matthew Sag has suggested that the origins of the fair use doctrine go back farther than the decision in *Folsom v Marsh*. See M Sag, 'The Prehistory of Fair Use' (2011) 76 *Brooklyn Law Review* 1371.

[46] P Leval, 'Toward a Fair Use Standard' (1990) 103 *Harvard Law Review* 1105.

[47] 714 F.3d 694 (2013).

the four factors and relevant jurisprudence allow for a broad rule of proportionality to be applied so that some decisions will favour copyright protection whereas other decisions will support fair use. The sub-doctrinal rule that the US courts have developed in order to apply the proportionality test is that of transformative use.

III. Copyright and the Robot Judge? The Fair Use Example

The problem with the legal singularity postulated by Alarie is that it cedes simply too much territory to an automated coded decision-making system. The difficulty that arises here is that the type of automated decision-making systems that have been contemplated in the literature are as Hildebrandt suggests, if-this-then-that (IFTTT) systems.[48] There is arguably a rigidity to such systems and the finer distinctions that need to be made in an applied area of law, keeping in mind copyright law's profoundly imperfect state of being, are that this allows too little room for complex multi-factoral decision-making where cases are ultimately decided by human judicial intuition and feel rather than pre-programmed commands.

Consider the following rudimentary dichotomy of statutory rules. On the one hand there are those statutory rules where the meaning is captured within the provision and can be almost mechanically applied to fact situations as they arise.[49] An example of this could be a hypothetical copyright statute which contains a rule stating that 'an infringement occurs once a substantial part of an original work is copied'. This could be considered a simple and prescriptive rule. Beyond the necessary definitions that underpin the concepts within the rule,[50] it requires little balancing and weighing of factors.

The second category is quite different. This category contains 'principles-based' statutory rules, such as the fair use rule described above. In contrast to the first category of rules set out above 'principles-based' statutory rules are not heavily prescriptive. Instead, they rely upon the use of a given set of principles to guide decision-making. There might well be no set hierarchy amongst the relevant principles and they may have to be weighed and balanced in their application in light of a fundamental underlying policy goal. This dichotomy is of course overly-simplistic, but it does highlight a broad divide amongst statutory rules.

Fair use is in effect, a 'principles-based' statutory provision as opposed to a prescriptive statutory rule. This has necessarily provided for a greater role for the judiciary to develop the law. A rule of this nature is fundamentally different to that which would fit neatly into the box of automated decision-making.

[48] See Hildebrandt, above n 11.

[49] The independent contractor or employee dichotomy almost fits neatly into this category. In the context of copyright law see *Redrock Holdings Pty Ltd & Hotline Communications Ltd v Hinkley* [2001] VSC 91 or *Beloff v Pressdram* [1973] RPC 756.

[50] In this instance, the questions of law that would arise would be as to the meaning of 'substantial part', 'original work' and 'copied'. When these questions are settled then the provision may be applied in light of the rules of statutory interpretation. Given the nature of legislative drafting it is more likely than not that such key phrases as 'substantial part' and 'original work' would be defined in the statute. In other words, the first category of statutory rules is prescriptive and their boundaries are tightly defined.

The key difficulty that principle-based rules pose for automated decision-making systems is that they are highly discretionary. They often require complex balancing acts and most often the decisions made here are controversial. For example, the seminal case of *Universal v Sony* produced a split 5–4 decision in the Supreme Court of the United States. In the section below, using the fair use doctrine as an example, I suggest that there are three main difficulties that will face automated decision-making systems.

A. New Rules Involve Complex Compromises

In *Sony Corporation of America v Universal City Studios Inc*,[51] the Supreme Court of the United States used the fair use doctrine, enshrined in section 107 of the Copyright Act 1976 to find that time-shifting constituted a fair use of the copyright in the broadcasted programs. The emergence of the Betamax video-cassette recorder posed a significant challenge to the copyright industries because of the potential for home copying. It took eight years for the *Sony* case to make its way through the US federal court system to the US Supreme Court and for the latter to rule that its uses were mostly protected as fair use.[52] Most importantly, a majority of the Supreme Court held:

> the sale of copying equipment, like the sale of other articles of commerce, does not constitute contributory infringement if the product is widely used for legitimate, unobjectionable purposes. Indeed, it need merely be capable of substantial non-infringing uses.[53]

In *Sony*, the majority looked to patent law to find a suitable rule of contributory liability that could be applied to copyright law.[54] Even then there was very little jurisprudence upon which the court could rely. Nonetheless, a compromise had to be fashioned between the technology industries, as represented by Sony, and the content industries. The rule that the US Supreme Court relied upon, and which was later raised in *Grokster*, is a compromise between competing concerns. What it is not, is a simple exercise in classifying a relationship as according to a pre-existing taxonomy.

What was at stake in *Sony* was the possibility that enforcing copyright as a strong property regime could foreclose the development of new and useful technologies. An automated machine learning system that is heavily reliant on past data might not necessarily grasp the true nature of the choice in a case like *Sony*. Moreover, in the absence of sufficient data upon which to conclusively decide, a machine learning system might opt for an enforcement of the existing law thereby favouring copyright owners and tacitly freezing the law in place.

A similar issue arose in *Campbell v Acuff-Rose*, where the US Supreme Court decided that 2-Live Crew's adaptation of Roy Orbison's song *Pretty Woman* was a transformative fair use. Here again the Supreme Court was called upon to fashion a compromise where two competing commercial interests came into use. The development of transformative

[51] *Sony Corporation of America v Universal City Studios Inc* 464 U.S. 417 (1984).
[52] See J Litman, 'The Story of Sony v Universal Studios: Mary Poppins Meets the Boston Strangler' (2006) in JC Ginsburg and RC Dreyfuss, *Intellectual Property Stories* (2005).
[53] *Sony*, 442.
[54] ibid.

fair use also represented a radical departure within the law of fair use. This decision permitted a commercial player, competing for a different audience demographic, to use the work of another author provided that it did so in a dramatically different way.

The problem that would arise here is that neither *Sony* or *Campbell* is entirely predictable based upon previous data. A difficult balancing act arises here. Statements employed in resolving one case can be applied and even misapplied in another case. The law is liable to be misdirected or at least to give rise to unintended consequences. This is a reality of any decision-making system, but a technology enhanced system, with exceptionally quick dispute resolution capabilities, could generate a vast amount of jurisprudence very quickly without necessarily having the benefit of reflection and review that is enjoyed in the modern legal system.

B. Concepts are Inherently Contestable

There is a basic framework that has now emerged around transformative use cases. In essence a first creator produces a work in which copyright subsists. A second creator comes along and then uses that work to create a second work. Under a traditional fair use analysis, the transformative nature of the second work is one of the key elements in the four factor test. Moreover, in cases like *SunTrust Bank v Houghton Mifflin*[55] it is apparent that transformative use effectively colours the entire fair use analysis. In *SunTrust*, the Eleventh Circuit noted the 'special import' of a work's transformative nature in relation to the purpose of the use. At issue in *SunTrust* was the parody novel *The Wind Done Gone* (TWDG) which took a substantial part of the earlier novel *Gone With The Wind* (GWTW). The Court noted that though GWTW was entitled to the greatest protection as a creative work, this factor was to be 'given little weight in parody cases'.[56] As with *Campbell v Acuff-Rose*, the work in *SunTrust* was a highly transformative parody.

However, the same observations cannot be made about the works in question in *Cariou v Prince*. In *Cariou*, the artist Richard Prince used elements of photographs taken by Patrick Cariou to create a series of paintings. The Second Circuit found that many of the photographs were transformative fair uses. The works in *Cariou* often involved placing parts of the pre-existing works in different and unusual situations, but they left the latter largely intact. As such, the demarcation line between transformative uses and infringing derivative works needs to be spelled out with greater clarity.[57] As with *SunTrust*, the Second Circuit in *Cariou* gave great weight to the first factor in that it established transformative use, and less weight to the other three factors. In relation to the nature of the protected work and the effect on the market, the Second Circuit stated 'just as with the commercial character of Prince's work, this factor may be of limited

[55] 68 F 3d 1257 (1 1th Cir, 2001).

[56] *SunTrust*, 268 F.3d 1257, 1271.

[57] See T Cotter, 'Transformative Use and Cognizable Harm (2010) 12(4) *Vanderbildt Journal of Entertainment and Technology Law* 701 making the argument that transformative uses and derivative works have an uncomfortable overlap and that this concern has been neglected in the relevant case law.

usefulness where, as here, the creative work of art is being used for a transformative purpose'.[58]

The problem that arises here is that concept of transformative is highly contestable. What one court might view as transformative another court might not. It is not at all clear that a machine learning system could do a better job. The difficulty lies in the fact that there is a degree of artistic appreciation involved in the assessment of the works in question. *Cariou* is a case where the Court was cognisant not just of the works produced by the second artist, but also his intentions.

C. Rules Contain Hidden Values

It is also noticeable in the fair use case law that there appears to be a good faith/bad faith dichotomy present in transformative use cases. For example, in *SunTrust*, Alice Randall's attempt to directly challenge the racism of Gone With The Wind was viewed by the Eleventh Circuit almost in terms of good faith. In contrast, in *Salinger v Colting*,[59] Colting's stated desire to write a 'sequel' to *Catcher in the Rye* and his later recanting was viewed by both the District Court and the Second Circuit as somewhat 'bad faith' conduct. Though the express terms 'good faith' and 'bad faith' are not used in the jurisprudence there is quite evidently some concern with the nature of the second author's conduct and their intentions.

In part, good faith conduct helps to explain the difference between cases where the line between liability and permitted free use is exceedingly thin. Yet, this is more than a mere issue of inconvenient obiter remarks, it goes to the heart of why cases like *Salinger v Colting* should be cases of infringement whereas cases like *SunTrust* warrant protection as transformative uses. Good faith is also relevant to the free speech question that lies as an undercurrent within transformative use cases. This was most directly addressed in *SunTrust*, perhaps in part because that case brought up the hot button issues of racial prejudice and slavery.

Could a machine learning system analyse large quantities of data and identify hidden values? This is not outside the realms of possibility and it is perhaps here that machine learning has great potential. However, again, this feature of machine learning capabilities only arises where there is a substantial amount of data upon which to base an analysis. In the absence of significant quantities of data, the human knack for intuition and fair play seems a superior quality.

IV. Conclusion

The idea of a legal singularity is promising. However, the premise upon which it is based is deeply flawed. There are two key problems that have been outlined in this chapter. The first is that rapid advances in technology that approach a point of singularity will not be

[58] *Cariou*, 710.
[59] *Salinger v Colting* 641 F Supp 2d 250 (SDNY, 2009); *Salinger v Colting* 607 F 3d (2nd Cir, 2010).

confined in their application to legal decision-making systems. They will permeate all aspects of life and take away some of the areas in which human labour has thrived. This will deprive the law of its human subject thereby creating new difficulties. The second is that machine learning systems are heavily data dependent. Yet, there are many areas of law in which novel questions arise. It is here that human systems and reasoning have proved resilient and adaptable. There is no guarantee at all that machine learning could produce outcomes like the *Sony* or *Campbell v Acuff-Rose* decisions. For these reasons the legal singularity should be treated with scepticism.

11

Capacitas Ex Machina: Are Computerised Assessments of Mental Capacity a 'Red Line' or Benchmark for AI?

CHRISTOPHER MARKOU AND LILY HANDS*

> That which exists does not conform to various opinions, but rather the correct opinions conform to what exists.
>
> Maimonides, *The Guide for the Perplexed* (1190)[1]

> [M]ost of the harm computers can potentially entrain is much more a function of properties people attribute to computers than of what a computer can or cannot actually be made to do.
>
> Joseph Weizenbaum, *On the Impact of Computers in Society* (1972)[2]

Mental disorders affect more than one billion people worldwide, with a substantial 'treatment gap' preventing all but a fraction from receiving adequate or, indeed, any mental health care.[3] The World Health Organization (WHO) estimates that untreated mental disorders account for '13% of the total global burden of disease'[4] and by 2030 'depression will be the leading cause of disease burden globally'.[5] Because responsibility for providing health services is typically vested in national governments, there is also a 'legislative gap'.[6] The WHO further reports '[t]here is no national mental health

* Faculty of Law, University of Cambridge. We gratefully acknowledge the support of the ESRC through its funding for the UKRI-JST Joint Call on Artificial Intelligence and Society.

[1] Maimonides, in M Friedlander (ed), *The Guide for the Perplexed*, 2nd edn (Dover, 1956) 1, 96a.

[2] J Weizenbaum, 'On the Impact of Computers in Society: How does one insult a machine?' (1972) 176 *Science* 4035, 614.

[3] R Kohn, S Saxena, I Levav and B Saraceno, 'The treatment gap in mental health care' (2004) 82 *Bulletin of the World Health Organisation* 11; *cf* D Vigo, G Thornicroft and R Atun, 'Estimating the true global burden of mental illness' (2016) 3 *The Lancet Psychiatry* 2.

[4] World Health Organization, 'Global burden of mental disorders and the need for a comprehensive, coordinated response from health and social sectors at the country level' (2011) EB130/9, apps.who.int/gb/ebwha/pdf_files/EB130/B130_9-en.pdf.

[5] World Health Organization, 'Global burden of mental disorders'; *cf* J-P Lépine and M Briley, 'The increasing burden of depression' (2011) 7 *(Supplement 1) Neuropsychiatric Disease and Treatment* 3.

[6] World Health Organization, 'Mental disorders affect one in four people' (*World Health Report*, 4 October 2001), www.who.int/whr/2001/media_centre/press_release/en/.

legislation in 25% of countries with nearly 31% of the world's population'.[7] While both the treatment and legislative gap present structural challenges to the provision of mental health services, the concept of mental disorder itself remains fiercely contested and eludes cogent definition.

Generally, mental disorders are believed to affect the structure and chemistry of the brain and catalyse changes in human behaviour, emotion and cognition.[8] In A History of Psychiatry, Shorter recounts what separated the biological turn in modern psychiatry from earlier attempts to understand and rationalise the workings of the human mind:

> What made the first biological psychiatry distinctive from previous humoral theories was not the belief that psychiatric illness possessed an underlying neural structure – physicians since the Ancients have believed that – but the desire to lay bare the relationship between mind and brain through systematic research.[9]

It is thus unsurprising that at the outset of the artificial intelligence (AI) enterprise in the mid-twentieth century, medical researchers started using computers to investigate the role of neurochemistry in human psychology and behaviour, identifying chemicals such as serotonin and noradrenaline as important variables in a range of mental disorders.[10] As Cobb observes:

> This nuanced view was quickly transformed into something far more definite, and by the 1980s the idea that low serotonin levels might directly cause depression had taken root, and became known as the chemical imbalance theory of depression.[11]

While the chemical imbalance theory also remains contested, and mental disorder a frustratingly protean concept,[12] Liddle suggests five common symptomatic dimensions: reality distortion, disorganisation, psychomotor, mood and anxiety.[13] In clinical practice, a patient is typically assessed through structured face-to-face clinical interviews and questionnaires (discussed below). These questionnaires provide a clinician with a rough heuristic for assessing the disposition and affect of a person, but do not constitute a positive 'diagnosis'[14] due to the subjectivity of interpreting and classifying behaviours[15]

[7] World Health Organization, 'Mental Health Legislation & Human Rights' (2003) *Mental Health Policy & Service Guidance Package*, www.who.int/mental_health/policy/services/7_legislation%20HR_WEB_07.pdf.

[8] *cf* BR Hergenhahn and TB Henley, *An Introduction to the History of Psychology*, 7th edn (Wadsworth, 2013).

[9] E Shorter, 'Chapter 3: The First Biological Psychiatry' in *A History of Psychiatry* (Wiley, 1998) 69.

[10] BJ Deacon and GL Baird, 'The Chemical Imbalance Explanation of Depression: Reducing Blame at What Cost?' (2009) 28 *Journal of Social and Clinical Psychology* 4; JR Lacasse and J Leo, 'Antidepressants and the ChemicalImbalance Theory of Depression: A Reflection and Update on the Discourse' (2015) 38 *The Behaviour Therapist* 7.

[11] M Cobb, *The Idea of the Brain: A History* (Princeton University Press, 2020) 306.

[12] *cf* M Foucault in J Khalifa (ed), *History of Madness* (J Murphy and J Khalifa tr, Routledge, 2006); J Ussher, *Women's Madness: Misogyny or Mental Illness?* (University of Massachusetts Press, 1992); L Bondi and E Burman, 'Women and Mental Health: A Feminist Review' (2001) 68 *Women and Mental Health* 6; W Schultz and N Hunter, 'Depression, Chemical Imbalances, and Feminism' (2016) 28 *Journal of Feminist Family Therapy* 4.

[13] P Liddle, *Disordered Mind and Brain: The Neural Basis of Mental Symptoms* (Royal College of Psychiatrists, 2001) 3–24.

[14] T Weaver, P Madden and V Charles et al., 'Comorbidity of substance misuse and mental illness in community mental health and substance misuse services' (2003) 183 *The British Journal of Psychiatry* 4; SM Hartz, CN Pato and H Medeiros, et al., 'Comorbidity of Severe Psychotic Disorders With Measures of Substance Use' (2014) 71 *JAMA Psychiatry* 3.

[15] JS Strauss, 'Diagnosis and reality: a noun is a terrible thing to waste' (2005) 38 *Psychopathology*; JS Strauss, 'Subjectivity and Severe Psychiatric Disorders' (2011) 37 *Schizophrenia Bulletin* 1.

and their ethnocultural relativity.[16] These factors, along with the circular hierarchy of medical knowledge,[17] the frequency of co-morbid disorders (i.e. schizophrenia and anxiety), and limits to current understanding, make the task of creating reliable diagnostic tools in psychological and psychiatric contexts uniquely challenging.[18] Among these challenges are the frequent co-morbidity of disorders,[19] stigma associated with mental health,[20] and the overarching challenge of differentiating between normal/abnormal psychopathology.[21] As Duffy et al. observe:

> Identifying a prototypical characteristic clinical description of a psychiatric illness is a challenge in of itself, given that illnesses rarely emerge fully formed as it were and our diagnostic criteria (which vary across taxonomies) are constantly undergoing 'consensus based' revision.[22]

The fundamental challenge of the psychiatric enterprise can thus be understood as recursively hypothesising what constitutes 'neurotypical' and 'aberrant' psychopathology, devising linguistic conceptions and diagnostic criteria for differentiating between them, and selecting the most appropriate treatment for ameliorating symptoms. The day-to-day challenge of the clinician tasked with diagnosing or treating the mentally disordered is that clinical observations are largely defined by those diagnostic criteria and various 'checklist' style assessments that provide a framework for selecting between existing definitions or 'labels' of mental disorder.[23] At face value, then, the systematic

[16] SM Manson, 'Culture and Major Depression: Current Challenges in the Diagnosis of Mood Disorders' (1995) 18 *Psychiatric Clinics of North America* 3; RJ Castillo, *Culture and Mental Illness: A Client-centered Approach* (Thomson Brooks, 1997); T Abdullah and TL Brown, 'Mental illness stigma and ethnocultural beliefs, values, and norms: An integrative review' (2011) 31 *Clinical Psychology Review* 6.

[17] O Bodenreider, 'Circular hierarchical relationships in the UMLS: Etiology, Diagnosis, Treatment, Complications and Prevention' (2001) *AMIA Annual Symposium Proceedings* 57.

[18] CC Bennett and TW Doub, 'Expert Systems in Mental Health Care: AI Applications in Decision-Making and Consultation' in DD Luxton (ed), *Artificial Intelligence in Behavioural and Mental Health Care* (Academic Press, 2016).

[19] KA Halmi, M Eckert and P Marchi, 'Comorbidity of Psychiatric Diagnoses in Anorexia Nervosa' (1991) 48 *Archives of General Psychiatry* 8; AA Khan, KC Jacobson, CO Gardner, CA Prescott and KS Kendler, 'Personality and comorbidity of common psychiatric disorders' (2005) 186 *The British Journal of Psychiatry* 3; PF Buckley, BJ Miller, DS Lehrer and DJ Castle, 'Psychiatric Comorbidities and Schizophrenia' (2008) 35 *Schizophrenia Bulletin* 2.

[20] KO Conner, VC Copeland, NK Grote, G Koeske, D Rosen, CF Reynolds and C Brown, 'Mental Health Treatment Seeking Among Older Adults With Depression: The Impact of Stigma and Race' (2010) 18 *The American Journal of General Psychiatry* 6; ER Pedersen and AP Paves, 'Comparing perceived public stigma and personal stigma of mental health treatment seeking in a young adult sample' (2014) 219 *Psychiatry Research* 1; JM Aultman, 'Psychiatric Diagnostic Uncertainty: Challenges to Patient-Centered Care' (2016) 18 *AMA Journal of Ethics* 6.

[21] JC Wakefield and MB First, 'Clarifying the Boundary Between Normality and Disorder: A Fundamental Conceptual Challenge for Psychiatry' (2013) 58 *The Canadian Journal of Psychiatry* 11; SM Hack, A Muralidharan, CH Brown, AL Drapalski and AA Lucksted, 'Stigma and discrimination as correlates of mental health treatment engagement among adults with serious mental illness' (2019) *Psychiatric Rehabilitation Journal*.

[22] A Duffy, GS Malhi and GA Carlson, 'The challenge of psychiatric diagnosis: Looking beyond the symptoms to the company that they keep' (2018) 20 *Bipolar Disorders* 5, 410.

[23] PR MIller, R Dasher, R Collins, P Griffiths and F Brown, 'Inpatient diagnostic assessments: 1. Accuracy of structured vs. unstructured interviews' (2001) 105 *Psychiatry Research* 3; MB First, HA Pincus, JB Levine, JBW Williams, B Ustun and R Peele, 'Clinical Utility as a Criterion for Revising Psychiatric Diagnoses' (2004) 161 *The American Journal of Psychiatry* 6; P Fusar-Poli, M Cappuciati, G Rutigliano, et al., 'At risk or not at risk? A meta-analysis of the prognostic accuracy of psychometric interviews for psychosis prediction' (2015) 14 *World Psychiatry* 3.

and iterative nature of psychiatric assessment and the classification of mental disorder into diagnostic categories lends itself to algorithmic formalisation and computerisation.

A key interface between law and psychiatry occurs when a person's legal right to make certain decisions is brought into question by reason of their mental state. In these circumstances, courts are called upon to determine whether a person has the 'mental capacity' to make the relevant decision(s).[24] Capacity is conceptually related to, but distinct from, a medical diagnosis of mental disorder, because the latter requires that a professionally diagnosed mental impairment is causing a (legally-defined) functional inability to make the decision(s). The relationship between a diagnosis of mental disorder, its functional consequences for individual decision-making capabilities, and the line between juridical capacity and incapacity, are accordingly complex and contested by medical professionals, and lawyers.[25] The gravity of capacity decisions makes them a particularly acute manifestation of state power to infringe on individual liberty and autonomy. As Kong observes:

> The importance of choice in our lives makes the value of autonomy a core pillar of liberal society. Despite its alleged universal importance, the right to make decisions about one's life has been extended to individuals with mental impairments only very recently. With this shift comes a challenge to understand what it means to exercise autonomy in the context of impairment and disability.[26]

The legal definition of incapacity has also been shown to influence the practice of psychiatry, with varying historical outcomes. For example, in their systemic review of international mental health legislation, Nys et al. report:

> [D]espite the importance of capacity in every-day life, in the psychiatric context the main focus has been on capacity as a formal legal category. According to this approach, by drawing a line between those who were deemed competent and those who were deemed incompetent, whole groups of people (e.g. minors, psychiatric patients, involuntarily committed patients, persons with legal representatives) were deemed incapable for all legal purposes.[27]

The interrelation of capacity with wider questions of criminal culpability has also led some to examine the potential of neuro-imagining to support claims of insanity or diminished responsibility, with the latter considered 'one of the more plausible avenues by which neuroscience may contribute to the law'.[28]

[24] *cf* H Buchanan, 'Mental Capacity, Legal Competence and Consent to Treatment' (2004) 97 *Journal of the Royal Society of Medicine* 9; D Okai, G Owen, H McGuire and S Singh, 'Mental capacity in psychiatric patients: Systematic review' (2007) 191 *The British Journal of Psychiatry* 4; S-L Bingham, 'Refusal of treatment and decision-making capacity' (2012) 19 *Nursing Ethics* 2.

[25] J Dawson and G Szmukler, 'Fusion of mental health and incapacity legislation' (2006) 188 *British Journal of Psychiatry* 504; C Kong, *Mental Capacity in Relationship: Decision-Making, Dialogue, and Autonomy* (Cambridge University Press, 2017) 1–17.

[26] Kong, *Mental Capacity in Relationship* 1.

[27] H Nys, S Welie, T Garanis-Papadatos and D Ploumpidis, 'Patient Capacity in Mental Health Care: Legal Overview' (2004) 12 *Health Care Analysis* 329–30.

[28] MS Pardo and D Patterson, *Minds, Brains, and Law: The Conceptual Foundations of Law and Neuroscience* (Oxford University Press, 2013) 17; *cf* A Popma and A Raine, 'Will future forensic assessment be neurobiologic?' (2006) 15 *Child and Adolescent Psychiatric Clinics of North America* 2.

Although the task of psychological assessment and diagnosis still requires a human interlocutor, computers are gradually enabling the identification and diagnosis of mental disorders using brain devices, fMRI imaging, genetic engineering, and AI.[29] Automation is also starting to be applied to a range of legal processes, including the task of adjudication. Yet these interrelated phenomena impact how 'mental incapacity' is juridically interpreted and applied. Whilst claims that machines will replace doctors and judges are likely exaggerated,[30] the more pertinent – and often overlooked – question is whether they ought to do so. In particular, the centrality of mental capacity to legal personhood, human rights and dignity merits serious consideration of both real and near-term technological developments. This means identifying and verifying the technical proficiency of systems, but also raising the question of so-called 'red lines' for the use of 'intelligent' tools in sensitive contexts such as medicine and the courts. Put more crudely, we might ask: should a computer decide whether someone lacks capacity? This question is philosophical in the sense that it engages fundamental issues about personhood and the exercise of human rationality. Ultimately, however, we regard it as an imperative public policy question bearing – directly and indirectly – on numerous legal rights and processes of governance. Following Joseph Weizenbaum, the contention here is that mental capacity should be regarded as an uncontroversial context for 'red lining' or closely regulating the use of algorithmic decision systems.

This chapter traces the history of computers in medicine, focusing on the rise of Expert Systems (ES) in the mid-twentieth century, the rise of connectionist AI research in its latter half, to the development of Automated Mental State Assessment (AMSA) and related bio-cognitive interfaces. It examines theoretical and practical problems for implementing these systems in the real world, and how psychiatry is likely to be impacted in the near term by technological advances. It then examines whether and how computational reasoning could or should operate in the context of capacity decisions in England and Wales, and identifies challenges and opportunities for future research.

I. Artificial Intelligence and Expert Systems in Medicine

Medicine has remained one of the most promising AI domains since the formalisation of AI as a field of study.[31] Due in part to the generalisability of medical applications, but also their vast commercial potential, researchers have explored a variety of ways to have

[29] G Meynen, 'Neurolaw: recognizing opportunities and challenges for psychiatry' (2016) 41 *Journal of Psychiatry & Neuroscience* 1; FX Shen, 'The Overlooked History of Neurolaw' (2016–17) 85 *Fordham Law Review* 667.

[30] Deakin and Markou this volume, *cf* IR Kerr and C Mathen, 'Chief Justice John Roberts is a Robot' (2014) University of Ottawa Working Paper, dx.doi.org/10.2139/ssrn.3395885; J Morison and A Harken, 'Re-engineering justice? Robot judges, computerised courts and (semi) automated legal decision-making' (2019) 9 *Legal Studies* 4.

[31] MH Klein, JH Greist and LJ Van Cura, 'Computers and Psychiatry: Promises to Keep' (1975) 32 *Archives of General Psychiatry* 7; P Szolovits (ed), *Artificial Intelligence in Medicine* (Westview Press, 1982); Amisha, P Malik, M Panathia and VK Rathaur, 'Overview of Artificial Intelligence in Medicine' (2019) 8 *Journal of Family Medicine and Primary Care* 7; CC Bennett and TW Doub, 'Expert Systems in Mental Health Care: AI Applications in Decision-Making and Consultation' in DD Luxton (ed), *Artificial Intelligence in Behavioural and Mental Health Care* (Academic Press, 2016).

computers assist doctors with their work. The longer term goal, however, has been the creation of an 'intelligent' diagnostic system – or 'Robot Doctor' – capable of making the right medical decisions in the real world and in real time.[32] The feasibility of this goal initially came into view when the first proper AI program was written in 1956 by Allen Newell, Herbert Simon and Cliff Shaw. Their program, Logic Theorist, validated the premise that computers could be designed to emulate aspects of human decision-making using logico-mathematical methods to 'mechanise' deductive reasoning.[33] Able to solve the first 38 of 52 problems in Whitehead and Russell's *Prinicipia Mathematica*[34] – and in one case identify a simpler proof than the one in the book – Logic Theorist was considered by some to be 'proof positive that a machine could perform tasks heretofore considered intelligent, creative and uniquely human'.[35]

But Logic Theorist was not just a captivating demonstration of the nascent potential of AI; it helped catalyse a new theory of mind premised on the information processing model, known as the Computational Theory of Mind (CTM) or computationalism. CTM generally refers to the view that 'intelligent behaviour is causally explained by computations performed by the agent's cognitive system (or brain)' and that biological cognition is most adequately explained as information processing. As Pinker explains:

> … beliefs and desires are information, incarnated as symbols. The symbols are the physical states of bits of matter, like chips in a computer or neurons in the brain … The computational theory of mind thus allows us to keep beliefs and desires in our explanations of behavior while planting them squarely in the physical universe.[36]

Historian of AI Pamela McCorduck observes that for its creators, Logic Theorist was 'as central to understanding mind in the twentieth century as Darwin's principle of natural selection had been to understanding biology in the nineteenth century'.[37] Three years later, the team behind Logic Theorist debuted the General Problem Solver, which was designed with the explicit goal of mincing the observed behaviour of human subjects in trying to solve logic and other problems.[38] Although it has faced sustained critiques,[39] CTM is established as the mainstream view of cognition, and has become the basis for contemporary neuroscience-inspired AI research.[40]

[32] RS Ledley and LB Lusted, 'Symbolic Logic, probability, and value theory aid our understanding of how physicians reason' (1959) 130 *Science* 3366.

[33] J Haugeland, *Artificial Intelligence: The Very Idea* (MIT Press, 1985).

[34] AN Whitehead and B Russell, *Principia Mathematica*, 1st edn (Cambridge University Press, 1910) *cf* I Newton in IB Cohen and A Whitman (eds), *The Principia: Mathematical Properties of Natural Philosophy* (University of California Press, 1999).

[35] P McCorduck, *Machines Who Think: A Personal Inquiry into the History and Prospects of Artificial Intelligence*, 2nd edn (CRC Press, 2004) 167.

[36] S Pinker, *How The Mind Works* (Penguin, 1998) 25.

[37] McCorduck, *Machines Who Think* 153.

[38] A Newell, JC Shaw and HA Simon, 'Report on a General Problem-Solving Program' (1959) *Proceedings of the International Conference on Information Processing*; *cf* McCorduck, *Machines Who Think* 123–36.

[39] J Fodor, *The Language of Thought* (Thomas Y Crowell, 1975); H Putnam, *Representation and Reality* (MIT Press, 1988); J Searle, 'Is the Brain a Digital Computer?' (1990) 64 *Proceedings and Addresses of the American Philosophical Association* 21; J Searle, 'Minds, Brains, and Programs' (1990) 3 *Behavioral and Brain Sciences* 417.

[40] D Hassabis, D Kumaran, C Summerfield and M Botvinick, 'Neuroscience Inspired Artificial Intelligence' (2017) 95 *Neuron* 2; U Hasson, SA Nastase and A Goldstein, 'Direct Fit to Nature: An Evolutionary Perspective on Biological and Artificial Neural Networks' (2020) 105 *Neuron* 416.

A. The Justification and Development of Medical Expert Systems

While Logic Theorist was an impressive, albeit limited, proof of concept, its limitations must be considered in view of the fact it was never intended for use in real-world decision-making contexts. Yet the potential of tools like it was not lost on researchers, and would gradually coalesce into the development of so-called Expert Systems (ES).[41] ES are essentially software 'programs for reconstructing the expertise and reasoning capabilities of qualified specialists within limited domains'.[42] ES were developed by formalising the knowledge of domain experts (ie, doctors, lawyers) into a knowledge base from which inferences about the present or future could be made. This knowledge base constituted the facts and associations that a program 'knows' about a particular domain. Reviewing the essential components of medical ES, Ravuri et al. explain:

> The knowledge base consists of diseases, findings, and their relationships. A finding can be a symptom, a sign, a lab result, a demographic variable such as age and gender, or a relevant piece of past medical history. Each edge between a finding and a disease is parametrized by two variables: evoking strength and frequency. Each of these variables has an associated score on a scale of 1 to 5, that is assigned by physician experts using their own clinical judgment and supporting medical literature.[43]

The subject of the facts and information encoded into the knowledge base determined the area of knowledge, or the 'domain' of the ES. These facts or 'domain expertise' could then be represented in various ways including the use of hardcoded rules, a decision tree or a factor table.[44] As Feigenbaum and McCorduck explain, domain expertise is decomposable into two categories:

> The first type is the facts of the domain – the widely shared knowledge … that is written in textbooks and journals of the field, or that forms the basis of a professor's lectures in a classroom. Equally important to the practice of the field is the second type of knowledge called heuristic knowledge, which is the knowledge of good practice and good judgment in a field. It is experiential knowledge, the 'art of good guessing', that a human expert acquires over years of work.[45]

By using an inference engine (a software interface) to query the knowledge base, a user could call upon a wealth of domain expertise contained in an ES knowledge base and use it to inform more consistent decisions. The rules contained in a knowledge base

[41] McCorduck, *Machines Who Think* 419–71.

[42] F Puppe, *Systematic Introduction to Expert Systems: Knowledge Representations and Problem-Solving Methods* (Springer-Verlag, 1993) 3; PS Sell, *Expert Systems – A Practical Introduction* (Macmillan, 1985) 3–19.

[43] M Ravuri, A Kannan, GJ Tso and X Amatriain, 'Learning from the experts: From expert systems to machine-learned diagnosis models' (2018) 85 *Proceedings of Machine Learning Research* 1, 4.

[44] B Chandrasekaran, 'Generic Tasks in Knowledge-Based Reasoning: High-Level Building Blocks for Expert System Design' (1986) *IEEE Expert* 23; R Studer, VR Benjamins and D Fensel, 'Knowledge engineering: Principles and methods' (1998) 25 *Data & Knowledge Engineering* 1–2.

[45] E Feigenbaum and P McCorduck, *The Fifth Generation: Artificial Intelligence and Japan* (Addison-Wesley, 1983) 76–77.

usually took the form of conditional 'if/then' statements, with 'then' usually referring to some probability.[46] To use a medical example: if a patient has symptom x, then the probability of disease y is 7.4 per cent (for instance). By formalising a wide array of medical knowledge into conditional rules, it was possible, at least in principle, to calculate a variety of a probabilistic clinical recommendations and standardise procedures and interventions. Feigenbaum's enthusiasm is indicative of that among computer scientists of the era that machines could not only be designed to replicate discrete tasks, but the broader spectrum of biological intelligence:

> We have the opportunity at this moment to do a new version of Diderot's Encyclopedia, a gathering up of all knowledge-not just the academic kind, but the informal, experiential, heuristic kind.[47]

B. Expert Systems in Psychology & Psychiatry

Perhaps the best-known example of a medical ES, MYCIN, was designed to assist doctors with diagnosing blood-borne diseases and proposing appropriate antibiotic treatments.[48] MYCIN's 'knowledge' was represented by approximately two hundred conditional rules – each capturing a discrete slice of knowledge about blood diseases compiled from consultations with human experts and translating their expertise into mathematical expressions.[49]

After the initial promise of MYCIN a variety of ES were developed for use in fields including geology, engineering, and law, to varying degrees of success.[50] However, while the development of ES in mental health contexts significantly lagged behind their uptake in physiological medicine, psychiatrists and psychologists were among the first to recognise the potential of ES as adjuncts to clinical decision-making[51] and a number of ES were developed for specific mental health applications.[52] Their development was in part motivated by practical problems (a shortage of psychiatrists and the cost of psychiatric treatment), but also indications that patients were less inhibited in self-reporting behaviours to a computer than to a human psychotherapist.[53]

[46] Sell, *Expert Systems* 13–19; BG Buchannan and EH Shortliffe (eds), *Rule-based Expert Systems: The MYCIN Experiments of the Stanford Heuristic Programming Project* (Addison-Wesley, 1984).

[47] Feigenbaum and McCorduck, *The Fifth Generation* 229.

[48] EH Shortliffe, 'MYCIN: A Knowledge-Based Computer Program Applied to Infectious Diseases' (1977) *Proceedings of the Annual Symposium on Computer Application in Medical Care* 66; BG Buchannan and EH Shortliffe (eds), *Rule-based Expert Systems* 3–19.

[49] HL Dreyfus and SE Dreyfus, 'From Socrates to Expert Systems: The Limits of Calculative Rationality' (1984) 6 *Technology in Society* 3, 230–33.

[50] P Harmon, R Maus and W Morrissey, *Expert Systems: Tools and Applications* (Wiley, 1988); S Tzafestas (ed), *Expert Systems in Engineering Applications* (Springer, 1993); P Leith, 'The Rise and Fall of the Legal Expert System' (2010) 1 *European Journal of Law & Technology* 1.

[51] RA Morelli, JD Bronzino and JW Goethe, 'Expert Systems in Psychiatry' 157.

[52] RL Spitzer and J Endicott, 'Can the Computer Assist Clinicians in Psychiatric Diagnosis?' (1974) 131 *Psychiatry* 5; D Servan-Schreiber, 'Artificial Intelligence in Psychiatry' (1986) 174 *Journal of Nervous and Mental Disease* 4.

[53] Servan-Schreiber, 'Artificial Intelligence in Psychiatry' 191.

C. Computer-Assisted Psychiatric Diagnosis

DIAGNO, developed at Columbia University in the 1960s–70s, was one early computer-assisted psychiatric diagnosis tool.[54] Using 39 clinical observation scores processed through a decision tree, DIAGNO proposed differential psychiatric diagnoses to clinicians. Although the system claimed comparable performance levels in diagnosing mental disorders, it was never used in clinical practice. Other examples of computer-assisted diagnosis in psychiatry include PARRY, an early 'chatbot' that simulated the symptoms of a patient with paranoid schizophrenia using computer mediated dialogue.[55] When challenged to a version of the 'Turing Test' psychiatrists were able to differentiate between patient transcripts and those produced by PARRY in 48 per cent of cases, roughly consistent with guessing.[56] The first such example of an ES for use in clinical psychiatry contexts would not, however, arrive until 1984 with the development of EMYCIN (Essential MYCIN). This system – which purported to 'solve problems in any domain' – provided clinicians with psychopharmacological 'advice' on the management of depression.[57]

D. Clinical Decision Support Systems (CDSS)

Despite the limited real-world application of psychiatric ES like EMYCIN and DIAGNO, confidence in their diagnostic validity saw aspects of their algorithmic deductive reasoning incorporated into existing Clinical Decision Support Systems (CDSS).[58] CDSS, as the name implies, provide contextually appropriate 'alerts, reminders, prescribing recommendations, therapeutic guidelines, image interpretation, and diagnostic assistance'.[59] This does not mean, however, that all CDSS are in some sense 'intelligent'. Rather, CDSS use hard-coded rules that visual or auditory alarms, but do not contain any probabilistic rules nor mechanisms for inferential reasoning. Most CDSS tools do, however, embody the basic principles of ES by providing contextually relevant diagnostic information.

[54] RL Spitzer and J Endicott, 'DIAGNO: A Computer Program for Psychiatric Diagnosis Utilizing the Differential Diagnostic Procedure' (1968) 18 *Archives of General Psychiatry* 6; RL Spitzer and J Endicott, 'DIAGNO II: Further Developments in a Computer Program for Psychiatric Diagnosis' (1969) 125 *The American Journal of Psychiatry* 7S.

[55] KM Colby, FD Hilf and S Weber, 'Artificial Paranoia' (1972) 2 *Artificial Intelligence* 1.

[56] AP Saygin I Cicekli and V Akman, 'Turing Test: 50 Years Later' (2001) 10 *Minds and Machines* 463, 500–01.

[57] B Mulsant and D Servan-Schreiber, 'Knowledge Engineering: A Daily Activity on a Hospital Ward' (1984) 17 *Computers and Biomedical Research* 71.

[58] K Kawamoto, CA Houlihan, AE Balas and DF Lobach, 'Improving clinical practice using clinical decision support systems: a systematic review of trials to identify features critical to success' (2005) *British Medical Journal* 330; MA Musen, B Middleton and RA Greenes, 'Clinical Decision Support Systems' in EH Shortliffe and JJ Cimino (eds), *Biomedical Informatics: Computer Applications in Health Care and Biomedicine* (Springer, 2014); ATM Wasylewicz and AMJW Scheepers-Hoeks, 'Clinical Decision Support Systems' in P Kubben, M Dumontier, and A Dekker (eds), *Fundamentals of Clinical Data Science* (Springer, 2019).

[59] W Crosby and AA Sanousi, 'Reasons For Physicians Not Adopting Clinical Decision Support Systems: Critical Analysis' (2018) 6 *JMIR Medical Informatics* 2, 1.

One example is the controversial Texas Medication Algorithm Project (TMAP).[60] TMAP, which commenced in 1997 and is still used today, is a CDSS employing a decision-tree to assist psychiatrists by providing detailed guidelines for the treatment and medication management of patients with bipolar disorder, schizophrenia, and depressive disorders. As with ES, CDSS – and TMAP in particular – have a mixed track record of usefulness.[61] Most CDSS are developed according to strict evidence-based guidelines derived from expert opinion and/or statistical averages that generalise interventions into a 'one size fits all' approach at the expense of individualised treatment. In real-world contexts the therapeutic benefit and awkward integration of CDSS into clinicians' workflows is often at odds with the aetiology of mental disorders.[62] Moreover, it has long been observed by clinicians that treatments that have proven successful in research and trials do not always generalise well to the wider population, and evidence-based guidelines on which they are based are often out-of-date by the time they are implemented.[63]

E. The Challenge of Medical Knowledge Engineering

The biggest impediment to the development of medical ES or CDSS is that of knowledge engineering: how do we formalise domain expertise, that is often tacit and innate,[64] into a knowledge base that can be practically updated and maintained? Davis helpfully summarises the domain-specific challenges of capturing medical knowledge:

> To build expert systems is to attempt to capture rare or important expertise and embody it in computer programs. It is done by talking to the people who have that expertise. In one sense building expert systems is a form of intellectual cloning. Expert system builders, the knowledge engineers, find out from experts what they know and how they use their knowledge to solve problems. Once this debriefing is done, the expert system builders incorporate the knowledge and expertise in computer programs, making the knowledge and expertise easily replicated, readily distributed, and essentially immortal.[65]

[60] AL Miller, JA Chiles, JK Chiles, L Crimson, AJ Rush and SP Shon, 'The Texas Medication Algorithm Project (TMAP) schizophrenia algorithms' (1999) 60 *Journal of Clinical Psychiatry* 10; T Suppes, AC Swann, AB Dennehy, ED Habermacher, M Mason, ML Crimson, MG Toprac, AJ Rush, SP Shon and KZ Altshuler, 'Texas Medication Algorithm Project: development and feasibility testing of a treatment algorithm for patients with bipolar disorder' (2001) 62 *Journal of Clinical Psychiatry* 6; TA Moore, RW Buchannan, PF Buckley, JA Chiles, RR Conley, ML Crimson, SM Essock, M Finnerty, SR Marder, DD Miller, JP McEvoy, DG Robinson, NR Schooler, SP Shon, TS Stroup and AL Miller, 'The Texas Medication Algorithm Project antipsychotic algorithm for schizophrenia: 2006 update' (2007) 68 *Journal of Clinical Psychiatry* 11.

[61] JS Ash, DF Sittig, EM Campbell, KP Guappone and RH Dykstra, 'Some Unintended Consequences of Clinical Decision Support Systems' (2007) *AMIA Annual Symposium Proceedings*; RT Sutton, D Pincock, DC Baumgart, DC Sadowski, RN Fedorak, KI Kroeker, 'An Overview of Clinical Decision Support Systems: Benefits, Risks, and Strategies for Success' (2020) 3 *NPJ Digital Medicine* 17.

[62] Mulsant and Servan-Schreiber, 'Knowledge Engineering'; S Kharait, D Marc, W Crosby and AA Sanousi, 'Reasons For Physicians Not Adopting Clinical Decision Support Systems'.

[63] P Shelke and JM Grimshaw, 'When should clinical guidelines be updated?' (2001) 323 *British Medical Journal* 155; LM García, AJ Sanabria, EG Álvarez, et al, 'The validity of recommendations from clinical guidelines: a survival analysis' (2014) 16 *Canadian Medical Association Journal* 1211.

[64] *cf* M Polanyi, *The Tacit Dimension*, rev edn (University of Chicago Press, 2009).

[65] R Davis, 'Amplifying expertise with expert systems' in PH Winston and KA Prendergast (eds), *The AI Business: Commercial Uses of Artificial Intelligence* (MIT Press, 1984) 18.

While the theoretical feasibility of ES came into sharper view with the development of new techniques for computationally imputing domain expertise, so too did the scale of the challenge of developing them for use in real-world medical contexts.[66] As Nelson et al. observe: 'although data collected from biomedical research is expanding at an almost exponential rate, our ability to transform that information into patient care has not kept at pace'.[67] Developing a useful medical ES was thus ultimately a task of combinatorial complexity,[68] as no matter how many rules are created to capture and encode domain expertise, there would always be exceptions requiring the creation of more rules, and thus the formalisation of further domain expertise. This leads to a problem of infinite regress: how do we represent the absolute state of the world, but simplify it in such a way that it remains usable without the need for potentially infinite rules?

II. Automating Psychological Assessment and Diagnosis

At its most fundamental, psychiatry explores the link between human physiology and behaviour.[69] While there is much that remains unknown about the human body, much less is known about the human brain – the body's central processing unit – and its relation to the human mind (the 'mind body problem').[70] Indeed, much of the psychiatric enterprise is deeply subjective: identifying behaviours, describing their presentation, and classifying them within fuzzily defined categories. However, the process of psychological assessment is not merely a pattern matching routine, and the experience of psychological disorder is not something that can be atomised into constituent parts and recombined using formal rules to form a valid diagnosis. As Feigenbaum and McCorduck conclude:

> The expert is simply not following any rules! He is doing just what Feigenbaum feared he might be doing – recognizing thousands of special cases. This, in turn, explains why expert systems are never as good as experts. If one asks the experts for rules, one will, in effect, force the expert to regress to the level of beginner and state the rules he still remembers, but no longer uses. If one programs these rules into a computer, one can use the speed and accuracy of the computer and its ability to store and access millions of facts to outdo a human beginner using the same rules. But no amount of rules and facts can capture the understanding an expert has when he has stored his experience of the actual outcomes of tens of thousands of situations.[71]

[66] HL Dreyfus and SE Dreyfus, 'From Socrates to expert systems: The limits of calculative rationality' (1984) 6 *Technology in Society* 3.

[67] As Nelson et al observe, 'Although data collected from biomedical research is expanding at an almost exponential rate, our ability to transform that information into patient care has not kept at pace'. CA Nelson, AJ Butte and SA Baranini, (2019) 10 *Nature Communications* 1, 1.

[68] *cf* S Aaora and B Barak, *Computational Complexity: A Modern Approach* (Cambridge University Press, 2009).

[69] MM Bradley and PJ Lang, 'Measuring Emotion: Behavior, Feeling and Physiology' in RD Lane and L Nadel (eds), *Cognitive Neuroscience of Emotion* (Oxford University Press, 2000).

[70] C McGinn, 'Can We Solve the Mind-Body Problem?' (1989) 98 *Mind* 391; J Kim, *Mind in a Physical World: An Essay on the Mind-Body Problem and Mental Causation* (MIT Press, 1998); T Crane and S Patterson (eds), *History of the Mind-Body Problem* (Routledge, 2012).

[71] Feigenbaum and McCorduck, *The Fifth Generation* 184–85.

Domain expertise, particularly the kind required in medical contexts, was thus proving resistant to logical formalism. But while the problem of knowledge engineering presented significant obstacles for the development of ES, there was also the broader question of what domain knowledge was worth, in the absence of the wisdom needed to apply it:

> Part of learning to be an expert is to understand not merely the letter of the rule but its spirit ... he knows when to break the rules, he understands what is relevant to his task and what isn't ... Expert systems do not yet understand these things.[72]

Whilst the ability to excavate a variety of observations is the basis of clinical observation, the positive identification of a particular symptom (ie, anhedonia) is itself insufficient to constitute a valid diagnosis. A person may be justifiably sad without being depressed, and anxious without having a diagnosis of generalised anxiety disorder. For instance, Damasio demonstrates that emotions like anxiety are intrinsic to certain decision-making processes, and should not be seen as a deficiency of the individual or a priori evidence of rationality.[73] Similarly, 'emotional intelligence' – a type of socially oriented cognition – may be an important predictor of real-world success independent of cognitive intelligence (ie, IQ).[74] However, some argue that the conscious experience of emotion is a red herring: a distraction from the essence of what emotion is.[75] Generally, these researchers tend to examine the biological (central or peripheral) substrates of emotion in animals and humans.[76] Others, however, consider conscious experience of emotion to be a core component of the emotion construct – part of the range of phenomena that must be described and explained.[77] But this divergence of views about emotion derives from a central philosophical problem in psychology: is it possible to objectively verify the nature or qualia (sensory experiences of abstract qualities such as temperature, texture, colour, sound and softness) of subjective experience?[78]

A. AI and Medicine

Despite the practical and conceptual challenges facing their development and implementation, there has been sustained focus on developing computer-assisted diagnostic tools for use in real-world contexts since the inception of AI research.[79] Several factors

[72] ibid.

[73] AR Damasio, *Descartes' Error: Emotion, Reason, and the Human Brain* (GP Putnam, 1994).

[74] P Salovey and JD Mayer, 'Emotional Intelligence' (1989) 9 *Imagination, Cognition, and Personality* 185; *cf* KC Petrides, M Mikolajczak, S Mavroveli, et al., 'Developments in Trait Emotional Intelligence Research' (2016) 7 *Emotion Review* 4.

[75] RD Lane, 'Neural Correlates of `Conscious Experience' in G Matthews, M Zeidner and RD Roberts (eds), *Emotional Intelligence: Science and Myth* (MIT Press, 2004).

[76] G Modinos, MK Kempton and S Tognin, 'Association of Adverse Outcomes With Emotion Processing and Its Neural Substrate in Individuals at Clinical High Risk for Psychosis' (2020) 77 *JAMA Psychiatry* 2.

[77] LF Barrett, B Mesquita, KN Ochsner and JJ Gross, 'The Experience of Emotion' (2007) *48 Annual Review of Psychology* 373.

[78] L Chumley, 'Qualia and Ontology: Language, Semiotics, and Materiality: An Introduction' (2017) 5 *Signs and Society* S1, *cf* DC Dennett, 'A History of Qualia' (2020) 39 *Topoi* 5.

[79] J Yanase and E Triantahyllou, 'A systematic survey of computer-aided diagnosis in medicine: Past and present developments' (2019) 138 *Expert Systems with Applications* 112821.

have motivated this, including the complexity of the medical diagnosis process itself, the availability of vast and complex clinical data and diagnostic knowledge (ie, diagnostic rules), and continued performance improvements in various AI and data science techniques.[80] The scope of this research is now immense, with AI techniques helping uncover new insights about everything from fundamental aspects of protein folding[81] to human brain interfaces.[82] Yet even at the smaller scale, computers – intelligent or not – are transforming the nature and delivery of care (eg, by enabling telemedicine), increasing the efficiency of care delivery, lowering its cost, and improving outcomes.

The concurrent development of diagnostic metrics such as the Hamilton Anxiety Rating Scale,[83] the definition of psychological disorders in diagnostic manuals such as the DSM and ICD,[84] and the enactment of specific mental health laws, made psychiatry an increasingly data-intensive domain, but one with unique challenges for computation and ES.[85] Almost as soon as they became available, researchers explored how to develop software programs to automate aspects of psychological assessment and diagnosis.[86] From simple true/false questionnaires to complex psychological profiling, early academic curiosity about the potential of computers in medicine quickly became a wave of commercial research into automating diagnosis,[87] medication management[88] and psychotherapy,[89] among other things. Some of this literature was social-scientific, and examined the reflexive use of computers in clinical settings by considering the reliability, validity, user acceptance, and cost-effectiveness of automated assessments over conventional therapeutic interventions.[90] Due to the sensitivity of medical records, and

[80] EJ Topol, 'High-performance medicine: the convergence of human and artificial intelligence' (2019) 25 *Nature Medicine* 44.

[81] G-W Wei, 'Protein structure prediction beyond AlphaFold' (2019) 1 *Nature Machine Intelligence* 336.

[82] M Lebedev, 'Brain-machine interfaces: an overview' (2014) 5 *Translational Neuroscience* 99.

[83] M Hamilton, 'The Assessment of Anxiety States by Rating' (1959) 32 *British Journal of Medical Physiology* 1.

[84] *American Psychiatric Association, Diagnostic and Statistical Manual of Mental Disorders*, 5th edn (American Psychiatric Publishing, 2013); World Health Organization, *ICD-10: The ICD-10 Classification of Mental and Behavioural Disorders: Clinical Descriptions and Diagnostic Guidelines* (World Health Organisation, 1992).

[85] MB First, 'Computer-Assisted Assessment of DSM III R Diagnoses' (1991) 21 *Psychiatric Annals* 1; *cf* J Paris and J Phillips (eds), *Making the DSM-5: Concepts and Controversies* (Springer, 2013).

[86] *cf* DN Osser, 'New Psychopharmacology Algorithms' (2015) 37 *Psychiatric Times* 5; WB Schwartz, 'Medicine and the Computer – The Promise and Problems of Change' (1970) 283 *New England Journal of Medicine* 1257; RA Morelli, JD Bronzino and JW Goethe, 'Expert Systems in Psychiatry: A Review' (1987) 11 *Journal of Medical Systems* 2/3.

[87] M Bauer, S Monteith, J Geddes, MJ Gitlin, P Grof, PC Whybrow and T Glenn, 'Automation to optimise physician treatment of individual patients: examples in psychiatry' (2019) 6 *The Lancet* 4; DM Low, KH Bentley and SS Ghosh, 'Automated assessment of psychiatric disorders using speech: A systematic review' (2020) 5 *Laryngoscope Investigative Otalaryngology* 1.

[88] DL Labovitz, L Shafner, MR Gil, D Virmani and H Hanina, 'Using Artificial Intelligence to Reduce the Risk of Nonadherence in Patients on Anticoagulation Therapy' (2017) 47 *Stroke* 5; A Eggerth, D Hayn and G Schreier, 'Medication management needs information and communications technology-based approaches, including telehealth and artificial intelligence' (2019) *British Journal of Clinical Pharmacology*.

[89] C Naugler and DL Church, 'Automation and artificial intelligence in the clinical laboratory' (2019) 56 *Critical Reviews in Clinical Laboratory Science* 2; A Haleem, M Javid and IH Khan, 'Current status and applications of Artificial Intelligence (AI) in Medical Field: An Overview' (2019) 9 *Current Medicine Research and Practice* 6.

[90] MJ Pazzani, S Mani and WR Shankle, 'Acceptance of rules generated by machine learning among medical experts' (2001) 40 *Methods of Information in Medicine* 5; CL Chi, WN Street and DA Katz, 'A decision support system for cost-effective diagnosis' (2010) 50 *Artificial Intelligence in Medicine* 3; CM Cutilo, KR Sharma, L Foschini, S Kundu, M Mackintosh, KD Mandl, 'Machine intelligence in healthcare – perspectives on trustworthiness, explainability, usability, and transparency' (2020) 3 *NPJ Digital Medicine* 47.

the role of psychiatrists as expert medical witnesses, both lawyers and judges were quick to identify privacy and human rights issues.[91] Dworkin, for instance, observed:

> The medical record is at the core of the confidential doctor-patient relationship. It usually contains personal, sensitive information and any unauthorised disclosure by the doctor has legal and professional consequences.[92]

More recent research identifies a number of medico-legal and ethical issues about the breadth of data collection conducted by companies engaged in health care and biomedical research.[93] Yet with nearly 60 years of research into the equivalency and validity of computerised diagnostics over traditional clinical interviews and psychological assessments, the tentative consensus is that automation benefits clinical assessment in an aggregate sense.[94]

B. Logical AI (1936–2000)

At their core computers are ultimately symbol manipulating machines. The symbols they manipulate are strings of 1s and 0s organised into patterns that correspond to words, sentences, images, and so forth. A computer can accordingly copy, transfer, delete, or write a string of symbols in a specific place, compare symbols in two different places, and search for symbols that match defined criteria. The most impressive breakthroughs and performance leaps in computing involved the optimisation of elaborate routines involving these basic tasks. The work of British computer science Alan Turing, however, helped revolutionise not only understanding of computers, but raised the question of whether computation offered a lens for understanding biological intelligence.[95]

The classical view of the brain assumed that biological cognition in general, and language processing specifically, involved the manipulation of symbols according to various rules.[96] This paradigm, in turn, oriented the formative years of AI research towards the 'Logical AI' approach or 'symbolicism'. The logical approach was oriented

[91] RS Sternberg, J Chapman and D Shawkow, 'Psychotherapy Research and the Problem of Intrusions on Privacy' (1958) 21 *Psychiatry* 2; BB Boyer, 'Computerized Medical Records and the Right to Privacy: The Emerging Federal Response' (1975–76) 25 *Buffalo Law Review* 37; DF Linnowes, 'Must Personal Privacy Die in the Computer Age?' (1979) 65 *American Bar Association Journal* 1180.

[92] G Dworkin, 'Access to Medical Records. Discovery, Confidentiality and Privacy' (1979) 42 *The Modern Law Review* 1, 88.

[93] J Powles and H Hodson, 'Google DeepMind and healthcare in an age of algorithms' (2017) 7 *Health and Technology* 351; TJ Rohringer, A Budkhkar and F Rudzicz, 'Privacy versus artificial intelligence in medicine' (2019) 96 *Artificial Intelligence in Medicine* 1; WN Price II and IG Cohen, 'Privacy in the age of medical big data' (2019) 25 *Nature Medicine* 37.

[94] BK Kiluk, DE Sugarman, C Nich, CJ Gibbons, S Martino, BJ Rounsaville and KM Carroll, 'A Methodological Analysis of Randomized Clinical Trials of Computer-Assisted Therapies for Psychiatric Disorders: Toward Improved Standards for an Emerging Field' (2011) 168 *The American Journal of Psychiatry* 8.

[95] AM Turing, 'On Computable Numbers, With an Application to the Entscheidungsproblem' (1936–7) s2–42 *Proceedings of the London Mathematical Society* 230; A Turing, 'Systems of Logic Based on Ordinals' (1939) s2–45 *Proceedings of the London Mathematical Society* 161; *cf* G Dyson, *Turing's Cathedral: The Origins of the Digital Universe* (Penguin, 2013).

[96] N Chomsky, *Cartesian Linguistics: A Chapter in the History of Rationalist Thought* (Harper & Row, 1966); JA Fodor, *The Language of Thought* (Thomas Y Crowell, 1975); ZW Pylyshyn, *Computation and Cognition: Towards a Foundation for Cognitive Science* (MIT Press, 1984).

by the possibility of creating a universal symbol system that could demonstrate discrete aspects of human biological intelligence.

The overarching hypothesis of the logical AI approach was that the creation of intelligent machines was not only possible, but was only possible by developing a universal symbol system. Newell and Simon, creators of Logic Theorist, boldly proclaimed that 'symbols lie at the root of intelligent action' and the thesis that the brain was primarily a symbol manipulation device was popularised by AI researchers, cognitive scientists, and philosophers. The logical approach, however, divided opinion among researchers. John Searle and Karl Lashley, for instance, argued that science has often analogised the brain to the technology of the day. Descartes likened the brain to a water clock, whereas Gottfried Leibniz explained the brain in terms of a factory. Others criticised the logical approach on the basis that there was no physiological evidence in the brain to suggest that a symbol is the atomic unit of biological cognition in the way it is with computation.[97]

Chess has often served as a proxy for understanding human intelligence in AI research. As Claude Shannon, one of the erstwhile 'godfathers of AI' remarked:

> Although of no practical importance, the question [of computer chess] is of theoretical interest, and it is hoped that … this problem will act as a wedge in attacking other problems of greater significance.[98]

A major validation of the connectionist AI approach would come in 1996, when IBM's Deep Blue became the first computer to defeat a reigning chess world champion. To achieve victory, however, Deep Blue relied upon traditional search and planning techniques, which were far from the bleeding edge of technological innovation.[99] Deep Blue approaches chess by planning many moves ahead and testing the contingencies of every combination – a technique known as a 'decision tree'. Deep Blue's 'chess expertise' was rooted in its ability to not only generate and test a vast amount of potential moves, but 'prune' its decision tree to simplify the branches, and speed up calculations, and 'reason' through approximately 200 million potential moves every second before selecting the optimal one. Practically, however, Deep Blue could only 'play chess' according to the static parameters of the game, and could not cope with a shift in those parameters.

While Deep Blue had the capacity to plan and test vast combinations of moves and counter-moves,[100] it could not generalise its chess 'expertise' beyond the defined parameters of its 'world' – the 64 positions of the chess board. If another row was added, Deep Blue's 'expertise' was not adaptable to the alien world of a chess board comprised of 82 positions. In a clinical setting, the flexibility of intelligence requires human decisions to be made time-sensitively and on the basis of incomplete or contradictory information. The logical AI approach, whilst impressive in narrow domains, was not suited to dealing with such a chaotic and unstructured 'real world'.

[97] P Smolensky, 'Connectionist AI, symbolic AI, and the brain' (1987) 1 *Artificial Intelligence Review* 95.
[98] C Shannon, 'Programming a Computer for Playing Chess' in D Levy (ed), *Computer Chess Compendium* (Springer, 1988) 2; *cf* N Ensmenger, 'Is chess the drosophila of artificial intelligence? A social history of an algorithm' (2012) 42 *Social Studies in Science* 1.
[99] M Newborn, *Kasparov versus Deep Blue: Computer Chess Comes of Age* (Springer, 1997).
[100] Newborn, *Kasparov versus Deep Blue* 73–89.

C. Connectionist AI (2000–Current)

After decades of over-promising and under-delivering, and no less than two 'AI Winters' in the late twentieth century, AI research pivoted from the logic-based approach that dominated its early period, towards the methodological pluralism of embodied, situated, and/or dynamical AI methods premised on Machine Learning (ML) and various probabilistic techniques.[101] This current approach – connectionism – incorporates elements of systems-thinking, cybernetics, and autopoiesis.[102] However, the move to connectionist models inspired by the human brain was largely one of necessity, as the limited success of ES had laid plain the limitations of using mathematical expressions to replicate the specificity, adaptability, and extensibility of human intelligence needed in the real world.[103] In other words, for AI to be not only useful but reliable in complex decision-making, it needed to contain domain expertise (specificity), but remain flexible (adaptive), to 'make sense' of the real-world, adapt to it, interact with it, and 'reason' within it on the basis of incomplete information.[104] As Cobb concludes, this was easier said than done:

> Since the 1950s our ideas have been dominated by concepts that surged into biology from computing – feedback loops, information codes, and computation. But although many of the functions we have identified in the brain generally involve some kind of computation, there are only a few fully understood examples, and some of the most brilliant and influential theoretical institutions about how nervous systems might 'compute' have turned out to be wrong.[105]

Deep Blue was premised on the logical AI approach, its successor, Watson, used connectionist models to tackle everything from the 'moonshot' goal of curing cancer to drug discovery and patient management.[106] In an impressive test of its credentials, Watson featured on the American game-show *Jeopardy!* in 2011 where it defeated longtime champions in another highly publicised demonstration. But while, IBM's chess playing computer, Deep Blue, could plan and suggest a move, it could not physically make it – requiring a human to actually move the chess piece. Watson, however, used advances in NLP to answer verbal questions in real-time competition.

[101] B McMullin, 'Thirty Years of Computational Autopoiesis: A Review' (2004) 10 *Artificial Life* 3; *cf* E Alpaydin, *Machine Learning* (MIT Press, 2016); I Goodfellow, Y Bengio and A Courville, *Deep Learning* (MIT Press, 2016).

[102] *cf* A Clark and R Lutz (eds), *Connectionism in Context* (Springer, 1992); P Babbar, A Singhal, K Yadav and V Sharma, 'Connectionist Model in Artificial Intelligence' (2018) 13 *International Journal of Applied Engineering Research* 7.

[103] T Ching, DS Himmelstein, BK Beaulieu-Jones, et al, 'Opportunities and obstacles for deep learning in biology and medicine' (2018) 15 *Journal of the Royal Society Interface* 141; F Cabitza and J-D Zeitoun, 'The proof of the pudding: in praise of a culture of real-world validation for medical artificial intelligence' (2019) 7 *Annals of Translational Medicine* 8.

[104] M Ravuri, A Kannan, GJ Tso and X Amatriain, 'Learning from the experts: From expert systems to machine-learned diagnosis models' (2018) 85 *Proceedings of Machine Learning Research* 1.

[105] M Cobb, *The Idea of the Brain: A History* (Princeton University Press, 2020) 6.

[106] H Kantarjian and PP Yu, 'Artificial Intelligence, Big Data, and Cancer' (2015) 1 *JAMA Oncology* 5; HY Chen, E Argentinis and G Weber, 'IBM Watson: How Cognitive Computing Can Be Applied to Big Data Challenges in Life Sciences Research' (2016) 38 *Clinical Therapeutics* 4.

i. *Watson and the AI Health Revolution*

While Watson proved highly adept at *Jeopardy!*, even surprising its developers with the complexity and nuance of some of its answers, the system neither 'thought' or 'reasoned' like a person. Instead, Watson brute-forced its way to victory, using raw processing power to conduct what amounted to a vast Google search using NLP and various probabilistic techniques to identify the optimal answer according to its internal error-correction metrics, not what Watson in any sense knew was the 'right' one. In a piece for *Slate Magazine*, one of the *Jeopardy!* Champions who faced Watson opined:

> IBM has bragged to the media that Watson's question-answering skills are good for more than annoying Alex Trebek. The company sees a future in which fields like medical diagnosis, business analytics, and tech support are automated by question-answering software like Watson. Just as factory jobs were eliminated in the 20th century by new assembly-line robots, Brad and I were the first knowledge-industry workers put out of work by the new generation of 'thinking' machines. 'Quiz show contestant' may be the first job made redundant by Watson, but I'm sure it won't be the last.

While *Jeopardy!* helped put Watson on the map, it also bolstered confidence amongst IBM executives that the system would usher in a new era of smart medicine. Practically this meant:

> … helping healthcare organizations apply cognitive technology to unlock vast amounts of health data and power diagnosis. Watson can review and store far more medical information – every medical journal, symptom, and case study of treatment and response around the world – exponentially faster than any human.[107]

In principle, at least, the refocusing of AI research around connectionist models has made it possible to individualise treatment in a way that the logical AI approach and ES could not. The use of ML and Deep Learning (DL) techniques allows for the development of systems that are in some sense able to 'learn' from empirical clinical data, in that they are able to store large amounts of data, recursively analyse it and extract valuable insights from it. It is through this recursive process of optimisation that an ML model can draw inferences from seemingly unrelated variables that human doctors may not be aware of. This has the benefit of allowing for both the discovery of 'new' knowledge from among clinical data and the refinement of existing knowledge and practice in real-world contexts.[108]

Nevertheless, the connectionist paradigm has not been able to get around the often time-sensitive nature of clinical care in the real-world, as well as the problem of non-ergodicity. Decisions made in clinical settings, and their consequent actions (ie, treatment), influence a patient's future state (ie, observations), and simultaneously transform the 'world' and the ensuing options available. Despite copious investment and hyperbole that Watson would revolutionise health care, IBM has realised that its

[107] PWC, 'What doctor? Why AI and robotics will define New Health' (June 2017), www.pwc.com/gx/en/industries/healthcare/publications/ai-robotics-new-health/ai-robotics-new-health.pdf.

[108] CC Bennett and TW Doub, 'Data mining and electronic health records: Selecting optimal clinical treatments in practice' (2010) *International conference on data mining* (DMIN) (pp 313318).

most powerful technology is no match for the realities of real-world medicine[109] and, without delivering on any of the promises made at its launch in 2014, has quietly scaled back its Watson Health division.

D. Affective Computing (AfC) and fMRI

Affective Computing (AfC) is a growing multidisciplinary field encompassing computer science, engineering, psychology, education, neuroscience, and many other disciplines. It explores the affective dimensions of human interactions with technology, how affective sensing and generation can help quantify aspects of human affect, and the design of affective software using various computer vision and acoustic sensing techniques. In recent years AC systems and advanced data analytics have been used in legally sensitive contexts such as immigration decisions (human rights, International law)[110] and the screening of job applicants (employment/administrative law).[111] Meanwhile, forensic psychologists have explored numerous techniques for the diagnosis and treatment of psychopathy – a diagnosis prevalent amongst those not only subject to capacity decisions, but to criminology more broadly. As DeLisi et al. explain:

> In addition to its theoretical and empirical significance, psychopathy is also critically important in practice and should be included in every handbook of every practitioner position in the juvenile and criminal justice systems … For virtually any research question centering on antisocial behavior, psychopathy is relevant. And it should, for it is the unified theory of crime.[112]

This 'computational turn' in the evaluation and treatment of mental disorder has accordingly made the quantification of psychopathology a primary goal. This has seen various methods for fusing the subjective insights of traditional clinical observation and evaluation with the seemingly objective and 'rational' logic of computation.[113] One particularly fruitful area of overlap has been between neuroscience researcher and neuro-imaging, leading some legal scholars to speculate on a forthcoming 'neurolaw' revolution and the use of fMRI and data science more generally in forensic psychology and treatment.[114] Critics, however, have highlighted empirical concerns about the reproducibility crisis in neuroscience, and the ethics of premising legal regimes on neuroimaging.[115]

[109] E Strickland, 'How IBM Watson Overpromised and Underdelivered on AI Health Care' (*IEEE Spectrum*, 2 April 2019), spectrum.ieee.org/biomedical/diagnostics/how-ibm-watson-overpromised-and-underdelivered-on-ai-health-care.

[110] P Molnar and L Gill, 'Bots at the Gate: A Human Rights Analysis of Automated Decision-Making in Canada's Immigration and Refugee Systems' (2018), citizenlab.ca/wp-content/uploads/2018/09/IHRP-Automated-Systems-Report-Web-V2.pdf.

[111] RA Calvo and S D'Mello (eds), *Affect Detection: An Interdisciplinary Review of Models, Methods, and their Applications* (IEEE Transactions on Affective Computing, 2010).

[112] M DeLisi, J Tostlebe, K Burgason, M Heirigs and M Vaughn, 'Self-Control Versus Psychopathy: A Head-to-Head Test of General Theories of Antisociality' (2018) 16 *Youth Violence and Juvenile Justice* 1, 267–68.

[113] AF Beavers and JP Slattery, 'On the Moral Implications and Restrictions Surrounding Affective Computing' in M Joon (ed), *Emotions and Affect in Human Factors and Human-Computer Interaction* (Academic Press, 2017).

[114] KD Phillips, 'Empathy for Psychopaths: Using fMRI Brain Scans to Plea for Leniency in Death Penalty Cases' (2013) 37 *Law & Psychology Review* 1.

[115] C-P Hu, X Jiang, R Jeffrey and X-N Zuo, 'Open Science as a Better Gatekeeper for Science and Society: A Perspective from Neurolaw' (2018), psyarxiv.com/8dr23/.

i. Neuroimaging Evidence in Court

Two Italian cases demonstrate the convergence of medico-legal factors relevant to adjudications of mental capacity. In 2009, an Italian appellate court reduced the sentence of a murderer, Abdelmalek Bayout, on the basis of neuroimaging evidence and on the presence of certain genetic variations, including the 'low activity' version of the MAO-A gene. In mitigation, the trial court reduced what was to be a 12-year prison sentence by three years on the basis of mental illness. After a detail report from clinicians, the appellate court further reduced the sentence by another year. In 2011 a Milanese court also relied on neuroimaging and genetic testing to reduce a murder sentence from life in prison to 20 years.[116] The court admitted EEG (electro-encephalogram) and VBM (Voxel Based Morphometry) – which both record varying levels of electrical activity in the brain – as evidence that the defendant displayed an 'unfavourable' genetic pattern in women which was associated with impulsivity and aggressiveness. At trial, expert testimony was given that 'these alterations (of brain structures) have to be considered in causal relation to the psychiatric symptomatology of the murderer'.[117] Both cases are examples of a more widespread phenomenon in which structural or functional brain imaging results are cited as evidence in the courtroom, alongside other evidence, in order to support claims that a defendant was mentally disordered.[118]

The question of whether findings from cognitive neuroscience can be used as evidence in the courtroom (in the form of expert testimony) is thus a central question of the interdisciplinary area between cognitive neuroscience and law, known as 'neurolaw' or 'neuroscience and the law'.[119] Judges must assess the scientific validity and reliability of the cited scientific evidence in order to decide its admissibility. This constitutes a significant challenge, since judges may have limited training in science.[120] Nonetheless, the comparative success of specialist mental health courts evidences how narrow specialist training can improve therapeutic outcomes.[121]

[116] F Turone, 'Medical tests help reduce sentence of woman accused of murder' (2011) 343 *British Medical Journal* 343.

[117] KD Phillips, 'Empathy for Psychopaths: Using fMRI Brain Scans to Plea for Leniency in Death Penalty Cases' (2013) 37 *Law & Psychology Review* 1.

[118] NA Farhany, 'Neuroscience and behavioral genetics in US criminal law: an empirical analysis' (2015) 2 *Journal of Law and the Bioscience* 3.

[119] E Picozza (ed), *Neurolaw: An Introduction* (Springer, 2016); CJ Kraft and J Giordano, 'Integrating Brain Science and Law: Neuroscientific Evidence and Legal Perspectives on Protecting Individual Liberties' (2017) *Frontiers in Neuroscience*; V Tigano, GL Cascini, C Sanchez-Castañeda, P Péran and U Sabatini, 'Neuroimaging and Neurolaw: Drawing the Future of Aging' (2019) 10 *Frontiers in Endocrinology* 217.

[120] WM Grove, RC Barden, HN Garb and SO Lilienfeld, 'Failure of Rorschach-Comprehensive-System-based testimony to be admissible under the Daubert-Joiner- Kumho standard' (2002) 8 *Psychol Public Policy Law* 2.

[121] J Bernstein and T Seltzer, 'Criminalization of People with Mental Illnesses: The Role of Mental Health Courts in System Reform' (2003) 7 *University of the District of Columbia Law Review* 143; E Turpun and H Richards, 'Seattle's mental health courts: early indicators of effectiveness' (2003) *26 International Journal of Law and Psychiatry* 33; F Davidson, E Heffernan, D Greenberg, T Butler and P Burgess, 'A Critical Review of Mental Health Court Liaison Services in Australia: A first national survey' (2016) 23 *Psychiatry, Psychology and Law* 6; L Rubenstein and PT Yanos, 'Predictors of mental health court completion' (2019) 30 *The Journal of Forensic Psychiatry & Psychology* 6.

E. Automated Mental State Detection (AMSD)

While the connectionist paradigm may yet help yield insights into the genetic aspects of mental disorder, more recent approaches are starting to focus in on the detection of human mental states. Given that disturbances in communication is a symptom common to many severe mental illnesses,[122] researchers have zeroed-in on communication as the locus for 'objectively' identifying a person's mental state. As Coehen and Elvevåg observe:

> In schizophrenia, for example, the incoherent discourse – a disjointed flow of ideas, loose associations between words or digressions from the topic – frequently appears during spontaneous speech, and is important for diagnosis, treatment monitoring and prognostic considerations.[123]

CTM has also oriented researchers to the development of tools to objectify communications – including natural language – and automate detection of human mental states.[124] Automated mental state detection (AMSD) is conceptually rooted in cognitive psychology, affective sciences, social psychology, study of nonverbal behaviour, and psychophysiology. Its technical roots, however, are in engineering and computer science, specifically sensors and wearable devices, and digital signal processing (ie, computer vision, acoustic modelling, ML/DL).

The psychological ambitions of AMSD are grounded in theories that posit mental processes as embodied. Embodied theories of cognition and affect hypothesize that mental states are not restricted to the confines of the mind, but also the body.[125] One of the most direct examples of a mind-body link is the hyper-activation of the sympathetic nervous system during fight-or-flight responses.[126] There are also well-known relationships between facial expressions and affective states,[127] for example, furrowing one's brow during experiences of confusion.[128] There is also a long history of using bodily/physiological responses to investigate cognitive processes like attention and cognitive load. For example, the study of eye movements (oculesics) has become an invaluable

[122] *cf* C Hymas, 'AI used for first time in job interviews in UK to find best applicants' *The Telegraph* (27 September 2019) www.telegraph.co.uk/news/2019/09/27/ai-facial-recognition-used-first-time-job-interviews-uk-find.

[123] AS Cohen and B Elvevåg, 'Automated Computerized Analysis of Speech in Psychiatric Disorders' (2015) 27 *Current Opinion in Psychiatry* 3, 3.

[124] S Abdullah and T Choudhury, 'Sensing Technologies for Monitoring Serious Mental Illnesses' (January–March 2018) *IEEE MultiMedia*; SK D'Mello, 'Automated Mental State Detection for Mental Health Care' in D Luxton (ed), *Artificial Intelligence in Behavioural and Mental Health Care.*

[125] M deVega, A Glenberg and A Graesser (eds), *Symbols, Embodiment, and Meaning* (Oxford University Press, 2008); P Ekman, 'An argument for basic emotions' (1992) 6 *Cognition & Emotion* 34; M Wilson, 'Six views of embodied cognition' (2002) 9 *Psychonomic Bulletin and Review* 625; LW Barsalou, 'Grounded cognition' (2008) 59 *Annual Review of Psychology* 1); L Shapiro, *Embodied Cognition*, 2nd edn (Routledge, 2019).

[126] J Larsen, G Berntson, K Poehlmann, T Ito and JCacioppo, 'The psychophysiology of emotion' in M Lewis, J Haviland-Jones and L Barrett (eds), *Handbook of Emotions*, 3rd edn (Guilford, 2008).

[127] JA Coan, 'Emergent ghosts of the emotion machine' (2010) 2 *Emotion Review* 3; J Lenge, J Dalegem, D Borsbroom, GA van Kleef and AH Fischer, 'Toward an Integrative Psychometric Model of Emotions' (2020) 15 *Perspectives on Psychological Science* 2.

[128] C Darwin, *The Expression of the Emotions in Man and Animals* (John Murray, 1872).

tool for investigating visual attention,[129] while electroencephalography has long been used as an index for mental workload.[130]

The close mind-body relationship is unsurprising once one considers that both cognition and affect inform human actions. Simply put, we think and we feel in order to act. If the human body is the agent of action, monitoring observable bodily changes can provide critical insights into unobservable mental states. This key idea underlies the automated detection approach, which attempts to infer mental states from bodily responses.

i. Emotion, Mood and Affective State Detection

A person's affective state and mood are primary factors in the diagnostic evaluation and identification of mental disorders.[131] Trzepacz and Baker describe affect as 'the external and dynamic manifestations of a person's internal emotional state' and mood as 'a person's predominant internal state at any one time'.[132] Because of their centrality to mental disorder more broadly, they are also important variables in mental capacity assessments and the characterisation of a person's rationality viz an index decision. In real-world settings, the Mental State Examination (MSE) is a standardised questionnaire used by clinicians:

> Psychiatric signs and symptoms are not necessarily mysterious or daunting, especially if approached systematically … The role of the MSE in the investigation of psychiatric problems is analogous to that played by the physical examination in the investigation of somatic problems […]
>
> The psychiatric MSE is the component of the psychiatric evaluation that includes observing the patient's behavior and describing it in an objective, non-judgmental manner. Like the physical examination, the MSE seeks to reveal signs of illness. Like the physical examination, the MSE is termed the objective portion of the patient evaluation, even though the elicited data carry with the clinicians' ability, style, and training.[133] [original emphasis]

Whereas affect is a broad term encompassing both moods and emotion, moods are understood to be more transitory and having only background influence on consciousness. Emotion, then, is understood to be more brief and acute, experienced at the forefront of consciousness and helping prepare the sympathetic nervous system for both physical and cognitive action (ie, the startle response). Recent AMSD research

[129] H Deubel and WX Schindler, 'Saccade target selection and object recognition: Evidence for a common attentional mechanism' (1996) 36 *Vision Research* 12; K Rayner, 'Eye movements in reading and information processing: 20 years of research' (1998) 124 *Psychological Bulletin* 3; Z Zhu and Q Ji, 'Robust real-time eye detection and tracking under variable lighting conditions and various face orientations' (2005) 98 *Computer Vision and Image Understanding* 1.

[130] C Berka, DJ Levendowski, MN Lumicao, et al, 'EEG correlates of task engagement and mental workload in vigilance, learning, and memory tasks' 2007) 78 *Aviation, Space, and Environmental Medicine Supplement* 1; *cf* JN Gledd, 'The Enigma of Neuroimaging in ADHD' (2019) 176 *The American Journal of Psychiatry* 7.

[131] HM Salsman, J-S Lai, HC Hendrie, et al., 'Assessing Psychological Well-Being: Self-Report Instruments for the NIH Toolbox' (2015) 23 *Quality of Life Research* 1.

[132] P Trzepacz and R Baker, *The Psychiatric Mental Status Examination* (Oxford University Press, 1993) 39.

[133] P Trzepacz and R Baker, *The Psychiatric Mental Status Examination* 4.

has focused on detecting emotions rather than moods, particularly the so-called 'basic emotions': anger, surprise, happiness, disgust, sadness, and fear.[134] Crivelli and Fridlund, however, deconstruct the Western foundations of the basic emotions framework, and conclude that 'many of BET's recent modifications are inconsistent in ways that may render it impossible to test and immune to falsification'. They instead suggest that 'the behavioral ecology view of facial displays, as an externalist and functionalist approach, resolves the quandaries and contradictions embedded in BET's precepts and extensions'.[135]

While there remains little conceptual agreement about the nature of emotion and its biological roots, research into attention and 'mind wandering' are particularly relevant for mental capacity assessments (discussed below) and mental wellbeing more generally.[136] Attention, or the lack thereof, is a relevant factor from the time a person undergoes an MSE right up until their ability to understand, retain, and weigh the consequences of a decision where capacity is in question.

Furthermore, research has indicated that individuals with dysphoria (ie, depression, fatigue) and ADHD have elevated levels of mind wandering across a variety of tasks. So whilst in principle, automated detection of mind wandering may be of therapeutic value in helping people with their day to day routines,[137] it could theoretically be used to assess the current state of a person's attention at the specific time they are making a decision, or are asked if they understood something (ie, their rights). Thus, automated detection of mind wandering as people go about their daily routines has the potential to provide valuable information into the attentional processes implicated in mental health, and questions of capacity in particular.

F. Human Brain Interfaces (HBI)

Measurement, it is often said, is a precursor for meaningful change. The science and practice of mental health care has much to gain from fully automated systems that purport to offer long-term and in-depth diagnostic insights into a person's mental state in a variety of contexts. AMSD can be integrated within the overall mental healthcare system at multiple levels, such as CDSS, ambulatory monitoring, and psychotherapeutic chatbot apps, for instance. The preceding overview has by necessity been selective and

[134] P Ekman, 'Basic Emotions' in T Dalgleish and M Power (eds), *Handbook of Cognition and Emotion* (Wiley, 1999); J Sabini and M SIlver, 'Ekman's basic emotions: Why not love and jealousy?' (2005) 19 *Cognition and Emotions* 5; D Keltner, JL Tracy, D Sauter and A Cowen, 'What Basic Emotion Theory Really Says for the Twenty-First Century Study of Emotion' (2019) 43 *Journal of Nonverbal Behavior* 195.

[135] C Crivelli and AJ Fridlund, 'Inside-Out: From Basic Emotions Theory to the Behavioral Ecology View' (2019) 43 *Journal of Nonverbal Behavior* 161.

[136] KW Brown and RM Ryan, 'The benefits of Being Present: Mindfulness and its role in Psychological Well-being' (2003) 84 *Journal of Personality and Social Psychology* 4.

[137] G Shaw, and L Giambra, 'Task unrelated thoughts of college students diagnosed as hyperactive in childhood' (1993) 9 *Developmental Neuropsychology* 1; J Smallwood and JW Schooler, 'The science of mind wandering: Empirically navigating the stream of consciousness' (2015) 66 *Annual Review of Psychology* 487518.

precludes exploring embedded technologies such as Human Brain Interfaces (HBI) in mental health[138] and other medical contexts such as restoring human sight.[139]

For now, we can say that AMSD presents a range of privacy and human rights challenges that cut to the core of human identity and what science claims to reveal about the human condition. At the time of this writing there is no AMSD deployed in clinical use, but this will soon change. Successive breakthroughs and performance leaps are enabling new ways of having machines detect naturalistic experience across a wider range of mental states, in more real-world contexts, leveraging increasingly small, wearable, and potentially biologically embedded technologies. While there is reason for optimism about the potential upsides, it must be couched in the realities of commercial data collection and its attendant impact on privacy, autonomy, and human rights, among other things. There is also the question of generalisability across different populations, and the over-arching problem of the reproducibility crisis in contemporary neuroscience and AI research. The imminent feasibility of AMSD and other technologies for objectifying human experiencing and offering insights to the puzzle of phenomenal consciousness leads us to our next question.

III. IF Computers Can Make Medical Decisions, THEN Should They?

The preceding parts briefly reviewed the application of computers to medicine, with a specific focus on the development of Expert Systems (ES), Clinical Decision Support Systems (CDSS) in mental health contexts, to the advent of Automated Mental State Detection (AMSD) and brain devices. They highlighted that the task of building a 'decision support' system using mathematical formalisms is one of immense complexity, and it was ultimately the recognition of that complexity that impeded the development and take-up of medical ES in real-world contexts, and psychiatry in particular. Despite the optimism of early researchers, no machine could demonstrate the full spectrum of abilities used by a human judge or psychiatrist – despite the vast formalisation of knowledge in both domains (ie, case reports, clinical data) and the structurally algorithmic nature of legal reasoning. That is to say, although both doctors and judges have written a lot of things down that a computer could now read, no computer could be programmed to emulate the full range of things a judge or doctor did.

The history of AI and Medicine is one largely characterised by bold ambitions, tantalising promises, good intentions, but also spectacular hubris. The purpose of the present study, therefore, is not to re-litigate that history or hubris, but propose how we can

[138] AS Widge, DD Dougherty and CT Moritz, 'Affective Brain-Computer Interfaces As Enabling Technology for Responsive Psychiatric Stimulation' (2014) 1 *Brain-Computer Interfaces* 2; *cf* M Pham, S Goerging, M Sample, JE Huggins and E Klein, 'Asilomar Survey: Researcher Perspectives on Ethical Principles and Guidelines for BCI Research' (2018) 5 *Brain-Computer Interfaces* 4.

[139] MS Beauchamp, D Oswalt, P Sun, et al, 'Dynamic Stimulation of Visual Cortex Produces Form Vision in Sighted and Blind Humans' (2020) 181 *Cell* 4; *cf* S Wells, 'Electrifying Brains May Be The Key to Restoring Sight – Study' (*Inverse*, 15 May 2020) www.inverse.com/innovation/brain-stimulation-helps-blind-see.

learn from it. We suggest that the ideological contours of AI research help sharpen a critique of the normative justifications and potential use-contexts for current and near-term 'AI' systems: specifically, so-called Automated Decision Making (ADM) systems, which leverage an array of analytical and probabilistic techniques to reanimate the goal of building computer programs to emulate aspects of human decision reasoning, and ultimately the need for human decision makers at all.[140] The history of AI is thus all the more instructive, as it appears to be repeating itself.

A. Automated Decision Making (ADM)

ADM systems have proliferated at a remarkable pace – with often lamentable results.[141] From medicine[142] to public policy[143] and immigration[144] to criminal justice[145] the ubiquity and consequential contexts in which ADM is used makes it hard to deny Pasquale's observation that 'authority is increasingly expressed algorithmically'.[146] This algorithmic-turn in decision-making means it is essential to critically appraise the ideological suppositions, power dynamics, and normative claims of algorithmic authority. This means not getting sandbagged by what Powles and Nissenbaum call the 'captivating diversion' of bias:

> … the preoccupation with narrow computational puzzles distracts us from the far more important issue of the colossal asymmetry between societal cost and private gain in the roll-out of automated systems. It also denies us the possibility of asking: Should we be building these systems at all?[147]

While these questions are relevant to broader questions of this chapter, the focus will shortly turn to the prospective application of ADM – or what we might call AI more

[140] M Whittaker, K Crawford et al, 'AI Now Report 2018', ainowinstitute.org/AI_Now_2018_Report.pdf; *cf* V Eubanks, *Automating Inequality* (St Martins Press, 2018).

[141] GL Ciampaglia, A Nematzadeh, F Menczer and A Flammini, 'How algorithmic popularity bias hinders or promotes quality' (2018) 8 *Scientific Reports* 15951; A Lambrecht and CE Tucker, 'Algorithmic Bias? An Empirical Study into Apparent Gender Based Discrimination. In the Display of STEM Career Ads' (2018), papers.ssrn.com/sol3/papers.cfm?abstract_id=2852260.

[142] WN Price II, 'Regulating Black-Box Medicine' (2017–18) 115 *Michigan Law Review* 1; VH Buch, I Ahmed and M Maruthappu, 'Artificial Intelligence in Medicine: Current Trends and Future Possibilities' (2018) 68 *British Journal of General Practice* 668.

[143] L Andrews, 'Public administration, public leadership and the construction of public value in the age of the algorithm and "big data"' (2018) *Public Administration* (online first); M Oswald, 'Algorithm-assisted decision-making in the public sector: framing the issues using administrative law rules governing discretionary power' (2018) 376 *Philosophical Transactions of the Royal Society A* 2128.

[144] P Molnar and L Gill, 'Bots at the Gate: A Human Rights Analysis of Automated Decision-Making in Canada's Immigration and Refugee Systems' (2018), citizenlab.ca/wp-content/uploads/2018/09/IHRP-Automated-Systems-Report-Web-V2.pdf.

[145] J Angwin and J Larson, 'Bias in Criminal Risk Scores is Mathematically Inevitable' (*ProPublica*, 30 December 2016), www.propublica.org/article/bias-in-criminal-risk-scores-is-mathematically-inevitable-researchers-say; K Hannah-Moffat, 'Algorithmic risk governance: Big data analytics, race and information activism in criminal justice debates' (2018) *Theoretical Criminology* (online first).

[146] F Pasquale, *The Black Box Society* (Harvard University Press, 2015) 8.

[147] J Powles and H Nissenbaum, 'The Seductive Diversion of "Solving" Bias in Artificial Intelligence' (*Medium*, 7 December 2018), medium.com/s/story/the-seductive-diversion-of-solving-bias-in-artificial-intelligence-890df5e5ef53.

generally – on the assessment of a specific subset of legal questions related to the assessment of mental capacity under the law of England and Wales. First, however, we review the contributions of American computer scientist Joseph Weizenbaum; specifically, his criticism of twentieth century AI research, and the prospect of computers replacing human decision makers.

B. Weizenbaum's ELIZA Experiments

One of the earliest Natural Language Programming (NLP)[148] applications was developed by computer scientist Joseph Weizenbaum at MIT from 1964–66. His program, ELIZA, was an early 'chatbot' designed to simulate human conversation by using pattern matching and substitution techniques to maintain the illusion that the program 'understood' conversations. In reality, ELIZA had no way to contextualise events and could not engage in conversation about anything other than what it was provided explicit instruction sets for. In her historical analysis of ELIZA and its influence on AI research, Bassett explains:

> ELIZA consisted of a language analyzer and a script or set of rules … like those that might be given to an actor … to improvise around a certain theme. The resulting bot was designed to undertake real interactions with human interlocutors based on 'simulation' or 'impersonation'.[149]

One script ELIZA could run was called DOCTOR, which Weizenbaum designed to emulate 'the responses of a non-directional psychotherapist in an initial psychiatric interview'[150] and prompt the user to explain their feelings. Like most logic-based systems of its day, DOCTOR used various rules for structuring interactions between a Rogerian psychoanalyst and patient. Rogerian psychotherapy was considered to be particularly suited to this task as it relied upon mirroring techniques where the therapist repeated statements back to a patient.[151] This had the effect of bounding the conversational parameters in such a way that dialogue was 'open' at one end (human participant) and 'closed' at the other (DOCTOR). Even when the admitted modesty of Wizenbaum's NLP ambitions are taken into account, it is evident that ELIZA had many limitations. The program was (and remains)[152] easy to 'trick', can be made to loop recursively, and 'persuaded' into nonsensical answers in much the same way Microsoft's AI chatbot, Tay, was 'trained' to parrot racist inflammatory and offensive remarks by Twitter users in 2016.[153]

[148] PM Nadkarni, L Ohno-Machado and WW Chapman, '*Natural Language Processing: An Introduction*' *(2011) 18 Journal* of the American Medical Informatics Association 5.

[149] C Bassett, 'The computational therapeutic: exploring Weizenbaum's ELIZA as a history of the present' (2019) 34 *AI & Society* 803.

[150] J Weizenabaum, 'ELIZA – A Computer Program For the Study of Natural Language Communication Between Man and Machine' (1966) 9 *Communications of the ACM* 1, 188.

[151] JCS Cheung, 'Behind the mirror: what Rogerian "Technique" is NOT' (2014) *13 Person Centred & Experiential Psychotherapies* 4.

[152] Eliza, the Rogerian Therapist, psych.fullerton.edu/mbirnbaum/psych101/Eliza.htm.

[153] R Metz, 'Microsoft's neo-Nazi sexbot was a great lesson for makers of AI assistants' (*MIT Technology Review*, 27 May 2018), www.technologyreview.com/s/610634/microsofts-neo-nazi-sexbot-was-a-great-lesson-for-makers-of-ai-assistants; MJ Wolf, K Miller and FS Grodzinsky, 'Why we should have seen that coming: comments on Microsoft's tay "experiment", and wider implications' (2017) 47 *ACM SIGCAS Computers and Society* 3.

Much to Weizenbaum's chagrin, ELIZA was considered one of the first programs to pass the 'Turing Test', a claim Weizenbaum roundly rejected.[154] Indeed, the earliest responses to ELIZA indicate just how optimistic some clinicians were about the all-conquering potential of computers in medicine, even if they did not yet envision the wholesale replacement of human therapists. One such response is illustrative:

> Because of the time-sharing capabilities of modern and future computers, several hundred patients an hour could be handled by a computer system designed for this purpose. The human therapist, involved in the design and operation of this system, would not be replaced, but would become a much more efficient man since his efforts would no longer be limited to one-to-one patient-therapist ratio as now exists.[155]

WR Ashby, a leading British cybernetician and trained psychiatrist, was similarly enthused:

> I cannot claim … to have justified cybernetics to the psychiatrist, but I hope I have given sufficient evidence to show that cybernetics is a worthwhile study, and that further research in it offers excellent prospects. It is my belief that this new science will lead us steadily forwards, first to an increased understanding of how the brain works, and then to those therapeutic advances that we are all awaiting so impatiently.[156]

C. Weizenbaum's Critique of Computerised Decision-making

It was responses to ELIZA such as the ones above that motivated Weizenbaum to publish the book *Computer Power and Human Reason* in 1976.[157] In it he made his ambivalence about computer technology (and technologists) clear; qualified the material and theoretical limits of computation; and observed a widening schism in perception regarding what digital technologies, and AI in particular, could actually do. He had made this basic point several years earlier in the 1972 article 'On the Impact of Computers in Society', excusing the misunderstanding of the lay public, but excoriating fellow computer scientists for their complicity in misrepresenting the potential of computers:

> The nonprofessional has little choice but to make his attributions of properties to computers on the basis of the propaganda emanating from the computer community and amplified by the press. The computer professional therefore has an enormously important responsibility to be modest in his claims. This advice would not even have to be voiced if computer science had a tradition of scholarship and of self-criticism such as that which characterizes the established sciences.[158]

[154] M Boden, *Artificial Intelligence and Natural Man* (Basic Books, 1977) 96–97; McCorduck, *Machines Who Think* 225.

[155] KM Colby, JB Watt and JP Gilbert, 'A Computer Method of Psychotherapy: Preliminary Communication' (1966) 142 *Journal of Nervous and Mental Disease* 2, 152.

[156] WR Ashby, 'The Application of Cybernetics to Psychiatry' (1954) 100 *Journal of Mental Science* 418, 124; G Bateson, 'The Cybernetics of "Self": A Theory of Alcoholism' (1971) 34 *Psychiatry* 1; *cf* A Pickering, 'Psychiatry, synthetic brains and cybernetics in the work of W. Ross Ashby' (2009) 38 Journal of General Systems 2.

[157] Weizenbaum, *Computer Power and Human Reason: From Judgment to Calculation* (Freeman, 1976).

[158] Weizenbaum, 'On the Impact of Computers in Society' 614.

Weizenbaum asserted that his own accomplishments with ELIZA were misconstrued in a way that overstated the all-conquering potential of computers and the 'brain = machine' metaphor of CTM:

> This joining of an illicit metaphor to an ill-thought out idea then breeds, and is perceived to legitimate, such perverse propositions as that, for example, a computer can be programmed to become an effective psycho-therapist.[159]

Wiezenbaum was particularly troubled by the optimism of experienced professional therapists that DOCTOR could be scaled up into a 'auto-therapist' (perhaps now realised in the form of 'virtual therapist' chat-bot apps).[160] But Weizenbaum's stated ambition for DOCTOR was to 'demonstrate that the communication between man and machine was superficial'[161] and push back against what he regarded as 'the hubris so bombastically exhibited by the artificial intelligentsia'.[162] Weizenbaum lamented that psychologists and psychiatrists – experts in the domain of human to human interaction – could '… view the simplest mechanical parody of a single interviewing technique as having captured anything of the essence of a human encounter'.[163]

Weizenbaum's broader conclusion, however, was that this enthusiasm was only possible from those who had pre-formed a view of the world as machine, cognition as an 'information process',[164] the brain as a 'meat machine',[165] and the human attached to it as a set of biological systems that could be atomised, studied, explained, and ultimately: controlled. Yet the 'hubris' that most troubled Weizenbaum lay in the goal at the heart of AI research: the attainment of Artificial General Intelligence (AGI). He thought that AGI was not just technically infeasible, but a pernicious fantasy that had captivated public understanding, and corroded the attention of his colleagues from more soluble and practical problems. He also bemoaned that hagiographical accounts of computationalism were so quickly made the orthodoxy of modern science. His lingering fear, however, seems to be one informed by his own experiences of fascism: one where the computationalist worldview promoted by AI researchers would lead to a world where man had no choice but to 'yield his autonomy to a world viewed as machine'.[166]

Although Weizenbaum's critique focused on what computers could do (technically), the question of what they ought to do (practically) clearly preoccupied him most. His critique was based on an a priori distinction: 'There is a difference between man and machine, and … there are certain tasks which computers ought not be made to do, independent of whether computers can be made to do them.'[167] In his view, because

[159] Weizenbaum, *Computer Power and Human Reason* 206.

[160] JR Moore and M Caudill, 'The Bot Will See You Now: A History and Review of Interactive Computerized Mental Health Programs' (2019) 42 *Psychiatric Clinics* 4.

[161] J Epstein and WD Klinkenberg, 'From Eliza to Internet: a brief history of computerized assessment' (2001) 17 *Computers in Human Behavior* 3, 296.

[162] Weizenbaum, *Computer Power and Human Reason* 221.

[163] ibid, 3.

[164] YN Harari, *Homo Deus: A Brief History of Tomorrow* (Vintage, 2018) 220–80.

[165] McCorduck, Machines Who Think, 85–110; *cf* S Aaraonson, 'The Ghost in the Quantum Turing Machine' in SB Cooper and A Hodge (eds), *The Once and Future Turing: Computing the World* (Cambridge University Press, 2016).

[166] Weizenbaum, *Computer Power and Human Reason* 9.

[167] ibid, x.

machines were ontologically removed from human experience, he cautioned that AI – while theoretically possible – should not be allowed to make decisions or provide advice that requires, among other things, the compassion and wisdom developed through human experience.[168] This was because machines' inexperience with 'domains of thought and action' would be a barrier

> … to the way humans relate to one another as well as to machines and their relations to man. For human socialization, though it is grounded in the biological constitution common to all humans, is strongly determined by culture. And human cultures differ radically among themselves.[169]

Weizenbaum also rejects suggestions that a machine could be designed with capabilities to acquire human experience by embodying computation in the form of robotics:

> [T]he deepest and most grandiose fantasy that motivates work on artificial intelligence … is nothing less than to build a machine on the model of man, a robot that is to have its childhood, to learn language as a child does, to gain its knowledge of the world by sensing the world through its own organs, and ultimately to contemplate the whole domain of human thought.[170]

For Weizenbaum, computer technology, as with all sciences, are ultimately self-validating systems, and science 'proceeds by simplifying reality'.[171] Through the process of design and development, computers may be used to further simplify and/or precisely define problems and corresponding 'solutions' within narrowly circumscribed (ie, computationally bounded) environments, but they do so to the exclusion of all data exogenous to the specific task they are instructed to perform. That is to say, computers do not in any meaningful sense 'share' human experience, even if they might 'interact' with it within circumscribed contexts, such as 'smart' medical devices (ie, electrocardiograph) and 'human brain interfaces', discussed in a subsequent section.[172]

To illustrate this point, Weizenbaum recounts a parable about a police officer coming across a man on his hands and knees searching for his lost keys beneath a lamp post. The officer asks the man what he is searching for and he replies that he lost his keys over there, pointing to a dark alley. 'So why are you looking for them under the streetlight?' the officer asks, to which the man replies 'because the light is so much better over here'. Weizenbaum concludes that scientific enquiry can similarly only look where it already has light. Yet 'only two things' matter regarding the nature of scientific enquiry: 'the size of the circle of light that is the universe of one's inquiry, and the spirit of one's inquiry. The latter must include an acute awareness that there is an outer darkness, and that there are sources of illumination of which one as yet knows very little'.[173]

Despite the funding that had begun flowing into computer science departments and AI research, Weizenbaum was something of an apostate amongst his contemporaries

[168] ibid, 204.
[169] ibid, 223–24.
[170] ibid, 227.
[171] ibid, 16.
[172] J Alberto Costa e Silva and RE Steffen, 'The future of psychiatry: brain devices' (2017) 69 *Metabolism*.
[173] Weizenbaum, *Computer Power and Human Reason* 127.

for opposing their increasingly bold claims that a computer could 'emulate' or 'replace' human decision making:

> The very asking of the question, 'What does a judge (or a psychiatrist) know that we cannot tell a computer?' is a monstrous obscenity. That it has to be put in print at all, even for the purpose of exposing its morbidity, is a sign of the madness of our times ... [the critical issues] cannot be settled by asking questions beginning with 'can'. The limits of the applicability of computers are ultimately stable only in terms of oughts. What emerges as the most elementary insight is that, since we do not now have any ways of making computers wise, we ought not now to give computers tasks that demand wisdom.[174]

Weizenbaum lamented that the human obsession with mastering the boundaries of what could be effectively computed would inevitably blind humanity to what lies beyond those boundaries, and diminish the capacity to understand or accept the limitations of computation. Whereas Nobel laureate Eugene Wigner famously touted 'the unreasonable effectiveness of mathematics in the physical sciences' as a mystery demanding an explanation, Weizenbaum retorted that '[b]elief in the rationality-logicality equation has corroded the prophetic power of language itself. We can count, but we are rapidly forgetting how to say what is worth counting and why'.[175] Weizenbaum's humanist critique was one ultimately premised on the conflation of knowledge with meaning, process with purpose, and subverting the Enlightenment quest for knowledge with the relentless pursuit of quantification and calculation.

IV. Mental Capacity in England and Wales

There has long been acknowledgment that legal provision should be made regarding individuals with reduced capacity to make decisions. Since the fourteenth century the predecessors to the High Court of England and Wales had jurisdiction over adults who were in some way incapable of giving consent under the doctrine of parens patriae, a Royal Prerogative recognising the duty of the state to citizens who cannot speak for themselves.[176] Often this arose in determining whether decisions made by the individual were effective at law and due to the necessity of managing property and affairs and consenting to medical care. In the 1980s work began on replacing piecemeal and restricted legislation concerning mental incapacity, resulting in the Mental Capacity Act 2005 (MCA). This process partly coincided with the passage of the Human Rights Act 1998, which enshrined relevant rights including the right to a fair trial, the private and family life, and freedom of expression.[177] More recently, there has been

[174] ibid, 227.
[175] ibid, 16.
[176] G Ashton (ed), *Court of Protection Practice 2016* (Jordan Publishing, 2016) 31; *cf* R Johns, 'Who decides now? Protecting and empowering vulnerable adults who lose the capacity to make decisions for themselves' (2007) 37 *The British Journal of Social Work* 3, 557–64, 558. The High Court has more recently asserted that the inherent jurisdiction extends to capacious but vulnerable adults: *cf Re PS* [2007] EWHC 623 (Fam) at para 3 per Munby J; *KC & Anor v City of Westminster Social and Community Services Department and Anor* [2008] EWCA Civ 198 at para 56 per Roderic Wood J.
[177] Human Rights Act 1998.

greater recognition that people with disabilities are vulnerable to neglect, abuse and exploitation,[178] and a concomitant widening of oversight of capacity in the context of, for example, informal deprivations of liberty.[179]

There has also been increased concern to reflect a modern climate emphasising autonomy and non-discrimination. Since the 1990s the courts have explicitly recognised that their responsibility arises because, and only because, 'the reduced capacity of the individual requires interference with his or her personal autonomy'.[180] Even before the introduction of the MCA's presumption of capacity and permissive stance towards unwise decisions, the bench recognised that the law on decision-making should look to capacity rather than rationality, reflecting a concern with protecting plural, incommensurable moral values that exist amongst the population, and safeguarding people from excessive interference in their decision-making.[181]

A. The Mental Capacity Act (MCA)

The MCA empowers the Court of Protection, made up of existing judicial officeholders,[182] to decide whether a person lacks capacity in relation to a decision or decisions on particular matters. As a starting point, patients are assumed to have capacity to make medical or other decisions unless explicitly proven otherwise. A person lacks capacity in relation to a matter if at the material time they are unable to make a decision about that matter for themselves (the so-called 'functional' test), because their mind or brain is impaired or disturbed in its functioning (the 'diagnostic' test).[183] A person will be unable to make a decision if they cannot understand, retain, use or weigh the information relevant to the decision, or if they cannot communicate their decision.[184] It does not matter whether the impairment or disturbance is permanent or temporary,[185] and a lack of capacity cannot be established merely by reference to the person's age or appearance, or a condition or aspect of their behaviour which 'might lead others to make unjustified assumptions about' their capacity.[186] A person's capacity is assessed as at the time of making the determination[187] on the balance of probabilities.[188]

[178] *cf* G Ashton (ed), *Court of Protection Practice 2016* (Jordan Publishing, 2016) 38.

[179] *cf P v Cheshire West and Anor and P&Q v Surrey County Council* [2014] UKSC 19, [2014] AC 896; Mental Capacity Act 2005, s 21A and Schedule A1.

[180] *G v E & Others* [2010] EWHC 2042 (Fam) at para 18.

[181] J Coggon and J Miola, 'Autonomy, Liberty, and Medical Decision-Making' (2011) 70 *Cambridge Law Journal* 523–47, 527, citing *In Re T (Adult: Refusal of Treatment)* (1993) Fam 95 at 116–17.

[182] Mental Capacity Act 2005, s 46.

[183] Mental Capacity Act 2005, s 2(1). Section 2(1) generally only applies to people over the age of 16: see ss 2(5) and 18(3). The diagnostic test has come under significant criticism because of its potential for discrimination against people with disabilities: see eg General Comment No 1 (2014) issued by the Committee on the Rights of Persons with Disabilities, 'Article 12: Equal Recognition before the Law', www.ohchr.org/en/hrbodies/crpd/pages/gc.aspx. Such criticism is beyond the scope of this chapter as, even if the diagnostic test were not included in s 2 of the MCA, medical evidence will almost universally contribute to capacity assessments (see below).

[184] Mental Capacity Act 2005, s 3(1).

[185] ibid, s 2(2).

[186] ibid, s 2(3).

[187] ibid, s 2(1).

[188] ibid, s 2(4).

Any person, including the person who is alleged to lack capacity, may apply to the Court of Protection for a capacity determination.[189] However, in practice, most capacity determinations are made by care and treatment teams rather than the court.[190] This is because the Court of Protection can decide whether a third party's act in relation to a person has been or will be lawful because of the person's incapacity.[191] For example, a member of a person's care or treatment team will not incur additional liability for an act which they reasonably believed to be in that person's best interest, if they took reasonable steps to establish a reasonable belief that the person lacked capacity.[192] Leaving capacity determinations to clinicians has its own issues. As Sessums et al. observe:

> … many clinicians lack formal training in capacity evaluation. The practical consequence is that clinicians regularly fail to recognize incapacity and generally question a patient's capacity only when the medical decision to be made is complex with significant risk … or if the patient disagrees with the physician's recommendation.[193]

Nonetheless, as matters currently stand, the Court of Protection is intended to provide a forum only for resolution of disputed or difficult cases and complex decisions, such as where a person challenges a decision that they lack capacity, or where professionals or family members disagree about an individual's capacity.[194] Once a lack of capacity is established, the court can either make a decision on the person's behalf in keeping with their best interests, or appoint a deputy, such as the Public Guardian, to do so.[195] The Court of Protection has power to make almost[196] any order relating to the person's personal welfare and property, including interventions as grave as the deprivation of liberty[197] and forced medical procedures.[198]

[189] Although some applicants will require court permission: see Mental Capacity Act 2005, s 50.

[190] Ruck Keene, Kane, Kim, and Owen, 'Taking capacity seriously? Ten years of mental capacity disputes before England's Court of Protection', p 60, citing *N v ACCG* [2017] UKSC 22 at para 38 per Baroness Hale.

[191] Mental Capacity Act 2005, s 15.

[192] ibid, s 5. This provision does not apply to some deprivations of liberty (see ss 4A-4B) or where there is a valid advance decision to refuse treatment: see Mental Health Act 2005 ss 5(4), 24–26. There are additional conditions for acts which restrain a person: see Mental Capacity Act 2005, s 6. Persons making decisions in relation to a person who lacks capacity must have regard to the MCA's Code of Practice, prepared by the Lord Chancellor: see Mental Capacity Act 2005, s 42.

[193] LL Sessums, H Zembrzuska and JL Jackson, 'Does This Patient Have Medical Decision-Making Capacity?' (2011) 306 *Journal of the American Medical Association* 4, 420.

[194] Code of Practice, paras 8.16–8.25. See also *G v E and others* [2010] EWHC 2042 (COP) (Fam); N Greaney, F Morris and B Taylor, *Mental Capacity: A Guide to the New Law*, 2nd edn (Law Society, 2008) 57. The MCA Code of Practice further provides that cases involving withdrawal of life support, bone marrow donation, non-therapeutic sterilisation and doubts or disputes about best interests should be brought before the court. Conversely, the expectation is that most matters relating to the property and affairs of P will require intervention by the court. See MCA Code of Practice, paras 8.4, 8.18–8.24; Butler, *A Practitioner's Guide to Mental Health Law* 241.

[195] Mental Capacity Act 2005, ss 15, 16.

[196] See specific exclusions and conditions related to family relationships, the Mental Health Act, voting, and research: Mental Capacity Act 2005, ss 27–34.

[197] See Mental Capacity Act 2005 ss 17, 21A and Schs A1 and AA1. (Note amendments in 2019 requiring that medical and capacity assessments be completed by those with appropriate experience and knowledge: see Mental Capacity (Amendment) Act 2019.)

[198] Mental Capacity Act 2005, ss 27–34. Applications for one-off welfare orders and those concerning deprivation of liberty are those most likely to raise issues of capacity: see A Ruck Keene, NB Kane, SYH Kim, and GS Owen, 'Taking capacity seriously? Ten years of mental capacity disputes before England's Court of Protection' (2019) 62 *International Journal of Law and Psychiatry* 56–76, 61.

B. The Process of Capacity Determinations[199]

The process of making responsible and evidence-based capacity assessments is neither simple nor straightforward. The consensus among clinicians is that responsible capacity assessments should consider capacity relative to certain decisions and actions, and as fluctuating over time and context. There are four primary dimensions to capacity assessments: (1) the capacity to make and express a choice; (2) the capacity to understand relevant information; (3) the capacity to appreciate the character of the situation and potential consequences; and (4) the capacity to retain and weigh information rationally.[200] The extent to which risk should be factored in remains unresolved in the relevant literature.[201]

The approach of courts in England and Wales is broadly similar to that of most European judicial systems; it assumes that adults have capacity to make competent decisions unless explicitly proven otherwise. Yet the presumption of capacity can create its own problems and is rebuttable in cases where a person's autonomy is in question. There is no situation, however, where a mentally disordered person is considered to be ipso facto incompetent.[202] Generally, a variety of methods are used in clinical contexts to elicit a person's decision-making capacity and assess either their competence or incompetence, a classification that is critical for determining the appropriate course of treatment, and whether it is administered in or out of hospital. Yet capacity assessments are not binary in nature. An assessment of mental capacity can lead to the diagnostic conclusion that an incompetent person still has sufficient understanding and insight to make their own decisions in a functional sense. Thus, in the interests of respecting individual autonomy, assessing mental capacity is preferred over competence when a person's decision-making is called into question.

In England and Wales, mental capacity assessment guidelines are jointly provided by the British Medical Association and the Law Society to help health and legal professionals, as well as to all those persons involved in the care of people with suspected mental impairment.[203] These guidelines define capacity as being related not to the outcome of the decision itself, but to the thought process of the decision. The basic procedural

[199] Adapted from A Ruck-Keene, K Edwards, A Eldergill and S Miles, *Court of Protection Handbook: A User's Guide*, 2nd rev edn (Legal Action Group, 2017) 54–57.

[200] Nys et al., 'Patient Capacity in Mental Health: An Overview' 331.

[201] AE Buchanan and DW Brock, *Deciding for Others: The Ethics of Surrogate Decision Making* (Cambridge University Press, 1989); RLP Berghmans, 'Capacity and Consent' (2001) 14 *Current Opinion in Psychiatry* 491; G Davidson, L Brophy and J Campbell, 'Risk, Recovery and Capacity: Competing or Complementary Approaches to Mental Health Social Work' (2016) 69 *Australian Social Work* 2; J Vess, T Ward and PM Yates, 'The Ethics of Risk Assessment' in KD Browne, AR Beeech, LA Craig and S Chou (eds), *Assessments in Forensic Practice: A Handbook* (Wiley, 2017).

[202] LA Craig, I Stringer and RB Hutchinson, 'Assessing Mental Capacity and Fitness to Plead' in KD Browne, AR Beech, LA Craig and S Chou (eds), *Offenders with Intellectual Disabilities: Implications for Practice: Assessments in Forensic Practice: A Handbook* (Wiley, 2017).

[203] Law Commission 'Mental Incapacity: Report No. 231' (1995) HMSO.

structure for determining whether someone has mental capacity under the MCA can be outlined in a series of questions as follows:

I. Decisions precedent to the determination of capacity

(a) Do the circumstances require a person to make a decision in connection with their own affairs, care or treatment?
(b) Should a formal assessment be initiated with respect to the decision?
   (i) Is there evidence to suggest that the presumption of capacity might be rebutted?
   (ii) Is the decision significant, complex, controversial, or involve placing the person at risk, or is capacity disputed?[204]
   (iii) Does anyone other than the person have a financial interest in any matter concerning the person?[205]
(c) Should the assessment be carried out by a professional only, or should there be an additional determination by the court?
   (i) Is there a conflict of opinion about the person's capacity between professionals, carers, family and or the person themselves?[206]
   (ii) Does the case involve withdrawal of life support, bone marrow donation, non-therapeutic sterilisation or a doubt or dispute about best interests?[207]

II. Has the applicant shown[208] on the balance of probabilities that the person does not have capacity to make the decision?[209]

(a) **Diagnostic test**: Is it more probable than not that the person has an impairment of, or disturbance in the functioning of, the mind or brain? A specific diagnosis may be given weight, but not necessarily.[210] Likewise, a lack of any specific diagnosis may preclude a finding of disturbance or impairment.
(b) **Functional test**: Is it more probable than not that the person is unable to make a decision for themselves in relation to the matter?[211]
   (i) Is the person unable to understand the information relevant to the decision, including by means of an explanation given to them that is appropriate to their circumstances?[212]

[204] R Jones, *Mental Capacity Act Manual*, 7th edn (Sweet & Maxwell, 2016) 1–029.
[205] 'Court of Protection Form COP3' (Assessment of capacity), www.gov.uk/government/publications/make-a-report-on-someones-capacity-to-make-decisions-form-cop3.
[206] MCA Code of Practice, paras 8.16–8.25.
[207] MCA Code of Practice, paras 8.4, 8.18–8.24.
[208] The burden of proof lies on the person asserting a lack of capacity and the standard of proof is the balance of probabilities: Mental Capacity Act 2005, s 2(4) and see *KK v STC and Others* [2012] EWHC 2136 (COP) at para 18.
[209] The effective judicial outcome appears to be 'the decision should be made by the person' or 'the decision should be made by someone else'.
[210] See below on the assessment of evidence relevant to incapacity.
[211] Mental Capacity Act 2005, s 2(1).
[212] ibid, s 3(1)(a); Court of Protection Form COP3 (Assessment of capacity), available at www.gov.uk/government/publications/make-a-report-on-someones-capacity-to-make-decisions-form-cop3 (accessed 4 March 2019).

(ii) Is the person unable to retain the information relevant to the decision for the time it takes to make the decision?[213]

(iii) Is the person unable to use or weigh the information relevant to the decision as part of the process of making the decision?[214]

(iv) Is the person unable to communicate their decision by any means at all?[215]

(c) **Causal nexus**: Is the inability to make a decision because of the impairment or disturbance?[216]

C. Capacity as a Legal Construct

Although the process for determining mental incapacity under the MCA can be laid out as a series of questions, the actual substance of each question introduces significant complexity and uncertainty. In *Re B*, Dame Elizabeth Butler-Sloss commented that '[t]he general law on mental capacity is, in my judgment, clear and easily to be understood by lawyers. Its application to individual cases … is infinitely more difficult to achieve'.[217] Much of the difficulty arises from the fact that mental capacity is not an objective, scientific, or materially observable fact. Rather, it is a legal, clinical, ethical and social construct[218] contingent on social and political contexts in just as the disciplines, professions and practices involved in assessing mental capacity are.[219]

History provides stark glimpses into how law and science have categorised normativity and what it means to be neurotypical or neurodivergent.[220] In relation to the diagnostic test, the categorisations of mental disorders change over time and are revised on the basis of scientific advances and social change, so that what was once considered

[213] Mental Capacity Act 2005, s 3(1)(b); Court of Protection Form COP3 (Assessment of capacity), available at www.gov.uk/government/publications/make-a-report-on-someones-capacity-to-make-decisions-form-cop3 (accessed 4 March 2019); R Jones, *Mental Capacity Act Manual*, 7th edn (Sweet & Maxwell, 2016) 1-049.

[214] Mental Capacity Act 2005, s 3(1)(c); Court of Protection Form COP3 (Assessment of capacity), available at www.gov.uk/government/publications/make-a-report-on-someones-capacity-to-make-decisions-form-cop3 (accessed 4 March 2019).

[215] Mental Capacity Act 2005, s 3(1)(d); Court of Protection Form COP3 (Assessment of capacity), available at www.gov.uk/government/publications/make-a-report-on-someones-capacity-to-make-decisions-form-cop3 (accessed 4 March 2019).

[216] It is not clear whether the inability to decide must be 'a' reason, the primary reason, or the only reason.

[217] *Re B (Adult: Refusal of Medical Treatment)* [2002] EWHC 429 (Fam) at para 14 per Butler Sloss LJ.

[218] P Case, 'Negotiating the domain of mental capacity' (2016) 16 *Medical Law International* 174–205, citing B Secker, 'Labeling Patient (In)Competence: A Feminist Analysis of Medico-Legal Discourse' (1999) 30(2) *Journal of Social Philosophy* 295–314; R Pepper-Smith, W Harvey and M Silberfeld, 'Competency and Practical Judgment' (1996) 17(2) *Theoretical Medicine* 135–50; J Craigie, 'Against a Singular Understanding of Legal Capacity: Criminal responsibility and the Convention on the Rights of Persons with Disabilities' (2015) 40 *International Journal of Law and Psychiatry* 6–14; and N Banner, 'Unreasonable Reasons: Normative Judgements in the Assessment of Mental Capacity' (2012) 18 *Journal of Evaluation in Clinical Practice* 5, 1038–44.

[219] Para 14 of the General Comment No 1 (2014) Committee on the Rights of Persons with Disabilities, 'Article 12: Equal Recognition before the Law', www.ohchr.org/en/hrbodies/crpd/pages/gc.aspx.

[220] For a review tracing the background of the large collection of documentary records on the relationship between high intelligence and mental illness assembled by Adele Juda during the Nazi-era and published in 1953 *cf* Wiedemann, W Burgmair and MM Weber, 'The highly gifted persons study by Adele Juda 1927–1955: pinnacle and end of psychiatric genius research in Germany' (2007) 91 *Sudhoffs Archiv* 20–37; *cf* P Chambers, *Bedlam: London's Hospital for the Mad* (The History Press, 2019).

an illness is no longer so considered, or new pathologies are introduced to, or indeed removed from, the diagnostic lexicon.[221] Discussing challenges to the compilation of the DSM V, Cobb remarks:

> These views change not least because the boundaries of mental health are partly socially determined – in the 1980s homosexuality was removed from the drafts of an earlier version of DSM only after a huge battle. In most cases, the causes of mental health problems are hard to explain in terms of brain function or chemistry … Our understanding of the origins of mental health problems, and how to treat them, remains profoundly unsatisfactory.[222]

So too are the functional criteria for capacity ostensibly descriptive while in reality reflecting normative and subjective positions. The legal evolution of the concept[223] and competing interpretations of capacity is one form of evidence for its constructive nature.[224] For example, the Idiots Act 1886 distinguished between 'lunatics', 'idiots' and 'imbeciles', with the Mental Deficiency Act 1913 adding the categories of 'feeble-minded people' and 'moral defectives'.[225] Change to the legal connotation and definition of incapacity has come from scientific developments (such as changes in accepted knowledge about psychiatric conditions, and advances in treatments), but also, importantly, social contestation and more subtle shifts within judicial understandings. For example, nineteenth century assessments focused on the presence or absence of delusions, but by the late 1900s, this was replaced by considerations about the individual's reasoning ability and intellect.[226]

D. Determining What Information is Relevant to the Decision

While history is particularly instructive, proof that capacity still remains an irreducibly complex and normative construct comes from a close examination of contemporary jurisprudence. The term 'mental capacity' simply has no precise legal meaning, as the test varies according to the particular circumstances of the alleged incapacity and the nature of the decision to be made.[227] Accordingly, the concept of capacity is inherently

[221] An example of social change influencing medical understandings of mental illness is the psychiatric approach to gender and sexual diversity in recent decades; *cf* J Drescher, 'Out of DSM: Depathologizing Homosexuality' (2015) 5 *Behavioral Sciences* 4; S Carr and H Spandler 'Hidden from history? A Brief Modern History of the Psychiatric "Treatment" of Lesbian and Bisexual Women in England' (2019) 6 *Lancet Psychiatry* 4.

[222] Cobb, *The Idea of the Brain* 304.

[223] See eg the current debates regarding the inclusion of the diagnostic test, reflecting increased social and normative emphasis on non-discrimination against people with disabilities: General Comment No 1 (2014) issued by the Committee on the Rights of Persons with Disabilities, 'Article 12: Equal Recognition before the Law', www.ohchr.org/en/hrbodies/crpd/pages/gc.aspx.

[224] P Case, 'Negotiating the domain of mental capacity' (2016) 16 *Medical Law International* 3–4.

[225] HW Ballantine, 'Criminal Responsibility of the Insane and Feeble Minded' (1918/1919) 9 *Journal of the American Institute of Law and Criminology* 485; HG Simmons, 'Explaining Social Policy: The English Mental Deficiency Act of 1913' (1978) 11 *Journal of Social History* 3.

[226] P Bartlett, 'Sense and nonsense: sensation, delusion and the limitation of sanity in nineteenth-century law' in L Bently and L Flynn (eds), *Law and the Senses: Sensational Jurisprudence* (Pluto Press, 1996) 21–41.

[227] GR Ashton, M Marin, AR Keene, and M Terrell, *Mental Capacity: Law and Practice*, 3rd edn (Jordan Publishing, 2015) 4–5; cf R Cairns, C Maddock, A Buchanan, AS David, P Hayward, G Richardson, G Szmukler, and M Hotopf, 'Prevalence and predictors of mental incapacity in psychiatric in-patients' (2005) 187 *The British Journal of Psychiatry* 4.

protean, with as much variability in the test for capacity as there are decisions to be made and people to make them. For example, the information relevant to a decision ostensibly includes:

(a) the nature of the decision;
(b) the reason why the decision is needed; and
(c) the reasonably foreseeable consequences of deciding one way or another; or failing to make the decision.[228]

However, this represents unbounded and almost infinite combinations of facts, necessitating a finely tuned and well justified evaluation of which evidence is relevant, which values are at stake, and, if they conflict (such as where carers and doctors disagree on capacity), how they should be resolved. Background issues may have a legitimate claim to be taken into consideration, including underlying behavioural issues which affect the determination of capacity; cultural, religious and ethnic considerations; family or personal circumstances, including any conflicts of interest; and what the person has decided in the past.

The fact a purported decision is 'unwise' may also be relevant. However, incapacity does not necessarily follow from the making of an unwise decision.[229] A lack of wisdom, and the weight afforded to it, will depend on the unique circumstances of each case and all the other relevant factors in the factual matrix.[230] Determining the relevance of a lack of wisdom is not a deterministic juridical task. In cases where a judge must consider the relevance of a lack of wisdom, they must consider the wisdom of an index decision (diagnostically) but its concordance with a holistic understanding of the persons psychology, worldview, culture, and ultimately the unique circumstances of their case and all the other relevant factors in the factual matrix. For example, the Court of Protection has occasionally decided on the basis of a lack of wisdom evident in the decision, particularly, but not necessarily exclusively, where there is a marked contrast between the unwise nature of the impugned decision and the person's former attitude to the conduct of his affairs at a time when his capacity was not in question. Whilst all practicable steps must be taken to help the person make the decision without success,[231] the nature of the help which must be provided will depend on the condition of the person, the available resources and the nature and urgency of the decision to be taken.[232] In some cases, a patient's lack of engagement or cooperation with the assessment may itself indicate that a patient is unable to understand the information relevant to a decision.[233]

Although the court has developed general tests for common 'types' of case involving similar facts, cases often defy such categorisation because they involve a form of capacity that is inextricably act-specific. To take one example, the court has recognised that

[228] Mental Capacity Act 2005, s 3(4); MCA Code of Practice para 4.16.
[229] Mental Capacity Act 2005, s 1(4): 'A person is not to be treated as unable to make a decision merely because he makes an unwise decision'.
[230] *D v R (the Deputy of S)* [2010] EWHC 2405 (COP) at para 40 per Henderson J.
[231] Mental Capacity Act 2005, s 1(3).
[232] R Jones, *Mental Capacity Act Manual*, 7th edn (Sweet & Maxwell, 2016) 1–014.
[233] *Re P* [2014] EWHC 119 (COP) at para 26 per Cobb J.

capacity to consent to sexual relations has to be assessed in relation to the particular kind of sexual activity in question; to take but one example, the risk of pregnancy is irrelevant in the case of same-sex sexual activity.[234] Deconstructing what information is relevant can present acute difficulty even in cases involving the most basic decisions. For instance, although diagnosis, treatment, prognosis and risks are the general areas of information relevant to a decision about medical treatment, Berg, Appelbaum and Grisso noted that they encountered quite significant difficulty in making the value judgments necessary to define which specific elements of a blood test it was essential for a patient to understand.[235]

E. The Nature of the Decision and the Threshold for Capacity

Even before the information relevant to the decision can be defined, the nature of the decision itself must undergo a process of characterisation. This is because the nature of the decision is highly fact-sensitive: 'In some circumstances, having understood and retained relevant information, an ability to use it will be what is critical; in others, it will be necessary to be able to weigh competing considerations.'[236] The Court of Protection has emphasised that the decision will itself determine whether capacity relates to an act, a person or a set of circumstances,[237] and whether the threshold for capacity is more or less difficult to pass.[238] This latter criterion has a normative aspect, because slight variations in the seriousness and complexity of a decision can have a significant impact on the determination of capacity.[239] More complex decisions require greater capacity; the degree or extent of understanding is relative to the particular transaction which it is to effect.[240] Moreover, in some cases, the degree or nature of the individual's impairment will mean that the decision will be characterised as more complex than it is for most people.[241] As to seriousness, it requires an assessment not only of the decision's magnitude, but also the nature of the risk, the effect which its occurrence would have upon the life of the person, the importance of the benefits sought to be achieved (for example by medical treatment), the alternatives available, and the risks involved in those alternatives.[242] In one case, gifting a house to one child before death was considered, by analogy, as significant as making a will.[243] The assessment of seriousness is 'fact-sensitive, and sensitive also to the characteristics' of the person.[244] But it is

[234] *A Local Authority v TZ* [2013] EWHC 2322 (COP) at paras 24 and 31 per Baker J.

[235] JW Berg, PS Appelbaum and T Grisso, 'Constructing Competence: Formulating Standards of Legal Competence to Make Medical Decisions' (1996) 48 *Rutgers Law Review* 345, 348–9.

[236] *IM v LM* [2014] EWCA Civ 37.

[237] *cf PC and Anor v City of York Council* [2013] EWHC (Civ) 478 at paras 16–18 per McFarlane LJ.

[238] *cf Re T* [1992] 4 All ER 649 at 661 per Lord Donaldson MR; *Re MB* [1997] 2 FLR 426 at 436 per Butler Sloss LJ.

[239] *cf Re T* [1992] 4 All E.R. 649 at 661 per Lord Donaldson MR.

[240] *Beaney (deceased) Re* [1978] 2 All E.R. 595, in the context of capacity to execute an instrument.

[241] *Local Authority X v MM and KM* [2007] EWHC 2003 (Fam) at per Munby J.

[242] *Montgomery v Lanarkshire Health Board* [2015] UKSC 11 at para 89, in the context of medical treatment.

[243] *Re Beaney* [1978] 1 WLR 770; [1978] 2 All ER 595.

[244] *Montgomery v Lanarkshire Health Board* [2015] UKSC 11 at para 89 per Lord Kerr and Lord Reed (Lords Neuberger, Clarke, Wilson and Hodge agreeing).

an irreducibly normative task. For example, the courts have tended to characterise the decision to marry as having a relatively low threshold for capacity, because marriage may enrich the lives of people even though they are of limited or borderline capacity.[245] These fine (and often normative) distinctions are evidence that mental capacity is by its nature 'in the eye of the beholder', regardless of the test that is set out in the legislation[246] or major developments in medical understanding and diagnosis. The identity of the beholder is therefore highly relevant as a matter of individual impact and public policy.

F. The Manner of Deciding

The court must, in some sense, adjudicate the acceptability or otherwise of the reasoning behind a purported decision. Today, the functional test is most often decided on P's ability to 'use and weigh' information.[247] 'Use and weigh' cases tend to involve third parties questioning P's risky or potentially self-harming conduct, such as the refusal of blood transfusions by a Jehovah's Witness, the refusal of intravenous feeding by a person diagnosed with anorexia nervosa,[248] or objections to pregnancy-related medical interventions such as abortion, induction and caesarean sections.[249] These cases reflect social disagreement about the status that should be given to certain beliefs, reasons and values in the context of the purported decision.[250] This requires the court to reconcile compliance with the principles of the MCA, which include the presumption of capacity and the right to make unwise but capacious decisions,[251] with addressing public policy matters and the legitimate underlying concerns in the relevant case.

The court's reliance on the 'use and weigh' criterion to make controversial findings of incapacity may be precisely because 'use and weigh' represents a 'rather amorphous standard'.[252] The court is placed in the position of making a complex normative judgment regarding 'what decision processes could reasonably follow from the information provided, and whether a person's beliefs, values and emotions affect how this information is handled in reasonable or appropriate ways'.[253] The court ostensibly looks to the rationality of the purported decision, based on P's beliefs and values, and, if the decision rationally follows from the values and beliefs, whether the beliefs and values are themselves rational. But rationality is a polysemous notion with a wide range of connotations and no singular definition within any academic domain.[254] The outcome is often

[245] *A, B & C v X & Z* [2012] EWHC 2400 (COP) at para 30 per Hedley J, citing *Sheffield City Council v E & Anr* [2005] 2 WLR 953 at para 144.

[246] A Ruck Keene, 'Is mental capacity in the eye of the beholder? (2017) 11(2) *Advances in Mental Health and Intellectual Disabilities* 30–39.

[247] Kong, *Mental Capacity in Relationship: Decision-Making, Dialogue, and Autonomy* 21.

[248] See e.g. Cheshire & Wirral Partnership NHS Foundation Trust v Z [2016] EWCOP 56.

[249] See eg *St George's Healthcare NHS Trust v S* [1998] 3 All ER 673.

[250] Ruck Keene, Kane, Kim, and Owen, 'Taking capacity seriously? Ten years of mental capacity disputes before England's Court of Protection' 70; Kong, *Mental Capacity in Relationship: Decision-Making, Dialogue, and Autonomy* 113; Banner, 'Unreasonable reasons: normative judgements in the assessment of mental capacity' 1040.

[251] See Mental Capacity Act 2005, s 1.

[252] P Bartlett, *Blackstone's Guide to the Mental Capacity Act 2005*, 2nd edn (Oxford University Press, 2008) 51.

[253] Banner, 'Unreasonable reasons: normative judgements in the assessment of mental capacity' 1042.

[254] J Craigie, 'Competence, Practical Rationality and what a Patient Values' (2011) 25 *Bioethics* 6; *cf* J Raz, 'The Myth of Instrumental Rationality' (2005) 1 *Journal of Ethics & Social Responsibility* 1.

a function of the weight given to different outcomes by the individual adjudicator,[255] informed by the social context of the issue and the legislative framework. In this sense, it is the judge's own assessment of the complex and constantly changing social context that will determine 'what counts as good and valid inferential reasoning', and therefore whether the person has understood, retained, and appropriately used or weighed the information relevant to the decision.[256]

The case law evidences some differences in the standard required for procedural and substantive rationality which are ill-defined and inconsistent, apparently for purely public policy reasons.[257] For example, if irrational beliefs are part of an organised religion or other generally socially accepted irrational belief system, the court may not make a finding of incapacity.[258] It is instructive to compare the examples of Jehovah's Witnesses refusing blood transfusions based on a religious belief generally being respected as a legitimate influence,[259] and people with anorexia nervosa being characterised as unable to weigh information when they purport to refuse treatment which will result in their gaining weight.[260] To accommodate the latter type of case, the court has held that a person will not be able to use and weigh information if the process of making the decision is so dominated by a factor such as a compulsive disorder, phobia, confusion, shock, fatigue, pain or drugs that the decision is not a 'true' decision.[261] Judgments reflect social considerations and societal biases as much as they reflect matters of law and medicine.[262]

G. Judicial Discretion in Capacity Determinations

Because of its 'uncertain penumbra' and the almost limitless information relevant to any particular decision, the Court of Protection has emphasised that it adopts a 'pragmatic' approach to the application of section 3 of the MCA.[263] However, in the difficult and borderline cases which the Court of Protection is called upon to adjudicate, whether a person has capacity is 'complex and ultimately based on a judgment involving interpretation'.[264] The discharge of the burden of proof 'depends on the weight and value

[255] D'Amato and Anthony, 'Can/Should Computers Replace Judges?' 11 *Georgia Law Review* 1277–1301 (1977) 1297.

[256] Kong, *Mental Capacity in Relationship: Decision-Making, Dialogue, and Autonomy* 113.

[257] J Craigie and L Bortolotti, 'Rationality, Diagnosis, and Patient Autonomy in Psychiatry' in JZ Sadler, KWM Fulford and CW van Staden (eds), *The Oxford Handbook of Psychiatric Ethics, Volume 1* (Oxford University Press, 2014).

[258] *cf Nottinghamshire Healthcare NHS Trust* [2014] EWHC 1317 (COP) at paras 34 and 35 per Mostyn J.

[259] cf MCA Code of Practice, para 3.10.

[260] *cf A NHS Foundation Trust v Ms X* [2014] EWCOP 35.

[261] *Re MB (Medical Treatment)* [1997] 2 FLR 426 at 431; *Re Trust A v H (An Adult Patient)* [2006] EWHC 1230 (Fam) at para 22 per Potter P; *Re T (Adult: Refusal of Treatment)* [1992] 4 Ell ER 649.

[262] L Roth, A Meisel and CW Lidz, 'Tests of Competency to Consent to Treatment' (1977) 134 *American Journal of Psychiatry* 3, 283.

[263] *RB v Brighton & Hove City Council* [2014] EWCA Civ 561 at para 42 per Jackson LJ.

[264] C Lennard, 'Fluctuating capacity and impulsiveness in acquired brain injury: the dilemma of decisions under the Mental Capacity Act' (2016) 18 *Emerald* 229–39, 231 citing NF Banner and G Szmukler, '"Radical interpretation" and the assessment of decision-making capacity' (2013) 30 *Journal of Applied Philosophy* 4, 379–94.

which the judge attaches to the various strands of evidence' as a result of assessing the credibility or reliability of the evidence.[265] The fact that adjudication of capacity cannot be purely technical[266] or reduced to a set of static criteria or procedural principles[267] leaves a significant zone of judicial discretion and appreciation.

Unsurprisingly, a 'defining feature' of medical jurisprudence is its evolution through judge-made law. Landmark cases are often light on legal authority, draw explicitly from non-legal norms, and explicitly adjust the dominant rules, standards, and principles over time.[268] This can sometimes give the impression that the jurisprudence lacks legal rigour or consistency. However, as Jackson LJ stated in RB, the MCA asks judges to apply its provisions to 'the unforeseen vicissitudes of human life' and decisions are not models to be followed, but merely 'examples, which may or may not illumine any new problem which arises'.[269] It is also worth remembering that only contested and complex cases tend to come before the court; accordingly, they 'tend to be acutely difficult, not admitting of any obviously right answer'.[270] As Banner[271] notes, there is simply no comprehensive evaluative standard by which the assessor can differentiate capacity-undermining pathological influences from legitimate but unusual influences such as religious doctrine or the value one places on one's own life. Definitively isolating a 'principled and soundly applicable theory' of mental incapacity that both accommodates plural views and non-arbitrarily ensures the genuinely incapacitated are appropriately protected[272] is impossible.

H. The Need for Reflexivity in Claims Concerning Values, Ethics and Policy

As a socially constructed concept, capacity is concerned with a primarily ethical domain.[273] The inescapable presence of orienting value frameworks in capacity assessment, and consequent need to exercise discretion, requires courts to demonstrate 'articulatory-disclosive rationality' by expressing the conceptions of goodness which bear on their decision.[274] This kind of reasoning requires the assessor to explain, clarify and elaborate the surrounding implicit moral landscape and the qualitative values

[265] A Ruck Keene (ed), *Assessment of Mental Capacity: A Practical Guide for Doctors and Lawyers*, 4th edn (British Medical Association and Law Society, 2016) para 4.2.8.

[266] Case, 'Negotiating the domain of mental capacity' 177.

[267] Lennard, 'Fluctuating capacity and impulsiveness in acquired brain injury: the dilemma of decisions under the Mental Capacity Act', 231, citing NF Banner and G Szmukler, 'Radical interpretation' and the assessment of decision-making capacity' 379–94.

[268] Coggon, 'Mental capacity law, autonomy, and best interests: An argument for conceptual and practical clarity in the Court of Protection' 408.

[269] *RB v Brighton & Hove City Council* [2014] EWCA Civ 561 at para 48 per Jackson LJ.

[270] ibid at para 40 per Jackson LJ.

[271] N Banner, 'Unreasonable Reasons: Normative Judgements in the Assessment of Mental Capacity' (2012) 18 *Journal of Evaluation in Clinical Practice* 5, 1038–44.

[272] *cf* Coggon and Miola, 'Autonomy, Liberty, and Medical Decision-Making' 528.

[273] Case, 'Negotiating the domain of mental capacity' 177.

[274] Kong, *Mental Capacity in Relationship: Decision-Making, Dialogue, and Autonomy* 135.

reflected there.[275] To maintain legitimacy as reasoned applications of the law, capacity determinations must be 'explicitly reflective and aware of the underlying concepts and values at stake, so that proper democratic debate can be had about how capacity assessments are undertaken'.[276] Anyone assessing capacity – including courts – must thus be both aware of the values of the person under assessment and also reflexively self-aware of their own values.[277]

Capacity assessments also require an awareness of and ability to articulate and evaluate broader questions of public policy. In *CC v KK*,[278] Baker J found that it is 'not necessary for a person to demonstrate a capacity to understand and weigh up every detail of the respective options, but merely the salient ones'. Relevantly, what is 'salient' sometimes requires judges to draw a line between capacity and incapacity on the basis of public policy effects. For example, in cases involving the issue of whether the person has capacity to consent to sexual relations, it has been observed by the court that, 'if only for public policy reasons' the reasonably foreseeable consequences of contraception decisions do not extend to considerations of the realities of parenthood, because that would set the bar for reasonable foreseeability among the general population too high, and risk social engineering in capacity cases.[279] Public policy may also be relevant to the way the court frames the decision, as discussed above with regard to marriage. Such considerations require a reflexive understanding of both the society to whom capacity law generally applies, and the potential impact of a particular capacity assessment on that society.

A significant tension in the law of mental incapacity is the extent to which expert evidence should be relied upon. In deciding capacity under the MCA, courts do not necessarily accept that psychiatric evidence is determinative of the legal question of whether the individual in question has the relevant decision-making capacity.[280] On the one hand, the evidence of psychiatrists is likely to be determinative of the issue of whether there is an impairment of the mind for the purposes of section 2(1) of the MCA, and 'medical – in particular psychiatric – expertise is routinely called upon both within and outside the court setting to determine complex questions of capacity'.[281] However, the court has often emphasised that the decision as to capacity is not ultimately a 'medical' question, but a judgment for the court to make.[282] This position recognises that capacity is not a purely medical construct but rather a socio-legal-medical issue involving different perspectives, of which the judge is the ultimate arbiter.[283]

[275] Kong, *Mental Capacity in Relationship: Decision-Making, Dialogue, and Autonomy* 135.
[276] ibid, 230.
[277] Ruck Keene, Kane, Kim, and Owen, 'Taking capacity seriously? Ten years of mental capacity disputes before England's Court of Protection' 70; A Ruck Keene, 'Is mental capacity in the eye of the beholder?'.
[278] [2012] EWHC 2136 (COP) per Baker J.
[279] *A Local Authority v Mrs A* [2010] EWHC 1549 COP at para 63.
[280] Ruck Keene, Kane, Kim, and Owen, 'Taking capacity seriously? Ten years of mental capacity disputes before England's Court of Protection' 70.
[281] Ruck Keene, Kane, Kim, and Owen, 'Taking capacity seriously? Ten years of mental capacity disputes before England's Court of Protection' 59.
[282] *King's College Hospital HS Foundation Trust v C and V* [2015] EWCOP 80; [2016] COPLR 50, 39 per.
[283] A Ruck Keene, 'Hard Capacity Cases: an English Perspective and a Plea for Help' (2017), mhj.org.uk/2017/09/13/hard-capacity-cases-an-english-perspective-and-a-plea-for-help.

As the Court of Protection has observed about the 'use or weigh' criterion, 'only the court has the full picture. Experts are neither able nor expected to form an overview'.[284] In some cases, judges may override expert medical opinion, even where the person in question has a diagnosed mental disorder.[285] In particular, pathological narratives will be rejected if they conflict with the legal norms underpinning capacity assessment, such as where the experts have a flawed understanding of the burden or onus of proof.[286] In other cases, the judge's own assessment of the facts will differ from expert evidence.[287] For example, in *WBC v Z*[288] Cobb J found that the expert evidence contesting a young woman's ability to make her own welfare decisions was outweighed by the significance of Z's testimony and the judge's own interpretation and assessment of her behaviour.

Even if medical and non-clinical experts correctly apply the law of capacity, expert evidence is itself not immune to subjectivity. First, purely technical evidence such as brain scans cannot objectively establish whether someone has capacity (although such information can inform a diagnosis).[289] A clinician's assessment of capacity is therefore as much an interpretation of the mental state and condition of a person as judicial determinations are.[290] This is demonstrated by the significant number of cases in which expert evidence is in conflict. For example, the experts disagreed with one another in 43 per cent of reported Court of Protection cases between 2007 and 2017.[291] Secondly, treating professionals tend to be more concerned with diagnosis and prognosis than the severity and implications of the disability,[292] and can be affected by the so-called protection imperative and their close professional relationships within care teams.[293] The majority of expert evidence in capacity cases comes from psychiatrists,[294] and sometimes even a

[284] *A Local Authority v A* [2010] EWCOP 1549 at para 66 per Munby J. See also *ST v CC* [2012] EWCOP 2136 and *London Borough of Islington v QR* [2014] EWCOP 26.

[285] Ruck Keene, Kane, Kim, and Owen, 'Taking capacity seriously? Ten years of mental capacity disputes before England's Court of Protection' 69.

[286] Case, 'Negotiating the domain of mental capacity' 191.

[287] This appears statistically more likely where the judge hears from the person alleged to not have capacity. *cf* Ruck Keene, Kane, Kim, and Owen, 'Taking capacity seriously? Ten years of mental capacity disputes before England's Court of Protection' 65.

[288] [2016] EWCOP 4.

[289] With the exception of those in vegetative states, in which capacity will not generally be challenged. See Lennard, 'Fluctuating capacity and impulsiveness in acquired brain injury: the dilemma of decisions under the Mental Capacity Act' 234, citing R Mackenzie and J Watts, 'Can clinicians and carers make valid decisions about others' decision-making capacities unless tests of decision-making competence and capacity include emotionality and neurodiversity?' (2011) 16 *Tizard Learning Disability Review* 3, 43–51.

[290] GS Owen, F Freyenhagen, M Hotopf and W Martin, 'Temporal inabilities and decision-making capacity in depression' (2015) 14 *Phenomenology and the Cognitive Sciences* 1, 163–82 cited in Lennard, 'Fluctuating capacity and impulsiveness in acquired brain injury: the dilemma of decisions under the Mental Capacity Act' 234.

[291] Ruck Keene, Kane, Kim, and Owen, 'Taking capacity seriously? Ten years of mental capacity disputes before England's Court of Protection' 65; GS Owen, F Freyenhagen, M Hotopf and W Martin, 'Temporal inabilities and decision-making capacity in depression' (2015) 14 *Phenomenology and the Cognitive Sciences* 1, 163–82.

[292] Case, 'Negotiating the domain of mental capacity' 198.

[293] *PH v A Local Authority* [2011] EWHC 1704 (COP) at para 16 per Baker J.

[294] P Case, 'Dangerous Liaisons? Psychiatry and Law in the Court of Protection – Expert Discourses of "Insight" (and "Compliance")' (2016) 24 *Medical Law Review* 3, 360–78 cited in Ruck Keene, Kane, Kim, and Owen, 'Taking capacity seriously?' 62.

single psychiatrist, leading to a further epistemic narrowing of the evidentiary basis of decisions. As the tendency of medical opinion to be portrayed as objective fact tends to elide these subjectivities,[295] the principled, often de-pathologising[296] scrutiny offered by legal adjudication is essential.[297]

V. Computational Logic and the Essential Humanity of Capacity Assessments

A determination of incapacity is one of the most consequential legal decisions a judge can make. It is a determination that a person does not meet the conditions to exercise all the powers and liberties humans enjoy by virtue of their legal personhood. Incapacity is determined on the basis that an individual cannot, and indeed should not, decide according to reasoning processes which the adjudicator – representing society at large – deems acceptable. This kind of determination necessarily involves defining not just the nature of the human condition, but its boundaries, including the 'correct' exercise of intelligence, reason, and individual autonomy. The notion of legal personhood is therefore intrinsically, but not uncontroversially, linked to both embodying and employing 'reasonable and rational behaviour'. The very meaning of mental incapacity, let alone its application to individuals, remains highly contested. In the exercise of their inherent and statutory jurisdictions to assess mental capacity, courts are called on to apply a fundamentally imprecise concept to subjective evidence while resolving conflicts between individual autonomy, social norms, ethics and public policy. This is not a task assigned to junior judges, and at the highest level the Court of Protection was statutorily created specifically out of recognition of the complexity, sensitivity, and intersystemic nature of 'mental health law' and 'capacity' in particular.

A point should here be made about adjudication not only as an outcome, but a process which has its own effects on those involved. Just as the concept of capacity is socially mediated, the process of having one's capacity determined is also experienced as a social occurrence, because it alters one's legal rights in society. There is evidence that, in addition to resolving legal rights and duties, well-conducted assessments can be considered therapeutic interventions because they can improve mental capacity.[298] Further, the combination of judicial and medical authority, properly applied,[299] can provide much needed 'closure' for families and care teams while encouraging public confidence in case outcomes.[300] A socially reflexive, individualised and empathetic reasoning process, whereby there is an understanding of what the loss of capacity would mean for the unique individual and for society, may well make all the difference in the world.

[295] Case, 'Negotiating the domain of mental capacity' 204.
[296] ibid, 186–87.
[297] ibid, 204.
[298] M Hotopf, 'The assessment of mental capacity', in T Holland, MJ Gunn and R Jacob, *Mental Capacity Legislation: Principles and Practice* (RCPsych Publications, 2013) 30.
[299] ibid.
[300] Case, 'Negotiating the domain of mental capacity' 204.

The 'success' of a capacity determination should not be judged according to claims of 'accuracy', but in its ability to reflexively observe its own meaning both for the individual and for the society whose behaviours and rationality will in turn be bounded by them. But adjudicative 'success' also includes maintaining the social legitimacy of the mental incapacity paradigm, and the integrity of both law and medicine as normative institutions. It may require adjudicators to justify conflicting evaluative standards within and between cases. The meaning of mental incapacity is continuously re-constructed in the process of being applied to individual cases, alongside, and influenced by, legislative, social and medical interpretations of mental illness and incapacity.

VI. Conclusion: The Map is not Territory

The Polish-American scholar of semantics, Alfred Korzbyski, is best remembered for his idea that 'the map is not territory'.[301] By this he meant that human knowledge of the world is invariably limited by the nervous system and the natural languages humans have developed to explain it. As a consequence, Korzybski reasoned, no person can directly access reality, as it must ultimately be parsed and recombined by the human brain as a response to that reality.[302] We simply do not know what reality is, nor what gives rise to phenomenological consciousness.

Whilst our senses, beliefs, and experiences may help us 'map' the world in which we exist, no map, regardless of its cartographic precision, could ever truly represent the reality of the territory it claims to illuminate. When we do not know the territory well, or if it changes with regularity or in unpredictable ways, a map is little more than a heuristic, perhaps enabling us to chart a tentative course. However, without factoring in how changing conditions affect the journey, or the likelihood of reaching the destination, blind adherence to a map can lead to unforeseen and perilous destinations. Maps are thus ultimately only as good as their cartographers, and are only improved by re-drawing them on the basis of new explorations which allow us to revise our understanding of the territory and how to navigate it.

In diagnosing and treating individuals, doctors, clinicians and psychiatrists must rely on their tacit and innate knowledge as well as their socially conditioned expertise to locate the individual on a map of mental order and disorder. Whereas clinical guidelines and codes of best practice may well serve as a guide for how to interpret that map, the individual presentation of mental disorder, and the extent to which a person's behaviour aligns or diverges from normative expectations, means that this map is continuously drawn and re-drawn on the basis of scientific projections, public policy interests, and prevailing conceptions of normativity.[303] It is always tentative, contested

[301] A Korzybski, 'Science and Sanity: An Introduction to Non-Aristotelian Semantics (Library Publishing Company 1933).
[302] *cf* MSA Graziano, *Rethinking Consciousness: A Scientific Theory of Subjective Experience* (WW Norton & Co 2019); D Hoffman, *The Case Against Reality: Why Evolution Hid the Truth from Our Eyes* (WW Norton & Co 2019).
[303] M Foucault, *History of Madness.*

and incomplete. Accordingly, any map claiming to correspond to the human condition must be understood as an exercise in institutional cryptocartography.

In determining whether an individual has mental capacity, the task of courts is to draw a different map over the same territory. As this map partially overlaps with medical maps via the diagnostic test, the judicial process provides an opportunity to compare, discuss, and critically engage with the navigatory efforts of medical professionals, with judges applying their own expertise and tacit experiential knowledge. This increases the likelihood that an error in medical navigation (or, crucially, the map itself) will be corrected. The court's map has an additional functional aspect which, even if the navigations of medical professionals are accepted completely, may lead to a different destination. A similar dialogue occurs between the juridical map of mental capacity and the various 'social' maps of those affected by the court's decision. Dialogue does not mean that the juridical map is thereby perfected; it simply means that juridical, social and medical knowledge forms are able to recursively and critically inform and influence one another in an unceasing evolutionary process.

The juridical map is drawn and redrawn according to its *own* logic, as much as any other. Although the doctrine of precedent requires like cases to be decided alike, whether a person has the mental capacity to make a decision ultimately depends on a constellation of individual, social, and contextual factors, as well as the specific facts of their case. Synthesising these factors requires subjective judgement which cannot be based solely on the precedents set by previous cases or purely biological markers. The connotation of mental capacity is, therefore, uniquely protean as both a legal and medical construct, and resistant to the mathematical formalism required by existing AI and data science techniques. Parsing the chaotic and unstructured world involved in each case requires not only the deductive, probabilistic reasoning which machines excel at, but inductive reasoning which they struggle with.[304] Weizenbaum drew this distinction between the language and culture of computers and people nearly 45 years ago concurrent to the development of the Logical AI approach. The current AI paradigm (connectionism) has framed all of the foundational questions Weizenbaum posed through the lens of 'AI Ethics' – but rarely puts the question of what computers ought to do at the forefront of considerations. Rather, 'ethics' frames the use of AI in courts, hospitals, etcetera, as inevitable once various 'technical considerations' are solved. If capacity, like mental impairment, is socially contructed; how should 'historical data' about 'capacity' be defined, let alone algorithmically formalised? Both medicine and law are epistemic communities that have a culture and language of their own. These are rarely interoperable. Moreover, how would we formalise the domain expertise of doctors and judges regarding mental impairment and incapacity, and use that to inform anything approximating a coherent 'knowledge base' of factors that could identify 'capacity'?

The central problem with the validity or 'accuracy' of inductive inference is: are we are justified in accepting a hypothesis on the basis of observations that frequently

[304] F Bergadano, 'Machine Learning and the foundations of inductive inference' (1993) 3 *Minds and Machines* 51; P Spelda, 'Machine learning, inductive reasoning, and reliability of generalisations' (2018) 35 *AI & Society* 29.

confirm it? In the context of mental capacity, this problem is amplified just as it was in the development of medical ES. There is not just one rule to be tested, but a range of conditional and contingent rules that need to be continuously revised and expanded. While diagnostic evidence may in some cases confirm these rules, how do we restrict the space of inductive hypotheses so that it possible to select appropriate rules that will map onto future examples?

> The subject is not only inexhaustible, but also indeterminate, because it mutates as soon as it is conceived. Situations from past history that have produced their event and no longer exist can be considered completed. One's personal situation has the stimulating feature that its thought still determines what will become of it.[305]

The hypothetical assessment of mental capacity using ML/DL techniques and Bayesian inference runs the risk of generalising a definition of 'capacity' and ossifying a medical standard of capacity using statistical inference and pattern matching techniques to define 'normative' or neurotypical functioning. The claim that a machine could judge mental (dis)order and (in)capacity is, therefore, a claim that the legal singularity is possible: that a machine or algorithm can offer insight into the conditions under which an individual ought to be denied the exercise of certain freedoms considered fundamental to humanity. Those freedoms are conferred on the individual precisely because the person's community recognises, through law, that they are a person, that adult people generally have the ability to make certain decisions for themselves about their life and physical liberty, and that they should therefore generally be free to make such decisions for themselves. What these freedoms are, and the reasoning ability needed to exercise them, are continually socially determined and redetermined and, as Weizenbaum observed, differ between cultures. While there might be some benefits to machine assessment of incapacity applications in the aggregate – in speed of assessment, and a quantifiable probability of any one assessment being 'accurate' – machine assessment of incapacity would involve delegating a machine the ontological superiority to define human reason itself. As McQuillan warns, treating humans as 'knowable' through data which can be scraped from their existence is a philosophically and ethically flawed approach, with ultimately unpredictable effects:

> Data science does not only make possible a new way of knowing but acts directly on it; by converting predictions to pre-emptions, it becomes a machinic metaphysics. The people enrolled in this apparatus risk an abstraction of accountability and the production of 'thoughtlessness.[306]

Every mental capacity assessment represents an incremental answer to the question 'who should be able to exercise their rights as a full legal person?'. If we are to retain control over how we define and respond to human suffering and disorder, the answer should always and everywhere be given by us, not a machine. Just as it is argued that a

[305] K Jasper cited in K Lichtblau, 'Sociology and the Diagnosis of the Times or: The Reflexivity of Modernity' (1995) 12 *Theory, Culture & Society* 1, 25.
[306] D McQuillan, 'Data Science as Machinic Neoplatonism' (2018) 31 *Philosophy and Technology* 253.

'kill decision' should be made by a 'human in the loop' in the context of lethal autonomous weapons,[307] the essential humanity and consequence of capacity decisions on not just the individual, but their community, demands that capacity be not only defined, but assessed and imputed by members of that community. Anything else would result in a machine being elevated to the role of arbiter of human behaviour and experience within a social reality it cannot access.

[307] A Sharkey, 'Autonomous weapons systems, killer robots and human dignity' (2019) 21 *Ethics and Information Technology* 75; *cf* A Del Re, 'Lethal Autonomous Weapons: Take the Human Out of the Loop' (2017) Naval War College, apps.dtic.mil/dtic/tr/fulltext/u2/1041804.pdf.

GLOSSARY AND FURTHER READING

Abductive Reasoning

Abductive reasoning, also termed abduction and abductive inference, is a method of logical enquiry which starts with an observation, or series of observations, and attempts to identify the simplest and most probable conclusion from them.

Further Reading

Aliseda A, *Abductive Reasoning: Logical Investigations into Discovery and Explanation* (Springer, 2006).

Andreewsky E and D Bourcier, 'Abduction in language interpretation and law making' (2000) 29 *Kybernetes* 7/8.

Lipton P, *Inference to the Best Explanation*, 2nd edn (Routledge, 2004).

Lombrozo T, 'Explanation and Abductive Inference' in K Holyoak and R Morrison (eds), *Oxford Handbook of Thinking and Reasoning* (Oxford University Press, 2012).

Walton D, *Abductive Reasoning* (University of Alabama Press, 2014).

Affective Computing

Affective computing is the interdisciplinary study and development of computational systems that can identify, measure, interpret, and simulate aspects of human affective behaviour.

Further Reading

Calvo RA, S D'Mello, J Gratch and A Kappas (eds), *The Oxford Handbook of Affective Computing* (Oxford University Press, 2015).

Cambria E, 'Affective Computing and Sentiment Analysis' (2016) 31 *IEEE Intelligent Systems* 2.

Gōjçay D and G Yildirim, *Affective Computing and Interaction: Psychological, Cognitive and Neuroscientific Perspectives* (IGI Global, 2010).

Picard RW, *Affective Computing* (MIT Press 1997).

Scherer KR, T Bänziger and E Roesch, *A Blueprint for Affective Computing: A Sourcebook* (Oxford University Press, 2010).

Algorithms

An algorithm is a finite sequence of defined instructions used to solve a class of problems or perform a computation.

Further Reading

Christian B, *Algorithms to Live By: The Computer Science of Human Decisions* (William Collins, 2016).
Cormen TH, *Algorithms Unlocked* (MIT Press, 2013).
Lourdias P, *Algorithms* (MIT Press, 2020).
Kleinberg J and E Tardos, *Algorithm Design* (Pearson, 2013).
Talia D, *Big Data And The Computable Society: Algorithms And People In The Digital World* (World Scientific Publishing, 2019).

Algorithmic Decision Making (ADM)

Algorithmic Decision Making entails the use of algorithms to analyse, classify, sort, and interpret data to infer correlations, or more generally, to identify information useful to a decision.

Further Reading

Cobbe J and J Singh, 'Regulating Recommending: Motivations, Considerations, and Principles' (2020) *European Journal of Law and Technology*.
Eubanks V, *Automating Inequality: How High-Tech Tools Profile, Police, and Punish the Poor* (St Martin's, 2018).
Pasquale F, *The Black Box Society: The Secret Algorithms that Control Money and Information* (Harvard University Press, 2015).
Weizenbaum J, *Computer Power and Human Reason: From Judgement to Calculation* (WH Freeman & Co., 1976).
Yeung K and M Lodge (eds), *Algorithmic Regulation* (Oxford University Press, 2019).

Artificial Intelligence (AI) or Machine Intelligence

Artificial Intelligence is an umbrella term spanning numerous disciplines, oriented by the goal of developing computers to emulate aspects of biological intelligence, such as visual perception, speech recognition, decision-making or language translation.

Further Reading

Boden M, *Artificial Intelligence: A Very Short Introduction* (Oxford University Press, 2018).
Frankish K and WM Ramsey (eds), *The Cambridge Handbook of Artificial Intelligence* (Cambridge University Press, 2014).
Hayles NK, *How We Became Posthuman: Virtual bodies in Cybernetics, Literature, and Informatics* (University of Chicago Press, 1999).
Mitchell M, *Artificial Intelligence: A Guide for Thinking Humans* (Pelican, 2019).
Russell S and P Norvig, *Artificial Intelligence: A Modern Approach*, 3rd edn (Pearson, 2016).

Artificial Intelligence Safety

Artificial Intelligence Safety is an interdisciplinary research field examining the ethics, design, and implementation of computational systems, and strategies for mitigating their potentially harmful effects and negative externalities.

Further Reading

Amodei D, C Olah, J Steinhardt, P Christiano, J Schulman and D Mané, 'Concrete Problems in AI Safety' (2016) https://arxiv.org/abs/1606.06565.
Challen R, J Denny, M Pitt, L Gompels, T Edwards and K Tsaneva-Atanasova, 'Artificial intelligence, bias and clinical safety' (2018) 28 *BMJ Quality & Safety* 3.
Zerilli J, A Knott, J Maclaurin and C Gavaghan, 'Algorithmic Decision-Making and the Control Problem' (2019) 29 *Minds and Machines* 555.
Macrae C, 'Governing the safety of artificial intelligence in healthcare' (2019) 28 *BMJ Quality & Safety* 6.
Yampolskiy RV (ed), *Artificial Intelligence Safety and Security* (CRC Press, 2018).

Artificial General Intelligence (AGI)

Artificial General Intelligence (AGI) refers to a hypothetical computational system that has the capacity to understand, learn, and adapt to perform any intellectual task of a human being.

Further Reading

Bostrom N, *Superintelligence: Paths, Dangers, Strategies* (Oxford University Press, 2014).
Kurzweil R, *The Age of Spiritual Machines: When Computers Exceed Human Intelligence* (Viking Press, 1998).
Lovelock J, *Novacene: The Coming Age of Hyperintelligence* (Allen Lane, 2019).
Goertzel B and C Pennachin (eds), *Artificial General Intelligence* (Springer, 2007).
Russell S, *Human Compatible: Artificial Intelligence and the Problem of Control* (Penguin, 2019).

Autopoiesis

Originally derived from systems theory in evolutionary biology, autopoiesis in sociology refers to the idea that society is comprised of self-organising sub-systems that co-evolve alongside each other and thereby create the conditions for their continued existence.

Further Reading

Baxter HW, 'Niklas Luhmann's Theory of Autopoietic Legal Systems' (2013) 9 *Annual Review of Law and Social Science* 175.

Geyer F and J van der Zouwen, *Sociocybernetics: Complexity, Autopoiesis and Observation of Social Systems* (Greenwood Press, 2001).

Luhmann N, *Theory of Social Systems: Volumes I and II* (Stanford University Press, 2012/2013).

Maturana HR and FJ Varela, *Autopoiesis and Cognition: The Realization of the Living* (D Reidel, 1972).

Teubner G, *Law as an Autopoietic System* (Blackwell, 1993).

Bias + Explainability

In the context of AI research, bias refers to the ways in which an algorithm can be influenced – intentionally or unintentionally – by flaws in the selection, curation, and manipulation of statistical information, and explainability refers to the extent to which the outputs out of a statistical model can be explained.

Further Reading

Ananny M and K Crawford, 'Seeing without knowing: Limitations of the transparency ideal and its application to algorithmic accountability' (2016) 20 *New Media & Society* 3.

Belkin M, D Jsu, S Ma and S Mandal, 'Reconciling modern machine-learning practice and the classical bias–variance trade-off' (2019) 115 *Proceedings of the National Academy of Sciences of the United States of America* 32.

Burrell J, 'How the machine "thinks": Understanding opacity in machine learning algorithms' (2016) 3 *Big Data & Society* 1.

Castelvecchi D, 'Can we open the black box of AI?' (2016) *Nature* www.nature.com/news/can-we-open-the-black-box-of-ai-1.20731.

du Boulay B, T O'Shea and J Monk, 'The black box inside the glass box: presenting computing concepts to novices' (1981) 14 *International Journal of Man-Machine Studies* 3.

Hildebrandt M and K O'Hara (eds) *Life and the Law in the Era of Data-Driven Agency* (Edward Elgar, 2020).

Big Data

Big data generally involves the use of parallel computing tools to capture, curate, and process large, and often multiple, data sets at scale.

Further Reading

Barocas S and AD Selbst, 'Big Data's Disparate Impact' (2016) 104 *California Law Review* 671.
Kalyvas KR and MR Overly, *Big Data: A Business and Legal Guide* (CRC Press, 2015).
O'Neil C, *Weapons of Math Destruction: How Big Data Increases Inequality and Threatens Democracy* (Penguin, 2017).
Seely Brown K and P Duguid, *The Social Life of Information*, rev edn (Harvard Business Review Press, 2017).
van Dijck J, 'Datafication, Dataism and Dataveillance: Big Data Between Scientific Paradigm and Ideology' (2014) 12 *Surveillance & Society* 2.

Brain-Computer Interface (BCI)

A brain-computer interface is a computational device and biological interface enabling users to interact with computers through brain-activity.

Further Reading

Bandettini PA, fMRI (MIT Press, 2020).
D'Mello SK, 'Automated Mental State Detection for Mental Health Care' in DD Luxton (ed), *Artificial Intelligence in Behavioral and Mental Health Care* (Academic Press, 2016).
Guger C, B Allison and J Ushiba, *Brain-Computer Interface Research: A State-of-the-Art Summary 5* (Springer, 2017).
Haushalter JL, 'Neuronal Testimonial: Brain-Computer Interfaces and the Law' (2018) 71 *Vanderbilt Law Review* 1365.
Shih JJ, DJ Krusienski and JR Wolpaw, 'Brain-Computer Interfaces in Medicine' (2012) 87 *Mayo Clinic Proceedings* 3.

Characteristica Universalis

The Characteristica Universalis, or Mathesis Universalis, is a recurring idea in the work of German polymath Wilhelm Gottfried Leibniz involving the development of a universal symbolic language capable of expressing all mathematical, scientific, legal, and metaphysical concepts.

Further Reading

Centrone S, S Negri, D Sarikaya and PM Schuster (eds), *Mathesis Universalis, Computability and Proof* (Springer, 2019).
Davis M, The Universal Computer: *The Road from Leibniz to Turing*, 3rd edn (CRC Press, 2019).
Mittelstrass J, 'The Philosopher's conception of Mathesis Universalis from Descartes to Leibniz' (1979) 36 *Annals of Science* 6.
Smith B, 'Characteristica Universalis' in K Mulligan (ed), *Language, Truth and Ontology* (Kluwer, 1992).
Strogantz S, *Infinite Powers: The Story of Calculus – The Language of the Universe* (Atlantic Books, 2019).

Clinical Decision Support Systems (CDSS)

A clinical decision support system (CDSS) is a computational system designed to provide physicians and other health professionals with contextual information relevant to clinical decision-making tasks.

Further Reading

Berner ES (ed), *Clinical Decision Support Systems: Theory and Practice*, 3rd edn (Springer, 2018).
Bright TJ, A Wong and R Dhujati et al., 'Effect of Clinical Decision-Support Systems: A Systematic Review' (2012) 157 *Annals of Internal Medicine* 1.
Shortliffe EH and MJ Sepúlveda, 'Clinical Decision Support in the Era of Artificial Intelligence' (2018) 320 *Journal of the American Medical Association* 21.
Sutton RT, D Pincock, DC Baumgart, DC Sadowski, RN Fedorak and KI Kroeker, 'An overview of clinical decision support systems: benefits, risks, and strategies for success' (2020) 3 npj *Digital Medicine* 17.
Wasylewicz ATM and MJW Scheepers-Hoeks, 'Clinical Decision Support Systems' in P Kubbem, M Dumontier and A Dekker (eds), *Fundamentals of Clinical Data Science* (Springer, 2019).

Cognitive Computing

Cognitive computing is the interdisciplinary study and development of computerised models to simulate the human thought process – in part or in whole – in complex situations under high uncertainty.

Further Reading

Chen M, F Herrera and K Hwang, 'Cognitive Computing: Architecture, Technologies and Intelligent Applications' (2018) 6 *IEEE Access* 19774.
Gupta S, AK Kar, A Baabdullah and WAA Al-Khowaiter, 'Big data with cognitive computing: A review for the future' (2018) 42 *International Journal of Information Management* 78.

Hurwitz J, M Kaufman and A Bowles, *Cognitive Computing and Big Data Analytics* (Wiley, 2015).
Mallick PK, PK Patnaik, AR Panda and VE Balas, *Cognitive Computing in Human Cognition: Perspectives and Applications* (Springer, 2020).
Weiser M, R Gold, JS Brown, 'The Origins of Ubiquitous Computing Research at PARC in the Late 1980s' (1999) *IBM Systems Journal*.

Cognitive Science

Cognitive science is an interdisciplinary scientific field examining the mind and mental processes, and the nature, aspects and functions of biological cognition.

Further Reading

Boden MA, *Mind as Machine: A History of Cognitive Science, Volumes 1-2* (Oxford University Press, 2006).
Cobb M, *The Idea of the Brain: A History* (Profile Book, 2020).
Margolis E, R Samuels and SP Stich (eds), *The Oxford Handbook of Philosophy of Cognitive Science*, rev edn (Oxford University Press, 2017).
Plessner H, *Levels of Organic Life and the Human: An Introduction to Philosophical Anthropology*, M Hyatt (trans) (Fordham University Press, 2019).
Varela FJ, E Thompson and E Rosch, *The Embodied Mind: Cognitive Science and Human Experience*, 2nd edn (MIT Press, 2017).

Computational Complexity

Computational complexity is a subfield of theoretical computer science broadly oriented by the goal of classifying and comparing the practical difficulty of solving mathematical problems involving finite combinatorial objects.

Further Reading

Anora S and B Barak, *Computational Complexity: A Modern Approach* (Cambridge University Press, 2009).
Casti JL, *Complexification: Explaining a Paradoxical World Through the Science of Surprise* (Perennial, 1995).
Mandelbrot BB, *The Fractal Geometry of Nature* (Times Books, 1982).
Post DG and MB Eisen, 'How Long is the Coastline of Law? Thoughts on the Fractal Nature of Legal Systems' (2000) 29 *Journal of Legal Studies* 545.
Thurner S, R Hanel and P Klimek, *Introduction to the Theory of Complex Systems* (Oxford University Press, 2018).

Computation

Computation refers to any calculation involving both mathematical and non-mathematical steps according to a well-defined model (i.e. algorithm).

Further Reading

Copeland BJ, CJ Posy and O Shagrir (eds), *Computability: Turing, Gödel, Church, and Beyond* (MIT Press, 2013).
Dyson G, *Darwin Among the Machines* (Penguin, 2012).
MacCormick J, *What Can Be Computed? A Practical Guide to Theory of Computation* (Princeton University Press, 2018).
Moore C and S Mertens, *The Nature of Computation* (Oxford University Press, 2011).
Turing AM, *Collected Works of AM Turing: Volumes 1-4* (JL Britton, RO Gandy, DC Ince, PT Saunders and CEM Yates (eds), Elsevier 1992).

Computationalism

Computationalism is the mainstream view of cognitive science that intelligent behaviour is causally explained by computations, and that cognition is roughly equivalent to computation.

Further Reading

Google for Education, 'Exploring Computational Thinking' https://edu.google.com/resources/programs/exploring-computational-thinking/.
Miłkowski M, 'From Computer Metaphor to Computational Modeling: The Evolution of Computationalism' (2018) 28 *Minds and Machines* 515.
Piccinini G, 'Computationalism in the Philosophy of Mind' (2009) 4 *Philosophy Compass*.
Piccinini G, *Physical Computation: A Mechanistic Account* (Oxford University Press, 2015).
Scheuz M (ed), *Computationalism: New Directions* (MIT Press, 2002).

Computational Lingustics

Computational linguistics is an interdisciplinary field involving statistical techniques and rule-based modelling of natural language to form a computational perspective, and the study of appropriate computational methods for solving linguistic questions.

Further Reading

Chomsky N, *Syntactic Structures* (Moulton & Co., 1957).
Clark A (ed), *The Handbook of Computational Linguistics for Natural Language Programming* (Wiley, 2012).
Hausser R, *Foundations of Computational Linguistics: Human-Computer Communication in Natural Language*, 3rd edn (Springer, 2014).
Mitkov R (eds), *The Oxford Handbook of Computational Linguistics* (Oxford University Press, 2005).
Oettinger AG, 'Computational Linguistics' (1965) 72 *The American Mathematical Monthly* 2.

Computational Theory of Mind (CTM)

The Computational Theory of Mind (CTM) is a family of views that understand the human mind as an information processing system, and that consciousness and cognition are a form of biological computation.

Further Reading

Chiao JY, *Philosophy of Computational Cultural Neuroscience* (Routledge, 2020).
Denning PJ and M Tedre, *Computational Thinking* (MIT Press, 2019).
Horst S, 'Symbols and Computation A Critique of the Computational Theory of Mind' (1999) 9 *Minds and Machines* 347.
Pinker S, *How the Mind Works* (WW Norton & Co., 1997).
Putnam H, *Representation and Reality*, rev edn (Bradford Books, 1991).

Computer Programming

The process of developing instruction sets which specify how a computer should perform a particular task.

Further Reading

Abelson H, GJ Sussman and J Sussman, *Structure and Interpretation of Computer Programs*, 2nd edn (MIT Press, 1996) www.web.mit.edu/alexmv/6.037/sicp.pdf.
Friedman DP and M Wand, *Essentials of Programming Languages*, 3rd edn (MIT Press, 2008).
Knuth DE, *The Art of Computer Programming, Volumes 1-4a* (Addison Wesley, 2011).
Shiffman D, *The Nature of Code: Simulating Natural Systems with Processing* (Self-Published 2012) www.natureofcode.com/.
Warren Jr HS, *Hacker's Delight*, 2nd edn (Addison Wesley, 2012).

Consciousness

A state of awareness or reflexive sentience of internal and external existence and their differentiation.

Further Reading

Critchlow H, *Consciousness* (Ladybird, 2018).
Dennett DC, *From Bacteria to Bach and Back: The Evolution of Minds* (WW Norton & Co, 2017).
Graziano MSA, *Rethinking Consciousness: A Scientific Theory of Subjective Experience* (WW Norton & Co, 2019).
Kahnemann D, *Thinking, Fast and Slow* (Penguin, 2012).
Seager W, *Theories of Consciousness: An Introduction and Assessment*, 2nd edn (Routledge, 2016).

Connectionism

Connectionism is part subfield, part ideology, within cognitive science attempting to explain biological intelligence using artificial neural networks – simplified algorithmic models of the brain.

Further Reading

Bechtel W and A Abrahamsen, *Connectionism and the Mind: An Introduction to Parallel Processing in Networks* (Blackwell, 1990).
Gárdenfors P, *Conceptual Spaces: The Geometry of Thought* (MIT Press, 2004).
Hinton GE, 'How Neural Networks Learn from Experience' (1992) 267 *Scientific American* 3.
Marcus GF, *The Algebraic Mind: Integrating Connectionism and Cognitive Science* (MIT Press, 2003).
Pinker S and A Prince, 'On Language and Connectionism: Analysis of a Parallel Distributed Processing Model of Language Acquisition' (1988) 28 *Cognition* (1–2).

Convolutional Neural Network (CNN)

A Convolutional Neural Network (CNN) is a class of deep neural networks that use convolution – a mathematical operation whereby two figures produce a third function expressing how the shape of one is modified by the other – in place of general matrix multiplication in at least one layer of the neural network.

Further Reading

Aggarwal CC, *Neural Networks and Deep Learning: A Textbook* (Springer, 2018).
Buckner C, 'Empiricism without Magic: Transformational Abstraction in Deep Convolutional Neural Networks' 2018 195 *Synthese* 12.
Kalchbrenner N, E Grefenstette and P Blunson, 'A Convolutional Neural Network for Modelling Sentences' (2014) https://arxiv.org/abs/1404.2188.
Kim M-Y, Y Xu and R Goebel, 'Applying a Convolutional Neural Network to Legal Question Answering' in M Otake, S Kurahashi, Y Ota, K Satoh and D Bekki (eds), *New Frontiers in Artificial Intelligence* (Springer, 2017).
Krizhevsky A, I Sutskever and GE Hinton, 'Imagenet Classification with Deep Convolutional Neural Networks' (2012) 25 *Advances in Neural Information Processing Systems* 1097.

Cybernetics

The interdisciplinary study of systems capable of receiving, storing, processing and retrieving information for purposes of control.

Further Reading

Gerovitch S, *From Newspeak to Cyberspeak: A History of Soviet Cybernetics* (MIT Press, 2002).
Hayles KN, *How We Became Posthuman: Virtual Bodies in Cybernetics, Literature, and Informatics* (University Of Chicago, 1999).
Malapi-Nelson A, *The Nature of the Machine and the Collapse of Cybernetics: A Transhumanist Lesson for Emerging Technologies* (Palgrave, 2017).
Mirowski P, *Machine Dreams: Economics Becomes a Cyborg Science* (Cambridge University Press, 2008).
Pickering A, *The Cybernetic Brain: Sketches of Another Future* (University of Chicago Press, 2010).

Dataism

A set of beliefs whereby the universe gives greater value and support to systems, individuals, and societies that contribute most heavily and efficiently to data processing.

Further Reading

Brooks D, 'The Philosophy of Data' (*The New York Times*, 4 February 2013) www.nytimes.com/2013/02/05/opinion/brooks-the-philosophy-of-data.html.
Harari YN, *Homo Deus: A Brief History of Tomorrow* (Harper Collins, 2017).
Lohr S, *Data-ism: Inside the Big Data Revolution* (Harper Collins, 2015).
Peters T, 'The Deluge of Dataism: A New Post-Human Religion?' (2017) 56 *Dialog* 3.
van der Meulen S and M Bruinsma, 'Man as "aggregate of data"' (2019) 34 *AI & Society* 343.

Data Science

Data Science is an offshoot of statistics focused on extracting knowledge from data sets, preparing and storing it for analysis.

Further Reading

Hildebrandt M, 'Law as computation in the era of artificial legal intelligence: Speaking law to the power of statistics' (2018) 68 *University of Toronto Law Journal* 1 Supplement.
Kelleher JD and B Tierney, *Data Science* (MIT Press, 2018).
McQuillan D, 'Data Science as Machinic Neoplatonism' (2018) 31 *Philosophy & Technology* 253.
Rowntree D, *Statistics Without Tears: An Introduction for Non-Mathematicians* (Penguin, 2018).
Spiegelhalter D, *The Art of Statistics: Learning from Data* (Pelican, 2019).

Decision Support Systems

A decision support system (DSS) is a computer system used to supplement human decision-making processes in the context of an organisation or business.

Further Reading

Adelman L, *Evaluating Decision Support and Expert Systems* (Wiley, 1992).
Goodman-Delahunty J, P Anders Granhagm, M Hartwig and EF Loftus, 'Insightful or Wishful: Lawyers' Ability to Predict Case Outcomes' (2010) 16 *Psychology, Public Policy, and Law* 2.
Landauer TK, *The Trouble with Computers: Usefulness, Usability, and Productivity* (MIT Press, 1996).
Marakas GM, *Decision Support Systems in the 21st Century*, 2nd edn (Pearson, 2003).
Suzuki K and Y Chen (eds), *Artificial Intelligence in Decision Support Systems for Diagnosis in Medical Imaging* (Springer, 2018).

Deductive Reasoning

Deductive reasoning, also termed deductive logic, is a method of logical enquiry for reasoning from one of more premises to reach a logically valid conclusion.

Further Reading

Boole G, *An Investigation of the Laws of Thought: On Which Are Founded the Mathematical Theories of Logic and Probabilities*, rev edn (Dover, 2012).
Clark HH, 'Linguistic processes in deductive reasoning' (1969) 76 *Psychological Review* 4.
Hughlings IP, *The Logic of Names: an Introduction to Boole's Laws of Thought* (HardPress, 2020).

Leiter B, 'Legal Formalism and Legal Realism: What is the Issue?' (2010) 16 *Legal Theory* 111.
Rips LJ, *The Psychology of Proof: Deductive Reasoning in Human Thinking* (MIT Press, 1994).

Deep Learning (DL)

Deep Learning (DL) is a subfield of Machine Learning (ML) involving the use of artificial neural networks and representational learning.

Further Reading

Bansal N, A Sharma and RK Singh, 'A Review on the Application of Deep Learning in Legal Domain' in J MacIntyre, I Maglogiannis, L Iliadis and E Pimenidis (eds), *Artificial Intelligence Applications and Innovations* (Springer, 2019).
Chalkidis I and D Kampas, 'Deep Learning in Law: Early Adaptation and Legal Word Embeddings Trained on Large Corpora' (2019) 27 *Artificial Intelligence and Law* 171.
Goodfellow I, Y Bengio, *A Courville and F Bach, Deep Learning* (MIT Press, 2017).
Kelleher JD, *Deep Learning* (MIT Press, 2019).
Marcus G and E Davis, *Rebooting AI: Building Artificial Intelligence We Can Trust* (Ballantine, 2019).

Economics of Artificial Intelligence

The social scientific study of the production, distribution, and consumption of goods and services related to the development of Artificial Intelligence (AI) and the automation of various processes.

Further Reading

Agrawal A, J Gans and A Goldfarb, *Prediction Machines: The Simple Economics of Artificial Intelligence* (Harvard Business Review Press, 2018).
Athey S, 'The Impact of Machine Learning on Economics' (2018) www.gsb.stanford.edu/sites/gsb/files/publication-pdf/atheyimpactmlecon.pdf.
Brooks C, C Gherhes and T Vorley, 'Artificial intelligence in the legal sector: pressures and challenges of transformation' (2020) 13 *Cambridge Journal of Regions, Economy and Society* 1.
van de Gevel AJW and CN Noussair (eds), *The Nexus Between Artificial Intelligence and Economics* (Springer 2013).
Varian H, 'Artificial Intelligence, Economics, and Industrial Organization' (2018) NBER Working Paper No. 24839 www.nber.org/papers/w24839.

Expert Systems (ES)

A computer containing a database comprised of mathematical representations of knowledge in expert domains (ie, law, medicine) designed to assist with complex decision-making tasks.

Further Reading

Coats PK, 'Why Expert Systems Fail' (1988) 18 *Financial Management* 3.
Dreyfus H and S Summer, 'Why Expert Systems Do Not Exhibit Expertise' (1986) 1 *IEEE Expert* 2.
Jackson P, *Introduction to Expert Systems*, 3rd edn (Addison Wesley, 1999).
Liebowitz J (ed), *The Handbook of Applied Expert Systems* (CRC Press, 2019).
Martins GR, 'Overselling of Expert Systems' (1984) 30 *Datamation* 18.

Game Theory

Game Theory is the interdisciplinary study of how the interacting choices of economic agents produce outcomes on the basis of preferences.

Further Reading

Erickson P, *The World the Game Theorists Made* (University of Chicago Press, 2015).
Gintis H, *The Bounds of Reason: Game Theory and the Unification of the Behavioral Sciences* (Princeton University Press, 2009).
Pastine I, *Game Theory: A Graphic Guide* (Icon Books, 2017).
Skyrms B, *The Stag Hunt and the Evolution of Social Structure* (Cambridge University Press, 2004).
von Neumann J and O Morgenstern, *The Theory of Games and Economic Behavior*, rev edn (Princeton University Press, 2007).

Global Catastrophic Risk

The interdisciplinary study of hypothetical future events which could harm human society on a global scale and strategies to ameliorate societal risks.

Further Reading

Bostrom N and MM Ćirković (eds), *Global Catastrophic Risks* (Oxford University Press, 2011).
Ord T, *The Precipice: Existential Risk and the Future of Humanity* (Bloomsbury, 2020).
Sheckelford GE, L Kemp and C Rhodes et al., 'Accumulating evidence using crowdsourcing and machine learning: A living bibliography about existential risk and global catastrophic risk' (2020) 116 *Futures* 102508 www.x-risk.net/.
Torres P, Morality, *Foresight & Human Flourishing: An Introduction to Existential Risks* (Pitchstone, 2017).
Turchin A and D Denkenberger, 'Classification of global catastrophic risks connected with artificial intelligence' (2020) 35 *AI & Society* 147.

Governmentality

Governementality, coined by French philosopher Michel Foucault, is a portmanteau of 'government' and 'rationality'.

Further Reading

Bevir M (ed), *Governmentality After Neoliberalism* (Routledge, 2016).
Dean M, *Governmentality: Power and Rule in Modern Society* (Sage, 1999).
Inda JX, *Anthropologies of Modernity: Foucault, Governmentality, and Life Politics* (Wiley, 2005).
Introna LD, 'Algorithms, Governance, and Governmentality: On Governing Academic Writing' (2015) 41 *Science, Technology, & Human Values* 1.
Rose N, P O'Malley and M Valverde, 'Governmentality' (2006) 2 *Annual Review of Law and Social Science* 83.

Heuristics

A heuristic is any approach to problem solving that involves a practical method that is not guaranteed to be optimal or perfect, but is nonetheless useful for reaching an immediate or short-term goal.

Further Reading

Baron J, *Thinking and Deciding*, 4th edn (Cambridge University Press, 2007).
Cyert RM and JG March, *A Behavioral Theory of the Firm* (Martino Fine Books, 2013).
Gilovich T, DW Griffin and D Kahneman (eds), *Heuristics and Biases: The Psychology of Intuitive Judgment* (Cambridge University Press, 2002).
Simon HA, *Administrative Behavior: A Study of Decision-making Processes in Administrative Organisations*, 4th rev edn (Free Press, 1997).
Tversky A and D Kahneman, 'Judgment under Uncertainty: Heuristics and Biases' (1974) 185 *Science* 4157.

History of Artificial Intelligence

The retrospective study of the intellectual, philosophical, scientific, economic, and sociological factors related to the research and development of intelligent machines and their impact on society.

Further Reading

Feigenbaum EA and P McCorduck, *Fifth Generation: Artificial Intelligence and Japan's Computer Challenge to the World* (Michael Joseph, 1984).
McCarthy J, ML Minksy, N Rochester and CE Shannon, 'A Proposal for the Dartmouth Summer Research Project on Artificial Intelligence' (31 August 1955) jmc.stanford.edu/articles/dartmouth.html.
McCorduck P, *Machines Who Think: A Personal Inquiry into the History and Prospects of Artificial Intelligence*, 2nd edn (Routledge, 2004).
Newborn M, *Deep Blue: An Artificial Intelligence Milestone* (Springer, 2003).
Wooldridge M, *The Road to Conscious Machines: The Story of AI* (Pelican, 2020).

History of Computation

The retrospective study of the intellectual, philosophical, scientific, economic, and sociological factors related to the research and development of computing machines.

Further Reading

Brooks Jr FP, *The Mythical Man-Month: Essays on Software Engineering*, 2nd edn (Addison Wesley, 1995).
Ceruzzi PE, *Computing: A Concise History* (MIT Press, 2012).
Kidder T, *The Soul of A New Machine* (Back Bay, 2011).
Markoff J, *What the Doormouse Said: How the Sixties Counterculture Shaped the Personal Computer Industry* (Viking Books, 2005).
O'Mara M, *The Code: Silicon Valley and the Remaking of America* (Penguin, 2019).

Inductive Reasoning

Inductive reasoning, also termed induction and inductive inference, is a method of reasoning where the premises are understood to supply some evidence for the truth of the conclusion.

Further Reading

Brewer S, 'Exemplary Reasoning: Semantics, Pragmatics, and the Rational Force of Legal Argument by Analogy' (1996) 109 *Harvard Law Review* 5.
Heit E and CM Rotello, 'Relations between inductive reasoning and deductive reasoning' (2010) 36 *Journal of Psychology: Learning, Memory, and Cognition* 3.
Weinreb LL, *Legal Reason: The Use of Analogy in Legal Argument*, 2nd edn (Cambridge University Press, 2016).
McAbee ST, RS Landis and MI Burke, 'Inductive Reasoning: The Promise of Big Data' (2017) 27 *Human Resource Management Review* 2.
Popper K, *The Logic of Scientific Discovery*, 2nd edn (Routledge, 2002).

Intelligence

The ability to perceive or infer information and retain it as knowledge that can be applied towards adaptive behaviours within an environment.

Further Reading

Clark A, *Natural Born Cyborgs: Minds, Technologies, and the Future of Human Intelligence* (Oxford University Press, 2004).

Godfrey-Smith P, *Other Minds: The Octopus and the Evolution of Intelligent Life* (William Collins, 2017).

Hawkins K and S Blakeslee, *On Intelligence* (Times Books, 2004).

Hernández-Orallo J, *The Measure of All Minds: Evaluating Natural and Artificial Intelligence* (Cambridge University Press, 2017).

Searle J, 'Minds, Brains, and Programs' (1980) 3 *Behavioral and Brain Sciences* 417.

Juridical Interpretation

Juridical Interpretation refers to the reasoning methods judges use to interpret the law, particularly constitutional documents or statutes (*cf* heuristics).

Further Reading

Bongiovanni G, G Postema, A Rotolo, G Sartor, C Valentini and D Walton (eds), *Handbook of Legal Reasoning and Argumentation* (Springer, 2018).

Deakin S, 'Juridical Ontology: The Evolution of Legal Form' (2015) 40 *Historical Social Research/ Historische Sozialforschung* 1.

Guthrie C, JJ Rachlinski and AJ Wistrich, 'Blinking on the Bench: How Judges Decide Cases' (2007-2008) 93 *Cornell Law Review* 1.

Cahill-O'Callaghan R, *Values in the Supreme Court: Decisions, Division and Diversity* (Hart Publishing, 2020).

Weinreb LL, *Legal Reason: The Use of Analogy in Legal Argument*, 2nd edn (Cambridge University Press, 2016).

Law

A matter of longstanding definitional debate, Law generally refers to a system of rules created and enforced through social or governmental institutions for the purposes of regulating and coordinating human behaviour.

Further Reading

Hildebrandt M, *Law for Computer Scientists and Other Folk* (Oxford University Press, 2020).
Howarth D, *Law as Engineering: Thinking About What Lawyers Do* (Edward Elgar, 2014).
Llewellyn KN, *The Bramble Bush: The Classic Lectures on the Law and Law School* (Oxford University Press, 2008).
Luhmann N, *Law as a Social System* (KA Ziegert (trans) F Kastner, R Nobles, D Schiff and R Ziegert (eds), (Oxford University Press, 2004).
Supiot A, *Homo Juridicus: On the Anthropological Function of Law* (Verso, 2007).

Legal Autonomy

The capacity of the legal system to 'self select' its internal mode of operations and determine normative expectation for political, economic, and social order.

Further Reading

Baxter H, 'Autopoiesis and the "Relative Autonomy" of Law' (1997–1998) 19 *Cardozo Law Review* 6.
Capps P and HP Olsen, 'Legal Autonomy and Reflexive Rationality in Complex Societies' (2002) 11 *Social & Legal Studies* 4.
Deggau H-G, 'The Communicative Autonomy of the Legal System' in G Teubner (ed), *Autopoietic Law: A New Approach to Law and Society* (Walter de Gruyter, 1988).
Hildebrandt M and A Rouvroy (eds), *Law, Human Agency and Autonomic Computing* (Routledge, 2011).
Rottleuthner H, 'A Purified Sociology of Law: Niklas Luhmann on the Autonomy of the Legal System' (1989) 23 *Law & Society Review* 5.

Legal Expert Systems (LES)

A computer designed to encode the 'domain expertise' of human lawyers and judges into a 'knowledgebase' and represent them with various mathematical expressions that can be accessed on-demand to assist with legal-decision making tasks.

Further Reading

Greinke A, 'Legal Expert Systems: A Humanistic Critique of Mechanical Legal Interface' (1994) 1 *Murdoch University Electronic Journal of Law* 4.
Leith P, 'The Rise and Fall of Legal Expert Systems' (2010) 1 *European Journal of Law and Technology* 1.
Stevens C, V Barot and J Carter, 'The Next Generation of Legal Expert Systems – New Dawn or False Dawn?' in N Bramer, M Petridis and A Hopgood (eds), *Research and Development in Intelligent Systems XXVII* (Springer, 2011).

Susskind R, *The Future of Law: Facing the Challenges of Information Technology* (Oxford University Press, 1996).
Zeleznikow K and D Hunter, 'Rationales for the Continued Development of Legal Expert Systems' (1992) 3 *Journal of Law and Information Science* 3.

Legal Personality

A legal person is any human or entity recognised as having the freedom to enter contracts, own and sell property, sue and be sued, and so forth.

Further Reading

Gunkel DJ, *Robot Rights* (MIT Press, 2018).
Kukri VAJ and T Pietrzkowski (eds), *Legal Personhood: Animals, Artificial Intelligence and the Unborn* (Springer, 2017).
Solum LB, 'Legal Personhood for Artificial Intelligences' (1992) 70 *North Carolina Law Review* 4.
Teubner G, 'Digital Personhood? The Status of Autonomous Software Agents in Private Law' (2018) dx.doi.org/10.2139/ssrn.3177096.
van der Meulen S and M Bruinsma, 'Man as "aggregate" of data' (2019) 34 *AI & Society* 343.

Leibniz, Gottfried Willhelm (1646–1716)

German polymath and one of the foremost mathematicians and natural philosophers of the Enlightenment; most prominently remembered for conceiving differential and integral calculus independently of Issac Newton.

Further Reading

Antagonazza MR, *Leibniz: An Intellectual Biography* (Cambridge University Press, 2009).
Anognazza MR (ed), *The Oxford Handbook on Leibniz* (Oxford University Press, 2018).
Garber D, *Leibniz: Body, Substance, Monad* (Oxford University Press, 2009).
Hoeflich MH, 'Law & Geometry: Legal Science from Leibniz to Langdell' (1986) 30 *American Journal of Legal History* 2.
Jolley N (ed), *Cambridge Companion to Leibniz* (University of Cambridge Press, 2008).

Logic

A systematic method of reasoning conducted or assessed according to strict principles of validity.

Further Reading

Ashley K, *Modeling Legal Arguments* (MIT Press, 1990).
Copi IM, C Cohen and DE Flage, *Essentials of Logic*, 2nd edn (Routledge, 2006).
Hodges W, *Logic: An Introduction to Elementary Logic*, 2nd edn (Penguin, 2001).
Smith P, *An Introduction to Formal Logic*, 2nd edn (Cambridge *University Press, 2020).*
Tarski A, Introduction to Logic and to the Methodology of Deductive Sciences (Dover Publications, 1995).

Logic and Law

The application of logical methods to the systematic study and analysis of legal phenomena, particularly legal reasoning.

Further Reading

Artosi A, B Pieri and G Sartor (eds), *Leibniz: Logico-Philosophical Puzzles in the Law* (Springer, 2013).
Bench-Capon T and H Prakken, 'Introducing the Logic and Law Corner' (2008) 18 *Journal of Logic and Computation* 1.
Glenn HP and LD Smith (eds), *Law and the New Logics* (Cambridge University Press, 2017).
Prakken H, *Logical Tools for Modelling Legal Argument: A Study of Defeasible Reasoning in Law* (Springer Science, 1997).
Prakken H and G Sartor, 'Law and logic: A review from an argumentation perspective' (2015) 227 *Artificial Intelligence* 214.

Machine Ethics

Machine Ethics, also termed AI Ethics, is a subfield of philosophy, engineering, and Artificial Intelligence concerning the compatability and alignment of machine behaviours with ethical principles.

Further Reading

Anderson M and SL Anderson (eds), *Machine Ethics* (Cambridge University Press, 2011).
Cockelbergh M, *AI Ethics* (MIT Press, 2020).
Dubber MD, F Pasquale and S Das (eds), *The Oxford Handbook of Ethics in AI* (Oxford University Press, 2020).
Weizenbaum J, *Computer Power and Human Reason: From Judgement to Calculation* (WH Freeman & Co., 1976).
Yampolskiy R, 'Artificial Intelligence Safety Engineering: Why Machine Ethics Is a Wrong Approach' in VC Müller (ed), *Philosophy and Theory of Artificial Intelligence* (Springer, 2012).

Machine Learning (ML)

Machine Learning (ML) is a technique within Artificial Intelligence research involving the study and design of algorithms that automatically adapt their mathematical parameters over time to improve performance at a task.

Further Reading

Alarie B, A Niblett and A Yoon, 'Regulation by Machine' (2016) dx.doi.org/10.2139/ssrn.2878950.
Alpaydin T, *Machine Learning: The New AI* (MIT Press, 2016).
Deisenroth M, AA Faisal and CS Ong, *Mathematics for Machine Learning* (Cambridge University Press, 2020).
Kleinberg J, H Lakkaraju, J Leskovec, J Ludwig and S Millainathan, 'Human Decisions and Machine Predictions' (2018) 133 *The Quarterly Journal of Economics* 1.
Lehr D and P Ohm, 'Playing with Data: What Legal Scholars Should Learn About Machine Learning' (2017) 51 *UC Davis Law Review*.

Mathematics

Mathematics, although eluding cogent definition, generally refers to the abstract science of numbers, quantity, and space; either as abstract concepts (pure mathematics) or as applied to specific disciplines such as physics or Artificial Intelligence (applied mathematics).

Further Reading

Du Sautoy M, *What We Cannot Know: Explorations at the Edge of Knowledge* (Fourth Estate, 2016).
Graham RL, DE Knuth and O Patshnik, *A Foundation for Computer Science*, 2nd edn (Addison-Wesley, 1994).
Hofstadter DR, *Gödel, Escher, Bach: An Eternal Golden Braid*, rev edn (Basic Books, 1999).
Rosenthal D, D Rosenthal and P Rosenthal, *A Readable Introduction to Real Mathematics*, 2nd edn (Springer, 2019).
Shapiro S (ed), *The Oxford Handbook of Philosophy of Mathematics and Logic* (Oxford University Press, 2007).

Mathematical Universe Hypothesis (MUH)

A speculative 'theory of everything' wherein external physical reality is a mathematical structure, and all structures that exist physically are said to exist mathematically.

Further Reading

Greene B, *The Hidden Reality: Parallel Universes and the Deep Laws of the Cosmos* (Alfred A Knopf, 2011).
James G, 'Some comments on "The Mathematical Universe"' (2009) arxiv.org/abs/0904.0867.
Penrose R, *The Road to Reality: A Complete Guide to the Laws of the Universe*, rev edn (Vintage, 2005).
Tegmark M, *Our Mathematical Universe: My Quest for the Ultimate Nature of Reality* (Penguin, 2015).
Tegmark M, *Life 3.0: Being Human in the Age of Artificial Intelligence* (Penguin. 2018).

Medical Expert Systems

A computer designed to encode the 'domain expertise' of human doctors and clinicians into a 'knowledgebase' and represent them with mathematical expressions that can be accessed on-demand to assist with medical diagnosis, treatment, and patient management.

Further Reading

Bassett C, 'The computational therapeutic: exploring Weizenbaum's ELIZA as a history of the present' (2019) 34 *AI & Society* 803.
Buchannan BG and EH Shortliffe (eds), *Rule-based Expert Systems: The MYCIN Experiments of the Stanford Heuristic Programming Project* (Addison-Wesley, 1984).
Metaxiotis KS and JE Samouilidis, 'Expert systems in medicine: academic illusion or real power?' (2000) 2 *Information Management & Computer Security* 8.
Ravuri, A Kannan, GJ Tso and X Amatriain, 'Learning from the experts: From expert systems to machine-learned diagnosis models' (2018) 85 *Proceedings of Machine Learning Research* 1.
Yanase J and E Triantahyllou, 'A systematic survey of computer-aided diagnosis in medicine: Past and present developments' (2019) 138 *Expert Systems with Applications* 112821.

Natural Language Processing (NLP)

Natural Language Processing (NLP) is a subfield of linguistics, computer science, and artificial intelligence examining the interaction of computer and human natural languages, with a particular focus on developing computers to process, analyse, and understand natural language data.

Further Reading

Eisenstein J, *Introduction to Natural Language Processing* (MIT Press, 2019).
Francesconi E, S Montemagni, W Peters and D Tiscornia (eds), *Semantic Processing of Legal Texts: Where the Language of Law Meetings the Law of Language* (Springer, 2010).

Jurafsky D and JH Martin, *Speech and Language Processing: An Introduction to Natural Language Processing, Computational Linguistics, and Speech Recognition*, 2nd edn (Prentice Hall, 2008).
Pinker S, *The Language Instinct: How the Mind Creates Language* (William Morrow and Co., 1994).
Winograd T, *Understanding Natural Language* (Academic Press, 1972).

Neuroscience

A multidisciplinary branch of biology spanning physiology, anatomy, chemistry, biology, psychology and mathematics that examines the fundamental and emergent properties of neurons and neural circuits in the brain.

Further Reading

Bear MF, B Connors and M Paradiso, *Neuroscience: Exploring the Brain*, 4th edn (Jones and Bartlett, 2015).
Beecher-Monas E and E Garcia-Rill, *Fundamentals of Neuroscience and the Law* (Cambridge Scholars Press, 2020).
Bickle J (ed), *The Oxford Handbook of Philosophy and Neuroscience* (Oxford University Press, 2009).
Pardo MS and D Patterson, *Minds, Brains, and Law: The Conceptual Foundations of Law and Neuroscience* (Oxford University Press, 2015).
Rippon G, *The Gendered Brain: The New Neuroscience the Shatters the Myth of the Female Brain* (Vintage, 2020).

Philosophy of Mind

A branch of philosophy examining the nature of the human mind (i.e. mental states, functions, properties and consciousness) and its relation to the physical body.

Further Reading

Du Sautoy M, *The Creativity Code: Art and Innovation in the Age of AI* (Oxford University Press, 2019).
Fodor JA, *Psychosemantics: The Problem of Meaning in the Philosophy of Mind* (MIT Press, 1988).
Heil J, *Philosophy of Mind: A Contemporary Introduction*, 3rd edn (Routledge, 2013).
Hofstadter D, *I Am A Strange Loop* (Basic Books, 2007).
Kim J, *Philosophy of Mind*, 3rd edn (Westview Press, 2011).

Provability

A form of modal logic used to investigate what mathematical theories can express in a restricted language about their provability predicates.

Further Reading

Davis M, *Computability and Unsolvability* (Dover, 1985).
Garey M and DS Johnson, *Computers and Intractability: A Guide to the Theory of NP-Completeness* (WH Freeman & Co., 1979).
Pápay G and T Hey, *The Computing Universe* (Cambridge University Press, 2014).
Turing A, 'On computable numbers, with an application to the Entscheidungsproblem' (1937) 2 *Proceedings of the London Mathematical Society* 1.
van Leeuwen J, *Handbook of Theoretical Computer Science* (Elsevier, 1988).

Rule of Law

The Rule of Law generally refers to the authority and influence of law in society, with particular regard to its role as a constraint on individual and institutional behaviour, and where all are considered equally subject to the conditions it imposes on individual and collective behaviours.

Further Reading

Bayamlioğlu and R Leenes, 'The "rule of law" implications of data-driven decision-making: a techno-regulatory perspective' (2018) 10 *Law, Innovation and Technology* 2.
Bingham T, *The Rule of Law* (Allen Lane, 2010).
Hildebrandt M, 'Algorithmic Regulation and the Rule of Law' (2018) 376 *Philosophical Transactions of the Royal Society A* 2128.
Nemitz P, 'Constitutional democracy and technology in the age of artificial intelligence' (2018) 376 *Philosophical Transactions of the Royal Society A* 2133.
Tamanaha BZ, *On The Rule of Law* (Cambridge University Press, 2004).

Surveillance Capitalism

Surveillance capitalism refers to a market driven process whereby the primary commodity is the ambient capture, storage, analysis of personal data for commercial or institutional purposes.

Further Reading

Gray D and SE Henderson (eds), *The Cambridge Handbook of Surveillance Law* (Cambridge University Press, 2019).
Lyon D, *The Culture of Surveillance: Watching as a Way of Life* (Polity Press, 2018).
Shapiro C and HR Varian, *Information Rules: A Strategic Guide to the Network Economy* (Harvard Business Review, 1998).

Webb M, *Coding Democracy: How Hackers Are Disrupting Power, Surveillance, and Authoritarianism* (MIT Press, 2020).
Zuboff S, *The Age of Surveillance Capitalism: The Fight for a Human Future at the New Frontier of Power* (Profile Books, 2019).

Technological Singularity

The Technological Singularity – or more simply, The Singularity – is a hypothesised point in the future whereby technological growth, particularly as it relates to machine intelligence, becomes uncontrollable, irreversible, and results in unforeseeable changes to human existence.

Further Reading

Callaghan V, J Miller, R Yampolskiy and S Armstrong (eds), *The Technological Singularity: Managing the Journey* (Springer, 2017).
Joy B, 'Why the Future Doesn't Need Us' (*Wired*, 4 January 2000) www.wired.com/2000/04/joy-2/.
Kurzweil R, *The Singularity Is Near: When Humans Transcend Biology* (Viking, 2005).
Shanahan M, *The Technological Singularity* (MIT Press, 2015).
Searle J, 'What Your Computer Can't Know' (2014) LXI *The New York Review of Books* 15.

Theory of Computation

In computer science and mathematics, the theory of computation is a subfield examining how efficiently problems can be solved using algorithms, and ultimately the fundamental capabilities and limitations of computers.

Further Reading

Feynmann RP, in T Hey and RW Allen (eds), *Feynman Lectures On Computation* (Westview Press, 2000).
Lewis FD, Essentials of Theoretical Computer Science cse.ucdenver.edu/~cscialtman/foundation/Essentials%20of%20Theoretical%20Computer%20Science.pdf.
Petzold C, *Code: The Hidden Language of Computer Hardware and Software* (Microsoft Books, 2000).
Sipser M, *Introduction to the Theory of Computation* (PWS Publishing, 1997).
Stuart T, *Understanding Computation: From Simple Machines to Impossible Programs* (O'Reilly, 2013).

Transhumanism

Transhumanism is a philosophical movement that advocates for revolutionising the human condition through the development and implementation of sophisticated technologies to enhance cognition, physiology, and various biological capabilities.

Further Reading

Burden D and M Savin-Baden, *Virtual Humans: Today and Tomorrow* (Chapman and Hall, 2019).
Cave S, *Immortality: The Quest to Live Forever and How It Drives Civilisation* (Biteback, 2013).
Frischmann B and E Sellinger, *Re-Engineering Humanity* (Cambridge University Press, 2018).
Ross B, *The Philosophy of Transhumanism: A Critical Analysis* (Emerald, 2020).
Winner L, 'Are humans obsolete?' (2002) 4 *Hedgehog Review* 3.

Turing Test

The Turing Test, developed by British computer scientist and mathematician Alan Turing in 1950, is a proposal for determining a machine's ability to exhibit aspects of intelligent behaviour equivalent to, or indistinguishable from, that of a human.

Further Reading

Copeland BJ, 'The Turing Test' (2000) 10 *Minds and Machines* 519.
Levesque HJ, *Common Sense, the Turing Test, and the Quest for Real AI* (MIT Press, 2018).
Moor JH, *The Turing Test: The Elusive Standard of Artificial Intelligence* (Springer, 2003).
Volokh E, 'Chief Justice Robots' (2019) 68 *Duke Law Journal* 1135.
Warwick K and H Shah, 'Can machines think? A report on Turing test experiments at the Royal Society' (2016) 28 *Journal of Experimental & Theoretical Artificial Intelligence* 6.

INDEX

abductive reasoning 285
ADM systems 6, 16, 32–3, 260–1
affective computing (AfC) 254, 285
affective state detection 257–8
AGI (artificial general intelligence) 3–4, 14, 18, 208, 263, 287
AI *see* **artificial intelligence**
AI crime 180–2
AI ethics 142, 281, 304
AI Judges 4–5, 6–7
Alarie, Ben 5, 18, 107–8, 115–22, 128–30, 135, 137–8, 209, 211, 224, 225, 227
Aletras, Nikos 215, 218
algocracy 3, 130–2
algorithmic accountability 117–22
algorithmic decision-making 96, 102–5, 286
see also **ADM systems**
algorithmic dissimulation 129, 130
algorithmic governmentality 22, 94–105, 123
algorithmic interactions 128–30
algorithms
definition 286
explainability 49, 66
further reading 286
law as 55–65
learning by 55–6, 73
objectivity 114, 120
predictability 121–2
and public policy 129
rationality 93
and reflexivity 113–15, 129–30
reliability 121
success of 62
transformative potential 162
AMSD (automated mental state detection) 256–9
Annas, Julia 168
ANNs (artificial neural networks) 37–8, 44–5
'any difference that makes a difference' 8
Appelbaum, Paul S. 273
Archer, Margaret 110
Arendt, Hannah 34
Aristotle 171
artificial general intelligence (AGI) 3–4, 14, 18, 208, 263, 287
artificial intelligence (AI) *see also* **Legal AI; machine learning (ML)**
automation of legal tasks 209–20
autonomy 180, 181
availability of legal tools 213–14
as 'black box' systems 179–80, 226
capabilities of legal tools 214–16
civil liability 204
connectionist models 15, 32, 252–4
constructive liability 198–9, 200
crime 178, 180–2, 189, 196–200, 202–4
criminal gap 197–200
criminal law extension 202–4
criminal liability for 178
definition 286
economics of 297
errors 226
ethics 281
'exceeding human capabilities' 3–4, 5, 208
see also legal singularity
further reading 287
governance of 142
Hard Crimes 178, 189, 196–200, 202–4
history of 299–300
innocent agency doctrine 197, 199–200
irreducibility of culpability 181–2
judges, replacement of 219–21
legal clarification 138–9
and legal functions 137–41
legal personality 25–6, 201–2
legitimacy of legal tools 216–20
limits of in law 49–55
logic-based approach 14, 32, 250–1
meaning of 206–7
and medical expert systems 241–7
and medical research 238
and medicine 248–50
mens rea 191–2
natural and probable consequences doctrine 197–8
novel issues 227
and psychiatry 249–50
punishment 177–204
affirmative case 185–7
alternatives to 196–204

costs of 200–2
culpability-focused limitations 187–96
Eligibility Challenge 188–92
reality of 194–6
retributivist limitations 187–96
reducibility of culpability 181–2, 192–4
regulatee use of 138–40
regulator use of 140–1
regulatory responsibilities 141–59
balance of interests 148–9
coherentism 153–5
commons 143–6
community values 146–8, 150, 151
expectations 155–9
institutions 155–9
rule of law 149–53
resistance to 136
for rule compliance 139–41
safety 287
strict liability 189–91
strong AI 14, 25, 180 *see also* artificial general intelligence
Turing test for 207
unpredictably 179
weak AI 14
Artificial Intelligence Safety 287
artificial moral agency 173, n46
artificial neural networks (ANNs) 37–8, 44–5
Asaro, Peter 185
Ashby, W. Ross 262
assisted conception 156
automated decision-making systems *see* **ADM systems**
automated mental state detection (AMSD) 256–9
automated systems 161–75
automation bias 162, 169
automation of legal tasks 209–20
automation of psychological assessment and diagnosis 247–59
autonomous artificial moral agents 173–4
autonomy, legal 302
autonomy of artificial intelligence 180, 181
autonomy of systems 163
autopoiesis 252, 288
axiomatic conception of law 12–14, 17

Re B (Adult: Refusal of Medical Treatment) 270
B2B (business to business) relationships 80
backpropogation 39, 60
Bacon, Francis 8
Baker, Robert 257
Balganesh, Shyamkrishna 228
banking regulation 80
Banner, Natalie 276
bar codes 90
Barbrook, Richard 4
Baroni, Marco 53
Basic Emotion Theory (BET) 258
Bassett, Caroline 261–2
Bateson, Gregory 8
Bauman, Zygmunt 88–9
Bayern, Shawn 147–8
Bayout, Abdelmalek 255
BCI (brain-computer interfaces) 289 *see also* **human brain interfaces**
Beer, David 96, 114
Beer, Stafford 113, 133
Bennett Moses, Lyria 136
Berg, Jessica Wilen 273
Berns, Thomas 123
BET (Basic Emotion Theory) 258
bias
ADM systems 260
automation bias 162, 169
definition 288
further reading 288
machine learning (ML) 120, 122
Big Data 20, 31, 34, 49, 50, 93, 289
binary coding 8, 10–11
bio-surveillance 91–2
biotechnology 90
bits 7
'black boxing' of law 6–7
blockchain-based smart contracts 81–2
Bolander, Thomas 119
Boole, George 10
Bostrom, Nick 171, 172
Bourdieu, Pierre 6
brain-computer interfaces (BCI) 289 *see also* **human brain interfaces**
Branting, Karl 5
Bratman, Michael E. 191
Breivik, Anders 194
Brennan-Marquez, Kiel 221
Brewer, Scott 13
Brown, James 48–9
Brownsword, Roger 116
Burwell v Hobby Lobby Stores 202
business to business (B2B) relationships 80

Californian Ideology 4
Cameron, Andy 4
Cameron, William 80
Campbell effect 73–4
Campbell v Acuff-Rose 227, 229, 232–3
Cariou v Prince 230, 233–4
Carter, David J. 48–9
Casey, Brian 186
Cashwell, Glyn 218, 219

Catcher in the Rye (Salinger) 234
CC v KK 277
CDSS (Clinical Decision Support Systems) 245–6, 290
characteristica universalis 11, 14–16, 289–90
chatbots 211, 245, 261
Chomsky, Noam 42, 53
Citizens United v Federal Election Commission 202
Clarke, Roger 209, 212
Clinical Decision Support Systems (CDSS) 245–6, 290
CNN (Convolutional Neural Networks) 45, 294–5
Cobb, Matthew 238, 252, 271
Cobbe, Jennifer 103–4
code-driven law 67–83
code-driven normativity 71–4
cognitive computing 90, 290–1
cognitive science 291
Cohen, Alex S. 256
Cohen, Julie 93, 152
coherentism 153–5, 156
commons 143–6, 157–9
community values 146–8, 150, 151
COMPAS system 68, 120, 212
complementarity 163
complementary artefact intelligence 209
computation 7–8, 292, 300, 309
computational complexity 247, 291
computational legalism 70, 75–6
computational linguistics 292–3 *see also* natural language processing
Computational Theory of Mind (CTM) 8, 16–19, 242, 293
computationalism 17–18, 242, 292
computer programming 293
computer-assisted psychiatric diagnosis 245
computerised decision-making 262–5
connectionism 15, 32, 252–4, 294
consciousness 225, 257, 259, 280, 294
constitutional principles 70
constructive liability 198–9, 200
consultative democracy 85–6
contestability of judicial decisions 217
contract law 12, 17, 69
convolution 39
Convolutional Neural Networks (CNN) 45, 294–5
copyright law
  exclusion 228–9
  fair use doctrine 223–4, 229–31, 232–4
  and legal singularity 224–7, 231
  as a property system 228–31
  and technological singularity 226
  transformative use 230, 232–4
corporate culpability 189
corporate legal personality 201–2
corrective justice 77
countability and control 83
countersurveillance 99–101
Covid-19 pandemic 91–2, 102
creativity 223, 226
crimes against humanity 158
criminal law 70, 202–4
criminal liability for artificial intelligence 178
Crivelli, Carlos 258
CTM (Computational Theory of Mind) 8, 16–19, 242, 293
culpability
  of artificial intelligence 181–2, 188, 192–4
  corporate 189
cybernetics 252, 295

Damasio, Antonio 166
Danaher, John 3, 130, 131
Darling, Kate 187
data partitioning and weighting 60–4
data protection legislation 101, 103
data science 49, 282, 296
dataism 125, 295
DataLex 213
dataveillance 145–6
Davis, Randall 246
Day, Ron 97, n57
Deakin, Simon 135–6, 226–7
Dean, Jodi 86
decision trees 78
decision-making
  algorithms 96, 102–5 *see also* ADM systems
  computerised 262–5
  systems 69, 224 *see also* ADM systems
decision-support systems 69, 245–6, 296
deductive reasoning 242, 245, 296–7
Deep Belief Networks 44–5
Deep Blue 119, 251
deep learning (DL)
  abstraction 52
  data 51–2
  definition 297
  further reading 297
  generalisation 51–2
  inference 52
  and law 107–8
  learning 52–3
  and natural language processing (NLP) 44–5
  non-hierarchical language 53–4
  overview 38–9
DeepMind 119
Deleuze, Gilles 88–9

democracy
and algorithmic governmentality 94–8
consultative 85–6
and decision making 104
and internet 86–7
and rule of law 77
Deng, Li 41
Descartes, René 251
desert constraint on punishment 184, 188
***Devs* (TV series)** 87, n9
Dewey, John 13
DIAGNO 245
diagnostic systems 242
digital computation 7–8
digital lifeworld 89–90, 94
direct democracy 86–7
disambiguation of requirements 73
distributive justice 77
Diver, Laurence 70, 75
DL *see* **deep learning**
DOCTOR (ELIZA script) 261, 263
double contingency 74–5
Dreyfus, Hubert 217
driverless cars 151
DSM (Diagnostic and Statistical Manual of Mental Disorders) 271
Duff, Antony 190
Duffy, Anne 239
Dworkin, Ronald 75–6, 250

economics of artificial intelligence 297
ecosystems 145
elections 218
Eligibility Challenge 188–92
ELIZA 261–3
Elvevåg, Brita 256
emerging technologies 156
empirical approaches to NLP 42–4
employment status classification 56–64
EMYCIN 245
enigmatic technologies 93
error correction 55–6, 59–60
ES *see* **expert systems**
Espeland, Wendy 127
Esposito, Elena 74
Essential MYCIN 245
'essentially digital governance' 2–3
ethical agency 167–9
Ethics Guidelines for Trustworthy AI (European Commission) 142
European Court of Human Rights judgments 215, 218
expert systems
definition 297
further reading 298
justification and development 243–4
legal 14–15, 17, 32, 216, 302–3
limitations of 214–15
medical 241–7, 306
psychiatry 244
psychology 244
uses of 211
explainability
algorithms 49, 66
definition 288
further reading 288

Facebook 95
fair use doctrine 223–4, 229–31, 232–4
fake news 87
Feigenbaum, Edward 243, 247
Feinberg, Joel 195
financial crisis of 2008 80, n47
financial sector 80
financial trading 129
Fintech 142
Fisher, Eran 96–7
fMRI (functional magnetic resonance imaging) 254
Fodor, Jerry A. 8
Folsom v Marsh 230
Foot, Philippa 195
formalisation of requirements 72–3
Foucault, Michel 91–2, 95, 96, 98, 100, 123
Fourth Industrial Revolution 1–2
Fridlund, Alan J. 258
Fullerian principles of legality 152
functional magnetic resonance imaging (fMRI) 254

Gabor, Dennis 74
'GAFAM' group 87
game theory 298
General Problem Solver 242
generativity 3
genomic coding 151
global catastrophic risk 298
Goffman, Erving 129, 130
Goldsworthy, Daniel 107–8, 118, 119
***Gone With The Wind* (Mitchell)** 233, 234
Goodhart effect 73–4
government 3
governmentality 123–4, 299 *see also* **algorithmic governmentality**
Green, Leslie 162
Grisso, Thomas 273
group interests 97

Habermas, Jürgen 5–6
habit acquisition 165

habit reversal 166–7
habitual agency 162, 165–70
Hallevy, Gabriel 177, 197–8
Hard AI Crimes 178, 189, 196–200, 202–4
Harkens, Adam 119
Harlow, Carol 103–4
Hart, HLA 6, 15, 182, 194–5, 218
HBI (human brain interfaces) 258–9 *see also* **brain-computer interfaces**
Henderson, Stephen 221
hetrotopias 100
heuristics 243, 299
Hidden Markov Models (HMMs) 43–4
hierarchical language 53–4
Hildebrandt, Mireille 6–7, 34–5, 217, 218, 219, 220–1, 224
HMMs (Hidden Markov Models) 43–4
Hobbes, Thomas 8, 9
Hohfeld, Wesley Newcomb 223
Holmes, Oliver Wendell 12–13, 107, 221
homo documentus 97, n57
Hoye, J. Matthew 93
Hu, Ying 177
human agency 145–6
human brain interfaces (HBI) 258–9 *see also* **brain-computer interfaces**
human development 145–6
human dignity 147, 150
human existence, essential conditions for 145, 150
Human Fertilisation and Embryology Act 1990 156
human override 151
human rights 77, 147, 150, 250
hypernudging 93

Idiots Act 1886 271
IJOP (Integrated Joint Operations Platform) 88, n10
image recognition 39
individual autonomy 97
inductive reasoning 281, 300
inference 52, 54–5, 94–8
information retention 55–6, 58–9
information technology 90
Innis, Harold 131
innocent agency doctrine 197, 199–200
instrumentality 76, 77–8
Integrated Joint Operations Platform (IJOP) 88, n10
integrity of law 75–6
intellectual property 228
intelligence 207, 208, 209, 301
intelligent diagnostic systems 242
international law 158–9
internet and democracy 86–7
internet intermediaries 103, 148
inverse reinforcement learning (IRL) 162, 164–5
irreducibility of culpability 181–2

Jackson, Dan 79–81
Jia, Robin 53
JT International SA v Commonwealth of Australia 229
judges, replacement of 219–21 *see also* **AI Judges**
judicial decisions
contestability of 217
on elections 218
and machine learning (ML) 215
judicial oaths 217–18
juridical interpretation 301
juridical reasoning
mathematical formalisation 5–6, 33–5, 49–50
purpose of 13–14
jus cogens 158
justice 76–8

Kaiser Aetna v United States 228
Kant, Immanuel 168
Katz, Daniel Martin 79–81
Kavenna, Joanna 88
Kerr, Ian 217, 218, 219, 221
Kitchin, Rob 91, 114, 123
knowledge engineering 246–7
Kong, Camillia 240
Kontingenzbewältigung 75
Koops, Bert-Jaap 149
Korzbyski, Alfred 280
Kuhn, Thomas 49
Kulynych, Bogdan 116

LaFave, Wayne R. 190
Lake, Brenden M. 53
Landes, William 228
Langdell, Christopher Columbus 12–13
language 71
Laplace, Simon 87, n9
Lashley, Karl 251
law *see also* **contract law; copyright law; criminal law; international law; private law; public law; smart law**
as algorithm 55–65
automation of 115–32
axiomatic conception of 12–14, 17
'black boxing' of 6–7
and *characteristica universalis* 14–16
code-driven 67–83
computability of 205–6, 210–11
and deep learning (DL) 107–8

definition 301
efficiency of 115–16
further reading 302
integrity of 75–6
and legal singularity 227
limits of AI in 49–55
and logic 304
and machine learning (ML) 31
mathematisation of 11
and natural language processing (NLP) 45–9
opacity 121–2, 130–2
optimisation of 62–3, 116
predictability 122
problematisation of 124–6
quantification of 126–8
rationalisation of 126–8
and reflexivity 111–13
as a social institution 6
and society 108, 122
and technology 35
Turing Completeness 17
LbD (legal by design) 79–82
learning 52–3
by algorithms 55–6, 73
legal advice 213–14
Legal AI 109–10 *see also* **artificial intelligence; LegalTech**
and algorithmic interactions 128–30
and automation of law 116–17
and law's function 117–22
and law's role in society 122–32
and legal reasoning 119–20
limitations of 118–22
objectivity 120
optimisation 118
predictability 121–2
problematisation of law 124–6
quantification of law 126–8
rationalisation of law 126–8
reliability 120–1
technical systems 122
legal autonomy 302
legal axioms 12–14
legal by design (LbD) 79–82
legal certainty 21, 75–9
legal complexity 79
legal computability, limits of 32–4
legal effect 72
legal ethics 219
legal expert systems (LES) 14–15, 17, 32, 302–3
legal interpretation 77–8
legal norms 72
legal personality 25–6, 201–2, 303
legal protection by design (LPbD) 79, 82–3
legal realism 13–14
legal reasoning
classification 56–8
data partitioning and weighting 60–4
employment status classification 56–64
error correction 55–6, 59–60
information retention 55–6, 58–9
and Legal AI 119–20
and machine learning (ML) 119–20
legal singularity 5–6, 18–19, 33, 34–5, 107–8, 109–10, 117, 132–3, 206, 208
and automation of legal tasks 209–12
and copyright law 224–7, 231
and rule of law 137–8
legal texts 45–9
legalism 70, 75–6
LegalTech 4, 16, 31–2, 109–10, 115–16 *see also* **Legal AI**
'legislation as code' movement 209–10
Leibniz, Gottfried Wilhelm
and artificial intelligence 9–12
binary coding 10–11
the brain 251
characteristica universalis 11
digital computers 11–12
further reading 303
law 11, 12–14
universal language 9–12
Leibniz Dream 11, 14
Lemley, Mark 186, 228
leprosy 91
LES (legal expert systems) 14–15, 17, 32, 302–3
Leval, Pierre 230
Levy, Frank 211, 219
Lewis, David 187
Liang, Percy 53
Liddle, Peter 238
linguistics 42
Lippe, Paul 79–81
liquid surveillance 88–9
Liu, Yang 41
lively data 91
logic 303–4
Logic Theorist 242, 243, 251
logic-based approach to artificial intelligence 14, 32, 250–1
Lowrie, Ian 93
LPbD (legal protection by design) 79, 82–3
Lucas critique 73–4
Luhmann, Niklas 75
Lukes, Steven 150
Lupton, Deborah 91
Lyon, David 88–9

Mac Síthigh, Daithí 103
McCarthy, John 14

McCarty, L. Thorne 14
McCorduck, Pamela 242, 243, 247
machine ethics 142, 281, 304
machine intelligence *see* **artificial intelligence**
machine learning (ML) *see also* **artificial intelligence**
  application of 15–16
  and artificial neural networks 37–8
  automation of legal tasks 211–12, 215, 216
  bias 120, 122
  definition 305
  design constraints 73
  further reading 305
  and judicial decisions 215
  and law 31
  learning algorithms 73
  and legal reasoning 119–20
  limitations of 118–22, 215–16
  and natural language processing (NLP) 47
  objectivity 120
  open-ended inference 54–5
  overreach 64–5
  predictability 121–2
  and reflexivity 118
  reliability 120–1
  sentiment analysis 47
  and Society 5.0 2
  supervised learning 35–7
  unsupervised learning 35–7, 62
machine-readable laws 209–10
Mackenzie, Adrian 114
Mackenzie, Donald 129–30
McQuillan, Dan 18
Mann, Steve 100–1
Manning, Christopher 41–2
'the map is not territory' 280–1
mapping 61
Marcus, Gary 38, 53, 54
Markou, Christopher 135–6, 226–7
Marx, Gary 99
Massive Online Legal Analysis (MOLA) 80–1
mathematical universe hypothesis (MUH) 17–18, 305–6
mathematics
  definition 305
  further reading 305
  unreasonable effectiveness of 17
Mathen, Carissima 217, 218, 219, 221
MCA (Mental Capacity Act) 266–7
media manipulation 87
medical decision-making 259–65
medical expert systems 241–7, 306
medical knowledge engineering 246–7
medical research 238
medicine 248–50
Mehozay, Yoav 96–7
mens rea 191–2
mental capacity 240–1, 255, 265–79
  assessments 268–70, 279–80, 282–3
  decisions on 271–5
  expert evidence 277–9
  functional test 266, 269–70, 274
  and inductive inference 281–2
  judicial discretion 275–9
  as a legal construct 270–1
  maps of 281
  and public policy 277
  reflexivity 276–80
  threshold for 273–4
  'use and weigh' criterion 274, 275, 278
Mental Capacity Act (MCA) 266–7
Mental Deficiency Act 1913 271
mental disorders 237–41, 280–1
mental health legislation 237–8, 266–7, 271
Mental State Examination (MSE) 257
Merton, Robert 110, 141
Metro-Goldwyn-Mayer Studios v Grokster 227, 232
Miller, Peter 124, 125
ML *see* **machine learning**
Model Penal Code 190
MOLA (Massive Online Legal Analysis) 80–1
Monaghan, Jeffrey 93
Montesquieu 72
Montoyo, A. 46
moral agency 146, 147
moral change 161, 165, 167–9
moral holidays 169–70
moral perfectionism 172–3
moral realism 171–3
moral risk 162
moral scrutiny 6–7
moral stances 163–5
moral Turing test (MTT) 173, n46
moral values 162–5
Morison, John 119
Morozov, Evgeny 4
MSE (Mental State Examination) 257
MTT (moral Turing test) 173, n46
MUH (mathematical universe hypothesis) 17–18, 305–6
Mulligan, Christina 186
mutuality case law 60–2
MYCIN 244

nanotechnology, biotechnology, information technology and cognitive technology (NBIC) 90
natural and probable consequences doctrine 197–8

natural language generation (NLG) 51
natural language interpretation (NLI) 51
natural language processing (NLP)
automation of legal tasks 211–12
and deep learning (DL) 44–5
definition 306
and empiricism 42–4
further reading 306–7
and law 45–9
and machine learning (ML) 47
and natural language understanding (NLU) 50–1
rationalist approaches to 41–2
sentiment analysis 46–7
text summarisation 47–8
topic modelling 48–9
natural language understanding (NLU) 50–1
naturalism 172
NBIC (nanotechnology, biotechnology, information technology and cognitive technology) 90
NELL (Never-Ending Language Learning system) 53
Nelson, Charlotte A. 247
neo-liberalism 125
neural networks 53 *see also* **artificial neural networks**
neuroimaging 255
neuroscience 254, 255, 307
Never-Ending Language Learning system (NELL) 53
New Zealand 209–10
Newell, Allen 242, 251
Niblett, Anthony 211
Nissenbaum, Helen 122, 260
NLG (natural language generation) 51
NLI (natural language interpretation) 51
NLP *see* **natural language processing**
NLU (natural language understanding) 50–1
Nolan, Jason 100–1
non-hierarchical language 53–4
normativity 71–4
Norvig, Peter 207
nudging 93, n42
Nys, Herman 240

O'Malley, Pat 140–1
open-ended inference 54–5
optimisation systems 118, 132
O'Reilly, Tim 3
Overdorf, Rebekah 116, 118, 132

pancomputationalism 18
PARRY (psychiatric chatbot) 245
Parsons, Talcott 75
Pasquale, Frank 3, 93, 116, 133, 218, 219, 260
personalisation 94
philosophy of mind 307
Piccini, Gualtiero 18
Pinker, Steven 242
plague 91–2
Plato 171
political organisation 97–8, 104
Popper, Karl 110
Posner, Richard 4, 228
Pound, Roscoe 13
power, the 'how' of 96
Powles, Julia 122, 260
predictions 73–4
***Principia Mathematica* (Whitehead & Russell)** 242
principles-based statutory rules 231–2
privacy 101–2, 149, 250
private law 69
private use of technological management 152
problematisation of law 124–6
property rights 228–9
Proust, Marcel 166
provability 307–8
psychiatry
and artificial intelligence 249–50
assessment 238–41
diagnosis 245
expert systems 244
psychology
assessment and diagnosis 247–59
expert systems 244
public decision-making 96, 98, 104
public law 70
public policy
and algorithms 129
and mental capacity 277
public services 85
punishment
of artificial intelligence
affirmative case 185–7
alternatives to 196–204
costs of 200–2
culpability-focused limitations 187–96
Eligibility Challenge 188–92
reality of 194–6
retributivist limitations 187–96
desert constraint 184, 188
theory of 182–5

quantification of law 126–8
quarantine 91–2
Quinton, Anthony 135

Radbruch, Gustav 76
radical uncertainty 74–5, 78
radiofrequency identification (RFID) 90
Rahmani, Adel 48–9
rationalist approaches to NLP 41–2
Ravuri, Murali 243
Rawlings, Richard 103–4
RB v Brighton & Hove City Council 276
Re B (Adult: Refusal of Medical Treatment) 270
reality 49, 123, 280
recidivism 68
reducibility of culpability 181–2, 192–4
reflexivity
  and algorithms 113–15, 129–30
  and law 111–13
  and machine learning (ML) 118
Řehůřek, Radim 48
Remus, Dana 211, 219
resistance to algorithmic governmentality 98–105
respondeat superior 189
retributivist limitations on punishment for artificial intelligence 187–96
reversibility 151
RFID (radiofrequency identification) 90
Rieder, Bernhard 93
risk assessment 156
risk management 151
robots 148, 150, 186–7, 201
Rogerian psychotherapy 261
Rose, Nikolas 124, 125
Rouvroy, Antoinette 123
rule of law 35, 70, 72, 78, 137–8, 149–53, 308
rule skepticism 13–14
rules as code 210–11, 214–15
Russell, Bertrand 242
Russell, Stuart 164, 207

Salinger v Colting 234
Sartor, Giovanni 5
Schoenfeld, Karel Menzo 72
Schütze, Hinrich 41–2
Searle, John 251
Seaver, Nick 113, 126
sentiment analysis 46–7
Sessums, Laura L. 267
Shannon, Claude 7–8, 251
Shaw, Cliff 242
shift registers 12
Shorter, Edward 238
Simmonds, Nigel E. 119
Simon, Herbert 242, 251
Simpson, Gerry 159
singularity *see* **legal singularity; technological singularity**
small claims 219
smart cities 91
smart contracts 67, 68–9, 81–2
smart law 4–5
smart policing 70
smart regulation 67
smart sentencing 70
Smith, Richard J. 10
Society 5.0 1–4
socio-moral change 167–9
Sojka, Petra 48
solutionism 4, 132–3
Sony Corporation of America v Universal City Studios 227, 229, 232, 233
sousveillance 100–1
speech recognition 39
speech-driven normativity 71
Spiegelhalter, David 15–16
State of Wisconsin* v *Loomis 6, n43
Stevens, Mitchell 127
Strathern, Marilyn 73–4
strict liability 189–91
strong AI 14, 25, 180 *see also* **artificial general intelligence**
subjectivity analysis 46–7
SunTrust Bank v Houghton Mifflin 233, 234
superintelligence 18, 25, 171–2
supervised learning 35–7
Supiot, Alain 35
Surden, Harry 218
surveillance 99–105, 129, 145–6
surveillance capitalism 87–94, 308–9
surveillant assemblages 91
Susskind, Daniel 211
Susskind, Richard 211

Tarski, Alfred 14
taxation 128–9, 138, 224
technological singularity 224, 225–7, 309
technology of government 95
'techno-regulation' 3
Tegmark, Max 4, 16, 17–18, 33
Terman, Lewis 207
Texas Medication Algorithm Project (TMAP) 246
text summarisation 47–8
text-driven normativity 72, 77–8
TextRank 48
'the map is not territory' 280–1
theory of computation 309
Thomas, Matt 47
Thompson, Kevin 98

TMAP (Texas Medication Algorithm Project) 246
top-down incorporation strategies 164
topic modelling 48–9
totalitarianism 34
transhumanism 310
Trzepacz, Paula 257
Turing, Alan 173, 250
Turing test 207, 310

ubiquitous computing 90–1
United Nations Security Council 158–9
Universal Product Code (UPC) 90
unsupervised learning 35–7, 62
UPC (Universal Product Code) 90

Vallor, Shannon 146
value-alignment problem 163
van Dijck, José 125–6
Vinge, Vernor 225, 226, 227
Volokh, Eugene 4–5, 216–17

Waddington, Matthew 210
Waldron, Jeremy 77, 217
Walker, Neil 159
Warnock Report 156
Watson (computer system) 15, 252–4
WBC v Z 278
weak AI 14
Wechsler, David 207
weighting 60–4
Weiser, Mark 90
Weizenbaum, Joseph 217, 241, 261–5, 281
Wellman, Barry 100–1
Wheatley, Martin 142
Whitehead, Alfred North 242
WHO (World Health Organization) 237–8
Wigner, Eugene 265
Winner, Langdon 114
Wittgenstein, Ludwig 71
World Community Grid 80, n48
World Health Organization (WHO) 237–8
Wu, Tim 102, 209, 212

Yeung, Karen 93–4
Yi-Jing 10
Yoon, Albert H. 211

Zed **(Kavenna)** 87–8
Zittrain, Jonathan 3
Zuboff, Shoshana 92–3, 99

www.ingramcontent.com/pod-product-compliance
Ingram Content Group UK Ltd.
Pitfield, Milton Keynes, MK11 3LW, UK
UKHW020237290926
15470UKWH00002B/593